T0366389

DUMBARTON OAKS
MEDIEVAL LIBRARY

Jan M. Ziolkowski, General Editor

MEDIEVAL LATIN LIVES OF MUHAMMAD

DOML 51

Medieval Latin Lives of Muhammad

Edited and Translated by

JULIAN YOLLES

and

JESSICA WEISS

DUMBARTON OAKS
MEDIEVAL LIBRARY

HARVARD UNIVERSITY PRESS
CAMBRIDGE, MASSACHUSETTS
LONDON, ENGLAND
2018

Printed in the United States of America

Library of Congress Cataloging-in-Publication Data
Names: Yolles, Julian, editor, translator. | Weiss, Jessica (Translator of Medieval Latin lives of Muhammad), editor, translator.
Title: Medieval Latin lives of Muhammad / edited and translated by Julian Yolles and Jessica Weiss.
Other titles: Dumbarton Oaks medieval library ; 51.
Description: Cambridge, Massachusetts : Harvard University Press, 2018. | Series: Dumbarton Oaks medieval library ; 51 | Text in Latin with English translation on facing pages ; introduction and notes in English. | Includes bibliographical references and index.
Identifiers: LCCN 2017047234 | ISBN 9780674980730 (alk. paper)
Subjects: LCSH: Muḥammad, Prophet, –632—Biography. | Christians—Attitudes—History—To 1500. | Biography—Middle Ages, 500–1500. | Christianity and other religions—Islam.
Classification: LCC BP75.3 .M43 2018 | DDC 297.6/3 [B]—dc23 LC record available at https://lccn.loc.gov/2017047234

Contents

CONTENTS

Introduction

Throughout the Middle Ages, Christian believers told tales about Muhammad and the rise of Islam. They did so to inform, warn, and entertain Christian audiences. This volume brings together a set of such accounts that traces the biographical tradition of Muhammad as it evolved in the medieval West. These stories were all written in or translated into Latin, the chief literary and intellectual language of medieval Europe. With one exception, all texts in this collection were composed as stand-alone, independent works. To supplement them, we have included a passage dealing with Muhammad from Theophanes's early ninth-century chronicle. The Latin translation of this Greek work was widely available throughout much of Western Europe and is vital in understanding later developments. These texts help to explain the origin of many persistent clichés about Muhammad, and to document ways in which Western perceptions of Islam have influenced literature, theology, and religious debate and polemic. In this introduction, we identify the principal stages of Latin literature about Muhammad and Islam and situate the texts in their historical and literary contexts.

History of Muhammad and *Tultusceptru* from the Book of Lord Metobius

Medieval Europe had two main points of contact with Islam. In the East, the Byzantine Empire bordered on Muslim lands. In the West, Muslims had settled since the early eighth century in an area of the Iberian Peninsula they called *al-ʾAndalus.* The earliest Christian accounts of the rise of Islam originated from within these two areas, Eastern and Western, where Christians frequently encountered Muslims.

Muslim conquests extended beyond the Arabian Peninsula, not long after the death of Muhammad in 632 CE. The earliest Christian polemics presented Islam as a heresy and its prophet as a figure who combined elements from Jewish and Christian scripture.[1] Such tracts explained to a Christian audience affinities between the Qurʾān and the Bible, while the label "heresy" enabled Christians to turn to the antiheretical writings of the Church Fathers for strategies in dealing with Islam.

Sometimes a Christian monk is credited with having introduced Muhammad to the Old and New Testament.[2] The alleged involvement of such a holy man was especially momentous for later Christian-Muslim diatribes and parallels early Islamic biographical traditions on the life of Muhammad, in which various ascetic figures play key roles in confirming his status as prophet. A monk named Baḥīrā, "well versed in the knowledge of Christians," recognized the young Muhammad as a prophet.[3] The Christian Waraqa ibn Nawfal translated portions of the Bible into Arabic and told Muhammad's wife, Khadīja, about her husband's visitations from Gabriel.[4]

Another strand of invective placed Muhammad and his followers outside the Christian fold entirely and viewed them as harbingers of the Antichrist within a Christian eschatological framework. One such text that was transmitted to the Latin West at an early stage is the so-called *Apocalypse* attributed to Methodius. Originally written in Syriac—presumably in Palestine, which had come under the rule of Islam—toward the end of the seventh century, it was soon translated into Greek. By 727, it reached Merovingian Gaul in Latin.[5] A narrative concerned with the end of times, it relates how the sons of Ishmael will come forth to wreak destruction upon the earth. Their dominion will be ended by a Roman emperor.

In Spain, Muslims had been present since 711, when conquests of the Iberian Peninsula began. Their expansion into Gaul was halted at the Battle of Tours in 732. Two eighth-century Latin chronicles from Spain viewed Muhammad and his followers as rebels against the Eastern Roman Empire during the reign of the Byzantine emperor Heraclius.[6] While these two chronicles presented Byzantine perspectives on the rise of Islam, the first extant Latin writings reflecting local Christian interactions with Muslims and Islam in Spain date to around a hundred years later.

In the 850s, an anti-Islamic resistance movement arose in Córdoba among Christian monks and clergy. They became known as the "Martyrs of Córdoba" after they had been executed. One of their main supporters was the cleric Eulogius of Córdoba, who extolled the virtues of the martyrs. His writings include a life of Muhammad, the earliest to survive in Latin, that he claimed to have found in Leyre in Northern Spain in 848. This account, known as the *Historia de Mahomet,* depicts Muhammad as an instrument of the

devil and a precursor of the Antichrist. To impugn its title character, this "History of Muhammad" draws on a Muslim biographical tradition in which the prophet married Zaynab, the wife of his adopted son Zayd.[7]

Eulogius belonged to a small circle of clergy and educated laymen who composed polemical works and actively promoted resistance to Islam. Other associates include Paulus Albarus, a noble layman who penned a treatise supporting the Córdoban movement and attacking Islamic teachings, and John of Seville, who appended a brief biography of the Muslim prophet to a letter to Paulus Albarus.[8] By the mid-ninth century, a small collection existed of Latin texts written by and for Christians who possessed a relatively detailed knowledge of Islam.

The next account in this volume may belong to a similar milieu. Transmitted in a late-tenth-century manuscript from Spain under the enigmatic title *Tultusceptru de Libro domini Metobii* (*Tultusceptru* from the Book of Lord Metobius), it describes a monk named Ozim. Bishop Osius entrusted this Spanish monk with the task of bringing a group of apostate satraps back to the Christian fold. Upon Ozim's arrival among them, an evil angel appeared, renamed him Muhammad, and taught him words loosely resembling the Islamic call to prayer, which the narrator identifies as a demonic invocation. The motif of Muhammad as a Christian monk entrusted with missionary responsibilities would become popular several centuries later.

Thus, by the ninth and tenth centuries, Christian polemical writings in Latin had emerged in Spain. Their strategy of refuting Islam by composing and disseminating tendentious biographies of Muhammad appealed to their audiences. Be-

cause Christianity depended on the biographical accounts in the gospels, an attack that took the form of a biography of a religious leader would have seemed a natural tactic. Yet the choice also reflects knowledge that Islam accorded great importance to the life of Muhammad. Alongside the Qurʾān, transmitted deeds, sayings, and teachings of the prophet were viewed as principal sources for Islamic theology and law.

Anastasius the Librarian, *Chronicle* of Theophanes

Whereas the Spanish lives of Muhammad enjoyed a limited diffusion in Europe, the model for all subsequent treatments was an early-ninth-century account from Byzantium translated into Latin later in the ninth century. The Byzantine monk Theophanes (ca. 759/60–818), later called the "Confessor," wrote an important early account of the life of Muhammad and the rise of Islam.[9] It forms part of a world chronicle, begun by George Synkellos, that spanned the creation of the world up to the accession of the Roman emperor Diocletian in 284 CE. Theophanes continued this historical work up to his own time, ending in 812/13 CE.

Theophanes's account of the rise of Islam appears in the section on the reign of the Byzantine emperor Heraclius (610–641), who reconquered territories lost to the Sassanian Persians before losing them again to the Muslims.[10] The Byzantine writer takes as his starting point what he believes to be the year of Muhammad's death and narrates the origin of Islam and the beginning of the Byzantines' encounters with Muslims.[11] The central figure is described as a "ruler and false prophet of the Arabs and Saracens." His rise is at-

tributed above all to the support he received from Jews, who considered him to be the Messiah. Despite perceiving their error, they continued to support him out of fear and urged him to plot against the Christians. The idea of Islam as an anti-Christian Jewish conspiracy would prove momentous for the development of Christian anti-Islamic polemic.

Equally significant is the appearance of the character known as the "pseudo-monk."[12] When Muhammad travels to Palestine and obtains Jewish and Christian scriptures, he suffers from what Theophanes describes as an epileptic seizure. Both the notion that Muhammad cobbled together elements of the Jewish and Christian holy texts to create his own and the materialist explanation of the visitations he received from the angel Gabriel as epileptic episodes become major motifs in later treatments. The account ends with a description of Muhammad's doctrine, crucially described as a "heresy" and therefore considered a distortion of Christianity. The analysis focuses on the promised paradise that awaits those who fought for Muhammad, thus criticizing Islamic doctrines of *jihād* and paradise, topics that became favorites among anti-Islamic authors.[13] The influence of Theophanes's account on Western perceptions of Islam depends on its translation into Latin between 871 and 874 by Anastasius the Librarian (b. before 817–d. ca. 879), who probably procured a Greek manuscript of Theophanes's chronicle during his attendance of the Fourth Council of Constantinople in 869–70.[14] Far from providing an integral rendering of Theophanes's work, however, Anastasius selectively combined three chronicles by Nikephoros, George Synkellos, and Theophanes, aptly dubbing it *Chronographia tripartita* (Three-Part Chronicle). He dedicated the transla-

tion to his friend and collaborator John the Deacon, to serve as the basis for an ecclesiastical history planned by John but never written.[15]

Anastasius discards Theophanes's lists of Orthodox bishops and patriarchs and adds instead the pontifical years of the Catholic popes. The major divergences between his translation and the Greek text result from variants in his Greek manuscript. The most significant of these is the depiction of the monk-figure consulted by Khadīja, Muhammad's wife, as an adulterer.[16]

Embrico of Mainz, *Life of Muhammad*

The first extensive work about Muhammad from Western Europe appeared in the late eleventh century in the intellectual circles around the cathedral school of Mainz on the Rhine. A long poem composed in elegiac couplets with internal rhyme, known as leonine verse, Embrico of Mainz's *Life of Muhammad* aimed to entertain while providing instruction and became popular north of the Pyrenees for several centuries.[17]

Embrico's name and affiliation with Mainz are known from a brief verse biography that praises the poet for his erudition and piety and tells us that he wrote the poem while he was still a student.[18] Although the verse biography states that he also wrote in prose, no other works attributed to him are extant.[19] The *Life* is dedicated to a certain Godebold, "mirror for the most eminent men," who suggested the topic by asking the writer to explain the origin of Islam.[20] Various identifications of the poet and his dedicatee have been proposed to date and localize the poem. Sug-

gested dates range from 1040[21] to 1137.[22] The most probable, namely 1073 to 1090, involves identifying the author with a treasurer of the cathedral of Mainz who later became provost of the cathedral, and Godebold with another cleric who served as provost of the same cathedral shortly before Embrico.[23] Through verbal correspondences between the *Life* and a confessional poem written by a bishop, Embrico has been identified with the bishop of Würzburg (1127–1146).[24] The chief obstacle to this identification is that the verse biography fails to specify the office of bishop among the "honors" enjoyed by Embrico.

Whoever the poet was, his work is set in the later fourth century.[25] Its main protagonist is an unnamed deceiver who aspires to become patriarch of Jerusalem by assuming the guise of a wonderworker *(magus)*.[26] When the Roman emperor Theodosius, divinely alerted to the deception, thwarts his plans, the mage retreats in exile to Libya to plot his revenge. There he murders the local governor with the help of a household slave named Mammutius. After convincing the populace to proclaim Mammutius their king, the mage tricks them into believing that the former slave is a prophet. Having founded a new religion based on sexual debauchery, Mammutius is punished by God with epilepsy. The mage explains the fits as resulting from the angel Gabriel translating his soul to heaven. In describing Mammutius's heavenly voyage, the mage claims that through the prophet's intercession his followers could be absolved of their sins by washing themselves with water. Eventually, Mammutius meets his end when he is devoured by pigs. This episode leads the mage to prohibit the consumption of pork. In one final indictment of their credulity, Mammutius is interred in a

tomb cleverly suspended by magnets, which his followers believe to be a miraculous phenomenon.[27]

Embrico's poem resembles the account presented by Theophanes mainly in mentioning Muhammad's epilepsy. The poet introduced additional fantastical elements that would become set motifs in later polemical traditions on the life of the prophet, such as the "miracles" performed by the mage and the wondrous tomb of Muhammad. Other new additions betray some knowledge of Islamic practices and traditions, including the parody of the celestial ascent (the *miʿrāj*), the mockery of ritual ablution, and the explanation for the prohibition against the consumption of pork. For information on Muhammad, Embrico may have relied upon pilgrims returning from the Holy Land, Mainz's Jewish community (which survived until shortly before the First Crusade), or contacts with Christian Spain.

Although this verse *Life of Muhammad* probably predates the First Crusade (1095–1099), its subsequent popularity indicates that it met a need for a Christian response to Islam. Embrico used a genre-bending approach to this problem. His *Life of Muhammad,* the antithesis of the saint's life, has been called a work of antihagiography.[28] Whereas saint's lives abound in miracles, Embrico's life of the antisaint is replete with the black magic of the mage, including potions, sleeping spells, and prognostication.

Walter of Compiègne, *Poetic Pastimes on Muhammad*

Within a few decades, another versified life appeared, it too in elegiac couplets, though without rhyme. It presented a different version of Islam and Muhammad. The author was

Walter of Compiègne, probably until 1131 a monk at Marmoutier Abbey in Tours, and thereafter prior of St. Martin in Chartres.[29] Early in his poem he tells us of having heard the story at Marmoutier from Garnerius, who later became abbot of the same abbey (1137–1155). Garnerius himself had been told the tale by Paganus of Sens (identified with an abbot of the cloister of Our Lady of Étampes), who had learned it from a nameless converted Muslim.[30] Thus at least six years and perhaps many more passed between when the poet heard the story, thirdhand, and when he composed his *Poetic Pastimes on Muhammad,* possibly at the request of his abbot.[31] The poem dates from between 1137 (the beginning of Garnerius's abbacy) and the second half of the twelfth century (the earliest manuscript witness). More specific outer limits have been suggested by scholars who detect the influence of Peter the Venerable's writings on Islam (d. 1156, see below), or who argue that the poem's relative lack of polemical undertones could not have been a product of the hostile climate immediately preceding the Second Crusade (1147–1149).[32]

The poem contains many motifs found in Embrico, but it adheres more closely to the narrative presented by Theophanes. Unlike Embrico's poem, Walter's narrative centers on Muhammad, who manages his master's merchant activities. One day, Muhammad encounters a hermit who claims that a demon has taken hold of him and will cause him to subvert the New Covenant. When his master dies, Muhammad persuades his widow to marry him. After suffering an epileptic episode, he tells his new bride that he received a divine revelation from the angel Gabriel. In a fulfillment of the hermit's prediction, Muhammad claims to have been

asked to preach a new covenant. He tricks the populace with false miracles, some closely resembling those described by Embrico. After his death, he is similarly interred in an iron casket suspended in midair, a miracle that his followers attribute to their prophet's power.

In Walter's poem, all traces of Embrico's mage and his black magic have disappeared. Muhammad is presented as a strong, learned, and autonomous character. The Christian monk of earlier traditions appears as a hermit who does not teach but figures only incidentally in the plot, since Muhammad is sufficiently learned in Christian teachings to create his doctrine on his own.

Like Embrico's poem, the *Poetic Pastimes* seek to entertain and edify rather than supply historical information. Thus, while Walter demonstrates familiarity with Theophanes, he does not set the narrative in any historical framework. Instead, the poem may be understood as a sort of elegiac comedy and akin to Old French fabliaux, given its picaresque presentation of Muhammad as a wily slave.

Adelphus, *Life of Muhammad*

By increasing contacts between Christians from Western Europe and Muslims, the First Crusade offered access to new sources on the origin of Islam and the life of Muhammad. In a mid-twelfth-century account, a speaker claims to have stopped over in Antioch (near the modern city of Antakya in Turkey) on the return voyage from Jerusalem to interview a local Greek about the rise of Islam.[33]

Antioch had been conquered in the First Crusade and remained in Frankish hands until well into the thirteenth cen-

tury. In addition to the Frankish descendants of the crusaders, the city was home to a variety of Greek- and Arabic-speaking Christians, as well as Armenians and Georgians. It boasted a long tradition of religious polemic, of which the author demonstrates awareness.[34]

If Embrico's poem drew an implicit connection between Islam and early Christian heresies, "Adelphus" introduces a figure named Nestorius, who is probably intended to be identified with the fifth-century heresiarch thought to have denied Christ's divinity. This Nestorius assumes the familiar role of the Christian monk. He accepts into his tutelage a young swineherd (later revealed to be Muhammad) who had been led to his cell by an evil spirit. Yet according to this account, Muhammad was already an accomplished mage and necromancer; together with Nestorius, he commingles and corrupts the Old and New Testaments to form a new and unholy whole. Although the precise nature of the resulting doctrine is passed over, this narrative pays special attention to the relationship between Muhammad and his preceptor and their collaborative creation of the Qurʾān. After gathering followers by means of miracles, Muhammad murders his master to acquire sole rule. As in Embrico, Muhammad meets his end consumed by pigs. This event not only explains Muslim abstention from pork but also lends special irony, given Muhammad's early career as a swineherd.

Beyond the numerous parallels with Embrico's poem, the notable innovations of the Adelphus account may reflect the Levantine context on which it claims to draw.[35] The sole manuscript attributes the text to one "Adelphus," but the identity of the author remains unclear.[36] What little can be known about the author must be inferred from the text. He

seems to have enjoyed a fairly extensive education in classical Latin authors and the Bible and to have had the resources and leisure to travel to Jerusalem either as a pilgrim or as part of a Crusade.

Apology of al-Kindī

By the mid-twelfth century, readers in the Latin West interested in Islam and the life of Muhammad could turn to several literary treatments in verse, inform themselves with a few stray comments dispersed among chronicles, or peruse histories of the First Crusade.[37] A systematic polemical treatment that rested on the Qurʾān and the biographical tradition of Muhammad was still lacking. Eventually Peter the Venerable (1092–1156), an abbot of Cluny for thirty-four years and a major figure in European politics, set about filling this lacuna. To gain access to Islamic texts, Peter journeyed to Spain in 1142/3 together with his secretary, Peter of Poitiers, and assembled a group of translators with a sufficient grasp of Arabic.[38] The team included Robert of Ketton and Hermann of Carinthia, both of whom had translated scientific works from Arabic into Latin; a certain Master Peter of Toledo, probably a Mozarab; and a Muslim, known only as Muhammad.[39] From these scholars he commissioned the first translation of the entire Qurʾān into Latin as well as translations of a lengthy polemical work known as the *Apology of al-Kindī* and several shorter writings on the genealogy of Muhammad and Islamic doctrine. These Latinizations are collectively referred to as the *Toledan Collection* or *Islamo-Latin Corpus.*[40]

The so-called *Apology of al-Kindī* was originally composed

in Arabic and consists of two letters, the first written by a Muslim named ʿAbd Allāh ibn Ismāʿīl al-Hāshimī, the second by a Christian introduced as ʿAbd al-Masīḥ ibn Isḥāq al-Kindī.[41] A short prologue explains that the two letters were written in Baghdad by members of the court of al-Maʾmūn (813–834). This caliph had invited the pair to engage in a religious debate. Accordingly, the Muslim attempts to convert his interlocutor by explaining why Islam is preferable to Christianity, to which the Christian replies with an extensive point-by-point rebuttal and an exhortation to convert to Christianity.

For unknown reasons, the authors' names have been altered from the original and appear to have been changed to stock names that clearly identify the religious affiliation of the persons they refer to, inasmuch as they translate to "Servant of Allāh, son of Ishmael, of the Hāshimite tribe," and "Servant of Christ, son of Isaac, of the Kindite tribe."[42] The author of the prologue must have written after the time when the letters were supposedly composed and may also have added an epilogue at the end of the Christian's letter, in which al-Maʾmūn is presented as adjudicating the debate.[43]

The Muslim's letter is written in a conciliatory tone intended to invite his correspondent to convert to Islam. He expresses his extensive knowledge of Christianity and experience with various Christian groups, as well as his admiration for monks of their faith. The latter portion of the text largely consists of a summary of Islamic teachings, focusing on the Five Pillars of Islam (confession of faith, prayer, alms, fasting, and pilgrimage) and concluding with a long series of Qurʾānic quotations on the Islamic portrayal of paradise and the fate that awaits unbelievers. The letter also includes

a refutation of fundamental Christian doctrines on the Trinity and Christ's divine nature.

The Christian's reply picks up on these doctrinal criticisms by defending the Trinity with scriptural evidence and dialectical reasoning. The letter-writer then proposes to inquire into the life of Muhammad, ostensibly in order to determine whether the facts of his life accord with the prophets of the Judeo-Christian tradition. The author's earlier hostile statements to Islam, however, suggest that his aim is to present a tendentious biography that discredits Muhammad's prophetic status, and thereby the revelations he claimed to have received that formed the basis of Islam. This proved to be the most popular section of the *Apology* among Latin Christians. It offered a wealth of information on the life of Muhammad. Although it set these details in a Christian polemical framework, it drew on genuine Islamic traditions. In addition, it furnished an accessible means of understanding the origins of Islam and attacking its fundamental premises.[44]

When discussing Muhammad's teachings and their origin, the Christian refers to a personage named Sergius. Once a monk, this character had been excommunicated for unnamed sins.[45] Wishing to regain the favor of his former brethren, he converts Muhammad, who had up to that point been an idolater, to Nestorian Christianity. In the process, Sergius changes his own name to Nestorius. Later, the Christian also mentions as Muhammad's teacher a figure called John Baḥīrā. With the aid of Sergius-Nestorius and John Baḥīrā, Muhammad is presented as having woven together and distorted elements of the Old and New Testament into a twisted version of the originals. This tack holds

to a shrewd polemical strategy, in that it inverts Qurʾānic accusations that Christians had corrupted and distorted their scriptures.[46]

Some have questioned whether the text represents a genuine epistolary exchange framed by a later prologue and epilogue, positing instead that both letters were penned by a single, Christian writer who composed the first letter as a straw man for the second, much longer one.[47] The prologue and the epilogue may also have been written by this same author, or added by a later redactor.[48] The most cogent arguments supporting this theory of single authorship note the short length of the Muslim's missive, its effusive praise of Christians and Christianity, and the fact that the brief summary of Islam it contains focuses on elements especially favored among anti-Islamic polemicists, such as the Islamic portrayal of paradise.

Moreover, scholars have differed widely on the dating of the *Apology* and on the identification of the precise religious affiliation of the Christian author. The outer limits of the composition of the Arabic text are the caliphate of al-Maʾmūn (813–834) and the composition of a work on chronology by al-Bīrūnī (ca. 1000), the first author who displays knowledge of the *Apology*.[49] The text has been variously dated from the early ninth century to the early tenth. Likewise, the author has been identified as West Syrian Christian,[50] Melkite,[51] or East Syrian Christian.[52] The current dominant opinion holds that the correspondence was written during the ninth century (during or shortly after the caliphate of al-Maʾmūn) by a single, Christian author, who may have had ties with East Syrian Christianity.[53] The letters were probably written for a Christian monastic community

in or around Baghdad and were subsequently subject to redaction under circumstances that are as yet unclear.

To complicate matters, the Latin translation includes at the end of the Christian's letter a section that is absent from all but two Arabic manuscripts. In this passage, the author explains his purpose and refers his Christian audience to an earlier work he had written against the heresy of Arius.[54] This section is probably the work of a later redactor, given that it does not fit organically with the rest of the Christian's letter and seems designed primarily to mention the sacraments.[55] Nevertheless, it demonstrates the importance of the Latin translation, which preserves the fullest version of the *Apology*.

In a letter to Bernard of Clairvaux, Peter the Venerable claimed that the Latin translation had been made by a Master Peter of Toledo, whose work was later polished by Peter the Venerable's secretary, Peter of Poitiers.[56] A rubric in some manuscripts indicates that this translation was completed in the year of the Christian reconquest of Coria, in 1142.[57] It has been suggested that Master Peter ought to be identified as Peter Alfonsi, a Spanish Jew who converted to Christianity and was baptized in 1106.[58] Alfonsi composed an influential polemical dialogue against Judaism, which also contains a chapter on Islam.[59] The chief argument against the identification with Peter of Toledo is the fact that, while Alfonsi also demonstrates knowledge of the *Apology* in his *Dialogue against Jews,* some elements in his discussion differ from the Latin translation commissioned by Peter the Venerable.[60]

The Latin translation enjoyed a reasonable popularity, with eleven extant manuscripts ranging from the mid-

twelfth to the sixteenth century. It diverges substantially from the Arabic text in various ways: errors and misunderstandings give rise to incoherent passages, while removals and additions are motivated by the translator's ideology and polemical intent.[61] For instance, the Latin describes East Syrian Christians, West Syrian Christians, and Melkites as "heretics"—a qualification absent in the Arabic.[62] In fact, the translator has consistently elided elements referring to Eastern Christianity, or replaced them with Catholicized versions.[63] In some cases, the changes made by the translator may have had inadvertent consequences. In a discussion of the textual transmission of the Qurʾān, Arabic examples are replaced by Latin ones; but where the Arabic merely lists a phonetic variant of the same word (*tābūt* versus *tābūh,* for the Ark of the Covenant), the Latin presents two completely different lexical items (*arcam* versus *arcem,* or "Ark" and "citadel"). This adaptation gives the misleading impression that texts of the Qurʾān showed greater variety than the Arabic *Apology* claims.[64]

Book of Nicholas and *Where Wicked Muhammad Came From*

After twelfth-century efforts to make materials on Islam available to a monastic and clerical audience, ostensibly for the purposes of mission and conversion, new polemical lives of Muhammad appeared in the thirteenth and fourteenth centuries. They arose amid turbulent developments within the Catholic Church that led to the establishment of an entirely new form of monasticism: the mendicant orders of Franciscans and Dominicans. These friars, no longer con-

tent to live in secluded communities, instead placed themselves in the bustle of urban life. Following Christ's example in leading a life of poverty and preaching, they soon developed educational centers. In them they trained novices to preach virtuous lifestyles to the common man and criticize backsliding monks and clergy, as well as to convert Jews, Muslims, and those they considered to be heretics.

Two anonymous polemical treatments of the life of Muhammad associated with the mendicants are included in this volume: the so-called *Liber Nycholay,* or "The Book of Nicholas," and the account here dubbed *Where Wicked Muhammad Came From,* after its incipit in the single surviving manuscript.[65] Though widely different in tone and overall thrust, these accounts share core elements: both were composed in a mendicant context (possibly by and for Dominicans in Italy), and both accounts contain a central character named Nic(h)olas. This figure developed out of the early tradition that associated Muhammad's prophetic career with a Christian monk. The name may derive from Nicolas of Antioch. One of the seven deacons of the apostolic period, he was considered the heresiarch who founded the Nicolaites. Members of this sect were reviled for their reported sexual licentiousness.[66] The identification of the Nicholas-figure as a member of the Catholic clergy with papal ambitions marks a significant shift in focus. Whereas earlier traditions associated the beginnings of Islam with Eastern Christian heresies, a further degeneration of those who had already been cast out of the Catholic fold, Islam was now presented as arising from the center of the Catholic Church.[67]

The source for Muhammad's connection with the

Nicholas-figure may be a remark in a ninth-century commentary on the Gospel of Matthew. There the exegete Pascasius Radbertus claims that the Saracens received the Gospel but were led astray by pseudo-apostles, specifically the disciples of Nicolas, and fashioned their own law by combining elements of the Old and New Testaments.[68] Another reference to the Nicholas-tradition appears in an eleventh-century school text (1086–1087), clearly drawing on the *Tultusceptru* narrative.[69] In response to the widespread identification of Muhammad with Nicolas, Peter the Venerable denies that the sect of the Nicolaites has any connection with the Muslims.[70]

The *Book of Nicholas,* in turn, identifies Nicholas with Muhammad, but indicates that this Nicholas lived after Emperor Constantine's conversion to Christianity, and is thus not associated with the pseudo-apostle Nicolas.[71] This version diverges from previous traditions by collapsing the Christian monk figure with Muhammad, who now becomes completely disassociated from Eastern Christianity and is instead made a member of the papal clergy ordered to convert Spain and Barbary to Catholicism. After Nicholas's ambitions of becoming pope are definitively thwarted, he devises an elaborate plan for revenge by founding a rival religion whose teachings are similarly based on the Old and New Testaments. Nevertheless, some of the precepts preached by Nicholas show knowledge of Islamic tenets, including circumcision, abstention from alcohol, the Islamic Feast of Sacrifice, fasting, and ritual cleansing.

The tone of the work differs markedly from the vitriol of most anti-Islamic polemics. Nicholas and his followers are presented positively, and the work ends on a remarkably

conciliatory note, focusing on the similarities of Christianity and Islam. The overall tone, moreover, is steeped in humorous irony: the sickly and ancient cardinal who is (ironically) rejuvenated upon being elected pope, the cardinal legate who founds a new religion in the lands he had been ordered to convert to Christianity, the Boccaccian tale of trickery in which two followers of Nicholas dispose of his body. Evidently, the purpose of the *Book of Nicholas* was not to provide accurate information on Islam, but to satirize the papal Curia.[72]

The *Book of Nicholas* is transmitted in two manuscripts, one from the late-thirteenth century, the other from the second half of the fourteenth century.[73] The earlier contains, immediately before the *Book of Nicholas,* a work chronicling Holy Roman emperors and popes, written by one Johannes Ruffus.[74] The juxtaposition of the two texts, correspondences in phrasing, and Ruffus's reference to Pope Agapitus II as the one who appointed one Nicholas ("who later was Machumetus") to be his successor, all suggest that Ruffus authored the *Book of Nicholas,* or at the very least that the texts are closely related.[75] Ruffus's history can be dated to 1261/62, and was probably written a little before the *Book of Nicholas.*[76] Little is known about Johannes Ruffus, and no other work of his survives. He must have been a friar, and may have been connected with the court of Manfred, king of Sicily and son of Frederick II, who was in all likelihood the addressee of Ruffus's chronicle. The chronicle demonstrates an intimate knowledge of Rome, while the *Book of Nicholas* also shows evidence of an Italian context.[77] A composition in Italy (possibly Rome) sometime after 1261/62 seems likely.[78]

Unlike the *Book of Nicholas, Where Wicked Muhammad Came From* (or *Qualiter,* in short, after the Latin incipit) sets the story in "the time of the apostles" and takes its point of departure from the pseudo-apostolic figure of Nicolas, who is immediately cast as the villain, with his description as "false" and "wicked," and compared to Judas. Nicolas intends to succeed Pope Clement I, but he is quickly cast out from the church and branded a heretic. Fueled by a desire to defame the church that rejected him and to lead its members astray, Nicolas continues to spread his heretical teachings, which include preaching communal possession of goods and wives. One of his chief disciples is a man named Maurus, or "Moor," who learns from him—among other things—necromancy and multilingualism. Eventually, the Church excommunicates Nicolas and imprisons him in a tower in Rome, where he dies. Maurus, however, inherits his teacher's thirst for revenge and sails to unspecified "Arab lands," where he takes up residence as a hermit on a mountain near a town that had recently converted to Christianity. He convinces a young camel herder named Muhammad to become his disciple, and together they plot for Muhammad to become king of the neighboring town.

Toward the end, a fanciful account of Muhammad's death is provided, in which he becomes enamored of a married Jewish woman. Rather than commit adultery with him, she devises a plot to kill Muhammad and dispose of his body in a way that would not incriminate her or endanger her people. The story shares elements with the *Book of Nicholas:* the prophet's adulterous affair leads to his demise, and the couple responsible for his death concoct a story that angels lifted him up to heaven and left only his foot behind. Yet

while the *Book of Nicholas* presented the husband as Muhammad's murderer, *Qualiter* focuses on the woman, who is identified as Jewish, and whose plan ultimately saves her and her people from certain death.

The text holds interest for its incorporation of new elements into existing traditions.[79] These include the distinction between Nicolas and Muhammad, the introduction of the figure of Maurus, and Muhammad's ascent to heaven. Embrico of Mainz had given a brief account of Muhammad's ascent, but the version in *Qualiter* is much more extensive and accords closely with a third text that survives in a thirteenth-century Latin version.[80]

Unlike the *Book of Nicholas,* the tone of *Qualiter* is far from conciliatory and recalls the invectives of earlier traditions, such as Theophanes, the Spanish lives, and the *Apology of al-Kindī.* This is especially true at the very end of the text, where the conclusion presents the devil as the inventor of Islam.[81] Thus, the text could not have been intended for missionary purposes aimed at converting Muslims; its vitriolic tone, combined with the legendary character of the narrative, indicates instead that it was probably meant to furnish materials for sermons, perhaps for the benefit of Dominican friars.[82] Ultimately, this text represents an attempt to understand Islam by locating its origins in a Christian context—with an utter disregard for chronology.[83] Like the *Book of Nicholas,* this life places Muhammad explicitly in a Moroccan setting, thus making the text relevant to a context in which the Moors were the dominant Muslims with whom Christians interacted.

The *Qualiter* account is preserved in a single manuscript that originated from the Dominican convent of Saint Cath-

erine in Pisa.[84] Some questions still surround the origins of the text and its relation to similar accounts. Given that it contains a narrative of Muhammad's ascent *(miʿrāj)* similar to the one translated in Spain by an Italian named Bonaventure of Siena, it may have been assembled in Spain within the same milieu, or represent an early Italian reception of Bonaventure's translation.[85] *Qualiter* also shows close similarities to a Castilian account attributed to Pedro Pascual, a thirteenth-century bishop of Jaén (d. after 1300), which probably derives from the Latin.[86] If this is true, we may date *Qualiter* to the final quarter of the thirteenth century: the bishop of Jaén claims to be writing in the year 1300, and the legend of the *miʿrāj* was not widely disseminated until after 1264.[87]

Conclusion

This volume covers nearly five centuries and a variety of regions. In this long literary tradition, we see the first encounters of Christians and Muslims in the Iberian Peninsula and in the Byzantine Empire; we engage with verse lives from France and Germany intended to entertain at least as much as to instruct, a conversation with a Greek interlocutor from the Crusader Levant, and an epistolary exchange translated from Arabic into Latin at the behest of a French abbot. Finally, we find two lives associated with Italy and the rise of the mendicant orders.

In these texts, we are exposed to the preoccupations of Western medieval readers and writers. A persistent motif in nearly all these lives is the figure of the Christian monk, frequently presented as instructing Muhammad in Christian

scripture and doctrine, or a twisted version of them. Sometimes, Jews are given prominent roles, either as early followers of Muhammad or as the cause of his demise. These Latin lives of Muhammad signal how medieval Christians viewed the relationship between Christianity, Islam, and Judaism. They tell as much about what they thought of Muslims and Islam as they do about their own interests and concerns.

We have provided our own translations of scriptural quotations since the wordings in our texts do not always accord with modern editions of the Bible or those of the Qur'ān. In the Notes to the Translations, however, we have used the revised Douay-Rheims translation of the Latin Vulgate and Pickthall's translation of the Qur'ān.[88]

We are grateful to Professor Wolf for his permission to provide here revised translations of the *History of Muhammad* and the *Tultusceptru* from the Book of Lord Metobius.[89]

Julian Yolles revised the *History of Muhammad* and *Tultusceptru* from the Book of Lord Metobius and translated the *Chronicle of* Theophanes, the *Apology of al-Kindī,* the *Book of Nicholas,* and *Where Wicked Muhammad Came From.* Embrico of Mainz's *Life of Muhammad,* Walter of Compiègne's *Poetic Pastimes on Muhammad,* and Adelphus's *Life of Muhammad* were translated by Jessica Weiss.

The authors wish to express their gratitude for the editorial assistance provided by the staff of the Dumbarton Oaks Medieval Library, with particular thanks to Noah Delwiche, Zachary Fletcher, Rebecca Frankel, Jessica Glueck, Jude

Russo, David Ungvary, and Elliot Wilson, who all proved immensely helpful in proofreading; to Winthrop Wetherbee and Danuta Shanzer, for their insightful comments; to Raquel Begleiter, whose supreme organization and sharp eye helped coordinate this project over several years; and finally, to Jan Ziolkowski, without whose generosity and support on every front this project could not have been completed.

Notes

1 See especially John of Damascus (675/6–749), who treats Islam in chapter 100 of his *On heresies* (*De haeresibus* or *Peri haireseōn*).

2 John of Damascus (*De haeresibus,* 100), identifies the Christian monk as an Arian heretic.

3 Ibn Hishām, *Sīrat Rasūl Allāh,* trans. Alfred Guillaume, *The Life of Muhammad: A translation of Isḥāq's Sīrat Rasūl Allāh* (Oxford, 1967), 79–81. It is unclear whether the Christian or the Muslim narrative appeared first; the name is in fact a Syriac honorific derived from the root "to prove, test." In the eighth or ninth century, various Christian elaborations of Baḥīrā's encounter with Muhammad appeared, collectively referred to as the *Legend of Baḥīrā* or the *Apocalypse of Baḥīrā.* For a detailed study of the tradition, see Roggema, *The Legend of Sergius Baḥīrā.*

4 Ibn Hishām, trans. Guillaume, 107.

5 For the Greek and the Latin texts, accompanied by English translations, see *Apocalypse Pseudo-Methodius,* trans. Benjamin Garstad, Dumbarton Oaks Medieval Library 14 (Cambridge, Mass., 2012).

6 The chronicles are known as "The Byzantine-Arabic Chronicle of 741" and "The Mozarabic Chronicle of 754," respectively. For the passages in question, see Di Cesare, *The Pseudo-historical Image,* 12–14.

7 For this tradition and its reception in Christian polemic, see Daniel, *Islam and the West,* 119–22.

8 For the relevant passages, see Di Cesare, *The Pseudo-historical Image,* 29–48.

9 On the life of Theophanes, see *The Chronicle of Theophanes Confessor,*

trans. Mango and Scott, xliii–lii; Treadgold, *The Middle Byzantine Historians,* 63–77.

10 There has been a long and vexed debate on the nature of Theophanes's "Eastern source(s)." It appears that, for the section on the life of Muhammad, at least, he may ultimately draw on Muslim Arabic sources, mediated and selected by a Christian source. For a recent discussion, see Conterno, *La "descrizione dei tempi" all'alba dell'espansione islamica,* 16–21, 76–79.

11 According to his reckoning, 622, corresponding to 629/30 in the Gregorian calendar, instead of the correct date of 632.

12 Unlike John of Damascus, who had claimed that Muhammad associated with an Arian monk, Theophanes recounts that he had been exiled on account of unspecified heresy.

13 See Daniel, *Islam and the West,* 172–76; Dronke, "La sessualità in Paradiso."

14 On the life of Anastasius, known as the Librarian (or Bibliothecarius), on account of his appointment as head librarian and archivist of the Church of Rome, see Arnaldi, "Anastasio Bibliotecario," and more recently his "Anastasio bibliotecario, antipapa"; Neil, *Seventh-century Popes and Martyrs,* 11–34.

15 On Anastasius's collections of translations and the role of John the Deacon (also known as John Immonides), see Forrai, "Anastasius Bibliothecarius and His Textual Dossiers."

16 Theophanes, c. 5 (and see the Notes on the Translations).

17 The poem is attested in sixteen manuscripts of varied provenance and date; twelve or thirteen date to as early as the twelfth century. For a description, see the edition in *La vie de Mahomet,* ed. Cambier, and more recently, González Muñoz, *Mahometrica,* 56–58.

18 The verse biography (henceforth *Vita auctoris*) was first published in Wattenbach, "Lateinische Gedichte aus Frankreich im elften Jahrhundert"; for more recent editions, see Cambier, "Embricon de Mayence (1010?–1077) est-il l'auteur de la Vita Mahumeti?" and González Muñoz, *Mahometrica,* 169–71. It is possible that Embrico authored the verse biography himself: although Guy Cambier disputes his authorship because the *Vita auctoris* speaks of the poet in the past tense, one could argue that he imagined posterity as his audience. See Cambier, "Embricon de Mayence," 471. González Muñoz challenges (*Mahometrica,* 35) the notion that the words *hec quod composuit carmina dum studuit* (*Vita auctoris,* l. 4) must indi-

cate that the poem was composed while Embrico was a student, offering the suggestion that it simply indicates that the poet studied the subject matter of his poem.

19 *Vita auctoris,* ll. 13–14: *Quem si vidisset quondam, Naso coluisset: / Prosa Sydonium, carmine Vergilium.* Ekkehart Rotter ("Embricho von Mainz und das Mohammed-Bild seiner Zeit," 128 n. 311) reads *Suetonium* ("Suetonius") for *Sydonium* (referring to Sidonius Apollinaris), unconvincingly arguing that the former is more likely to be regarded as a master of prose. However, in addition to poetry, Sidonius Apollinaris was known in the Middle Ages for his nine books of letters. For Apollinaris's popularity as a stylistic model, see Peter von Moos, "Literarkritik im Mittelalter: Arnulf von Lisieux über Ennodius," 933.

20 Embrico of Mainz, *Life of Muhammad,* ll. 73–78.

21 This date (maintained by Manitius, *Geschichte der lateinischen Literatur des Mittelalters,* 2:582–87, and Cambier, "Embricon de Mayence," 473–78) involves the identification of the author with an Embrico who was later archbishop of Augsburg. Cambier's far-fetched argument that the poem refers to events occurring in Constantinople during the 1030s was convincingly questioned in Southern, *Western Views of Islam,* 30n.

22 The latest possible date would be in the early part of the twelfth century, since several manuscripts are not much older, while the *Poetic Pastimes* of Walter of Compiègne, which may have been influenced by Embrico's poem, can be reliably dated to after 1137 (see below).

23 Rotter and Staab, "Anhang: Der Autor Embricho," 123–37.

24 González Muñoz, *Mahometrica,* 39–42.

25 Cambier speculates that the reason for Embrico's chronological error may lie in the unknown sources of the chronicle of Michael the Syrian (*Embricon de Mayence,* 13–14). As for the geographical error, Thomas Burman suggests that Embrico may have set his *Life of Muhammad* in Libya due to a confusion of Yathrib, the ancient name for Medina (sometimes represented as Thrib), with Tripoli in Libya (Tolan, *Sons of Ishmael,* 163 n. 23). Rotter produces a parallel from the literary production surrounding the cathedral of Mainz: in 1060 to 1062, a certain Gozwin, schoolmaster of the cathedral school at Mainz and provost of St. Maria ad gradus in Mainz, authored a *Life of St. Theonest,* in which Theodosius and Ambrose are likewise implicated ("Embricho von Mainz und das Mohammed-Bild," 96–97).

26 As John Tolan points out (*Sons of Ishmael,* 8), the name Magus would have held associations with the biblical figure Simon Magus, later deemed a heresiarch and progenitor of the corrupting practice of simony, or the buying and selling of ecclesiastical offices (see Acts 8:9–24).

27 The floating tomb may have been Embrico's invention or he may merely have been the first to record the legend. For an extensive discussion of the legend, which was widely diffused until well into the eighteenth century, see Tolan, *Sons of Ishmael,* 19–34, who views the legend within the context of hagiographical motifs of miracles occurring after a saint's death. Since, according to Embrico, Muhammad was not a real saint, the posthumous miracle is likewise a trick.

28 For the notion of Embrico's poem as an antihagiography, see Tolan (*Sons of Ishmael,* 2–18), and Stella, "Le versificazioni latine delle vita di Maometto."

29 The identities of all these figures were suggested by Hans Prutz and have been generally accepted by scholars: Prutz, "Über des Gautier von Compiègne 'Otia de Machomete.'"

30 *Poetic Pastimes,* ll. 5–14.

31 On the dating of the poem, see Cambier, "Quand Gautier de Compiègne composait les Otia de Machomete."

32 For the former suggestion, see Cambier, "Quand Gautier de Compiègne composait les Otia de Machomete," 538; for the latter, see González Muñoz, *Mahometrica,* 70–71.

33 Bischoff, "Ein Leben Mohammeds."

34 (Ps.-)Adelphus, 1.

35 Bischoff suggests ("Ein Leben Mohammeds," 111) that it may have been a local legend in Antioch that Muhammad's preceptor was not an East Syrian monk, but rather Nestorius the heresiarch himself, given Nestorius's connection with Antioch. Edeltraud Klueting observed that the motif of the Christian preceptor's murder is also found in William of Tripoli ("Quis fuerit Machometus? Mohammed im lateinischen Mittelalter," 303–4).

36 Bischoff ("Ein Leben Mohammeds," 106–7) drew attention to a Benedictine abbot named Adelphus, to whom the fifteenth-century writer Johannes Trithemius ascribed, in addition to a number of sermons, a *Contra Sarracenos liber* ("Book against the Saracens"). Nonetheless, it is not clear whether this text is to be identified with the account attributed to Adelphus, and if so, how reliable Trithemius's information regarding its author

is. It may instead be possible that the attribution derived from a scribe's misunderstanding of the text, in which the Greek interlocutor addresses the author as *adelphe,* Greek for "brother" or "friend."

37 The history of the First Crusade authored by Guibert of Nogent presented a treatment of the life of Muhammad. See Guibert of Nogent, *Dei Gesta per Francos,* ed. R. B. C. Huygens, Corpus Christianorum: Continuatio Mediaevalis 127A (Turnhout, 1996), 1.244–416.

38 For Peter the Venerable's journey to Spain, and the question of whether or not his project to translate Arabic works on Islam predated the journey, see Bishko, "Peter the Venerable's Journey to Spain."

39 Peter the Venerable, *Contra sectam Saracenorum,* ed. and trans. Irven M. Resnick, *Peter the Venerable. Writings against the Saracens* (Washington, D.C., 2016), 17.

40 The former, more traditional designation has fallen out of favor, given that there is no direct evidence linking the translation activities with the city of Toledo specifically, other than the involvement of Peter of Toledo; instead, it seems that the translations may have been made at Nájera, and from there en route to Salamanca. See Bishko, "Peter the Venerable's Journey to Spain," 167–69; Tolan, *Sons of Ishmael,* 47. For a recent translation of Peter the Venerable's writings on Islam, see *Peter the Venerable. Writings against the Saracens,* trans. Resnick.

41 Not to be confused with the ninth-century philosopher Yaʿqūb ibn ʾIsḥāq al-Ṣabbāḥ al-Kindī. The Arabic text was first printed in *The Apology of El-Kindi,* ed. Tien. This edition has been superseded by a critical edition: *Dialogue islamo-chrétien sous le calife Al-Maʾmūn,* ed. Tartar.

42 The Hāshimite tribe was the tribe of Muhammad (encompassing also the Quraysh tribe), while the Kindites were a famous Christian Arab tribe.

43 al-Maʾmūn's pronouncement that Islam is the true faith has, unsurprisingly, not made it into the Latin translation. However, a close look at the oldest Latin manuscript (Paris, Bibl. de l'Arsenal, MS 1162) reveals that it was included but later erased.

44 Large extracts from the Latin translation were used by Vincent of Beauvais in the mid-thirteenth century (where the two letters appear in inverse order), mostly focusing on the life of Muhammad. See *Speculum Historiale,* Book 24.

45 As Roggema points out (*The Legend of Sergius Baḥīrā,* 58), the name Ser-

gius, presumably referring to a popular saint, was added by Christians, who perceived Baḥīrā to be an honorific title rather than a name. In the *Apology,* the Sergius-Baḥīrā figure has been separated into two figures: Sergius-Nestorius and John Baḥīrā.

46 See, for example, Q 2:75; 5:13; 5:41. This is known as the doctrine of *taḥrīf* ("corruption").

47 Most notably Abel, "L'Apologie," 502–3, followed by Griffith, "The Prophet Muḥammad," 107–8, and Tolan, *Saracens,* 301 n. 96. Tartar, however, maintained that the first letter was indeed written by a Muslim (*Dialogue,* 45–61).

48 While the prologue appears in most of the Arabic manuscripts, the epilogue is extant in a single Arabic manuscript (both appear in the Latin), and is probably a later addition.

49 He mentions the names of the two authors and quotes a passage from al-Kindī's letter: al-Bīrūnī, *Kitāb al-āthār al-bāqiya ʿan al-qurūn al-khāliya,* ed. E. C. Sachau (Leipzig, 1878), 205. For the passage, see also Samir, "La version latine," 34. Rachid Haddad's claim (*La Trinité divine chez les théologiens arabes,* 41), followed recently by Laura Bottini ("*The Apology of al-Kindī,*" 585), that this al-Kindī was mentioned earlier by ʾAbū Ḥayyān al-Tawḥīdī (d. 1023) in his *Kitāb al-Imtāʿ wa-l-muʾānasa,* must be discarded. As D. S. Margoliouth already pointed out ("The Discussion between Abu Bishr Matta and Abu Saʿid al-Sirafi on the Merits of Logic and Grammar," 89), the al-Kindī mentioned by al-Tawḥīdī must be the more famous philosopher Yaʿqūb ibn ʾIsḥāq al-Ṣabbāḥ al-Kindī rather than the apologist, given the philosophical nature of the debate in question. See more recently Adamson, *al-Kindī,* 17–18.

50 Massignon, "al-Kindī, ʿAbd al-Masīḥ," 1080–81; d'Alverny, "Deux traductions," 87–96.

51 See Van Koningsveld, "The Apology," 82–83, who linked the Apology to the thought of the early-ninth-century Melkite bishop of Ḥarrān Theodore ʾAbū Qurra.

52 So argued by Georg Graf and supported by Georges Troupeau and Thomas Burman: Graf, *Geschichte,* 2:141–45; Troupeau, "al- Kindī, ʿAbd al-Masīḥ," 120–21; Burman, "The Influence of the Apology of Al-Kindi," 199.

53 For overviews, see Troupeau, "al- Kindī, ʿAbd al-Masīḥ," 120–21; Bottini, "*The Apology of al-Kindī,*" 585. At the very least, the Muslim appears to

treat the Christian as an East Syrian by appealing to the authority of the East Syrian catholicos Timothy I and commending East Syrian Christians ("Nestorians") for their skill in debate, adding that Muhammad praised this sect in particular (*ES* 10–11). Werner Caskel pointed out a passage that contradicts the central East Syrian tenet denying the Virgin as the bearer of God *(theotókos),* and suggests that, unless the passage was added at a later date, the author may have been an East Syrian convert to Orthodox Christianity (Caskel, "*Apologia del Christiamismo,*" 154). The Latin translator certainly appears to have considered the Christian to be an adherent of East Syrian Christianity—while at the same time eliminating these elements and references—since the Latin presents the Muslim writing to the Christian that the "Nestorians" are "akin to you" (*ES* 11), a phrase that is absent from the Arabic.

54 *RC* 255–65.

55 So argued in González Muñoz, *Exposición,* xlii–xliii.

56 Peter the Venerable, *Epistola de translatione sua,* ed. Glei, 22.

57 For the rubric, see González Muñoz, "La versión latina," 28.

58 See *Dialogus contra Iudaeos,* ed. Mieth, 1–2. James Kritzeck raised the possibility but summarily dismissed it: *Peter the Venerable,* 64, citing Monneret de Villard, *Lo studio dell'Islām in Europa nel XII e nel XIII secolo,* 14. In his review of Kritzeck's book, Allan Cutler proposes to keep the possibility open: "*Peter the Venerable and Islam* by James Kritzeck," 190. For a more recent proponent of the identification, see van Koningsveld, "La apología de Al-Kindî en la España del siglo XII," 107–29.

59 The *Dialogus contra Iudaeos.*

60 For instance, Alfonsi identifies the monk Sergius as a West Syrian ("Jacobite"), while the Latin translation of the *Apology* presents him as an East Syrian ("Nestorian"). See *titulus quintus* in Peter Alfonsi's *Dialogus contra Iudaeos,* ed. Klaus-Peter Mieth, *Diálogo contra los Judíos* (Huesca, 1996), 91–103.

61 The most significant divergences are mentioned in the Notes to the Translations; for a fuller discussion, see Gonález Muñoz, "Consideraciones sobre la versión latina," 43–70.

62 *ES* 11; see also *RC* 97, where the translator has added a parenthetical remark on "Nestorian heretics."

63 For example, by referring to the East Syrian catholicos Timothy I as a

bishop, or by having the Christian explicitly identify himself as catholic: see *ES* 11 and *RC* 38, respectively.

64 *RC* 104.

65 Norman Daniel referred to this life as the "Pisan text" (*Islam and the West,* 416), while John Tolan dubbed it *Iniquus Mahometus* or "Deceitful Muḥammad" (see his "*Iniquus Mahometus,* 'Deceitful Muḥammad'").

66 See Acts 6:5; Apoc 2:6. For their reportedly wanton behavior, see especially Jerome, *Epistulae* 147, ed. Isidorus Hilberg, Corpus Scriptorum Ecclesiasticorum Latinorum 56:1 (Vienna, 1996), c. 4, 319–20.

67 For early studies of the motif of Muhammad as a member of the Curia, see d'Ancona, *La leggenda di Maometto in Occidente;* Doutté, *Mahomet cardinal.* See more recently Daniel, *Islam and the West,* 104.

68 This was observed by Marie-Thérèse d'Alverny ("La connaissance," 237). For the passage in question, see Pascasius Radbertus, *Expositio in Matheo libri XII,* ed. Beda Paulus, Corpus Christianorum: Continuatio Mediaevalis 56B (Turnhout, 1984), c. 11.446–61, 1163; Di Cesare, *The Pseudo-historical Image,* 49–51.

69 Master Siguinus, *Ars lectoria,* ed. Joseph Engels, C. H. Kneepkens, and H. F. Reijnders (Leiden, 1979), 124.

70 Peter the Venerable, *Summa totius haeresis,* ed. and trans. Resnick, 3.

71 *Book of Nicholas* 1.

72 González Muñoz, "*Liber Nycholay,*" in *Christian-Muslim Relations,* 4:650–53.

73 Paris, BnF lat. 14503, fols. 352r–54r, and Rome, Vat. Reg. lat. 627, fols. 17v–18v. The first was compiled in Avignon in the second half of the fourteenth century and contains the entire *Corpus Islamo-latinum* as well as Mark of Toledo's translation of the Qur'ān. For a description of the manuscripts, see González Muñoz, "*Liber Nycholay,*" 6–7.

74 The title of this work is *Liber de historiis veteribus et modernis imperatorum et pontificum romanorum* ("Book on ancient and modern histories of emperors and Roman pontiffs"), which has been edited in Sommerlechner, "Der *Liber de istoriis.*"

75 For the passage, see Sommerlechner, "Der *liber de istoriis,*" 301. For the similarities in phrasing, see González Muñoz, "*Liber Nycholay,*" 38–39; Sommerlechner is more cautious in attributing the *Book of Nicholas* to Johannes Ruffus, asserting that, as a "timeless" work directed against the

Curia, it could also have been composed by a later scribe ("Der *liber de istoriis,*" 247).

76 González Muñoz, "*Liber Nycholay,*" 39.

77 Nicholas's rival to the papal see, John, is specifically identified as a "cardinal bishop of the titular church of San Lorenzo in Damaso," while the name *Marzucus,* who figures in the *Book of Nicholas* as the husband of Nicholas's adulterous disciple, is of Italian origin. See the *Book of Nicholas,* 3 and 25–26, respectively, and the Notes to the Translations.

78 Fierro ("La visión") emphasizes the text's connection with Spain and North Africa and suggests that the *Book of Nicholas* demonstrates a familiarity with a specific reformist movement within Islam, that of the Almohad caliphate, which ruled large portions of the Maghreb in North Africa and al-Andalus in about 1127–1269. Some of the evidence adduced for this connection, however, ignores the preexisting polemical traditions on Islam to which the *Book of Nicholas* refers. For example, the Qurʾān written in golden lettering described in the *Book of Nicholas* (7) is a trope that goes back to Embrico of Mainz (ll. 671–78), rather than referring to a book owned by the founder of the Almohads, the Mahdī Ibn Tūmart (Fierro, "La visión," 156).

79 Case in point being its absence in Michelina Di Cesare's otherwise excellent repertory of medieval Latin texts on Muhammad: Di Cesare, *The Pseudo-historical Image.* For discussions of this text, see González Muñoz, "Dos versiones"; Tolan, *Sons of Ishmael,* 22–23; Tolan, "*Iniquus Mahometus.*"

80 Embrico of Mainz, 900–954. This independent text may derive from a lost Arabic original incorporating elements from Qurʾānic passages and hadith on the *isrāʾ* (night journey from Mecca to Jerusalem) and *miʿrāj* (ascent to heaven via a ladder). The Latin version was translated by Bonaventure of Siena in 1264 from a now lost Castilian version by the Jewish physician Abraham of Toledo. For a bibliography, consult Echevarria, "*Liber scalae Machometi.*"

81 *Qualiter* 44. For good measure, the statement is repeated in the manuscript's *explicit.*

82 González Muñoz, "Dos versiones," 598.

83 A good example of Michelina Di Cesare's category of the "legendary Muhammad" (see *The Pseudo-historical Image,* 8–10).

84 Camillo Vitelli, who cataloged the manuscript, tentatively dated it to

the fifteenth century, but after consulting the manuscript we concur with Mancini's earlier dating. See Vitelli, "Index codicum latinorum," 353; Mancini, "Per lo studio," 328.

85 González Muñoz argues ("Dos versiones," 595) that the *miʿrāj* account in *Qualiter* depends on the *Liber scale* translated by Bonaventure of Siena, which found a wide reception in Europe thereafter; it would therefore not be necessary to postulate that *Qualiter* was composed in Spain.

86 In the past, some have posited a common source, while others have argued that *Qualiter* draws on Pascual's account: Mancini, "Per lo studio," 327–28; Cerulli, *Nuove ricerche sul Libro della Scala,* 253. More recently, the prevailing opinion is that Pascual drew instead on the Latin account: González Muñoz, "Dos versiones," 596–98; *Sobre la se[c]ta mahometana: Pseudo Pedro Pascual,* ed. Fernando González Muñoz (Valencia, 2011), 18–23; Tolan, "*Iniquus Mahometus,*" 655.

87 González Muñoz grants that doubts about the dating remain, since (Ps.-)Pascual exists only in sixteenth- and seventeenth-century manuscripts and the dating to 1300 could have been fabricated ("Dos versiones," 598).

88 *The Vulgate Bible: Douay-Rheims translation,* ed. Swift Edgar (Cambridge, Mass., 2010–2013); *The Meaning of the Glorious Qur'an: Text and Explanatory Translation,* trans. Muhammad M. Pickthall (Elmhurst, N.Y.: 1999).

89 Millet-Gérard, *Chrétiens mozarabes,* 126–27; Colbert, *The Martyrs of Córdoba*, 336–38; Wolf, "The Earliest Latin Lives of Muḥammad," 89–101 (repr. in *Medieval Iberia. Readings from Christian, Muslim, and Jewish Sources,* ed. Constable, 48–50). The *History of Muhammad* was also copied in a later ninth-century chronicle, the so-called *Cronica profetica* or *Chronicle of Albelda.* For a modern translation, see Yves Bonnaz, *Chroniques Asturiennes (fin IXe siècle)* (Paris, 1987), 5–6.

HISTORY OF MUHAMMAD

Historia de Mohamet

Exortus est Mahmeth haeresiarches tempore Heraclii imperatoris, anno imperii ipsius septimo. In hoc tempore Isidorus Hispalensis episcopus in catholico dogmate claruit, et Sisebutus Toleto regale culmen obtinuit; ecclesia beati Euphrasii apud Iliturgi urbem super tumulum eius aedificatur, Toleto quoque beatae Leocadiae aula miro opere, iubente praedicto principe, culmine alto extenditur. Obtinuit praedictus Mahmeth nefandus propheta principatum annis decem, quibus expletis, mortuus est, et sepultus in inferno in saecula saeculorum.

2 Exordia vero eius fuerunt talia. Quum esset pusillus, factus est cuiusdam viduae subditus; quumque in negotiis cupidus foenerator discurreret, coepit Christianorum conventibus assidue interesse, et ut erat astutior tenebrae filius, coepit nonnulla <e> collationibus Christianorum memoriae commendare, et inter suos brutos Arabes cunctis sapientior esse. Libidinis vero suae succensus fomite, patronam suam iure barbarico inire congressus est; mox erroris spiritus in speciem vulturis ei apparens, os aureum sibi ostendens, angelum Gabrielem esse dixit, et ut propheta in gente sua appareret impetravit.

3 Quumque repletus esset tumore superbiae, coepit inaudita brutis animalibus praedicare, et quasi ratione quadam,

History of Muhammad

The heresiarch Muhammad rose up in the time of the emperor Heraclius, in the seventh year of his reign. At that time, Bishop Isidore of Seville excelled in Catholic doctrine, and Sisebut held the throne in Toledo, the capital of the realm. A church in honor of the blessed Euphrasius was built over his tomb in the city of Iliturgi. Furthermore, in Toledo the church of the blessed Leocadia was enlarged with a high roof of wonderful workmanship by order of Sisebut. The aforementioned wicked prophet Muhammad held power for ten years and when that time had passed, he died and was buried in hell forever.

Muhammad's beginnings were these. When he was a lit- 2
tle boy, he was put in the charge of a certain widow. When, as an avaricious usurer, he was rushing around on business, he began assiduously to attend gatherings of Christians, and, as he was a most shrewd son of darkness, began to commit some <of> the words of the Christians to memory and became wiser than all among his fellow uncivilized Arabs. Fueled by lust, he had relations with his patroness, as was lawful among those barbarians. Soon after, the spirit of error appeared to him in the form of a vulture displaying its golden face to him. It said it was the angel Gabriel and persuaded him to manifest himself as a prophet among his people.

And since he was swollen with pride, he began to preach 3
unheard-of things to these brutish creatures and conveyed

ut ab idolorum cultu recederent, et Deum corporeum in caelis adorarent, insinuavit. Arma sibi credentibus assumere iubet, et quasi novo fidei zelo, ut adversarios gladio trucidarent, instituit. Occulto quoque Deus iudicio—qui olim per prophetam dixerat: *"Ecce ego suscitabo super vos Chaldaeos, gentem amaram et velocem, ambulantem super latitudinem terrae, ut possideat tabernacula non sua, cuius equi velociores lupis vespertinis, et facies eorum ventus urens"*—ad arguendos fideles et terram in solitudinem redigendam, nocere eos permittit. Primum namque fratrem imperatoris, qui illius terrae ditionem tenebat, interimunt, et ob tantum triumphum victoriae gloriosi effecti, apud Damascum Syriae urbem regni principium fundaverunt.

4 Psalmos denique idem pseudopropheta in honore insensibilium animalium composuit, vitulae scilicet rufae memoriam facientes; araneae quoque muscipulae ad capiendas muscas historiam texuit; upuppae namque et ranae edictiones quasdam componit, ut foetor unius ex eius ore eructaret, garrulitas vero alterius ab eius labiis non sileret. Alios quoque ad condimentum sui erroris in honorem Ioseph, Zachariae, sive etiam genitricis Domini Mariae, stilo suo digessit.

5 Quumque in tanto vaticinii sui errore sudaret, uxorem vicini sui nomine Zeid concupivit, et suae libidini subiugavit. Quod ille maritus eius sentiens exhorruit, eamque prophetae suo, cui contradicere non valebat, praetermisit; ille vero quasi ex voce Dominica in lege sua adnotari praecepit:

to them under the guise of reasonable argument that they should abandon the cult of idols and worship a corporeal God in heaven. He ordered those who believed in him to take up arms and, as if with newfound zeal of faith, he taught them to cut down their adversaries with the sword. With some secret judgment, God—who had once said through his prophet: *"For behold I will raise up over you the Chaldeans, a bitter and swift people, wandering over the breadth of the earth, to take possession of tents that are not their own, whose horses are swifter than wolves at night, and whose appearance is like the burning wind"*—so as to rebuke those of the true faith and to reduce the land to emptiness, God permitted this people to inflict injury. First they killed the brother of the emperor who held dominion over the land, and on account of this triumph they became boastful and set up the beginnings of their kingdom in the Syrian city of Damascus.

Then this same false prophet composed psalms in honor 4
of irrational animals, for instance, commemorating a red heifer. He also wove a story of a spider web, a trap for catching flies. He composed certain utterances of the hoopoe and the frog so that the stench of the one might belch forth from his mouth and the babbling of the other might never be silent on his lips. To season his error he composed others in his own style in honor of Joseph, Zacharias, and even the mother of the Lord, Mary.

And while he strove hard in the great error of his proph- 5
ecy, he lusted after the wife of a certain neighbor of his by the name of Zayd, and subjected her to his lust. Her husband, realizing this, was horrified and released her to his prophet, whom he could not refuse. Muhammad commanded that it be noted in his law as if from the voice of the

"Quumque mulier illa displicuisset in oculis Zeid, et eam repudiasset, sociavimus eam prophetae nostro in coniugium, quod ceteris in exemplum, et posteris fidelibus id agere cupientibus, non sit in peccatum."

6 Post cuius tanti sceleris factum mors animae et corporis illius simul appropinquavit. Quod ille interitum sibimet imminere persentiens, quia propria virtute se resurrecturum nullo modo sciebat, per angelum Gabrielem, qui ei in specie vulturis saepe apparere solitus erat, resuscitaturum tertia die praedixit; quumque animam inferis tradidisset, solliciti de miraculo quod eis pollicitus fuerat, ardua vigilia cadaver eius custodire iusserunt. Quem quum tertia die foetentem vidissent, et resurgentem nullo modo cernerent, angelos ideo non adesse dixerunt, quia praesentia suorum terrerentur. Invento mortuo salubri consilio, privatum custodia cadaver eius reliquerunt; statim vice angelica ad eius foetorem canes ingressi latus devoraverunt. Quod reperientes factum, residuum cadaveris eius humo dederunt; et ob eius vindicandam iniuriam, annis singulis canes occidere decreverunt: ut merito cum eo habeant illic participium, qui hic pro eo dignum meruerunt subire martyrium.

7 Digne ei quidem accidit ut canum ventrem tantus ac talis propheta repleret, qui non solum suam sed multorum animas inferis tradidisset. Multa quidem et alia scelera operatus est, quae non sunt scripta in libro hoc; hoc tantum scriptum est, ut legentes quantus hic fuerit agnoscant.

Lord, saying: "Since that woman was displeasing in the eyes of Zayd and he repudiated her, we joined her to our prophet in marriage, as an example to the others and to future followers wishing to do the same that it not be reckoned a sin."

After the commission of such an enormity, the death of 6
Muhammad's soul and of his body approached simultaneously. Sensing that his destruction was imminent, because he knew that he would in no way be resurrected on his own merit, he predicted that he would be resuscitated on the third day by the angel Gabriel, who had been in the habit of appearing to him in the guise of a vulture. When he had given up his soul to hell, they gave orders to guard his body with an arduous vigil, apprehensive about the miracle that he had promised them. When on the third day they saw that he was rotting, and discerned that he would not by any means rise again, they said the angels were not present because they were frightened by the presence of the people. Having come up with a serviceable explanation about the dead man, they left his cadaver unguarded, and immediately instead of angels, dogs followed his stench and devoured his flank. Learning of the deed, they surrendered the rest of his body to the earth. And in vindication of this injury, they ordered dogs to be killed every year so that they, who on his behalf deserved to undergo worthy martyrdom here, might rightly share in his lot there.

It was appropriate that such a great prophet fill the stom- 7
achs of dogs, a prophet who had surrendered not only his own soul, but those of many, to hell. Indeed, he performed many other such sins that are not recorded in this book. This much is written so that those reading may take the measure of the man.

TULTUSCEPTRU
FROM THE BOOK OF LORD METOBIUS

Tultusceptru de Libro Domini Metobii

Papa Osius episcopus dum angelum domini vidisset ad se loquentem . . . qui angelus dixit illi: "Vade et dic ad satrapes meos qui stant in Erribon quorum dedi dura facie et indomabile corde velut silice velut habitantes qui sunt in eremo, ad quos ego mitto te ad gentem apostatricem. Recesserunt a me patres eorum, praevaricati sunt pactum meum; filii autem eorum perseverant <in> inpudicitiis et negotiis periurantibus nomen meum, sed vade et dic eis: 'Qui audit audiat et qui quiescit quiescat, quoniam ecce domus domini exasperata est.' Et dic eis: 'Nolite esse increduli sed fideles.'"

2 Et dum ambularet ut enarraret verba domini ad eos infirmatus est et vocatus a domino. Et praecepit unum de monachis suis cui nomen erat Ocim ut pergeret in Erribon ut loqueretur ad eos verba quae angelus domini praeceperat loquere ad papam Osium episcopum; qui puer <cui> nomen erat Ozim dum audisset verba doctoris sui quae narraverat ei angelus domini . . . dum pergeret et diceret satrapum eorum ad quem ordinatus fuerat . . . dum ascenderet in Erribon invenit angelum tentationis stantem in arborem ilicis, habentem similitudinem angeli.

3 Sic dixit illi angelus malignus qui stabat ante eum: "Quis vocaris?" Ille respondit: "Ozim vocor qui missus sum a papa Osio doctore meo ut enarrem verba quae mihi locutus est

Tultusceptru from the Book of Lord Metobius

Father Osius the bishop, when he had seen the angel of the Lord speaking to him. . . . The angel said to him: "Go and speak to my satraps who dwell in Erribon, to whom I have given hard faces and hearts indomitable as flint, like those living in the desert; I send you to them, to a people who apostatized. Their fathers receded from me. They violated my pact. Their children have persisted <in> shameless acts and in business dealings that perjure my name. But go and tell them, 'he who will hear, let him hear, and he who will be still, let him be still. For lo, the house of the Lord is wrathful.' And say to them: 'Be not unbelievers but believers.'"

2 When Osius set out to speak the words of the Lord to them, he became ill and was summoned by the Lord. And he ordered one of his monks whose name was Ocim to go forth to Erribon and speak to them the words that the angel of the Lord had ordered Father Bishop Osius to speak. The boy, <whose> name was Ozim, heard the words of his teacher, the words which the angel of the Lord had narrated to him . . . and set off to tell their satrap to whom he had been sent. . . . When he went up to Erribon, he found, standing by an oak tree, an angel of temptation who resembled an angel.

3 The evil angel who stood before him said to him: "What is your name?" Ozim responded: "I am called Ozim. I have been sent by my teacher Father Osius to speak the words

quod ei angelus domini praeceperat loqui hacc; sed quia vocationis dies invenit eum, nunc spiritus eius caelestia regna vocatus est." Sic locutus est angelus malignus dicens ei: "Ego sum angelus qui missus sum ad papam Osium episcopum, sed dicam tibi verba quae praedices satrapum eorum, ad quos missus es." Et dixit ei: "Non vocaris Ozim sed Mahomad."

4 Et illi inposuit nomen angelus qui se illi ostendit et praecepit illi dicere ut credant: *"alla occuber alla occuber situ leila citus est mohamet razulille."* Et non sciebat ille monachus quia daemones invocabat, quia omnis *alla occuber* advocatio daemonum est, quia iam cor eius praevaricatus fuerat ab inmundo spiritu et verba quae ei dominus narraverat per doctorem suum oblivioni traditum fuerat. Et dum esset vas Christi factum est vas Mamonae ad perditionem animae suae, unde et omnes <qui> in errore conversi sunt et eos qui persuasione suaserunt manipula incendii nuncupantur.

that he spoke to me, for the angel of the Lord had ordered him to speak these words, but the day of his summons came and his spirit was called to the celestial kingdom." Then the evil angel spoke, saying to him: "I am the angel who was sent to Father Bishop Osius. I will tell you the words that you are to preach to the satraps to whom you are sent." And he said to him: "You are not called Ozim but Muhammad."

The angel who had revealed himself to him imposed this 4
name on him and ordered him to say, so that the satraps might believe: *"Alla occuber alla occuber situle ilacitus est mohamet razulille."* The monk did not know that by so doing he was invoking demons, for every *alla occuber* is a summoning of demons, because already his heart had been turned away by the unclean spirit and the words that the Lord had narrated to him through his teacher had been lost to oblivion. And so, although he was a vessel of Christ, he became a vessel of Mammon to the ruin of his soul, and all who converted to this error and those whom they induced to do so by persuasion, are said to be sheaves for burning.

CHRONICLE OF THEOPHANES

Anastasius the Librarian

Theophanis Chronographia

Mundi anno VICXXII, divinae incarnationis anno DCXXII, anno vero imperii Heraclii vicesimo primo, Iohannes papa Romanus habebatur. Hoc etiam anno Muamed Saracenorum, qui et Arabum, princeps et pseudopropheta moritur promoto Abubacharo, cognato suo, ad principatum suum. Ipsoque tempore venit auditio eius, et omnes extimuerunt.

2 At vero decepti Hebraei in principio adventus eius aestimaverunt esse illum qui ab eis expectatur Christus ita, ut quidam eorum, qui intendebant ei, accederent ad ipsum et eius religionem susciperent, Mosis inspectoris dei dimissa. Erant autem numero decem qui hoc faciebant, cum ipso quoque degebant usque ad caedem eius. Porro, cum aspicerent eum comedentem de camelo, cognoverunt quod non esset quem aestimabant; et haesitabant quid agerent, et religionem eius dimittere formidantes miseri docent eum contra nos Christianos illicita et conversabantur cum ipso.

3 Necessarium autem reor enarrandum de generatione huius ita. Ex una generalissima tribu oriundus erat, Hismahelis videlicet, filii Abrahae. Nizarus enim, Hismahelis pronepos, pater eorum omnium ducitur. Hic gignit filios duos, Mudarum scilicet et Rhabian. Mudarus gignit Curasum et Kaison et Theomimen et Asadum et alios ignotos. Hi omnes habitabant Madianiten heremum et in ea nutriebant pecora in tabernaculis conversantes. Sunt autem et his interiores,

Chronicle of Theophanes

In the year 6122 since the world's creation, 622 since the divine incarnation, and the twenty-first year of Heraclius's rule, John was elected pope in Rome. In this year also died Muhammad, ruler and false prophet of the Saracens, also known as Arabs, after appointing his relative ʾAbū Bakr as his successor. In this same period rumor of him spread, and everyone became afraid.

2 At his first appearance, the Hebrews were deceived and thought that he was the Messiah they expected, so that some of them, who were well-disposed toward him, followed him and accepted his religion, while giving up that of Moses, who had seen God. Those who did this were ten in number, and they remained with Muhammad until his murder. But as soon as they saw him eating camel meat, they realized that he was not the man they thought he was, and they were unsure what to do; as they, wretches, were afraid to give up his religion, they taught him unlawful behavior toward us Christians and remained with him.

3 I think it is necessary to explain his ancestry in detail. He came from a widespread tribe, that of Ishmael the son of Abraham, for Ishmael's great-grandson Nizār is considered to be the father of all Arabs. He had two sons, Muḍar and Rabīʿa. Muḍar begat Quraysh, Qays, Tamīm, ʾAsad, and others, who are unknown. All of them lived in the desert of Midian, kept cattle, and dwelt in tents. There are also some

qui non sunt de tribu ipsorum, sed ex Iectan: videlicet hi qui vocitantur Ammanitae, id est Homiritae. Quidam sane ipsorum negotiabantur in camelis suis.

4 Cum autem inops et orphanus praedictus esset Moamed, visum est sibi ad quamdam introire mulierem locupletem et cognatam suam, nomine Chadigan, mercennarius ad negotiandum cum camelis apud Aegyptum et Palaestinam. Paulatim autem fiducia penes ipsam percepta mulierem, quae vidua erat, et accepit eam uxorem, et habuit camelos illius atque substantiam.

5 Cumque veniret in Palaestinam, conversabatur cum Iudaeis et Christianis. Capiebat autem ab eis quasdam scripturas. Porro habebat passionem epilepsiae. Quo comperto huius coniux oppido tristabatur, utpote nobilis et quae se huiusmodi copularit, egeno scilicet et epileptico. Procurat vero ipse placare illam taliter dicens quia "Visionem quamdam angeli Gabrielis dicti contemplor et haud ferens huius aspectum mente deficio et cado." Ipsa vero, cum haberet adulterum quemdam propter infidelitatem ibidem exulem habitantem, amicum suum, indicavit ei omnia et nomen angeli.

6 At ille volens eam reddere certam dixit ei: "Veritatem locutus est, etenim iste angelus mittitur ad cunctos prophetas." Ipsa ergo prima suscepto pseudomonachi verbo credidit ei et praedicavit id aliis mulieribus contribulibus suis, prophetam eum esse; et taliter ex feminis fama venit ad viros, primo dumtaxat ad Abubacharum, quem et successorem dimisit. Et tenuit haeresis eius partes Aethribi postremo per bellum. Nam primum quidem occulte annis decem, et bello similiter decem, et manifeste novem.

who live deeper in the desert than they, but are not of their tribe, but of that of Joktan: those who are called Yemenites, that is, Ḥimyarites. Some of them conducted trade by camel.

Since the aforementioned Muhammad was an orphan 4
and poor, he decided to go to a certain wealthy woman, a relative of his named Khadīja, to be hired to conduct trade by camel in Egypt and Palestine. Gradually he gained the trust of that woman, who was a widow, and he married her, and acquired her camels and property.

When he went to Palestine he associated with Jews and 5
Christians, and got hold of certain writings from them. Then he suffered an epileptic seizure, and when his wife found out about this she became very upset, since she was noble and had now joined herself in marriage to a man who was both poor and an epileptic. He took care to put her at ease with the following words: "I witness a kind of vision of the angel called Gabriel, and since I cannot bear the sight of him, I faint and collapse." Now, she had befriended a certain adulterer who had been living there in exile on account of his unfaithfulness, and she intimated to him every detail, including the name of the angel.

Wanting to reassure her, he said to her: "He has spoken 6
the truth, for this is the angel sent to all the prophets." Upon hearing this statement of the false monk, she was the first to believe Muhammad, and proceeded to proclaim to the other women of her tribe that he was a prophet. In this way, the rumor reached the men through the women, but ʾAbū Bakr first of all, whom he also sent forth as his successor. At last his heresy took hold of the remaining parts of the land of Yathrib through war. First it was practiced in secret for ten years, by war for another ten, and openly for nine.

7 Docuit autem auditores suos quod qui occidit inimicum vel ab inimico occiditur in paradisum ingrediatur. Paradisum vero carnalis cibi ac potus et commixtionis mulierum perhibebat fluviumque vini ac mellis et lactis et feminarum—non praesentium sed aliarum—et mixturam multorum annorum futuram et affluentem voluptatem nec non et alia quaedam luxuria et stultitia plena, compati tamen invicem et auxiliari patienti.

8 Porro eodem anno natus est in Oriente David, filius eius, eademque die natus est Heraclius, filius Heraclii iunioris, qui et Constantinus appellatus est, et baptizatus est a Sergio patriarcha.

Muhammad taught those who listened to him that he who killed an enemy or was killed by one would enter paradise. He said that paradise was one of earthly food and drink and intercourse with women, and that there was a river of wine, honey, and milk, and that there would be intercourse that would last many years and continuous pleasure with women—not those of this world, but others—as well as other things full of lust and foolishness. Yet he also taught them to have sympathy for one another and to help those who suffer. 7

In the same year a son, David, was born to Heraclius in the East, while on the same day Heraclius, the son of the younger Heraclius (also called Constantine), was born and baptized by Patriarch Sergius. 8

LIFE OF MUHAMMAD

Embrico of Mainz

Vita Mahumeti

Heu! Quot sunt stulti miseranda fraude sepulti
contemptaque Dei cognitione rei,
qui Christum spernunt cuius miracula cernunt—
quem Dominum solum iam tremit omne solum.
Unde magis gentes se damnant insipientes
quod Christum rident dum sua regna vident.
Nam qui viderunt hunc passum nec potuerunt
credere, stultitia sic redimunt vitia.
Sed ne delinquam, quoniam modo taliter inquam,
neve tuendo reos sim reus inter eos,
Christum sprevisse crimen contendo fuisse;
sed qui desipuit, sic veniale fuit.
At scelus est triste non nunc tibi credere, Christe,
utque loquar tuto, nec veniale puto.
nam facinus tale, tam dirum, tam capitale,
quis dignum venia crederet esse pia?
Hos autem dignos aeterna morte malignos,
iudice me capiet atque vorax rapiet
infimus infernus, nec qui satiatur Avernus.
Vixque potest scribi quid patiantur ibi:
ignis eos torret—ad quod mihi iam cutis horret,
res equidem sonitu, res gravis admonitu.
Illos infestant miseros vicibusque molestant
igneus inde vigor, frigoris inde rigor,

Life of Muhammad

Alas! How many fools are buried in a pitiable lie! Sinners who have scorned the knowledge of God reject Christ although they see his miracles—a lord who alone makes the whole earth tremble. The foolish peoples damn themselves even more because they laugh at Christ although they see his realms. For those who saw him suffering, and could not believe, atone for their sins with their stupidity. But so as not to err, while speaking now on this subject, and so as not to gaze at sinners while being one of them, I hold that to have rejected Christ was a crime, but the foolishness of this makes the sin pardonable. But it is a sad crime not to believe in you now, Christ, and to be safe I would say that I do not think it can be pardoned. For who would think that an offense of this sort, so dreadful, so capital, would deserve compassionate forgiveness? These evil men deserve eternal death, in my judgment: the deep, hungry inferno, insatiable Avernus, will seize them and bear them away.

It is scarcely possible to set down what they suffer there: fire scorches them—my skin already shivers, for me the matter is fearsome to hear or to call to mind. Blazing fire on one side and stiff frost on the other will in turn harass

nam sic damnantur ut frigora nunc patiantur,
alternaque vice sulphura mixta pice.
Vermis eos rodit quos omnipotens Deus odit
poenaque fit pravis multiplicata gravis.
Ignis ibi spissus quem taetra revolvit abyssus.
Numquam grata dies est ibi, nulla quies!
Ultima—quid servo?—res huic accedit acervo
cunctis praefatis plus miseranda satis:
semper lugere, cruciatus fine carere
—hoc vere gravius et miserabilius!
Quae cum narrare nullus queat aut numerare,
cur ego dinumero cum careant numero?
Sed male secura gens, flebiliter peritura,
perfidia tabens, nil rationis habens,
si posset scire sic se debere perire,
haec puto desereret et sibi consuleret.
Linqueret errorem te, Christe, sequens meliorem
consuleretque sibi vota ferendo tibi.
Sed sunt pagani, qui spe luduntur inani,
qui quodcumque volunt pro deitate colunt.
Nec gens errore seducitur ista minore,
de qua proposui scribere ceu potui.
Ipsa Iovis mundum, fratris negat esse profundum,
Plutoni Stygium detrahit imperium.
Et reputat vanam rem cum Iunone Dianam,
nec facit eximium Palladis ingenium.
Martem cum Venere dicit deitate carere
et negat esse deum cum Proteo Nereum.
Divos campestres, vel montanos vel agrestes,
nobiscum superos esse putat miseros.

and torment them, for they are condemned to suffer cold alternating with sulfur mixed with pitch. The worm will gnaw those hated by omnipotent God. Harsh punishment is multiplied for the depraved. There the black abyss whirls thick fire. There is never pleasant daylight there, no rest! To this heap is added a last matter—why do I delay—much more pitiable than the ones mentioned above: perpetual mourning, no end to tortures—this is indeed more oppressive and more pitiful!

When no man can tell of or count these things, why do I enumerate things that lack number? An unwisely carefree people that will perish woefully wastes away in faithlessness, lacking reason. If they could know that they must perish in this fashion, I think they would abandon these ways and act to their own advantage. They would leave their error, following you, Christ, a better choice, and by praying to you they would act to their own advantage.

But pagans exist, deceived by empty hope, who worship whatever they please as a god. And this people, about whom I undertake to write as I am able, have been seduced by an error that is at least as great. They deny that the world belongs to Jove, the depths to his brother; they steal Pluto's Stygian empire from his grasp. They deem Diana and Juno alike to be vanity, nor do they consider Athena's genius to be great. They say that Mars and Venus lack divinity and deny that Nereus and Proteus are gods. They consider the rural divinities, whether of the mountains or the field, to be

Quicquid et antiquae fuit olim fraudis ubique
horum sub titulis viluit his populis.
Haec execrantur et eos, haec qui venerantur.
Nos quoque confutant et miseros reputant
vivere, dicentes sicut faenum comedentes,
aeque Iudaeos Christicolasque reos.
Se dicunt sapere sed nos ratione carere
et nos sicut eos dicimus esse reos,
sic insensatos nos illi seque beatos,
dicentes vere se Dominum colere,
qui Deus in caelo iusto regat omnia zelo.
Sed gens revera non colit hunc misera.
Hinc si quaeratur quis sit quem sic veneratur,
nomen habet Mahumet, quo duce fisa tumet.
Illi cunctorum cessit cultura deorum,
qui tenet ut proprium perfidiae solium.
Expulit errores error novus iste priores,
et Mahumet soli sunt data regna doli.
At tu summorum speculum, Godebolde, virorum,
quod fuerit quaeris principium sceleris
primaque tantorum fuerit quae causa malorum.
Praecipis, expediam; praecipis, et faciam,
conveniens esse quoniam reor, immo necesse,
ut quaecumque sciam quae iubeas faciam.
Quodsi dignatur Deus ut coeptum peragatur,
dum tua iussa sequor, sic lege nostra, precor,
ne transcribantur aut a multis videantur!
Nostra timent vitia publica iudicia.
Haec sed omittamus et ad inceptum redeamus,
quod, rogo, iudicio perlege propitio!

wretched gods, as we do. Whatever ancient deceit existed at a remote time everywhere under these names has no worth for these peoples. They abominate those things and the people who revere them. And they also refute us and consider both Jews and Christians miserable sinners who, they say, live as animals eating straw. They say that they themselves are wise and that we are mad and that we are sinners, just as we say they are. They say that we are senseless and they are blessed, and that they truly worship the Lord who is God in heaven and rules all things with zeal for justice. But in truth this wretched people does not worship him.

Therefore if someone asks who it is that they worship in this way, his name is Muhammad, and trusting in this leader they swell with pride. The worship of all gods yielded to him who holds the throne of faithlessness as his own. This new error drove out the earlier errors, and the realms of deceit were given to Muhammad alone.

But you, Godebold, mirror for the most eminent men, ask what was the beginning of this sin and what was the first cause of such great evils. You command, I will dispatch; you order, and I will perform, since I think it is fitting, or rather necessary, that to the extent of my knowledge I should do what you order. But if God grants that this plan be carried out, while I am following your orders, read my words but, I pray, let them not be copied or seen by many people! My shortcomings fear public judgments. But let us skip this and return to the project at hand, which I beg you to read through with favorable judgment.

Plus nocet, ut nostis, ad cuncta domesticus hostis,
et res ipsa docet qualiter ille nocet.
Nam male devotus quidam, baptismate lotus,
plenus perfidia vixit in ecclesia,
per magicas fraudes quaerens hominum sibi laudes
ut sua per studia corruat ecclesia.
Quod dum celabat et caute dissimulabat,
ceu lupus ecclesiis sedit in insidiis,
dulci sermone ficta quoque religione
blanditus populo sub fidei titulo.
Falsus ad hoc testis accesserat horrida vestis,
fota cibis raro marcida paene caro.
Qui procul a ludo fugiens ibat pede nudo,
obstipo rite cuncta loquens capite.
Quando pergebat coram, sua labra movebat
ut sanctum teneat quisquis eum videat.
Sed, suspirando, si tolleret hic aliquando
summissos oculos concitet ut populos,
tunc exaltabat palmas vocemque levabat—
non pro se maerens sed populi miserens.
Nam de se tutus nihil est vel pauca locutus,
tantum pro populo corde rogans tremulo.
Illius unde fidem plebs admirans sacra pridem
in Hierosolymis est prope capta dolis.
Nam cum transisset pater illius urbis et isset
in caelum, subito corpore deposito,
tunc exaltari magus hic et pontificari
adspirans avide se tamen haec pavide
dixit facturum nisi sciret non nociturum
si praesul fiat, cum Deus hoc cupiat:

As you know, an enemy in one's own house does more harm in every way, and the matter at hand teaches how it harms. For a certain man, lacking in devotion but cleansed by baptism, lived in the church, though completely faithless, seeking men's praises for himself through magic deception and bringing the Church's ruin by his efforts.

As long as he concealed and carefully dissimulated this, he lay in wait for the Church like a wolf, flattering the people with his sweet discourse and his pretended observance under the name of faith. His rough garment bore false witness to this, and also his almost rotting flesh, rarely nourished with food. He kept far away from amusement and would walk barefoot, uttering all statements with suitably downward-bent head. When he walked in public, he would move his lips so that whoever saw him would hold him to be a holy man. But whenever, with sighs, he would raise his lowered gaze to rouse the people, then he would lift up his palms and raise his voice—not as a man grieving for his own sake, but having pity on the people. For he played it safe and spoke little or nothing on his own behalf, rather he only pleaded on the people's behalf with a trembling heart.

For this reason the holy populace at Jerusalem long ago was amazed at his faith and were almost taken in by his tricks. For when the patriarch of that city passed away and went to heaven after a sudden death, this mage then aspired eagerly to be exalted and to act as pontiff. However, he said that he feared to do this unless he knew that he would do no harm if he became a prelate, since God desired this:

"Nil equidem gravius quam sarcina nominis huius,
ad quod pondus," ait, "me Deus ipse trahit."
Sed Deus inspector cordis iustus quoque rector,
ut pius utque scius, consuluit melius.
Nam quod praefatus cupiebat homo sceleratus
Christo displicuit nec fieri potuit.
Tunc rex invictus Theodosius et benedictus,
hostis perfidiae, filius Ecclesiae,
summus erat regum. Sub quo sacra sanctio legum
praedictante pio floruit Ambrosio.
Hic cum scivisset quod tantus praesul obisset,
festinans abiit qua pater hic obiit.
Et tandem multo cum luctu patre sepulto,
Christum supplicibus consuluit precibus
ut sibi monstraret quem digne pontificaret.
Cui sic insonuit vox et eum monuit:
"Ne credas turbae, latet hostis ut anguis in urbe!"
Vox ut conticuit, rex tacitus stupuit.
Quid sit miratur, tamen ignorans veneratur
Et replicat monitus talibus attonitus.
Sed cito plebs solvit quae rex dubitata revolvit.
Simplex delirum nam rapit ipsa virum
et, velut invitum, secum pertraxit iniquum
ante fores regis. Simplicis ergo gregis
dum male consultus fremit hic sine lege tumultus,
rex quaerit strepitus quid velit insolitus.
Cui quidam fatur: "Plebs te prodire precatur."
Rex sicut petitur, protinus egreditur.
Quem magus egressum cernens stupet et cito gressum
flexit nam vere tunc voluit fugere.

"For my part, I find nothing more oppressive than the burden of this title, to which burden," he said, "God himself is compelling me." But God who sees into the heart and governs justly, since he is compassionate and discerning, had a better plan. For what that wicked man desired was not pleasing to Christ and could not happen.

At that time the unconquered and blessed King Theodosius, the enemy of faithlessness, the Church's own son, was the most exalted of kings. Under his rule the holy ordinance of the laws flourished through the preaching of holy Ambrose. When Theodosius learned that the great prelate had died, he hastened to the place where that father had died. And when that father had at last been buried with much mourning, he asked advice of Christ with suppliant prayer, pleading to be shown who deserved to be made pontiff. A voice sounded forth to him and warned him thus: "Don't believe the throng, an enemy lies hidden in the city like a serpent!" And when the voice fell silent, the king was astonished and said nothing. He wondered what it could be, but nevertheless, without knowing, he worshipped, and he thought over the warnings again, astounded by them.

But soon the common people resolved the king's doubtful hesitation. For simple as they were, they seized that madman and, as though he were unwilling, they dragged that scoundrel along with them up to the king's door. And so while the ill-advised and lawless tumult of the simple flock sounded, the king asked what was the meaning of this unusual clamor. Someone said to him: "The common people are begging that you come out." Just as he was asked, the king went directly out.

When the mage saw that the king had come out, he was silent, and he quickly turned away for then he truly did wish

Nec quid vidisset, scio, propter quod timuisset.
Hoc patet: invitus hunc fuit intuitus.
Nam nota palloris dat in ipso signa timoris.
Unde libens fugeret si populus sineret.
Qui sic dicebat luctanti quem retinebat:
"Quamvis lucteris, tu pater urbis eris!"
Utque retraxerunt, hunc pontificem petierunt
laudantes equidem verba virique fidem.
Pro quo de more dum perstrepit aula favore,
infremuit subitus et favor insolitus:
nam non humanis ululatibus, immo profanis,
ut plebs conticuit, ipsa domus fremuit,
huc quia venerunt toto quaecumque fuerunt
mundo daemonia, turba magi socia.
Audiit ut tantum plebs murmur vociferantum,
sternitur atque tacet, dum stupefacta iacet.
Quam rex signavit signoque crucis revocavit
atque rogans Dominum reddat ut his animum
aulam mundavit populumque Deo reparavit,
et male praesagum talibus inde magum
vocibus affatur: "Quid nunc tua fraus operatur,
insidiosa lues? Haec tua facta lues!
Nam qui damnosum sibi te scit et insidiosum,
cum te discutiet tunc male percutiet!
Utque Deus verus tibi sit magis inde severus,
nunc ego parco tibi, sed patieris ibi
perpetuo digne quando cruciaberis igne.
Qua veniam cupies nec tamen invenies.
I procul, immitis! Dignissima victima Ditis!
Eminus hinc fugias! Quod nisi iam facias,

to flee. I know he saw nothing that should have caused him to fear. This is evident: he did not wish to see the king. For the mark of his paleness signaled his fear. Hence he would willingly have fled the place if the people had let him.

The people spoke thus to the struggling man that they were holding: "Although you struggle, you will be the city's father!" And as they held him back they sought to make him pontiff, praising the man's words and his faith insistently. And while the hall was resounding with applause for him in the usual way, a sudden and unusual applause roared forth: for it was not with human cries, but with unholy ones, that the building itself roared as the common people fell silent, because all the world's demons had come to this place, a multitude of allies for the mage.

When the common people heard such a great rumbling of shouting voices, they were subdued, and stunned, they remained passive in silence. The king made the sign of the cross and with this called them back, and, begging the Lord to restore their courage, he cleansed the hall and returned the people to God, and he addressed the wickedly prophetic mage thus: "What has your deceit achieved now, you insidious corrupter? Your deeds are corruption itself! For he who knows that you are ruinous and treacherous to him will strike you severely when he dispels you! And so that the true God may be the more severe with you on this account, I will spare you now, but you will suffer there when you will be tortured with eternal fire as you deserve. There you will desire forgiveness but you will not find it. Go far away, you cruel man! You richly deserve to be a victim of Pluto! May you flee far from here! If you do not do so soon,

quae sit nostrorum sententia iudiciorum,
tunc volo comperias. Ergo cito fugias."
Inde suis fatur: "Iubeo procul hic rapiatur!"
Mox, igitur, rapitur atque foras trahitur.
Sic dolus antiquus, sic pestis, et hostis iniquus
fallere non potuit, fallere quos voluit.
Qui tamen abstractus et longius ire coactus,
hanc ignominiam dixit in Ecclesiam:
"Ipse reportabo, neque sic, sed centuplicabo.
Vestra sit eximia nunc licet ecclesia
sentiet illa minas nostras—patiendo ruinas:
cum sua posteritas victa mihi meritas
exsolvet poenas et—uti desidero, plenas."
In quo praesagus—heu!—fuit iste magus.
Si quaeris testem, paganam respice pestem.
Cuius nequitiae signa manent hodie.
Nam gens exosa Christo, gens perniciosa,
gens Mahumet parens et ratione carens,
certat adhuc stultum defendere sedula cultum.
Cur perit illa, scio, perpete supplicio.
Causa mali talis magus iste fuit specialis,
quem pro perfidia depulit ecclesia.
Qui pulsus, dira flagrans exaestuat ira,
et rabida vadens perditione madens
in Libyam cursus detorquet, ut impius ursus.
Et tunc in Libya floruit ecclesia.
Africa florebat et Christo vota ferebat.
Sed bene quem coluit—Heu!—cito deseruit!
Nam modo, praedicta, veniens magus, urbe relicta,
hanc quoque rite piam saevit in ecclesiam.

I desire that you learn the verdict of our judgments. Therefore, may you flee quickly." And then he said to his men: "I order you to take him far away!" Soon, therefore, he was seized and brought outside.

And so the ancient deceiver, the corrupter, the wicked enemy was not able to trick those whom he wished to trick. Although they had dragged him out and forced him to go far away, he told of this disgrace for the Church: "I myself will come back, and not thus, but multiplied a hundredfold. Although your Church is great now it will nevertheless feel my threats—it will suffer great losses: since its vanquished posterity will pay to me the deserved punishment—in full, as I desire."

Alas! In this that mage was prophetic. If you want a witness, look at the scourge of the pagans. The signs of the mage's wickedness remain today. For a people loathing Christ, a ruinous people, a people obeying Muhammad and lacking reason, strives stubbornly to this day to defend its foolish worship. For this reason, I know, they perish with eternal punishment.

This mage was the special cause of such evil, a man whom the Church had expelled for his faithlessness. He had been driven away, and so he seethed and blazed with dreadful anger, and, drunk with frenzied damnation, he departed and changed course and went to Libya, like a reckless bear. In those days, the Church was flourishing in Libya. Africa was prospering and praying to Christ. It worshipped him well, but—Alas!—deserted him quickly! For as soon as the mage came to Africa, after leaving the aforementioned city behind, he raged also against the African Church, correct in its devotion.

Hic etenim sancte se vivere finxit, ut ante.
Quod bene dum simulat, arte malum cumulat.
Nam meditans caedes animarum consulis aedes
—hostis—ut hospes init. Consul eum recipit;
hospite gaudebat quia tam reverenter habebat
omnes Christicolas utpote caelicolas.
Unde magum fovit cuius ieiunia novit,
et vidit ritus atque sacros habitus.
Nam vivebat ita sceleratus simplice vita
simplex apparens et, quasi, felle carens,
quod flos illarum dictus fuit ecclesiarum.
Nullus enim poterat scire magus quod erat.
Quare praefatus dives magis hunc veneratus
dilexit, timuit, utque pium tenuit.
Cui bene credebat, hic servum dives habebat
nomine Mammutium, cuius id officium
res dispensare domini super haec vigilare.
Haec lex officii curaque Mammutii.
Qui procuravit et supra cetera cavit,
ut sic praefato serviat ipse mago
quod sibi cuncta daret quae vellet, nulla negaret,
et quae praeciperet omnia mox faceret.
Hunc magus amplectens et amicitia sibi nectens,
multis blanditiis atque veneficiis,
alligat ut captum quia Mammutium videt aptum
materiam fieri proposito sceleri.
Haec igitur verba iactabat voce superba:
"Nunc sodes quaere quod placet eligere!
Elige! Lecta dabo quaesitaque multiplicabo.
Et quicquid quaeres, me tribuente feres!"

Here he again feigned a holy life, as before. And while he successfully deceived, with skillful artifice he piled up evils. Planning the slaughter of souls, he—the enemy—entered the house of a consul as a guest. The consul who received him rejoiced in the guest because he reverently held all Christians to be denizens of heaven. For this reason he cherished the mage whose fasting he knew and whose observances and holy demeanor he saw. For this wicked man appeared to live a simple life and, as it were, to lack venom, so that he was said to be the flower of those churches. Indeed, no one knew that he was a mage. And for this reason that rich man esteemed him highly, loved him, respected him, and considered him devout.

And that rich man had a trusted servant by the name of Mammutius, whose duty it was to administer the properties of his master and to watch over them. This was the rule of his duty and his care. And Mammutius procured and was careful above all else to serve the mage also. He would give him everything that he wanted, denying him nothing, and he would perform all the mage's commands without delay. The mage embraced this man and bound him to himself with friendship, with much poisonous flattery as though captive, because he saw Mammutius as a suitable tool for the crime he was planning.

Therefore he proudly boasted: "Now please choose what you like! Choose! I will give you what you choose and I will multiply the things you seek. Whatever you seek I shall bestow on you, and you will have it!" When the mage made

Ut magus haec pactus fuit, illo stetit stupefactus
quaerens quid cupiat, quid sibi conveniat.
Et tandem dixit: "Pater, ad tua verba revixit
mens mea. Quod quaero si fieri potero,
nil aliud certe, rogo, contingat mihi per te
quam liber fieri praesidio celeri."
Ad quae praedictus respondit homo sceleratus:
"Compos ceu quaeris muneris huius eris.
Sed male me noscis, qui talia munera poscis.
An mihi difficile quod minimis facile?
Esset enim pronum tibi quemlibet hoc dare donum.
Sed tibi me vere plura libet facere.
Nam cum persona decet ut sint consona dona:
parva decent humiles; magna, mihi similes.
Consul eris per me—dixi tibi cetera ferme
quae dare proposui, sed melius tacui.
Et tamen hoc veniet. Sed quod dixi, modo fiet!"
Contra Mammutius intulit haec citius:
"Si tibi servus ero, non altera munera quaero;
nam bene liber ero, si tibi serviero."
At magus ut novit, sua mox praestigia movit,
et sic inmeritum Mammutii dominum
morbo percussit tantisque doloribus ussit
quod sibi mors levior, vita foret gravior.
Cumque moraretur nec tam subito moreretur,
quod non prompta fuit mors magus indoluit,
et secum fatur: "Nisi protinus hic moriatur,
tunc ego nil valeo, sed quid agam, teneo."
Hoc tacite dicto, replicat mox, sicut Erichtho,
sub recti specie murmura nequitiae.

this offer, Mammutius stood dumbfounded at this, wondering what he wanted, where his interests lay. At last he said: “Father, my mind has come alive again at your words. If I could become what I seek to be, then I certainly beg nothing other through your power than to become free with your swift assistance.”

At this the wicked man responded: “You will possess this reward as you wish. But you do not know me well, since you ask for such gifts. Or are things that are easy for the least of men difficult for me? It would have been easy for anyone to give you this gift. I want to do much more for you. For it is fitting that gifts be appropriate to the person: small things are appropriate for the humble; great things, for the likes of me. You will be consul through me—I nearly told you the other things that I planned to give you, but it is better that I kept silent. This too will come, however. But what I have said, will be done now!” And Mammutius quickly responded thus: “If I shall be your slave, I shall not ask for other gifts; for I will be free enough, if I am to serve you.”

But when the mage knew this, he soon implemented his sleight of hand, and he struck the innocent master of Mammutius with such an illness and burned him with such intense pains that death would have been gentler: life was more oppressive for him. And since the consul was lingering and did not die so suddenly, the mage was annoyed that the death was not quick, and he said to himself: “If this man does not die immediately then I am powerless, but I have a plan.”

When he had said this silently, with the appearance of an upright man he soon repeated, like Erichtho, the murmurs

Et surgens nocte subtraxit lumina docte
ut facerent tenebrae tale nefas celebre,
et quasi defunctos somno ligat ordine cunctos.
Quo facto, propius criminis it socius,
et sic exsertis umero tenus ipse lacertis
infirmum manibus conterit et genibus.
Huius et absque mora cum naribus obstruit ora
quae tunc spiramen vix movet. Ipse tamen
guttur ei fregit mortemque subire coegit,
reddens pro donis talia dona bonis.
Ergo redit gaudens et dicit, in hoc sibi plaudens:
"Nunc facto scelere, me puto proficere."
At postquam luxit Phoebus mundoque reduxit
luminis officium, consulis exitium
servis detegitur. Sed ubi multis aperitur,
fugit ab ore color insolitusque dolor
omnes confundit: hic flens sua pectora tundit.
Hic crines lacerat; quemque dolor macerat.
Hic gemit, hic plangit, omnes unus dolor angit.
Tunc quoque patroni mors miseranda boni
non solum flentes fertur movisse clientes,
flebant assidue sed simul hunc viduae,
et, luctu plenum, super omnia, vulgus egenum.
Maerebantque piae quaelibet ecclesiae:
omnis sanctorum cum clero grex monachorum.
Princeps, plebs humilis tunc fuit in lacrimis.
His quoque praefatus accessit homo sceleratus,
qui lacrimando madens inque dolendo cadens
exemplum flendi factus fuit atque dolendi,
quare nullus eum credidit esse reum.

of wickedness. Then he rose at night, and he cunningly removed the lights so that darkness made the unspeakable act notorious, and he bound each in turn with sleep as though dead. When this was done, he went nearer, a partner in crime, and when he had bared his arms up to his shoulders, he himself crushed the sick man with his hands and knees. Without delay he blocked the sick man's nose and mouth, although by that time he was barely breathing. In spite of this he himself broke the consul's throat and forced him to undergo death, repaying his generous gifts in this fashion. Then he returned happily and, congratulating himself on this, said: "Now that the crime has been performed, I think that I am making progress."

But after Phoebus shone and returned to the world the service of his light, the death of the consul was revealed to the slaves. But when it was disclosed to many, color fled from faces, and unaccustomed grief dismayed everyone: one man beat his chest weeping. One man tore his hair; everyone was worn down by grief. One man groaned, another mourned, one grief choked all. They also say that the pitiable death of the good lord stirred the feelings not only of his weeping vassals, but at the same time that widows mourned him constantly, and, above all, the impoverished masses were full of grief. Every devout church mourned: the whole flock of holy monks, together with the clergy. The ruler and the humble people were then in tears. To these was added the aforementioned sinner; streaming with tears and fainting with grief, he became an example of weeping and grieving, and for this reason no one thought that he was guilty.

Sed vir honoratus postquam fuerat tumulatus,
et dolor ut sedit, mens sua cuique redit.
Tunc magus inceptis magis insistebat ineptis
taliter afficiens arteque decipiens
consulis uxorem quod vix pateretur amorem
ni servum proprium nomine Mammutium,
quamvis invitum, festinet habere maritum.
Pro quo, praesagum consulit illa magum.
Cui, quasi prudenter, magus intulit haec reverenter:
"Istud si faceres, tu tibi consuleres.
Sed bene coepisti, si feceris ut voluisti.
Haec auctore Deo consilioque meo."
Illa redit gaudens et iam quodvis scelus audens,
dummodo Mammutium possit habere suum.
Impatiensque morae mox libertatis honore
donans Mammutium, detrahit officium
illi servile pro quo sibi reddit herile.
Atque suum dominum constituit famulum
nempe maritali taeda rituque iugali
huic se subposuit—heu!—quia depuduit.
Quod quamvis dicam, fateor tamen ipse pudicam
hanc et matronam rite fuisse bonam,
sed dolus antiquus, magus hanc decepit iniquus,
cui nec erat dirum mortificasse virum.
Sic ubi primatus iam fulsit honore beatus,
consul Mammutius, dives et eximius,
ad se damnatum vocat ille suum sceleratum
quem sic alloquitur: "Ecce tuus potitur
Mammutius per te promissis rebus aperte.
Consul dicor ego, me tamen esse nego.
Nam domini more nostro fungeris honore.
Noster honor tuus est, quippe, tuus meus est.

But after the man of high office had been buried, and as grief settled, everyone returned to his senses. Then the mage continued with his inappropriate plans by influencing and deceiving the consul's wife so that she could scarcely endure her love if she did not hasten to have her own slave by the name of Mammutius as her husband, even though he was unwilling. For this purpose, she took counsel with the prophetic mage. The mage, as if being prudent, responded deferentially: "If you do this, you will act in your own interest. And you have begun well, if you have done as you desired. I say this on God's authority and my own advice." She went away joyfully, ready to dare any crime, as long as she could have her Mammutius. Impatient at the delay, she soon granted Mammutius the honor of freedom, and she took away his duty as a slave and instead made him a master. She established a servant as her own lord, indeed, with the torch of marriage and the conjugal rite she subordinated herself to him—Alas!—because she lost her shame. Although I relate this, I myself do nevertheless acknowledge that this woman was chaste, a good and pious matron, but she was deceived by the ancient trickery of the wicked mage who had had no fear of killing her husband.

Thus when he was already happily distinguished by the office of command, Mammutius the consul, rich and great, called to himself that damned man, his own accomplice in crime, and said to him: "See how your Mammutius openly possesses the things that you promised. I am said to be a consul, but I deny that I am. For you will discharge my office as a master. My office is yours and, indeed, yours is mine.

Tu praedictabis, Pater, et facienda notabis
Praeceptoque tuo pareo continuo."
"Per me maiorem," magus inquit, "habebis honorem
si tibi quae iubeo, feceris, ut iubeo.
Haud ablactatum sed nunc de matre creatum
sume tibi vitulum! Res lateat populum!
Sumptum claudemus et nutriri faciemus
ut nulli pateat qua vitulus lateat.
Res tamen ut vere possit sine teste latere,
est opus arte mea. Fiet enim cavea
omnibus ignota sic et de luce remota
ut, quid ibi fiat, sol neque luna sciat.
Illic ponatur vitulus sed ne videatur!
Solus ibi lateat; nil nisi nos videat.
Neve repentina se prodat vox vitulina,
ne possit prodi, debet in ima fodi.
Curaque sit prima quod sic fodiatur in ima
aures ne populi vox feriat vituli!
Nos duo pascemus illum solique sciemus.
Nec res proficiet si vaga turba sciet.
Ast oculus quintus vitulum si viderit intus,
quintum post oculum scire putes populum.
Ergo fac celes et nulli dicta reveles!
Debes ipse tui calliditate frui!"
Mammutius stabat et respondere parabat,
sed magus hunc cohibet atque loqui prohibet.
"Non est dicendum nunc," inquit, "sed faciendum."
Quare Mammutius se rapit hinc citius
et iam nil fatur, solum facit et meditatur
compleat ut rite singula sollicite

You will instruct, Father, and will indicate what to do, and I will obey your command immediately."

"By my agency," the mage said, "you will have a higher office if you obey my commands, as I order. Take up a calf, not one that has been weaned but one that has just now been born of its mother! Conceal this affair from the people! When you have taken the calf, we will lock it up and feed it so that no one will know where it is hidden. Nevertheless, if this matter is to really have no witnesses, my art will be needed. A cave will be dug so unknown to all and so removed from the light that neither the sun nor moon will know what is done there. There we will place the calf, but let it not be seen! Let it be hidden alone there; it will see nothing but us. So that no sudden cry from the calf can betray it, so that no sound can be heard, we must dig down deep. Let our first task be to dig so deep that the calf's voice will not strike the ears of the people! We two will feed it, and we alone will know. Our cause will not advance if the fickle mob knows. If a fifth eye sees the calf inside, after the fifth eye you may assume that the people know. Therefore conceal it and tell my words to no one! You yourself should make use of your cunning!"

Mammutius stood there and prepared to answer, but the mage prevented him, forbidding him to speak. "It is not time for words," he said, "but for actions." Hence Mammutius quickly left the place and said nothing more, only acted and reflected so as to correctly carry out with care each

quae magus aptari praeceperat atque parari.
  Quaesivit vitulum. Res latuit populum.
Fodit speluncam, qualis, puto, non fuit umquam:
  caecam, terribilem, daemoniis habilem,
quae fuit infernis vicina, remota supernis
  et Stygio ritu taetra, timenda situ.
Carcere damnatus tali, vitulus modo natus
  clauditur et crebris pascitur in tenebris.
Paverunt usque magus illum Mammutiusque.
  His solis patuit res, alios latuit.
Soli paverunt vitulum solique scierunt,
  cum iam taurus erat qui vitulus fuerat.
Quem si spectares, taurum vix esse putares:
  dixisses potius: "daemonis est socius!"
Nam non taurina fuit illi, sed peregrina
  monstri forma novi nec simulanda bovi,
cornibus horrendus, plus rhinocerote timendus.
  Ignea lux oculi terror erat populi.
Horruit ipsarum quasi spinis forma genarum.
  Huic habuit nares bestia nulla pares.
Terribilis flatus, patulus fuit oris hiatus.
  Et rictus atri forma fuit baratri.
Vertex cristatus et equino more comatus.
  Colli magnifica formaque terrifica
exstabatque toris pectus sublime decoris
  —et conformis ibi vix fuit ipse sibi.
Neu ponam dorsum vel cetera membra seorsum.
  Dorso, poplitibus, cruribus et pedibus,
silvis exstanti fuit, ut puto, par elephanti.
  Et si quis quaerat, belua talis erat.

thing the mage ordered him to make ready. He procured the calf. The matter was concealed from the people. He dug a cave, such as, I think, there never has been: lightless, frightening, fit for demons, close to hell and far from the celestial regions, foul like Styx, fearsome in its location. The newborn calf was shut in, condemned to this prison, and it was fed in the thick darkness. Even the mage himself and Mammutius were afraid of it. The plan was known to them alone, and hidden from others. They alone fed the calf, and they alone knew when what had been a calf became a bull.

If you had seen it, you would scarcely have thought it to be a bull: you would have declared: "It is in league with demons!" For its shape was not a bull's, but that of a strange new monster not to be compared with a bull, fearsome with its horns, more terrifying than a rhinoceros. The fiery light of its eye was a terror for the people. Its very cheeks bristled as if with spines. No other beast had nostrils like these. Its breath was terrible, its mouth gaping open. Its jaws were like the black inferno. It had a tuft on its head like a horse's mane. Its neck was splendid but terrifying, and its rippling chest had a lofty beauty—something in which it was scarcely consistent with itself. I will not treat its back and its other members individually. As far as its back, knees, shins and feet, I think it was like an elephant standing taller than the jungle itself. If anyone asks, the beast was like this.

Interea flenda res accidit atque dolenda:
filius ecclesiae, rex obiit Libyae.
Qui dum vivebat suus orbis pace vigebat.
Non ibi nequitia sed pia iustitia.
Quid foret impietas nullius noverat aetas,
sed quid simplicitas, quid pietas, bonitas.
Nullus crudelis; in quemquam quisque fidelis
perfidiae vitium cavit ut exitium.
Fecerat hoc legis rigor et mens strenua regis.
Quo regnante, pia floruit ecclesia.
Ille velut custos, defendens undique iustos,
hostis, qua poterat, impietatis erat.
Desolatarum spes ille fuit viduarum,
amplectens miseros ceu proprios pueros,
illis solamen illis fuit ipse iuvamen,
esse sui similes quosque putans humiles.
Sic bonus ille bonis et amator religionis,
luctus materia fit moriendo pia.
O vere, pietas vix luctus dat sibi metas!
Flet robur iuvenum debilitasque senum.
Flet pietas matrum, maeret reverentia patrum
flentque simul teneri cum patribus pueri.
Africa maerebat, quia pro se quisque dolebat,
omnis Christicola, miles et agricola.
Par quoque servorum luctus fuit et dominorum;
maerebant inopes quique tenebat opes.
Maerebat clerus monachorum grexque severus
et quisquis coluit rite Deum doluit.
Nam tutela boni fuit huius vita patroni,
quo moriente, pia corruit ecclesia.

Meanwhile a sad and grievous thing happened: the King of Libya, the Church's own son, passed away. While he lived his region thrived and was at peace. There was no wickedness there, but justice with devotion. No one of any age had known what impiety was, but all knew simplicity, piety, and goodness. No one was cruel; everyone was true to everyone else and as wary of the vice of faithlessness as of death itself. The firmness of the law and the king's strong spirit achieved this. While he reigned, the devout Church flourished. He was like a guardian, defending just people everywhere, and wherever he was able, he was an enemy of impiety. He was the hope of destitute widows, he embraced the lowly as his own children, being for them a consolation and a help. He considered humble people his own peers.

And since he was so kind to virtuous people and a lover of religion, his death became a subject for pious grief. Truly, piety scarcely sets limits to its sorrow! Strong young men wept, and weak old men wept. Devout mothers wept, and respectable fathers grieved. Tender boys wept together with their fathers. Africa grieved, since each person mourned for himself, every Christian, knight and peasant. It was just as grievous for slaves as for masters; the poor and the rich mourned. The clergy mourned, and the austere band of monks and whoever worshipped God correctly grieved. For the life of this lord was a defense of the good, and when he died the devout church collapsed. The sad fates of both king

Sic lacrimis usque tristes casus utriusque
regis et ecclesiae flentur ubique pie.
Ergo, nimis multo cum luctu rege sepulto,
signant in tumulo scripta sub hoc titulo:
"TRES LUCTUS CAUSAE SUNT HOC SUB MARMORE CLAUSAE:
REX, DECUS ECCLESIAE, SUMMUS HONOR PATRIAE."
Ast ubi tantorum torrens abit ille dolorum,
instituit dubia concilium Libya
qua disceptatur, procerum quis constituatur,
quis sit rex Libyae, digna salus patriae.
Sic inter proceres regno dum quaeritur heres,
Mammutio socius haec ait ille suus:
"I, precor, et solito properans velocius ito
et pete concilium consiliis dubium!
Cum liceat fari tibi, fac me, quaeso, vocari,
nam scio me vere sic tibi proficere.
Sed loquerer plura, nisi forte forent nocitura.
Haec quoque dum moneo, te male detineo."
Omnia Mammutius mox ad verbum facit huius:
se rapit inde cito, plus properans solito.
Nil expectabat: fugientis more volabat,
donec concilium venerat in medium.
Qua sceleris diri murmur iam coepit oriri,
dum culmen rerum quisque cupit procerum.
Qui mox immitis iniissent iurgia litis,
venisset medius ni cito Mammutius.
Nam cum post verba, praeludia litis, acerba,
arma viri caperent castraque perstreperent,
inter dementes populos et in arma furentes
exiliit medius concito Mammutius,
et sic sedavit proceres et conciliavit.
Quos ubi composuit et populus siluit,

and the Church were mourned continually with tears in devotion everywhere. Therefore, when the king had been buried with great grief, they inscribed the following text on his tomb: "THERE ARE THREE REASONS FOR GRIEVING ENCLOSED UNDER THIS MARBLE: THE KING, THE CHURCH'S GLORY, AND THE COUNTRY'S SUPREME HONOR."

As soon as that torrent of intense grief abated, Libya, in its doubt, convened a council to discuss which of the nobles was to be made King of Libya, a fitting salvation for the country. While an heir for the kingdom was sought thus among the nobles, Mammutius's ally said this to him: "Go more quickly than usual, I pray, and seek the assembly that hesitates to adopt a plan! When you are permitted to speak, please have me called upon, for this way I know that I can truly benefit you. I would say more, were it not that what I say might cause harm. Even while I give you this advice, I am holding you back to ill effect."

Mammutius soon performed everything according to his request: he rushed off from that place, making more haste than usual. He waited for nothing: he went flying like a man trying to escape, until he had arrived at the assembly. There people had begun to mutter about a dreadful crime, since each of the leading nobles desired the pinnacle of power. They soon would have begun the invectives of a bitter dispute, if Mammutius had not quickly arrived in their midst. For when the men were seizing their weapons after bitter words, the prelude to a dispute, and the camps were filled with noise, Mammutius quickly stepped into the midst of the frenzied people afflicted with the mad desire for war, and he calmed down the nobles and reconciled them.

When he had calmed them and the crowd was silent, af-

paulo cunctatus sic dicitur esse profatus:
"Gaudeo composita iurgia praeterita:
quo tamen ex facto me nequaquam modo iacto.
Sed venisse volo, quod loquor absque dolo.
Gaudeo venisse, sed plus vos composuisse
per quos iustitia floret in hac patria,
per quos nostrorum stat, crescit culmen honorum,
per quos eximia pace viget Libya.
Vos tales vere decet omnes sceptra tenere,
et decet eximium quemlibet imperium.
Sed regni munus, mos exigit ut ferat unus:
una domus geminos non patitur dominos.
Nam scio regi rex est, quod crimina legi,
concordem socium non habet imperium.
Sed tamen, ut rite sit rex unus sine lite
—si cupitis celeri consilio fieri
et mihi communi consensu creditis uni—
hoc ego monstrabo consiliumque dabo.
Nosco virum quendam, non personam reverendam,
sed contemptibilem, sed misero similem.
Et tamen est plenus hic religionis egenus:
simplex et sapiens quaeque futura sciens,
et, puto, sermone sapientior est Salomone
namque prophetia sunt sua consilia.
Iste requiratur ut iudicet atque loquatur
quid recte fiat, quid male conveniat."
Ille perorabat et dicere plura parabat.
Plura loqui cuperet, si populus sineret.
At partes aeque sic vociferantur utraeque:
"Mammutius taceat! Dictaque res placeat."

ter a slight hesitation, he is said to have spoken thus: "I am delighted that your previous disputes have been calmed: but I do not in any way boast of this fact. But I am glad to be here, which I say honestly. I am happy to have come, and even happier to have calmed you, men who make justice flourish in this country, who make the pinnacle of our honor hold its place or even rise further, who cause Libya to thrive in perfect peace. As such, you are all fit to hold the scepter, and each fit for the distinguished command. But custom demands that the duty of ruling be borne by one man: one house cannot endure two masters. For I know that a king is to another king, what crimes are for the law, and supreme power cannot have an amicable partner. But nevertheless, so that there may rightly be one king without an argument—if you wish to achieve this with an efficient plan and if you will trust me alone in common agreement—I will reveal and grant this advice to you. I know a certain man, whose person is not awe-inspiring, but rather is contemptible, a poor wretch. Nevertheless, this indigent person is full of religion: he is pure and wise and he knows the future, and, in my opinion, he is wiser in his discourse than Solomon, for his advice is prophecy. Let us ask this man to judge and say what should rightly be done, and what would not be to our advantage."

He was finishing his speech and preparing to say more. He wanted to say more, had the mob let him. But both bands shouted out in the same fashion: "Let Mammutius be

Tunc male sensatus laudans haec dicta senatus,
quis sit quem mittat, iam minime dubitat
proque viro mirae virtutis protinus ire:
orant Mammutium. Sed rogat hic socium.
Cui procerum mille datur optio deligit ille
quendam, qui fatuus esset et ingenuus.
Ergo recesserunt pariterque magum petierunt,
quem multum rogitant et prece sollicitant
ut veniat secum quo iudicet omnibus aequum
conciliumque regat. Sed magus ipse negat
istud se facere, dicens se nolle docere,
immo quod taceat si quis eum doceat.
Hoc quoque dicebat et multotiens repetebat
in turba procerum scire nihil miserum.
Qui tamen oratus tandem multumque rogatus,
flectitur, ut nolens et velut inde dolens.
Quodque foret laeta sibi mens male fraude sueta,
per tristes habitus dissimulat penitus.
Cumque sibi stratum vidisset equum phaleratum,
"Quid mihi cum phaleris?" dixit homo sceleris,
"Quis mihi stravit equum? Nihil illi credite mecum!
Sit procul omnis equus: nil mihi tale decus.
Aut ferar his binis pedibus, vel si peregrinis,
bis binis asini more ferar Domini."
Ergo legati, iuxta verbum scelerati,
conantur facere quod iubet et propere
huic asinum quaerunt ipsumque superposuerunt.
Quo facto, redeunt et celeres abeunt.

silent! We have decided to act on his words." Then the senate praised these words with bad judgment, and they did not hesitate even for a moment as to whom they should send: they begged Mammutius to go quickly to fetch this man of amazing virtue. But he asked for someone to accompany him. He was given the choice of one thousand nobles, and he chose one who was foolish and naïve.

Therefore they withdrew and went to seek the mage together, whom they beseeched and begged, pleading, that he come with them so that he could judge what was right for all and guide the assembly. But the mage refused to do so, saying that he did not want to instruct them, but rather that he would be silent if someone would instruct him. He also said and repeated many times that he knew of no contemptible man in the crowd of nobles. Nevertheless, when they had begged and pleaded a great deal with him, his will was bent at last, as if he were reluctant and even pained by it. His mind, accustomed to evil and deceit, was glad, but he dissimulated this completely in his sad bearing. And when he saw that a horse adorned with trappings had been saddled for him, the sinful man said "What do I want with trappings? Who has saddled this horse for me? Believe me, I want nothing to do with him! Far be it for me to have any horse: such a distinction is alien to me. I will either go on my own two feet, or if on other feet, then I will go on the four feet of a donkey, as the Lord did." Therefore the messengers, following the sinner's words, tried to do as he ordered and speedily sought a donkey for him and put him on top of it. When this was done, they departed quickly on their return journey.

Sed, praedictante sibi nequitia, magus ante
taurum de cavea solverat interea,
concilium quando iussus petiit properando
dictus Mammutius ille, suus socius.
Et frontem tauri titulo praecinxerat auri
sic ducens illum lumen ad insolitum.
Ceu moveat bella fera territa luce novella,
exsiliens mugit et velut aura fugit.
Unde mora parva cito proxima transvolat arva,
nullius miserens, singula quaeque terens.
Nulli parcebat: homines et rura premebat.
Aeque stravit oves pervalidosque boves,
sternebatque sata tumido calcans pede prata,
nec quod taurus erat esse memor poterat.
Ergo damnosus multis, et prodigiosus
innumerum populum contrahit ad speculum,
cum iam praefatus diro magus omine natus
concilium subiit quo properans abiit.
Et medius procerum stabat, confusio rerum,
hostis iustitiae, formula nequitiae.
Stans humilis vultu, spectandus paupere cultu.
Sicut ovis tacuit—quod populo placuit!
Unde rogabatur ab eis quod et ipse loquatur,
et regem solus deligat ipse dolus.
Cumque videretur dicturus, ubique siletur,
ut queat audiri vox scelerata viri.
Ille gemens primo suspiria traxit ab imo
pectore, flens subito, more sibi solito.
Attollensque manus sua volvit in ore profanus
murmura sollicite, pauca loquens tacite.

But as wickedness dictated to him, the mage had in the meantime released the bull from his confinement, while his ally, Mammutius, was making haste for the assembly, as ordered. And the mage had hung a golden tablet around the bull's forehead and led him, adorned in this fashion, to the unfamiliar light. The beast, frightened by the new kind of light, leapt forth with a bellow as though waging war, and fled like the wind. Thus in a short while he swiftly crossed the nearest fields having mercy on no one, crushing everything. He spared no one: he attacked the men and the fields. He laid low the sheep and the strongest cattle alike. He plowed down the crops, treading on the them with his proud hoof, and he could not remember that he was a bull.

The monstrous creature was harmful to many, and he had drawn countless people to behold the sight, when the mage of ill-omened birth made haste and reached the assembly. He was standing in the middle of the nobles, this confounder of affairs, this enemy of justice, this paragon of wickedness. Standing with a humble expression on his face, he attracted attention with his poor attire. He was silent like a sheep—and the people loved it! Therefore they begged him to speak, and they let deceit itself acting alone choose a king. And when they saw he was about to speak, there was silence everywhere, so that the man's sinful voice could be heard. First, he groaned and then sighed from the depths of his chest, and then he suddenly wept, as he was wont to do. And raising up his hands the unholy man turned his own mutterings around in his mouth with anxious care, speaking few words and softly. Afterward he knelt, and his

Inde genu flectit, laqueos mens perfida nectit
 ut credatur ei sub specie fidei.
Quod plebs miratur—simplex—et conlacrimatur.
 Et sic, esse reum nescia, laudat eum.
Indignum laudis commendat, nescia fraudis,
 quam sceleratus ibi praeparat ille sibi.
Qui postquam lacrimis maduit dicturus opimis.
 Cetera prosequitur tristis et haec loquitur:
"Pro vestris rebus ego curo quibusque diebus
 nam mihi vos hodie curaque cotidie.
Pro vobis oro. Vobis prodesse laboro.
 Vester semper ero qualibet, ut potero.
Sed quia nunc istis pro rebus consuluistis
 personam vilem, me, misero similem,
memet confundo si solus consilium do:
 si solus dedero, iure protervus ero.
Quare de caelo vobis mihi nota revelo.
 Sensus et ista meus non dabit, immo Deus.
Digne regnabit taurum quicumque iugabit,
 qui iuga non tulerit ferreque nescierit.
Quem Deus eligat, hunc homo diligat et veneretur!
 Placat namque Deum, quisquis amabit eum.
Cur habeat signum tamen haec electio dignum!
 Absolvam leviter—si placet—et breviter:
haec gens aequatur et tauro consimilatur,
 nam genus hoc hominum vix patitur dominum.
Sed rex prudenter Libyam reget atque potenter,
 qui taurum melius subiugat et levius.
Hic confirmabit et iustitiam solidabit,
 noxia mutabit et nova iura dabit,
et qua regnabit, mala quaelibet inde fugabit.
 Florebitque pia pace sub hoc Libya."

treacherous mind set snares so that he would be believed for his show of faith. This amazed the people—simple as they were—and they cried along with him. And they praised him, unaware that he was a sinner. They commended him, though he deserved no praise, in ignorance of the deception that the wicked man was preparing there for them.

When, later, he was about to speak, he shed abundant tears. He continued sadly, saying: "I am concerned with your affairs each and every day, for you are my concern today and every day. I pray for you. I strive for your benefit. I will always be yours wherever you wish, as best I can. But since you now ask advice in these matters from me, a commoner, like to the wretched, I myself become confused if I give advice alone: if I give advice alone, I will rightly be called reckless. For this reason, I reveal to you things known to me from heaven. My understanding will not tell you these things, but rather God will. The man who deserves to reign is he who yokes a bull that has borne no yoke and does not know how to bear them. Whomever God elects, let people love and revere him! For whoever loves God's elect, pleases God. And for this reason let this choice have a worthy sign as well! I will sum up nimbly—if you wish—and also briefly: this people is equated and compared to a bull, for this race of men scarcely endures a master. But that king will wisely rule Libya with great power who can yoke a bull more skillfully and gently. This man will strengthen and consolidate justice, he will change harmful laws and give new ones, and he will chase all evils from his realm. And Libya will flourish in devout peace under this man."

Dixerat et multus sequitur sua verba tumultus:
applaudunt iuvenes, nec tacuere senes.
Esse sibi facile putat hoc robur iuvenile
sed longum senium, cui dedit ingenium,
dicebat secum: "Matura scientia mecum
et virtus iuvenum vincitur arte senum.
Cur ego despero? Cur non regnum mihi quaero?
Si vetat hoc senium, suadet at ingenium.
Ars compensabit quod vis mihi parva negabit,
dum, quicquid facio, cauta regat ratio."
Sic omnes proceres regnum sperasse videres:
vi propria iuvenes, calliditate senes.
Iam regio tota tauri formidine mota.
Pars metuens fugitat; magna pavens latitat.
Sed qui fugerunt ita conventum subierunt,
ut sibi concilium conferat auxilium.
Esseque dicebant, pro quo trepidi fugiebant,
monstrum terribile, paene bovi simile,
quod, parcens nulli, vix turbae cederet ulli
quaque furens rueret, omnia destrueret.
Ad quod conventus pavet omnis, et ipsa iuventus
monstrum pertimuit atque pavens tremuit.
Tunc magus hortatur quod ad hoc monstrum veniatur,
utque magus voluit, obvia turba ruit.
Quae procul ingentem cernens taurum venientem
horruit. Eximii spe tamen imperii,
illud qui captat, se totum quilibet aptat
cum iam magnificus taurus et horrificus
stat medius, miro circumdatus undique gyro.
Ast ubi turba stetit, ista magus repetit:

He had spoken, and a great commotion followed on his words: the young men applauded, and the old men were not silent. The strong, young men thought that this would be easy for them. But long-lived, old men, to whom skill has been granted, said to themselves: "Mature wisdom is with me and the strength of young men is defeated by the skill of old men. Why then should I despair? Why should I not seek the realm for myself? If old age forbids this, talent, however, persuades me. Craft will compensate for what my little strength denies to me, as long as cautious reason guides my actions." You would have seen all the nobles expecting thus to rule the realm: the young because of their own strength and the old because of their cunning.

Now the whole region was already stirred up by fear of the bull. Some fled in fear; a great many, frightened as well, were in hiding. But then those who fled made an agreement that the council should bring them aid. And they said that what the fearful were fleeing was a terrible monster, somewhat like a bull, which would spare no one, would scarcely yield to any band, and wherever it rushed in raging, would destroy everything.

At this, the whole assembly was afraid, and the young men themselves feared the monster and trembled in their fear. Then the mage exhorted them to attack this monster, and, as the mage wished, a band rushed out to meet it. But when they saw the huge bull coming from a distance they shuddered. Nevertheless whoever had hope of seizing of the distinguished command prepared himself completely now that the magnificent and horrific bull was standing surrounded on all sides by a circle of amazed men. And where the band stood, the mage repeated this: "Go on! Whoever

"Eia! Rex esse qui vis, modo regna capesse!
Imperii dotes quaeris? Habere potes!
Qui iugat hunc taurum, capiat, me iudice, laurum,
atque, iubente Deo, terra sit haec sub eo."
Vocibus his plausus datur. Et nullus, tamen, ausus
appropiare fuit; quisque sibi timuit.
Sed taurus stabat in seque fremens dubitabat
quid potius faceret, quos prius impeteret.
Nam fore credebat hostes quoscumque videbat.
Quos circumspiciens, caedis in hos sitiens,
in se bacchatur et in orbem crebro rotatur,
stabat enim dubius quo ruat ipse prius.
Hic—quod dicendum reor et minime reticendum—
strenuus effrenis prosiluit iuvenis.
Haec ait ad taurum: "Nisi victus des mihi laurum,
nobiliter moriar laudeque sic potiar.
Te feriente, mori magno mihi fiet honori:
haec tibi laus feritas, sed mihi strenuitas."
Inde per obliquum vadens ut fallat iniquum,
per cornu propere temptat eum rapere
et, puto, cepisset nisi belua cauta fuisset.
Quae dum cauta fuit, obvia tota ruit
atque, velut certo gauderet in hoste reperto,
huic inhiat soli forma cruenta doli.
Quo viso, iuvenis, velut aurae flamine lenis
percussus, rubuit nec tamen extimuit.
Qui quamvis nosset quod non evadere posset
ni citius fugeret ac sibi consuleret,
intrepidus restat. Tantum virtus sibi praestat
ut malit cadere quam timide fugere.

wants to be king must seize his kingdom now! You seek the empire as your dowry? You can have it! Whoever yokes this bull, in my judgment, will win the laurel, and, as God commands, may this land be subject to his rule." They applauded his words. No one, however, dared to go closer; everyone feared for himself. The bull, for its part, stood and bellowed to itself and wondered what to do, whom to attack first. For it believed that everyone it saw would be its enemy. It looked around at them, thirsting for their destruction, and was frenzied like a Bacchant, spinning around again and again inside the circle, for it was in doubt where to charge first.

Then—something that should be said and not passed over in silence—a brave, headstrong young man leaped forward. He said this to the bull: "If I cannot conquer you and win the laurel, I will win praise by dying nobly. To die pierced by your horn will be a great honor for me: your fame will be of savageness, mine will be of bravery."

Then approaching at an angle so as to trick the wicked bull, he tried to seize it swiftly by the horn, and I think he would have, if the monster had not been on its guard. But since it was on its guard, it rushed to meet him at full force and, as though rejoicing that it had found a clear enemy, that bloodthirsty paragon of trickery ravened at him alone.

When the youth saw this, as if struck by a breath of gentle wind he flushed but did not panic. When he knew that he could not escape, except by fleeing quickly to save himself, he stood his ground fearlessly. His virtue was so exceptional that he preferred to die rather than flee in fear. He

Armis ergo carens, animi sed robore clarens.
Quae natura dedit, laetus ad arma redit
bellaque sic captat ad quae sua membra coaptat:
dextra fuit gladius, laeva manus clipeus.
En, alter Scaeva, nuda sine tegmine laeva!
Qualia sustinuit, qualia non timuit!
Ense carens stabat nec inermis adhuc trepidabat.
O mira mirum strenuitate virum!
Quem vix laude pari reor umquam posse notari.
Cui mors grata fuit, vivere dum potuit.
Maluit ergo mori quam succubuisse timori,
se gaudens populo sic fieri speculo.
Tunc fera feralis—tamquam cursum iuvet alis—
in iuvenem rapitur qui miser opprimitur.
Et citius dictu letali corruit ictu.
Ut taurus vidit quod iuvenis cecidit,
tunc ita saevit in hunc quasi victo diceret: "I nunc
et me fac scribi succubuisse tibi!
Sic potiere meo per saecula longa trophaeo!"
Sed iuvenis vita despoliatus ita
—pro dolor—exspirat. Quem belua pessima gyrat,
sic ludens in eo sicut in hoste leo.
At variae gentes dicebant ista videntes:
"Venit revera caelitus ista fera,
iureque regnabit, illam quicumque domabit."
Sed iuvenem miserum iam penitus lacerum
taurus ut aspexit, per circum cornua flexit
atque suos dominos forte videt geminos.
Quaque sibi notos videt illos stare remotos
hac abiit propere, sed populus fugere

lacked weapons but his mighty spirit shone. He gladly returned to the weapons that nature gave him and he made war with his own limbs: his right hand was his sword, his left, his shield. Lo, another Scaeva, with his left hand bare without covering! O what he bore, O what he did not fear! He stood there without a sword and though weaponless did not fear. What a remarkable man of amazing bravery! I think he can scarcely ever be mentioned with sufficient praise. Death was pleasing to him, although he could have lived. He preferred to die rather than to succumb to fear, and rejoiced to see himself become a model for the people.

Then the savage beast—as though its motion were aided by wings—rushed against the youth, who was miserably overpowered. Quicker than speech he fell to the deadly blow. When the bull saw that the young man had fallen, it raged against him as if saying to the defeated youth: "Go now and make them write that I have succumbed to you! Thus will you possess my trophy through the long ages!" But the youth, who had thus been robbed of his life—alas!—breathed his last breath. That dreadful beast spun him around playing with him as a lion does with his prey. And different people said as they looked on: "This beast has truly come from heaven, and whoever conquers it, will rightly rule."

But when the bull saw that the wretched youth was already completely mangled, he spun his horns around the circle and by chance spotted his two masters. And he went hastily to the place where he saw the familiar men standing

coepit ab hac parte, magica male lusus ab arte.
Cum mox Mammutius, ille magi socius,
nil patiendo metus procedit ab agmine laetus
egreditur solus—fraus, scelus, ipse dolus,
perfidiae zelus! Aderat iam taurus, anhelus,
et sibi praelatas saepe sed ante datas
ore manus lambit dominumque frequentius ambit,
quem, sicut voluit, Mammutius tenuit.
Callidus ergo iugum petit afferri sibi dudum
oblatumque fuit, quod bovis imposuit
victor cervici. Taurus patienter amici
tactum sustinuit, quem dominum timuit.
Dum sic Mammutius feritatem mitigat huius,
accedunt trepidi mox proceres stupidi
scriptaque legerunt propter quae plus stupuerunt.
Signis namque novis frons titulata bovis
auro fulgebat carmenque novum retinebat.
Quod qui viderunt tale fuisse ferunt:
"HUNC DEUS ELEGIT, QUI ME SERVIRE COEGIT,
SIC EGO MISSUS EI SUM PIETATE DEI."
Postquam viderunt proceres quae scripta fuerunt,
Mammutium rapiunt et dominum faciunt.
Tunc fragor e castris quasi bellicus intonat astris;
bellum civile nil sonuit simile:
dixisses fractas ipsas caeli cataractas.
Omnia si ruerent, non aliter fremerent.
Tanta fuit gentis vox indiscreta furentis
dum sibi Mammutium constituit dominum.
Ille reluctatur, et in obluctando profatur:
"Non aequum facitis! Cur ita me rapitis?

some distance away, but the people began to flee from this area, evilly deceived by the mage's craft. Soon Mammutius, the mage's accomplice, feeling no fear, gladly stepped out of the line—he went out alone—deceit, sin, trickery itself and zeal for faithlessness! The bull, panting, approached and licked with his mouth the hands that had often been offered to him before and circled his master again and again. And Mammutius held him, as he wished. Next he cleverly asked the yoke to be brought to him. They brought it, and he put it on the bull's neck and became the victor. The bull patiently tolerated the touch of its friend, because it feared him as master.

And while Mammutius thus tamed its ferocity, the astonished nobles soon came closer in fear, and they read the inscription, which astounded them even more. For the bull's brow bore an inscription in fresh letters that shone in gold and held a strange verse. Those who saw it reported that it read: "GOD CHOSE THIS MAN, WHO HAS FORCED ME TO SERVE. THUS I HAVE BEEN SENT TO HIM BY GOD'S DEVOTION." And after the nobles saw the writing they seized Mammutius and made him their lord. Then the warlike clamor from the camps resounded to the stars; no civil war sounded like that: you would have said that the heaven's own cataracts had burst open. If everything had come crashing down, it would have sounded just the same. So great was the raging mob's brash sound when they made Mammutius their master. He fought against them, and in his struggle exclaimed: "You are doing an injustice! Why do you seize me

Numquam quaesivi nec regna tenere cupivi.
Non aequum facitis et, puto, nil sapitis.
Sed si perstatis ut vos mihi vim faciatis,
ex desiderio non fruar imperio."
Unde magis raptus sceptris regalibus aptus
solus clamatur sicque corona datur.
Mammutius fit rex per quem sacra deperiit lex.
Ordine nam tali venit origo mali.
Hos igitur fastus illi dederat suus astus,
cuius perfidia saucia flet Libya.
Cum iam regnaret vir iniquus et imperitaret,
tunc sic aggreditur hunc magus et loquitur:
"Te benefactorum memorem decet esse meorum
—quid sis, quid fueris, si memor huius eris—
et mihi dona dabis et me, nisi fallor, amabis
et, sicut spero, non tibi vilis ero.
Nunc igitur si vis ut homo faveat tibi quivis,
fac quod ego iubeo, par eris inde Deo.
Sic tibi summa dabo, sic te super astra levabo.
Est mihi terrarum regna dedisse parum.
Per me summus eris, per me Deus efficieris,
si, quae te moneo, feceris, ut iubeo.
Lex mutandorum gravis est evangeliorum!
Quae sensu vacuos nos putat et fatuos
dum nos moechari prohibet vel luxuriari,
et cognatorum destruit ipsa torum.
Multaque praeceptis vetat aut confirmat ineptis,
quae tu damnabis dum magis apta dabis.
Nam tu moechandum statues venerique vacandum.
Luxuriet penus sitque soluta venus!

like this? I have never sought nor have I desired to rule. You are doing an injustice and, I think, in ignorance. But if you are determined to use force on me, then I will not rule out of desire." And so they seized him, and they exclaimed that he alone was fit for the royal scepter, and the crown was bestowed in this manner.

Mammutius became king, and he destroyed the sacred law. For the evil originated in this order. His own trickery thus gave him arrogance, and because of his faithlessness wounded Libya weeps. When this wicked man was in power and governing, then the mage approached him and spoke thus: "It is fitting that you recall my services to you—what you are, what you have been, if you remember this—you will give me gifts and you will love me, if I am not mistaken, and I expect that you will not hold me in contempt. Now therefore if you want anyone to treat you with devotion, do as I order, and you will be equal to God. Thus I will give you the highest things, and thus I will raise you above the stars. For to have given you earthly realms is too little for me. Through me you will be the highest, through me you will be made God, if you do the things I advise, as I command.

"The harsh law of the gospels must be altered! This law supposes that we are foolish or lack judgment when it prohibits us to commit adultery and to indulge ourselves, and when it prohibits marriage between relatives. It forbids or it encourages with its inept commandments many things that you will condemn when you give more suitable commandments. For you will decree adultery and free time for sex. Let food be abundant and let there be free love! You should

Sed tua decreta debes hac claudere meta:
ut modo sit licitum quicquid erat vetitum.
Sic tibi maiorem populi—sine fine—favorem
conciliare potes si mea verba notes.
Nil magis est oneri quam stricta lege teneri.
Ergo, fac liceant omnia quae libeant!
Qualiter hoc fieri possit ratione doceri
arguta poteris si mihi parueris.
Argue scriptorum vitiose dicta priorum
et male scripta prius, corrige nunc melius.
Quae careant menda sine crimine trade legenda.
Cetera deride non bene digna fide!
Illi scripturae debemus credere iure
(iureque suscipio) quae favet arbitrio.
Contra, scripturam, quae dat legem nocituram,
iuste despicio, nam nocet arbitrio.
Arbitrium latum sub libertate creatum
si legem statuas protinus evacuas,
si non omne licet quod libertas mihi dicet
quae sub lege suum non habet arbitrium.
Ergo decet regem tantum talem dare legem
ut quicquid libeat hoc etiam liceat.
Sic, sic magnus eris, sic perpete pace frueris!
Hoc facti titulo, iure placens populo."
Cui rex tantorum grates referens monitorum
intulit: "Eximia sunt tua consilia
et tua doctrina, nobis penitus peregrina
nota tibi soli, venit ab arce poli!
Per te divina mundo lucet medicina:
nam loqueris video cuncta docente Deo.

sum up your decrees with this saying: let everything that had been forbidden be permitted now. This way you can attain greater favor among the people—and without end—if you heed my words. There is no greater burden than to be bound by a strict law. Therefore, permit everything that pleases!

"You can learn how to do this with convincing reasoning, if you obey me. Assert that the sayings of previous scriptures are flawed and correct what was written poorly earlier, so that it will be better now. Let the statements without flaws be read without sin. Deride the rest as unworthy of belief! We should rightly trust that scripture (and I rightly adopt it) that is favorable to our own power of judgment. On the contrary, I rightly despise a scripture that promulgates a harmful law, for it harms our own power of judgment. You immediately void the wide-ranging choice that comes from liberty, if you establish a law—if not everything is allowed that liberty will propose to me—for, if she is subject to the rule of law, she lacks her own freedom to dispose. Therefore it is only fitting that a king decree as a law that whatever pleases is also permitted. Thus, thus will you be great, thus will you enjoy perpetual peace! With this as a pretext for the deed, you will give legal satisfaction to the people."

The king thanked him for his valuable advice and responded: "Your counsel is exceptional, and your teaching, which is completely foreign to us and known only to you, comes from the citadel of heaven! Through you, divine medicine for the world shines forth: for I see that all your sayings are God's teachings. For this reason I beg, lying at your

Quare prostratus precor ut modo sim tibi gratus
sicut et ante fui quando minus valui.
Tu me fecisti dominum; tu regna dedisti.
Sed nunc amplificas et data magnificas.
Sic mecum stabis et adhuc pater, insinuabis
per quod ego facere nil videar temere.
Ergo mihi suade faciendaque singula trade
et mihi te speculum, te facias oculum.
Semper, uti scisti, feci quicquid voluisti.
Nunc si praeteream quae iubeas, peream!
Africa parebit his quae tua lingua docebit
Et tibi discipulus totus erit populus!"
Ad magicos nutus rex quaeque nefanda secutus.
Sicut pollicitus est, ita sollicitus
omnia complevit. Sacras leges abolevit
et "quicquid libuit, hoc licitum" statuit.
Addit et hoc sceleri nolentes hoc revereri
rebus privari suppliciisque dari.
Ad quae decreta, gens Afrorum, male laeta
gaudet et insanit dum mage flenda canit.
Multiplicans laetas voces lascivior aetas,
laetatur scribi cuncta licere sibi.
Iamque puellaris chorus et plausus popularis
solum Mammutium praedicat eximium.
Extuleratque virum quasi sacratum, quasi mirum,
aura favoralis, semper amica malis.
O gens confusa, magico male dogmate lusa!
O socianda feris, o miseranda, peris.
"Libera sum!" dicis. Libertas haec inimicis
nostris eveniat nosque, precor, fugiat!

feet, that I may please you now just as I did earlier when I had less power. You made me a lord; you gave me kingdoms. But now you extend them, increasing your gifts. Thus you will stand by my side, and, as ever a father, you will show me how not to seem to do anything recklessly. Therefore advise me and entrust each task to me and make yourself my mirror and my eye. As you know, I have always done whatever you wished. If I fail now to do as you order me, may I perish! Africa will obey the teachings of your tongue, and the whole people will be your pupils!"

At the mage's nod the king followed every wicked command. And just as he had promised, he carefully performed everything. He abolished the sacred laws and decreed "whatever pleases is permitted." He added to this crime that those refusing to revere this law should be deprived of property and punished. At these decrees, the people of Africa, happy in their wickedness, rejoiced and raved, while they sang of things that should rather be lamented. Those of a more lascivious age multiplied happy voices, rejoicing that it was written that everything was permitted to them. And now the chorus of girls and the people's applause preach that only Mammutius is great. And the breeze of favor, always a friend to evil men, exalted the man as though sacred, as though wondrous.

O confused people, sadly deceived by the mage's doctrine! He has brought you down to the level of animals, and you perish miserably. "I am free!" you say. Let our enemies have this freedom, and let us, I pray, escape it! Such freedom

Libertas talis vobis erit exitialis,
quae vos damnabit suppliciisque dabit.
Dum tibi consultum credis, genus o male stultum,
quo gaudens raperis? Laeta canens moreris!
Dum nunc exultas, poenas cumulas tibi multas,
et iuxta meritum tendis ad interitum.
Ergo prurigo Veneris scelerum fit origo.
Africa dum temere polluitur Venere
sollicitans nuptas ruit effrenata voluptas,
nullaque virgo fuit nubere quae potuit.
Aspernata torum mulier vaga legitimorum
quodlibet esse pium credit adulterium.
Omnes ardebant: vir et uxor idem faciebant.
Caeca fuit iuvenum, caeca libido senum,
quare plerumque sexum confudit utrumque
incertumque genus fecit iniqua Venus.
Sic homo confusum rationis perdidit usum.
Non faciendo secus quam rude quodque pecus.
Nil fuit humanum nisi constitit esse profanum;
qui minus hoc timuit, sanctior ille fuit.
Ut scelus irrepsit, honor et reverentia cessit,
quae commisceri non poterant sceleri.
Quare laudari coeptus fuit et celebrari
omnis concubitus lege sacra vetitus.
Dum tibi, Natura, rapuerunt vi tua iura,
femina quaeque parem, mas subigendo marem.
Mox, contra morem, frater premit ipse sororem.
Nupta soror fratri victima fit baratri.
Incestat matrem sua proles, filia patrem.
Sic quicquid libuit lege nova licuit.
Heu! Quot prudentes facti sunt insipientes
nequitiaeque favent, dum sua damna pavent!

will be your destruction. It will condemn and punish you. While you think you are provided for, you evil and foolish people, where will this glee carry you? You will die chanting happy verses! While you exult now, you heap up many punishments for yourself, and you court the destruction that you deserve.

Thus the itch of sex was the origin of their sins. While Africa was recklessly defiled by Venus, unbridled sensuality rushed in tempting married women, and no virgin could be found whom one could take in marriage. The straying women refused the beds of legitimate husbands and believed that any adultery was an act of devotion. All were on fire: husband and wife did the same. The lust of the young men was blind, and that of the old men also. For this reason unjust Venus confused both sexes, more often than not, and made gender uncertain. Thus man lost his use of reason. He was confused and acted no differently from every base animal. Nothing was human unless it was plainly taboo; whoever was less inhibited, was holier. As sin crept in, honor and respect ceased, since they were not compatible with sin. For this reason they began to praise and practice every sexual act forbidden by sacred law. While they stole from you, Nature, your laws by force, woman mounted woman, and man, another man. Soon, contrary to custom, the brother got atop his own sister, the sister, as wife of her brother, fell victim to the abyss. Son committed incest with his mother, daughter with father. Thus whatever was pleasing was permitted under the new law. Alas! How many cautious people were made fools and favored wickedness, fearing harm to

Regis enim terror quosdam sed publicus error
plures post vitia traxit in exitia.
Pauci constantes solique Deo famulantes,
dum meliora docent ut populum revocent,
confirmaverunt exemplo quod docuerunt.
Nam vel supplicio, vel prece, vel pretio
crebro temptari poterant sed non superari.
Qui mox suppliciis expositi variis,
poenas spreverunt quas multas sustinuerunt.
Quidam verberibus, pars quota carceribus
mundum vicerunt, quidam flagris perierunt.
Ille famen patitur, ille siti moritur.
Quidam truncati, quidam sunt igne probati,
vectibus hic foditur aut oleo coquitur.
Ille coronatur quia vivus decoriatur.
Hic sectus periit astraque sic subiit.
Ille triumphavit quia corvos in cruce pavit.
Hic imbrem rapidum sustinuit lapidum,
tigribus oblati quidam vel praecipitati.
Vicerunt alii supplicio gladii.
Cuncta relinquentes quidam Dominumque sequentes,
in se crudeles dum metuunt homines,
invia silvarum peragrant rabiesque ferarum
illesos patitur, quos homo persequitur.
Qui sic inventi modo vivunt omnipotenti;
nacti morte sua gaudia perpetua.
Sed sibi vindictam Dominus memor esse relictam
Mammutium subito percutit et merito:
nam male pro gestis rapit hunc epileptica pestis,
quae vexet miserum pro numero scelerum.

themselves! Some people were dragged into vice and then destruction by fear of the king, but most followed the general misconception.

The few steadfast people who served God alone, while teaching better things in order to call the people back, confirmed with their example what they taught. For they could often be tempted by punishment, entreaties, or payment, but they could not be overcome. They soon suffered various tortures, but they scorned the many punishments they suffered. Some conquered worldliness by receiving blows, and many others in prisons, while others were flogged to death. One suffered hunger, while another died of thirst. Some were dismembered, while others were tried by fire. Others were pierced with bars or cooked in oil. Another earned the [martyr's] crown because he was skinned alive. Another perished cut into pieces and thus ascended to the stars. Another conquered by becoming food for ravens on the cross. Another suffered a swift rain of stones. Some were offered to the tigers or thrown down headlong from high places. Others conquered by the sword's punishment. Some left everything and followed the Lord, and since they feared men's cruelty toward themselves, they traversed pathless woods, and the beasts' ferocity left them unharmed, although they were pursued by men. Those who were found to have done thus now live for omnipotent God; they have attained eternal bliss with their death.

But God was mindful that vengeance was his, and so he struck Mammutius suddenly and deservedly: for owing to his evil deeds epilepsy seized him, and it harried the

Cumque flagellaret Deus illum quo revocaret,
non potuit sapere prae nimio scelere.
Sed velut effrenis equus haud retinetur habenis,
sic ob supplicia plus abit in vitia.
Sic solet iratus Dominus punire reatus
ut, quamvis feriat, plus homo desipiat.
Qua lue damnatum magus ut videt hunc sceleratum,
introrsus gemuit nec modice doluit.
Neve tamen tristis rebus videatur in istis,
caute dissimulat hoc quod eum stimulat.
Quod bene dum celat, ad maius crimen anhelat.
Ad quam nequitiam sic parat ipse viam
ut, quotiens caderet rex exanimisque iaceret,
cum rex deficeret, vim scelus acciperet.
Certe nimirum reputabitur hoc fore mirum,
si quando legitur. Ordine nos igitur
mandemus chartae magus haec qua fecerat arte.
Cuius laetitia nil nisi nequitia.
Nam quasi plaudebat, rex quandocumque dolebat,
laudes rite Deo multiplicans ideo:
quod respexisset populum cui praeposuisset
regem magnificum, moribus angelicum,
quique putaretur defunctus, cum raperetur
in caelum totiens, summa Deus quotiens
regni tractaret vel cum nova iura crearet.
Dixit enim per eum cuncta patrare Deum.
Quare deceptas monuit gentes et ineptas
ut lacrimas teneant et minime doleant,
immo laetentur regemque magis venerentur,
cum videant in eo complacuisse Deo.

wretched man in accordance with the number of his sins. He was unable to perceive, due to his excessive sin, that it was God striking him in order to call him back. Rather like an unbridled horse that is not held back by the reins, because of his punishment he retreated further into vices. When God is angry, he usually punishes sins in such a way that the more he strikes the sinner, the more foolish the sinner grows.

When the mage saw this wicked man condemned to this pestilence, he groaned inwardly and grieved considerably. Nevertheless, so as not to appear sad for this reason, he cautiously disguised what motivated him. While he concealed this well, he panted to commit a greater crime. He prepared a way for new wickedness such that whenever the king would fall down and lie unconscious, even though the king had fainted away, the sin would gain force. Surely this will be thought amazing when it is read. Therefore, let us entrust to parchment now in due order the trickery by which the mage did these things. His delight was in evil and in nothing else.

For, as it were, he applauded whenever the king was afflicted, and he accordingly multiplied his praises of God, because God had shown concern for the people over whom he had installed a magnificent king of angelic character, who would be thought dead, when he was carried off to heaven, whenever God was treating the highest affairs of the realm or when he was making new laws. He even said that God accomplishes all things through him. For this reason, he warned the foolish and gullible people to hold back their tears and not to grieve, but rather to rejoice and increase their veneration toward the king, since they saw that they had pleased God through him.

Sed gens polluta magicum mox dogma secuta,
ipsa suum proprium vergit in exitium.
Nempe suo more cum rex, urgente dolore,
vi subita caderet exanimisque foret,
Vulgus, seductum, vertens in gaudia luctum,
unde prius gemuit, hinc modo concinuit,
mente virum captum quia dicit ad aethera raptum
ut det iura solo praesideatque polo.
Plebs ita gaudebat et, ut inquam, laeta canebat.
Sed magus interea cogitat ad scelera.
Qui cum praesciret tempus quo morbus abiret
ut regi vita iam redeat solita,
tunc excludebat omnes solusque manebat,
fingens mysterium se celebrare pium.
Cumque recessisset dolor et rex convaluisset,
mox magus hunc docuit, suetus ut ante fuit,
atque suum virus instillat homo sibi dirus
ut pereat misera plebs lue mortifera.
Sed rex progressus, morbum pallore professus,
taliter orditur et populis loquitur:
"Festiva laude, gens electissima, plaude
nam tua complacita sunt superis merita!
Hoc tu fecisti, tu vere promeruisti,
quod cunctis adeo caelitibus placeo!
Quodque meum cursum totiens ego dirigo sursum
convenit ascribi, gens benedicta, tibi!
Sed quia plorastis me quando dolere putastis,
discite quam gratus sit meus ille status.
Cum velut amentem me cernitis atque dolentem,
in caelum rapior nilque mali patior.

The depraved people soon followed the mage's teaching and headed to their own destruction. For in fact when the king, compelled by pain as he often was, would fall down with sudden force and lie unconscious, the multitude, under the mage's sway, transformed their grief into joy. What had made them groan, now made them sing, because they said that the demented man had been snatched up to ethereal heights in order to give laws to the earth and to rule the heavens. And so the people rejoiced and, as I say, sang happily.

But in the meantime the mage planned more sins. Since he knew in advance the moment when the disease would subside and normal life would return to the king, he would shut everybody out and remain alone, pretending that he was devoutly celebrating a mystery. And when the pain diminished and the king improved, the mage soon instructed him, as he was already accustomed to do, and the ill-omened man instilled his poison into the king so that the wretched people would perish in lethal depravity.

When the king came out, his pallor announcing his illness, he began to speak thus to the people: "Applaud, most chosen people, with festive praise, for your good deeds have pleased those in heaven! It is your doing, and with your merits, that I so please all those in heaven! And that I so often travel heavenward must be ascribed to you, blessed people! But because you wept when you thought that I was in pain, hear how pleasing that condition is to me. When you see me looking as though crazed and in pain, I am snatched up to

Nam tunc sanctorum fruor alloquio superorum
condignasque Deo delicias habeo.
Quippe meos visus ibi delectat paradisus,
glorior hymnificis laudibus angelicis.
Nunc feror in Plaustrum, nunc inde relabor ad austrum,
ignea quem gelidum zona facit calidum,
inde, renitentes stellas mundumve sequentes,
hisque noto pariter quae via, quod sit iter.
Hinc mea miratur mens cum caelum rapiatur
unde queant superi tam stabiles fieri
ut non volvantur simul immo nec moveantur.
Talia cum videam, creditis ut doleam.
Hic tunc languesco sed ibi gaudens requiesco,
qua sine lite quies, qua sine nocte dies.
Hunc tamen ad mundum mihi cum fuerit redeundum
tunc certe doleo tam cito quod redeo.
Nam bona tantarum cum desero deliciarum
vix patior reditum carnis ad introitum.
Unde recusarem reditus et non remearem
nec mundum peterem, vos nisi diligerem.
Vos! Mihi sudoris vos estis causa laboris!
Quare percipite, gens mea, sollicite
quid modo vidissem cum raptus ad alta fuissem,
et, quod ego promo, disce, fidelis homo!
Mundum damnamus si vos prius excipiamus;
si vos excipimus, omnia despicimus.
Quid colat, humanum nescit genus ut male sanum.
Nescit quid faciat, multa licet faciat.
Vos, genus electum, vos nil sapitis nisi rectum!
Vos verum sapitis, membra sacri capitis!

heaven where I suffer no evil. For then I enjoy the conversation of the saints above, and I possess delights fit for God. There indeed I enjoy the view of paradise, and I glory in the hymn-like praises of the angels.

"At one time I am lifted up to the Plow, and at another I slide down from there to the south, (icy itself, but rendered torrid by a fiery belt), from there to the stars, either the unyielding ones or those that follow the earth, and by these stars alike I mark the path, the journey. Then whenever the sky moves swiftly my mind is amazed to observe that the heavenly ones can become so stable that they are not whirled around at the same time and indeed are not even moved. When I see such things, you believe that I am in pain. At those times I languish here, but I rest in joy in the place where there is rest without strife, where there is day without night.

"Nevertheless when I must return to this world, as soon as I get back I am certainly in pain. For since I leave behind the enjoyment of so many delights it is difficult to endure returning to enter the flesh. I would refuse to return and not come back to seek the world, were it not that I love you. You! You are the cause of my sweat and toil! Therefore listen attentively, my people, to what I have seen just now when I was carried off to heaven, and learn what I reveal to you, O my faithful!

"We would condemn the world if we were first to make an exception for you; if we make an exception for you, we show contempt for everything. The human race, as though mad, does not know what it should worship. It does not know what to do, although it does many things. You, chosen race, you know nothing but right! You know the truth, limbs of

Illi constringunt se legibus, et sibi fingunt
et nova iura creant in quibus et pereant.
Vos superis grati. Vos, libertate beati,
vos Deus innocuos aestimat esse suos!
Illi sublati nunc essent et reprobati,
venissent media ni mea consilia.
Nam cum damnandae gentes essent miserandae,
sic mea, quod decuit, lingua locuta fuit:
'Coetus caelestis, quia nil nescire potestis,
quam sit magnifica religio Libyca,
vos ipsi scitis. Sed, quaeso, notare velitis
hanc gentem noviter nosse salutis iter,
et discernatis quod honor sacrae novitatis,
cum vix extremam contigerit Libyam,
tam cito diffundi non possit ad ultima mundi.
Quod nemo docuit, discere quis potuit?
Unde precor genti sano doctore carenti
detur adhuc spatium quo redimat vitium.
Sed si ridebunt postquam sacra nostra videbunt,
ni cito paeniteant, iudice me, pereant
et sic damnentur ut perpetuo crucientur!'
Hic ubi conticui, sic superis placui
quod mihi decretus locus est sine fine quietus,
et quotiens redeam, sceptra poli teneam,
par ego viventi per saecula Cunctipotenti,
cum quo solus ego quaeque regenda rego.
Ergo gaudete praeceptaque nostra tenete
cum multo studio, quippe procul dubio
vos exaltabo, mihi vos ego consimilabo,
hic mihi si meritis consimiles eritis.

the sacred head! Other peoples limit themselves with laws, and they deceive themselves. And they create new laws in which they also perish. You are pleasing to those in heaven. God esteems you, blessed with freedom, to be his own blameless people!

"They would have been removed and condemned, if I had not intervened with my advice. For since we must have pity on condemned peoples, my tongue spoke thus, as was fitting: 'O heavenly assembly, since there is nothing that you can fail to know, you yourselves know how magnificent the Libyan religious devotion is. But please consider that this people has only recently come to know the path of salvation, and understand that the honor of this new worship, since it has only just arrived in distant Libya, cannot be so quickly disseminated to the furthest parts of the world. Who could learn what no one has taught? Therefore, I beg that for the people who are lacking a sound teacher a space of time still be granted in which they may redeem this flaw. But if they laugh after they have seen our sacred rites, unless they quickly repent, if I am judge, may they perish and be condemned to perpetual torture!'

"And then when I was silent, I so pleased those in heaven that a place of rest without end was decreed for me, and whenever I return, I will wield the scepters of the heavens, as an equal to the Omnipotent who lives on through the ages without end, and with him, I alone govern all that must be governed. Rejoice therefore, and follow our commandments with great zeal, for without a doubt I will exalt you and make you equal to myself, if here you will be similar to me in your merits.

Sed plene purus vix esse potest moriturus.
Propter carnis onus dum nequit esse bonus—
nemo sub hoc onere valet, inquam, labe carere—
unde subesse scio vos alicui vitio.
Quare, pollutis haec sit via prima salutis:
ut post peccata quisque lavetur aqua.
Nempe sacramentum veniae dabit hoc elementum!
Sed vere sacrum tale sit ut lavacrum.
Quisquis purgari bene vult et purificari
sic se sanctificet et quater haec replicet:
'Quicquid deliqui, Mahumet, purgator iniqui,
dilue sacratam, deprecor, hanc per aquam!'
Taliter ablutis summae dabo dona salutis:
regni perpetui semper honore frui.
Pluribus instruerem vos, si modo tempus haberem,
nam dum protrahitur sermo, dies rapitur.
Corde sed intento, mea gens, retinere memento,
sicut disposui, singula quae docui!
Et libertatis ita iacturam caveatis,
liber ut in proprio quisque sit arbitrio!
Nam si sic vultis nostris insistere cultis
carnis post obitum tunc dabo pollicitum."
Haec postquam dixit, gens simplex laude canora
intonat, adiectis plausibus absque mora
inque modum tonitrus tantus ferit aethera clamor
quantum Iunonis sub Iove nescit amor.
Quid facis his monitis, scelerum caput, hostia Ditis,
brutos atque rudes dum laqueare studes?
Sed metuis, credo,—crudelis et impie praedo!—
ne solus pereas. Quod, rogo, ne timeas!

"But it is scarcely possible for a mortal to be completely pure. And while owing to the burden of the flesh a mortal cannot be good—and I declare that no one can fail to slip up under this burden—hence I know that you have submitted to some vice. For this reason, let this be the primary path to salvation for the polluted: that after sins each be washed with water. Surely this element will provide the sacrament of pardon! But let this rite be like a bath. Whoever wishes to be purged well and cleansed let him sanctify himself thus and repeat this four times: 'In whatever I have transgressed, Muhammad, cleanser of sin, wash it away, I pray, with this sacred water!' To those who have washed themselves thus I will grant the gifts of highest salvation: to enjoy the honor of the perpetual kingdom forever. I would teach you more things, if only I had time, but while my speech drags on the day is snatched away. But, remember, my people, to hold in your attentive hearts everything that I have taught just as I have prescribed! And beware loss of liberty, so that each person may be free in his own judgment! For if you wish to maintain our observances in this manner, then after the death of the flesh I will give you what I promised." After he said this, the simple people thundered with singing praise and applauded without hesitation, and like thunder such a great clamor pierced the sky that Juno's love under Jove did not know so great a din.

What are you doing with this advice, chief of sinners, victim of Pluto, while you strive to trap the uninformed and the brutish? You fear, I believe,—cruel and wicked robber!—to perish alone. I beg you not to fear this! For you

Nam tu privatus non ibis et incomitatus,
immo turba tua non erit exigua.
Nec multis annis tua saeviet ista tyrannis,
nec tua quod quaerit vita perennis erit.
Ultio divina, dum tu gaudes, inopina
iam te praeveniet nec leviter feriet.
Sicque repente cades—generalis et unica clades!
iamque patet Ditis aula tuis meritis;
te, membrum Satanae, chaos absorbebit inane.
Et, quasi te sitiat, Tartarus omnis hiat.
Eia! Laetare neque desistas cumulare
quod tibi post obitum fructificet geminum.
Et tibi, gens stulta, superest confusio multa
nec tibi laetitia semper erit socia.
Cursu namque brevi spatium decurritur aevi;
post quod finitum, vadis ad interitum.
Cumque tuo Mahumet, Plutonis victima fies
errorisque tui praemia percipies.
Cum iam crevisset fraus et dolus invaluisset
nec sceleri metas poneret impietas,
tunc destructarum clamores ecclesiarum
et Mahumet facinus intuitus Dominus,
saevit in auctorem sceleris tantumque furorem
dignis persequitur suppliciis. Igitur
solis ad auroram rex primam lucis ad horam
egreditur tacite, forte carens comite.
Et meditans ibat quid agat, quae dogmata scribat,
et quid cras doceat unde suis placeat.
Sed mors instabat quae cras vixisse negabat
praeveniens hodie dogmata perfidiae.

will not go destitute and unaccompanied, rather your band will not be small. This tyranny of yours will not rage for many years, nor will your life be eternal, though it seeks that. For while you rejoice, divine vengeance will overtake you suddenly and will not strike lightly. And thus suddenly you will fall—a general and singular destruction! Soon Pluto's hall will be open to your deeds and empty chaos will absorb you, O limb of Satan. All Tartarus gapes open as though thirsting for you. Go on! Rejoice and do not stop accruing what afterward will bear the fruit of a twofold demise. Deep confusion lies in store for you, foolish people, and you will not always be happy. For the span of life elapses in a brief course; when it is done, you go to your death. And with your Muhammad, you will become a victim of Pluto, and you will receive the rewards of your error.

When the deception had spread and the trickery had gained force and impiety put no reins on sin, then the Lord perceived the clamor of the ruined churches and Muhammad's sin, and he attacked the perpetrator of the crime and persecuted such monstrous madness with deserved punishment. At dawn, at the first hour of the sun's light, the king went out silently and, as it happened, he was unaccompanied. He walked meditating on what to do, what doctrines to compose and what to teach tomorrow in order to please his followers. But death was imminent, which would deny him life tomorrow and forestall today the teachings of faith-

Nam quae verba daret populo dum rex agitaret,
corripuit solita pestis eum subita.
Et cadit exsanguis torpens, quasi frigidus anguis,
nec, sicut voluit, esse nocens potuit.
Viscera constringens, intus dolor aestuat ingens.
Aestuat interius nec minus exterius.
Omnia torpebant: manus, os, pes, lingua rigebant.
Totus diriguit, totus iners iacuit.
Guttur praeclusum linguae vocis negat usum,
stabant et vacua lumina luce sua.
Quid moror? Immensus dolor abstulerat sibi sensus,
iamque subacta fere, vita parat fugere:
quod portendebant spumae quibus ora madebant,
et male continuus flatus et exiguus.
Sic, absente mago, tenet hunc dum mortis imago,
accurrere sues—digna repente lues!
Qui rapidus sic grex quasi spernens quod foret hic rex
totus in hunc properat et miserum lacerat
ac vitae reliquum quod adhuc sustentat iniquum
exhaurit leviter; ille gemit graviter.
O, tandem moritur! Morienti Styx aperitur,
et Stygius latro mergitur in baratro.
Et quia damnavit animas et corpora stravit,
nil parcens animae, corporibus minime,
nunc ipsum porcus, animam depascitur Orcus,
et sordis propriae volvitur in sanie.
Iureque damnatus, in utroque ferens cruciatus,
poenarum genera sustinet ad scelera.
Cum magus audisset quoniam rex solus abisset
ac praeter solitum protraheret reditum,

lessness. For while the king was considering what words to give the people, his usual illness came over him suddenly. He fell down pallid and lay motionless like a cold snake, and he was not able to do harm as he wished. An intense pain stewed inside him, contracting his guts. He seethed on the inside and no less on the outside. His every limb was motionless: his hands, mouth, feet, tongue were stiff. He was completely rigid, and he lay inert. His throat was blocked, denying his tongue the use of his voice, his eyes were emptied of their light. Why do I delay? The immeasurable pain deprived him of his senses, and the life in him, already almost subdued, prepared to flee: the foam that wet his mouth warned as much, along with his faint and interrupted breathing.

Thus, in the mage's absence, while the image of death held the king, pigs suddenly ran up—an affliction he deserved! The swift herd, as though scornful that this man should be king, all rushed against him and tore up the wretch and dispatched easily the remaining life that still sustained the wicked man, and he groaned grievously. O, at last he was dead! Styx was opened to the dying man, and the Stygian thief was submerged in the abyss. And because he damned souls and laid low bodies, not sparing soul nor bodies in the least, the pigs now fed on his body, and Orcus, on his soul, and he rolled in the discharge of his own filth. Rightly condemned, he suffered tortures in both body and soul, and he suffered the punishments that corresponded in kind to his sins.

When the mage heard that the king had gone out alone and that his return was taking longer than usual, he went

solus eum sequitur. Quo dum velocius itur,
cernitur in media rex cecidisse via.
Ultor adhuc stabat grex et regem lacerabat
ac si lege cibi sit datus ille sibi.
Sed, veniente mago, cessit porcina vorago
atque caput scelerum deseruit, lacerum.
Tunc, fons peccati, magus ad corpus lacerati
accessit propius quid faceret dubius.
Sed quid ad haec faceret nisi fleret flensque doleret?
Flens igitur gemuit nec modice doluit.
At cum sentiret dolor hic quod inanis abiret,
et quod flere suum cederet in vacuum,
secum dicebat: "Quando pater Hectora flebat,
numquid ei lacrimae profuerant?—Minime!
Ergo cum luctus nullos faceret sibi fructus,
corde quidem doluit, flere tamen posuit.
Tu quoque depone fletum simili ratione:
hunc etenim lacrimis amodo non redimis."
Talibus armatus monitis magus et recreatus
vultus composuit, et lacrimas tenuit
atque reportavit corpus lectoque locavit,
arte licet sera membra fovens lacera.
Ad quod miscetur quodcumque valere videtur:
sucus laureolae flosque tener violae.
Implebantque domum tus, balsama, nardus, amomum;
ex quibus ignotum fecerat antidotum,
et membris cunctis regalibus inde perunctis,
vestibus ornat eum. Tendit enim laqueum
quo deceptorum capiat mentes populorum,
gaudens fraude sua non nisi continua.

alone after him. As he went along swiftly, he saw that the king had fallen in the middle of the road. The avenging herd was still standing there and tearing at the king as though he had been given to it as its rightful food. But when the mage approached, the whirling herd of pigs yielded and abandoned the chief sinner, mutilated.

Then the mage, that fount of sin, approached the body of the mangled man and hesitated as to what to do. But what should he do in this situation except weep and, in weeping, grieve? Therefore he wept and groaned and grieved intensely. But when he felt that this grief was futile, and that his crying was yielding to emptiness, he said to himself: "When Priam mourned his son Hector, were the tears of any use to him?—None at all! Therefore since mourning did not benefit him at all, in his heart he grieved indeed, but he stopped his weeping. You too should cease weeping for the same reason: for indeed you cannot ransom him with your tears now."

Armed with this advice and refreshed, the mage composed his expression and stopped his tears, and he carried the body back and placed it on the bed. He ministered to the torn limbs with skill, although too late. For this purpose he mixed whatever seemed to be effective: the sap of a laurel shoot and the tender violet flower. Incense, balsam, nard, amomum filled the house; from these he had made an unknown antidote, and when he had anointed all the king's limbs with this mixture, he adorned him with his vestments. For he held a snare with which to trap the minds of the gullible people. He did not rejoice in his trickery unless it could continue.

Rege perornato, mox ore suo scelerato
regales famulos convocat et populos,
quos sic affatur: "Lux haec sollemnis agatur
qua caelos hodie rex petiit Libyae.
Rex est ille quidem caelestis factus ibidem
utque suos pueros, nos, vocat ad superos.
Nam dilatatus licet eius sit dominatus,
non tamen inde minus noster erit dominus.
Immo suos Libycos non ut servos sed amicos,
conservando teget atque fovendo reget.
Sed quid turbatur cor vestrum dum meditatur
et causam quaerit cur pater hic dederit
porcis rodenda sua membra nimis reveranda?
Quam caro sit vilis, mors docet haec humilis.
Hoc ut monstraret et aperte significaret,
ipse pati voluit nosque per hoc monuit
quam fragiles simus. Sed quamvis carne perimus,
post mortem reliqua spes tamen est aliqua,
fit quia nostrarum mors ipsa salus animarum.
Et quando morimur, tunc Mahumet sequimur.
Qui sublimabit cunctosque sibi sociabit
qui sua complere iussa volunt opere.
Cuius mandatis hoc addimus ut caveatis
porcina temere vos dape polluere.
Nec puto dicendum cur istud sit faciendum,
cum per se pateat quod satis hoc doceat."
Ex hoc gens illa contempta carne suilla,
pollutum credit de sue quisquis edit.
Et quia porcorum grex regem rosit eorum,
dicta superstitio venit ab hoc odio.

When he had finished dressing up the king, he used his sinful mouth to summon the king's servants and the peoples, and he said to them: "Let this day be passed in solemn manner, for the King of Libya has gone home to heaven today. There he indeed has become King of Heaven, and he summons us, as his own children, up to the heavenly ones. For although his dominions have expanded, he will not be less our lord for this reason. Rather he will preserve his Libyans, protecting them not as servants but as friends, and he will rule ministering to them.

"But why is your heart troubled when you consider and seek a reason why this father has given his own revered limbs to the pigs to gnaw on? This humble death teaches how base the flesh is. He wished to suffer this way so as to illustrate and openly symbolize that teaching, and he warns us thus how fragile we are. But although we perish in the flesh, after death some hope still remains, since death itself becomes the salvation of our souls. And when we die, then we follow Muhammad. He will lift up and unite to himself all who wish to fulfill his commandments in their deeds. To his commandments we must add that you must beware of polluting yourself rashly by eating pork. Nor do I think I must say why we must do so, since it is evident that he taught this sufficiently." For this reason that people rejects pork and considers whoever eats it as polluted. Since a herd of pigs gnawed on their king, this superstition comes from that hatred.

Tunc sua praecepta gaudens Magus esse recepta
   rerum gestarum credidit esse parum
ni consummaret scelus et quasi sanctificaret.
   Quod plenus scelere, sic parat efficere:
construxit fanum, fanum non, immo profanum.
   Cuius pro foribus sculptile marmoribus
carmen habebatur, quod tale fuisse putatur:
   "HIC BENE QUOD PETITUR PER MAHUMET DABITUR."
Hac in structura nihil exstabat sine cura.
   Tota domus pretio fulsit et ingenio:
marmore candebat Pario quacumque patebat,
   sed marmor Parium vicit opus varium.
Nam si vixisset opus atque loqui potuisset,
   "Materiam vici!" diceret artifici.
Taliter ornatum fanum fuit atque paratum.
   Sed si quis quaerit quanta domus fuerit,
cum procul hinc statur, mons aureus esse putatur
   in tantum spatii continet et pretii.
Plus mirareris si forsitan ingredereris;
   fulgor enim lapidum te faceret stupidum.
Qui sic ornabant opus auri, quod variabant,
   sicut nocturnum lucida stella polum.
Hic opus elatum solo, magnete paratum,
   in medio steterat et velut arcus erat.
Sub quem, portatur Mahumet tumuloque locatur,
   qui, si quis quaerat, aere paratus erat.
Et quia revera magnes sibi contrahit aera,
   in qua rex iacuit tumba levata fuit
et sic pendebat, quod vis lapidum faciebat.
   Ergo, rudes populi prodigium tumuli

Then the mage rejoiced that his teaching was accepted, but he thought that his achievements were too small unless he could consummate his crime, and, as it were, make it holy. Full of sin, he prepared to accomplish this: he constructed a temple, not a holy place but an unholy one. Outside its marble doors a verse was chiseled, which is thought to have been such: "WHAT IS SOUGHT IN THE RIGHT SPIRIT HERE WILL BE GIVEN THROUGH MUHAMMAD." The whole structure had been prepared with great care. The whole building shone with great expense and craftsmanship: it gleamed with Parian marble, wherever it was open to view, but the varied workmanship surpassed the Parian marble. For if the workmanship had been alive and could have spoken, it would say to the craftsman: "I have conquered the material!" The temple was decorated and prepared in this fashion. But if anyone should ask how large the building was, when one stands at a distance from it, it seems to be a golden mountain, so great is the space it occupies and its value. You would be more amazed if you should enter it; the gleaming of the stones would stun you. The stones adorn the gold work, to which they provide variation, just as a shining star in the night sky. The structure, raised off the ground using a magnet, stood in the middle and was like an arch. Under this, Muhammad is carried and placed in his tomb, which, should anyone ask, is made of bronze. And since indeed the magnet attracts the bronze, the tomb in which the king lies has been raised up and floats in this fashion, as a result of the stones' force. Therefore, when the uneducated people saw

postquam viderunt, rem pro signo tenuerunt,
   credentes miseri per Mahumet fieri
pondere res plena quod pendeat absque catena
   nec sit pendiculum quod teneat tumulum.
Hoc ubi viderunt stulti, Mahumet coluerunt,
   gente quod in Libyca fecerat ars magica.
Sed nos errorum quia causas diximus horum,
   Musa manum teneat! Et Mahumet pereat!

the wonder of the tomb, they took it to be a miracle, believing wretchedly that Muhammad had made a heavy thing hang without a chain and that there was no hanger that supported the tomb.

When the fools saw what the mage's craft had accomplished among the Libyan people, they worshipped Muhammad. But since we have told the causes of those errors, Muse, stay your hand! And may Muhammad perish!

POETIC PASTIMES ON MUHAMMAD

Walter of Compiègne

Otia de Machomete

Quisquis nosse cupis patriam Machometis et actus,
otia Walterii de Machomete lege.
Sic tamen otia sunt, ut et esse negotia credas:
ne spernas, quotiens "otia" fronte legis.
Nam si vera mihi dixit Warnerius abbas,
me quoque vera loqui de Machomete puta.
Si tamen addidero vel dempsero, sicut et ille
addidit aut dempsit forsan, ut esse solet,
spinam devita, botrum decerpere cura.
Botrus enim reficit, vulnera spina facit.
Abbas iam dictus monacho monachus mihi dixit,
immo testatus est mihi multotiens,
quod quidam, cui nomen erat Paganus, honestus
clericus et Senonum magnus in ecclesia,
secum detinuit aliquanto tempore quendam
qui Machomis patriam gestaque dixit ei,
qui de progenie gentili natus et altus
Christi baptismum ceperat atque fidem.
Ergo se puerum didicisse legendo professus
quicquid scripturae de Machomete sonant.
Dixit eum genitum genitoribus ex Idumaeis
et Christi doctum legibus atque fide;
rhetor, arithmeticus, dialecticus et geometer,
musicus, astrologus grammaticusque fuit,
qui licet ut liber excelleret artibus istis,
ex servis servus ortus et altus erat.

Poetic Pastimes on Muhammad

If you wish to know about Muhammad's country and his deeds, then read Walter's poetic pastimes on Muhammad. These poetic pastimes are such that you might believe they are also serious: so do not scorn them, when you see "pastimes" on the front. For if the abbot Warnerius has told me the truth, then believe that I too am telling the truth about Muhammad. If however I have added or subtracted, just as perhaps he has added and subtracted, as is customary, avoid the thorn, take care to pluck the grape. The grape cluster refreshes, but the thorn wounds.

The aforesaid abbot said to me as one monk to another, or rather he testified to me many times, that a certain man named Paganus, a decent cleric and an important man in the Church of Champagne, spent some time with another man who told him of Muhammad's country and deeds. Although this man was born and raised a Gentile, he had accepted the baptism and the faith of Christ. For that reason he declared that as a boy he had learned by reading whatever has been written of Muhammad. He said that Muhammad's parents were Edomites, and that Muhammad was well-versed in the Christian laws and faith; he was an orator, a mathematician, an expert in dialectics and geometry, a musician, an astrologer, and a grammarian; but although he excelled at these arts like a free man, he was a slave, born of and raised by slaves.

Servus erat domini cuiusdam nobilis atque
castellis, opibus divitis et populo,
qui licet omnibus his et pluribus esset abundans,
more tamen gentis illius et patriae
merces mutandas, species quoque pro speciebus
longe per servos mittere suetus erat.
Sed magis arbitrio Machometis quaeque fiebant:
utilior reliquis plusque fidelis erat.
Illis temporibus et in illis partibus unus
vir fuit egregii nominis et meriti,
conversans solus inter montana rogansque
pro se, pro populo nocte dieque deum,
more prophetarum gnarus praenosse futura,
totus mente polo, carne retentus humo.
Vicinis igitur de partibus atque remotis
multi gaudebant eius adire locum,
consilio cuius, prece, dogmate quisque refectus
regrediebatur laetior ad propria.
Sic etiam Machomes devotus venit ad illum,
recte vivendi discere dogma volens.
Quo viso sanctus admoto lumine mentis
intus possessum daemone novit eum
et cruce se signans, "Possessio daemonis," inquit,
"Vas inmunditiae, fraudis amice, fuge!
Quid luci tenebrae vel quae conventio Christi
ad Belial? Tecum portio nulla mihi!"
His Machomes motus et scrutans intima cordis
et manuum, talem se reperire nequit.
Unde satis supplex humilisque requirit ab illo
quare tam graviter corripuisset eum.

He was the slave of a certain master, who was noble and rich in castles and money and slaves. Although his master was well supplied with all these things and more, as was the custom of that people and country, he used to send slaves far off to exchange merchandise and goods for other goods. However whatever took place was mostly at Muhammad's discretion: he was more capable and more loyal than the others.

In those days there lived in that region a man of exceptional reputation and worth. He lived alone in the mountains and spent day and night praying to God on his own behalf and the people's. Like the prophets he knew how to predict the future: his mind was drawn entirely toward heaven, but his flesh held him to the earth. For this reason, many from nearby and from faraway were glad to visit his retreat. Each was uplifted by his advice, his prayers and his teaching and returned to his own pursuits happier.

Muhammad, in his devotion, also came to him thus, wishing to learn the doctrine of living rightly. But when the holy man saw him and turned the light of his spirit toward him, he realized that inside he was possessed by a demon. He crossed himself and said, "O possessed man! Unclean vessel, friend of deceit, flee! What does darkness have to do with the light, or what agreement does Christ have with Belial? I will have nothing to do with you!"

Muhammad was upset by these words and, although he examined the depths of his heart and his hands, he could not find himself to be this sort of man. Therefore in suppliant fashion and very humbly he asked that man why he had made such a serious accusation against him. The holy man

Sanctus ei: "Vere possessio daemonis es tu:
lex nova, sacra fides te tribulante ruet,
coniugium solves, corrumpes virginitatem;
iudicioque tuo castus adulter erit
et lex legitimum damnabit, iniquus amicum
iustitiae, pietas impietate cadet.
Tu facies mentis ut circumcisio non sit,
ut redeat carnis, ut sacra cesset aqua:
utque loquar brevius, Adam veterem renovabis
atque novas leges ad nihilum rediges!"
Tunc Machomes constanter ait se malle cremari
quam per se leges ad nihilum redigi,
vir tamen ille dei nihilominus increpat illum
eque sua facie iam procul ire iubet.
Abscedens Machomes et sancti dicta revolvens
innumeras animo fertque refertque vices:
nam de se sancto plus quam sibi credere coepit
et sicut mentem, sic variat faciem
iamque satis posset advertere quilibet illum
non proprii iuris esse, sed alterius:
daemon enim ducebat eum quocumque volebat
permissuque dei prospera cuncta dabat.
Qui proprium tamen ad dominum de more reversus
exsequitur solitum sedulus obsequium:
conservos ad se vocat; adsunt. Imperat illis,
illius imperiis accelerando favent:
serica cum Tyriis et murice pallia tincta,
plurima praeterea, quae pretiosa putant,
de domini sumunt thesauris atque camelos
ex ipsis onerant; sic iter arripiunt.

said to him: "You are truly possessed by a demon. The new law, the holy faith will collapse under your onslaught. You will destroy marriage and you will corrupt virginity; in your judgment the chaste man will be an adulterer and the law will condemn the legitimate, the wicked man will condemn the friend of justice, reverence for god will be toppled by godlessness. You will get rid of the circumcision of the spirit, so that the circumcision of the flesh will return, and baptism cease: in short, you will restore the old Adam and you will reduce the new laws to nothing!" Then Muhammad insisted that he would rather be consumed by fire than have the laws be reduced to nothing through him, but that man of God accused him nevertheless and ordered him to go quickly far away from his sight.

As Muhammad departed, he weighed the holy man's words and brought them to his mind countless times, for he had begun to believe the holy man about himself more than he believed himself. As his mind changed, so his expression changed, and soon anyone would have been able to notice that he was not in control of himself, but rather another controlled him: a demon was leading him wherever it wished, and with God's permission the demon gave him good fortune in everything.

Nevertheless when he returned to his own master as usual, he attentively continued with his usual obedience. He called his fellow slaves to him; they came. He gave them orders; they hastened to obey his orders. They took silk gowns dyed with purple dyes from Tyre and from shellfish and many things that they thought were valuable from among the treasures of their master. They loaded them on the cam-

Aethiopas igitur, Persas Indosque petentes
merces mutandas mercibus instituunt.
Non sic ad votum Machometis cesserat umquam,
nec tantum domino proderat ante suo:
nam rediens commissa sibi duplicata reportat
quaedam, multa magis quam triplicata refert.
O, divinorum scrutator iudiciorum
quis queat esse? Malis plus sua vota favent!
Sed si credamus rationi Christicolarum,
quam sacra lex firmat, quam tenet alma fides,
retribuit deus ista malis propter bona quaedam,
quae quandoque mali, parva licet, faciunt.
Econtra nemo tam sancte vivit ad unum,
quin aliquando manu, mente vel ore cadat:
hic igitur premitur ut et hic deponat amurcam
quam de peccato contrahit exul homo.
Sic Iob, sic Machomes, bonus hic, malus ille, fuerunt;
nunc habet hic requiem, sustinet ille crucem.
Taliter Antiochus, Macchabei taliter; hii nunc
felices gaudent, nunc miser ille dolet.
Pressuras sancti sic omnes paene tulerunt,
ut dolor iste brevis gaudia plena daret.
Iam non turberis domino si iudice iustis
hic mala proveniunt vel bona saepe malis:
divitis esto memor, quem Lazarus ille rogabat,
cuius lingebat ulcera lingua canum:
dives inhumanus modo tormentatur in igne,
nunc Abrahae gaudet Lazarus in gremio.
Sic Nero, sic Decius, Dacianus, Maximianus
presserunt Christi tempore membra suo,

els; thus they set off. They sought out the Ethiopians, the Persians and the Indians and set about exchanging wares for other wares. Never had Muhammad's wishes been fulfilled thus, nor had he ever before made such a profit for their master: for when he returned he brought the double of certain wares entrusted to him, and of many wares, he brought back more than the triple.

Who can fathom God's judgments? The prayers of evil people have better outcomes! If we may trust the Christian arguments, which the sacred law supports and the kindly faith maintains, then God bestows these things on evil people owing to certain good deeds that at some time the evil men have done, though they be small. On the other hand, no one lives such a holy life in every respect without transgressing at some point in deeds, thoughts or words. He is afflicted here, so that here he will also rid himself of the residue of sin that man accumulates in his exile. Thus Job, thus Muhammad: one was good, the other evil: one is at rest now, while the other bears the cross; thus Antiochus, thus the Maccabees; the latter are content and rejoice now, but the former is in pain and miserable. Almost all the saints endured afflictions thus so that brief pain would bring them perfect joys. Now you will no longer be disturbed if, in the Lord's judgment, bad things often befall the righteous here or good things befall the wicked. Remember the rich man, from whom Lazarus begged, whose sores the dogs licked with their tongues: the heartless, rich man is now tortured in fire, while Lazarus rejoices in the bosom of Abraham. Thus Nero, thus Decius, Dacianus, Maximian, in their own times, persecuted the limbs of Christ, and head of these

et caput ipsorum, Christum loquor, in cruce misit
gens cui promissus et cui missus erat.
Ille resurrexit, ascendit, regnat et illuc
membra trahit secum iugiter ipse sua,
sic antichristos vermis qui non morietur
rodet et inferni flamma vorabit eos.
Talibus exemplis sta firmus, cum mala iustis
vel bona non iustis saepe venire vides;
nam quod de domino testatur lectio sacra,
iudicium iustis exerit hic patiens.
Quod quia tangendum visum fuit utile, noster
est intermissus ad modicum Machomes.
His intermissis redeuntes ad Machometem
texere propositum iam satagamus opus.
Tempus adest quo mortuus est dominus Machometis
et sine prole manet uxor et absque viro,
sed sicut domino Machomes fuit ante fidelis,
sic etiam domine subditur imperiis,
servit ei, dat consilium, procurat agenda:
plus solito domine multiplicantur opes.
Postquam post domini decessum transiit annus,
disponit iuvenis nubere iam domina
secretoque vocans Machometem tempore dicit:
"Sum iuvenis, sexu femina, res fragilis,
possideo servos, ancillas, praedia, villas,
sunt castella mihi, sunt etiam proceres,
sum viduata viro, natis et utroque parente:
ignoro prorsus qualiter ista regam.
Ergo tu, qui consilio callere probaris,
praemeditare mihi quae facienda probes.

limbs, that is Christ, was sent to the cross by the people to whom he had been promised and sent. Christ rose again, ascended, and reigns, and he himself carries his limbs away with him perpetually. Thus the worm that will not die will gnaw the Anti-Christs, and hell's flame will devour them. Hold fast to such examples when you see how often good fortune comes to people who are unjust, and misfortunes to the just; for, as Holy Scripture bears witness, the Lord patiently reveals his judgment to the just.

Since it seemed useful to touch on this, our Muhammad has been interrupted for a short while. After this interruption we return to Muhammad, and we will strive to weave the work already proposed.

The time came when Muhammad's master died, and his wife was still childless and now widowed. But just as Muhammad had been loyal to his master, he also obeyed the orders of his mistress. He served her, gave her advice, he performed duties, and her wealth multiplied more than usual. When the first year after his master's death had passed, Muhammad's young mistress was already planning to wed. And at a private moment she called Muhammad to her and said: "I am a young woman, a frail thing; I own slaves, maidservants, estates, villas, I have castles, and I even have nobles. I am a childless widow, and both my parents are dead. I am completely ignorant of the administration of all these assets. So since you have been proven to give clever advice, consider what you think that I should do. I beg that you

Utile consilium rogo provideas et honestum:
numquam laude carent haec duo iuncta simul.
Sit persona decens, sapiens et strenua, sit quae
non minuat nostrum nobilitate genus,
denique vir talis sit, ut esse per omnia dignum
illum me nemo iure negare queat."
Respondit Machomes: "Operam dabo nocte dieque,
forsitan inveniam qui deceat dominam.
Sed quia vix talis in multis invenietur,
quod quaeris longo temporis esse reor.
Non diffido tamen, quia si deus ista futura
praevidit, non est cur remanere queant."
His dictis Machomes abscedens pervigil instat
si quo forte modo ducere possit eam.
Transierant vix octo dies, cum subdolus ille
veracem simulans praemeditatus adest.
Vultum dimittit, oculos gravat, afficit ora,
mentitur facie religionis opus.
Pallidus apparet, ut quilibet hunc eremitam
aut anachoretam iudicet aut monachum;
talem se simulat, ut dicere vera putetur
cum dominam fallit falsa loquendo suam
rhetoricosque suis verbis miscendo colores
cum domina tamquam Tullius alter agit:
"Si iuveni nubas quem nobilis ordo parentum,
quem decus atque decor strenuitasque levet,
depopulator erit rerum fortasse tuarum;
vastabit villas, praedia destituet,
omnia consumet vivendo luxuriose.
Quae modo dives eras, ad breve pauper eris.

give me expedient and honorable advice, for if the advice is both of these things it will never want for approval. Let it be an attractive, wise and vigorous person, and let it be a person who is not less than my family in nobility, and finally let him be such a husband that no one can rightly deny that he is worthy of me in all respects."

Muhammad responded: "I will work at this by day and by night, and perhaps I will find someone worthy of my lady. But because such a man is scarcely to be found among many, I think that what you are looking for will take a long time. Nevertheless I have no doubt that if God intends for this to be, then nothing can prevent it."

After he had said this he departed and thought incessantly about whether there might be some way for him to marry her. Scarcely eight days had passed when that deceitful man made his plans and, pretending to be honest, approached her. He looked downcast, with a serious gaze, and he altered his face and gave the deceitful appearance of religious devotion. He appeared so pale that anyone would take him for a hermit or an anchorite or a monk; he pretended to be such a person so that he would seem to tell the truth while he deceived his mistress speaking lies, and, mixing the colors of rhetoric with his words, he spoke with his lady as if he were a second Cicero:

"If you marry a young man distinguished by nobility, good looks, fine manners and vigor, he might turn out to be a wastrel with your fortune, he will lay waste the estates, plunder the lands; he will consume everything with luxurious living. You are now rich, but will soon be poor. And worse, he

Quodque puto gravius, te spernens fiet adulter,
unde timens capiti non eris ausa loqui.
Quare consilium dominae me iudice non est
nobilis et iuvenis quaerere coniugium.
Sed iam de senibus tecum, puto, mente revolves:
'Ille vel ille senex est bonus, est sapiens,
congruit ille mihi, bene me reget et sapienter
omnia disponet: nubere quaero seni!'
Sed non hoc quaeras, quia non sibi convenienter
iunguntur iuvenis femina virque senex.
Illa colore viget, nitida cute, corpore recto;
pallidus, incurvus, sordidus ille tremit.
Illa iuventutis amplexus factaque quaerit
. . .
ille dolet, tussit, emungitur, excreat; illa
sanior et iuvenis paene nihil patitur.
Auditus, gustus, olfactus, visio, tactus,
integritas mentis in sene deficient,
sed, nisi turbetur casu natura, iuventus
sensibus his sanis laeta vigere solet.
Cum sibi dissimiles ita sint iuvenesque senesque,
cum sene quo pacto copula stet iuvenis?
Non igitur iuveni, qualem praediximus ante,
nec cuiquam vetulo conveniat domina.
Ut vulgare loquar, praesumo docere Minervam.
Non praesumo tamen: actito iussa mihi.
Et solet hoc multis contingere, res alienas
multotiens melius quam proprias agere,
et quod non fallat haec in me regula nosti,
namque tuis semper postposui propria.

may spurn you and commit adultery, and you may fear for your life and not dare to speak. Therefore in my opinion it is not wise for my lady, if I am to judge, to seek to marry a young nobleman.

"But now you are thinking about old men, I imagine: 'This old man or the other, is good, wise; he is suited to me, and he will rule me well and administer everything wisely. I want to marry an old man!' But you should not desire this, since it is not suitable for a young woman and an old man to be joined in marriage. She possesses healthy coloring, glowing skin, an upright body; he trembles, is pale, hunched, dirty. She seeks the embraces and deeds of youth; . . . he has pains, coughs, wipes his nose, spits. She is healthier and young and has almost no complaints. An old man lacks hearing, taste, smell, vision, touch and soundness of mind, while, unless nature is disturbed by an accident, youth is usually happily endowed with healthy senses. And since the young and the old are so different from each other, how can a young woman and an old man couple? Therefore, neither the young man of the sort I have already described nor just any miserable old man is appropriate for my lady.

"To speak plainly, I presume to teach Minerva. But I do not presume: I am following orders. And as often happens, many people do other people's business many times better than their own, and you know that this rule is not broken in my case, for I always put your interests before my own.

Dum tibi vir vixit, me nemo fidelior illi,
nemo tibi viduae me fuit utilior.
Cumque tibi maneam tam commodus atque fidelis,
cur dubites nostro credere consilio?
Quodque loquar dominae non mentem, non gravet aures,
cum cupiam tibi plus quam mihi proficere."
Illa refert: "Constat, Machomes, te vera locutum
et debere tibi credere me fateor.
Dic igitur quodcumque placet, quodcumque videtur
consilium: certe credere non renuam."
Tunc Machomes solito factus securior, illi
iam reserare parans abdita cordis ait:
"Quae modo sunt dominae dominique fuisse probantur:
ancillae, servi, praedia, prata, domus,
villarum reditus, terrarum commoda, cuncta
a puero semper nota fuere mihi.
Nullus de servis dominae sic omnia novit,
nullus ei tantum commodus esse potest.
Et nisi servili sub conditione tenerer,
nobilium nulli nuberet utilius."
Talibus auditis ut prudens atque modesta
responsum tali temperat illa modo:
"Consilium quod das nec prorsus dico probandum
nec prorsus dico quod reprobare velim.
Nam quod de iuvenum dixisti nobilitate,
ut patet in factis, nemo negare potest.
Vix etenim videas cum nobilitate iuventam,
quin sit contemptrix, prodiga, vana, procax.
Sic etiam constat te vera fuisse locutum
quod senis et iuvenis copula non deceat

While your husband was alive, no one was more loyal to him than I, and no one has been more useful to you in your widowhood than I. And since I am still so obliging and loyal to you, why do you hesitate to trust my advice? What I will say must not weigh heavy on my lady's mind or ears, since I seek to benefit you more than myself."

She replied: "I agree, Muhammad, that you have spoken the truth, and I confess that I ought to trust you. So say whatever you think right, whatever advice you think best: I will certainly not refuse to believe it." Then Muhammad felt more confident than usual, and he prepared to open up to her the secrets of his heart, and spoke thus: "Everything that is now my lady's and that had been my master's: the maidservants, the slaves, the estates, the pastures, the buildings, the revenues of the estates, the profits from the lands, all this has always been known to me from boyhood. None of my lady's slaves is so familiar with everything, none can be so profitable to her. And if I were not limited by my status as a slave, she would scarcely wed any nobleman to greater advantage."

Since the lady was prudent and modest, when she heard this she tempered her response thus: "I do not say that the advice you give should be adopted completely nor do I say that I wish to reject it entirely. For nobody can deny what you have said about young noblemen since it is evident from what they do. Indeed you can scarcely find youth coupled with nobility, unless it is haughty, prodigal, vain, licentious. Likewise, I agree that what you say is true: a union of an old man and a young woman is not fitting, and you demon-

et bene monstrasti disconvenientia, quare
iungi non debent: id placet idque probo.
Sed quod me dicis tibi nubere convenienter
nulla mihi ratio persuadere potest.
Si dominae servus iungatur, nemo tacebit,
ridendi causas omnibus ipsa dabo.
Clamabunt omnes, simul omnes improperabunt
et dicent omnes, femina virque simul:
'Quae solet esse super, nunc subiacet, et dominari
quae solet, ancillae nunc gerit officium!'
Quodque magis timeo, quoniam magis est pudibundum:
dicent me quondam subcubuisse tibi!
Quod si vel leviter submurmuret unus ad unum,
id quoque si sciero, me puto malle mori.
Est etiam procerum mihi copia, qui mihi debent
temporibus certis reddere servitia,
quos pudeat servire mihi, si nupsero servo.
Sic honor et nostrae sic minuentur opes.
Quin etiam servi conservum despicientes
nec tua curabunt nec mea iussa sequi.
Sic et quae spondes ex te mihi commoda perdam
quaeque putas per te damna cavere, feram."
Cautus ad haec Machomes aurem patienter habebat,
cordis in arcano singula verba locans,
oreque compresso modicum silet, ut videatur
responsum magni ponderis esse suum.
Inde levans oculos, sed et oris claustra resolvens:
"Crede mihi," dixit, "non nisi vera loquar.
Si libertati tibi me donare placebit,
quae metuis poterunt nulla nocere tibi.

strated well the incongruities owing to which they should not to be joined together: I agree and I approve of this.

"But when you say that I should marry you, no argument can persuade me. If the lady is joined to the slave, no one will be silent: I will become a laughingstock to all. There will be a general outcry, and accusations from everyone. All will say, women and men alike: 'She who was accustomed to be on top, now lies underneath, and she who was the mistress, now plays the part of a maidservant!' And what I fear even more, since it is more shameful: they will say that I had submitted to you in the past. If one man should whisper this lightly to another, and if I find out about it, I think I would rather die. For I have a band of nobles, who must render me services at certain times, and they will be ashamed to serve me if I marry a slave. Hence my honor and my wealth will diminish. For even the slaves will look down on their fellow slave and will not bother to follow your orders or mine. And so this way I will lose the profits that you promise to make for me, and I will suffer the losses that you think you can prevent."

Muhammad carefully and patiently gave ear to this, placing each of her words in his inmost heart. Then he shut his mouth and was silent for a while, so that his response would seem weightier. Then he lifted up his eyes and broke his silence: "Believe me," he said, "I will say nothing but the truth. If it please you to give me my freedom, you will not

Nobilis aut servus tibi vel mihi nemo resistet:
aut timor hos subdet aut sociabit amor.
Unde tuam nemo presumet laedere famam,
sed benedicetur nomen ubique tuum.
Divitiae crescent, augmentabuntur honores
et procerum solito maior erit numerus,
multiplicabuntur reditus, augebitur omne
quod minus esse solet, villula, vicus, ager.
Et quod promitto si non erit, excute dentes
aut fodias oculos aut mihi tolle caput!"
Tam magnis igitur promissis illa ligata,
si proceres laudent, nubere spondet ei.
Tunc Machomes gaudens exit festinus ab illa
ad proceres, ambit, munera magna parat.
Hunc trahit in partem, secreto postulat illum;
hunc sibi promissis allicit, hunc precibus,
aurum promittit, argentum, pallia, vestes,
quicquid amat mundus, quicquid habere cupit.
Rem tamen occultat nisi quis firmaverit ante
quod ferat ex toto corde iuvamen ei.
Postquam per partes Machomes sic quemque ligavit
ut nulli retro cedere iam liceat,
consilio prudens omnes conduxit in unum
et quo res tendat omnibus innotuit:
scilicet ut liber fiat laudantibus illis
et per eos dominae possit habere torum
iamque manu misso sibi reddere non gravet illos
antea quae domino debita reddiderant.
O caecum virus, quo turget iniqua cupido,
quo semel inbutus se quoque nescit homo!

suffer the damages that you fear. No noble man or no slave will put up resistance to you or to me: either fear will subdue them or love will bind them. Hence no one will dare to damage your reputation, but your name will be blessed everywhere. Your wealth will grow, your honors will increase, you will rule over more nobles, your revenues will be multiplied, everything that is now less will increase, farmhouses, villages, fields. And if what I promise does not happen, knock out my teeth, or gouge out my eyes, or chop off my head!"

She thus felt bound by such great promises, and she promised to marry him, if the nobles gave their consent. Then Muhammad rejoiced, and hastily left her behind and went to canvass the nobles, preparing great favors for them: he coerced one to his side; in secret he entreated another; he lured another to himself with promises, another with entreaties; he promised gold, silver, gowns, clothing, whatever the world loves, whatever it wishes to have. Nevertheless he hid this business, unless each person would confirm first that he would help him wholeheartedly. Afterward Muhammad bound each individually so that now no one was permitted to go back. With a clever plan he brought everyone together and made known to all where the matter was heading: namely that he would be manumitted with their consent, and with their agreement he could share his lady's marriage bed, and that when he was free they would be no worse off in rendering him the same services that they had rendered to his master before him.

O invisible venom with which evil greed swells, the man once tainted with this fails to know even himself! The

Hos ita caecavit nummi species, rubor auri,
quod faciunt dominam ducat ut ille suam.
Cuius erant domini fiunt ob munera servi,
libera subponunt colla manusque iugo.
Ad dominam properant et quod Machometis ab ore
audierant, illi persuadere student:
"Si dominus noster," dicunt, "tuus ille maritus
nobilis et sapiens non moreretur adhuc,
non tibi vicinus praesumeret ullus obesse;
externos etiam subderet ille tibi;
omnia curaret, disponeret omnia, nulla
morderet mentem sollicitudo tuam.
Sed quia mortuus est et te sine prole reliquit
atque remanserunt multa gerenda tibi,
est opus ut nubas, quia non potes absque marito
pondera curarum femina ferre diu.
Sed vivente viro constat quod casta fuisti,
post obitum cuius haec quoque fama manet.
Unde timebamus ne forte tibi statuisses
sic semper vitam ducere velle tuam.
Hac igitur causa convenimus, ut verearis
tot vel tantorum spernere consilium.
Nube viro, quia si de te non venerit heres
qui teneat terram te moriente tuam,
omnia quae tua sunt miserabiliter rapientur
particulamque volet quisque tenere suam,
immo si fuerit quis fortior, omnia tollet.
Si quis ei contra dixerit ense cadet
et nos aut poenis aut morte peribimus omnes,
si non ut servi subiciamur ei.

beauty of coins, the glitter of gold so blinded them that they enabled him to marry his own mistress. Because of his gifts his masters became his slaves, and they bowed their free necks and hands to the yoke.

They hastened to the lady and tried to persuade her of what they had heard Muhammad say: "If our lord," they said, "your noble and wise husband were still alive, no neighbor would dare get in your way; he would make even the people outside your realms serve you; he would take care of everything, administer everything, you would be free of worries. But because he is dead and has left you childless, and many things have been left to you to administer, you must marry, since you, as a woman, cannot sustain for very long the burdens of these cares without a husband.

"When your husband was alive, it was known that you were chaste, and you maintain this reputation even after his death. Hence we were afraid that perhaps you would decide to live thus forever. We have come together for this reason: so that you may hesitate to scorn the advice of so many important men. Take a husband, because if no heir should be born to you who will hold your lands when you die, everything that is yours will be miserably plundered, and each will wish to have his own small share, or rather if someone is stronger, he will take everything; if someone speaks against him, he will fall by the sword. And we will all succumb to either punishments or death, if we do not submit to him as

Quae mala iure tibi vertentur ad impietatem,
si nos contemnens nubere nolueris."
Illa refert: "Etsi non nubere proposuissem,
propositum pietas vinceret et ratio.
Sed constat mecum me nil proponere magnum,
quod non ex vestro pendeat arbitrio.
Ergo personam mihi quaerite convenientem,
quae mihi, quae vobis utilis esse queat.
Si tamen ille mihi fuerit minus utilis, opto
consilium vestrum non minus inde sequi!"
Hoc verbum statim rapuere loquentis ab ore,
quod procerum placitum spondeat illa sequi.
Tunc quidam, fortasse senex cui credere dignum
monstrabat gravitas canaque caesaries,
antiquos annos memorans et gesta priorum,
alloquiis dominam talibus aggreditur:
"Principio nullus servili conditioni
subditus est, omnis tunc homo liber erat.
Sed quia primus homo peccavit transgrediendo,
peccati poenae subditur omnis homo.
Unde recens natus, si vivat nocte vel una,
primi peccati sorde nec ille caret,
et nisi mundetur sacri baptismatis unda,
semper ei caeli ianua clausa manet.
Hoc quoque mundatis transgressio contulit illa,
quod peccare, mori nemo carere potest.
Qui nisi peccasset, potuisset utrumque cavere
et modo sub neutro posteritas gemeret.
Sed sub utroque gemit, et Ham contraxit ab illo
quod legitur nudum non tacuisse patrem.

slaves: these evils will rightly be attributed to your impiety, if you spurn us and refuse to marry."

She responds: "Even if I had not intended to marry, piety and reason would override my intentions. But it is true that I do not make any important plan that does not depend on your discretion. Therefore seek for me a suitable person, who could be useful to me and to yourselves. If however he were less useful to me, I will choose to follow your advice nonetheless."

As she spoke, they quickly snatched the phrase from her mouth in which she promised to follow the decision of the nobles. Then one of them, as it happened an old man, whose sobriety and flowing white locks proved that he was trustworthy, and who remembered olden times and the deeds of their ancestors, approached the lady with the following speech:

"In the beginning no one was subjected to slavery: all men were free. But because the first man sinned by disobedience every man is subject to the punishment for this sin. For this reason a newborn baby, if it lives for only one night, is not free from the filth of the first sin, and unless it is cleansed in the waters of holy baptism heaven's gate will remain closed to it.

"Even for those who have been cleansed, this transgression means that no one is free from sin and from death. If the first man had not sinned, he could have avoided both, and now his posterity would not groan under either. But it groans under both and Ham incurred this because it is read that he was not silent about his father's nakedness. But since

Sed quia fortasse dominae non venit ad aures,
non reor indignum si reseratur ei.
Cum genus humanum deus ob peccata sub undis
delesset solis octo superstitibus,
obdormisse Noe legitur, detecta pudenda
eius erant; vidit Ham sine veste patrem,
detulit ad fratres, fratres doluere, pudorem
patris texerunt. Nota fuere patri,
qui contristatus Ham subposuit maledicto
et semper servum fratribus instituit.
Ex hoc cepit homo causas homini dominandi,
ex hoc servile sumpsit habere caput.
Sed quia peccavit, Ham vel Chanaan modo servit,
qui sequitur, Iafeth, Sem quoque liber erit.
Nam si quis peccat, peccati servus habetur,
eque deo natus crimina cuncta fugit,
non peccando dei iam filius esse docetur
nec servus dici iure nec esse potest.
Hoc Iesus dicit et apostolus ille Iohannes,
hinc evangelio non mihi quaero fidem.
Hos quoniam testes constat non posse refelli,
liber erit merito quisque fidelis homo.
Est autem dominae servorum copia multa,
inter quos unus omnibus est melior,
qui bonus et sapiens, qui strenuus atque fidelis,
qui validus membris, qui specie nitidus
digne rex posset seu princeps quilibet esse,
si non ex servis eius origo foret."
Tunc velut ignorans quod de Machomete loquantur,
callida responsum dissimulando dedit:

this has perhaps not reached my lady's ears, I do not think it unworthy if I disclose it to her.

"When God had wiped out the human race under the waves owing to its sins leaving only eight survivors, Noah is said to have fallen asleep, with his genitals exposed; Ham saw his father without clothing; he reported it to his brothers; his brothers grieved; they covered the shame of the father. The father found out; he was distressed, and he put a curse on Ham making him forever a slave to his brothers.

"This caused man to become the master of man, and with this slavery began. But because Ham sinned, or Canaan, he is now a slave; Japheth who follows, and Shem also, is free. For if someone sins, he is considered the slave of sin, and he who is born of God flees all sins: by not sinning he shows that he is the son of God, and he cannot rightly be called a slave or be one. Jesus says so, and John the apostle too. Hence I ask you to trust the Gospel and not myself. Since it is agreed that these authorities are irrefutable, then a man of faith will deserve to be free.

"My lady has a large number of slaves, among whom one is better than all the others. He is good and wise, vigorous and loyal; he is strong-limbed, and elegant in appearance, and worthy to be any king or prince if his origin were not servile." Then, as though she did not know that they were speaking of Muhammad, she feigned slyly as she responded:

"Quem mihi laudatis, ignoro, sed exhibeatur
et fiat liber: sim sua sitque meus."
Praesentant proceres Machometem. Suscipit illa,
de servo liber protinus efficitur.
Tractatur de coniugio, consentit uterque
et modico lapso tempore conveniunt.
Gaudia, prandia, fercula, pocula, vasa, ministros,
pransores, citharas, cymbala, sistra, lyras,
pallia, cortinas, aurum, lapides pretiosos,
ornamenta domus quis numerare queat?
Auceps, venator non defuit, ardea, cygnus,
grus, pavo, mergus adest, ursus, aper, caprea.
Festivos egere dies, dum festa fuere.
Sed dolor infestat festa repente gravis.
Nam Machomes morbo, qui dicitur esse caducus,
arreptus dominae concidit ante pedes,
membra volutat humi, decurrunt ore salivae.
Iam quasi defunctum flet domus et domina
paeneque deficiens, nimio confecta dolore
quod spes quae fuerat de Machomete perit,
ad thalamum properat et claudens ostia post se
ut dare solamen nemo valeret ei,
ingeminat luctus, vestes a pectore scindit,
abrumpit crines, unguibus ora secat.
Interea Machomes animo flatuque resumpto
tristitiae causas quaerit et audit eas.
Et dominam quaerit; thalamos intrasse docetur,
praecipit ut veniat, ostia clausa vetant.
Tunc per se Machomes accedit et ostia pulsat,
quae pulsata diu vix reserantur ei.

"I do not know whom you praise to me but bring him forth and let him be free. Let me be his, and he, mine."

The nobles present Muhammad. She receives him, and by that act from a slave he is made a free man. They discussed marriage, both agreed, and when a short time had passed, they came together. Rejoicing, feasting, platters, drinks, vessels, servants, guests at table, cithers, cymbals, rattles, lyres, gowns, cauldrons, gold, precious stones, who could enumerate the ornaments of the house? The fowler, the hunter was not absent: heron, swan, crane, peacock, gull, bear, wild boar, roe. They kept festive days, while there were feast days. But suddenly oppressive pain disturbed the feast. For Muhammad was attacked by the so-called falling sickness and fell down at his lady's feet. His limbs flailed on the ground, and saliva ran down from his mouth. The household wept over him as though he were already dead, and the lady, almost fainting, crushed by excessive grief because the hope that she had for Muhammad was perishing, hastened to her chamber, closing the doors after her so that no one could comfort her. There she redoubled her laments, she ripped the clothing from her chest, tore her hair, scratched her face with her nails.

Meanwhile Muhammad had recovered his spirit and caught his breath and asked the reasons for her sadness and heard them. And he looked for the lady; he is instructed to enter her chambers; he orders her to come, but the closed doors forbid it. Then Muhammad approached on his own and pounded on the doors, and when he had knocked for a

Ingressus dominam solari temptat, at illa
nullum solamen ex ratione capit.
Blandiri dominae Machomes molitur, at illa
pro blandimentis evomit opprobria.
Commendat Machomes illius nobilitatem,
illi de servis exprobrat illa genus.
At Machomes, quamquam sibi sit patientia falsa,
pace tamen dominae sustinet opprobria,
scilicet ut longo tandem satiata furore
vel sic suscipiat quae rationis erunt.
Res ita provenit: dominae deferbuit ira,
unde fit in Machomen iam minus ipsa gravis.
Laetatus Machomes, supplex accedit ad illam
atque salutatam taliter alloquitur:
"Si servum velles audire tuum patienter—
nam Machomes dominae non nisi servus erit—
si velles, inquam, mihi credere, protinus omnis
ira dolorque tuo cederet ex animo."
"Dic," inquit, "patiar tantum si vera loquaris,
si me non temptes fallere more tuo!"
Respondit: "Nisi vera loquar, si fallere quaeram,
linguam fallacem gutture velle suo."
Propositae praebens assensum conditioni
annuit ore, manu. Protinus ille refert:
"Quod me sperasti nuper tormenta tulisse,
nulla fuit morbi passio, crede mihi.
De caelo virtus in me descendit et illam
immensam fragilis ferre nequivit homo.
Propterea cecidi spumans et membra volutans,
non quia passio me laeserit ulla mali.

long time, they were opened to him after much ado. He entered and tried to console the lady, but she took no solace from reasoning. Muhammad tried to flatter her, but she spit out insults in exchange for his flattery. Muhammad praised her nobility; she reproached his origins from slaves.

But although Muhammad's patience was false, he nevertheless bore the lady's insults in silence: this was clearly so that when she was sated by prolonged raging she would perhaps thus accept reasoning. And thus it turned out: the lady's ire cooled, and as a consequence she became less hostile to Muhammad. He gladly approached her as a suppliant, hailed her and said: "If you were willing to hear your servant out patiently—since for his lady Muhammad will be nothing but a servant—if you would please believe me, all your anger and grief would soon be dispelled from your mind."

"Speak" she said, "I will allow it only if you speak the truth, if you do not try to deceive me as usual!" He responded: "If I do not speak the truth, if I seek to deceive you, then tear my lying tongue from my throat." She agreed to the proposed condition; she assented with her mouth, with her hand. He replied immediately:

"In spite of your apprehension, the tortures that I recently experienced was no suffering from a disease, believe me. Power descended into me from Heaven, and fragile man is unable to bear that infinite power. For that reason I fell foaming and flailing my limbs, and not because I suffered

Sed nunc mandatis praebe caelestibus aurem,
quae mihi de caelo nuntius explicuit.
Sicut enim Gabriel archangelus ille Mariae
adventus Christi nuntius ante fuit,
sic ventura deus reserat mihi nunc per eundem,
et pietate prius et pietate modo.
Naturalis enim primos transgressio legis
infecit patres et genus omne suum.
Postea scripta dei digito Moysi data lex est,
quam mandante deo detulit ad populum.
Promisit populus domini se iussa tenere,
sed cito desiliit transgrediendo viam.
His igitur causis moriendi lege tenemur,
exilium patimur tartareasque cruces.
Sed deus has hominum poenas miserando recepit
naturam nostram virgine matre satus,
in cunis positus intra praesepe locatus,
contectus pannis vilibus et modicis—
esuriens panis! sitiens fons! divus egenus!—
praeter peccatum cuncta gerens hominis.
Ex infante puer, sed et ex puero iuvenescens,
denique vir factus discipulos habuit.
Vitandum vitium, virtutem dixit amandam,
respuit elatos suscipiens humiles,
coniugio docuit praeferri virginitatem,
de qua praeceptum non tamen ipse dedit,
coniugium castum mandavit, ut unus et una
consociarentur foedere legitimo.
Nam reliquo quocumque modo se quis macularet,
turpis eum dixit criminis esse reum.

harm from any disease. But now give ear to the celestial commandments that a messenger has revealed to me from heaven. Indeed just as the archangel Gabriel was once the messenger of Christ's advent to Mary, thus God reveals to me the future now through the same angel: in compassion back then, and in compassion now.

"For the transgression of the natural law stained the first fathers and their whole race. Afterwards a law written by God's finger was given to Moses, which at God's command he brought to the people. The people promised that they would obey the Lord's commandments, but quickly they went astray, deviating from the path. For this reason, we are bound by the law of death; we suffer exile and bear the tortures of Tartarus.

"But God took pity on man's sufferings and received our nature, sown in a virgin mother, placed in a cradle within a manger, dressed in a few worthless rags,—bread that itself is hungry! a thirsty fountain! a needy rich man!—except for sin he took on all things human. From an infant he became a boy, and from a boy a youth, and finally as a grown man he had disciples. He said that we must avoid vice, and love virtue; he scorned the proud and received the humble; he taught that virginity is to be preferred to marriage; nevertheless, he did not insist on virginity. He ordained a chaste marriage, that one man and one woman be brought together by a legitimate bond. For if anyone stained himself in any other way, he said that he was guilty of a shameful sin. He

Omnibus impendi sincerum iussit amorem,
omnibus ut cupiat quod sibi quisque cupit.
Hinc circumcidi carnem vetuit genitalem
usque modo, dicens: 'ista figura fuit.
Re praesente figura vacet, baptismatis unda
illi succedat, haec stet et illa cadat.
Agnus, ovis, vitulus et cetera signa recedant!
Quo sol resplendet non habet umbra locum.
Iam Pharisaeorum procul absint traditiones!
Lex vetus impletur lege vigente nova.'
Talia dum mandat constanter homo deus idem,
saevit Iudaeus et Pharisaeus ad haec.
Insidiantur ei, verborum retia tendunt,
se verbo Verbum fallere posse putant.
Quod quia non possunt, intendunt crimina falsa,
sed nisi cum voluit, fraus nihil illa fuit.
Nam contra dominum non est sapientia, non est
consilium, virtus, sermo vel ingenium.
Ergo cum voluit tentus fuit, aspera lenis
sustinuit, clavos, verbera, probra, crucem;
in cruce defunctus, terrae mandatus adivit
Tartara, confregit, cum spoliis rediit.
Discipulis visus est quadraginta diebus;
Thomae palpandum praebuit ipse latus
corporeumque cibum sumpsit cernentibus illis,
ut monstraretur vivere vera caro.
Denique iussit eos totum transire per orbem
et veram populis insinuare fidem,
ut credant, ut agant, ut sacro fonte laventur,
et salvi fient: sin alias, perient.

ordered sincere love to be lavished on all: each should desire for all what he desires for himself.

"Hence he forbid that the flesh of the genitals be circumcised up to now, saying, 'This was a symbol. At present let the symbol be without power. Let the water of baptism be the successor of that other; let the latter stand, let the former fall. Let the lamb, the sheep, the calf and the other signs be gone! Where the sun shines, the shadow has no place. Let the traditions of the Pharisees recede! The old law is filled out by a new valid law.' While the man, at the same time God, commanded such things firmly, the Jews and the Pharisees were enraged. They set ambushes for him; they spread nets of words, thinking that they could trick the Word with a word. Since they could not, they attempted false accusations, but unless God was willing, that deception was nothing. For there is no wisdom, no counsel, virtue, discourse, or talent that can oppose the Lord.

"Therefore since he was willing he was stretched out [on the cross]. Although gentle himself, he suffered cruelty: nails, blows, insults, the cross. When he died on the cross and had been committed to earth, he went to the regions of Tartarus; he broke them down and returned with the spoils. He appeared to his disciples for forty days; he himself gave his side to be touched by Thomas and he accepted bodily food with all looking on in order to show that the true flesh lived. Finally, he ordered them to travel the whole world and convince the peoples of the true faith, so that they believe, so that they act, so that they be washed in the sacred spring and saved: otherwise they will perish.

His dictis benedicit eis caeloque receptus
  promisso patris munere firmat eos:
spiritus inter eos in linguis venit et igne,
  ut per verba fluant quos sacer urat amor.
Ergo muniti linguis et amore calentes
  securi Christi nomen ubique ferunt.
Unde flagella, cruces, ignes, gladios patiuntur,
  sed poenis illos vincere nemo potest,
quin sibi collato virtutum munere reges
  et populos Christi subposuere iugo.
O nova res! Morum mutatio tanta fiebat,
  ut qui maior erat, gaudeat esse minor;
qui fuerat quondam nutritus deliciose,
  cum modico modicam pane requirat aquam;
qui prius ornari pretiosa veste solebat,
  nunc vili sacco frigida membra tegat.
Hic cibus, haec vestis ita strinxerat illa pudenda,
  quod vix inter eos quis nisi castus erat.
Virginis hic votum sibi fecerat, ille maritus
  servabat sancti foedera coniugii.
Tantam Christicolae tenuerunt religionem
  dum data lex noviter, dum novus ordo fuit.
Sed quod habere solet noviter novus ordo statutus,
  primitus ut vigeat, inde tependo ruat,
sic quoque religio decrevit christicolarum,
  ut quae summa fuit, postea corruerit:
invidiae surgunt, sibi quisque requirit honorem,
  et fratrem frater laedere non metuit.
Ebrius efficitur qui sobrius esse solebat,
  et parcus venter solvitur ingluvie;

"When he said these things, he blessed the disciples. He was received by heaven and strengthened his disciples with the promised gift of the father: the spirit came down among them in tongues and fire, so those burned by the sacred love would flow with words. Thus fortified with tongues and ablaze with love, they fearlessly bore the name of Christ everywhere. For this reason they suffered blows, crosses, fires, swords, but no one could conquer them with punishments and prevent them from using the gift of virtues conferred upon them to subject kings and peoples to the yoke of Christ.

"O new order! Such a great change of customs occurred that the greater man rejoiced to be lesser; the man once fed on delicacies now requires little water along with little bread; he who once dressed up in precious clothing now covered his cold limbs with vile sackcloth. This food, this clothing so restrained their genitals that there was scarcely anyone among them who was not chaste. Some made the vow of virginity to themselves, others preserved the bonds of holy matrimony as spouses.

"The Christians' observance was great while the law was newly received, while the order was new. But as usual when a new order is recently established just as it flourishes at first, afterward it cools down and collapses. Thus also the religious devotion of the Christians decreased, although it had been supreme, it collapsed afterward: jealousies arose; each sought high office for himself; and brothers did not fear to injure their brothers. Those who were usually sober, got drunk, and the sparing stomach was replaced by gluttony;

foedantur mentes et corpora commaculantur.
  Virgo ruit vitio, castus adulterio.
Nemo fidem Christo promissam servat; amorem
  nemo tenet castum; sic perit omnis homo.
Et quem iam Christus cruce, sanguine, morte redemit,
  ut redimat rursum non morietur item.
Sed tamen ex ipsa, qua praeditus est, pietate
  consilium statuit ne penitus pereat.
Legis onus minuet, tollet baptisma, decemque
  uxores unus ducere vir poterit:
scribere mandavit deus haec mihi per Gabrielem,
  cetera iussurus tempore quaeque suo.
His mihi de causis Gabriele superveniente,
  sicut vidisti, concido, spumo, tremo.
Qui simul abscedit, ego mox virtute resumpta
  gratulor arcani conscius angelici.
Tu quoque congaude, quia femina sola mereris
  divinum mecum noscere consilium."
His Machomes dominam sic decepisse putabat
  ut quicquid dicat credere non dubitet.
Sed nihil illa putans verbis fallacius istis,
  conviciis illum talibus aggreditur:
"Mendax, plene dolo, te sustinui patienter,
  expectando diu te mihi vera loqui!
Sed quia nunc video te non nisi falsa locutum
  contra promissum, quo mihi iunctus eras,
me vix abstineo quin excutiam tibi dentes,
  quin oculos fodiam, quin caput ense cadat."
Respondit Machomes: "Ut credas profero testem,
  de cuius dictis sit dubitare nefas.

minds were sullied, and bodies were also stained. The virgin was ruined by vice; the chaste man, by adultery. No one kept the faith promised to Christ. No one practiced chaste love; everyone was undone. And when Christ has once redeemed mankind with his cross, his blood, his death, he will not die the same way to redeem it again.

"But nonetheless out of his native compassion he establishes a plan so that man not perish completely. He will reduce the burden of the law, he will abolish baptism, and one man will be able to marry ten wives. God commanded me through Gabriel to write these things, and he will command other things, each in its own time. When Gabriel comes down to me for these purposes, just as you have seen, I fall down, I froth, I tremble. When he departs, I soon recover my strength and am glad to know the angelic secret. Rejoice with me too, because you are the only woman who deserves to know God's plan along with me."

Muhammad thought he had deceived his lady with these words so that she would not hesitate to believe whatever he said. But she thought that nothing could be more false and approached him with these insults: "Liar, full of trickery, I endured you patiently, hoping for a long time that you would speak truth to me! But now since I see you have spoken only lies, breaking the promise by which we were married, I can scarcely restrain myself from knocking out your teeth, from gouging out your eyes, from letting your head fall to the sword."

Muhammad answered: "So that you may believe, I offer a witness whose words it would be sacrilege to doubt. We all

Nos omnes scimus quod in isto monte propinquo
est quidam magni nominis et meriti,
a quo si quisquam quae sunt ventura requirat,
quicquid respondet indubitanter erit.
Non prece, non pretio nullove timore moveri
a vero poterit: firma columna manet.
Hic tibi quae dixi si deneget, omnia membra
per minimas partes, annuo, tolle mihi!"
Illa rapit verbum, sanctum commendat et: "Illum
cras," inquit, "dicta conditione petam."
Laudat et hoc Machomes et eum de nocte requirens
cuncta refert et post talia commemorat:
"Praeteriere, puto, iam tres aut quattuor anni,
ex quo sancta domus haec mihi nota fuit.
Tunc mihi dixisti quod me faciente peribunt
lex nova, sacra fides, coniugium, lavacrum;
his adiunxisti quam plurima, more prophetae
antea quam veniant notificata tibi.
Et si praevidit per me deus ista futura,
ut praedixisti, res ita proveniet.
Sic igitur Christi destructa lege fideque
in baratri poenas corruet omnis homo,
nam nisi qui fuerit baptismi fonte renatus,
ad Christi regnum nullus habebit iter.
Attamen haec aliter fieri fortasse valerent,
si nostris velles credere consiliis:
christicolis aliis destructis tu superesses
et Solymae templum discipulique tui,
et miserante deo modico de semine posset
Christi cultorum surgere magna seges."

know that in the nearby mountain there is a certain man, very famous and worthy, and if anyone asks of him what will come to pass, whatever he responds will happen without a doubt. He will not depart from the truth for any entreaties, at any price, or in fear of anything: he remains a steadfast pillar. If he denies to you what I have said, then I give you my consent to tear me limb from limb!"

She seized his phrase, praised the holy man and said: "I will seek him out tomorrow under the condition you specified." And Muhammad approved this decision also, and sought out the holy man at night. He told him everything and then reminded him: "I think three or four years have passed now since I first saw this holy house. At that time you said to me that, through my deeds, the new law, the sacred faith, marriage, and baptism would perish; to these you, like a prophet, added much more made known to you before it happens. If God foresaw that I would do this as you predicted, then it will so come about. Thus when Christ's law and faith have been destroyed, each man will descend to the punishments of hell, for unless he has been born again at the baptismal font, no one will have a path to the kingdom of Christ.

"But nevertheless, perhaps this could happen differently, if you were willing to believe my advice. When the other Christians have been destroyed, you would survive and so would the Temple of Jerusalem and your disciples, and through divine mercy from a small seed a great harvest of worshippers of Christ could arise." The holy man re-

Sanctus ad haec: "Iura te non evertere templum
quodque mihi parcas discipulisque meis
et faciam quaecumque voles, tantummodo non sint
adversus Christi iussa sacramque fidem."
Et Machomes: "Christo contraria multa videntur
quae dispensanter saepe licet fieri."
Sanctus ait: "Sic est, dic quod placet: impleo, tantum
servetur semen christicolae populi!"
Iuravit Machomes et subdidit: "Est mihi coniunx,
excellens fama, divitiis, genere,
qua nubente mihi venerunt prospera cuncta.
Sed cito turbavit gaudia nostra dolor,
improvisus enim morbus mihi contigit et me
seminecem stravit ante pedes dominae.
Illa repentino casu turbata simulque
tota domus flentes unguibus ora secant.
Sic iacui similis defuncto paene per horam
et rursus sumpto flamine convalui.
Et satagens maestos solari dissimulabam,
affirmans passum me nihil esse mali,
sed secreta dei mitti mihi per Gabrielem,
cuius virtutem ferre nequiret homo.
His illa non dante fidem te nomino testem;
laudat et idcirco cras tua tecta petet.
Haec tibi confiteor, haec antea dicere veni
quam veniat, ne tu dicta negare queas.
Haec et in occulto teneas cum venerit illa!
Quae si testeris tuque tuique ruent
et, quod iam dixi, sic christicolae perimentur,
ut iam non valeat surgere vestra fides."

sponded: "Swear that you will not topple the temple, and that you will spare me and my disciples, and I will do whatever you wish, if only it does not go against the Lord's commandments and the sacred faith." And Muhammad: "Many things seem to be contrary to Christ that often are allowed to happen by [divine] dispensation." The holy man said: "That is true. Say what you please: I will perform it, only let the seed of the Christian people be preserved!"

Muhammad swore to this, and he added: "I have a wife, distinguished in reputation, riches and birth, and when I married her, I achieved success in everything. But quickly pain disturbed our joys, for an unexpected disease befell me and laid me low, half-dead at my lady's feet. She was upset by the sudden turn of fortune, and she wept along with her whole household and all scratched their face with their nails. I lay thus like a dead man almost an hour, and then I caught my breath and returned to health.

And so, to console those who were sad, I covered this up by asserting that I had not suffered any evil but rather that God's secrets were sent to me through Gabriel whose power man is unable to bear. When she did not believe these words, I named you as a witness; she agreed and so tomorrow she will seek out your dwelling. I make this confession to you, I came to say these things before she arrives, so that you may not deny what I said. Conceal this when she comes! If you bear witness to this, you and yours will perish, and, as I have already said, the Christians will be destroyed so completely that your faith will not be able to rise up again."

Tunc sanctus Christi plus commoda quam sua pensans
dicere promittit quae Machomes monuit.
Regrediens Machomes aurorae praevenit ortum,
ne quis eum videat et referat dominae.
Iamque die facto montem petit illa prophetae,
nescia quod Machomes nocte fuisset ibi.
Omnia narrat ei, quae sit, cur venerit; ille
quae fuerat doctus a Machomete refert.
Illa redit gaudens tanto nupsisse marito,
qui mundi mutet iura iubente deo.
Iam veniam poscit: iam se peccasse fatetur,
quod iussis eius improba restiterit.
Iam veneratur eum; iam prorsus subditur eius
imperiis; iam se non reputat dominam.
Laetatur Machomes ita se vicisse prophetam,
ut per eum dominam sic sibi subdiderit,
et dicit: "Nosti tibi me non falsa locutum:
certam te fecit ille futura videns.
Nunc igitur quid agas te doctam convenit esse,
quando superveniet angelus ille mihi.
Sicut iam dixi, virtutem ferre nequibo,
sed tremulus, spumans protinus ipse cadam.
Tu vero statim me veste teges pretiosa,
donec item redeat angelus ad superos:
si quis enim videat me talem, nescius alti
consilii morbo me cecidisse putet."
Illa refert: "Pro posse geram quaecumque iubebis;
intendent in te mens, manus, os, oculi;
contra stare tibi praesumet nemo meorum,
nam tua sunt melius quam ea, quae mea sunt."

Then the holy man thought more of Christ's advantage than his own and promised to say what Muhammad had suggested. Muhammad returned, arriving before dawn, so that no one would see him and tell the lady. And when day broke, she headed for the prophet's mountain, unaware that Muhammad had been there that night. She told him everything, who she was, why she had come; and he replied as Muhammad had instructed him. She returned rejoicing that she had married so great a husband, who would change the world's laws at God's command. She asked forgiveness and said that she had sinned by insolently resisting his orders. Now she venerated him; now she submitted utterly to his orders; now she no longer considered herself his sovereign.

Muhammad was delighted to have so conquered the prophet and that through him he had made his lady subordinate to himself, and he said: "You know that I have not spoken falsely to you: that seer of future things has assured you. Now therefore you should be instructed what to do when the angel comes upon me. As I have already said, I will not be able tolerate his power, but I will fall down at once trembling and foaming. You, however, will cover me immediately in precious clothing, until the angel likewise returns to those above: for if anyone ignorant of the heavenly plan should see me in such a state, he would think that I had succumbed to a disease."

She replied: "I will perform to my best ability whatever you command; my mind, hands, mouth, and eyes will obey you; and none of my men will dare to stand in your way, for what you possess is better than what I have."

Hinc simulat Machomes vultum solito graviorem
et, velut e caelo venerit, alta sonat.
Sic risum vitat et verba moventia risum,
ut stupeat quisquis antea nosset eum.
Sub terra Machomes cameram fieri sibi fecit,
in quam praeter eum nullus haberet iter,
quam Machomem coniunx ideo fecisse putabat,
ut domino posset vivere liberius.
Sed vitulum niveum Machomes absconderat intus,
cuius erat potus Bacchus et esca Ceres,
qui sic doctus erat studio Machometis, ut eius
se genibus flexis sterneret ante pedes
et persistebat in terra sicut adorans,
donec surgendi signa daret Machomes.
Contigit ut fierent illic sollemnia quaedam,
ad quae convenit patria tota fere;
per se magnates, per se plebs, et muliebris
a maribus sexus dissociatus erat.
Femineus sexus in verbis semper abundat:
dixeris arcanum, vix reticere potest.
Sic uxor Machomis conventu dixit in illo
quae celanda sibi crediderat Machomes,
namque sui dum quaeque viri laudes memoraret,
omnibus ipsa suum praeposuit Machomen,
dicens: "In vestris quicquid laudabile constat,
longe praecellit in Machomete meo.
Quin etiam nova si qua deus disponit agenda,
angelus illa meo nuntiat ante viro.
Et quia coniugii nos castus amor facit unum,
nulla putat Machomes non retegenda mihi.

Then Muhammad simulated a face more serious than usual, and, as if he had come from heaven, he spoke of elevated things. He so avoided laughter and words provoking laughter that anyone who had known him before was amazed.

Muhammad commanded a subterranean chamber to be made for himself that no one could reach except himself; his wife thought that Muhammad had made it in order to be freer to live for the Lord. But Muhammad had hidden a snow-white calf inside, whose drink was Bacchus and food was Ceres, and Muhammad had taught it by his own effort to bend its knees and bow down before his own feet and to remain kneeling as though adoring him until he gave the signs for it to rise.

It happened that in that place there were certain celebrations, which were attended by almost the whole country; the people were divided into the common people and into those who were important, and the women were separated from the men. Women are always rich in words: if you have told a secret, they can scarcely keep silent. And so Muhammad's wife spoke at that gathering of the things that Muhammad had believed she would keep to herself. For while each woman was recounting the praises of her own husband she placed her own Muhammad before all the others, saying: "Whatever is considered praiseworthy in your husbands is far superior in my Muhammad. For if God orders new things to be done, an angel announces them in advance to my husband. And because the chaste love of marriage makes us one, there is nothing that Muhammad does not think should be revealed to me. Therefore, if you prom-

Unde fidem mihi si facitis secreta tenere
quae vobis dicam, mira futura loquar."
Affirmant omnes se nulla prodere causa,
donec eis Machomes ipsave praecipiat.
Tunc quicquid Machomes secretum dixerat illi,
ipsa revelat eis ordine quaeque suo.
Omnes mirantur, omnes hanc esse beatam
dicunt quod tanto sit sociata viro.
Finito festo redeunt ad propria quique
atque domi referunt dicta vel acta foris,
cumque referretur quorundam plurima virtus,
virtutum Machomis mentio maior erat.
Nec tamen ullus adhuc procerum secreta sciebat,
quae dominabus erant credita de Machome.
Quae licet illarum fidei mandata fuissent,
una nocte tamen non tacuere viris,
scilicet arcanis Machomen caelestibus uti
et ventura prius noscere quam veniant,
quod lex a Christo data dura nimis moderanda
per Machomen domino praecipiente foret,
multaque praeterea, quae supra diximus aut quae
sunt retegenda suo tempore sive loco.
Mirantur proceres super his secumque revolvunt
quidnam portenti talia significent:
hii dubitant fieri tot tantaque per Machometem,
hii dubitare putant de Machomete nefas,
nam dum respiciunt virtutes anteriores,
coguntur per eas his quoque ferre fidem.
Ne vero quisquam remaneret pendulus ultra,
de se dicturus ille vocatus adest.

ise me to keep secret what I say, I will speak of the wonders to come."

All affirmed that they would not reveal these things for any reason until Muhammad or she herself should command them to do so. Then she revealed to them each of the secrets that Muhammad had told her in appropriate order. Everyone was amazed, everyone said that she was blessed to be married to such a great man. When the celebration was over, everyone returned to his own affairs, and each recounted at home what had been said and done outside. And when they told of the great virtue of certain men, the account of Muhammad's virtues was greater. Nonetheless, none of the nobles knew yet the secrets about Muhammad that had been entrusted to their ladies. Although these things had been told to them in confidence, nevertheless together with their husbands at night they were not silent but said that Muhammad was familiar with heaven's secrets and knew the future before it happened, and also that the overly harsh law given by Christ was to be tempered by Muhammad at the Lord's command, and also many more things that we have mentioned above or that must be revealed at the proper place or time.

The nobles were amazed at this and pondered what this sort of portent could mean. Some doubted that so many great things were done by Muhammad; others thought that doubting Muhammad was sacrilege, for when they considered his previous virtues, they were compelled by these to believe the others also. But so that no one should remain in doubt any longer, he was summoned to speak about himself,

Excipiens illum summo conventus honore
surgit et in primo dat residere loco.
Tunc Machomes causam conventus quaerit et unus,
quem commendabat lingua, genus, probitas,
cycnea canities—quis enim praesumeret alter
aut sciret tanto reddere verba viro?—
hic igitur talis ac tantus supplice voce,
vultu demisso sic reverenter ait:
"O patriae custos, o spes, o gloria nostra,
nos omnes servos noveris esse tuos,
nec servos durum qui te dominum patiamur,
sed quos more patris corripiendo foves.
Propterea quotiens audimus grandia de te,
quisque velut proprio gaudet honore tuo.
Quae vero de te miranda modo referuntur,
extollunt caeli nomen ad alta tuum.
Nam si consiliis divinis participaris
et deus arbitrio tractat agenda tuo,
angelus aut deus es humano corpore tectus,
iam tibi divinus exhibeatur honor,
iam tibi donentur thymiamata, thura crementur,
ut te pacatum mundus habere queat."
Respondit Machomes: "Ne me iactare viderer,
propositum fuerat ista silere mihi.
Sed quae vult per me fieri divina potestas,
per me non fieri criminis esse reor.
Ergo locus certus et terminus instituatur,
in quo conveniant cum populo proceres,
ut referamus eis quae sit divina voluntas,
qualiter infirmis parcere provideat.
Longinquas igitur percurrat epistola partes
nuntia conventus temporis atque loci."

and he came. The assembly rose to their feet to receive him with the highest honor and gave him the foremost seat.

Then Muhammad asked the reason for the assembly, and a man replied who had his eloquence, his birth and his honesty to recommend him as well as his head of hair white like a swan—indeed who else would presume or would know how to reply to so great a man?—therefore this great and distinguished man responded deferentially, in the voice of a suppliant with a humble expression:

"O guardian of the fatherland, our hope and our glory, you know that we are all your servants, not slaves who endure you as a harsh master, but rather whom you nurture by correcting us as a father would. For this reason whenever we hear great things of you, each of us rejoices as if your honor were ours also. But the amazing things told of you now lift your name up to the heights of the heaven. For if you take part in divine assemblies and if God discusses things to be done at your discretion, then you are an angel or god clad in a human body. Let us now receive you with divine honors; let us now give you incense and let frankincense be burned, so that the world can keep you satisfied."

Muhammad answered: "My plan was to be silent about these matters so as not to seem boastful. But I consider it a sin to fail to accomplish what the divine power wills to bring about through me. Therefore let a definite time and place be established, where the nobles will come together with the people so that we can inform them of God's will and how it is his plan to spare the weak. Let a letter be sent out to distant regions announcing the time and place of the assembly."

Dictum laudatur, edictum mittitur; omnes
tam Machomis nomen quam nova fama movet.
Conventu facto Machomis facundia captat
aures et mentes gestibus, ore, manu,
unde satis miror si vel fuit unus in illis,
qui Machomis verbis nollet habere fidem.
Dixit quae supra iam me scripsisse recordor,
propter quod breviter sunt memoranda mihi,
quod Moyses redeat Christo cedente vetusque
ritus agatur item lege cadente nova,
quod sacramentum cessat baptismatis et quod
circumcidendi mos iterum redeat,
quod licite denas uxores ducere possit
unus et una decem possit habere viros.
Haec postquam dixit Machomes, et cetera quae se
dicere dicebat praecipiente deo:
"Ascendamus," ait, "montem quem cernitis illic,
fortassis nobis caelica verba sonent:
sic etenim quondam Moyses de monte refertur
in tabulis legem dante tulisse deo."
Haec praetendebat Machomes verissima, verum
sub specie veri decipiebat eos.
Nam prius occulte montem conscenderat ipsum,
in quo mel multum lacque recondiderat.
Montis enim culmen qua nescio foderat arte,
ut tuto liquidum quid retinere queat.
Mel igitur Machomes foveae commiserat uni,
altera lac tenuit, dum Machomes voluit.
Sic quoque caespitibus fovearum texerat ora,
ut nullus fossae posset habere notam.

His speech was approved, and the edict was issued; both Muhammad's name and the new rumors excited everyone. When the assembly was convened, Muhammad's eloquence captured ears and minds with his gestures, his mouth, his hand; hence I am quite amazed if there was even one among them unwilling to believe Muhammad's words. He said those things that I remember having written already above and hence I must mention them only briefly: that Moses would return, and Christ would yield to him; that the new law would yield and the old rite would be practiced; that the sacrament of baptism would cease and the custom of circumcision return again; that it would be legal for one man to marry ten women, and for one woman to have ten husbands.

After Muhammad said these things and other things that he claimed to say at God's command, he said: "Let us climb the mountain that you see over there, and perhaps words from heaven will sound forth for us. For thus long ago Moses, it is said, carried the law that God gave him down from the mountain on tablets."

Muhammad alleged that this was the perfect truth, but he deceived them with the appearance of truth. For he had first climbed that mountain secretly and hidden there large quantities of honey and milk. For he had dug out the top of the mountain—I don't know how—so that it could hold some liquid securely. Then Muhammad had put honey in one pit; the other held milk while Muhammad wished it. He had also covered the mouths of the pits with pieces of turf so that no one could notice the pits. Meanwhile the bull

Praeterea taurus, quem me memorasse recordor,
cuius erat potus Bacchus et esca Ceres,
haud procul a foveis mellis lactisque latebat,
leges confictas a Machomete gerens.
Huc igitur postquam Machomes, proceres populusque
venerunt, Machomes quemque silere iubet,
quo facto quasi consilium domini manifestat,
quid de mutandis legibus instituet.
Sed cum nonnullos super his dubitare videret,
immo perpaucos his adhibere fidem,
sic ait: "A domino devote signa petamus,
quae valeant servos certificare suos."
Tunc genibus flexis sternentes corpora terrae,
ex desiderio cordis ad astra volant,
cumque rogata diu pietas divina fuisset,
surgens surgendum significat Machomes.
Post haec assumptis secum senioribus, illuc
ducit eos, quo mel lacque recondiderat.
Erectis igitur oculis manibusque refertur
ad dominum tales exhibuisse preces:
"O pater omnipotens, qui verbo cuncta creasti
quique creata regis cuncta manens stabilis,
qui de te genitum fecisti sumere carnem,
qui mundo vitam mortuus ipse dedit
quique novae legis per eum mandata dedisti,
quae si quis servet, vivere semper habet.
Sed quia iam senuit mundus, vix illa tenere
quis valet; unde prope iam perit omnis homo.
Si placet ergo tibi legis mollire rigorem,
quod te facturum me docuit Gabriel,

that I recall having mentioned, whose drink was Bacchus and whose food was Ceres, was concealed not very far from the pits of honey and milk carrying the laws devised by Muhammad.

Therefore after Muhammad, the nobles and the people had arrived at that place, Muhammad commanded all to be silent. After this he revealed as if it were the Lord's plan what he was to establish concerning the laws that had to be changed. But since he saw that some doubted this, or rather that very few believed it, he said: "Let us ask devoutly for signs from the Lord that can convince his servants." Then on bended knees, prostrating their bodies on the earth, their hearts' desire transported them to the stars, and when they had prayed a long time for God's devotion, Muhammad rose up himself, thus giving the sign that they should rise. Then he took the elders with him and led them to the place where he had hidden the milk and honey. Then it is said that with raised eyes and hands he offered prayers to the Lord thus: "O Omnipotent Father, you created all things with a word; and you, while remaining stable yourself, guide all created things; you made your begotten son take on the flesh, who in turn died himself to give life to the world; and you gave the commandments of a new law through your son, thus giving eternal life to anyone who follows them.

"But since the world has already grown old, scarcely anyone is able to obey them; therefore nearly everyone now perishes. If you please, therefore, soften the law's rigor, as [the angel] Gabriel has taught me that you would do, then

digneris praeter solitum mundo dare signum,
per quod noscat in hac te sibi parte pium."
Sic prece finita Machomes inquirere coepit
nunc hunc, nunc illum dissimulando locum.
Post tamquam casu fossas devertit ad illas,
mel ubi lacque prius ipse recondiderat.
Porro caespitibus nunc hinc, nunc inde remotis,
altera fossarum mel dedit, altera lac.
Quo magis indicio pietas divina pateret:
dulcia mel superat, lacte quid albius est?
Attamen ut dubius Machomes probat ore saporem,
post illum gustant ordine quique suo.
Tunc extollentes voces et corda manusque
grates divinis laudibus accumulant
et Machomes lacrimis ficta pietate profusis
atque diu tonso pectore sic loquitur:
"Ecce videtis," ait, "quanta dulcedine mundum
et mundi leges conditor orbis agat.
Melle figuratur quod legis amara recedant,
lacte, quod ut genitos nos alat ipse suos."
His dictis rursus ita flesse refertur, ut omnes
illius exemplum moverit ad lacrimas.
Tunc ait: "Oremus, ut sicut montis in alto
Christum discipulis iura dedisse liquet
et sicut legem Moyses in monte recepit,
quae fertur digito scripta fuisse dei,
sic quoque nos scripto dignetur certificare,
qua genus humanum vivere lege velit."
Quo facto Machomes tanto clamore replevit
aera, quod caelos intonuisse putes.

you will see fit to give to the world a sign beyond the usual, so that the world may thereby know your devotion to it."

When the prayer was thus finished Muhammad began to seek, feigning, now in one place and now in another, here and there. Afterward, as though by chance he turned toward the ditches where he had earlier hidden the milk and honey himself. Then he moved the pieces of turf in one direction and the other, and one of the ditches gave honey, the other milk. By what sign could divine piety be more evident: honey surpasses sweet things, and what could be whiter than milk? Nevertheless, as though doubting, Muhammad sampled the taste with his mouth, and after him, each one tasted in turn. Then lifting up their voices and hearts and hands, they piled up thanks with God's praises.

And after Muhammad had spilled tears in feigned piety and beat his chest for a long time, he said: "Lo! You see with what great sweetness the creator of the universe drives on the world and the world's laws. Honey symbolizes that the bitterness of the law yields, and milk, that he himself will nourish us as his own children." After he said this, it is said that he wept again, so that his example moved everyone to tears. Then he said, "Let us pray, so that just as we know that Christ gave laws to his disciples on a mountaintop, and just as Moses received the law on the mountain, which is said to have been written with God's finger, thus also he may see fit to reassure us with something written; and may the human race be willing to live by this law!"

After this Muhammad filled the air with such a great clamor that you would have thought the heavens had thun-

Tunc taurus, quem nutrierat, quod iam memoravi,
qui iuxta gracili fune ligatus erat,
exsilit ad vocem Machometis, vincula rumpit
et domini pedibus stratus adorat eum.
Hic igitur leges cornu gestabat utroque
fictas et scriptas arte, manu Machomis.
Quo viso Machomes coepit simulare stuporem,
ac si non alio tempore nosset eum.
Tunc propius plebs et proceres accedere iussi
sollicite vitulum scriptaque perspiciunt.
Inveniunt illic ea, quae confinxerat ille
astutus Machomes mente, dolo, manibus:
ut sacramentum baptismi destituatur
circumcidendi lege levante caput;
ut Christi carnis et sanguinis occidat usus
et redeant aries, hircus, ovis, vitulus;
ut denas ducat uxores masculus unus
et pereant casti foedera coniugii.
Plurima praeterea Machomes scripsisse refertur,
quae mihi certa minus duco tacenda magis,
multaque multotiens non est replicare necesse,
quae scio saepe suis me meminisse locis.
Verum quis poterit exponere sufficienter,
quas laudes dederint plebs proceresque deo?
Virtutes etiam Machometis ad astra levabant,
quod sibi par hominum nullus in orbe foret,
et satis atque super tauri mirando decorem
de caelo missum quisque putabat eum.
Hinc quam detulerat legis mandata probantes,
obsequium spondent nutibus, ore, manu.

dered. Then the bull that I mentioned that Muhammad had reared, which was tethered nearby with a thin rope, leaped forth at the sound of his voice, and broke its chains, and lying at its master's feet adored him. The bull was carrying on each horn laws invented and written by Muhammad's craft and hand.

At the sight of the bull, Muhammad began to feign surprise, as if he had not known it at another time. Then when the nobles and the people had been ordered to come closer, they carefully scrutinized the calf and the writings. They found there those things that the cunning Muhammad had contrived with his mind, his trickery, and his hands: to abolish the sacrament of baptism, while the law of circumcision reared its head; to kill off the ritual use of Christ's flesh and blood, while bringing back the ram, the goat, the sheep and the calf; for one man to marry ten wives, while the bond of chaste marriage perished. In addition, it is said that Muhammad wrote more things, but I consider them to be less certain and so I prefer to pass over them in silence, and there is no need to go over many things many times, since I know I have often mentioned them in the appropriate places.

But who could give a sufficient account of the praises the people and the nobles gave to God? They praised the virtues of Muhammad to the stars claiming that no man in the world was equal to him, and when they had contemplated the bull's beauty more than sufficiently, each thought that it was sent from heaven. They approved of the commandments of the law that it had brought, and they swore obedience with nods, mouth, hands.

Exactis igitur sollemniter octo diebus,
laetus et admirans ad sua quisque redit.
Taurus cum solo solus Machomete remansit.
At Machomes illum clausit, ut ante fuit,
et pascebat eum, dum vixit, ut ante solebat,
se tamen excepto nemo videbat eum.
Cumque rogaretur Machomes quo taurus abisset,
per quem de caelo lex nova missa foret,
ad superos illum Machomes fingebat abisse,
unde petisse prius ima docebat eum.
Credebant quicquid Machometis ab ore sonabat,
ac si caelestis nuntius ille foret.
Credebant igitur quia taurus ad astra regressus
virtutum numero consociatus erat;
credebant Machomen terris ideo superesse
ut praesit mundo, cum deus astra regat.
His ita transactis modico post tempore, cum iam
gens sua tuta satis sub Machomete foret,
insurrexerunt in eos gens effera Persae,
omnia vastantes igne, fame, gladio.
Namque querebantur Idumaeos fraude tenere
iuris Persarum praedia, castra, domos,
quae nisi restituant, possessa minantur eorum
subicienda modis omnibus exitio.
Talibus auditis turbatur gens Idumaea
et contra Persas bella movere parant.
Attamen inter eos qui consilio meliores
esse videbantur, corde vel ore graves,
ante requirendum persuadent a Machomete
quam contra Persas tale quid incipiant.

Then after eight days had passed in ceremonies all returned to their affairs in happiness and amazement. The bull remained with Muhammad alone. But Muhammad shut him in, as he had been before and fed him, as long as he lived, as he did before, and nobody saw him except Muhammad. And when Muhammad was asked where the bull had gone who had brought the new law from heaven, Muhammad pretended that he had departed to those above, and he taught that he had first descended to the depths from there. They believed whatever Muhammad's mouth proclaimed as if he were a heavenly messenger. Therefore they believed that the bull had returned to the stars, to which he was akin by the number of his virtues; they believed that Muhammad remained on the earth in order to preside over the world, while God guided the stars.

A short time after this, when Muhammad's people had already been safe enough under his rule, the savage people of Persia rose up against them destroying everything with fire, hunger, the sword. For they complained that the Edomites were holding estates, camps, buildings that rightfully belonged to the Persians, and the Persians threatened that if they would not return these to them, then their possessions would be subjected to destruction by every means possible.

When the Edomites heard this, they were agitated, and they prepared to wage war on the Persians. Nevertheless those among them who seemed to have better advice and seemed to speak seriously or sincerely persuaded them that first Muhammad must be asked before beginning this sort of venture against the Persians.

Qui respondit eos non posse resistere Persis,
cedendum potius quod sibi iure petunt.
Tunc quidam iuvenes ingenti corde, lacertis
fortibus, instructi spicula dirigere,
muniti clipeis etiam fugiendo sagittis
hostes Parthorum more ferire suos,
sic aiunt Machomi: "Si sic dimittimus ista
quae repetunt Persae, tollere cuncta valent:
nam velut infirmos nos et pavidos reputantes,
a modicis tendent ad potiora manum
nostraque libertas periet, sic nostra manebunt
regis Persarum subdita colla iugo.
Sed deus avertat ut vivi sic pereamus
ne nostrae genti vivat in opprobrium.
Nam cur portamus pharetras, cur tela tenemus,
cur tegimur clipeis, spicula cur gerimus,
si sic uxores, si sic sine sanguine terras,
si sic servitio pignora nostra damus?
Per gladios veniant! Sit eis transire per hastas!
Mors gentem nostram vincere sola potest,
si vinci tamen est, ubi non animus superatur
sed caro sola iacet, dum cadit ense caput!"
Omnes collaudant dictum Machomenque precantur
ut contra Persas dux sit et auctor eis.
Opponit Machomes aetatis tempora longa,
vires consumptas corpore iam vetulo,
se bello modicum vel nullum ferre iuvamen,
quin magis ut senior ipse iuvandus erit.
Praeterea caeli dicebat abesse favorem,
quo sine nil vires, nil valet ars hominum.
Has propter causas dicit se bella cavere,
ne quibus esse velit utilis, his noceat.

Muhammad responded that they could not resist the Persians, but rather should cede what the Persians rightly sought for themselves. Then certain young men of great courage and strong arms, who were skilled in aiming their javelins, and who, when protected by their shields, knew how to pierce their enemies with arrows in the Parthian manner, even when fleeing, said to Muhammad: "If we thus relinquish what the Persians seek, then they can carry off everything, for they will think we are weak and fearful, and, starting from the small things, they will reach for the greater things. Our liberty will come to an end, and thus our necks will be placed under the Persian king's yoke.

"But may God save us from perishing alive in this fashion so that this fact not live on as a reproach against our people. For why do we carry quivers? Why do we have javelins? Why are we protected by shields? Why do we carry spears, if we thus give up our wives, our lands, our children to slavery without bloodshed? Let them advance through swords! Let it be their task to pass through spears! Only death can conquer our people, if one is conquered when the spirit is not defeated, but the flesh alone is fallen, when the head falls by the sword!"

Everyone praised the speech and begged that Muhammad act as commander against the Persians and be their leader. Muhammad argued against them citing his advanced age, the exhausted force of his already aged body, and said that he could be of little or no help in a war but rather as an old man himself required assistance. Moreover he said that heaven was not in favor, and without this human strength and skill could achieve nothing. For all these reasons, he said he was wary of wars lest he do harm to those whom he wants to benefit.

Ad quod dum tamquam victi ratione silerent,
sic Machomi quemdam verba dedisse ferunt:
"Quod dominus noster Machomes excusat inire
proelia, ne iuvenes impediat senior,
dicimus econtra iuvenum minus acta valere,
si non consilium dirigat illa senum.
Unde necesse reor ut sis quoque corpore praesens,
ut gens nostra tuum currat ad arbitrium.
Praeterea scimus te tot non esse dierum,
quin bene, si sit opus, arma movere queas.
Scimus et audacem, melior te nemo fuisse
creditur: haec semper fama tui maneat.
Quodque negas caelum nobis ad bella favere,
ob culpam nostri criminis esse reor;
sed constat quoniam deus est summae pietatis,
parcens peccanti, si bene paeniteat.
Sic de flente Petro, sic de latrone beato,
sic de Mattheo pagina sancta docet:
hi peccaverunt graviter, sed paenituerunt,
unde dei pietas cuncta remisit eis.
Sic et nos culpas nostras punire parati
omnia spondemus quae facienda iubes:
carnem tormentis quantislibet afficiemus
extensis sursum mentibus et manibus.
Sic Ninivitarum non desperamus ad instar,
placandam nobis, si qua sit ira dei.
Si magis hircorum, taurorum vel vitulorum
victima delectat, sacrificemus et haec.
Quod cum fecerimus, qua te ratione retardes
a servis dominus, a genitis genitor?

At this they were silent, as though they had been conquered by reason. They say that a certain man tricked Muhammad in this way: "In response to our lord, Muhammad, who declines to enter battle so that as an elder he not get in the way of the young men, we say, to the contrary, that the actions of young men achieve less if the advice of their elders does not guide them. Therefore I think it is necessary that you also be present in body so that our people may advance speedily at your discretion. Moreover we know that you are not so full of days that you cannot wield weapons well, if it is necessary. We know also that you are brave, and it is believed that no one has been better than you: may your reputation remain so forever!

"You deny that heaven will look favorably on us in these wars, but I think this is the fault of our sin; it is agreed, however, that God is supremely compassionate and that he spares the sinner if he repents sincerely. The holy page teaches thus concerning Peter's weeping, concerning the blessed thief, and concerning Matthew: they committed grievous sins, but they repented, and therefore God's compassion forgave them for everything. We are likewise prepared for our sins to be punished thus, and we promise to obey all your orders. We will inflict on the flesh as many tortures as you please with our minds and our hands directed toward heaven. And so we do not despair if we must appease God's anger like the Ninevites. Or if he delights rather in the sacrifice of goats, bulls or calves, we will sacrifice these too. And when we have done this, what reasoning may hold you, our master, back from your slaves, or you, our father,

Si placet, uxores, infantes, tota supellex
  sit commissa tibi, cum pueris sedeas.
Des modo consilium, nos proelia sustineamus.
  Nos feriant hostes, nos feriamus eos!
Si superemus eos, laus sit tua; si superemur,
  stultitiae nostrae deputet omnis homo."
Hoc laudant omnes. Machomes plorasse refertur
  quod sic quisque suum tendit ad interitum.
Attamen assensum faciens se spondet iturum
  sicque datur pugnae terminus atque locus.
Dicitur hoc Persis, verum nihilominus ipsi
  insistunt, rapiunt, excruciant, perimunt.
Terminus advenit, locus insinuatur, adesse
  Persae non metuunt, hostis utrimque ruit,
pugnant, oppugnant telis, mucronibus, hastis—
  sed socios Machomis bella premunt gravius.
Porro cernentes Idumaei se superari
  a Persis bello, viribus et numero,
dimittunt Machomen loculos aurumque ferentem,
  quae natis reddat coniugibusque suis,
ne si forte patres perimantur sive mariti,
  paupertas matres opprimat et pueros.
Dumque redit Machomes, quorundam templa deorum
  temporis antiqui cernit et intrat ea;
in quibus argentum, loculos aurumque reponens,
  quae servanda sibi gens sua tradiderat;
exiit ac claudens signat simul ostia post se.
  Et sic ad dominas tendit et ad pueros,
tendit et ad reliquum vulgus, quod inutile bello
  dimissum fuerat haud procul in casulis.

back from your children? If you please, let our wives, children, all our household goods be entrusted to you; you may stay with the children. Merely give us your advice, we will wage the battles. Let the enemies strike us, let us strike them! If we defeat them, the praise will be yours; if we are defeated, everyone will attribute it to our foolhardiness."

Everyone approves of this. Muhammad is said to have wept because with this plan each was headed for his own destruction. Nevertheless, he assents and promises to go forth, and thus a place and time was given for the battle. The Persians are told this, but in spite of this they press on, plunder, torture, destroy. The time comes, they occupied the place; the Persians do not fear to appear, the enemy falls on both sides. They fight, they resist with javelins, swords, spears—but war takes a heavier toll on Muhammad's allies.

Then the Edomites realized that they had been defeated by the Persians in battle, in strength and in number, and so they sent Muhammad away with treasure boxes and gold, to return to the women and children so that if by chance their fathers or husbands perished, the mothers and children would not be crushed by poverty. And on his journey Muhammad saw the temples of certain gods of ancient times and entered them; he deposited the silver, treasure boxes and gold that his people had entrusted to his keeping and he emerged closing, locking, and sealing the doors behind him. And thus he heads to the ladies and children and to the remaining throng of people who had been sent back as useless for warfare, and who were not far away in

Eius enim gentis mos dicitur iste fuisse
et fortassis adhuc istud idem faciunt,
ut si quando procul vadunt ad bella gerenda,
ducant vel portent mobile quicquid habent.
Ergo dum Machomes et vulgus inutile bello
stat procul, eventum nosse rei cupiens,
astute Machomes cunctis blanditur, ut aetas,
ut genus, ut sensus huius et huius erant,
dicens: "O comites, vestri mihi cura relicta
et iuvenum pietas debilitasque senum
et fragilis sexus monet et movet intima cordis,
usibus ut vestris commoda provideam.
Scitis quod nostris ad bella volentibus ire
adversus Persas, ut facerent vetui.
Quod non fecissem, si non divinitus illud
praescissem vetitum praecipiente deo.
Et quoniam vetitum divinum praeterierunt,
omnes, ut timeo, destruet ira dei.
Sed vos insontes quid poenae promeruistis,
infans, mater, anus, verna, puella, senex?
Ergo deus vobis parcet vestraeque puellae
et pueri thalami foedere convenient
taliter, ut denas sibi copulet unus, et una,
si libeat, denos copulet ipsa sibi.
Nec tamen ille deo mandante putetur adulter
nec reputetur ob hoc criminis illa rea:
cultor enim terrae si multos seminat agros,
messibus e multis horrea multa replet,
sic et ager quando multis versatur aratris,
si fuerat sterilis, fertilis efficitur.

small shelters. For it is said to have been the custom of that people, and perhaps they still do likewise, that whenever they go forth to wage war they bring or carry whatever moveable property they have.

Therefore when Muhammad and the throng that was unfit for warfare stood nearby, wanting to know the outcome of the matter, Muhammad cleverly flattered everyone in accordance with the age, the birth, the sensibility of each, saying: "O my companions, your care has been left to me. The piety of the young and the weakness of the old and of the weaker sex advises and moves the depths of my heart to provide supplies for your use.

"You know that when our people wished to go to war against the Persians, I forbid them to do so. I would not have done so, if it were not that I had foreknowledge from divine sources that this was forbidden by God's command. And since they went against the divine prohibition, I fear that God's anger will destroy them all. But you who are innocent, what punishment do you deserve, the infant, the mother, the old woman, the slave, the girl, the old man?

"Therefore God will spare you, and your girls and boys will come together in the marriage bond thus: one man will couple with ten women, and one woman, if she wishes, will couple with ten men. And yet the man will not be considered an adulterer, since God commands it, nor will the woman be guilty of an offense: for if a farmer sows many fields, from his many harvests he fills many granaries, and if the field had been barren then, when it is turned over by many plows, it will thus be made fertile. Thus the man will

Sic gignet multos multis e matribus ille,
illa vel ex uno semine concipiet.
Nam si de tot erit natura frigidus unus,
alter erit calidus et sobolem faciet
sicque volente deo sine fructu nulla manebit
nec sterilis metuet arboris ulla rogum."
Dum sic sermonem Machomes protendit ad omnes,
nuntius unus adest solus et ipse malus:
omnibus occisis se clamat ab hostibus unum
esse reservatum tanta referre mala.
Exoritur luctus, clamor tentoria replet,
plorantum caelos tollitur usque sonus:
"Vir!" matrona sonat, "Pater!" infans, sponsa: "Marite!"
flet genitor genitum, vernula flet dominum.
Tunc Machomes inquit: "Deus hoc praeviderat esse;
non aliter decuit. Parcite iam lacrimis!
Quin magis oremus omnes domini pietatem,
ut nos et nostros nostraque cuncta regat.
Et quibus abstraxit solacia tanta virorum,
vobis vel loculos reddere sustineat."
His dictis praecedit eos ad templa deorum,
in quibus ipse prius abdiderat loculos.
Tunc velut ignorans girabat, denique tamquam
munere divino repperit introitum.
Ingrediens reperit loculos et signa quibusque
in loculis monstrant singula cuius erant.
Femina quaeque sui cognoscit signa mariti
et recipit iuris quod patet esse sui.
Inde maritantur iuxta legem Machometis
et vivunt omnes eius ad arbitrium.

engender many from many mothers, and the woman will conceive perhaps from one seed. For if of so many men one should by nature be cold, another will be warm and will produce offspring, and thus, by God's will, no woman will remain without fruit, and no woman will fear being thrown on the pyre like a sterile tree."

When Muhammad had given this speech to everyone, only one messenger returned, with bad news: everyone had been killed, and the enemy had spared him alone to report the great misfortune. Mourning broke out, noise filled the tents, and the sound of the mourners rose to the heavens. "Husband!," says the matron, "Father!" the infant, "Groom!" says the bride. The father weeps for his son; the poor little slave for his master.

Then Muhammad says: "God had foreseen this: no other outcome would have been fitting. Now hold your tears! Let us all rather pray that the Lord's compassion guide us and our families and all our affairs. And although he snatched from you the great comfort of your husbands, may he allow at least your treasure boxes to be returned to you." When he had said this, he led them to the temples of the gods where he had hidden the treasure boxes earlier. Then, as though he did not know, he turned one way and another, and at last he found the entrance, as though by divine favor. He entered and found the treasure boxes and the signs on each indicating the owner. Each wife recognized her husband's signs and received what was obviously hers by right.

From that time on they were married according to Muhammad's law and they all lived according to his discretion.

Plurima pax illic viguit Machomete vigente,
pacatis cunctis hostibus arte sua.
Unde deum Machomen reputabant atque per illas
partes illius nomen erat celebre.
Transactis igitur in tanta pace diebus,
qui spatium vitae Machomis extiterant,
mortuus est Machomes et praemia digna recepit
inferni poenas, ut tenet alma fides.
At sua gens, credens quod spiritus eius ad astra
transisset, metuit subdere corpus humo.
Instituens igitur operis mirabilis arcam,
intus eum posuit quam melius potuit.
Nam sicut fertur, ita vas pendere videtur,
intra quod Machomis membra sepulta iacent,
ut sine subiecto videatur in aere pendens,
sed nec idem rapiat ulla catena super.
Ergo si quaeras ab eis, qua non cadat arte,
fallentes Machomis viribus hoc reputant.
Sed vas revera circumdatur undique ferro
quadrataeque domus sistitur in medio,
et lapis est adamas, per partes quattuor aedis
mensura distans inde vel inde pari,
qui vi naturae ferrum sibi sic trahit aeque,
ut vas ex nulla cedere parte queat.
Sic igitur Machomen divo venerantur honore
et venerabuntur dum deus ista sinet.
Urbs, ubi dicuntur Machometis membra sepulta,
non sine portento Mecha vocata fuit:
nam Machomes immunditiae totius amator
moechiam docuit, moechus et ipse fuit.

Then there was a lasting peace while Muhammad thrived, since he pacified all the enemies with his skill. Hence they thought that Muhammad was God, and his name was famous in those parts.

When the days of Muhammad's life had passed in complete peace, he died and he received the rewards he deserved: hell's punishment, as our gentle faith holds. But since his people believed that his spirit had migrated to the stars, they were afraid to bury his body in the ground. Therefore they made a coffin with amazing workmanship and put him inside as they were best able. For it is said that the container where Muhammad's limbs rest in burial seems to hang in such a way that it appears to be hanging in the air with nothing beneath it and no chain to pull it upward. Therefore, if you ask them by what craft it does not fall, they will mistakenly attribute this to Muhammad's power. But in truth the container is covered on all sides with iron, and it stands in the middle of a square building; and there is a diamond stone, at an equal distance from one side and the other in four parts of the building, which by the power of its nature attracts the iron in such a balanced way that the container is not drawn toward any part. Thus they venerate Muhammad with divine honor, and they will continue to venerate him as long as God allows it.

The city where Muhammad's limbs are said to be buried is called Mecca, and this is a portent, since Muhammad loved all sorts of uncleanness and taught adultery and was

Sic ob praeteritos actus vel signa futura
multis imponi nomina saepe solent:
sic est dicta Babel, quod eam qui constituebant
dum per eam vellent scandere summa poli,
his deus indignans linguas confudit eorum,
ut linguam nemo nosceret alterius.
Sic, reor, Aegyptus tenebrae sonat, obtenebrata
et ducis et populi corda futura docens.
Plenius haec dicit Moyses: ego taedia vito.
Tu Moysen, si vis cetera nosse, lege.

himself an adulterer. For it is because of past deeds or future signs that names are customarily given to many things. Thus Babel is named because its founders wanted to climb to the top of the heaven through it, and so God in his indignation confused their languages so that no one would know anyone else's language. Thus Egypt means darkness, which teaches us that the hearts of the leader and his people would be darkened. Moses says more about this; I will avoid tediousness. Read Moses, if you wish to know the rest.

LIFE OF MUHAMMAD

Adelphus

Life of Muhammad

Graeci omnium paene artium aut inventores aut scriptores, quorum urbana facetia de veteri utre in novum vas deducta plurima Latina turget pagina, nil tam fabulose editum reliquere, in quo non pura veritas intus—quasi tecta—reperiatur, si eo lumine, quod ab ipsorum silice Latina vigilantia cudebat, curiose investigatur. Quorum nimirum Graecorum ex sententia, qua ipsi cum Saracenis disceptare solent, hoc, quod stili officio commendare in praesens disposui, quasi unus de curiosis cyclicis collegi. Collegi autem hac occasione.

2 Dum frequenter Saracenos monstrum quoddam Machomet horrendum vocis sono, utpote qui bacchanalia colunt, invocantes et pro deo adorantes audissem vehementique admiratione perculsus Antiochiam ab Hierosolymis in redeundo advenissem, Graeculum quendam tam Latinae quam Saracenae linguae sciolum super huiusmodi conveni et, quod vel unde illud monstrum oriundum credere deberem, omni qua poteram cautela sciscitatus sum. Nec deerat mihi eius prompta loquacitas, quam naturale et domesticum in Saracenos auxerat odium. Est enim aeterna inimicitia inter fidei sacrarium et paganismum, inter templum Dei et idolum, et qui de ancilla illum, qui de libera natus est, persequitur.

Life of Muhammad

The Greeks, who are the inventors of almost all the arts, or the writers whose urbane cleverness, extracted from an old wineskin into a new container, fills many a Latin page, have left behind nothing composed in so fantastical a manner that the pure truth inside—hidden, as it were—could not be found, if one searches carefully with the light that Latin vigilance struck from their flint. It is of course from the ideas of these Greeks, with which they are accustomed to debate with the Saracens, that I have assembled what I have undertaken to entrust at present to the office of the pen, like one of the diligent writers of the epic cycle. I have assembled it on the following occasion.

When I had often heard the Saracens calling with the 2
sound of their voice, like those who celebrate Bacchic rites, on a frightful monster, a certain Muhammad, and worshipping him as god, and when, struck by intense wonder at this, I had arrived at Antioch on my way back from Jerusalem, I approached a certain Greek on such matters, who knew something of both Latin and the Saracen language, and I inquired as cautiously as I could what I should believe that monster to be or where it had arisen. He was ready and willing to speak, incited even more by his natural, inborn hatred for the Saracens. For there is an eternal enmity between the sanctuary of the faith and paganism, between God's temple and an idol, and the man born of a handmaid attacks him who was born of a free woman.

3 Quid igitur? Graeculus magna aviditate loquendi suis interim dilatis negotiis,—quae miratus rogabam studiosus disserere—orditur in haec verba: "Primum, o Adelphe, oportet te omni absque ambiguitate cognoscere illos, qui se hoc nomine gloriantur, non vere dici vel esse Saracenos. Agareni enim et sunt et rite dicuntur. Illud enim, si historia ab Abraham ad nos usque revolvatur, a nemine ignoratur. Nimirum separatio est filiorum Abraham, scilicet Isaac, qui utique Saracenus eo, quod de Sara processit, dicitur, a quo XII patriarchae patres filiorum Israhel iure paterno et nomine Saraceni nemo est qui nesciat; relinquitur ergo, quatinus nullus dubitet Ismahelem filium Agar Agarenum et, ex eo qui processerint, Agarenos et esse et iure vocari. Non sunt utique illi, de quibus loqui instituimus, vel secundum carnem vel secundum spiritum filii liberae sed ancillae. Igitur in praesenti sermonis, quem a me exigis, collatione Agarenos, non Saracenos eos nominare satius duco. Sed haec hactenus; deinceps de monstro horrendo Machomet quod interrogas absolvam.

4 "Postquam gloriosa veneratione dignissimus huius Antiochenae sedis princeps et protoapostolus Petrus hanc dilectam sibi patriam sancti spiritus semine ipso seminante abunde fecundam reliquit et exigente communi ecclesiae utilitate, qua semper totus fervebat, ipse caput ecclesiae orbis et urbium caput atque dominam Romam adiens praesignatum a magistro gloriosissimum caelo martyrii

What next? The Greek, who had in the meantime put off his business out of his great eagerness to speak,—which amazed me, and I begged him with interest to speak—began with these words: "First, Adelphus, you should know without any ambiguity that those who boast of this name, cannot truly be called, nor are they, Saracens. Indeed, they are Hagarenes and are rightly so called. If we go back over history from Abraham up to our time, no one can fail to realize this. Of course, there is a distinction between the sons of Abraham: Isaac, clearly, is necessarily called a Saracen, because he proceeds from Sarah, and from him the twelve patriarchs, fathers of the sons of Israel by their paternal right and name are Saracens, as no one fails to know; it remains therefore as nobody may doubt that Ishmael the son of Hagar is a Hagarene, and those descended from him are Hagarenes and are rightly so called. For those of whom we undertake to speak, are by no means, either according to the flesh or according to the spirit, sons of the free woman, but rather sons of the handmaid. Therefore in the present discourse, which you request of me, I think it more appropriate to call them Hagarenes and not Saracens. But enough of this; next I will answer your question about the terrible monster Muhammad. 3

"Peter, the foremost of the apostles and the founder of this see of Antioch, most worthy of glorious veneration, made his homeland, so beloved by him, abundantly fertile by sowing it with the seed of the Holy Spirit. And when the common advantage of the Church required, which always motivated him strongly, he himself the head of the Church, on his way to Lady Rome, the capital of the world and its cities, brought the most glorious trophy of martyrdom 4

trophaeum devexit, humani generis inimicus sanctae fidei unitati sanctaeque invidens religioni zizania inter triticum sparsit, unde pessima malorum omnium radix prodiit et pullulavit, scilicet haeresis multiformis tam nefaria quam varia, tam maculans quam maculosa, radix una sed rami innumerabiles, una belua sed capita plura. Unde beatus Paulus prophetans ait, 'post discessum meum introibunt in vos lupi rapaces, lupi graves.' Inde et in Canticis Canticorum praecantatur: 'Capite mihi vulpeculas, quae demoliuntur vineas.' Inter quos huiusce radicis innumerabiles ramos, inter inimici zizania, inter vulpeculas demolientes, inter lupos graves emersit ante nostram memoriam in hac ecclesia surculus fructuum spem enecans, erepsit vineam Christi demolita vulpecula, apparuit ovile Domini dilanians lupus omni atrocitate immanior nova utpote sua haeresi armatus: Nestorius haereticus.

5 "Qui si non ultra modum, ultra mensuram, ultra id quod oportet sapere scientiam extenderet, si se infra terminum observandae fidei contineret, si inviolatae et inviolandae trinitati blasphemiam non exhiberet, novimus et fatemur, quia laudis locus non parvus sibi in ecclesia pateret. Nunc vero, quia, quod plus iusto volebat, ex malo erat, non laudi sed errori eius nos invidere quisque intelligat. Cuius haeresis sententia quia ratione caret, melius deputo eam te prorsus ignorare quam inde quicquam disputare. Saepe enim

down from heaven, as the master had prophesied that he would. When the enemy of the human race saw this, he envied the unity of the Holy Faith and Holy Religion and scattered tares among the wheat, and from these the most detestable root of all evils shot up and sprang forth, that is, heresy in its many forms, as vile as it is varied, which stains just as it is stained. The root is one, but the branches are innumerable; it is one beast but has many heads. Blessed Paul made a prophecy on this, saying, 'after my departure, voracious wolves will appear among you, dangerous wolves.' And it is also sung in the Song of Songs: 'Catch for me the little foxes that destroy the vineyards.' Among the innumerable branches of this root, among the enemy's weeds, among the destructive little foxes, among the oppressive wolves, before our memory, in this Church a shoot emerged that killed hope of harvest, the little fox arose who destroyed Christ's vineyard, a wolf appeared that savaged the sheepfold of the Lord, more frightful than any atrocity, armed with new heresy all his own: Nestorius the heretic.

"If he had not extended knowledge beyond the mean, be- 5
yond the measure, beyond that which one should know, if he had contained himself within the boundary of the faith to be practiced, if he had not blasphemed against the Holy Trinity, inviolate and not to be violated, we realize and confess that the place for his praise in the Church would not be small. Now however, because what he desired immoderately was in fact evil, let everyone understand that we look askance at him not because of his praise but because of his error. As to the idea behind this heresy, since it lacks reason, I think it better that you be in complete ignorance of it than that you discuss it at all. For it often happens that

contingit id obesse si scitur, quod nil obest, verum prodest si nescitur. Igitur, qui tunc temporis regendae ecclesiae praesidebant, posteaquam praefatum Nestorium reiecto ovium indumento confesse lupum deprehendebant et secreto atque publice correptum nequaquam resipiscere velle cognoscebant, huiusmodi membrum anathema fieri et ab ecclesiae corpore proici communi sententia statuebant, quippe quia 'corrumpunt mores bonos colloquia mala,' 'uvaque livorem ducit ab uva,' et 'grex totus unius scabie cadit et porrigine porci.' Habito itaque consilio longinquo Nestorius deputatur exilio, scilicet in partes Agarenorum in silvam densissimam montis Libani, in locum horroris et vastae solitudinis, in locum, qui ab hominum frequentia remotior visus est, quatinus vel solus ad salutis iter paenitentia ductus rediret vel solus ibidem deperiret.

6 "In qua nimirum horrifera eremo cum per aliquot annos nil suum meditans latitasset nullumque suae nequitiae socium vel factorem multis temporibus habuisset, ecce humani generis inimicus solum eum condolens periturum, quem captivavit, et iniquitatis complices et perditionis suae consortes arte, qua cunctis insidiatur, paravit, quasi assumptis septem spiritibus nequioribus se diceret, 'revertar in domum unde exivi.' Fiebant namque novissima hominis illius peiora prioribus. Reperit ilico adversarius noster, qualiter semen, quod seminaverat in Nestorio, multiplicatum cresceret in multorum perditione. Quidam vero porcarius cum in eadem silva porcos pascendo longius aberrasset, casu vel

something is an obstacle if it is known that would be no obstacle, but rather a benefit, if it were not known. Therefore, those who ruled the Church at that time, after they caught the aforesaid Nestorius, who had rejected sheep's clothing and admitted he was a wolf, and they knew that although he was censured privately and publicly he had no wish to come to his senses, they decreed by common agreement that this sort of a limb should be excommunicated and cut off from the body of the Church, since 'evil discourses corrupt good customs,' 'the grape is bruised by the grape,' and 'the whole herd falls with the scales and scurf of one pig.' And so when counsel had been taken, Nestorius was assigned to a distant exile, namely, in the region of the Hagarenes, in the thickest wood of Mount Lebanon, in a fearful, vastly deserted place, in a place that seemed to be remote from human population so that, alone, he would either do penance and return to the path of salvation, or perish alone in the same place.

"Naturally, in this frightful, deserted place when he had 6
been hiding for some years, meditating on nothing of his own, and when he had had for a long time no ally or agent of his own wickedness, lo, the enemy of the human race, feeling sorry that the man he had captured should perish there alone, with the art by which he lies in wait for all, furnished accomplices in his wickedness and partners in his perdition, as though, having taken in seven spirits more wicked than himself he might say 'I will return to the house which I have left.' For the last state of that man was worse than his first. Our adversary discovered there a method by which the seed that he had sown in Nestorius could multiply and grow into the perdition of many. For when a certain swineherd had wandered far into the same wood so that his pigs could

quod verius est maligni ductu spiritus ad Nestorii cellam devenit. Solus uterque solo reperto de praesentia gaudebat alterius. Coepit porcarius diligenter de Nestorio sciscitari, quis vel unde esset quave de causa in id loci devenisset. Quod dum Nestorius propria dissimulata culpa, ut in talibus solet, suam defendendo partem astuta digressione exposuisset, porcarium, quatinus frequenter ad se veniret, rogatum dimisit. Id porcarius magno studio se facturum et promisit et male verax adimplevit sicque brevi socios reddidit usus et frequentia, quos actuum compares fecit nequitia. Erat enim porcarius ille artis nequissimae, mentis callosae, necrologicae vir peritiae, diabolicae alumnus doctrinae, magus super omnes,

'quem non herba nocens nec vox occulta fefellit.'

7 "Vide, si par convenit pari, cum talis iungitur tali. Vide quam facile in talibus noster insidiator quod voluit fecit. Nam cum crebro consedissent et de multis uterque de suis multa sermocinando contulissent, advertit Nestorius porcarium promptuli esse ingenii adeo docilem et affectuosum et totius disciplinae admodum capacem iuvenem; id, inquam, advertit et, quatinus litteras a se disceret, summopere hortari coepit. Placuit iuveni affectus et exhortatio Nestorii et omni qua poterat vigilantia, omni assiduitate litterarum

graze, by chance, or more accurately, by the guidance of the wicked spirit, he arrived at Nestorius's cell. Each one, being alone, and having found a person who was alone rejoiced at the presence of the other. The swineherd began carefully to inquire of Nestorius who he was and where he was from, and why he had arrived at that place. When Nestorius had explained this, without imputing blame to himself, as happens in such cases, defending his own part with clever digressions, he sent away the swineherd, after first having begged him to visit him often. The swineherd promised with great zeal that he would do so and, being truthful for evil purposes, fulfilled his promise, and thus in a short time frequent contact made them partners, whom wickedness made fellows in action. For that swineherd had an exceedingly wicked craft, and a very wily mind. He was a man well-versed in necromancy, a student of diabolical teaching, a peerless magician,

> 'whom neither harmful plant nor hidden voice has escaped.'

"Consider how two equals were united, when such men 7
were joined together. Consider how easily our deceiver did as he wished with such men. For when they had often sat together and when each had recounted many of his own affairs in conversation, Nestorius noticed that the swineherd was a young man with a ready mind and was so docile and warmly disposed and able to grasp his whole teaching; he noticed this, I say, and he began to persuade him with great effort to learn reading and writing from him. Nestorius's attention and encouragement pleased the youth, and he took up the practice of reading with all the attentiveness and per-

exercitium arripuit nec tamen a cura porcorum cessavit. Mirum prorsus, per triennium eatenus in litteris profecit, ut non solum magistro in his, quae ab eo didicerat, non cederet, verum priorem sua adinventione multomagis augeret errorem. Vetus itaque novumque testamentum ita duorum miscuit et pravavit ars virorum, ut, quod Nestorius suo perdito intellectui attemperare nullatenus poterat, porcarius scilicet Machometa vel subvertendo vel iuxta patriae suae perditissimam ritum interpretando suo sensui vindicaret. Sic nimirum figmentum, inventio, ars et interpretatio utriusque alterius roboratur errore. Alteri uterque existebat mirabilis: ille quod usu tenebat, iste quod noviter addiscebat; ille quod in ecclesia pridem sophistice contendebat, iste quod noviter diabolice inveniebat; ille propter quod deicitur, iste propter quod assumitur; ille quia solitarius, iste quia porcarius; ille per haeresim, iste per mathesin. His igitur moribus, his artibus facile coaluere, qui sibi in perpetuum multisque in futurum nocuere, novi erroris praedicatores, nequissimi ritus initiatores, animarum innumerabilium supplantatores.

8 "Nam dum Nestorius saepius a Machometa gentis suae fidem inquireret percepissetque Agarenos nec Christicolas fore nec idolatras, sed quodam ignoto cultu circumductos omne quod liberet licitum sibi aestimare, omne quod viderent aeque deum, aeque sanctum putare, facile eos suae

severance that he could, without ceasing to care for the pigs. Amazingly enough, in three years' time he had made so much progress in letters that not only was he not inferior to his teacher in what he had learned of him, but rather he increased his teacher's previous error greatly by his own invention. And so the craft of the two men so mixed and twisted the New and Old Testaments that what Nestorius had not been able to make fit with his own depraved understanding, the swineherd Muhammad claimed for his own meaning either by ruining it or by interpreting it according to his own country's depraved rite. Thus, of course, the fiction, invention, craft, and interpretation of each were strengthened by the error of the other. Each was remarkable to the other: the one for what he customarily did, and the other for what he had newly learned; one with what he had long ago argued sophistically in the Church, and the other with what he had newly discovered in diabolic fashion; the one with what got him cast out, the other with what had caused him to be accepted; one because he was a hermit, the other because he was a swineherd; one by heresy, the other by learning. And so with these characters, with these crafts, they easily were united, men who harmed themselves for all eternity and many more in the future, the preachers of the new error, the creators of a most depraved rite, the stumbling blocks of innumerable souls.

"For when Nestorius had often asked Muhammad about 8
the faith of his people, he learned that the Hagarenes were neither Christians nor idolaters, but rather that, led astray by a certain unknown cult, they thought that everything that gives pleasure was permitted to them and everything that they saw was in equal share God to them, equally holy,

doctrinae cessuros cogitavit, quos nullius culturae veritas solidavit. Nec eum sua fefellit opinio. Huic consilio Machometam sibi socium iungere operae pretium ducens

discipulum dictis tandem compellit amicis:

'Et res et tempus et necessaria admodum ratio postulare videtur, quatinus, o fili, id, quod a me didiceras tuoque ingenio magna ex parte adauxeras, in actum publicae administrationis perferas. Fac igitur tibi nomen aeternum, arripe inter tuos praedicationis officium, annuntia veritatis verbum, ignorantes corrige, quatinus te docente, quid credendum quidve agendum sit, cognoscant, te ducente ad viam redire cogantur. Non tibi deest ad hoc exequendum sapientia, non sermo interpres, non eloquentia, non patriae linguae magna experientia. Sunt et reliqua tibi attributa: quid si non est tibi personae gravitas vel generis dignitas vel divitiarum prosperitas?

Illucesce tuis lumenque parentibus esto.

Nec tibi aberit, quicquid nostra ars et favor poterit.'

9 "Cui Machometa, 'Gratias,' inquit, 'pater, tuae piae devotioni et in praesens refero et in futurum referre nulla mihi aboleverit aetas, qui tale mihi nomen adoptas. Sed nosti, quia superbia hominum tales, qualis ego sum, audire dedignatur et extraneorum doctrina maiori auctoritate quam

and he thought that they would yield easily to his doctrine, since the truth of observance had not made them steady. And his belief did not deceive him. And since with this plan in mind he thought that it was worth the effort to make Muhammad his ally,

at last he compelled his student with friendly words:

'Both the matter and the time and a rather necessary reason seem to demand that you, my son, apply what you have learned from me and increased in large part by your own talent to the activity of public service. Therefore make an eternal name for yourself, take up the vocation of a preacher among your people, announce the word of truth, correct the ignorant so that, with you teaching them, they will know what to believe and what to do, and under your leadership they may be compelled to return to the path. You do not lack the wisdom to achieve this, nor the exegete's discourse, nor the eloquence, nor ample experience with the language of the country. You have other attributes also: so what if you do not have the respectability of person or the proper birth or prosperity in riches?

Light up your people, be a light to your relatives!

And you will not lack for whatever my skill and favor will be able to achieve.'

"To him Muhammad said, 'Father, I give thanks for your 9
pious devotion at present, and no age will let me forget to give thanks in the future since you wish to bring me such a name. But you know that people's pride makes them disdain to listen to men like myself, and that the teaching of foreigners is often listened to with greater authority than that of

domesticorum saepe auditur. Didici enim in schola tua, quia nemo propheta acceptus est in patria sua. Nemo igitur meorum me docentem susciperet tum superbia tum etiam invidia. Gravius quidem est, quod mihi imponis, quam ego solus portare praevaleam. Ergo, quod benigne in gentem meam excogitasti, ipse suscipe, ipse inchoa, ipse manum mitte, praedicare incipe, docere satage; in te doctrinae gravitas, personae dignitas, docentis auctoritas. Tibi quicquid dixeris creditur. Tuis verbis fides adhibebitur. Tibi itaque, pater, tibi dignius, quod mihi optas, nomen accrescet.

10 "'Verumtamen me, quantum in me, devotissimo utere nuntio et adiutore. Spero quippe, quia a proximis circumquaque civitatibus meo instinctu, meis monitis talisque viri fama nonnullos tuam ad doctrinam audiendam conduxero. Nec ignoro, quod, postquam te audierint, signum a te requirent, sine quo non facile post te convertentur. Hoc igitur omni cautela praevideatur, ne quid apud te incautum ab illis reperiatur. Binos quam maximos potero utres praeparabo, qui pridie, quam ad te turbae convenient, aqua repleti in secretiori parte cellulae tuae terrae infodiantur, quatinus, cum turbae te per triduum audientes siti vexantur, die tertia per te quasi virtute dei reficiantur. Hoc enim signo tuae doctrinae auctoritas magna ex parte roborata procedet.'

11 "Placuit enim tum Nestorio huiusce consilii argumentosa inventio. Placuit, inquam, utque festinantius his operam daret, Machometam hortatur. Nec moram egit Machometa.

the natives. Indeed, I have learned in your school that no prophet is accepted in his own country. None of my people would accept me as a teacher either out of pride or out of envy. Indeed what you put upon me is heavier than I can bear alone. Therefore, what you have thought out kindly for my people, take up and begin and handle yourself, begin to preach, undertake to teach, you have the seriousness for spiritual leadership, the personal dignity, a teacher's authority. Whatever you say is believed. People will confide in your words. Hence, you are worthier of the name that you choose for me, and you can make it grow.

"'Nevertheless, use me as a messenger and helper, the most devoted that I can be. For I expect that I will bring some men from the nearest surrounding cities to hear your teaching at my prompting, with my admonitions, and with the fame of so great a man. I realize that, after they hear you, they will seek a miracle from you, and that without this it will be difficult to convert them to your cause. Let us carefully plan in advance so that they not find anything in your quarters unprepared. I will make ready two sacks, as large as possible, full of water, which will be dug into the ground in a more secluded part of your cell the day before the masses come to you, so that, when the masses have been listening to you for three days and are suffering from thirst, on the third day you may quench their thirst as if by the power of God. By this sign, indeed, the authority of your teaching will be greatly strengthened and will be manifest.' 10

"Then indeed Nestorius was pleased with this plan that his partner had thought up in great detail. He was pleased, I say, and he encourages Muhammad to undertake this plan with greater haste. And Muhammad did not delay. For he 11

Est enim spiritus, quo agebatur, sine mora et requie. Porro civitates et loca circumquaque vicina adiens multos inde alloquitur et suscitat viros mixtae aetatis; memorat se invenisse hominem sanctum saluti eorum de caelo missum eosque, quatinus secum eum ad videndum et audiendum pergerent, arte omni qua noverat persuasit. Quod et factum est. Excitati namque fama tanti viri alii humana curiositate, alii spe si dixerim mutandae in melius conversationis, alii qualibet mobilitate animi, plures novarum rerum cupidi ad cellulam Nestorii nova doctrina, novo cultu, novo ritu et tam pravo quam novo perituri.

12 "O quam festinatur perditio! O quam caeco pede curritur ad periculum! O quam tortuosi praetenduntur laquei! O quam in profundam caditur foveam. O duplici, O multiplici, et omni errore decepta gentilitas!

Quo peritura ruis, quo caecus te rapit error,
Cladibus acta tuis, quo peritura ruis?

Nescis, quia novissima tua erunt peiora prioribus? Perpende, quid et quantum debes ei, qui hoc te munere beavit.

13 "Tandem igitur perventum est ad cellulam Nestorii, ubi cum gaudio laetitiaque susciperentur. Per tres continuos dies ad doctrinam Nestorii a mane usque ad vesperam impertaesi intendebant. Nec deerat versutus artifex, qui, quod foris audierant, intus in cordibus eorum plantare satagebat.

had a spirit which led him to act without delay and without rest. Then he went to the surrounding cities and towns, and he spoke to and inspired many men of all ages from those places; he said that he had found a holy man sent from heaven for their salvation, and he persuaded them with every trick that he knew to accompany him to see and hear this man. And they did so. For they were excited by the reputation of such a great man and went to Nestorius's cell: some did so out of human curiosity, others with hope, I would say, of changing to a better way of life, others with a certain restlessness of spirit, and many with desire for a new order. They were to perish with a new teaching, a new devotion, a new rite as depraved as it was new.

"O how hastily perdition approaches! How men run to- 12
ward danger on blind feet! What winding snares are set for them! How deep is the pit into which they fall! O Gentiles, deceived by double, or multiple, or any and all errors!

> Where do you rush, sure to perish, where does your
>   blind error carry you,
> compelled by your own calamity, on the verge of destruction, where do you rush?

Do you not know that your last state will be worse than your first? Consider carefully what and how much you owe to him who blessed you with this gift.

"At last, therefore, they arrived at Nestorius's cell, where 13
they were received with rejoicing and contentment. They paid indefatigable attention to Nestorius's teaching from sunrise to sunset for three days in a row. Nor did the clever craftsman fail to take pains to plant what they heard on the outside inside in their hearts. Therefore Nestorius's

Visa est ergo illis Nestorii doctrina admodum dulcis et omni auctoritate roborata et adeo saluti eorum proficua, ut foret prae omnibus magno affectu exposcenda. Tertia itaque die deficiente, quem secum adtulerant domi, victu et maxime eos urente siti, erat enim locus ille desertus et aridus, clamare coeperunt ad Nestorium, quatinus invocato deo suo aquam eis ad bibendum praeberet. Quid igitur? Promisit ille se in crastinum eis aquam abundanter daturum, sed una die ac nocte deo super hoc ait supplicandum. Nimirum sitientes vix ad diem usque expectantes summo diluculo ad cellam venere aquam postulantes. Simulata ille intus, quasi se de oratione nuper levaret, fatigatione acceptis per fenestram vasis singulorum de utribus, quos ad hoc absconderat, aquam ad sufficientiam cunctis latenter propinarat, quam utique illi divinitus datam credentes tam pro sanctuario quam pro siti avide laetanterque potabant. Habebant denique signum illud furtivum et magna admiratione et maximo suae doctrinae firmamento.

14 "O iterum iterumque omni caligine caecior gentilitas, quare tam concita mente furtivo signo credebas? Cur non saltem apertum et detectum poscebas? Certe certe non furtim sed palam Mosi virga fontem de petra elicuit sicque sitientibus ministravit. Nempe, quae lucem fugiunt, tenebrarum esse opera quis dubitet?

15 "Decepta vero et perdita hoc modo miserrima turba huic

doctrine seemed to them extremely sweet, and supported by all authorities, and so profitable to their salvation that it should be inquired about with great emotion above all things. And so on the third day, when the food that they had brought from home was running out, and when they were most burning with thirst, for that place was solitary and parched, they began to cry out to Nestorius to call on his god to provide them with water to drink. What next? He promised that for the next day he would give them water in abundance, but he said they must pray to God one day and one night for this. And since, of course, they were thirsty, they scarcely waited for day and at the break of dawn came to his cell demanding water. And Nestorius in his cell feigned weariness, as though he had recently gotten up from prayer, and, receiving the cups of the individuals through the window, from the bags that he had hidden there for this purpose, he gave sufficient water to all without being perceived. And they believed absolutely that this water had been given to him by God, and they drank it joyfully and eagerly both as a holy gift, and out of thirst. In sum, they regarded that deceptive miracle with great wonder as a most convincing support for his doctrine.

"O Gentiles, again and again blinder than all darkness, 14
why were your minds in such a hurry to believe this deceptive miracle? Why did you not at least demand one that was open and manifest? Verily, verily, it was not secretly but in the open that Moses's rod brought forth a spring from the rock, and thus he supplied the thirsty. For indeed, who would doubt that works that flee the light are works of darkness?

"But thus deceived and ruined, and initiated into this 15

cultui initiata sed non integre adhuc dedita redeundi ad sua licentiam a Nestorio postulavit. In cuius audientia

talibus alloquitur monitis Machometa magistrum:

'Horum, qui ad te confluebant, longe, pater, abhinc distat habitatio utpote trium aut amplius dierum spatio et est via laboriosa tum deserti difficultate tum etiam loci ariditate. Noli igitur eos ultra ad te usque veniendi labore vexare. Mihi si placet impone, quatinus tua ad illos posthac fungar legatione. Nec onerosum duco tuo parere imperio, tum quia tuis me tibi ligasti beneficiis, tum quia, quicquid illis evenerit, mihi evenisse volo, quicquid crediderint credam, quicquid coluerint colam. Restat igitur, ut, qui suam deposituri nova sunt conversatione novoque ritu initiandi, maiori ad hoc quam humana instituantur auctoritate. Supplica igitur deo tuo, quatinus fides, quam verbis apud nos astruis humanis, suo nutu, suis signis caelitus usque ad nos scripta perveniat. Neque enim Mosi dicenti sed litteris digito dei scriptis populus Hebraeorum corda praebuit.'

16 "His omnes assensere dictis tam Nestorius quam turba, quae convenerat, dicens alioquin se nolle patriae culturae renuntiare et novae legi adhaerere, nisi ea, quam Machometa dixit, auctoritate.

worship, but not yet completely given over to it, that most wretched crowd asked Nestorius for permission to return to their homes. In his audience,

Muhammad addressed his teacher with such warnings:

'Father, the dwelling place of those who have flocked to you is far from here, a space of three or more days, and the journey is toilsome both owing to the inaccessibility of the remote location and because of the dryness of the region. Therefore do not trouble them with the task of coming to you again. If you please, command me to play the role of your emissary to them. And I do not think it will be burdensome for me to obey your orders both because you have bound me to yourself by your favors, and also because, whatever happens to them, I will wish it had happened to me; whatever they believe, I will believe; and whatever they worship, I will worship. It only remains then, since they are to abandon their way of life and be initiated into a new way of life and a new rite, that they be instructed in this by a superhuman authority. Pray therefore to your god that the faith that you propagate among us with human words will arrive for us in written form with his consent with his own signs from heaven. For the Hebrew people did not give their hearts to Moses when he spoke, but to the letters written with God's finger.'

"Everyone agreed to this, both Nestorius and the crowd 16
that had come to that place, and they said that they did not want to renounce their ancestral worship and adhere to the new law, except with the authority that Muhammad mentioned.

His verbis, hoc consensu sua quisque revisit;
Solus cum solo tantum Machometa remansit

Nestorio non inscius. Habuit enim ad hoc non deserentem se magistrum, qua arte suo satisfaceret consilio.

17 "'Habeo,' inquit, 'O Nestori pater, habeo consilium satis ad inchoata, prout mihi visum est, utile, necessarium et probabile, quod tuae proferam electioni. Sit labor et cautio tua, immo tecum, si iusseris, mea, citius quam poteris quid agendum, quid vitandum, porro per omnia qualiter vivendum, qualiter sit credendum quidve adorandum, nominatim et discrete praefigere et digesto ordine chartae inscribere. Quam scripturam cornibus illigabis vitulae, quae biduo, ut non bibat, inclaudatur et tertia die emittatur. Videbis deinceps, quid sequatur.'

18 "Quod dum Nestorio placuisset, praesens enim erat ad artem, quam ille excogitaverat, parere consilio eius non distulit arreptaque citius charta perditissimi vivendi normam perditis et perituris Agarenis, quam hactenus servant, Nestorius et Machometa in commune scriptitarunt. Quod iste non poterat per haeresim, ille adiecit per mathesin.

19 "Postquam igitur duorum artibus perfecta in unum conscribuntur perversa praecepta, dies et locus astu praevidetur, quo Machometa apud suos legatione magistri fungeretur. Praevidetur, inquam, conventui locus paene unius

With these words, this agreement everyone returned to
his own affairs;
only Muhammad remained alone

with Nestorius, and he was not at a loss. He had indeed for this purpose a teacher who would not desert him to show him by what trick he should achieve his plan.

"He said, 'O father Nestorius, I have a plan for our under- 17
taking, quite, as it seems to me, useful, necessary and plausible, that I offer for your choice. Let the task and responsibility be yours—nay rather if you command, let them also be mine along with you, more quickly than you will be able to [alone], to set down specifically and clearly according to a careful scheme on parchment what to do, what to avoid, indeed all aspects of how to live, what to believe and how to worship. You will tie this document to the horns of a heifer that shall be shut up two days without drinking, and on the third day it shall be sent forth. Then you will see what follows.'

"Nestorius agreed to this, for he was inclined to the trick 18
that the other had thought up, and he did not delay to obey his advice, and Nestorius and Muhammad quickly took up parchment, and wrote there together a norm of utterly depraved living for the depraved and doomed Hagarenes, which they still follow. What Nestorius was not able to achieve by heresy, Muhammad added by his learning.

"Therefore, after the perverse commandments had been 19
perfected by the talents of the two men and drawn up as a whole, the day and place was carefully planned, on which Muhammad was to act as emissary to his people. They planned, I say, the place of the meeting scarcely one day's

itinere diei distans a cella Nestorii, ubi erat fons lucidus turbae confluenti adeo necessarius et pascuis pecorum uberrimus. Quid plura? Venit dies ab utrisque constituta, ruit obviam Machometae Agarenorum turba, quid vel de magistro vel per se referret, auditura. Cumque multis sermonibus ille diem protraheret, nonnullis ambagibus turbam detineret, ecce, sole iam a centro ad nonam vergente, vitulam a Nestorio emissam procul accurrentem adeo sitibundam, noverat enim ibi fontem, aspexere.

"Dumque stupefacti starent omnes, solus Machometa—sciebat quippe quid erat—

intrepidus stetit atque suos compellat amicos:

'Ecce, quod cupivimus iam tenemus, quod expectavimus iam videmus; ablatus est totius dubitationis locus. Vitula, quam accurrentem cernitis, nuntia dei venit; scripta, quibus vivamus, cornibus gerit et velocitas currentis magnam nobis innuit voluntatem mittentis.' Dum haec et itidem talia loqueretur, quibus stulta illorum corda ad hoc, quod voluit, redderet attenta et benivola—facile enim illis persuadebat—, iam super fontem venerat vitula; et siti, cuius impetus ferebatur, satisfaciens ripae genibus incumbebat et prospecta cornuum insolita specie sub unda ad singulos tactus reformidat. Magno itaque conamine circumdatam comprehendunt vitulam magnaque reverentia abreptam a cornibus scripturam legentes et, quae in ea habebantur, sibi propria

journey from Nestorius's cell, where there was the clear spring so necessary for the throng that came together and abundant pastureland for the livestock. What more? The day came that was established by both, the crowd of Hagarenes rushed up to meet Muhammad to hear what he would relate from his teacher or on his own. And when he had dragged out the day with different discourses, and detained the throng with several digressions, lo, when the sun was sinking down from the center to the ninth hour, they spied the heifer sent by Nestorius running up from a distance because it was thirsty and knew that there was a spring there.

"While everyone was standing there stunned, only Muhammad—he knew, naturally, what it was—

stood there fearlessly, and he called together his friends:

'Look, we have now what we have desired, we see now what we were waiting for; all room for doubt has been removed. The calf which you see running up is God's messenger; it carries on its horns the writings according to which we should live, and the speed of its running points to the great goodwill toward us of the one who sent it.' While he was saying this and other similar things, by which he rendered their foolish hearts receptive and well-disposed to his wishes—for he persuaded them easily—the calf had already come upon the spring; and, satisfying the thirst that was driving it on, kneeled at the edge of the spring, and, having glimpsed the unaccustomed appearance of its horns upon the water, recoiled from everyone's touch. And so they surrounded the calf and corralled it with great effort and reading the scripture taken from its horns with great reverence

veneratione servanda ponentes utpote caelitus missa nullamque ultra super hac doctrina dubitationem habuere.

21 "Verum Machometa clarus apud illos habebatur et magnus, sed multo clarior maiorque Nestorius. Unde plures ex Agarenis ad eum confluere eiusque magistratui adhaerere coeperunt. Miscebant se utique ad hoc malum malorum omnium germina, invidia scilicet et superbia. Coepit namque Machometa famae Nestorii invidere sibique soli id nomen magisterii optavit et honorem. Ad quod tali arte perventum est. Quadam itaque nocte, dum Nestorius et discipuli somno vinoque sepulti iacerent, Machometa tacite surrexit, cultrum e vagina dormientis cuiusdam condiscipuli eripuit, magistrum occidit, cultellum in vaginam, unde eripuit, cruentum recondit sicque cubitum perrexit. Cumque facto mane tanti facinoris auctor caute perquiritur, Machometa edicente et consiliante requisitum est inter omnes et, apud quem ferrum repertum est cruentum, suspensus laqueo licet innocens vitam finivit. Eligitur itaque Machometa a discipulis in locum Nestorii et, quod optaverat, fama, quae erat prius duorum, in Machometam pervenit solum. Statuit igitur ille quasi pro lege, quatinus nemo ex Agarenis vino utatur, quia per ebrietatem talia in Nestorium perpetrata sunt. Fecerat autem hoc, ut suam eo magis dissimularet culpam. Tamen hactenus ea lex apud illos servatur.

22 "Non longe post moritur rex Agarenorum de Babylonia et, quia filius sibi non erat, uxorem regni dimisit heredem. Nec mora, suscitatus Machometa spiritu, quo totus

and imposing on themselves obedience with their own veneration to the things found in it as though sent from heaven, they had no further doubt concerning this doctrine.

"They held Muhammad to be illustrious and great, but 21
Nestorius was considered greater and much more illustrious. Hence many of the Hagarenes went to him and began to follow his teaching. And in this evil, the seeds of all evils were mixed, that is, pride and envy. For Muhammad began to envy Nestorius's fame and to desire for himself alone the renown and honor for teaching. He attained it by such a trick. One night, while Nestorius and his disciples were lying buried in sleep and wine, Muhammad silently arose, snatched a knife from the sheath of a certain disciple while he slept, killed his teacher, hid the bloody dagger in the sheath from which he had snatched it and thus retired to bed. And when morning had come, and the author of this great crime was being sought, Muhammad spoke out and gave advice, and a search was carried out upon everyone, and the one who was found with the bloody knife in his possession was hanged by a noose and, though innocent, his life came to an end. And so Muhammad was elected by the disciples in Nestorius's place, and, as he had desired, the fame, which had belonged to the two men, came to be Muhammad's alone. Therefore he established, as it were, a law that none of the Hagarenes should drink wine, since this crime was committed against Nestorius due to drunkenness. He did this, however, in order to better disguise his guilt. Nevertheless, they observe this law to the present day.

"Not long afterward the King of the Hagarenes of Baby- 22
lon died, and, because he had no son, he made his wife heir to the realm. Without delay Muhammad was stirred to

agebatur, spiritu inquam confusionis et superbiae, qualiter reginae conubio simulque regno potiretur, propriae confisus arti cogitare coepit. Reperit ergo nequitiae suae adiutorem quendam, quem caute quid loqueretur instructum ad reginae direxit colloquium. Qui cum secreta reginae allocutione fungi permitteretur: 'Diu,' inquit, 'O regina, visionem quam videram ad te perferre neglexeram. Tertio autem durius admonitus, quae videram quaeque audieram, reticere tibi non audeo, sed tu ut me placanter audias exopto. Num tibi quicquam attulit fama super quodam Machometa, cuius meritis et labore nova et praecipua nostrae genti illata est secta? Etenim post illum multi de nostris abierunt. Hunc videlicet caelitus iussa es habere maritum regnique consortem. Ex quo etiam filium universo orbi imperaturum habebis.'

23 "Talibus acceptis primum regina

obstupuit; dubitavit enim, si vera referret.

Tandem sicut est animus mulieris in utramque partem facilis: 'Audieram,' inquit, 'de hoc Machometa, sed, quia sequestratus ab hominibus in solitudine suo nescio cui ignoto deo coepit vacare, haud certa consisto, an de talibus ultra velit curare,' simulque, ut in praesentiam eius duceretur, praecepit. Quo cum ille pervenisset et regina sermonem cum eo super coniugio habuisset: 'Novi,' inquit versipellis ille, 'te

action by the spirit that motivated him completely, the spirit, I say, of confusion and pride, and trusting in his own skill he began to consider how he could at the same time marry the queen and possess the kingdom. And so he found an accomplice in wickedness, whom he cautiously instructed in what to say and sent to speak with the queen. When this man was allowed a secret conversation with the queen, he said: 'For a long time, O Queen, I have neglected to relate to you a vision that I saw. However, since I have been warned for the third time more severely, I do not dare to fail to tell you what I have seen and heard, but I desire that you listen to me with favor. Has any rumor reached you concerning a certain Muhammad whose good works and toil have brought a new and outstanding sect to our people? For many of us have followed him. Clearly it is this man whom you are commanded by heaven to have as your husband and partner in kingship. From him you will have also a son who will rule the whole world.'

"When she heard this, the queen at first 23

was stunned; she doubted indeed, if he was telling the truth.

But in the end just as a woman's mind is easy to sway to both sides, she said: 'I had heard of this Muhammad, but because while living apart from men in his own retreat he began to worship who knows what unknown god, I think it quite uncertain that he still wishes to concern himself with such matters,' and at the same time she ordered that he be brought into her presence. When he arrived and the queen spoke with him about marriage, the cunning man said, 'I

mihi caelitus destinatam uxorem, sed nisi spe prolis promissae, vellem, si fas esset, destinatis reluctari. Verum quod futurum est qui resistere temptat, quin fiat, penitus errat.'

24 "Hac arte regia potitus uxore regio quoque sublimatur honore. Scilicet ut tanto gravior eius fieret casus, quanto altior erat, quem ascenderat, gradus. Postquam ergo in regno satis convaluit, praedictam sectam artibus auxit et evexit omnesque in regno suo eam colere, quos sponte non poterat, vi coegit. Fit itaque tum inter suos tam mirabilis, ut illum pro deo invocare placuerit. Tantum enim mathesis sua valebat.

25 "Ad ultimum, cum iam nequitiam suam terra diutius sustinere minime valeret, supplantator animarum, cui semper servivit, congruum vitae suae exitium finemque sibi condignum praevidit. Nam posteaquam visus est perpetuum sibi fecisse nomen, eo quod universum regnum ad suum flectebat errorem, cum die quadam venatum in silvam pergeret et a suis forte aberrasset, repente in porcorum gregem incidebat, a quibus membratim discerptus atque penitus consumptus est ita, ut nihil ex eo praeter dextrum brachium remaneret. Unde per universos Agarenos decretum est, ut ex illo nemo deinceps in perpetuum porcis utatur, quae lex apud illos hactenus integerrima servatur, eo quod rex illorum, ipse doctor et propheta eorum, a porcis consumebatur.

know that you are destined by heaven to be my wife, but, if it were not for the promised offspring, I would be willing to struggle against destiny, if it were allowed. Whoever attempts, however, to resist what will be, to prevent it happening, makes a serious error.'

"In this manner, he took possession of the royal wife and 24
was also elevated to royal rank. Of course, this was so that his fall would be the more severe, the higher the rank to which he ascended. Therefore after he had sufficiently established his power in the realm, he increased the aforesaid sect with his devices and exalted it, and everyone in his realm whom he could not compel by their own initiative to worship thus he compelled by force. And thus he became so admired by his own people that it was decided to call upon him as a god. So much power did his learning have.

"Finally, when the earth could scarcely support his wick- 25
edness any longer, the stumbling block of souls, whom he had always served, foresaw a suitable destruction for his soul and an end worthy of him. For after he was seen to have made an eternal name for himself by bending the whole realm to his own error, when one day he went hunting in the woods and had by chance wandered away from his companions, he suddenly came upon a herd of pigs who tore him limb from limb and consumed him so that nothing but his right arm remained. Hence it was decided by all the Hagarenes that from that day onward no one should ever consume pigs, and they follow this law perfectly up to the present day, because their king, their very teacher and prophet himself, was consumed by pigs.

"Et merito porcis rex contingebat edendus,
pascere qui porcos iuvenis persaepe solebat."

26 Iste est Machometa, qui ab Agarenis doctor honoratur, rex atque propheta vocatur et ut deus adoratur. Haec de Nestorio Agarenis Machometa, prout Graecus mihi retulit, dixisse sufficiat. Verum quisquis ista falsa putaverit, mihi cesset exprobrare, cum verius debeat vel suae ignorantiae vel Graecorum inventioni id imputare.

EXPLICIT AB ADELPHO COMPOSITUS.

"And deservedly did their king chance to be eaten by pigs,
who as a young man had very often put pigs out to graze."

This is Muhammad, who is honored as a spiritual leader 26
by the Hagarenes, is called king and prophet, and is adored as a god. Let it suffice to have said these things about Nestorius, the Hagarenes, and Muhammad, just as the Greek told me. But whoever thinks that these things are false, may he not accuse me, since he ought rather to blame it on his own ignorance or on the invention of the Greeks.

THE BOOK WRITTEN BY ADELPHUS ENDS HERE.

APOLOGY OF AL-KINDĪ

Apology of al-Kindī

Epistulae Saraceni et Christiani

In nomine Dei misericordis et miseratoris. Adiutorium tuum, O Domine. Tempore Abdalla Helmemun Emirhelmomini, fuit quidam vir de prudentissimis et excellentissimis, Eleheisimin, filii Alahabet, de familiaribus regis, notus in religione et probitate et in fide Maurorum perfectus atque profundus et implens mandata eius, manifestus in hoc tam in publicis quam in privatis. Et erat illi amicus de Christianis doctus et sapiens, ex Quinda oriundus, in fide Christianorum perfectus, et erat in servitio regis et proximus illi. Et erant amici carissimi adinvicem, alter in alterius mutua amicitia confidentes. Et erat Emirhelmomini Elmemun et omnes primates et adhaerentes regno eius scientes hoc. Horum duorum nomina aliqua de causa scribere recusavimus. Scripsit itaque Eleheisimin Christiano chartam, cuius exemplar hoc est.

Epistula Saraceni

2 A quodam filio cuiusdam ad quendam filium cuiusdam Christianum. Salus super te et misericordia Dei. Scriptum meum tibi cum pace et misericordia incipio aperire

Apology of al-Kindī

Letters of a Saracen and a Christian

In the name of God, the merciful and compassionate. May your aid, O Lord, be with me. In the time of ʿAbd Allāh al-Maʾmūn, the *ʾamīr al-muʾminīn,* there was a certain man among the most prudent and excellent courtiers of the king, a Hāshimite and an ʿAbbāsid, known for his piety, moral uprightness, and his complete and deep adherence to the faith of the Moors and to fulfilling its commands, clearly doing so both in public and private matters. He had a friend from among the Christians who was learned and wise, and came from Kinda; he was complete in his Christian faith, and was in the service of the caliph and in his inner circle. They were very dear friends to each other, each professing mutual affection for the other. And both the *ʾamīr al-muʾminīn* al-Maʾmūn and all of his courtiers knew this. I have decided not to give their names here for a reason I will not mention. And so the Hāshimite wrote a letter to the Christian, of which the following is a copy.

The Letter of the Saracen

From a certain son of a certain man to a certain Christian, 2
son of a certain man. May God's salvation and mercy be upon you. I begin my letter to you with peace and mercy, in

imitatione domini mei et domini prophetarum Mahumet, Dei nuntii (oratio Dei super eum et salus).

3 Sic enim venerabiles maiores nostri, certi et veridici, recitantes nobis praecepta prophetae nostri (super eum salus), retulerunt nobis quod hic mos eius fuerit. Aperiebat enim verbum suum omnibus hominibus cum pace et misericordia, quando eis scribebat, non discernens inter pauperem et divitem nec inter fidelem et incredulum. Dicebat namque: *"Missus sum in moderamine mentis et lenitate ad homines, et non sum missus in superbia et ferocitate."* Et testificatur deinde super hoc ubi dicit: *"Misericors sum hominibus et propitius."*

4 Et sic vidi facientes antistites nostros prudentes et consultos (orationes Dei super eos). Imitabatur enim doctrina eorum honestatem et nobilitatem sui generis et sollertiam animi et mentis venustatem, et sequebantur vestigia sui prophetae (orationes Dei super eos). Et non discernebant in hoc ut praeponerent aliquem alicui. Ego igitur, arrepto hoc itinere et huius doctrinae adepta honestate, illorum viam secutus, tibi hoc in libello meo cum pace et misericordia incipio ne forte, ad quem hic libellus meus pervenerit, dicat illum non esse meum.

5 Deinde compulsus ea quam erga te habeo dilectione, immo cum dominus meus meusque propheta Mahumet (oratio Dei super illum et salus) dixerit, "Amor Arabum credulitas et fides," ego vero parens nuntio Dei (super quo salus), fideliter amo te. Dignum namque est hoc tuae gloriae venerationi atque dilectionis honestati, maxime cum ex

imitation of my lord, and the lord of the prophets, Muhammad, messenger of God (God's prayer and salvation be upon him).

Indeed, this is how our venerable forefathers, speaking the truth, recited to us the teachings of our prophet (salvation be upon him), and told us that this was his custom. For, whenever he wrote to them, he began his words with peace and mercy to all, making no distinction between a poor man and a rich man, or between a believer and an infidel—for he said: "I have been sent with moderation of mind and kindness toward men, and I have not been sent with pride or savageness." Then he testifies to this when he says: "I am merciful and well-disposed toward men." 3

This is how I have seen our wise and learned sovereigns act (God's prayers be upon them). Their teachings reflected the honorable and noble nature of their lineage, a prudent spirit, and an elegant mind, following in the footsteps of their prophet (God's prayers be upon them). And they did not discriminate by placing one before another. I am therefore following in their path by undertaking this journey and accepting these honorable teachings, and I begin this booklet of mine with peace and compassion toward you, to prevent whomever this booklet of mine may reach from claiming that it is not mine. 4

Furthermore, I was driven by the affection that I feel for you—indeed, since my lord and prophet Muhammad (God's prayer and salvation be upon him), said, "Love is the belief and faith of the Arabs," in compliance with God's messenger (salvation be upon him) I love you faithfully. For this is what is worthy of the venerable nature of your glorious position and the sincerity of your friendship, especially since it 5

affectu intimo nostro amori te semper pronum fuisse pateat et dominus meus filiusque mei patrui Emirhelmomini te honorabiliter habuerit et sibi proximum fecerit et, in te confidens, de te bona dixerit. Unde tibi equidem volo quod mihimet ipsi et meae uxori filioque meo concupisco.

6 Ea propter puram exhortationem tibi impendens, nostrae fidei regulam, quam nobis Deus et omnibus quos creavit dari voluit, manifeste insinuo. Hinc enim Deus retributionis praemium nobis in regeneratione promittens, a iudiciali sententia in resurrectione mortuorum, benedictus et gloriosus, securos nos fecit, cum diceret: *"Plebs Abrahae perfecte Saracena."* Rursumque (magnus et gloriosus) in sacro suo eloquio dixit: *"Qui nostris signis crediderunt et Saraceni fuerunt."* Deinde diligenter subsequitur dicens: *"Nec Iudaeum nec Christianum, sed sincerum Saracenum fuisse."*

7 Idcirco et ego quae mihimet ipsi dedidero tibi quoque exoptans, dilectioni tuae compatior, eo quod disciplinae tuae multitudo et sanctae conversationis et sapientiae dignitas tuique generis nobilitas omnibus patet. Et quia omnes domesticos tuos meritis antecellis, ut maneas sicut permanere in tua fide consuevisti, in memet ipso dixi: ego patefaciam illi quod nobis Deus contulit et faciam illum scire illud, in quo constituti sumus, lenitate verbi atque honestate. Et sequar in hoc praeceptum quod me arguit atque prohibuit dicens: *"Nolite altercari cum legem habentibus nisi benigne atque pacifice."* Ego quippe nullatenus disceptabo tecum nisi honestate verbi et tenore locutionis atque sermonis moderamine. Fortassis conversus satisfacies veritati.

is clear from your own deepest sense of affection that you have always been disposed to my love, and since the *ʾamīr al-muʾminīn,* my lord and the son of my paternal uncle, has treated you with honor and invited you into his inner circle, and, trusting in you, has spoken well of you. Because of this I wish for you that which I desire for myself, my wife, and for my son.

In paying you these respects for the purpose of a genuine 6
exhortation, I hand to you in plain sight the rule of our faith, which God wished to give to us and to all he created. For it is on this account that God promised to us the reward of resurrection and kept us, blessed and glorious as he is, safe from the pronouncement of judgment during the resurrection of the dead, when he said: "The people of Abraham are perfectly Saracen." Again, he (great and glorious) said in his sacred scripture: "They who believed my signs and were Saracens." Then he adds more specifically: "He was neither Jew nor Christian, but purely Saracen."

For this reason I wish for you what I would give to myself, 7
and respond to your friendship, since the greatness of your learning and your dignified way of life, as well as your wisdom and noble lineage are plain to all. Since you exceed in your merits all your fellow courtiers, in that you persevere in your faith as you have become accustomed to do, I said to myself: I will show him what God has bestowed on me, and I will lay open to him with gentle and honest words the religion I have accepted. In doing so I will follow the precept that admonishes and rebukes me when it says: "Only debate with the People of the Book in a kind and peaceful manner." I, for my part, will only debate with you with fair words, in an even style, and with moderate speech. Perhaps you will convert and do justice to the truth.

8 Illud, obsecro, appetas quod tibi de verbo Dei refero, quod videlicet descendit supra Mahumet, prophetarum ultimo et domino filiorum Adam. Tandem igitur de hoc nequaquam desperans, expetivi a Domino, qui quos vult iustificat, et postulavi eum ut me causam tuae salutis faceret. Nam ipsum Dominum, qui benedicatur et exaltetur, in suae legis ordine invenio dicentem quoniam *"Qui apud Deum Saraceni."* Iterum priori verbo subiungit dicens: *"Qui appetit praeter Maurorum fidem, ab eo non recipitur et est in futuro damnandus."* Deinceps, benedictus et excelsus, coercenti nutu exprimit dicens: *"O vos, qui fideliter credidistis Deo, timete eum et nolite mori nisi effecti Saraceni."*

9 O tu, homo, auferat a te Deus infidelitatis stultitiam et cor tuum fidei splendori aperiat. Non ignores me multitudinis annorum aetatem percucurrisse et paene omnes fides generaliter scrutatum fuisse. Temptavi certe eas et multa de scripturis eorum a quibus tenentur revolvi. In scripturis denique vestris, scilicet, Veteris ac Novi Testamenti, quas Deus Iesu et Mosi et prophetis ceteris dedit, O Christiani, specialiter multum laboravi.

10 Vetus Testamentum hoc est: Lex, liber Iesu filii Nun, liber codicis Iudicum, liber Samuelis prophetae, liber codicis Regum, Psalmi David, Sapientia Salomonis, liber Iob, liber Isaiae, liber Ieremiae, liber Ezechielis, liber Danielis. Haec sunt omnes Veteres Scripturae. Novum vero Testamentum est hoc: in primis Evangelium, quod quattuor partibus dividitur; prima pars Evangelium decimatoris Matthei, secunda

I beg you, pursue that which I tell you about the word of God, which descended upon Muhammad, the last of the prophets and the lord of the children of Adam. Finally, since I did not despair of this in the least, I asked it of the Lord, who justifies whom he wishes, and I asked him to make me the cause of your salvation. I find that very same Lord (may he be blessed and exalted) saying in the course of his law, "They who are with God are Saracens." Again, to the earlier passage he adds, "He who pursues any faith but that of the Moors is not received by him, and he will be condemned in the future." Then, blessed and exalted, he says with a commanding gesture, "O you, who have faithfully believed in God, fear him and do not die unless you have become Saracens." 8

O Man, may God remove from you foolish unbelief and open your heart to the splendor of faith! You should be aware that I have progressed through a lifetime of many years and have investigated, in a general way, nearly every faith. Certainly, I examined them and read much from the scriptures of their adherents. I expended special effort on your scriptures, O Christians, that is to say, the Old and New Testament, which God gave to Jesus, Moses, and the other prophets. 9

The Old Testament is this: the Law, the book of Joshua son of Nun, the book of Judges, the book of the prophet Samuel, the book of Kings, the Psalms of David, the Wisdom of Solomon, the book of Job, the book of Isaiah, the book of Jeremiah, the book of Ezekiel, the book of Daniel. This is the whole of the Old Testament. The New Testament is this: first the Gospel, which is divided into four parts; the first part is the Gospel of Matthew the tax 10

pars Evangelium Marci filii sororis Symeonis, qui dicitur "claritas," tertia pars Evangelium Lucae medici, quarta pars Evangelium Iohannis filii Zebedaei. Horum quattuor virorum duo cum eo fuerunt, Mattheus scilicet et Iohannes. Alii vero duo de septuaginta discipulis, Marcus et Lucas. Deinde vidi Gesta Apostolorum, et enarrationes et actus, quae post ascensionem Christi Apostolus Lucas scripsit. Subsequuntur quattuordecim epistolae Pauli, quas ego perlegens et meditationi earum incumbens, de his cum Timotheo Episcopo disceptavi. Tu vero scis illum praeesse vestris omnibus tam dignitate principatus quam acumine scientiae et sensus.

11 Postea vero vidi quosdam, qui sequebantur haeresim trium haereticorum, qui ceteris maiores habentur, scilicet illam quae regia dicitur a Rege Marciano eo tempore quo disceptatio fuit inter Nestorium et Arium. Isti enim sunt Romani et Iacobiani et sunt omnibus deteriores in fide. Secunda haeresis illorum est, qui sequuntur sectam Cyrilli Alexandrini et Iacobi Syri et Severi alterius Syri, qui praeerat Antiochenae sedi. Tertia quoque haeresis Nestorianorum est, qui tibi proximi sunt et plane propinquiores illis qui veritati consentiunt; astutiores etiam in disputationibus magisque nobis consentientes in hoc quod credimus. Quorum sectam noster propheta Mahumeth praecipue laudasse videtur.

12 Veneratus est enim eos et pactum cum eis iniit, proposuitque tam ipse quam socii eius ut eos inter se cum benevolentia et modestia tractarent. Dedit etiam eis privilegia ut bene ageret cum illis, quando iam honorabiliter habebatur et

collector, the second part is the Gospel of Mark, the son of Symeon's sister, who is called "brightness," the third part is the Gospel of Luke, the physician, the fourth part is the Gospel of John, son of Zebedee. Of these four men two were with Jesus: Matthew and John. The others, Mark and Luke, were two of the seventy disciples. Then I saw the Acts of the Apostles, and the accounts and deeds which the apostle Luke wrote down after Christ's ascension. Then follow fourteen epistles of Paul, which I read and meditated upon, and afterward I debated about them with Bishop Timothy. You are aware that he surpasses all of you both because of the dignity of his office and because of the keenness of his knowledge and prudence.

Afterward, I saw certain people who followed the heresy 11 of three heretics, who are considered to be greater than the others: the heresy called "kingly" after King Marcian, in the time of the debate between Nestorius and Arius. These men are Romans and Jacobites, and their faith is worse than that of all the others. The second heresy is that of followers of the sect of Cyril of Alexandria and Jacob the Syrian and Severus the other Syrian, who is the prelate of the see of Antioch. The third heresy is that of the Nestorians, who are akin to you and clearly nearer to those who accord with the truth; they are more skilled in debates and accord more with what we believe in. Our prophet Muhammad appears to have praised their sect in particular.

He respected them and struck an agreement with them, 12 and both he and his companions proposed to treat them with kindness and dignity. He also granted them privileges in order to treat them well, at the time when he was already regarded with honor and was superior to the rest. Certainly,

ceteris praeminebat. Isti quippe haeretici, favore illius suffulti, cum ille iam apud homines magnus haberetur, commemorabant illi auxilia quae sibi ad adipiscendum ipsum honorem impenderant.

13 Monachi siquidem istius sectae annuntiabant illi, antequam Verbum Dei descenderet super eum, omne illud quod praestitit illi Deus et adeptus est. Idcirco saepe veniebat ad illos et diutinam cum eis collocutionem habebat, videlicet, quando proficiscebatur in Syriam et in ceteras regiones. De multis enim consulebat cum illis, unde et ipsi monachi et qui morabantur in monasteriis, diligentes eum et nomen eius exaltantes, praedicebant ceteris Christianis quod sublimandus esset a Deo. Propter quod Christiani, in amorem illius proni, referebant illi Iudaeorum calliditates et participatorum, qui vocantur Chorais, qui tres personas in Deo esse dicebant. Invidentes enim illi Iudaei et ipsi participatores dolose agebant cum eo et quaerebant ei malum. Christiani vero perfecte agebant in affectu dilectionis eius et eorum qui ei adhaerebant.

14 Tunc descendit Verbum super prophetam nostrum et testificatus est illi Deus in Alcorano, quod sonat "lex," et dixit: *"Sint vobis odibiliores omnibus hominibus participatores Corais, et qui ex Iudaeis crediderunt. Sint vobis amabiliores omnibus hominibus qui crediderunt et dicunt: 'Nos Christiani sumus,' eo quod in eis et monachi et presbyteri sunt et non superbiunt."* Noverat enim propheta per Verbum Dei, quod descenderat super eum, animos eorum et mentes et quia non fuerunt ex illis, qui

at the time when he was considered great among men, those heretics, strengthened by his support, recalled the assistance which they had rendered to him so that he might attain that position of honor.

In fact, monks of that sect reported to him all that God 13
had bestowed upon him and all that he had acquired before the Word of God descended upon him. For this reason he often came to them and held lengthy conversations with them, that is to say, at the time when he was going to Syria and to other regions. He sought their counsel on many matters, and because of this those very monks, as well as those who remained in their monasteries, loved him and exalted his name, preaching to the other Christians that he would be raised up high by God. For this reason, the Christians, who were inclined to love him, told him of the cunning of the Jews and of the polytheists called Quraysh, who claimed that there were three persons in God. Because they were envious of him, those Jews and polytheists were deceitful toward him, and sought to bring evil upon him. The Christians, on the other hand, acted completely in accordance with the affection they shared for him and his supporters.

Then the Word descended upon our prophet and God 14
testified to him in the Qurʾān, which means "law," and said: "Let the polytheists of the Quraysh be more hateful to you than all other men, as well as those among the Jews who believe. Let those who believe be dearer to you than all other men, they who say: 'We are Christians,' because among them are both monks and priests, and they are not prideful." For the prophet knew their hearts and minds through the Word of God, which had descended upon him, and that they were not among those who spoke up against him, who

contradicebant illi, qui habebant dolum et fraudem in corde suo. Sunt revera socii Christi, qui incedunt more eius et in lege eius persistunt. Renuebant enim proelia et sciebant sibi esse illicita, nec cum aliquo dolose agebant, nec alicui male volebant. Quaerebant quippe salutem et, pariter omnibus consulentes, nec odium nec dolum in corde retinebant.

15 Propheta itaque noster fecit eis pacta et privilegia et imposuit sibi et sociis suis ut in subiectione qua detinebantur bene cum illis ageret, monens eos in eadem doctrina persistere, cum revelaret illi Deus quod revelare voluit de illis et de sinceritate scripturae ipsorum. Nos vero confitentes et non negantes hoc, huic operi favemus, hanc legem sequimur, in hoc testamento perseveramus, huic veritati oboedimus.

16 Denique vidi monachos notos in sancta religione et sapientiae multitudine. Et ingrediens diversa loca et monasteria eorum et oratoria multa, prolixis etiam orationibus, quae septem diei horae nuncupantur, interfui. Sunt namque orationes noctis, et oratio primae et tertiae et meridiei et nonae et oratio somni. Et intuitus sum mirabilem eorum instantiam, quam habent in procidendo et adorando et facies terrae figendo et frontes percutiendo et interim manus saepe elevando ac retrorsum eas ligando, donec eorum perficiantur orationes. Hoc autem maxime faciunt in noctibus dominicae diei et sextae feriae ac sollemnitatum, in quibus solent vigilias celebrare. Sed et pedes suos adaptant in oratione et vigiliis et offerendis sacrificiis, tota insuper nocte psallendo.

had deceit and treachery in their heart. They are truly companions of Christ, who walk in his footsteps and abide by his law. They refused to engage in conflict and knew that it was unlawful for them, nor were they deceitful toward anyone, nor did they wish evil upon anyone. They sought salvation and, in their concern for all, held neither hate nor deceit in their hearts.

Our prophet therefore struck pacts with them and 15
granted them privileges, and required both himself and his companions to do good unto those who were in a state of subjugation, urging them to persist in the same teachings, since God would reveal to him that which he wished to reveal about them and the authenticity of their scripture. As for us, we confess and do not deny this, we are favorable to this task, we follow this law, we persevere in this testament, and we obey this truth.

Finally, I have seen monks well-known for holy obser- 16
vance and great wisdom. I visited various sites and monasteries of theirs, and many houses of prayer, and attended even the lengthy prayers called the seven hours of the day. For there are prayers of the night, and there is a prayer of the first hour, of the third, of midday, of the ninth hour, and of the hour of sleep. I witnessed their extraordinary perseverance, which they practice in prostrating themselves and worshipping, pressing their faces to the ground and striking their foreheads, and in the meantime often raising aloft their hands and binding them behind their backs until their prayers are completed. They do this especially on Sunday and Friday night, and on the nights of feast days, on which they are accustomed to celebrate vigils. They also move their feet in prayer, during the vigils and while offering sacrifices, all the while singing psalms the entire night.

17 His adiungunt ieiunia a mane usque ad vesperum, ita sibi mandata complentes memoriamque Patris et Filii et Spiritus Sancti saepius iterantes. Observant quoque dies afflictionis, quos et dies indulgentiae vocant, in quibus etiam nudis pedibus incedunt, induti laneis et cinere conspersi, et flentes multum uberes lacrimas ab oculis fundunt. Vidi quoque qualiter faciebant panem sacrificii et cum quanta reverentia et devotione praeparationi eius studebant, quantumque prolixe orabant ac supplicabant, quando panem illum in altari offerebant cum calice, in quo vinum est, in domo, quae vocatur domus sanctificationis. Et vidi qualiter in cellulis induebantur et celebrabant sex ieiunia, videlicet quattuor maiora et duo minora, et cetera. Haec omnia praesentialiter vidi et intellexi, et dum ea celebrarentur adfui.

18 Archiepiscopos quoque et episcopos in multitudine sapientiae et scientiae strenuitate memoratos inspexi, multum profundos in fide Christianorum et in perfectione religionis saeculo notos. Cum quibus etiam disputavi disputatione recta et inquisitione modesta sine iurgio et contentione, nec in aliquo cum eis egi violenter sive potestate sive generis nobilitate. Concessi enim eis in suis disceptationibus securitatem, ut quaecumque vellent libere loquerentur, non increpans eos neque despiciens in aliquo sermone locutionis meae, sicut solent disputare stolidi et insipientes et qui in nostra fide sunt rusticiores et genere obscuriores, qui non habent sensum neque fidem. Disputant namque cum

To this they add fasts from dawn until dusk, in this way fulfilling the commandments given to them and continuously reliving the memory of the Father, the Son, and the Holy Spirit. They also observe days of suffering, which they also call days of indulgence, in which they even walk on bare feet, clothed in wool and covered in ash, weeping and pouring forth plentiful tears from their eyes. I have also seen how they make the bread of sacrifice, and what great reverence and devotion they expended upon its preparation, and how long they chanted and prayed when they offered that bread on the altar, together with the chalice that contains the wine, in the house which is called the house of sanctification. I also saw how they dress in their cells and participate in six fasts, that is the four major and two minor fasts, and the remaining matters. All of this I saw and perceived in person, and I was present while these things were celebrated. 17

I also saw archbishops and bishops, renowned for their great wisdom and active knowledge, who were deeply immersed in the faith of the Christians and known to the world for their perfect religious observance. I also debated with them in a proper debate, inquiring respectfully without quarrel or contention, and I did not act forcefully toward them in any matter, either because of my position of power or my noble lineage. For I granted them security in their debates, so that they might freely speak whatever they wished, and I did not reproach them or look down upon them in any utterance of mine, as the stupid and foolish are used to do in debating, or those of our faith who are rather uncultivated and of obscure lineage, who have neither sense nor faith. They debate with strife and quarrel, using the 18

lite et altercatione et violentia potestatis absque sapientia et ratione. Ego autem quotiens volui disputare cum Christianis et de quibuslibet quaestionibus ac ratione fidei suae subtiliter indagare, ipsi suaviter et modeste et in nullo me de his quae quaerebam fallentes omnia mihi nota faciebant. Unde tam de interioribus eorum quam de exterioribus plenam cognitionem inveni.

19 Scripsi itaque tibi (quem Deus adiuvet), clarissimo sermone et praeparavi magna inquisitione et diligenti investigatione ac longi temporis meditatione quod tibi expedire noveram, ne forte me indoctum aut caecum in huiusmodi negotio aestimes, vel quicumque hoc meum scriptum perlegerit huius rei me ignarum putet. Omnia enim quae ad religionem Christianorum pertinent, diligenter animadverti.

20 Nunc igitur post hanc meam tuae fidei in qua degis cognitionem huiusque laboris prolixitatem, te (quem Deus salvet), ad meam fidem, quam mihi elegi, invito. Ero enim tibi certa fideiussione fideiussor paradisi et securitatis ab igne, si colueris unum Deum, qui est singulariter unitas atque soliditas, qui non habuit uxorem neque filium nec novit sibi aequalem. Ipse est enim species qua (gloriosus et excelsus) insinuavit se, cum non esset aliquid quod plus sciret de eo quam ipse de se. Ad hunc igitur colendum, cuius talis est species, te invitare permoveor. Et hic ego non addidi supra quod ipse de se praedicavit (sit memoria eius gloriosa et excelsa)—longe ab his qui ei participes faciunt. Nostra etenim plebs genus est patris nostri et vestri Abrahae, qui fuit perfecte Saracenus.

force of their position of power without wisdom or reason. As for me, whenever I wished to debate with Christians and to inquire carefully into any matter or issue pertaining to their faith, they explained to me all the things I asked about in a kind and respectful manner, without deception. In this way, I acquired a full understanding of both their internal and external features.

I have written to you (may God aid you) in an utterly clear 19
style, and I have prepared for you, through great examination, careful inquiry, and lengthy meditation that which I knew would be of use to you, to prevent you from thinking me ignorant or blind in such a matter, and to prevent anyone reading these writings of mine from considering me uninformed of these issues. Indeed, I have carefully taken notice of all that pertains to the religion of the Christians.

Now then, after this review of my knowledge of the faith 20
to which you adhere, and of my extended effort in this pursuit, I invite you (may God save you) to my faith, which I have chosen for myself. I will be to you a guarantor of paradise and of safety from the fire, with a sure guarantee, if you will worship the one God, who is a singular and indivisible unity, who has not had a wife or child, and who knows no equal to himself. For he is the very definition in which he (glorious and exalted) has revealed himself, since there was nothing that could know more about him than he knows about himself. I am strongly moved to invite you to worship him, whose definition is such. I have not added here anything beyond what he himself has proclaimed about himself (may his memory be glorious and exalted)—much in contrast with those who create "persons" in him. Our people are of the line of Abraham, both our and your forefather, who was truly Saracen.

21 Rursus igitur invito te ad testificationem et professionem Domini et domini mei, qui creaturis Dei est melior et sigillum prophetiae filiis Adam et electus a creatore saeculorum et novissimus prophetarum, Mahumet, filius Abdalla, Alchoresi natione, Eleheisimin genere, Alaptahi tribu, Etuhemi regione, possessor virgae et cameli et cisternae et intercessionis et dilectus a Deo gloriae. Locutus est enim cum Gabriele spiritu fideli, cum eum mitteret Deus ad nuntiandum et praedicandum hominibus iustificationem et fidei veritatem, ut ostenderet eum esse super omnem fidem, etiamsi participatores renuissent.

22 Vocavit autem omnes, orientales et occidentales, tam in terra quam in mari, tam in planis quam in asperis commorantes, cum misericordia et benignitate, cum suavitate mentis et moderatione eloquii et bonitate et longanimitate et lenitate. Idcirco humanum genus, praedicationi eius oboediens, testificatur quod ipse est nuntius, quem Deus creator saeculorum misit ad homines. Omnes vero nationes oboedientes ei adquieverunt veritati et aequitati, quae de ore et sana ipsius doctrina procedebant, certa ratione et aperto iudicio. Scriptura quippe data illi a Deo talis est qualis nec ab hominibus nec a daemonibus fieri potest. Unde tibi sit sufficiens testimonium certitudo advocationis ipsius.

23 Vocavit omnes ad colendum unum Deum singularem et solidum. Accedentes autem homines ad fidem eius subiecerunt se potestati eius, non renuentes neque superbientes, sed humiliter consentientes exultaverunt in illuminatione doctrinae ipsius. Et de eius nomine gloriantes, sese ceteris omnibus praetulerunt. Quisquis ergo eius prophetiam vel epistolam negaverit eiusque mandata neglexerit, inanis et

Again I invite you to testimony and profession of faith in the Lord and in my lord, who is better than all of God's creations and the final seal of prophecy to the children of Adam, chosen by the creator of the world and the last of the prophets, Muhammad, son of ʿAbd Allāh, of the people of Quraysh, of the clan of Hāshim, of the Abtaḥī tribe, from the region Tihāma, possessor of the rod, camel, well, and intercession, and beloved of glorious God. He spoke with Gabriel, a faithful spirit, when God sent him to announce and preach to men the justification and truth of faith, in order to demonstrate that he was above all faith, even if the polytheists denied it. 21

He called all men, both in the east and the west, both on the land and the sea, both dwelling in plains and mountains, with compassion and kindness, with sweet thoughts, moderate speech, with goodness, patience, and gentleness. For this reason the human race, obeying his preaching, testifies that he is the messenger whom God the creator of the world sent to mankind. All peoples who obeyed him rejoiced in truth and justice, which proceeded from his mouth and from his salutary teachings, by rational conviction and plain judgment. Indeed, to him was given by God a scripture such as cannot be created by men or demons. For this reason, let the truth of his calling be sufficient testimony for you. 22

He called upon all men to worship the one God, singular and indivisible. Those who went over to his faith submitted themselves to his power, neither resisting nor prideful, but with humble consent they exulted in the enlightenment of his teaching. Glorying in his name, they placed themselves above all others. Therefore, whoever denies his prophethood or mission, and ignores his precepts, will be vain and 23

vacuus erit. Propterea namque Deus credentibus illi omnia in regionibus subiecit diversasque nationes et populos eis prostravit, praeter illos qui eorum dictis et fidei crediderunt et testimonio consenserunt. Sicque ab effusione sui sanguinis liberati, honorem sibi et gloriam servaverunt. Ceteri vero tributarii nostri facti sunt. Hoc enim est testimonium verum (glorificet te Deus), quod Deus, antequam saecula crearet, testificatus est, videlicet, cum in throno scriptum esset: *"Non est deus nisi Deus, Mahumet nuntius Dei."*

24 Quapropter invito te ad quinque orationes, quas quicumque impleverit, petitione sua non fraudabitur, nec damnum aliquod pertimescet, eritque tam in hoc saeculo quam in futuro laudandus. Istae quippe orationes duabus institutionibus datae sunt, una quidem a Deo, altera a Dei nuntio. Sunt enim post cenam tres genuflexiones et duae in aurora et post meridiem duae et duae post solis occasum. Quicumque autem aliquid ex hoc dimiserit, a peccato immunis non erit, et oportet illum paenitere et subdi correptioni. Institutio vero orationis inter diem et noctem decem et septem genuflexionibus constat: in aurora duae, post meridiem quattuor, in vespera quattuor, post solis occasum quattuor, in prima cena ante comestionem duae, post cenam, quae vocatur "ultima," quando iam est alahatama, id est "densitas tenebrarum," duae. De hoc prohibuit Dei nuntius ut haec hora non vocetur alahatama. Dicit enim: "Alahatama nihil aliud est quam genuflexio camelorum, quando de agro collecti nocte accubare incipiunt."

25 Rursum invito te ad ieiunium mensis Ramazan, quod Deus iustus Iudex instituit et in eo Alcoran venire fecit. In quo mense de nocte praedestinationis testificatus est et nox

idle. For this reason God subjected to those who believe in him all things in the regions they inhabit, and subjugated the various nations and peoples to them, except those who believed in their words and faith, and yielded to their testimony. In this way they were saved from bloodshed and kept their honor and reputation intact. The rest were made to pay tribute to us. Indeed, this testimony is true (may God glorify you), since God attested it before he created the world, for on the throne is written: "There is no god but God, and Muhammad is the prophet of God."

For this reason I invite you to participate in the five prayers; whoever fulfills them will not be cheated of his request, he will not fear any loss, and he will be praiseworthy both in this world and the next. Those prayers were instituted in two ways: first by God, secondly by God's messenger. They consist of three prostrations after dinner, two at dawn, two at noon, and two after sunset. Whoever leaves anything out will not be free from sin, and he will have to repent and subject himself to rebuke. The institution of prayer consists of seventeen prostrations over the course of one day and night: two at dawn, four in the afternoon, four in the evening, four after sunset, two at the start of dinner before consumption, and two after dinner (called "the last"), when it is the time of *al-ʿatama,* which means "thickening of the shadows." With regard to this, God's messenger forbade that this hour be called *al-ʿatama.* He said: "*al-ʿAtama* is nothing but the prostration of camels, when they are gathered from pasture and begin to sleep at night." 24

Again, I invite you to participate in the fast of the month of Ramaḍān, which God instituted, being a just judge, and he caused the Qurʾān to appear during it. In that month, he 25

illa mille mensibus melior habetur. Ieiunabis in die ab omnibus cibis et potibus et concubitu usquequo solis lumen occidat et noctis ordo incipiat. Tunc comedes et bibes et concumbes per totam noctem, quousque filum album a nigro discerni possit. Hoc enim liberum et licitum est et vita tranquilla et suavis a Deo. Tunc vero, si puritate mentis ad celebrandam noctem praedestinationis pervenire merueris, ab omni malo et nunc et in futuro securus eris.

26 Dixit etiam Deus: *"Scripsi vobis ieiunium numeratis diebus sicut scripsi illis qui vos praecesserunt. Fortassis timebitis. Si quis infirmus est aut occupatus itinere, eundem dierum numerum alio tempore solvat. Illorum vero ieiunium qui ieiunare non potuerint, victu unius pauperis redimatur. Interim qui oboedierit, melius illi erit. Si enim ieiunaveritis et scieritis quod hominibus utile est—et iustificationis testimonia et Alfurcan—propriam mercedem habebitis. Quicumque tamen mensi Ramazan occurrerit ieiunet, praeter illos qui aut langore aut itinere detenti fuerint, quibus alio tempore idem dierum numerus exsolvendus imponitur. Deus enim vobis quod est facile vult et non quod difficile.*

27 *"Magnificate Deum super hoc quod iustificat vos, forsitan gratias agetis. Et, cum cultores mei te de me interrogaverint, prope ego sum ut exaudiam vocem deprecantis, cum clamaveris ad me. Illi autem audient et credent in me, forsitan prudenter agent. Dormire vero cum mulieribus in ieiunio licentiam vobis tribuo. Illae indumentum vobis sunt et vos similiter illis. Praescivit enim Deus quod*

bore testimony of the night of predestination, and that night is considered better than a thousand months. During the day you shall abstain from all food, drink, and intercourse, until the light of the sun sets and the time of night begins. Then you shall eat, drink, and have intercourse all through the night, until a white thread can be distinguished from a black one. This, a peaceful and pleasant life, is permitted and allowed by God. If you are worthy in your pureness of mind to celebrate the night of predestination, then you will be safe from all evil, both now and in the future.

God also said: "I have written to you about the fast of a 26
certain number of days, just as I have written to those who have gone before you. Perhaps you will fear. If anyone is weak or engaged in travel, let him fulfill the same number of days at a different time. Let the fast of those who are unable to fast be compensated by feeding one poor person. At any rate, it will be better for him who will obey. For if you will fast and know what is beneficial to people—both the testimonies of just conduct and *al-furqān*—you will receive your due reward. Nonetheless, let anyone who finds himself in the month of Ramaḍān fast, except those who will be prevented either by sickness or travel, to whom it is prescribed to fulfill the same number of days at a different time. For God wishes for you that which is easy, not what is difficult.

"Glorify God because he justifies you, and perhaps you 27
will give thanks to him. And, when my worshippers have questioned you about me, I will be near in order to lend my ear to your beseeching voice when you call out to me. They will hear and believe in me, and perhaps act with prudence. I grant you leave to sleep with women during the fast. They are a garment to you, and likewise you to them. God knew

circumcisuri essetis animas vestras et paenituit eum et liberavit vos. Adhaerete igitur illis et diligite hoc quod vobis scripsit Deus: comedite quoque et bibite, donec in aurora discerni possit filum album a nigro. Deinde perficite ieiunium usque ad noctem sine coitu mulierum. Eritis enim perseverantes in domibus orationum et non appropiabitis eis. Haec sunt praecepta Dei." Praeferebat enim nuntius Dei vespertinam cenam matutino cibo.

28 Iterum invito te ad domum Dei illicitam, quae in Mecha sita est, et videre illicitum nuntii Dei et considerare vestigia et loca ipsius et quomodo lapilli proiciuntur retro, quod vocatur alchimar, et involutionem linteoli circa renes, et quomodo osculatur angulus domus illius, et videre loca illa sacrata et multa mira, quae ab hominibus appetuntur.

29 Iterum invito te ad expeditionem divinam, quod est contra inimicos et adversum incredulos proficisci et expugnare participatores et haereticos in ore gladii, donec ad fidem Dei ingrediantur et testificentur quia non est deus nisi Deus et Mahumet servus ipsius et nuntius, aut tributum reddant.

30 Iterum invito te ad confessionem Dei, ad cuius nutum resuscitabuntur mortui. Qui iudicabit eos in iustitia, et bonis bona retribuet et malis mala, et faciet suum populum eos qui sibi oboedierunt et, confitentes singularitatem eius, testificati sunt quod Mahumet propheta est ipsius et nuntius, et crediderunt omnibus quae super eum descenderunt a Deo in excipiendo legem, videlicet, de paradiso, in quo multa bona praeparata sunt:

beforehand that you would circumcise your souls and he felt sorry for you, and gave you free rein. Remain with them, therefore, and love what God has written to you: eat and drink until dawn, when a white thread can be distinguished from a black one. Then you must complete the fast until the night, while abstaining from intercourse with women. You will persevere in houses of prayer and not approach them. These are the commandments of God." For God's messenger preferred the evening meal to that of the morning.

Again, I invite you to the forbidden house of God, which 28
is in Mecca, and to see the forbidden place of the messenger of God, and to look upon his footsteps and sites, and how stones are thrown backward, which is called *al-jimār,* and the wrapping of linen around the loins, and how they kiss the corner of that house, and to see all of those many sacred and wondrous sites that people visit.

Again, I invite you to participate in the holy campaign, 29
which consists of marching against the enemies and against the infidels, and defeating the polytheists and heretics with the edge of the sword, until they join the faith of God and testify that there is no god but God and that Muhammad is his servant and messenger, or until they pay tribute.

Again, I invite you to confess to God, at whose call the 30
dead will be resurrected. He will judge them with justice, rendering good things unto the good and bad things unto the bad, and he will make those who have obeyed him his people, those who confess to his single nature, who have testified that Muhammad is his prophet and messenger, and who have believed all that has descended upon him from God as he received the law, specifically concerning paradise, in which many good things have been prepared:

31 *"Cum habuerint armillas de auro et electro, eruntque vestimenta eorum serica" "et dicent: Gratias Deo, qui abstulit a nobis tribulationem";* nulla oppressio vel molestia eos tanget. *"Habebunt certum alimentum et fructus, et erunt in paradiso deliciarum exultantes et sibi invicem occurrentes honorificati. Discurretur per eos vasis argenti candidi cum vino, quibus bibentes delectabuntur. Non erit ibi luctus neque maeror. Habebunt mulieres venustis oculis," "Habebunt cenacula et supercenacula, sub quibus erunt flumina. Numquam enim Dei promissio fallit," "et dicetur eis: 'O cultores Dei, nolite hodie timere. Tristitia non appropinquabit vobis. Ingredimini paradisum vos et uxores vestrae, et estote securi. Discurretur per vos calathis et scutellis aureis et habebitis quod animae appetunt et concupiscunt oculi in secura mansione, in ortis et fontibus.'" "Erunt induti vestibus, quae omnia superant indumenta. Dedimus illis uxores pulcherrimas venustissimis vultibus. Ipsi vero securi varia fructuum sibi videbunt adduci. Ibi post primam mors alia non sequetur, et fecit eos securos a tormentis inferni. Haec est gratia Dei tui, ipsa est enim liberatio magna."*

32 Dixit etiam Deus (gloriosus et excelsus): *"Timentibus Deum optima erunt in ultimis. Aperientur eis portae horti Eden, ubi pariter discumbentes praecipient sibi afferri vinum et abundantiam fructuum. Et habebunt uxores oculis speciosissimas. Hoc eis promittitur in die iudicii. Victus ibi numquam deficiet."*

"When they will have armlets of gold and electrum, and their garments will be made of silk," "and they will say: Thanks to God, who has taken away our tribulation"; no anguish or suffering will harm them. "They will have continuous nourishment and fruit, and they will exalt in a paradise of delights and meet one another with dignity. Wine vessels made of shining silver will pass between them, from which they will drink and delight. There will be no grief or sorrow in that place. They will have women with comely eyes." "They will have dining rooms and additional dining rooms above them, beneath which will flow rivers. Never will God's promise fail them," "and it will be said to them: 'O worshippers of God, do not fear today. Sorrow will not approach you. Enter paradise, both you and your wives, and do not worry. Golden cups and trays will pass among you, and you will have what your hearts seek and what your eyes desire, in a safe dwelling, among gardens and springs.'" "They will be clothed in garments which surpass all other clothing. We have given to them the most beautiful wives with the comeliest features. Without any care they will look on as various fruits are being brought to them. In that place, another death will not follow the first, and this has freed them from anxiety about the torments of hell. This is the gracious gift of your God, for it is a great liberation." 31

God (glorious and exalted) also said: "The best things will come in the end to those who fear God. The gates of the Garden of Eden will be opened for them, where they will recline together and order wine and fruits to be brought to them in abundance. And they will have wives with the most remarkable eyes. This is promised to them on the day of judgment. At no point will they run out of sustenance there." 32

33 Dixit iterum Deus (gloriosus et excelsus), in descriptione paradisi: *"Sunt in eo duo fontes currentes. Opera Dei vestri semper in veritate manebunt. Sunt in eo de cunctis fructibus bis bina. Opera Dei vestri semper in veritate manebunt. Sunt in eo speciosissimae quas nec homines nec daemones attigerunt, ut margaritae fulgentes. Opera Dei vestri semper in veritate manebunt. An possunt retribui pro bonis nisi bona? Opera Dei vestri semper in veritate manebunt. Sunt praeter hunc duo horti, in quibus defluunt duo fontes. Opera Dei vestri semper in veritate manebunt. Sunt in eo pomorum arbores et palmae et mala punica. Opera Dei vestri semper in veritate manebunt. Sunt in eo bona peroptima, scilicet, pulcherrimae in tentoriis. Opera Dei vestri semper in veritate manebunt. Ante illos non eas tetigit homo neque daemon. Opera Dei vestri semper in veritate manebunt. Discumbunt in excelsis viridiariis super pomis primis. Opera Dei vestri semper in veritate manebunt. Sit nomen Dei tui gloriosum et venerabile. Opera Dei vestri semper in veritate manebunt."*

34 Et dixit (gloriosus et excelsus): *"Adducentur timentes Deum in paradisum per turmas et agmina congregati. Quibus, cum ostiarii ianuas aperuerint, dicent: 'Pax vobis, habemini suaviter, ingredimini et estote hic in perpetuum.'"*

35 Et dixit (gloriosus et excelsus): *"Feci eos occurrere gaudiis et delectationibus et dedi eis pro retributione paradisum eo quod patientiam habuerunt, in quo erunt discumbentes super pulvinaria, et non percutiet eos sol neque frigus, et super eos umbrae illius*

God (glorious and exalted) also said, in the description of paradise: "There are two flowing springs in it. Truly, the works of your God will always remain. In it there are two pairs of every fruit. Truly, the works of your God will always remain. In it there are the most beautiful women, shining like pearls, which neither man nor demon has touched. Truly, the works of your God will always remain. Can something other than good be given in recompense for good things? Truly, the works of your God will always remain. In addition to it there are two gardens, in which two springs flow. Truly, the works of your God will always remain. In it there are fruit trees, palm trees, and grenadines. Truly, the works of your God will always remain. All of its goods are excellent, specifically, the most beautiful women living in tents. Truly, the works of your God will always remain. Before the believers, no man or demon has touched these women. Truly, the works of your God will always remain. They recline in excellent pleasure gardens, on the first fruits. Truly, the works of your God will always remain. Let the name of your God always be glorious and venerable. Truly, the works of your God will always remain." 33

And he (glorious and exalted) said: "Those who fear God will be led to paradise and convened in squadrons and ranks. When the porters open the doors for them, they will say to them: 'peace to you and be comfortable, enter and remain here forever.'" 34

And he (glorious and exalted) said: "I have let them encounter joys and delights, and I have given them paradise in compensation for the fact that they have endured with patience, and they will recline there on couches, neither sun nor cold will harm them, and the shade of paradise will re- 35

permanebunt, per quos vasis argenteis et canistris discurretur. Similiter et vasculis modicis argenti et pixidibus ministrabitur eis et facient eos potare vasae, quasi commixti ginginberi. Fons in eo est, qui 'claritas' appellatur."

36 Iterum dixit (gloriosus et excelsus): *"Timentibus Deum, qui liberati sunt, dabuntur pomaria et horti et diversitas fructuum et uvarum et vasa mirabilia. Non audient ibi dolum neque mendacium. Haec est retributio Domini tui, quod est donum praemaximum."*

37 Et dixit (benedictus et excelsus): *"Timentes erunt in hortis deliciarum epulantes in his quae Dominus dabit eis. Dominus enim eorum liberabit eos a cruciatu inferorum, dicens illis: 'Comedite et bibite securi discumbentes in lectulis dispositis. Dedimus eis uxores pulcherrimas. Qui vero crediderunt eosque filii sui in fide secuti sunt, erunt pariter in eodem. Nihilque eis de suo malo opere imputabitur, et unusquisque secundum quod appetit obtinebit. Dedimus illis diversitates pomorum et quicquid carnis ad edendum concupiscunt et ut sibi propinent invicem. Ibi non erit iniquitas vel fraudulentia. Ministri sicut aurum fulgentes discurrent per eos ad serviendum parati. Supervenientes vero alterutrum et interrogantes dixerunt: "Nos eramus olim in nostra generatione benigni, unde largitus est nobis Deus suam gratiam et liberavit nos a cruciatu incendii, eo quod nos olim serviebamus illi. Ipse namque est magnus et misericors."'"*

38 Et dixit (benedictus et excelsus): *"Praecedentibus et festinantibus dentur mansiones in paradiso voluptatis. Pauci de primis et pauci de novissimis erunt super lectulis ordinatim dispositis,*

main over them, and silver vessels and baskets will pass between them. Likewise silver vessels of moderate size and saucers will be served to them, and vessels will serve them drink with a mixture of ginger. There is a spring in this place called 'clearness.'"

Again he (glorious and exalted) said: "To those who fear 36
God and who are set free orchards, gardens, a variety of fruits and grapes, and wondrous vessels will be given. They will hear there neither lies nor deception. This is the recompense of your Lord, which is the greatest gift of all."

And he (blessed and exalted) said: "Those who fear God 37
will feast in gardens of delights on what the Lord will give them. Their Lord will free them from the torment of hell, and say to them: 'Eat and drink without care, reclining on couches that are set out. I have given them the most beautiful wives. Those who have believed, and those who have followed them as their children in the faith, they will be together in the same place. None of their bad deeds will be counted against them, and each will receive that which he desires. I have given them varieties of fruits, whatever kind of meat they desire to eat, and I have granted that they pour drinks for one another. There will be neither injustice nor deceit there. Servants glittering like gold will run about among them, ready to serve them. Those who arrive will inquire and say to one another: "We were once kind among our people, therefore God has granted us his grace and freed us from the torment of fire, since we once served him. For he is great and merciful."'"

And he (blessed and exalted) said: "Let dwellings in the 38
paradise of delight be given to those who go before and hasten. There will be a few of the first-comers and a few of

semetipsos adinvicem intuentes, inter quos erunt ministri sine fine mansuri tenentes discos et conchas et vasa pretiosa. Numquam inde exibunt vel expellentur. Quicquid de pomis vel de carne volatilium voluerint, obtinebunt. Quibus adhaerebunt mulieres velut margaritae fulgentes, scilicet, sui operis praemium. Non erit illic dolus vel iniquitas, sed tantum pax et salus. Quicumque ex parte dextera sunt erunt in stramentis compositis et in lectulis pretiosis et umbra extensa et aqua praeterfluente et pomorum multitudine. Nos creavimus eas et volumus esse virgines illis qui ex parte dextera sunt, qui sunt pauci de primis et pauci de novissimis."

39 Haec est descriptio paradisi, quem praeparavit Deus credentibus in se et in nuntio eius, ubi praeparata sunt illis multa delectabilia edendi et bibendi et dormiendi cum mulieribus intactis, quae sunt velut lapides pretiosi sine fine splendentes. Et accipient omnia quae oculi eorum concupiscunt, et habebunt honorem et vitam, et sedebunt super toros induti mollibus et purpureis, ornati quoque armillis pretiosis et nitidis. Vultus eorum hilares et iocundi. Inter quos mares et feminae servientes perambulabunt et velut aurum rutilantes fragrabunt ut muscus et variae aromatum species. Bibent de fonte suavitatis et dicetur eis: "Avete in omni pace, comedite et bibite et delectamini, eo quod digni estis, cum omni securitate." Non audietur ibi horribile vel inhonestum. Et non esurient neque sitient amplius. Sunt in his epulis exultantes sine fine mansuri.

those who came last seated on couches arranged in order, gazing at one another, and among them will be servants who will remain without end to bear platters, cups, and precious vessels. They will never leave that place, nor will they be driven out. They will receive whatever kind of fruit or poultry they wish. Women will accompany them like shining pearls, as the reward of their labor. There will be no deception or injustice there, but only peace and well-being. Anyone who is on the right side will be on rugs spread out for them, on precious couches with extensive shade, water flowing by, and a great many fruits. We have created those women, and we wish them to be virgins for those who are on the right side, the few who are of the first-comers and of those who come last."

This is the description of paradise, which God has pre- 39
pared for those who believe in him and in his messenger, where the many delights of food, drink, and sleeping with unblemished women, who are like precious gems that sparkle without end, have been prepared for them. They will receive all that their eyes desire, and they will have both dignity and life, and they will be seated on couches, clothed in soft purple fabrics, and adorned with precious shining armlets. Their countenance will be joyous and pleased. Among them will walk both male and female servants, shining like gold and fragrant like musk and various kinds of spices. They will drink from sweet springs and it will be said to them: "Greetings with all peace; eat, drink, and be merry without cares, for you are worthy." Nothing terrible or dishonorable will be heard there, and no longer will they be hungry or thirsty, for they will continue to exult in this feast without end.

40 Infideles vero, qui participes faciunt Deo et pares illi attribuunt et prophetae Dei non credunt nec epistolam eius suscipiunt et praecepta Dei contemnentes adversus prophetam eius rebelles effecti sunt, deputabuntur Gehennae incendio eruntque in cruciatu et stridore ineffabili et igne sine fine inextinguibili. Quorum cutis quotiens ignis ardore consumitur, totiens ad nova iterum supplicia reparatur. Mansio eorum puteus abyssi. Potus omni felle amarior. Cibus de arbore quae appellatur azachum et est omni pessimo sapore deteriore. Eruntque sub ira Dei cum diabolo et angelis eius.

41 Dixit quoque Deus (gloriosus et excelsus): *"Qui non credunt mirabilibus Dei et prophetas et eos, qui veritatem praedicant, interficiunt, erunt in horribili cruciatu, quorum opera maligna nullo eis auxiliante super ipsorum capita redundabunt."*

42 Et dixit (gloriosus et excelsus): *"Qui non credunt Deo et prophetis ipsius et dicunt, 'Credimus quibusdam et quibusdam non credimus,' et ita excusationem quaerunt, ipsi certe sunt infideles, quibus praeparati sunt perpetui cruciatus."*

43 Dixit iterum Deus (gloriosus et excelsus): *"Qui non credunt, Gehennam incessabiliter sustinebunt. Morientur nec tamen a cruciatu liberabuntur."* Et dixit: *"Arbor azachum data est pro delectatione impiis. Ipsa est enim quae in profundo abyssi nascitur, cuius fructus quasi daemoniorum capita, de quo manducantes ventrem suum implebunt. Denique omnibus malis subicientur et semper ad inferni supplicia revolventur."* Rursum: *"Vae illis,"* inquit,

The infidels, who declare that God has associates and equals, who do not believe the prophet of God nor accept his mission, who despise God's commandments and have become rebels against his prophet, will be sent to the fire of Gehenna where they will be in torment and unspeakable wailing, and in endless, unquenchable fire. Every time their skin is consumed by the heat of the fire, it will be renewed for fresh punishments. Their dwelling is the pit of the abyss. Their drink is bitterer than any gall, and their food comes from the tree called *zaqqūm,* which is worse than the most terrible flavor. They will be subject to the anger of God, together with the devil and his angels. 40

God (glorious and exalted) also said: "Those who do not believe in God's miracles and who murder prophets and those who preach the truth will be in terrible torment. Their wicked deeds will be upon their own heads, with nobody there to aid them." 41

And he (glorious and exalted) said: "Those who do not believe in God and his prophets and say: 'Certain people we believe, and certain people we do not believe,' seeking an excuse in this way—they certainly are infidels, for whom eternal torment has been prepared." 42

Again, God (glorious and exalted) said: "Those who do not believe will suffer Gehenna without end. They will die and yet they will not be freed from torment." And he said: "The tree *zaqqūm* is given to the impious as their delight. It grows at the bottom of the abyss, and its fruits are like the heads of demons. They will fill their bellies by eating from this tree. Finally, they will be subjected to all manner of evil, and they will experience again and again the punishments of hell." Again he said: "Woe to them, from the fire and ex- 43

"ab igne et a malis novissimis, quae passuri sunt in inferno." Et dixit: *"Superius et inferius caligo, ignis, et tenebrae."* Et dixit: *"In die resurrectionis facies eorum, qui Deo non credunt, horribiles erunt atque nigerrimae. Numquid enim Gehenna mansio impiorum non est et eorum, qui nostris signis non credunt et damnandi sunt?"*

44 Et dixit: *"Qui non crediderunt detrudentur in infernum conglobati. Ad quem cum pervenerint et ministri portas aperuerint, dicent illis: 'Nonne ex vobis erant nuntii missi ad vos, qui vobis insinuantes praecepta Dei annuntiaverunt diei istius occursum?' At illi respondebunt dicentes, 'Ha,' sed verbum damnationis destinatum est impiis. Tunc dicetur eis: 'Intrate igitur Gehennae portas ad habitandum in ea sine fine. Haec domicilia praeparata sunt superbis.'" "Et dixerunt qui in igne submersi sunt ministris: 'Deprecamur vos, orate pro nobis Deum ut alleviet nobis cruciatum huius diei.' Ministri responderunt: 'Nonne vobis nuntii missi sunt habentes secum testimonia?' Dixerunt: 'Utique.' Iterum dixerunt ministri: 'Orate, sed quid oratio impiorum nisi error?' Et dixerunt: 'Numquid non vidistis disserentes de signis Dei, qui faciebant converti eos qui non credebant scripturae?' Ex hinc sentient pondus catenarum et vincula, eruntque salientes in igne et rursus fatigati in igne."*

45 Et dixit: *"Sustinebunt impii intolerabilem cruciatum et videbis impios, cum subiecti fuerint poenis, dicentes: 'An poterit hic haberi remedium?' Tunc videbis eos afflictione oppressos et timidis oculis*

treme evils, which they will suffer in hell." And he said: "Above and below there is gloom, fire, and darkness." And he said: "On the day of resurrection, the faces of those who do not believe will be terrible and utterly black. Surely Gehenna is the dwelling of the impious, and of those who do not believe our signs and deserve to be condemned?"

And he said: "Those who did not believe will be rounded 44
up and cast together into hell. When they arrive there, and the servants open the gates for them, they will say to them: 'Were there not messengers sent from among you, who made known to you God's commandments and announced to you the approach of this day?' They, however, will respond, 'Yes,' but the sentence of damnation has been passed on the impious. Then it will be said to them: 'Enter, therefore, the gates of Gehenna, to live there without end. These are the dwellings that have been prepared for the prideful.'" "And those who were submerged in the fire said to the servants: 'We beseech you, pray to God for us, that he may relieve us of this day's torments.' The servants responded: 'Have not messengers been sent to you, bearing their testimonies with them?' They said: 'Certainly.' Again, the servants said: 'Pray, but what is the prayer of the impious but a delusion?' And they said: 'Have you not seen those who discourse about the signs of God, which they performed to convert those who did not believe the scripture?' After that they will feel the weight of chains and shackles, and they will leap in the fire, and again be tormented by it."

And he said: "The impious will suffer unbearable tor- 45
ment, and when they have been subjected to punishment, you will hear them say: 'Will it be possible to receive relief here?' Then you will see them oppressed by their suffering

latenter aspicientes." Iterum dixit (benedictus et excelsus): *"Impii permanebunt in cruciatu Gehennae, ubi detrusi ulterius non respirabunt. Nos illis nihil iniuste fecimus, sed ipsi sibi impii extiterunt. Tunc impii vociferabuntur: 'Usquequo damnandi sumus, O Rex?' Dixit: 'Ita manebitis sine fine.'"* Et iterum dixit: *"Arbor azachum cibus est peccatorum, fervet in ventre sicut sulphur. Accipite illum et ad horribilia inferni loca deducite et super caput eius cruciatus et dolores infundite. Haec sunt enim opera quae faciebatis."*

46 Et dixit (gloriosus et excelsus): *"Afferte aquam amaram, quae viscera eorum disrumpat, eo quod dixerunt illis quos odio habuerunt: 'Nihil descendit a Deo.' Nos reddemus eis aliquantulum. Deus enim novit corda eorum. Quid erit cum angeli vobis occurrerint percutientes anteriora et posteriora eorum? Quoniam ipsi, quod ira Dei dignum erat, hoc dilexerunt et gratiam eius renuentes nihil de suis operibus lucrati sunt."* Deus vero tuus aliquando dixit non credentibus: *"'Ite ad illud propter quod mentiebamini, quod vos a flammis liberare non potest.' Vae non credentibus in die, qua nec permittentur loqui ut aliquam habeant excusationem."*

47 O tu, homo, numquid tam dulce ac mirabile eloquium audisti? Quantis modis invitat et mulcet et promittit et minatur et terret! Quantis modis advocat et mendaces et veraces et fideles et incredulos et confitentes et negantes et potentes et impotentes! Tu vero, si nihil aliud hinc adquisisses quam tantam sermonis dulcedinem, multum iam lucratus fuisses. Sic quoque sola ignis comminatio et inferni

and secretly casting fearful glances." Again, he (blessed and exalted) said: "The godless will remain in the torment of Gehenna, and once they have been cast there, they will have no respite. We have done nothing unjustly toward them, but they themselves were impious. Then the impious will shout: 'Until what time are we to be damned, O King?' He said: 'So you will remain without end.'" And again he said: "The tree *zaqqūm* is the food of the sinners, it is hot in the stomach like sulfur. Receive him and bring him to the terrible places of hell, and pour torments and afflictions on his head. These are the deeds which you will perform."

And he (glorious and exalted) said: "Bring bitter water to 46
rupture their innards, because they have said to those they hate: 'Nothing descends from God.' We will give them a little bit, for God knows their hearts. What will happen when the angels meet you, striking in front and behind? For they loved what deserved God's wrath and spurned his grace, and did not receive any benefit from their actions." Your God once said to the unbelievers: "'Go forth to that for which you lied, but which cannot free you from the flames.' Woe to the unbelievers on that day, on which it will not even be permitted to speak so that they might have some excuse!"

O Man, have you ever heard speech so sweet and won- 47
drous? In how many ways does it invite, soothe, promise, threaten, and terrify! In how many ways does it call out to liars and those who speak the truth, to the faithful and the unbelievers, the confessors and the deniers, the powerful and the weak! As for you, if you would have taken nothing else from this but the great sweetness of speech, you would already have benefited much. Likewise merely the threat of the fire and the terrible things of hell should be sufficient

horribilia tibi ad correctionem debent sufficere. Alioquin tuae culpae imputabitur ad damnationis interitum. Deus enim (gloriosus et excelsus) dixit: *"Facite illum reminisci et iterum reminisci, quoniam reminisci prodest credentibus."*

48 Nos autem iam tibi multa commemoravimus de scriptura quae a Deo descendit. Quae si cordis aure perceperis et credideris, absque dubio salvus eris. Si vero nolueris et in infidelitatis errore ac rebellione contra veritatem perdurare elegeris, immunes erimus a peccato, quoniam praecepta Dei aperte tibi insinuare curavimus. Veritas autem ipsa de te exigat ultionem.

49 Haec est enim fides nostra certa et constans, O tu—cuius cor Deus fidei suae splendore illuminet! Et haec sunt praecepta Dei et signa et lex. Tu ergo, si ad hanc fidem accesseris et professus ac testificatus nostra testificatione fueris et nostrae vocationi satisfeceris et ad praeceptorum decorem et secretorum cognitionem et ad legis benignitatem introieris, erimus in omnibus pares atque unanimes. Considera igitur quam bonum sit et hic habere gloriam et in futuro.

50 Propheta enim noster in die resurrectionis, cum unusquisque regum ac prophetarum occupatus fuerit circa seipsum, suos advocabit dicens: "Domus mea, domus mea, plebs mea, plebs mea." Et primo quidem exaudietur pro domo, deinde pro plebe. Misericors autem dicet angelis: "Ego verecundor non audire intercessionem electi et dilecti mei Mahumet." Tunc tibi tantum erit meriti quantum et mihi, et erimus fratres in fide sine ulla divisione. De hoc dixit Deus (gloriosus et excelsus, et sermo eius verus): "Fideles omnes

for you to change your ways. If not, your death and damnation will be considered your own fault. For God (glorious and exalted) has said: "Remind him again and again, for it is beneficial for believers to be reminded."

I have told you many things from the scripture that de- 48
scended from God. If you will perceive them with your heart's ear and believe them, you will undoubtedly be saved. If you will not, however, and if you choose to persist in the error of unbelief and rebellion against the truth, I will be free from sin, since I have made sure to inform you clearly of God's commandments. Let the truth itself exact vengeance from you.

This is our firm and steadfast faith, O you—may God il- 49
luminate your heart with the splendor of his faith! These are the commandments of God, the signs, and the law. If you come to this faith, confess and testify to it by our testimony, and give heed to our call and proceed toward the grace of the commandments, the knowledge of secrets, and the kindness of the law, we will be equals and in harmony in all things. Consider therefore how good it is to have glory both here and in the future.

On the day of resurrection, when each and every king and 50
prophet will be concerned with himself, our prophet will summon his own and say: "My house is my house, my people are my people." First he will be heard on behalf of the house, then on behalf of the people. The Merciful One will say to the angels: "I would be ashamed not to give heed to the intercession of my chosen and beloved Muhammad." Then your merit will be as great as mine, and we will be brothers in faith without any distinction. On this subject God (glorious and exalted) has said (and his words are true): "All the

fratres habentur." Nullus igitur tibi nocebit, nullus erit tibi molestus, nullus conviciabitur tibi, nullus iniuriam inferet. Decebit te quod et nos. Interim ad nostram meridiem, quam Deus sibi elegit, orationem facies. Quinque autem orationes perficies post tinctionem purificationis. Hoc, si sanus fueris, stando facies; si vero infirmus aut imbecillis, residendo; si vero itinere detentus, medietatem persolves.

51 Dixit quoque Deus (benedictus et excelsus): *"Instate orationibus et persolvite hezeque,"* quod interpretatur "augmentum," et est quarta pars decimae, scilicet, ex quadraginta unus. Hoc autem persolvitur in fine cuiusque anni et debet erogari maxime tui generis pauperibus et tuae cognationis necessitatem patientibus.

52 De mulieribus vero habeas quantum volueris sine ulla contradictione vel ignominia. Quamcumque scilicet duxeris duobus testibus et unius cuiuslibet tuitione, dabis ei in dotem quodcumque inter vos facilius convenerit. Legitimae uxores non sint tibi amplius quam quattuor, ex quibus dimittes quamcumque volueris, quandocumque volueris, causa sive taedii sive odii sive satietatis, et sit tibi licentia revocandi, quando volueris. Dixit etiam Deus (cuius memoria exaltetur): *"Dimissam uxorem non prohibeo revocari."* De ancillis tibi coniunges quantum manus tua possederit. Circumcideris vero ad suscitandam legem Abrahae dilecti Dei misericordis, et legem Ismahelis patris tui (orationes Dei super eos), et a pollutione somnii lavaberis.

53 Deinde ieiunium Ramazan adimplebis. Quod si forte hoc causa aut infirmitatis aut imbecillitatis aut itineris

faithful will be considered brothers." Therefore no one will harm you, no one will harass you, no one will reproach you, no one will bring injustice upon you. What is proper to us will then also be proper to you. In the meantime, you shall perform your prayer to our south, which God has chosen for himself. You will complete five prayers after the purifying bath. You shall do this standing up, if you are healthy; if, however, you are ill or weak, do so sitting down; if you are engaged in travel, you shall do half.

God (blessed and exalted) also said, "Persist in your prayers and pay the *zakāt,*" which means "increase," and is a fourth of a tenth, that is to say, one-fortieth. This is paid at the end of every year, and must be paid out to the poor, especially those of your family, and to your kinsmen who are in need. 51

You may have as many women as you wish without any reproach or disgrace. Give whatever you most easily agree upon as dowry to whom you wed, as long as there are two witnesses present and the guarantee of any one person. Let no more than four wives be lawful for you, any one of whom you may dismiss whenever you wish, either because of boredom, hatred, or saturation, and you may have the discretion of recalling her when you wish. God (may his memory be exalted) also said: "I do not forbid a dismissed wife from being recalled." You may be united with as many slave girls as are in your possession. You shall be circumcised to restore the law of Abraham, beloved by merciful God, and the law of Ishmael your father (prayers be upon them), and you shall cleanse yourself from nocturnal defilement. 52

Then you will complete the fast of Ramaḍān. However, if perchance illness, weakness, or travel should prevent you, 53

prohibuerit, alio tempore celebrabis. Deus enim vobis quod est facile vult et non quod difficile.

54 Si autem in sacramento periurabis, facies quod Deus iussit. Dicit enim Deus: *"Non iudicaberis secundum verba iuramenti, sed secundum quod intelligitur in iuramento. Est autem Deus misericors et propitius. Siquidem, O Saraceni, remedium periurii est decem de nostris mediocribus indumentum aut unius diei victum impendere aut captum a captivitate redimere. Qui nihil horum potuerit, tribus diebus ieiunet, et sic culpa periurii solvitur. Cavete tamen a periurio. Sic vobis Deus signa sua manifestat, forsitan honorabitis eum."*

55 Oportet te etiam peregre proficisci, quod Arabice dicitur alahagh, vulgari Latino romeria. Dicit enim Deus: *"Hoc debent homines Deo inter cetera, scilicet, alahagh, quod est proficisci in domum."* Hoc exigitur ab his qui possunt et ab his qui debitores non sunt et ab his qui ire proposuerunt et eundi posse habebunt. Sic etiam debent exercere expeditionem contra adversarios fidei, ut et prae manibus habeant lucrum in hoc saeculo et magnum praemium in futuro.

56 Deus autem leviter nobiscum agit, et nos ei propter fideles gratias agimus. Ipsum igitur (benedictum et excelsum) tam facilitate et alacritate quam severitate et austeritate sequamur. In fide quippe Saracenorum nihil aliud est quam tranquillitas et devotio cordis ad Deum et requies et fiducia in his quae nobis pollicitus est, scilicet, quando dabit nobis magnum retributionis praemium, et faciet nos possidere hortum deliciarum, ubi sine fine permanentes in perpetuum

you shall celebrate it at a different time, for God wishes what is easy for you, not what is difficult.

If you commit perjury in a sacred oath, you shall do what 54
God orders you, for God says: "You will not be judged according to the words of the oath, but according to what is understood by the oath, for God is merciful and benign. The compensation for perjury, O Saracens, is to provide clothing for ten of our people of small means, or food for one day, or to redeem from captivity one who has been captured. He who cannot do any of these should fast for three days, and so will his sin of perjury be absolved. Nonetheless, beware of perjury. In this way does God show his signs to you; perhaps you will honor him."

You must also go on pilgrimage, which is called *al-ḥājj* in 55
Arabic and *romeria* in the common Latin tongue, for God says: "This is what people owe God, among other things: *al-ḥājj,* which is to travel to the house." This is required of those who are able to do so, and of those who do not owe money and of those who have planned to go and will have the ability to go. In the same way they must also undertake the campaign against the opponents of the faith, so that they may have profit in their hands in this world, and a great reward in the next.

God deals gently with us, and we give thanks to him on 56
behalf of the faithful. Let us follow him (blessed and exalted) both with willingness and cheerfulness, as well as gravity and sternness. In the faith of the Saracens there is nothing but peacefulness and devotion to God, tranquility and faith in the things he promised us: that he will give us a great reward in repayment, and will allow us to possess the garden of delights, where we may remain without end and rejoice

gaudeamus, et in hoc saeculo de impiis infidelibus praestabit obtinere triumphum.

57 Ego autem iam declaravi tibi de verbis Dei excelsi quod est verbum veritatis, cuius eloquium fallere non potest nec promissio praeterire. Tu vero, carissime, aufer a te id in quo—pro dolor!—positus es infidelitatis et erroris et miseriae et calamitatis, et exue te ab illa commixtione ambiguitatis quam tu et ego novimus: videlicet, de Patre et Filio et Spiritu Sancto. Respue quoque culturam crucis, quae nec obest nec prodest. Decet enim tuam serenitatem et tuae nobilitatis generositatem ab hac ignominia et stultitia recedere, cum Deus (benedictus et excelsus) dicat: *"Deus participatoribus non dimittit, dimittit autem praeter hos, quibus sibi placuerit."*

58 Rursum (gloriosus et excelsus) dicit: *"Quam male credunt illi, qui Christum filium Mariae dicunt esse Deum. De hoc quippe ipse Christus dominus exprimit dicens: 'O filii Israel, Deum colite, Dominum meum et Dominum vestrum. Quoniam qui partes Deo attribuunt, paradiso privantur et in inferno truduntur. Impii vero nulla habebunt auxilia.'"*

59 Item: *"Quam male credunt qui dicunt Deum trinum, id est, tres deos. Non est enim deus nisi unus Deus. Quod si paenitentiam non egerint illi, qui infideles sunt et hoc sentiunt tradentur certe igni perpetuo, eo quod apropinquare nolunt Deo excelso et eius indulgentiam postulare. Deus enim est misericors et propitius. Christus vero filius Mariae non est nisi nuntius ante quem et alii nuntii iam venerant. Mater autem ipsius erat sancta et pariter manducabant. Vide ergo quae signa dedit eis ut crederent."*

60 Tu igitur desine ab illis prolixis orationibus et vehementer

forever, and that he will grant us victory over the impious infidels in this world.

I have already declared to you that the words of the exalted God are words of truth, whose pronouncements cannot deceive and whose promise cannot fail. Dearest one, abandon that state of unbelief and error, misery and ruin that you—what sorrow!—have adopted, and extract yourself from that dubious amalgamation of which both you and I are aware: that of the Father, the Son, and Holy Spirit. Reject also the worship of the cross, which neither harms nor benefits. It befits your peace of mind and your nobility to depart from this ignoble foolishness, since God (blessed and exalted) says: "God has no mercy on the polytheists, but apart from these, he has mercy on those he wishes." 57

Elsewhere he (glorious and exalted) says: "How mistaken are they who claim that Christ, son of Mary, is God! On this matter even Lord Christ himself says: 'O children of Israel, worship God, your lord and mine; for those who declare that God has parts are deprived of paradise and cast into hell. The impious will receive no aid.'" 58

Likewise, he says: "How mistaken are they who claim that God is threefold, that is to say, three gods! There is no god but the one God. If the infidels who believe this do not repent, they will certainly be handed over to the eternal fire, since they are unwilling to approach the exalted God and beg for his indulgence, for God is merciful and benevolent. Christ, son of Mary, is no more than a messenger, before whom there had been other messengers. His mother was holy, and they both ate food. Behold, therefore, what signs he has given to them, in order that they might believe." 59

Desist, therefore, from these long and intense prayers, 60

laboriosis et ab illa austeritate ieiunii et superstitione continentiae et longa calamitate et diuturno labore, quibus submersus haberis. Non enim proficit neque aliquid inde utilitatis adquiritur nisi lassitudo corporis et cruciatus animae. Ingredere vero ad hanc saluberrimam fidem, cuius via est facilis, credulitas sana, iter spatiosum, quam suis electis atque cultoribus Deus instituit et omne genus humanum a cunctis aliis legibus segregatum ad hanc specialiter invitavit. Fecit hoc gratuita pietate et benigna miseratione ut cum illis clementer ageret.

61 Ego itaque debitum purae dilectionis tibi adimplens, de omnibus quae ad salutem expediunt satisfecisse me arbitror, cupiens te et desiderans mecum uno animo et una mente sentire, idemque consilium et eandem fidem pariter obtinere, cum dominus meus dicat: *"Quoniam Legem Habentes et participatores, qui nolunt credere erunt perenniter in inferno. Ipsi pessimi sunt omnium hominum. Qui autem crediderunt et operati sunt iustitiam, omnium hominum optimi sunt et sunt apud Deum in hortis Eden perenniter permansuri, in quibus decurrunt flumina sine fine. Sunt autem acceptabiles Deo et Deus acceptabilis illis; hoc est illorum qui timent Deum."*

62 Rursum in alio loco scriptura dicit: *"Vos estis meliores omnibus populis, quos ab hominibus eduxi, et misericorditer egi vobiscum."* Opto igitur te esse de congregatione fidelium, qui Deo acceptabiles sunt et Deus acceptabilis illis, et sunt sanctiores omnibus hominibus. Expecto quoque ut sis de populo

from the rigorous fasts, the superstitions regarding chastity, from that drawn-out distress and continuous labor in which you are submerged. It does not benefit you, nor do you receive anything of use from it but exhaustion of the body and torment of the soul. Enter into this faith that brings salvation, whose way is easy, whose beliefs are wholesome, whose path is spacious, and which God has established for his elect and worshippers, and to which he has invited the entire human race, having separated them from all other religions in favor of this one alone. He has done this out of affection freely given, and out of kind compassion, so as to be merciful toward them.

Striving to fulfill my debt of pure friendship to you, I 61
think that I have sufficiently treated those things which lead to salvation, in my wish and desire for you to share a single heart and mind with me, and to have the same resolve and faith as I, since my Lord says: "For the People of the Book and the polytheists who are unwilling to believe will forever be in hell. They are the worst of all people. However, those who have believed and acted justly, they are the best of all people, and they will forever remain with God in the gardens of Eden, in which rivers flow without end. They are pleasing to God and God is pleasing to them; this is for those who fear God."

In another passage, scripture says: "You are better than 62
all people, you, whom I have led forth from the other people and treated with compassion." I wish for you to be part of the congregation of believers, who are pleasing to God and to whom God is pleasing, and who are holier than all other people. I also long for you to be part of the people

meliore ceteris hominibus, qui in hoc mundo omnium excellentissimus apparuit.

63 Quod si conatus fueris veritati resistere et contra hoc insipienter contendere et in infidelitate ac pertinacia, qua detineris, elegeris permanere, et illud quod tibi scripsimus negligens nostrae exhortationis consilio nolueris adquiescere, unde nos nullum a te praemium sive laudem exigimus, rescribe tu (quem Deus salvet) ea quae tuae fidei sunt, sine ullo timore et reverentia. Paratus sum enim audire tuam vocem et pati omnia quae dicuntur a te, oboediens et non denegans satisfacere veritati. Videbo autem quae a te proferantur et rescribantur, et faciam ea cum his conferri quae prae manibus habentur.

64 Et volo ut illud quod rescripseris aperte et intelligibiliter insinues, nullam afferens excusationem, quasi non audeas proferre quod sentis. Nos siquidem dedimus tibi licentiam et facultatem respondendi, ne forte, quod nostrum non est, iniuste erga te agere videamur. Idcirco disputa quod vis et dic quod vis et loquere quod vis et illud exerce quo tuam rationabiliter disputationem defendere valeas. Hac ergo securitate munitus, qua tibi quicquid volueris loqui permittimus, iustum inter nos et te iudicem elige, qui et iustum iudicium proferat et a veritate non deviet. Nos etenim rationi consentientes nullam tibi vim inferre volumus, dicente scriptura: *"Nihil violenter in fide."* Unde nec in aliquo te cogimus, sed ut placida et spontanea voluntate ad ea, quae nostra sunt, venias exhortamur. Vale.

that is better than all other people, which is shown to be the most excellent of all in this world.

However, if you should strive foolishly to resist the truth 63
and prefer to remain in the unbelief and stubbornness that holds you captive, and to disregard what I have written to you and to refuse to give in to my urgent advice, for which I ask no reward or praise from you, write to me in return (God save you) the tenets of your faith, free from any fear or deference. I am willing to listen to your voice and to bear your words, ready to obey the truth and not deny it. I will inspect what you utter and write, and I will make a comparison between it and what I hold in my own hands.

I also wish for you to reply openly and to inform me 64
clearly, and not to give any excuses, as though you do not dare to express what you believe. I have given you full license and opportunity of responding to prevent myself from appearing to act unjustly toward you, which is not in my nature. Debate what you wish, therefore, and say and express what you wish, and marshal that by means of which you might be able to defend your position in a rational manner. Safeguarded by the security in which I allow you to speak whatever you wish, choose a just judge for us, one who may be able to pronounce a just judgment and not stray from the truth. Since I accord with reason, I do not wish to bring any violence against you, since scripture says: "Do nothing violently in faith." For this reason I do not force you to do anything, but I urge you to come to our side out of your own untroubled free will. Farewell.

Rescriptum Christiani

In nomine Patris et Filii et Spiritus Sancti, misericordis et miseratoris. Ad quendam filium cuiusdam quidam filius cuiusdam Christianus, minimus servorum Christi. Salus a Deo et pietas et clementia et donum et misericordia in te specialiter veniat et super omne humanum genus eius benignitate atque humanitate generaliter descendat.

2 Vidi litteras tuas et gratias egi Deo super hoc, quod mihi impendit de consilio domini mei Emirhelmomini, et oravi Dominum, qui non defraudat deprecantem se, cum ei pura mente preces effuderit, ut prolonget vitam domini mei Emirhelmomini in abundantia bonorum et perpetuitate honoris et plenitudine securitatis.

3 Consideravi quoque tui (quem Deus honorificet) laboris benignitatem, qua mihi, scilicet, expressisti tuae dilectionis affectum, quodque mihi specialis amoris impendere studuisti. Et hoc quidem hucusque de te semper apud me constitit. Sed modo pleniori iudicio benignitatis tuae gratiam erga me recognoscens, tuae venerationis debitum implere non valeo. Tu vero in hoc secundum mores tuae probitatis et tui generis nobilitatem egisti. Ego autem ad Deum preces fundo, in cuius manu omne bonum est, ut det tibi praemium retributionis ex abundantia bonitatis suae et benefaciat tecum.

4 Plane diligenter egisti mecum, nihil praetermittens in tua exhortatione, unde et ego multas debeo tibi gratias agere, maxime cum sciam te hoc nonnisi puritate mentis et clara

The Reply of the Christian

In the name of the Father, the Son, and the Holy Spirit, the merciful and compassionate. A certain Christian, son of a certain man, and least among Christ's servants, to a certain son of a certain man. May salvation, piety, clemency, reward, and mercy come to you in particular from God, and may they also descend upon the entire human race in general, out of his benevolence and kindness.

I have seen your letter, thanked God for granting me the 2
advice of my lord the *ʾamīr al-muʾminīn,* and I prayed to the Lord, who does not deceive the one who prays to him, whenever he pours out prayers to God with a pure mind, that he may prolong the life of my lord the *ʾamīr al-muʾminīn* with an abundance of goods, continuous honor, and complete peace.

I have also considered your kind work (may God honor 3
you) in which you expressed your affection to me, and strove to bestow particular love upon me. And so, too, have my feelings always been toward you. But now, acknowledging with fuller discernment your graceful kindness toward me, I am unable to repay the debt of your reverence. In this enterprise you behaved in accordance with your moral soundness and the nobility of your family. But I pray to God, who has every good thing in his hand, to grant to you the reward of recompense out of his abundant goodness, and to do well unto you.

Clearly you have taken good care not to leave out any- 4
thing in your exhortation, and for this I must thank you, especially since I know that you have done so with nothing but pureness of mind and patent affection. In addition, I

dilectione fecisse. Praeterea legi et intellexi—intelligere te faciat Deus omne bonum!—quicquid in tuo libello subtiliter descripsisti, et de fide in qua constitutus es expressius declarasti, et de vocatione tuae exhortationis, qua me ad tuam legem invitare voluisti. Scio equidem quod hoc tam tuae benivolentia caritatis quam etiam pro amore, quem mihi a domino meo Emirhelmomini exhiberi novisti, facere curaveris. Idcirco iterum quas possum gratias ago, orans Deum ac supplicans ut qui potens est retribuat tibi pro me.

5 De hoc igitur quod me ad tuam fidem quam tenes et ad legem cui servis, quae secundum vos *alhanifia,* id est, conversio ab idolis vocatur, invitasti, et quod de plebe Abraham te esse dixisti, affirmans eum perfecte Saracenum, nos deprecamur Dominum nostrum Iesum Christum et salvatorem mundi, qui pollicitus est vera pollicitatione in suo sacro evangelio dicens, *"Cum steteritis ante reges et praesides, nolite praemeditari quemadmodum dicatis aut respondeatis, dabitur enim vobis in illa hora et inspirabitur quid loquamini,"* ut impleat in me suum sacrum promissum. Mea enim fiducia in ipso est. Adsit ergo mihi hoc certamen tecum aggredienti et pro fide ac lege ipsius dimicare parato, ut expedita et convenientia verba proferam et rationabili disputatione incedam. Ego enim de ipsius adiutorio confisus, quod suis semper impertiri solet electis, respondere tibi incipio.

6 Dixisti te scripturam Dei legisse et bibliothecam quae Novum et Vetus Testamentum continet sagaciter inspexisse. Nonne ibi in Lege, quae a Deo Mosi data est, primo libro, cui nomen Genesis, scriptum habetur quod Abraham descenderit cum parentibus suis in Aran et illic commoratus

have read and understood all that you have subtly written in your booklet—and may God grant you to understand all that is good!—what you have spoken frankly about the faith you observe, and about your urgent exhortation, with which you wished to invite me to your religion. I know that you have taken the pains to do so, both out of the kindness of your affection as well as because of the love you know my lord the *ʾamīr al-muminīn* has for me. For this reason I once again give all the thanks I can, praying and supplicating to God to repay you on my behalf, who alone is able to do so.

Concerning the fact that you have invited me to the faith 5
you hold and to the religion you serve, which is called by you *al-ḥanīfiyya,* that is to say, conversion from idolatry, and the fact that you have claimed to be of the tribe of Abraham, asserting that he was perfectly Saracen, I pray to our Lord Jesus Christ and savior of the world to fulfill in me his sacred promise, for he promised truly in his sacred gospel: "When you stand before kings and authorities, do not consider beforehand how you should speak or answer, for at that moment inspiration will be given to you on what you should say." My trust is in him. May he assist me as I proceed in this battle with you, ready to fight for his faith and religion, so that I may readily say the proper words and proceed with reasonable argumentation. Fully trusting in his aid, since he is always accustomed to bestow it upon his elect, I will begin my reply to you.

You said that you have read the scripture of God, and 6
that you have keenly analyzed the collection containing the New and Old Testament. Is it not written there, in the Law given by God to Moses, in the first book called Genesis, that Abraham went down to Ḥarrān with his parents and dwelled

est, et ibi apparuit ei Deus post nonaginta annos *"et credidit Deo et reputatum est ei ad iustitiam"?* Nos quoque accepimus quod Abraham post nonaginta annos descenderit in Aran et erat cultor idoli quod vocabatur Eleze. Ipsum enim idolum notum erat in Aran et colebatur sub nomine lunae, et habitatores Aran ei serviebant. Quae etiam cultura in progenies eorum permanet usque nunc, non latenter sed publice—praeter sacrificia quae faciunt de hominibus, quae in aperto facere timent. Colebat autem Abraham idolum cum parentibus et avis et populis terrae, sicut tu dixisti illam culturam esse alhanifia. Et nos invenimus in scripturis divinis alhanifia nomen impositum cultoribus idolorum. Sed idem postea conversus et unius Dei cultor effectus est.

7 Isaac quoque filius promissionis factus est possessor illius unitatis. Ipse est qui, oblatus Deo, redemptus est ariete. Sic enim praeceperat ei Deus dicens: "Tolle filium tuum, quem diligis, Isaac, et vade offerre illum holocaustum mihi in locum quem monstravero tibi." De stirpe vero Isaac, qui est filius Sarae liberae, processit Christus salvator mundi. Qua de causa fecit eum Abraham heredem unitatis.

8 Deinde Isaac Iacob filium suum, quem Deus Israel vocavit, eiusdem unitatis heredem reliquit. Iacob vero duodecim tribus. Haec successio non cessavit a filiis Israel, donec ingressi sunt Aegyptum diebus pharaonum causa Ioseph. Deinde paulatim decrescendo ac deficiendo non destitit quousque ita defecit, sicut defecerat in diebus filiorum Noe.

there, and that God appeared to him there after ninety years, and "he believed in God and it was credited to him as righteousness"? I, too, have heard that Abraham went down to Ḥarrān after ninety years, and that he was a worshipper of an idol called al-ʿUzzā. This was an idol that was known in Ḥarrān, and was worshipped under the name of the moon, and the inhabitants of Ḥarrān served it. This worship continues down to their descendants even to this day, not in secret but in public—unlike their human sacrifices, which they are afraid to perform in the open. Abraham worshipped this idol along with his parents, grandparents, and the tribes of his land, in accordance with what you called *al-ḥanīfiyya.* And I found that in the divine scriptures the term *al-ḥanīfiyya* is applied to idolaters. But the same Abraham later converted and became a worshipper of the one God.

Isaac, too, the promised son, became heir to that mono- 7
theism. He is the one who, after being offered to God, was replaced by a ram. For this is what God had ordered him: "Take up your son Isaac, whom you love, and go to offer him as a burnt offering to me, in the place that I will show to you." For from the line of Isaac, who is the son of the freeborn Sarah, descended Christ, savior of the world. For this reason Abraham made him the heir of monotheism.

Then Isaac left behind his son Jacob, whom God called 8
Israel, as the heir of the same monotheism. Jacob, however, left behind twelve tribes. This legacy continued among the children of Israel, until they entered Egypt in the days of the pharaohs on account of Joseph. Subsequently it did not cease, but gradually decreased and lessened, until it was reduced to what it had been in the days of the children of Noah.

9 Adam quippe protoplastus primus hanc unitatem cognovit. Deinde filius eius Seth, deinde Enos, qui coepit praedicare unitatem et adoravit eam. Denique non desiit haec successio de generatione in generationem usque ad Noe et ad filios eius. Postea vero paulatim coepit deficere usque ad Abraham, in quo, sicut dixi, reparata est. A quo etiam crevit usque ad Iacob, et inde coepit deficere usque ad Mosen, cui apparuit Deus in rubo ardente ut eum mitteret in Aegyptum. Moses autem excusabat se dicens: "Cur mittere me vis ad populum durae cervicis? Si interrogaverit me quod est nomen tuum, quid eis dicam?" Respondit Deus, "Haec dices filiis Israel: Ego sum qui sum, et in Hebraeo: Ehiehas Rahieh misit me ad vos," quod ita interpretatur, "Aeternus, qui non desinit esse, Deus patrum vestrorum, Deus Abraham, Deus Isaac, Deus Iacob misit me ad vos." Renovata est hoc in loco memoria unitatis, simulque revelatum est quoddam trium personarum mysterium, ubi dicit: *"Deus Abraham, Deus Isaac, Deus Iacob."*

10 In hac repetitione et unitas demonstratur et trinitas. Renovatur vero ipsa unitas, sicut insinuata erat ab initio. Ipse enim proculdubio unus trium personarum est. Ipse qui dicit, "Deus patrum vestrorum rursum," repetit "Deum" ter. Licet ergo hic intelligi tres deos an unum deum ter repetitum? Si dixerimus tres deos esse, erimus participatores et sermo noster inconveniens veritati. Si vero dixerimus unum deum esse ter repetitum, auferemus scripturae suum ius.

Of course Adam, the first-created, was the first to be- 9
come acquainted with monotheism; then his son Seth, and after him Enoch, who began to preach and practice monotheism. In short, this legacy continued from generation to generation all the way until Noah and his children. Later, however, it gradually began to decrease, until it reached Abraham, in whom, as I have said, it was renewed. From him it grew, until it reached Jacob, at which point it began to decrease until Moses, to whom God appeared in a burning bush to send him to Egypt. Moses, however, attempted to excuse himself by saying, "Why do you wish to send me to a stiff-necked people? If they ask me what your name is, what should I tell them?" God answered, "This you shall say to the sons of Israel: I am who I am, and in Hebrew: *Ehiehas Rahieh* has sent me to you," which means, "The eternal one, who does not cease to exist, the God of your fathers, the God of Abraham, the God of Isaac, and the God of Jacob has sent me to you." In this passage the memory of monotheism was renewed, and simultaneously a certain mystery of the three persons was revealed, when he said: "The God of Abraham, the God of Isaac, and the God of Jacob."

With these repetitions, both the Unity and the Trinity 10
are made clear. Monotheism, however, was renewed, as was indicated at the start. For he is without doubt one of the three persons. He himself says "the God of your fathers," and repeats the word "God" three times. Can this be understood to mean that here are three Gods, or that one God is repeated three times? If I were to say that there are three gods, I would be a polytheist, and my discourse would be at odds with the truth. But if I were to say that it is three times repeated that there is one God, I would take away from

Poterat enim dicere: "Deus patrum vestrorum, Abraham, Isaac, et Iacob." Superest ergo causa ad inquirendum ut, scilicet, dicatur mihi quare repeto ter dicens: "Deus Abraham, Deus Isaac, Deus Iacob." Ideo certe repetii quia magnum hic mysterium significavi. Ita est enim ac si dicerem: Deus pro certo unus Deus et tres personae. Tres igitur personae unus Deus habens tres personas.

11 Quae ergo veritas apertior aut quae lux splendidior hac re? Nisi forte sit aliquis volens contradicere veritati et sibimetipsi nocere, qui et oculos suos claudat et aures obturet ne videat vel audiat mysterium prophetis traditum et scripturae commendatum. Quod quidem tenentes legem hucusque prae manibus habent, sed non potuerunt illud intelligere, donec venit possessor mysterii, Christus Dominus noster, qui aperiens illud dedit nobis intelligere.

12 Nos siquidem scimus quoniam Abraham ab ortu suo usque ad nonaginta aetatis annos fuit hanif, id est, cultor idoli. Deinde credidit Deo et fuit semper fidelis. O tu, homo (quem Deus adiuvet), qui me ad fidem Abrahae et ad plebem eius invitas, utinam scirem ad quam utriusque fidei ipsius me invitare velis aut in quo genere utriusque vitae illius me esse praecipias, utrum quando idolatra erat cum omnibus parentibus suis in Aran aut quando exiens de Aran unum Deum cognovit et coluit et credidit ei atque mandatis eius oboediens migravit de terra sua Aran, quae erat civitas erroris et domus infidelitatis. Ego enim non aestimo congruere sapientiae et mirabili doctrinae tuae, maxime cum dixeris te

scripture its own authority. For it could have said: "The God of your fathers, Abraham, Isaac, and Jacob." The matter remains, therefore, for me to discuss why I repeat "God" three times: "The God of Abraham, the God of Isaac, and the God of Jacob." Certainly, I have repeated it because I have indicated a great mystery here. It is as if I said: "God is without doubt one God and three persons. The three persons are one God, who has three persons."

What truth is clearer or what light is more brilliant than this? Unless, perhaps, there is someone who wishes to deny the truth and bring harm to himself, one who shuts his eyes and plugs his ears to prevent himself from seeing or hearing the mystery that has been delivered to the prophets and entrusted to scripture. Those who hold on to the Torah have this mystery before them even now, but they have been unable to understand it until the arrival of the heir of the mystery, our Lord Christ, who revealed it to us and granted us to understand it. 11

I know that Abraham was a *ḥanīf*, that is, an idolater, from his birth until he was ninety years old. Then he believed in God, and he always remained faithful. O you (may God help you), who invited me to the faith of Abraham and to his tribe, I wish I knew to which of his two faiths you wish to invite me, or in which of the two manners of life you order me to be: when he was an idolater, along with all of his forefathers in Ḥarrān, or when he left Ḥarrān and learned of the one God, and worshipped and believed in him, and, obeying his commands, moved out of his country Ḥarrān, which was a city of error and an abode of faithlessness? I do not consider it befitting your wisdom and wondrous learning, especially since you claim to have read the scriptures and to have 12

legisse scripturas et in eis meditatum fuisse, ut me ad illud erroris et infidelitatis invites, in quo degebat Abraham, antequam unum Deum cognosceret.

13 Si vero ad illud me invitas, in quo fuit Abraham, quando *"credidit Deo et reputatum est illi ad iustitiam,"* haec certe invitatio multo magis pertinet ad Iudaeum, qui est filius Abrahae. Ipse enim est possessor hereditatis eius et hoc negotium illius est, tuum autem minime. Quare ergo hanc tibi iniuriam facis ut officium alienum usurpes, cum superius dicas te numquam a tramite iustitiae deviasse?

14 Quod autem Abraham Saracenum fuisse asseris, vide quam contrarius sis socio tuo Mahumet, qui se primum Saracenum esse testatur. Dicit enim in sua scriptura quoniam dictum est illi: *"Dic, iussus sum ut sim qui primus Saracenus fuit et non sis de participatoribus."* Numquid non vides eum esse primum Saracenum? Et hanc Saracenitatem numquid non ipse primus praedicavit? Ergo nec Abraham nec alii ante illum Saraceni fuerunt. Ipse enim confessus est primum se esse qui Saracenus fuit, et hoc satis est omnibus qui rationi adquiescunt.

15 Sed quia, sicut tibi superius dixi, de Abraham quis fuerit aut quid fecerit, ad Iudaeum pertinet, non ad te, cum pro Iudaeo loqui videaris et causam eius agere, quid facies apud iudicem, si Iudaeus suum prolocutorem te esse negaverit? Si vero concesserit, quid apud tuos facies? Meo igitur consilio totum hoc negotium dimittes, ne de his, quae ad te non pertinent, superflue occupatus esse videaris.

16 Porro de ipso uno Deo, ad cuius unitatem confitendam

meditated upon them, to invite me to the error and faithlessness in which Abraham remained until he came to know the one God.

However, if you invite me to the faith Abraham adhered 13
to when he believed in God, "and it was credited to him as righteousness," this is an invitation that properly belongs to a Jew, who is the son of Abraham. For it is the Jew who is the heir of Abraham's inheritance, and this is his task, not yours. Why then do you wrong yourself by laying claim to another person's task, even though you claimed earlier that you have never turned away from the path of justice?

As to the fact that you claim that Abraham was a Saracen, 14
see how you contradict your friend Muhammad, who testifies that he is the first Saracen? For he says in his scripture that it was said to him: "Say: 'I have been given commands in order that I might be the first one to be a Saracen,' and do not be one of the polytheists." Do you not see that he was the first Saracen? Was he not the first to preach this Saracen faith? Therefore neither Abraham nor anyone before him was a Saracen, for Muhammad himself confessed to being the first Saracen, and this is sufficient for all who submit to reason.

But since, as I have said before, who Abraham was or 15
what he did is relevant to the Jew and not to you, and since you appear to be speaking on behalf of the Jew and to be pleading his case, what will you do before the judge, if the Jew denies that you speak on his behalf? But if he grants you that role, what will you do before your own kind? My advice is to abandon this whole enterprise, so as not to appear unnecessarily concerned with things that do not concern you.

Now about the one God, whose unity you have so often 16

totiens me invitas, quaero a te, si tamen dicere potes qualiter hoc ipsum quod dicis et tam saepe repetis, "unus Deus," tu ipse intelligas. Primum igitur interrogo quot modis dicitur unum "unum." Cum autem hoc ostenderis, tunc sciemus quod vere dixeris te credere uni Deo. Quod si non potueris, audi a me, si placet, quoniam non potest dici nisi tribus modis unum "unum," hoc est, aut genere aut specie aut numero. Nullo enim alio modo hoc mihi dici posse videtur.

17 Ego autem tibi scribo sicut homini docto et intelligenti et de rebus subtiliter proponenti. Nec habeo te sicut aliquem ex illis qui, postquam ad subtilitatem quarumlibet quaestionum venerint et propter socordiam et hebitudinem ingenii nihil dicere potuerint, confusi verecundia, nihil aliud dicunt nisi "mirabilis Deus!" Et ego dico quia mirabilis Deus et mirabilis Deus usque in finem saeculi.

18 Quaero tamen ut mihi respondeas quo ex his tribus modis unum Deum intelligas, genere scilicet, an specie, an numero? Si dixeris illum esse unum genere, erit unum complectens diversas species. Hoc enim intelligitur unum genere, quod de pluribus speciebus praedicatur, quod nullatenus pertinet ad qualitatem Dei. Si vero dixeris unum specie, species similiter habet diversas res sub se, non unum singulare. Si unum quoque numero dixeris, eris contrarius tuis verbis, quibus dicis eum unum singularem et solidum. Ego vero non dubito quoniam, si quis te interrogaverit de te ipso dicens quot es, non poteris respondere <nisi> quod sis unus singularis. Quomodo ergo tuo sensu de Deo haec

invited me to confess, I ask you, if you are capable at least of answering how you yourself understand the following, which you so often repeat: "the one God." Firstly, I ask you in how many ways "one" is said to be "one." When you have showed me this, then we will know that you truly claim to believe in one God. But if you are unable to do so, hear from me, if you will, that "one" can only be called "one" in three ways, that is, either with respect to genus, species, or number. It seems to me that this cannot be described in any other way.

I write to you as to a learned and insightful man, who dis- 17
cusses things with subtlety. I do not consider you to be one of those who, when they come upon the finer points of a matter and are unable to say anything because of the stupidity and dullness of their intellect, are baffled with shame and are unable to say anything but "God is wondrous!" And I say to you that God is wondrous, and that God will be wondrous until the end of time.

Still, I ask you to answer me in which of the three ways 18
you understand there to be one God: with respect to genus, species, or number? If you say that he is one by genus, he will be one by encompassing various species. But that which is understood to be one by genus is predicated about many species, which does not at all fit with the nature of God. But if you say that he is one by species, a species also includes many different things under its heading, not just one thing. And if you say that he is one by number, you will contradict your own words, by which you call him singular and indivisible. I do not doubt that, if anyone were to ask you how many you are, you could not answer him but that you are one and singular. How then, in your opinion, can this property be

qualitas recipi potest ut non eum praeferas creaturae? Et utinam, cum dicis eum unum numero, non pronuntiares eum subiectum diminutioni et contrarietati! Numquid tu, homo, qui scripturas multas legisti et cum diversarum sectarum magistris totiens disputasti et tanta in diversis libris subtiliter indagasti, ignoras quoniam "unus singularis" in numero pars est numeri? Perfectio enim numeri est quae complectitur omnes species numeri. Ergo "unus" pars est numeri, et hoc est contrarium tuae sententiae.

19 Item si dixeris eum unum specie: sicut iam diximus, species habet diversas res sub se, non unum singulare. Quae si fuerint unum in substantia, oportet nos interrogare te an contradicas qualitati "unius" in numero, an "unum" illum, quem intelligis specie, eundem intelligis numero. Si autem dicis ista esse contraria, dicemus tibi quod definitio "unius" in specie apud sapientes, qui norunt definitiones verborum et sunt docti regulas dialecticae artis, est "nomen complectens diversos numeros." Definitio vero "unius" in numero "quod non complectitur nisi seipsum."

20 Numquid tu confiteris quoniam unus Deus est in substantia complectente diversum numerum, an praedicas eum esse unum individuum? Nam si eum intelligis unum esse numero, ignoras quid sit unum specie vel qualiter sit, et converteris ad illud quod dixeras primum, quoniam unus est numero. Hoc vero non praedicatur nisi de creaturis, sicut ante praediximus.

21 Si autem dixeris mihi: "Numquid tu praedicare poteris

predicated of God, which has the result that you do not place him above creation? I trust that, when you call him one in number, you did not declare him to be subject to demotion and contradiction! Surely, you, who have read many scriptures and have debated so often with teachers of various sects, and have carefully scrutinized so much in various books, are not unaware that "one," singular with respect to number, is still a part of number? For the essence of number encompasses all species of number. Therefore "one" is a part of number, and this contradicts your statement.

The case is similar if you say that he is one by species, as I 19
have already said; for a species includes various things under it, not just one thing. If those things are one in substance, then I should ask you whether you claim that this is different from the nature of "one" in number, or whether you understand this "one" in accordance with number as well as according to species. But if you say that those two things are different, I will say to you that the definition of "one" in accordance with species is, according to the wise, who know the definitions of words and have been taught the rules of the art of dialectic, "a concept that encompasses various numbers." However, the definition of "one" according to number is "that which encompasses nothing but itself."

Surely you do not assert that God is one in substance, en- 20
compassing various numbers, or do you declare him to be single and indivisible? For if you understand him to be one in number, you do not know what it is to be "one" according to species, or what its nature is, and you return to what you said first, that he is one in number. Yet this is only predicated of creation, as I have said before.

If you say to me: "Surely you cannot call God one in 21

Deum unum numero, cum superius dicas: unus in numero pars est numeri et non plenitudo?" Respondeo tibi quia nos praedicamus eum unum perfectum in substantia, non in numero, eo quod est in numero—scilicet personis—trinus. Ergo qualitas ipsius utroque modo perfecta est, cum eum unum praedicaverimus in substantia.

22 Est enim ille sublimior omnibus creaturis sensibilibus et insensibilibus, cui nihil simile est nec aliquid sibi commiscetur praeter ipsum. Simplex, incompositus, spiritualis, incorporeus, cuius substantia super omnia est sine complexione vel commixtione sive compositione. In numero quippe complectitur omnes species numeri. Numerus autem duobus modis dicitur, quia est aut par aut impar. Hi duo modi in his tribus habentur. Nam qualicumque modo praedicemus eum, non ei auferimus qualitatem plenitudinis, ut scias nos praedicasse Deum unum non sicut tu.

23 Ego puto quod haec mea responsio sufficere debeat lectoribus huius libri, si tamen consentire non renuerint veritati. Et nos quidem altioribus et subtilioribus verbis in hac disputatione uti possemus, maxime cum hoc exigat ipsa materia. Sed ne legentibus taedium aut obscuritas inferatur, plane et aperte loqui magis elegimus.

24 Te autem (quem Deus salvet) volo intelligere quia nos, ego scilicet et tu, in hoc certamine ita esse videmur ac si duo heredes de sibi relicta hereditate, quae pari iure utrique obveniat, contendentes. Cuius possessione, si ego, utpote a paternis moribus degenerantem te omnino indignum esse monstravero eamque totam mihi rationabiliter vindicare

number, since you have said earlier: 'One in number is part of number, and not a whole?'" I will answer that I call him completely one in substance, not in number, because he is threefold in number—that is, in persons. His nature, therefore, is perfect in each way, since I have called him one in substance.

For he is elevated above all creatures, both those with 22
senses and those without; and nothing is like him, and he does not associate with anything except himself. He is simple, not a compound, spiritual, incorporeal, whose substance is above all things, without association, mixing, or composition. In number he encompasses all species of number, for number is referred to in two modes: even and odd. These two modes are subsumed under this "three." In whatever manner I refer to him, I do not remove from him the nature of fullness, so that you may know that I do not refer to God as one in the same way that you do.

It is my opinion that this response of mine should suffice 23
for readers of this book, provided they do not refuse to accord with the truth. I could have used loftier and more refined words in this debate, especially since the very subject matter requires it; however, to prevent boredom or abstruseness from affecting the readers, I have instead chosen to speak clearly and openly.

I want you (may God save you) to understand that we— 24
that is, you and I—appear in this battle to be like two heirs fighting over an inheritance that rightly belongs to each of them. If I demonstrate you to be entirely unworthy of possessing this inheritance, since you have degenerated from your father's morals, and if I reasonably wish to claim the entire inheritance for myself, it should not seem surprising

voluero, non tibi debet mirum videri—nec rogo graviter accipias—si propter hoc aliquid durius me in hoc libro loqui contigerit.

25 Illud itaque quod dixisti quia Deus non habuit uxorem neque filium nec quemquam aequalem sibi, si rationi et regulae veritatis adquievisses, numquam de ore tuo procederet. Numquam enim hoc aliquis, qui vel leviter Christianus esset aut aliquid pietatis vel gravitatis haberet, cogitare potuit, sed ab illa scriptura, quae socium tuum electum et dilectum et amicum Dei fatetur, primo huius spurcissimi sermonis mentio nefanda processit. Haec namque et his similia contra Dei et Christi Domini maiestatem consilio et calliditate malitiosa Iudaeorum, qui de vobis toti mundo ludibrium facere cupiebant, ille libro suo apposuit. Quae nec in Novo nec in Veteri Testamento, quod utrumque te studiose legisse dixisti, ullatenus invenire potuisti. Auctores quippe ad hoc habuit Vehben, filium Muniae, et Abdalla, filium Celehmin, et Chabin, Iudaeos callidissimos totius boni inimicos, qui talia de Christianis in Alcorano scribi fecerunt. Absit enim a nobis ut Deum habuisse uxorem vel ex uxore filium fateamur. Nam ille, quem nos Filium Dei dicimus, Verbum aeternum ipsius est, per quod creata sunt universa.

26 Deus namque aeternus Verbo et Spiritu suo omnia vivificans numquam destitit esse potens et sapiens. Quod autem praedicatur a nobis clemens et misericors et Rex et Dominator et cetera, ex humano usu pro similitudine operum ista dicuntur. Propria vero definitio ipsius est: "Deus una

to you—and I ask you not to take this with indignation—if it should happen that I speak rather harshly in this book on account of this.

As to your statement that God did not have a wife, nor a son, nor anyone equal to himself, such words would never have left your mouth if you had submitted to reason and the rule of truth. Indeed, never has anyone, who was even a less than wholehearted Christian or had any modicum of piety or dignity been able to think this; rather, the unspeakable account of this most vile tale first proceeded from that scripture, which proclaims your friend to be the elect, the beloved, and the friend of God. He added these and similar things in his book, which are contrary to the majesty of God and Lord Christ, at the wickedly cunning instigation of the Jews, who desired to make a laughingstock of you for the entire world. And none of those things have you been able to find in any way in either the New or the Old Testament, both of which you claim to have read diligently. He had as authorities for this Wahb b. al-Munabbih, ʿAbd Allāh b. Sallām, and Kaʿb, most cunning Jews and enemies of all that is good, who were responsible for writing such things about Christians in the Qurʾān. Indeed, far be it from us to declare that God had a wife, or a son from a wife. For he, whom we call the Son of God, is his eternal Word, through whom all things were created. 25

For God is eternal, giving life to all things through his Word and Spirit, and has never ceased being powerful and wise. As to the fact that he is called merciful, compassionate, King, Lord, etc., these predications are taken from human use because of creation's similarity to him. However, the proper definition is: "God is simple with one substance, 26

simplex substantia, habens Verbum et Spiritum," id est, sapientiam et vitam omnia vivificantem.

27 Quaero autem utrum haec nomina, id est, "vivens" et "sapiens," substantiva sint an relativa, quae significent aliquid adiungi alicui. Substantiva quippe nomina sunt "caelum," "terra," "aer," "ignis," "aqua," et cetera quae ad aliquid aliud referri non possunt. Relativa ad aliquid, sicuti "sciens" et "scientia," "sapiens" et "sapientia," et his similia. Sciens enim scientia sciens est, et scientia non est nisi scientis, et sapientia sapientis est et sapiens nonnisi sapientia sapiens est. Ergo videndum est, quando "sapientia" vel "vita" de Deo praedicantur, si substantialiter aut accidentaliter praedicentur. Dicitur namque Deus etiam creator quia creavit, et cetera quae ad opera ipsius referuntur, postquam ea creavit—sicuti dicitur a nobis "dispositor" et "rector" vel "ordinator" omnium quae creavit. Sed numquid sicut dici potest fuisse aliquando sine creatura, dici etiam potest fuisse aliquando sine sapientia et vita? Quod intelligere absurdissimum est.

28 Unum autem e duobus confiteri necesse est: aut ipsum aliquando solum sine creatura fuisse, aut creaturam illi coaeternam esse. Ego vero existimo te illum execrari qui creaturam Deo coaeternam esse putaverit. Creditur tamen semper fuisse potens creare quod voluit et quando voluit. Quod si quis obiciat cum eo semper creaturam in praescientia fuisse, et ideo ipsum creatorem semper extitisse, potest etiam dicere secundum hoc resurrectionem mortuorum iam factam

having the Word and the Spirit," that is, wisdom and life that gives life to all.

I ask you whether these words, that is, "living" and "wise," 27
are substantive or relative, in that they signify that something is joined to something else. Substantive words are "heaven," "earth," "air," "fire," "water," and other things that cannot be used to refer to something else. Relative words refer to something else, such as "knowledgeable" and "knowledge," "wise" and "wisdom," and similar things. A knowledgeable person is knowledgeable through knowledge, and knowledge only belongs to one who is knowledgeable, and wisdom belongs to the wise, and a wise person is only wise through wisdom. When "wisdom" or "life" is being predicated of God, we should see, therefore, whether they are predicated substantively or accidentally. God is called a creator because he created, and so with other predications that refer to his creations, after he created them—just as he is called by us an "arranger," "helmsman," or "regulator" of all that he created. Yet surely he cannot be said to have at one point been without wisdom or life, in the way that he can be said to have been without creation? To think this would be most senseless.

It is necessary to declare one of these two things: either 28
that he was at one point without creation, or that creation is coeternal with him. But I think you would decry the person who thinks that creation is coeternal with God. All the same, he is believed to have always been able to create what he wished and when he wished. But if someone were to argue that creation was always with him in his foreknowledge, and that for this reason he has always been a creator, then, in accordance with this, one could also say that the resurrection of the dead has already taken place, and that the just

esse et iustos in vitam aeternam, impios in ignem aeternum intrasse, quod totum adhuc in praescientia est.

29 Redeamus igitur ad id quod ratio exigit et intellectui patet: alia scilicet dici de Deo secundum essentiam naturalem, alia secundum operationum qualitatem. Dicitur enim secundum operum qualitatem "propitius," "indultor," "misericors," "gubernator." Secundum naturalem vero essentiam, "sapiens" et "vivens." Quia ergo semper sapiens et vivens fuit, sapientia et vita illi coaeterna sunt. Hac igitur ratione probatur quod Deus unus, habens Verbum et Spiritum, tribus personis per se existentibus constat, quas complectitur una substantia divinitatis.

30 Deum itaque colimus unum in substantia, trinum in personis, sicut Lex et prophetae et omnis divina pagina illum nobis insinuant. Primum namque, cum vellet creare hominem, in libro Genesis Moses sic eum introducit loquentem: *"Faciamus hominem ad imaginem et similitudinem nostram,"* non: "Faciam hominem ad imaginem et similitudinem meam." Et in alio loco eiusdem libri: *"Non est bonum esse hominem solum. Faciamus ei adiutorium simile sibi."* Rursus in eodem: *"Ecce Adam factus est quasi unus ex nobis,"* non: "Quasi ego." Et alibi: *"Venite, descendamus et confundamus linguam eorum,"* et non dixit: "Descendam et confundam."

31 Ita Moses, aspirante Deo, mysterium nobis trium personarum in divinitate monstravit. Numquid ergo possum dimittere verbum et mysterium quod mihi Moses propheta Dei insinuavit signisque et mirabilibus, quae nonnisi a Deo

have entered into the eternal life, and the unfaithful into the eternal fire, since all of this is already in his foreknowledge.

Let us return to that which reason demands and is clear 29
to the intellect: that some things are predicated of God in accordance with his natural essence, other things in accordance with the character of his actions. For in accordance with the character of his actions he is called "kind," "lenient," "merciful," "governor." In accordance with his natural essence, however, he is called "wise" and "living." And because he has always been wise and living, wisdom and life are coeternal with him. By this reasoning it is proven that God is one, having the Word and the Spirit, and consists of three persons that exist independently, encompassed by a single divine substance.

We worship, therefore, a God who is one in substance, 30
but threefold in persons, just as the Law, the prophets, and every sacred page indicates him to us. For in the beginning, when he wished to create man, Moses portrays him in the book of Genesis as saying the following: "Let us create a man in our image and likeness," not as saying: "Let me create a man in my image and likeness." And in a different passage of the same book: "It is not good that man is alone. Let us create a helper like him." Elsewhere in the same book: "Behold, Adam has been created like one of us," not: "like me." And elsewhere: "Come, let us go down and confound their language," and he did not say: "Let me go down and confound."

In this way, Moses, with God's inspiration, showed to us 31
the mystery of the three persons in the divinity. Surely I cannot dismiss the words and mystery indicated to me by Moses, prophet of God, and confirmed by him with signs and

esse poterant, confirmavit, et socio tuo adquiescere, qui sine sensu, sine intellectu, sine ratione, carens etiam signis et miraculis est? Ipse enim dixit: *"Deus unus est singularis solidus."* Deinde contra hoc ipsum loquens, dicit Christum Spiritum Dei et Verbum. Delirus enim et amens modo Deum ternificat, modo unificat. Nihil quippe intelligens secundum sui pessimi cordis aestimationem, quod sibi videbatur fingebat, quod iustum vel aequum esse tuae prudentiae videri non puto.

32 Daniel propheta ad Nabuchodonosor dictum a Deo esse commemorat: *"Tibi dicimus, Nabuchodonosor,"* non: "Tibi dico." Ista igitur, quae sive in Mose sive in Daniele sive in aliis pluraliter dicta inveniuntur, proculdubio divinae trinitatis mysterium nobis annuntiant. Quod, ut plenius monstraretur, narrat Moses quod apparuit Dominus Abrahae ad ilicem Manbrae in specie trium virorum, quos sicut unum adoravit et sicut uni locutus est dicens: "Domine, si inveni gratiam in oculis tuis, ne transieris servum tuum." Statimque in uno eodemque ipso sermone mysterium Trinitatis designans adiungit: *"Sed afferam pauxillum aquae et laventur pedes vestri et requiescite sub arbore."*

33 Moses quoque in Lege ait: *"Audi Israel: Dominus Deus tuus Deus unus est."* Et David mysterium Trinitatis insinuans: *"Verbo, inquit, Dei caeli firmati sunt et spiritu oris eius omnis virtus eorum."* Numquid apertius nos ipsi vel aliquis hoc possemus exprimere? Idem quoque in alio loco: *"Benedicat nos Deus, Deus noster, benedicat nos Deus."* An David rex et

miracles, which could only have been performed by God? And surely I cannot acquiesce to your friend, who has no sense, understanding, or reason, and also lacks signs and miracles? He himself said: "God is one, singular, and whole." Then he contradicts this, and calls Christ the Spirit of God and the Word. This raving and senseless man now makes God threefold, and then he makes him one. Since he did not understand anything, in accordance with the worth of his most wicked heart, he fabricated whatever he wished, and I do not think that this appears just or right to your prudent judgment.

The prophet Daniel recounts to Nebuchadnezzar that 32
God said: "We say to you, Nebuchadnezzar," not: "I say to you." These things, which are found in abundance in Moses, Daniel, and others, announce to us beyond any doubt the mystery of the divine trinity. And to demonstrate this even more fully, Moses recounts that the Lord appeared to Abraham at the holm oak of Mamre in the form of three men, whom he venerated as one, and addressed as one: "Lord, if I have found grace in your eyes, do not pass by your servant." Immediately following this, in this very same address, he references the mystery of the Trinity when he says: "But I will bring some water and may your feet be washed, and rest yourselves under the tree."

Moses also says in the Torah: "Listen, Israel: The Lord 33
your God is one God." And David refers to the mystery of the Trinity when he says: "By the word of the Lord were the heavens made; and all the host of them by the breath of his mouth." Surely neither we ourselves, nor anyone else, could express this more clearly? David also says in a different passage: "May God bless us, our God, may God bless us." Was

propheta tantus a tribus diis se benedici poscebat? Isaias etiam ipsum Dominum sic loquentem inducit: *"Et nunc Dominus misit me et Spiritus eius."*

34 His et aliis similibus Scripturae Sanctae testimoniis edocti, unum in essentia, trinum in personis Deum credimus, et confitemur praecepta et testimonia Divini Eloquii, non transgredientes nec aliquid in eis augentes aut minuentes vel pro arbitrio mutantes aut corrumpentes, sicut tu nobis obicis et socius tuus mentitur. Quod omnis homo rationabilis scripturas nostras legens intelligit, et quam iniuste atque impudenter talia dicatis advertit.

35 Ut autem de mysterio Sanctae Trinitatis aliquid iterum dicamus, illud Isaiae testimonium non omittam, quod se in visione positum, vidisse commemorat seraphin iuxta thronum Dei clamantes alterum ad alterum et dicentes: *"Sanctus, sanctus, sanctus Dominus Deus exercituum, plena est omnis terra gloria eius."* Quid enim aliud datur intelligi, dum singulari numero ter "sanctus" repetitur, nisi ut unus et singularis Deus in tribus personis ab omnibus adoretur? Ita enim sancti angeli eum ab initio laudaverunt et sine fine laudabunt.

36 Sed quia nisi prolixus esse timerem, innumeris scripturarum testimoniis super hoc te pluviare possem; sufficiat me hactenus aliqua commemorasse, quae idcirco praecipue tibi commemoranda putavi, quia scripturas sanctas studiose te legisse dixisti. Pauca itaque ista tibi sufficiant, utpote homini docto et qui de paucis plura perpendere novit.

David, such a great king and prophet, asking here to be blessed by three gods? Isaiah, too, portrays the Lord as saying the following: "And now the Lord and his Spirit have sent me."

Instructed by these and similar testimonies in holy scripture, we believe that God is one in essence, but threefold in persons, and we confess the teachings and testimonies of the Holy Writ, without transgressing, adding, removing, altering, or corrupting anything as we deem fit, as you accuse us of doing, and as your friend lies about us. Any rational man who reads our scriptures understands this, and notices how unjustly and shamelessly you claim these things. 34

To mention something else concerning the mystery of the Holy Trinity, I will not omit Isaiah's testimony, in which he recounts having seen in a vision seraphim calling to each other by the throne of God, and saying: "Holy, holy, holy Lord God of hosts, all the earth is filled with his glory." When the word "holy" is repeated three times in the singular, what else should be understood but that God is worshipped by all as one single God in three persons? For this is how the saintly angels have praised him from the beginning, and how they will praise him without end. 35

If I were not afraid to be verbose, I could shower you with innumerable testimonies from the scriptures about this matter; but let it suffice to have recounted to you some things which I thought especially worthy to recount to you, because you said that you have read the holy scriptures diligently. Let these few testimonies suffice for you, since you are a learned man capable of considering the majority of things based on a few testimonies. 36

37 Post hanc igitur manifestatam a nobis veritatis cognitionem, qua tibi aperte ostendi quomodo sit Deus unus trinus et trinus unus, invito te ad ipsum unum verum Deum colendum et adorandum, non ad illud horribile et irrationabile et absurdum et abominabile ad quod me invitandum insipienter elaborasti. Siquidem oportet te, secundum quod pollicitus es, adquiescere veritati. Veritas enim Deus est. Quaeso ergo te, considera vim verborum ac proprietatem sententiarum perpende, et videbis quoniam non invito te nisi ad unum Deum, qui in tribus personis est unus, perfectus cum Verbo suo et Spiritu, et ita est unus trinus et trinus unus, et non tres dii, sicut tuus socius nobis imponit in Alcorano, dicens nos tres deos colere et sic loquens: *"Quam male credunt, qui dicunt unum Deum tres deos esse, cum non sit Deus nisi unus. Qui, si ab hoc non recesserint, horribili cruciatui subiacebunt. Cur non agunt paenitentiam, supplicantes Deo ut indulgeat illis?"*

38 Utinam ego scirem qui sunt illi de tribus sectis Christianorum superius a te commemoratis, qui dicunt unum Deum tres deos esse, cum nullus inter Christianos haereticus apparuerit qui unum Deum tres deos esse dixerit! Nec te etiam, qui multas haereticorum sectas audisti et qui multa legisti, talem aliquem vel audisse vel vidisse crediderim, nedum nos, qui "Catholico" nomine gloriamur, hoc—quod absit—umquam vel cogitare potuerimus, nisi forte tu illos intelligere velis qui sunt de secta Marconii et dicunt tres sphaeras esse, a quibus regitur mundus, et vocant eas tres deos, quorum unus est pius, alter iustus, alter iniustus. Isti certe nec Christiani sunt nec Christiani vocantur. Omnes vero

Having clearly demonstrated to you this true knowledge by which the one God is threefold, and the threefold God is one, I invite you to worship and venerate that same one true God, and not that horrifying, irrational, absurd, and detestable worship you have expended such efforts to invite me to. Indeed, it is proper for you to submit to the truth, as you promised; for God is the truth. Therefore I ask you, consider the force of my words and weigh carefully the proper signification of my statements, and you will see that I invite you to nothing else but the one God, who is one in three persons, complete with his Word and Spirit, and so he is one and threefold, threefold and one, and not three gods, as your friend accuses us in the Qurʾān, claiming that we worship three gods, and saying: "How wrongly do they believe, who say that the one God is three gods, since there is no God but the one. If they do not depart from this, they will be subject to horrible torture. Why do they not repent, beseeching God to forgive them?" 37

Would that I knew about the three sects of Christians you mentioned earlier, who claim that the one God is three gods, even though there has never been a heretic among the Christians who has claimed that the one God is three gods! Nor would I believe that even you, who have heard and read much about many sects of heretics, have ever heard or seen any such person, let alone that we, who glory in the name "Catholic," could have ever even conceived of such a thing—God forbid!—unless, perhaps, you mean those of the sect of Marcion, who claim that there are three spheres through which the world is governed, and who call those spheres three gods, of which one is pious, another is just, and another is unjust. Indeed, they are neither Christians nor are 38

Christiani et qui "Christiano" nomine gloriantur longe sunt a trium deorum opinione sacrilega, negantesque et anathematizantes quicumque vel tale quid cogitaverint. Credunt unum Deum habentem Verbum et Spiritum sine discretione et divisione unitatis.

39 Tuus autem socius in Alcorano sic loquitur dicens: "Christus Iesus, filius Mariae, nuntius est Dei, et Verbum et Spiritus a Deo missus in Mariam. Credite in Deum et in nuntium eius, nec dicatis tres deos et erit vobis melius." Vide ergo tu qualiter hic dicat Deum habere Verbum et Spiritum, et iubeat te credere unum Deum habentem Verbum et Spiritum, et qualiter demonstrat tibi quoniam Christus homo est perfectus, Verbo Dei corporatus et unitus? Numquid apertius Christi incarnatio ab aliquo poterit declarari? Postea vero sequitur dicens: *"Non dicatis vel cogitetis tres deos esse in Deo, fugite hoc, plane melius vobis erit."* Quomodo autem vel de quibus hoc dixerit vel quos deos coli prohibuerit, nihil ad nos, qui nec pagani sumus nec Marconiani.

40 Sed redeamus ad illam superiorem tuam invitationem, qua me totiens ad tui prophetae testificationem et legem suscipiendam vocasti. Si enim vera et utilia sunt quibus me credere et adquiescere exhortaris, nec me nec aliquem sanae mentis vel rationis refragari convenit quin diligenter investigatae et inventae veritati libentissime adquiescam. Si vero falsa et inutilia esse probantur, nec te in eis remanere oportet, nec alios ad ea ullatenus invitare. Nam, si hoc feceris, et

they called Christians. All Christians, and all who glory in the name "Christian," are far removed from the sacrilegious doctrine of three gods, since they argue against and strike with anathema anyone who has even conceived of such a thing. They believe in one God, having the Word and the Spirit, without distinction or division of its unity.

However, your friend says the following in the Qurʾān: 39
"Jesus Christ, son of Mary, is God's messenger, and the Word and Spirit have been sent by God to Mary. Believe in God and in his messenger, and do not say that there are three gods, and it will be to your benefit." See how he says that God has the Word and the Spirit, and orders you to believe in the one God, having the Word and the Spirit, and how he shows you that Christ is a perfect man, having become flesh and unified with the Word of God? Surely Christ's incarnation could not have been declared more openly by anyone else? Later, he follows this up with: "Do not say or think that there are three gods in God; avoid this, and surely it will be to your benefit." What he meant by this, or about whom he was speaking, or which gods he forbade to worship, does not pertain to us in any way, since we are neither pagans nor followers of Marcion.

But let us return to your invitation made earlier, when 40
you so often called upon me to bear witness to your prophet's law and to accept it. If what you urge me to believe and give assent to is true and beneficial, it is not right for me, or anyone of a healthy mind and in possession of reason, to resist freely assenting to a truth that has been sought after with much care, and which has now been found. But if it is proven to be false and not beneficial, you should not continue to believe it, nor should you invite others to do so any

tuae animae hostis efficieris, et de his quos ad tanta mala induxeris rationem Deo reddere compelleris.

41 Videamus ergo, si placet, et amicabiliter ac pacifice, sine pertinaci patrocinio defensionis, investigemus causam istius hominis, cuius me prophetiae adquiescere rogas, diligenter omnia perscrutantes et ab initio usque ad finem eius quis fuerit, quid egerit consideremus, in nullo a veritate ad mendacium declinantes. Quanto enim in hoc negotio gravior pendere causa videtur, tanto expressius ac studiosius totius rei inquisitioni debemus intendere.

42 Numquid tu nescis et nos omnes quod homo iste pupillus fuit in sinu patrui sui Abdamenef, qui cognominatur Abdemutalla, in cuius tuitione pater ipsius moriens eum commendaverat, eratque tutor et curator illius? Ipse vero postea cultor fuit idolorum, quae vocantur Elleth et Alaze in Mecha, cum omni domo et generatione sua, sicuti in sua scriptura testificatur dicens ita dictum sibi fuisse: *"Nonne tu fuisti pupillus et collectus es? Et in errore et iustificatus es? Et pauper et ditatus es?"*

43 Ita ergo vixit usque quo pervenit ad servitium camelorum Hadigae, filiae Huleit, cuius factus fuerat mercennarius, et proficiscebatur cum camelis in Syriam et in alia loca, donec duxit eam uxorem, interveniente causa quam tu scis. Postquam vero se divitem factum eiusdem mulieris opibus vidit, conatus est super gentem et patriam suam regnum arripere. Sed dum hoc ad effectum prout cupiebat non posset perducere, praesertim cum paucos adhuc fautores haberet, arte

longer. For, should you do this, you will become an enemy of your own soul and will be forced to render an account before God for those you have led to such evils.

Let us take a look, if you wish, and let us inquire in a friendly and peaceful manner, and without resorting to constant defensiveness, into the motives of that man, whose prophecies you ask me to accept, and let us carefully go over every detail and consider from beginning to end what sort of man he was, what things he did, at no point straying from the truth into lies. For the weightier the matter appears to be, the more we ought to pay close and careful attention to an investigation of the entire matter. 41

Surely you are aware, as we all are, that that man was an orphan in the care of his uncle ʿAbd Manāf, called ʾAbū Ṭālib, to whose care his father entrusted him upon his deathbed, and that he was his protector and caretaker? Muhammad himself subsequently became a worshipper of the idols, which are called al-Lāt and al-ʿUzzā in Mecca, together with his entire household and tribe, to which he testifies in his book when he says that the following was said to him: "Were you not an orphan and taken in? And did you not stray, and were you not pardoned? And were you not poor, and were you not made wealthy?" 42

In this way did he live until he hired on to become the caretaker of the camels of Khadīja, the daughter of Khuwaylid, and left with her camels for Syria and other places. Finally he married her—and you know what motivated him. After he had seen to making himself wealthy with the riches of that woman, he tried to obtain the crown of his people and country. But since he could not realize his desire, especially because he had yet few supporters, he used his great 43

et ingenio magno usus est, ut—qui rex esse non poterat—prophetam se Dei esse et nuntium simularet. Tu vero (quem Deus salvet) scis quantum hoc displicuerit omni parentelae et generationi eius, quae vocatur Chorais.

44 Cumque hoc modo prophetae nomen sibi usurpasset, ingressus est ad homines, qui tanto facilius qualibet astutiae machinatione decipi poterant, quanto longius ab omni sapientia et usu civilitatis totiusque humanae prudentiae honestate per agros et villulas sequestrati. Quid Dei nuntius vel propheta esset, vel in quo cognosci deberet, denique quid inter veritatem et mendacium, inter fatuitatem distaret et sapientiam discernere nesciebant. Ad hos decipiendos cuiusdam astrologi, cuius postea nomen et causam dicemus, ope et consilio non mediocriter confortatus, homines pestiferos et viarum insidiatores, fugitivos quoque et homicidas sibi aggregavit. Quos etiam ad devia silvarum, ad cacumina montium et ad proxima fontibus loca circumquaque mittebat, insidiari scilicet negotiatoribus et iter agentibus, ad interficiendum eos et diripiendum tam camelos quam cetera quae ducebant, vel alia quae negotiationis vel necessitatis causa portabant.

45 De ipso etiam scimus quod primo tempore prophetiae suae, cum de Civitate veniret ad Mecham et inveniret hominem camelum habentem, eundem illi camelum abstulit, et cum iam quinquaginta trium annorum esset, tali beneficio praedicationis suae primordia dedicavit. Habuit autem ibi quadraginta de suis, qui ei affuerunt, custodientes eum ab illis de Mecha, quos valde infestos habebat, eo quo ipsi omnes artes eius et maleficia nossent. Oderant quippe illum

skill and talent to pretend that—as he could not be a king—he was a prophet and messenger of God. But you (may God save you) know how much this displeased his family and his entire tribe, which is called Quraysh.

When he had claimed for himself the title of prophet he 44
approached such men as could easily be deceived by any kind of clever contrivance, since they lived isolated in their fields and small country houses, lacking any kind of wisdom, education, and nobility proper to human prudence. They did not know what a messenger of God or a prophet was, or how he ought to be recognized—in short, how to tell the difference between truth and lies, folly and wisdom. To deceive them, he gathered pernicious men, highway robbers, fugitives, and murderers around him, with no small amount of help and advice from a certain astrologer, whose name and life we will discuss later. He sent them in every direction, even to pathless wildernesses, to the summits of mountains, and to places near springs, to lie in ambush for merchants and travelers, in order to kill them and to snatch away their camels and everything else they brought with them, or any other things which they carried for trade or out of necessity.

We also know about him that in the early period of his 45
career as a prophet, while he was going to Mecca from Medina, he encountered a man in possession of a camel; he took the camel from him and, when he reached the age of fifty-three, he dedicated the early period of his prophetic activity to this bounty. He had at that point forty of his men with him, guarding him from the Meccans, whom he considered his archenemies since they knew all of his tricks and crimes. Indeed, they hated him extremely, since he used to

nimis, quia, cum latro et pestifer esset, prophetam se Dei esse stultis hominibus mentiebatur.

46 Abiit autem in civitatem quae destructa habebatur, quam ex maiori parte Iudaei pauperes inhabitabant. In quam cum ingrederetur, volens ostendere iustitiae suae regulam et prophetiae modum, pupillis cuiusdam carpentarii filiis domum abstulit et in ea mesquidam fecit.

47 Deinde misit in prima sua expeditione Hanzetan, filium Abdimelic, cum equitatu triginta virorum ad silvas regionis Iuheinen rapere camelos Chorais, quando revertebantur de Syria. Cumque illi occurreret Hebegel, filius Hissen, in trecentis viris de Mecha, dispersis ubique qui cum eo erant, nullum certamen ausus committere fugit. O tu (quem Deus salvet), ubi sunt modo signa prophetiae? Si enim vere propheta fuisset, hoc ei magis contingere deberet quod Deus per Mosen populo suo promittit dicens: *"Quomodo persequebatur unus mille et duo fugarent decem milia?"* Sicut etiam Iosue filium Nun fecisse legimus, cum introduceret populum in terra promissionis.

48 Ex hoc igitur duobus modis probamus illum non esse prophetam, quia, si propheta fuisset, nec quod futurum erat eum latere potuisset, nec ille, qui missus erat ab illo, tam facile ab idolorum cultoribus victus et fugatus esset. Custodiretur enim ab angelis, sicut invenimus custoditum fuisse Iosue, quando apparuit ei angelus in similitudine armati ducis et Iosue dixit ei: "Noster es an adversariorum?" Et ille: "Princeps," inquit, "sum exercitus Domini et modo veni." Procidens autem Iosue in faciem suam super terram adoravit et

falsely declare to fools that he was a prophet of God, even though he was a robber and criminal.

46 He left for a city that was thought to be in ruins, and which was inhabited for the most part by indigent Jews. When he entered the city, wishing to demonstrate his standard of justice and manner of prophecy, he took the house from the orphaned sons of a certain carpenter, and built a mosque inside it.

47 On his first mission he sent Ḥamza b. ʿAbd al-Muṭṭalib with thirty horsemen to the woodlands of Juhayna to steal camels from the Quraysh, when they were returning from Syria. But when he encountered ʾAbū Jahl b. Hishām with three hundred Meccans, his own men dispersed in all directions and he fled, not daring to engage in battle. O you (may God save you), where are now the marks of a prophet? For if he had truly been a prophet, what God promised to his people through Moses ought to have happened to him instead, when God said: "How did one man pursue a thousand, and two men drive off ten thousand?" Just as we read that Joshua, the son of Nun, did, when he led his people into the promised land.

48 We can prove, therefore, that he is no prophet, since, if he had been a prophet, the future could not have been hidden from him, nor could Ḥamza b. ʿAbd al-Muṭṭalib, who was sent by him, have been defeated and put to flight by idolaters so easily, for he would have been guarded by angels, just as we find that Joshua was protected when an angel appeared to him in the appearance of a commander-in-arms and Joshua said to him: "Are you one of ours or one of the enemies?" And he said: "I am the commander of the Lord's host and have just arrived." Joshua fell prostrate on the floor

dixit: "Quid praecipit Dominus servo suo?" Respondit: "Solve calciamentum de pedibus tuis, locus enim in quo stas terra sancta est." Et fecit ita Iosue, in quo facto magnum mysterium est.

49 Sed cum hic respondere non possis, veniamus ad secundam ipsius expeditionem. Ibi forsitan respondebis. Post haec in secunda expeditione misit Hugaida, filium Alaharachi, filii Amuthallabi, sicut tu novisti, in sexaginta militibus, ut esset duplex numerus primo coetui, nec facile ab aliquo terreri possent, ad loca proxima Algafati. Cui occurrit Ebezephin cum suis militibus. Inter quos tanta extitit effusio sanguinis quantam ipse novisti. Ego autem nullum ibi ab angelis adiutum esse audivi, cum dicatur in Alcoran quod angelus Gabriel in similitudinem equitantis super albam equam, habens viridia vestimenta, comitatus fuerit filios Israel, cum eos persequeretur Pharao in quadringentis curribus usque ad mare. Cumque venissent filii Israel ad medium maris, ecce Gabriel, equitans super equam, secutus est vestigia eorum dicens, "Venio ad liberandum vos," et submersus est Pharao et socii eius, et liberati sunt filii Israel. Tu autem et socius tuus vacui estis ab huius angelicae defensionis praesidio.

50 Sed veniamus ad tertiam expeditionem, in qua, cum missus esset Zaid, filius Ebihacad, similiter non longe ab Algafati, in viginti viris, nec invenisset camelos (iam enim altera die transierant), spe sua et desiderio frustratus, inanis et vacuus rediit. Hic etiam omnino prophetica gratia defuisse cognoscitur. Si enim gratiam prophetiae habebat, cur non,

and said: "What does the Lord order his servant to do?" He responded: "Take off your sandals, for the place on which you stand is hallowed ground." Joshua did so, and in that act a great mystery lies hidden.

However, since you cannot respond to this, let us proceed 49
to his second campaign. Perhaps then you will respond. After these events, he sent ʿUbayda b. al-Ḥārit b. ʿAbd al-Muṭṭalib on his second campaign, to a place close to al-Juḥfa, with sixty soldiers, as you know, so that the number of soldiers would be doubled from the previous group, and they would not easily be frightened away by anyone. They encountered ʾAbū Sufyān with his soldiers. Between them there was great bloodshed, as you know. But I have not heard that anyone there was aided by angels, even though it is said in the Qurʾān that the angel Gabriel, with the appearance of a horseman riding a white mare and wearing green garments, accompanied the sons of Israel when Pharaoh pursued them with four hundred chariots all the way to the sea. When the sons of Israel had come halfway across the sea, lo! Gabriel, riding a mare, followed in their wake, and said, "I have come to set you free," and Pharaoh and his companions were submerged, and the sons of Israel were freed. You, however, and your companion are without this kind of angelic protection.

However, let us proceed to the third campaign. After Saʿd 50
b. ʾAbī Waqqāṣ was sent once again to a place close to al-Juḥfa, with twenty men, and did not find any camels (for they had already passed by the day before), he returned empty-handed, disappointed in his hope and desire. In this, too, Muhammad's prophetic grace is shown to have been lacking. For if he had the grace of prophecy, why did he not

sicut Samuel de asinabus patris Saul inveniendis, iste de camelis amittendis et inani militum suorum labore praescius erat? Haec est enim prophetiae norma, qua praesciuntur futura, sicut Deus ea solet manifestare prophetis.

51 Licet autem tres istae expeditiones sufficere possint ad convincendam falsitatem tui prophetae, non tamen alias ipsius, quas per se facere voluit, "probitates" tacebimus, illam, scilicet, primam commemorantes, qua egressus est ad capiendos camelos Chorais, quando venit ad locum qui dicitur Gueden. Ubi cum invenisset Muhzen, filium Guhf Elmuhni, et non praevaleret adversus eum, rediit vacuus. Iterum secundo per semetipsum exiit donec venit Barath, quae est in via Sem, ut invaderet camelos Chorais. In quo loco resistens ei Humeie, filius Halaph, inanem ad propria remeare coegit. Tertio exiit per semetipsum, donec veniret Iambo, quaerendo iterum camelos Chorais, qui erant apud Sem et quibus insidiabatur in redeundo, et quamvis tunc pro eis acriter dimicaret, tandem confusus abscessit.

52 Tu igitur (quem Deus adiuvet) considera et diligenter adverte si huiusmodi expeditiones ad Dei prophetam debeant pertinere, in quibus nihil aliud quam fraus et violentia et humani sanguinis effusio et quicquid prorsus latrones et viarum insidiatores faciunt agebatur. Quae enim distantia est inter istum et illum pessimum grassatorem et itinerantium strangulatorem, Behic Elgurmi, cuius scelerata fama ad dominum nostrum Emirhelmomini et ad nos usque manavit? Ad quod te nihil respondere posse sicut nec ad alia superiora non miror, maxime cum tota vita prophetae istius ab initio

know beforehand that they would miss the camels and that the soldiers' efforts would be in vain, just as Samuel knew about finding the she-asses of Saul's father? Such is the pattern with prophecies by which the future is known beforehand, since God is accustomed to reveal it to prophets.

Although these three campaigns would suffice to prove 51
that your prophet was false, still we will not pass over his other "good deeds" in silence, which he wanted to commit in person. The first we will mention occurred when he had gone to capture the camels of the Quraysh and had come to the place called Waddān. There he met Mahshī b. ʿUmar al-Ḍamrī and, being no match for him, returned empty-handed. He left for a second time in person and arrived in Būwāṭ, which is on the way to Syria, to assail the caravans of the Quraysh. There ʾUmayya b. Khalaf opposed him and forced him to return to his own land empty-handed. He left for a third time in person and arrived in Yanbuʿ, once again in search of the camels of the Quraysh, which were in Syria. He lay in ambush for them on his return voyage, and although he fought fiercely for them, at last he left defeated.

Consider therefore (may God help you) and pay close at- 52
tention as to whether such campaigns ought to apply to a prophet of God, campaigns in which nothing but deception, violence, and human bloodshed was practiced—indeed, whatever thieves and highway robbers commit. What difference is there between him and that terrible robber, Bābik al-Khurramī, who strangled travelers, and whose infamous crimes have even reached our ears and those of our lord the *ʾamīr al-muʾminīn?* I am not surprised that you are unable to say anything in response to this, just as to any of the things mentioned above, especially since that prophet

usque ad finem in huiusmodi sceleribus consumpta sit. Fueruntque expeditiones ipsius viginti sex praeter insidiarum assultus, qui fiebant nocte ac die. Quarum novem ipsemet fecit, reliquas sociis imperavit.

53 Faciebat etiam—quod peius est!—ut, si qui ei in istis suis maleficiis contradicerent vel in aliquo eum reprehenderent, statim eos, ubicumque sibi contingeret, aut per se aut per suos, dormientes sive vigilantes, proditorie iugularet. Sicuti fecit quando misit Abdalla, filium Ragaha Alenzari, ad interficiendum Ezir Iudaeum, filium Dedan, in loco qui dicitur Haibari, et improvise trucidavit eum. Misit quoque Zelin filium Ahamir Algambri solum ad Imenhachil, senem Iudaeum, quem dormientem securum in lecto suo ideo iugulari fecit, quia se ab illo vituperatum dicebat.

54 O tu (quem Deus salvet), quis umquam—non dico propheta sed qui vel in modico qualemcumque Dei notitiam haberet—talia fecisse auditus est? An non poterat aliter de Iudaeo illo suas iniurias vindicare nisi dormientem confoderet—quod non solum apud Deum sed et apud omnem creaturam ipso auditu super omnia mala horribile est? Certe quod de brutis animalibus ipsa humani cordis naturalis affectio fieri detestatur, adeo ut pullos avium in nido repertos nullatenus occidere pro lege teneat, iste de hominibus faciebat. Unde igitur hoc illi nisi ex diaboli parte, qui proditor et homicida primus ab initio extitit, inesse poterat? Quod et humano et divino iudicio omnes impietates exsuperat. Ubi

of yours spent his entire life in committing crimes of this nature, from beginning to end. He had twenty-six campaigns, in addition to the ambushes, which took place both at night and during the day. Nine of these he carried out himself, the others he delegated to his companions.

He also—and this is even worse!—would treacherously 53
assassinate anyone who opposed him in these crimes of his or in any other matter, wherever he found the opportunity, killing them either in their sleep or when they were awake, and either doing so himself or through his agents. This he did when he sent ʿAbd Allāh b. Ruwāḥa al-ʾAnṣarī to assassinate al-Yusayr b. Rizām, a Jew, in the place called Khaybar, and he killed him in a surprise attack. Muhammad also sent Sālim b. ʿUmayr al-ʿUmarī alone to ʾAbū ʿAfak, an old Jew. Muhammad arranged for him, as he was sleeping peacefully, to be killed in his bed, since he claimed to have been slandered by him.

Tell me (may God save you), who has ever been said to 54
have perpetrated such acts—I say nothing of a prophet, just someone who possesses to a moderate degree any kind of knowledge of God? Had he no other way of exacting revenge upon that Jew for his injury than to stab him in his sleep—a deed horrible beyond all evils to hear of, not only for God but for all of creation? Indeed, he did to humans the very thing that natural human kindness cannot stand to see happen to dumb animals, inasmuch as it is considered unlawful, as it were, to kill hatchlings found in a bird's nest! Where could this nature of his have come from, if not from the devil, who was the first betrayer and murderer from the beginning? According to both human and divine judgment, this is the worst of all godless acts. What was that you were

est quod paulo ante dicebas eum in sua scriptura dixisse: "Missus sum ad homines cum pace et misericordia"?

55 Sed prosequamur, ut coepimus, prophetae vitam. Et licet quae dicturi sumus minora superioribus videantur, aliqua iterum de suis "bonis operibus" proponamus. Ipse enim est qui misit Abdalla, filium Chassin Elacedi, ad hortum filii Haamir, qui vocatur Nahla, in duodecim viris de comitatu suo, ut annuntiarent illi qualiter se haberent Chorais. Quibus cum occurrisset Gomar, filius Halarami, habens secum camelos Chorais et negotiationes multas, quas attulerat de Elihemen, percutientes eum, camelos et omnia quae portabant tulerunt et dederunt quintam partem Mahumet.

56 Sic quoque et de filiis Phenica factum est ab illo, quia, cum eos audisset multas habere divitias et quiete atque innocenter vivere, venit et obsedit eos, donec subderentur ei. Quibus, licet interveniente Abdalla, filio Ebissuruch, vitam relaxaverit, omnia tamen quae illorum fuerant tulit et quintam partem sibi retinuit.

57 Haec et his similia—quae, si per singula dicerentur, possent fatigare legentem—tu vide si prophetae Dei opera sunt. Nam illam ridiculosam ipsius expeditionem superfluum puto retexere, in qua, cum ei, praeciso labro, dens etiam inferiorum medius excussus fuisset, insuper et a Gutheba, filio Abihacad, in fronte et facie vulnera suscepisset, filius Chumeimae dextrum cum umero bracchium paene illi sustulerat, nisi a Talha, filio Hubeitalla, qui ibi digitum perdidit, defensus evaderet. Cui tamen digitum, quod satis prophetam decuisset, non restituit, ostendens quam alienus sit

saying just a little earlier, that he said in his book: "I have been sent to mankind with peace and compassion"?

But let us continue discussing the life of your prophet, as we have begun to do. Although what we are about to say may seem to be of lesser importance than what we have already said, let us recount once again some of his "good deeds." For he himself sent ʿAbd Allāh b. Jaḥsh al-ʾAsadī to the garden of Ibn ʿĀmir, called Nakhla, accompanied by twelve of his men, in order to report what the situation of the Quraysh was. When they came upon ʿAmr b. al-Ḥaḍramī, who was bringing camels of the Quraysh with him along with much merchandise, which he brought from Yemen, they struck him down and carried off the camels and all they were carrying, giving a fifth portion to Muhammad. 55

So he did also with the sons of Phenica, when he heard that they possessed much wealth and lived peacefully and innocently, he went to them and laid siege until they surrendered to him. And although he allowed them to live (because of the intervention of ʿAbd Allāh b. ʾUbayy b. Sallūl), still he took all that was theirs and kept a fifth portion for himself. 56

Consider carefully whether these things—as well as other similar things that would tire the reader if they were mentioned individually—are the acts of a prophet of God. I consider it superfluous to recount that laughable campaign of his, in which his lip was cut, his lower middle tooth was knocked out, and he also was wounded on his face by ʿUtba b. ʾAbī Waqqāṣ, and Ibn Qamiʾa would have cut off his right arm and shoulder, if he had not been protected by Ṭalḥa b. ʿUbayd Allāh, who lost a finger. As he did not restore his finger, which would have been fitting for a prophet, he demonstrated how different he was from the one who, according 57

ab illo, qui, sicut Evangelium narrat, etiam inimico abscisam auriculam reddidit. Iste vero nec amico, qui se pro illo morti obiecerat, in aliquo subvenire potuit. Et ubi erant angeli, qui olim cum prophetis semper fuisse leguntur, eosque a persecutoribus defendisse, sicut Heliam ab Achab, Danielem et socios eius a Nabuchodonosor, multosque alios, quos enumerare longum est?

58 Ego autem mirari non sufficio quo pacto tibi persuasum sit Dei esse nuntium vel prophetam hominem cuius, ut breviter eius facinorosam vitam demonstrem, nulla fuit alia operatio vel meditatio quam homines interficere, aliena diripere, incestus et adulteria perpetrare. Qui etiam tale dedecus in scriptura prophetiae suae sibi facere non erubuit ut diceret datum renibus suis a Deo quadraginta viros in coitu potentissimos fortitudine libidinis adaequare. Ubi quoque inter cetera rebus odoriferis et mulieribus super omnia se delectari dicit.

59 Sed ut etiam de his aliqua nominatim dicamus, nonne ipse, cum adamasset Zaineb, filiam Gaissi, uxorem Zaidi, et non posset eam habere, Deum illi in Alcorano introduxit loquentem ita: *"Cui dedit Deus et ego illi, faciam virum tuum retineri super te. Tu autem timebis Deum et celabis quod facturus est. Et si times hominem, magis time Deum."* Iterum ad seipsum loqui Deum faciens, *"Cum,"* inquit, *"compleverit Zaidi vir eius votum suum cum ea, tunc eam dabimus tibi, ut non sit aliquid difficile fidelibus in tali negotio, cum completum fuerit quod ad rem pertinet et quod praecipit Deus. Nihil enim est prophetae difficile in eo*

to the Gospel, restored an ear that had been cut off, even to his own enemy. Yet Muhammad could not even come to the aid of his friend, who had thrown himself in death's way on his account. And where were the angels, who, as we read, in earlier times always accompanied prophets and protected them from their attackers, as Elijah was protected from Ahab, Daniel and his companions were protected from Nebuchadnezzar, and many others, whom it would take too long to mention?

It does not cease to amaze me how you can be convinced 58
that he is God's messenger or prophet, when his every activity and thought (to briefly summarize his life of crime) was devoted to killing people, stealing what belonged to others, and committing incest and adultery. He even felt no shame in committing such a disgraceful act in the book of his prophecy as to say that God had granted that in sexual stamina his loins could equal forty of the most potent men in coitus. There he also says, among other things, that he delights, above all, in fragrances and women.

Let us go into more detail about some other things: when 59
he was in love with Zaynab, daughter of Jaḥsh, and the wife of Zayd, and he was unable to have her for himself, did he not in the Qurʾān present God as saying to him: "For the one to whom I have given favor, I will cause your husband to remain with you. You shall fear God, and keep secret what he will do. If you fear man, fear God all the more." Presenting God as speaking to him once again, he says: "Once Zayd, her husband, has brought to an end his vow toward her, then we will give her to you, since in such matters nothing is difficult for the faithful, once what is proper and commanded by God has been fulfilled. For a prophet, nothing that has been

quod Deus illi instituit. Praeceptum namque Dei est praedestinatio praedestinata."

60 Quid vero turpius dici potest quam quod de sua uxore, quae vocabatur Aissa, ipse fecisse dicitur? Haec enim, cum pulchra esset et libidini dedita, diligebatur a Zaphagan, filio Almuathan Ethsulemi qui et consuetudinarium cum ea stuprum gerebat, ipso Mahumet sciente et consentiente. Cumque multi inde loquerentur et testificarentur, maximeque Musatha, filius Ephebe, filii Abdemutalla, et Hazen, filius Zebith, et Abdalla, filius Zurul, et Hamia, filia Gahs, ad ultimum vero Hali, filius Abitalib, princeps et nobilis inter suos. Inde eum liberius argueret dicens copiam esse mulierum nec decere tantum hominem a muliercula dehonestari dignamque esse repudio confirmaret, respondit nullam sibi adeo caram vel dilectam, utpote quam virginem acceperat et adhuc iuvencula videbatur, non se inde curare nec propter hoc mulierem sibi habilem dimissurum, unde usque hodie odium est in Arabia inter generationem Aissae et generationem Hali. Postmodum vero dicit in Alchoran mulierem illam esse innocentem, et hoc sibi divinitus revelatum.

61 Fuerunt autem uxores eius quindecim ingenuae et duae ancillae. Prima Hadiga, filia Huleit. Secunda Aissa, filia Ebibecr, et ipse est Abdalla qui cognominatur Ihatic, filius Abinahaf. Tertia Zodatuh, filia Zama. Quarta Hafcetu, filia Gumar; ista est quam diligebat Aissa. Quinta Umecelme,

arranged by God is difficult, for God's order is a predestined decree."

60 What rumor is more scandalous than what he is said to have done concerning his wife, who was called ʿĀʾisha? She was loved, since she was beautiful and given to lust, by Ṣafwān b. al-Muʿaṭṭal al-Sulamī, who regularly committed adultery with her, with the knowledge and consent of Muhammad himself. Afterward, many people began to gossip and declare themselves witnesses, particularly Masaṭṭah b. Uṭāṭa b. ʿAbd al-Muṭṭalib, Ḥassān b. Thābit, ʿAbd Allāh b. Sallūl, Ḥamna daughter of Jaḥsh, and finally, ʿAlī b. ʾAbī Ṭālib, a noble prince among his people. When ʿAlī b. ʾAbī Ṭālib criticized Muhammad rather freely, saying that there was an abundance of women and that it was improper for such a great man to be dishonored by a mere girl, and asserted that she deserved to be cast aside, Muhammad responded by saying that there was no woman who was so dearly beloved by him, for he had taken her in when she was a virgin and still looked extremely young, and that he was not concerned about this matter and would not on that account repudiate a woman fit for him. For this reason there exists in Arabia even today hate between the tribe of ʿĀʾisha and that of ʿAlī. However, afterward Muhammad wrote in the Qurʾān that the woman was innocent, and that this was revealed to him by divine revelation.

61 He had fifteen freeborn women and two handmaidens. The first was Khadīja, daughter of Khuwaylid. The second was ʿĀʾisha, daughter of ʾAbū Bakr; his name was ʿAbd Allāh, and he was known as ʿAtīq b. ʾAbī Quḥāfa. The third was Sawda, daughter of Zamʿa. The fourth was Ḥafṣa, daughter of ʿUmar; she was the one most liked by ʿĀʾisha.

cuius nomen Hind, filia Abuimei; ipsa est seducta mater infantium, de qua dixit Mahumet quod auferret ab ea zelum, quando discessit ab eo ad matrem suam, fugiens uxorem Gaiere; quam postea revocavit dans ei vestes et ornamenta et duas armillas, ipsa vero accepit hoc de possessione huius saeculi et futuri. Sexta Zaineb, filia Gaissi, uxor Zaidi, cui ipse misit portionem carnis ter et ipsa respuit, unde et ipse indignatus est in eam; propter illam quoque in alias uxores iratus proposuit se ad nullam earum ingressurum per unum mensem; ingressus est tamen vicesimo nono die. Septima altera Zaineb, filia Hazima Alihilelia. Octava Humgebiba, et ipsa est Rambla, filia Euicephien, soror Maoia. Nona Emmamona, filia Alharati. Decima Zaphia, Iudaea Albastria, filia Hai, filii Ahptab, quam docuit gloriari super alias uxores suas, quae improperabant ei Iudaismum, et ut diceret eis: "Ego sum, cuius pater es Aaron, patruus Moses, maritus Mahumet." Undecima Ephatima Alchilevia, filia Azahac, de qua dicitur quod fuit Gambra. Duodecima Ezudeit Alchilevia. Tertiadecima Egumeia, filia Zillaia. Quartadecima filia Noem Alquindia. Quintadecima Elmulaica, filia Cahap Alleizia. Sextadecima Meria mater Abraham filii sui. Septimadecima Reihana, filia Simeonis, Iudaea Cretensis. Haec sunt uxores socii tui.

62 O quam longe est ab ista impura et turbulenta doctrina

The fifth was ʾUmm Salama, called Hind, daughter of ʾAbū ʾUmayya; she, a mother of young children, was seduced by Muhammad, who said that he would remove all jealousy from her when she left him to go to her mother, fleeing from the wife of Gaiere. After he called her back he gave her clothing, jewels, and two armbands; she accepted this as a dowry for both this life and the next. The sixth was Zaynab, daughter of Jaḥsh, wife of Zayd; three times he sent her a portion of meat, and she refused; for this reason he felt insulted by her. Because of her, he also became angry at his other wives, and angrily declared that he would not visit them for one month; nonetheless, he visited them on the twenty-ninth day. The seventh was another Zaynab, daughter of Khuzayma, a Hilalite. The eighth was ʾUmm Ḥabība, also called Ramla, daughter of ʾAbū Sufyān, and sister of Muʿāwiya. The ninth was Maymūna, daughter of al-Ḥārith. The tenth was Ṣafiyya, a Jew from Baṣra, daughter of Ḥuyay b. ʾAkhṭab, who was reproached for being Jewish, and whom Muhammad taught to boast about herself above all his other women, and to say to them: "I am the one, whose father is Aaron, whose uncle is Moses, and whose husband is Muhammad." The eleventh was Fāṭima, a Kilabite, daughter of al-Ḍaḥḥāk, who is said to be ʿAmra. The twelfth was Ezudeit, a Kilabite. The thirteenth was Ḥanna, daughter of Dhū al-Liḥya. The fourteenth was the daughter of al-Nuʿmān, a Kindite. The fifteenth was Malīka, daughter of Kaʿb, a Laythite. The sixteenth was Māriyya, mother of his son ʾIbrāhīm. The seventeenth was Rayḥāna, a Jewish woman from Crete and daughter of Shamʿūn. These were the wives of your friend.

O, how far removed from this filthy and tempestuous 62

Christianae disciplinae pia et sancta religio, quae per gloriosum Paulum Apostolum ad Dei amorem et sanctae castimoniae expeditissimam philosophiam omnes homines invitans dicit: *"Qui habet uxorem, cogitat quae sunt mundi, quomodo placeat uxori; qui autem sine uxore est, cogitat quae Dei sunt, quomodo placeat Deo."* Et iterum: *"Volo autem vos sine sollicitudine esse."* Et ipse Dominus in Evangelio: *"Nemo potest duobus dominis servire, aut enim unum odio habebit et alterum diliget, aut uni adhaerebit et alterum contemnet."*

63 Ut enim cetera dimittamus quae hinc rationabiliter dici possent, si una sola uxor a Dei amore impedit hominem, quomodo qui tantas habebat et totus in earum libidine versabatur—praedes quoque et homicidia et insidias ac cetera, quae superius enumerata sunt, mala omni tempore exercebat—officium prophetae congrue adimplere poterat? Officium namque prophetae non aliud est quam ieiunare, orare, praedicare et his similia bona opera facere. Quibus miror si homo tantis flagitiis subditus umquam potuit vacare.

64 Verum hactenus de gestis eius dixisse sufficiat, quae idcirco in medium adduximus, ut ex ipsis quod Dei propheta esse non possit qui talem vitam duxerit monstraremus. Quod si quis obiciat multos male vixisse sed tamen bene docuisse, qualiter etiam vester propheta docuerit videamus. Consideremus diligenter si vel propheta iure dicatur vel si doctrina eius aliorum prophetarum doctrinae, quos veros prophetas esse cognovimus, concordare videtur. Quia si eis consonare et dictis eorum vel praeceptis similia docuisse

teaching is the pious and sacred religion of Christian teaching, which invites all men through the glorious apostle Paul to the love of God and to the most beneficial philosophy of sacred chastity, saying to them: "He that is married cares for the things that are of the world, how he may please his wife; he, however, who is unmarried, cares for the things that are of God, how he may please God." Elsewhere: "But I want you to be without worry." The Lord himself says in the Gospel: "No man can serve two masters: for either he will hate the one, and love the other; or else he will hold to the one, and despise the other."

Passing over whatever else could reasonably be said on 63
this subject, if only one wife can hinder a man in his love for God, how can a man who has so many wives and is completely occupied by his lust for them—who, moreover, at all times engages in looting, murder, treachery, and other evils mentioned above—properly fulfill the office of a prophet? For the office of a prophet consists of nothing but fasting, praying, preaching, and performing similar good works. I would be surprised if a man dedicated to such crimes could ever have found time for these things.

But enough now about his deeds, which we have men- 64
tioned to demonstrate through them that a man who has led such a life cannot be a prophet of God. If, however, someone should object that many have lived badly and yet taught well, let us see how your prophet has taught. Let us consider carefully whether he should justly be called a prophet, and whether his teachings are in harmony with those of the other prophets, whom we recognize as true prophets. For if he is proven to be in harmony with them and to have taught things similar to their words and precepts, we will rightly

probatur, merito illum recipiendum iudicabimus. Si autem ab eis dissidet, constat quia falsus est et ab omnibus respuendus.

65 Primo igitur quid sit propheta videamus. Propheta est ignota praedicens, sive de praeteritis sive de futuris. Quod autem verum dicat de praeteritis, quomodo poterit ei credi nisi per signa atque miracula? Inde enim Mosi credimus de praeteritis quod signa et miracula faciendo etiam vera dixisse cognoscitur de futuris. Eum igitur merito prophetam dicimus, qui quod de praeteritis vera narraverit, signis manifestis et caelestibus confirmavit.

66 Sed prophetia de futuris duobus modis habetur: dum ea quae futura sunt aut in longum tempus praevidentur aut in proximum. De proximo quippe Isaias prophetabat, quando obsessa a Sennacherib Hierosolyma, Ezechiae regi eiusdem Sennacherib interitum praedicebat et quod ipse Ezechias de infirmitate sua convalesceret auctis sibi quindecim annis. De longinquo vero quando dicebat: *"Ecce virgo concipiet et pariet filium"* et cetera multa. Et Ieremias destructionem templi in proximo videbat et restitutionem in longum. Et Daniel Nabuchodonosor quae futura erant de proximo dicebat, quando ei visiones et somnia exponebat. De longinquo vero quando Iudaeis quod Christus ab eis occidendus esset et quod sacerdotium et unctio et cetera sacra eorum in adventu eius cessarent annuntiabat. Similiter et alii prophetae.

67 Scimus autem quod olim, quando prophetae fuerunt, non statim quicumque hoc nomen usurpasset etiam auctoritatem habebat, sed longa et diuturna vitae sanctitate, signis

consider him to deserve to be received into their company. If, however, he is in discord with them, it is certain that he is false and deserves to be rejected by all.

Let us first analyze what a prophet is. A prophet is one who predicts the unknown, be it the past or the future. Is it not true that what he says about the past can only be believed because of signs and miracles? For this reason, we believe Moses concerning the past, since he is confirmed to have spoken the truth about the future by performing signs and miracles. Therefore we deservedly call him a prophet, since he confirmed by clear, heavenly signs that he told the truth about the past. 65

There are two kinds of prophecy about the future: either the near future is being foreseen or the distant future. Isaiah prophesied about the near future, for when Jerusalem was occupied by Sennacherib, he predicted to Hezekiah the death of Sennacherib, as well as that Hezekiah himself would recover from his illness and be given another fifteen years. However, it was the distant future that he predicted when he said: "Behold a virgin shall conceive, and bear a son," et cetera. Jeremiah saw the destruction of the Temple in the near future, and its restoration in the distant future. Daniel spoke to Nebuchadnezzar of the near future when he explained his visions and dreams. However, it was the distant future he predicted when he announced to the Jews that Christ would be killed by them, and that the priesthood, the unction, and the rest of their sacred rites would cease upon his arrival. So it is also with the other prophets. 66

We know, however, that a long time ago, when there were prophets, not everyone who laid claim to this title had immediate authority, but only after first being confirmed by 67

quoque et miraculis, a principibus et populo Dei primitus comprobatus huius nominis gloriam obtinebat. Nam et Dominus Iesus Christus prophetiae gratiam magnum quid esse sciens, licet creator et omnipotens Deus aeternaliter sit quod super omnia est, prophetam tamen et se ipse dixit et ab aliis dictus est, et hoc verum esse futura multa praedicendo monstravit. Quae iam cum ex maiori parte impleta videmus, pauca quae restant implenda nullatenus dubitamus. Praedixit enim, verbi gratia, de proximo Lazari resurrectionem, Petri negationem, suam etiam passionem et resurrectionem. De longinquo autem Templi destructionem, Iudaeorum calamitatem, martyrum pro suo nomine passiones, sed et falsorum prophetarum seductiones.

68 Tu ergo, si potes, ostende quibus signis, quibus miraculis, quibus sanctis operibus propheta tuus prophetiae honorem meruerit. Si dixeris eum multa praeterita enarrasse—veluti scilicet, de Adam, de Noe, de Abraham, de Mose et Christo—, utinam, sicuti apud nos erant, ipse ea veraciter praedicaret et non per multa mendacia delirans totam paene scripturae sanctae veritatem subverteret!

69 Quantum ergo ad praeterita, iam de ordine prophetarum cecidit, qui tot mendaciis veritatem corrupit. Sane si volueris eum munire fabulis illis, quas de Zhemuth et de camelo et de dominis elephantis et his similibus in scriptura sua posuit, te ipsum testem adhibeo quod fabulae istae, antequam

the rulers and the people of God on account of a long and enduring holiness, as well as signs and miracles, did one acquire this glorious title. The Lord Jesus Christ also knew how great the grace of prophecy was; even though the creator and omnipotent God is eternally above all things, nevertheless he, too, called himself a prophet and was so called by others, and demonstrated this to be true by predicting many future events. Since we see that for the most part those events have come to fulfillment, we have no doubts concerning the few that still remain to be fulfilled. He predicted, for example, the resurrection of Lazarus in the near future, Peter's denial, and even his own passion and resurrection. In the distant future he predicted the destruction of the Temple, the downfall of the Jews, the passions of martyrs for the sake of his name, and also the deception of false prophets.

Show us, therefore, if you can, through what signs, what 68
miracles, what holy works your prophet had earned the honor of prophethood. If you should say that he has recounted many past events—as, for instance, concerning Adam, Noah, Abraham, Moses, and Christ—, would that he had spoken truthfully about them, the way they were in our tradition, and that he had not almost completely subverted the truth of sacred scripture by madly telling a host of lies!

With respect to prophesying the past, he has already 69
fallen from the rank of prophets, since he has marred the truth with so many lies. Of course, if you wish to defend him with the tales he inserted in his writings about the Thamūd, the camel, and the lords of the elephant, and similar tales, I call upon you yourself as a witness that, before even his grandfather was born, those tales were being sung by old

avus eius nasceretur, a vetulis et mulierculis in lanificiis et textriniis per totam Arabiam cantabantur. Sed et si aliquas fabulas forsitan ad suum libitum composuit, quae numquam auditae sunt, nullatenus ei credendum est, quia et hoc a quolibet facile potest fieri et ipse iam in aliis mendax probatus est.

70 De futuris vero quod nihil dixerit nec te ipsum ignorare puto, maxime cum in tota scriptura eius nihil tale inveniatur. Unde etiam quantum ad futura a prophetali gratia exclusus, iam nec signis nec miraculis nec prophetia nec vita inter prophetas esse merebitur. Nam illud totum quod de paradiso quasi praedixisse videtur ad nihil aliud nos cogit nisi ut dicamus eum ita mentiri de futuris, sicut probatus est mentitus fuisse de praeteritis.

71 De signis vero et miraculis quod non sint illi data a Deo, ipse sibi ita dictum a Deo testis est dicens: "Nisi sciremus eos tibi non credituros, sicut nec aliis crediderunt, daremus tibi signa et prodigia." Patet ergo tam ratione quam auctoritate—si tamen non renuas adquiescere veritati—illum non esse prophetam.

72 Iterum forsitan dices quia, nisi esset propheta, numquam ad talem potentiam pervenisset, maxime cum socii eius pauci essent numero quando pugnavit contra regem Persarum, qui erat fortissimus atque potentissimus, et obtinuit triumphum. Quasi vero semper illi, qui Dei cultores sunt, hostes suos superet et non inveniantur etiam in scriptura sacra pauci idolatrae multos Israelitas fugasse. Sed et illi qui semper vincunt non propter sua merita vincunt, sed quia illi

wives and maidens in weavers' shops throughout all of Arabia. Even if perhaps he composed certain tales at his own discretion, which had never been heard, in no way should he be believed, since this could easily be done by anyone, and he has already been proven to be a liar in other matters.

I do not suppose that even you are unaware of the fact 70
that he has spoken nothing about the future, especially since no such things are to be found in his entire book. Since he is deprived of prophetic grace even with regard to predicting the future, he will not deserve to be considered among the prophets, neither on account of signs, miracles, prophecies, nor for his life. With respect to all that he appears to have predicted, as it were, about paradise, he merely forces us to proclaim that he lies about the future just as much as he is proven to have lied about the past.

About the fact that signs and miracles were not granted 71
to him by God, he himself bears witness that God spoke to him thus: "If I did not know that they would not believe you, just as they did not believe others, I would give you signs and prodigies." It is clear, therefore, both through reason and authority, that he is not a prophet—provided that you do not refuse to give in to the truth.

You may, in turn, say that if he had not been a prophet he 72
would never have arrived at such power, especially since his allies were few in number when he fought against the king of the Persians, who was very strong and powerful, and he was victorious. As if those who worship God always defeat their enemies, and as if even in sacred scripture a few idolaters are not found to have put to flight many Israelites. However, those who are always victorious are not so because of their own merit, but because their opponents are worthy

contra quos dimicant tali poena digni sunt. Sicuti per Mosen dicitur ad filios Israel: *"Non ideo quia dilexit vos Deus super alias gentes dedit vobis potestatem interficere et devastare illas, sed propter nequitiam et impietatem eorum."*

73 Item inveniuntur ipsi filii Israel propter peccata sua multotiens a gentibus victi et captivati fuisse. Numquid ergo Nabuchodonosor idolorum cultor, quia Templum Dei destruxit et Hierusalem vastavit, idcirco propheta fuit? Nihil enim mirum est Persarum gentem idolatram et spurcissimam a Mahumet victam esse, non quia ipse melior illis erat, sed quoniam ipsi hoc promeruerant ut a sibi consimili diabolo punirentur.

74 Redeamus tamen adhuc et videamus quale sit illud quod sibi dicit Deum dixisse: "Nisi sciremus eos tibi non credituros, sicut nec aliis crediderunt, daremus tibi signa et prodigia." Et quidem de Iudaeis, quod aliqui signis Mosi non crediderunt, dici potest. Hoc tamen ad Arabes quid pertinebat, qui nec prophetam viderant et ideo nec signa prophetica contempsisse umquam potuerant? Cuius autem impudentiae est dicere illos signis eius non credituros, qui non sine signis tantum sed et sine aliquo alicuius boni indicio, quod nec pecora facere deberent, pessimae vitae homini crediderent?

75 Quia ergo illum tam philosophicis rationibus quam divinis auctoritatibus, sua etiam confessione, ab omni prophetali gratia extraneum esse probavimus, restat ut quales sint fabulae, in quibus contra id quod supra dixerat signa se fecisse asserit, videamus. Dicitur itaque ibi quod aliquando audiens ululantem lupum dixerit sociis se ex voce eius

of such punishment. Just as was said by Moses to the sons of Israel: "God has given you the power to kill other peoples and to lay waste to them not because he loves you more than them, but because of their wickedness and impiety."

Likewise, the sons of Israel are found to have been de- 73
feated and captured by the Gentiles many times because of their sins. Surely Nebuchadnezzar, an idolater, was not a prophet because he destroyed God's Temple and laid waste to Jerusalem? Therefore it is in no way surprising that the idolatrous and vile Persian people was defeated by Muhammad, not because he was better than they, but because they deserved to be punished by a devil similar to themselves.

However, let us return for now and analyze the meaning 74
of the statement he claims God uttered to him: "If I did not know that they would not believe you, just as they did not believe others, I would give you signs and prodigies." This could also be said about the Jews, since some did not believe Moses's signs. Yet how did this relate to the Arabs, who had not seen a prophet and therefore could never have despised prophetic signs? What shamelessness to claim that they would not believe his signs, since they believed a man who had led a horrible life, not only without signs, but also without any token of good! This is something not even cattle should do.

Since we have proven, by means of both philosophical 75
reasoning and divine authority, that he was devoid of any prophetic grace (even by his own confession), it remains for us to consider the nature of the tales in which he claims, contrary to what he had said earlier, that he performed signs. There it is stated that one day he heard a wolf howling, and that he said to his companions that he could tell

intelligere quod lupus ille inter alios maior et princeps omnium esset, sciscitansque ab eis utrum vellent lupo illi aliquid accidere, quod transgredi non posset, illisque se nolle respondentibus ait: "Ergo dimitte illum et cavete ab eo," et ipso innuente ei tribus digitis, lupus fatigatus abscessit.

76 O signum propheticum et res admirabilis, in qua philosophi et sapientes obstupescunt! Nonne similiter potuit dicere quod lupus eum in illa voce prophetam esse signaret? Quis enim inde illum posset arguere, cum quid inter se lupi dicant homines nesciant? Certe mihi parum videtur quicumque hanc fabulam fecerit in componendis fabulis doctus fuisse, cum multo urbanius, si aliquid intelligeret, eam componere potuisset.

77 Sicut et de quodam alio lupo ibi refertur quod, cum allocutus fuisset Vehben, filium Euz Elheslemi, statim factus sit Saracenus. Ubi si leonem pro lupo ille fabularum compositor posuisset, multo elegantior fabula extitisset. Sed non inmerito fabulis suis praecipue lupos intexuit, qui more luporum rabidus et cruentus semper incessit. Qui etiam bovem Zorai domino suo locutum fuisse dixit et quod super ubera ovis Humemabet mulieris manum suam posuerit. Item quod ipse praeceperit arbori et statim adoravit eum, quod tamen Saraceni ipsi falsum esse testantur.

78 Item dicit quod, cum Zaineb Iudaea, uxor Zelem, filii Muslim Iudaei, in ove assa venenum sibi apposuisset, scapula ovis locuta sit ei, "Noli me comedere, quia veneno

from the howling that the wolf was greater than the other wolves and their leader. When he inquired whether they wished for something to happen to the wolf from which it would not be able to recover, and they answered that they did not, he said, "Then let him go and beware of him," and when he motioned toward the wolf with three fingers, it left exhausted.

O what a prophetic sign, and what a remarkable event, for which both philosophers and wise men are at a loss of words! Might he not just as well have claimed that the wolf signaled with his howling that he was a prophet? Who could have argued with him, since nobody knows what wolves say to one another? Indeed, whoever came up with this tale seems to me to have been poorly versed in making up tales, since he could have made it much wittier, if he had had any sense. 76

Just as it is said that a certain other wolf spoke to Uhbān b. Aws al-Sulamī, who immediately became a Saracen. If the writer of the tale had put a lion instead of a wolf, the tale would have been much more elegant. However, he did not include wolves in his tales undeservedly, for he always walked around ferociously and bloodied, in the manner of wolves. He also said that the ox of Darīkh spoke to its master, and that he placed his hand on the udder of the sheep of the woman Umm Maʿbad. He also claimed that he had given orders to a tree and that it immediately worshipped him, which the Saracens themselves, however, declare to be false. 77

He also claimed that when Zaynab, a Jewish woman and wife of Sallām, the son of the Jew named Muslim, had served him poison on roasted lamb, the lamb cutlet spoke to him, "Do not eat me, for I have been prepared with poison," and 78

confecta sum," et ipse noluit comedere; comedit autem inde Ebereu, filius Mazuz, et mortuus est. Vellem scire utrum ipse solus an omnes, qui cum eo aderant, vocem illius scapulae audierint. Si enim ille solus audivit, quare socium suum inde comedere permisit? Si vero omnes audierunt, mirum est quod ille comedere ausus fuit, nisi forte de suo propheta sperans quod etiam mortuum resuscitare potuerit.

79 Resuscitavit enim Helias filium viduae. Et Heliseus filium Sunamitis, et ossibus Helisei tactum cadaver mortui stetit supra pedes suos, quod totum in Veteris Testamenti scriptura reperitur, in qua nos et Iudaei, licet inimici, concordamus. Aut si propheta erat, quare non confidens de virtute prophetica venenum etiam contemnebat, cum constet in supra dicta scriptura filios prophetarum herbam mortiferam comedisse sed Heliseo benedicente in nullo laesos fuisse?

80 Christus quoque Dominus in Evangelio suis discipulis dixit quod, si mortiferum quid biberent, nihil eis noceret. Qui tam in isto quam in ceteris miraculis adeo claruerunt ut eos licet pauperes, humiles, piscatores et per omnia huic mundo despectos, reges, principes, philosophi, divites, potentes, omnes denique terrarum populi, nationes, linguae, tribus, fortes, sapientes, fastum, delicias, honores et quaecumque in mundo sunt contemnentes, ad fidem et cultum unius verae Christianae fidei sequerentur. Haec sunt signa veri prophetae.

81 Iterum narratur ibi quod aliquando miserit manum suam in caverna, unde exierunt aquae, de quibus ipse bibit et socii eius et pecora eius, quod magis de Mahumeth, filio Azari, narrari solet. Cum tamen de utroque apud Saracenos

he did not wish to eat of it. However, al-Barraʾ b. Maʿrūr ate of it, and died. I would like to know whether he alone heard the voice of the cutlet, or all those present. If he alone heard it, why did he allow his companion to eat? If, however, all heard it, it is surprising that he dared to eat, unless perhaps he hoped that his prophet could also resurrect the dead.

For Elijah resurrected the son of a widow, and Elisha the 79
son of the Shunammite woman; and when a corpse was touched by the bones of Elisha, it stood upright on its feet—all of which is found in the Old Testament, in which we are in agreement with the Jews, even though they are our enemies. Moreover, if he was a prophet, why did he not trust in his prophetic power and defy the poison, since it is known that, in the passage mentioned above, the sons of prophets ate poison but suffered no harm at all due to Elisha's blessing?

The Lord Christ also said to his disciples in the Gospel 80
that if they would imbibe any poison, it would not harm them. They have become so well-known through these and other miracles that kings, princes, philosophers, the rich, powerful—in short, all of earth's peoples, nations, languages, tribes, the strong, the wise, followed them to the faithful worship of the one and only Christian faith, even though they were poor, lowly, fishermen, despised by this world in every respect, and in so doing they left behind all delights, honors, and whatever else belongs to this world. These are the signs of a true prophet.

It is also said that he once stretched out his hand into 81
a hollow, and water poured forth from which he, his companions, and his cattle drank—a story that is usually told about Muhammad b. ʾIsḥāq. In both cases, however, this is

incertum et frivolum habeatur, ipse quoque ista omnia mendacissima esse testatur, cum in maiori scriptura sua dicat signa sibi non esse data. Et cum iterum loquitur dicens: "Non sum missus nisi in virtute gladii: et qui non susceperit meam prophetiam, occidatur aut reddat tributum, pretium pro infidelitate sua, et dimittatur."

82 Unde vero apertius et manifestius, ipso teste, falsa esse illa omnia comprobantur quam ex suis iterum dictis, quibus in Alcorano sic loquitur: "Quicquid inveneritis pro me scriptum, conferte illud cum Alcoran et, si ei non concordaverit, scitote quia innocens sum ab illa scriptura et non est mea." Ergo secundum istam regulam signa illa omnia respuenda sunt, quae nullatenus inveniuntur.

83 Nam illud tam ridiculum nobis quam lamentabile suis est quod, cum praecepisset eis ut mortuum se non sepelirent, eo quod tertia die assumendus esset in caelum, ipsique praeceptum observantes magnis hoc desideriis expectarent, et iam a secunda feria, in qua mortuus fuerat, usque ad vesperam quartae feriae longa expectatione fatigati, nihil aliud in eo quam foetoris magnitudinem magis ac magis excrescere cernerent, tandem, sicut retulit Humbran, nudum eum proiecerunt.

84 Gumbran tamen, filius Elhuzain, dixit quod lotus et tribus vestibus indutus sepultusque sit per manus Hali, filii Abitalib, et Alfadl, filii Alahabet, filii Abdemutalla, patrui sui. Fertur enim quod per septem dies morbo pleuretico aegrotaverit et amiserit sensum, septimo vero die convaluerit et iratus est Hali, filius Abitalib, eo quod perdiderat sensum

considered dubious and trifling by Saracens, for he himself is a witness to the fact that all of it is a pack of lies, since he says in his principal work that no signs were given to him. So is it when elsewhere he says: "I have been sent only by the virtue of the sword; and he who does not accept my prophecy should either be killed or render tribute, a price for his lack of faith, and be allowed to leave."

Where are all those things more openly and clearly proven to be false—by his own testimony—than, once again, in his own words when he says the following in the Qurʾān: "Whatever writings you find attributed to me, compare them to the Qurʾān and, if they are not in agreement, know that I have no part in them and that they are not mine." Therefore, in accordance with this rule, all those signs are to be cast aside, which are nowhere to be found in the Qurʾān. 82

The following is as laughable to us as it is lamentable to his followers: when he ordered them not to bury him when he died, because he would be taken up to heaven on the third day, they obeyed his command and awaited this event with great desire; and when they were tired of the long wait, lasting from the day after he died until the evening of the fourth day, and observed only his stench growing worse and worse, at last they cast him out naked, as Humbran relates. 83

However, ʿImrān b. al-Khuzāʿī says that he was washed and clothed in three garments and buried by the hands of ʿAlī b. ʾAbī Ṭālib and al-Faḍl b. al-ʿAbbās b. ʿAbd al-Muṭṭalib, his uncle. There is an account that for seven days he suffered from a cardiac condition and lost his senses, but regained his health on the seventh day and was angry with ʿAlī b. ʾAbī Ṭālib, because he had lost his senses, and he said so to him. 84

et dixit hoc ei. At ille iussit nullum amplius remanere secum in domo nisi Halahabet, filium Abdemutalla. Alia vero die septima mortuus est et intumuit venter eius et retro curvatus est minimus digitus eius, et fuit obitus eius secunda feria, duodecimo die mensis Rabeg primi, anno sexagesimo tertio vitae ipsius, postquam aegrotare coepit quarto decimo die.

85 Mortuo vero Mahumet, omnes ab eo decepti reversi sunt statim unusquisque ad suam, quam ante tenuerant, sectam sive idolatriam sive quamlibet aliam, praeter paucos suae cognationis, qui expectabant se successuros in regno. Eo tempore fuit Ebubecr, filius Abicahaf, vir prudens et callidus, qui non multo post regnum adeptus est, quod vehementer displicuit Hali, filio Abitalib, quousque rex adeo illum obsequiis et blandimentis mitigavit ut etiam regnum ei post se delegaret. Illos quoque qui aversi fuerant a secta Mahumet omni ingenio et astutia ad eam revocans iterum eos stultitiae mancipavit. Quidam enim timore, quidam spe honoris et facultatum, alii alterius cuiuslibet lucri causa, omnes tamen ficte et simulatorie non ex animo redierunt.

86 Puto autem te (quem Deus salvet) optime recordari quid dominus meus Emirhelmomini aliquando, cum essemus ei astantes et quidam quererentur de aliquo, qui videbatur esse Saracenus et non erat, coram omnibus responderit. Dixit enim ita: "Ego miror quod de isto solo quasi aliquid novum mihi dicatis, cum sciam non istum solum sed multos alios nobiliores et probiores in palatio meo Saracenos non esse.

He ordered that no one be allowed to remain with him, except for al-ʿAbbās b. ʿAbd al-Muṭṭalib. However, he died seven days later: his belly swelled up, and his little finger curved backward, and his passing took place on a Tuesday, on the twelfth day of the first month of Rabīʿ al-ʾAwwal, in the sixty-third year of his life, fourteen days after he began to grow ill.

After Muhammad died, all those who had been deceived by him returned immediately to the sect they had followed before, whether it was idolatry or something else, except for a few of his kinsmen, who hoped to succeed his kingship. During that time there was a prudent and clever man called ʾAbū Bakr b. ʾAbī Quḥāfa, who acquired the kingdom not much later. This greatly displeased ʿAlī b. ʾAbī Ṭālib, until the king assuaged him with indulgences and favors, even to the point of bequeathing the kingdom to him. With every kind of device and trick, he even brought back those who had turned away from Muhammad's sect, once again enslaving them to foolishness. Some returned out of fear, some out of hope for honor and riches, others for any other kind of profit—all, however, with feigned and insincere intentions. 85

I think you (may God save you) remember very well what my lord the *ʾamīr al-muʾminīn* once said in front of everyone when we were in his presence and some people issued a complaint about a man who appeared to be a Saracen yet was not. He said the following: "I am surprised that you report to me about this man alone, as if it is something unheard of, even though I know that he is not the only one, but that there are many more noble and upright men in my palace who are not Saracen. Indeed, all present themselves 86

Ostendunt quidem se esse sed non sunt. Est enim, inquit, mos paene omnium ut, sicut de Iudaeo proverbium dicit: Iudaeus nisi postquam efficitur Saracenus Iudaeus non est; vix aliquis suam legem, nisi prius aliam acceperit, diligat.

87 "Ego autem de hoc quid aliud debeo vel possum facere quam quod dominus meus Mahumet ipse faciebat? Nam illi hoc etiam contigit ut fere omnes et maxime, qui ei proximiores et familiares esse videbantur, non nisi deceptorie et simulate legem eius tenerent, adeo enim spernebatur ab eis et quicquid dicebat pro nihilo habebant, odientes eum in cordibus suis, ut quadam die volentes eum occidere expectarent in quadam valle, quatinus transeunte illo terrificarent subito mulam eius ut praecipitatus interiret. Qui tamen numquam propter hoc eis se iratum monstravit. Eius igitur exemplo omnes istos qui, sive de Christianis sive de Iudaeis sive de paganis, Saracenos se esse dicunt in regno meo et non sunt, numquam ad aliud cogam. Scio namque quod nullus Christianus qui timore Saracenus fit in Saracenitate permanebit, similiter et de aliis sentio. Quid ergo amplius possum facere? Videat Deus et iudicet. Hoc solum faciam ut semper maledicam eis." Haec quidem ille ita dixit te ipso praesente et audiente, quod tanto melius te recordari puto quanto recentius et paene nuper hoc ab ipso dictum, omnes qui erant in palatio audierunt.

88 Vita vero Mahumeth, de qua superius dicebamus, sexaginta tribus annis extitit, quorum in prophetia viginti tres expendit: decem in Mecha, tredecim in Civitate. Haec omnia, quae de ipso retuli, tu ipse melius nosti, utpote qui ab

as Saracens, yet they are not. This is customary," he said, "among nearly all men, just as the proverb about the Jew goes: a Jew is not a Jew until after he becomes a Saracen; almost nobody likes his own religion, unless he has first accepted another one.

"As for me, what should I, or can I, do in this situation, 87
other than what my lord Muhammad himself did? It happened that nearly everyone, and especially those who seemed to be the closest and most friendly to him, only held to their religion in a deceitful and feigned manner; in fact, they despised him and disdained everything he said to such an extent that they, filled with hate for him in their hearts, wished to kill him, and one day lay in ambush for him in a certain valley, in order to frighten his mule as soon as he passed by, so that he would be thrown headlong to his death. Regardless, he did not act angry toward them. In accordance with his example, I will never force anyone in my kingdom who claims to be a Saracen but is not—whether this concerns Christians, Jews, or pagans—to be something else. For I know that no Christian who becomes a Saracen out of fear will remain in the Saracen faith—and likewise with other religions. What more can I do? Let God consider and judge. The only thing I will do is curse them forever." He said this in these words, while you were present and listening, and I believe you will remember this all the better because all who were in the palace heard these words spoken recently and only just the other day.

The life of Muhammad, about which I have spoken 88
above, lasted for sixty-three years, twenty-three of which he spent as a prophet: ten years in Mecca, thirteen in Medina. All that I have reported, you yourself know even better,

illo edoctus es qui ista omnia transtulit, cum transtulisset Legem. Haec sunt quae fecit Mahumet a principio usque ad finem.

89 Sed iterum si forte dixeris non debuisse me reprehendere illum si proelia commisit, si se aliquando vindicavit, cum hoc inveniantur fecisse Iosue et ceteri multi prophetae, scias aliud esse quod fit praecipiente Deo, aliud quod homo praesumit. Deus enim hoc illis praecipiebat, de cuius praecepto quodcumque sit, quandocumque sit, ubicumque sit, non licet homini iudicare. Ergo, inquis, nec Mahumet debet hinc reprehendi, siquidem et illi talia Deus praecepit. Unde tamen probas quod Deus illi praecepit? Deus enim ille, si Deus fuit, in aliquo se Deum esse ostendere debuit. Secundum ea vero quae superius ostendimus, nec signis nec miraculis hoc ostendit.

90 Nos igitur illum Deum fuisse non credimus, nam, si Deus esset, numquam sine miraculis legem daret. Quod enim de Deo credimus, tam in Novo quam in Veteri Testamento, signis et miraculis nobis commendatum et confirmatum est, nec alium umquam pro Deo habebimus nisi illum unum et verum qui, quotiens legem dare voluit, signis hanc divinis et mirabilibus confirmavit. Propheta vero tuus quis fuerit vel unde venerit nescio, cum dicatur mihi a Domino meo Iesu Christo quod in Iohanne Baptista finis sit omnium prophetarum.

91 Illud quoque prudentiae tuae nullo pacto convenire arbitror quod invitare me voluisti ut scilicet dimitterem sacrosancta et spiritualia Domini mei Iesu Christi praecepta, ex

since you were taught by the person who compiled all of those stories, after he had compiled the Law. From beginning to end, these are the things that Muhammad did.

However, if you were to say that I should not criticize a man for fighting battles if he has justified himself, since Joshua and many other prophets can be found to have done so, you should know that it is one thing for something to happen because God orders it, but another thing entirely for man to take it upon himself. For it was God who gave them the command, and it is not up to man to judge it, no matter the command, or when or where it is issued. You say that for this reason Muhammad, too, should not be criticized, since God commanded him. Yet how do you prove that it was God who commanded him? That God, if God he was, ought to have revealed himself to be God in some way. In accordance with what I have demonstrated above, he did not do so either with signs or with miracles. 89

For this reason, we do not believe that he was God, for, if he had been God, he would never have given a law without miracles. Indeed, that which we believe about God, both in the Old and the New Testament, has been entrusted to us and confirmed with signs and miracles, and we will never consider anyone else to be God except for the one and true God, who, whenever he wished to issue a law, confirmed it with divine and miraculous signs. Concerning your prophet, on the other hand, I have no idea who he is or where he comes from, since it was said to me by the Lord Jesus Christ that John the Baptist was the last of all prophets. 90

I also do not think that it befits your sound judgment to wish to invite me to leave behind the sacred and spiritual teachings of my Lord Jesus Christ, in which he does not 91

quibus ipse mihi non illam sordidissimam, quam descripsisti, paradisum tuam, sed aeternam angelorum vitam in caelestibus promittit, et accederem ad impurissimos et pecuales ritus, non a Deo—quod absit!—immo a spiritu fornicationis et castrimargiae miserrimis et carnalis faeculentiae servis infelicissimis persuasos, quorum, sicut de similibus Paulus Apostolus dicit, *"Deus venter est et gloria in confusione ipsorum,"* qui nonnisi terrena, caduca, ventri et libidini congruentia sapiunt nec sapere possunt. Excaecavit enim eos spiritus inmunditiae, qui aeternam putredinem et vermes immortales hereditabunt, quia porcorum more semper in stercore et foetore libidinis volutantur.

92 Ego enim mirari non sufficio quomodo persuaderi potuerit non dico alicui sapienti, sed vel qui per somnium aliquid humani cordis se habere putaret, istum fuisse prophetam, cum eius et vita et doctrina ita contraria sint non solum divinae religioni, verum etiam humanae honestati, ut ipsa quoque bruta animalia paene hoc intelligere possint. Sed ut iterum aliquid mitius dicamus, quis umquam sanctorum et divinorum nuntiorum quos a Deo missos esse cognovimus, in terrore gladii se missum asseruit? Quis ita facinorose vixit? Quis denique tantas spurcitias docuit? Aut quis ita ventri et libidini genus humanum prostituit?

93 Iterum tamen ad praecepta eius diligentius inspicienda revertamur, quae ego nescio ad quam legem pertinere videantur. Duas enim leges a Deo accepimus: unam gratiae, alteram iustitiae. Lex gratiae a Christo data est, lex iustitiae a Mose. Lex gratiae talia iubet: diligite inimicos vestros, bene-

promise me that most foul paradise of yours, but instead the eternal life of angels in the heavens, and to wish me to adopt the most unclean and beastly rites, enjoined on the most miserable and most unhappy servants of carnal filth not by God—far be it!—but rather by the spirit of fornication and gluttony, "whose God is their belly, and whose glory is in their shame," as the apostle Paul says about similar people, who know only earthly, fleeting things, fit for their belly and their lust, and cannot possess true knowledge. The spirit of uncleanliness has blinded them; they will inherit eternal rot and undying maggots, since they perpetually wallow like pigs in the mire and stench of lust.

I cannot but wonder how anyone—not just a wise man, 92
but even someone who thought, as in a dream, that he had some semblance of human prudence—could have been persuaded that this man was a prophet, since both his life and teachings are so opposed not only to divine religion, but also to human honesty, that even brute animals could almost perceive this. However, to speak a little less harshly, which one of the holy and divine messengers, of whom we are certain that they have been sent by God, has ever claimed to have been sent as a terror with a sword? Which one of them has lived such a criminal life? Who, finally, has taught such filth? Or who has prostituted the human race in such a way to gluttony and lust?

Let us return, however, to analyzing his teachings in more 93
detail—teachings of which I have no idea to which law they seem to belong. For there are two laws that we have received from God: one of grace, the other of justice. The law of grace was given by Christ, the law of justice by Moses. The law of grace commands the following: love your enemies, do

facite his qui vos oderunt, et cetera huiusmodi. Lex iustitiae oculum pro oculo, dentem pro dente, usturam pro ustura, percussuram pro percussura, et cetera quae ad talionem pertinent reddi imperat. Harum duarum nullam socii tui esse manifestum est. Multo enim antequam ipse emergeret, una a Christo, altera a Mose data est.

94 Cum igitur istae duae tantummodo leges hominibus datae sint, quarum altera divina, altera humana magis esse videtur, ista tertia lex a socio tuo inventa, quid erit nisi diabolica? Diabolo enim inspirante, maxime hanc subito nescio unde emersisse cognoscimus, quae nec humana nec divina esse probatur. Sed inter utrumque prodigiosa facie nunc hoc nunc illud videri volens et se nunc illam nunc istam esse confingens, nullum alium nisi diabolum, qui se inter Deum et homines semper medium facere nisus est, imitatur.

95 Sed forsitan dices inde probari hanc legem esse divinam, quia, cum Mahumet idiota et sine litteris esset, nullatenus eam scribere vel annuntiare hominibus nisi divina virtute potuisset. Maxime cum ipse ibi dicat quia nec homines nec diabolus talem scripturam facere possint. Et iterum: *"Si in aliquo de hac lege dubitatis, producite testes vestros absque Deo et conferte sententias cum sententiis."* Et iterum: *"Si hanc legem fecissemus descendere super montem, inclinaret se mons ipse et adoraret eam prae timore Dei."* Et alia multa frivola et nihil rationis habentia, quae tu aperta et manifesta signa prophetiae socii tui esse dicis, quibus probetur esse vera. O signa mirabilia in istis verbis Mahumet! O signa comparanda Mari Rubro diviso

well unto those who hate you, etc. The law of justice commands that an eye be given for an eye, a tooth for a tooth, a burn for a burn, a blow for a blow, and so forth about matters that pertain to retribution. It is clear that neither of these two laws is that of your companion. One was given by Christ, the other was given by Moses long before he arose.

Since therefore only those two laws were given to human- 94
kind, of which one is divine, the other seemingly more human, why should this third law, invented by your friend, be anything but diabolical? Indeed, this law especially we understood to have come about suddenly from some place or other at the devil's instigation, since it is proven to be neither human nor divine. Wishing to appear now as this one, now as that one, unnaturally in between both, and shaping itself in the likeness now of one, now of the other, it imitates none other than the devil, who has always attempted to hold the middle ground between God and mankind.

Perhaps you will say this law is proven to be divine on ac- 95
count of the fact that Muhammad, being uneducated and unlettered, could not have written it down or proclaimed it to mankind without divine power, especially since he himself states that neither man nor the devil could fabricate such scripture. Elsewhere he states: "If you doubt this law in any way, bring forth your witnesses, apart from God, and compare their statements." Elsewhere: "If I had let this law descend to the top of a mountain, then even the mountain would have prostrated itself and venerated it for fear of God." There are many other such paltry and irrational statements, which you claim to be clear and manifest signs of the truthfulness of your friend's prophetic vocation. O what miraculous signs are in those words of Muhammad! Signs

et soli ad imperium Iosue stanti et Christi praecepto mortibus imperanti! Immo vere magna tam veritatis quam virtutis inopia, quae tibi haec sola argumenta, immo deliramenta, omni ratione et virtute vacua dereliquit.

96 Verumtamen ne solis verbis agere videamur, non tibi, quaeso, sit grave si in certamine positi dicamus quod quidem non modo tibi placeat sed forsitan, Deo volente, postmodum prodesse valeat. Grave namque infirmo est cum vulnus aperitur, sed postea gratum esse incipit, cum sanitas inde consequitur. Ita enim tu loqueris quasi nescias vel numquam audieris unde et quomodo vel per quem prophetae tui mysteria exordium habuerint. Nullo enim modo quicquid tu dicas ignorare te crediderim, quod dicere volo et quod aliis ut cognoscant expono; tibi autem ut recognoscas ad mentem reduco.

97 Tu igitur (quem Deus salvet!) noli dissimulare, sed, sicut audisti, recognosce quia Sergius monachus, cum in monasterio graviter peccasset et propter hoc excommunicatus et expulsus fuisset, venit ad regionem Tuhemiae, et exinde usque ad Mecham descendens, ubi erant duo populi, unus cultor idolorum et alter Iudaicus, invenit ibi Mahumet, qui colebat idola. Volensque aliquid facere unde monachis illis qui eum expulerant placeret et reconciliari mereretur (erant enim haeretici Nestoriani, qui dicunt Mariam non peperisse

worthy of comparison with the parting of the Red Sea and the sun standing still at Joshua's command and Christ's command to the dead to rise up! On the contrary, it is a truly great dearth of both truth and virtue that has left you with only these arguments—or rather delusions devoid of all reason and virtue.

However, so as not to appear to be merely debating, do 96
not take offense if in the heat of battle I say something that might not only please you, but perhaps, God willing, also have the potential to benefit you afterward. Indeed, it is painful for an injured person to have his wound opened, but afterward, when his health is restored by the procedure, it begins to be agreeable to him. You speak in such a way as if you do not know or have never heard from where or how or through whom your prophet's mysteries found their beginning. In no way whatsoever, whatever you may say, would I believe you to be ignorant of the things I wish to say, and which I tell others in order that they may be aware; however, so that you might take cognizance of them once again, I will remind you of them.

You then (may God save you) should not pretend not to 97
know, but just as you have heard, should take notice again of the fact that, after he had sinned grievously in his monastery and had been excommunicated and driven away because of this, the monk Sergius came to the region of Tihāma and went down all the way to Mecca, where there were two peoples, one of idolaters and the other Jewish, and that he found Muhammad there, who was an idolater. Wishing to perform some deed by which he might regain the favor of the monks who had driven him out (for they were Nestorian heretics, who claim that Mary did not give birth to God but only to a

Deum nisi hominem tantum), omni studio et conamine persuadebat ei ut ab idolis recederet et Christianus Nestorianus esset. Quod cum effectui mancipasset, discipulus eius factus est Mahumet, et ille se propter hoc Nestorium nuncupavit. Et ita factum est ut ab isto monacho aliqua de Veteri et Novo Testamento edoctus, ipsa in Alcorano suo fabulose et mendose intexeret. Hoc etiam ille persuasit ut in Alcorano poneret dictum a Deo quod monachi et presbyteri Christiani familiariores ei esse deberent, quia non superbiunt.

98 Cum vero cognovissent Iudaei quod multi et etiam ipse Mahumet ad qualemcumque quasi umbram Christianitatis illum monachum sequerentur et paene illud, quod postea factum est per Mahumet, per istum Nestorium iam consummatum esset, prosilierunt tres longe superius a nobis commemorati Iudaei, id est, Vheben, filius Muniae, Abdalla filius Celemin et Chabin, qui cognominabatur Alhahabarc. Et timentes ne in veram Christianitatem quandoque Mahumet incideret, accesserunt ad eum et malitiosa calliditate socios vel discipulos eius se esse in hac secta dicentes, eique omnia, quae turpia vel nequiora in Alcorano sunt, scribere persuadentes, usque ad finem eius cum eo semper fuerunt.

99 Post mortem vero Mahumet, cum, sicut diximus, unusquisque redisset ad sectam suam et successisset in regno Ebubecr, Hali quoque, filius Abitalib, licet nobilior eo sub ipso maneret. Praedicti Iudaei, volentes iterum turbare omnia, persuadebant Hali dicentes: "Quare, cum sis fortis et nobilis, non te in prophetam elevas sicut fecit socius tuus

human), he persuaded Muhammad with all zeal and effort to denounce the idols and to be a Nestorian Christian. When he accomplished this, Muhammad became his disciple, and because of this Sergius called himself Nestorius. And so it happened that Muhammad, having been taught some things from the Old and New Testaments, interwove them in a fantastic and deceptive way into his Qur'ān. He also persuaded Muhammad to insert a saying of God into the Qur'ān that monks and Christian priests should be on more friendly terms with him, since they are not proud.

When the Jews found out that many people, as well as 98
Muhammad himself, were following that monk as if he were some kind of shadow of Christianity, and that that which was later accomplished by Muhammad was nearly accomplished by that Nestorius, the three Jews whom I mentioned above stepped forth: Wahb b. Munabbih, ʿAbd Allāh b. Sallām, and Kaʿb, who was called al-'Aḥbār. Because they feared that at some point Muhammad would encounter true Christianity, they went to him and, in their wicked cunning, claimed that they were fellows or students of his in this sect, and persuaded him to write all of the scandalous and vile things in the Qur'ān, and they stayed with him continuously until his death.

However, after Muhammad's death, when, as I said ear- 99
lier, each had returned to his own sect and 'Abū Bakr had succeeded Muhammad's rule, ʿAlī b. 'Abī Ṭālib remained under 'Abū Bakr's rule, even though he was more noble. The aforementioned Jews, wishing to turn everything into chaos once again, attempted to persuade ʿAlī with the following words: "Since you are strong and noble, why do you not elevate yourself to the status of prophet as your companion

Mahumet, qui erat Christianus Nestorianus, et erimus tecum, sicut fuimus cum illo adiuvantes te in omnibus?" Ille autem, utpote iuvenis et totius bonae doctrinae expers, facile adquievit. Iam enim quasi ad hoc praedoctus fuerat, siquidem aliquando, cum puer esset et vagabundus, ut illius aetatis est, quadam die per aliqua devia incederet, Nestorii illius pseudomonachi latibulum, unde ab eo Mahumet furtim responsa dabantur, offendit. At ille, cum se deprehensum esse videret, puerum tam minis quam blandimentis induxit ut hoc nulli hominum proderet. Itaque iam paene ad hoc incipiendum declinaverat Hali. Sed rex Ebubecr, hoc comperto, iuvenem ad se venire mandavit. Quem cum venisset tantis blanditiis et promissionibus delinivit ut ab huiusmodi incepto omnino desisteret, seque illi subditum in omnibus exhiberet.

100 Iudaei tamen non cessaverunt facere quod potuerunt. Nam accepto libro ab ipso Hali, quem reliquerat ei Mahumet, quicquid sibi visum est aut addiderunt aut detraxerunt aut mutaverunt. Ex quibus illud est unum: *"Dicunt Iudaei: Christiani nihil sunt; dicunt Christiani: sed Iudaei stulti sunt."* Item inter alia multa et fabulosa illud capitulum, ubi est fabula de formica, et aliud, ubi est fabula de ape, et aliud ubi de aranea narratur.

101 Qualiter vero scriptura ista non solum a Iudaeis sed etiam a multis aliis varie excepta, diverse intellecta, multiformiter exposita et tandem tota paene dilacerata sit ex aliqua parte non propter te, qui haec omnia melius nosti, sed propter alios dicam. Post quadraginta dies vel, sicut alii volunt, post sex menses ex quo regnare coeperat Ebubecr, vocavit Hali filium Abitalib et dixit ei: "Quare praesens non fuisti,

Muhammad did, who was a Nestorian Christian? We will be on your side, just as we were on his, aiding you in every way." He, being young and without any proper instruction, easily acquiesced. Indeed, in a way he had already been told to do so before, since once, when he was a boy and, as is common with boys of such age, was wandering about in an abandoned area, he had stumbled upon the hiding place of that Nestorian pseudo-monk, from where he used to offer secretive responses when Muhammad consulted with him. When he saw that he had been discovered, he persuaded the boy, both with threats and charms, not to betray him to anyone. In this way, he had nearly already set ʿAlī on this course. King ʾAbū Bakr, however, when he learned of this, ordered the young man to come to him. When he did, he lavished such sweet promises upon him that he desisted from this course altogether, and acted as his subordinate in every way.

The Jews, however, did not cease to do as much as they 100
could. Taking the book from ʿAlī, which Muhammad had left to him, they added, removed, or changed whatever they wished. The following is one of those instances: "The Jews say: 'Christians are nothing.' Christians say: 'Jews are fools.'" Likewise, among the many other fabulous things, there is the chapter with the tale of the ant, and another with the tale of the bee, and another with that of the spider.

In what manner that scripture was variously received, 101
variously understood, expounded in manifold ways and nearly wholly torn apart, not only by Jews but also by many others, I will tell of in part, not for your benefit, since you know all of this better than I do, but for others. After forty days, or, as others have it, six months after ʾAbū Bakr began ruling, he called ʿAlī b. ʾAbī Ṭālib and said to him: "Why

quando factus sum rex, et non cum aliis nobis astitisti, cum sis magnus princeps noster et nobilis?" Respondit Hali: "Quia occupatus fui in colligenda scriptura, sicut iniunxit mihi propheta." Et iam collegerat Eleage, filius Iuzef, multos codices et diminuerat multa in illis, sicque ceteri multi. Quidam enim legebant secundum Hali, scilicet familia et domestici et propinquiores eius, illam scripturam quae fuerat apud Chorais et quae prima illius fuisse dicebatur, quam tradiderat ei Nestorius monachus, quem vocavit aliquando Gabrielem, aliquando spiritum fidelem.

102 Alii vero legebant collectum a diversis hominibus. Multi vero secundum Arabem quemdam venientem nuper de solitudine, qui multa inde scripserat absque sensu et ratione. Alii secundum Zahefatin et Azihbin, alii secundum Hatuhil Enhail, alii secundum Hazim Elquef, alii secundum alios. Qui omnes in membranis et rotulis, quod unicuique videbatur, transtulerant. Alii iterum secundum Iben Muzod, qui dicebat: "Quicumque vult habere Alchoran recentem et sicuti descendit, purum et inviolatum, quaerat exemplaria filii Umemabeth mulieris." Est enim illius exemplar, qui ostendebatur semel in anno Mahumet, et in anno quo mortuus est, bis. Alii secundum Hubei filium Hagb, quod paene simile erat exemplari Iben Muzod. Erant itaque varii inter se et discordes, dicebantque cum legerent ad alterutrum: "Ego melius quam tu, sed tu deterius quam ego, et ego totum habeo sed tu nihil, sed tu nihil et ego totum." Hoc igitur

were you not present when I was made king, and why did you not stand before us with the others, since you are noble and a great prince among our people?" ʿAlī responded: "Because I was busy compiling the scripture, as the prophet commanded me." Already al-Hajjāj b. Yūsuf had compiled many codices and suppressed much that was in them, and so had many others. For some people read that scripture in accordance with ʿAlī, that is, his family, his household, and his kinsmen; this is the scripture that was among the Quraysh and which is said to have been the first one of Muhammad, which the monk Nestorius had handed over to him, whom he sometimes called Gabriel, sometimes a faithful spirit.

Others, however, read what was gathered by different 102
persons. Many read in accordance with a certain Arab, who had recently come from the desert, who had written many things that lacked both sense and reason. Others read in accordance with Zahefatin and Azihbin, others in accordance with Hatuhil Enhail, others in accordance with Hazim Elquef, others in accordance with others. All of them transmitted the text on parchment and scrolls, as each deemed fit. Some read the version of Ibn Masʿūd, who said: "Whoever wishes to have the new Qurʾān, just as it came down from above, pure and inviolate, let him seek the copies of the son of the woman ʾUmm ʿAbd." It is the copy of the book that was displayed once a year to Muhammad, and twice in the year in which he died. Others read the version of ʾUbayy b. Kaʿb, which was nearly the same as the copy of Ibn Masʿūd. They differed, therefore, and were at variance, and when they read, they said to each other: "I am better than you are, and you are worse than I am, and I have everything and you nothing, and you have nothing and I

modo aliis addentibus, aliis minuentibus, aliis mutantibus, aliis alio quolibet modo corrumpentibus, liber ille omni fide indignus effectus est.

103 Denique mortuo Ebubecr et succedente sibi Ozmen, filio Hafen, cui insidiabatur Hali, filius Abitalib, et quaerebat eum interficere, cum perlatum fuisset ad regem de diversitate scripturae et assiduis contentionibus et rixis quae propter eam fiebant, dicerentque illi sapientiores timere se ne hac de causa seditiones et discidium orirentur in regno, maximeque ne ex toto scriptura illa periret, praecepit rex omnes libros et chartulas undecumque colligi, licet tamen Hali Abitalib et Iben Muzod libros suos dare noluerunt. Reliqui vero collecti dati sunt in manus Zeidi, filii Zebith Alenzari, et Abdalla, filii Alahabet, ad redigendum omnia in unum codicem et emendandum, dictumque est illis: "Si contigerit vos in aliquo capitulo non posse concordare, scribite illud secundum exemplar et auctoritatem Chorais."

104 Quod et ipsi fecerunt sicuti, verbi gratia, quando invenerunt in quodam loco *arcam* et alius dixit *arcem* et alius *arcam,* tandemque secundum id quod habebat Chorais dixerunt, sic et de multis aliis. Facientesque quattuor similes codices, unum miserunt in Mecham, alium in Syriam, alium Aleirac, alium reliquerunt in Civitate. Sed ille qui ad Mecham missus fuerat incendio periit quando vastata est Mecha ab Ozeraio. Ille vero qui in Civitate remansit in diebus Gezit, filii Maoia, perditus est. Tertius, qui in Aleirac erat, a tempore

everything." In this way, as some added things, others removed things, others changed things, and others corrupted the text in some other way, this book ended up being completely untrustworthy.

When ʾAbū Bakr had died and was succeeded by ʿUthmān 103
b. ʿAffān, whom ʿAlī b. ʾAbī Ṭālib was conspiring to kill, news of the divergences of the scripture and the constant arguments and bickering surrounding them was brought before the king, and those wisest said to him that they feared that uprisings and discord would arise in the kingdom on this account, and especially that the scripture would disappear entirely. The king gave the order to gather all the books and leaves of parchment, yet ʿAlī b. ʾAbī Ṭālib and Ibn Masʿūd refused to hand over their books. However, all the other books were brought into the hands of Zayd b. Thābit al-ʾAnṣārī and ʿAbd Allāh b. al-ʿAbbās, for them to emend and redact into a single codex. They were told: "If it should happen that you cannot find agreement in a particular *sūra,* write it in accordance with the authoritative exemplar of the Quraysh."

And they did this, as when, for example, in a particular 104
instance they found *arcam* ("chest") and another copy read *arcem* ("citadel") and another *arcam,* and so, in the end, they copied down in accordance with what the Quraysh version read, and likewise in many other instances. When they had made four identical codices, they sent one to Mecca, another to Syria, another to Iraq, and the remaining one they left in Medina. The copy that was sent to Mecca, however, was lost in a fire when the city was sacked by ʾAbū Sarāyā. The one that remained in Medina was lost during the rule of Yazīd b. Muʿāwiya. The third copy, which was in Iraq, never

Almustar nusquam comparuit. Rex autem Ozmen, qui libros illos praeceperat fieri, quaecumque remanserunt in chartis praecepit comburi.

105 Ex his igitur varietatibus et mutationibus quae superius dictae sunt, contigit ut multa ibi capitula diversa inter se et sibi invicem contraria inveniantur, sicut, verbi causa, *Capitulum Bovis* et *Capitulum Vaccae,* de quibus dicitur quod *Capitulum Bovis* ante fuerit prolixius *Capitulo Vaccae,* nunc vero brevius. Dicitur etiam *Capitulum Sententiarum* corruptum esse et imperfectum. *Capitulum* quoque *Barathi* et *Elanfel* olim sine interpositione dicuntur fuisse; interpositionem dico quae ita ad initium uniuscuiusque capituli habetur: "In nomine Dei misericordis et miseratoris." Dicit quoque filius Muzod quod partes ibi quae dicuntur Mahuzeten a nescioquibus postea additae sint. Gomar vero cuidam qui multa inibi corruperat et abstulerat ita maledicit: "Non sit," inquit, "immunis a peccato qui hoc vel illud abstulit." Deinde sic prosequitur: "Quid enim nocebat ei, si Deus facile agebat cum hominibus? Venit enim Mahumet in lege spatiosa et lata." Et iterum dicit Hubei duo capitula inde ablata esse, *Capitulum Chonotu,* id est, orationis cuiusdam, et *Capitulum Almothati.* Sed de *Capitulo Almothati* dicitur quod Hali abstulerit illud. Dixit etiam Aissa, uxor Mahumet, Hali non istud solum sed multa alia abstulisse et paene totum demutasse, insuper prohibuisse homines ne legerent Alchoran, et propter hoc multos saepe verberasse.

106 Post multa iterum tempora Elehegeig, filius Iuzef, cum

appeared again after the rule of al-Mukhtār. King ʿUthmān, who had ordered those books to be made, ordered that whatever remained in leaves of parchment be burned to ashes.

Now it happens that, of those variants and changes men- 105
tioned above, many sūras are found to be different and at odds with one another, as, for example, the *Sūra of the Ox* and the *Sūra of the Cow,* of which it is said that the *Sūra of the Ox* was once longer than that of the *Cow,* but now it is shorter. It is also said that the *Sūra of Sentences* is damaged and incomplete. It is also said that once there was no separation between the *Sūrat al-ʾAʿrāf* and the *Sūrat al-ʾAnfāl;* I mean the separation that occurs at the beginning of each sūra, like so: "In the name of the compassionate and the merciful." Moreover, Ibn Masʿūd asserts that the sections called *al-muʿawwidhatān* were added later by someone or other. Indeed, ʿUmar curses a certain person who had corrupted and removed much from there, in the following manner: "Let not the one," says he, "who removed this or that be free from sin." He continues: "What disadvantage is it to him, if God acts kindly toward humans? For Muhammad came with a broad and wide religion." Again, ʿUbayy asserts that two sūras were removed from there, the *Sūrat al-Qunūt,* a certain person's prayer, and the *Sūrat al-Mutʿa.* However, it is said that ʿAlī was the one who removed the *Sūrat al-Mutʿa.* Even ʿĀʾisha, Muhammad's wife, claims that ʿAlī removed not only that passage but also many others, and almost completely altered the whole text, and, in addition, forbade men to read the Qurʾān, and that he often had many people whipped because of this.

When, after many years, al-Hajjāj b. Yūsuf began to rule, 106

regnare coepisset, iussit congregari omnes libros et chartas et volumina, confectoque ex eis uno codice ad suum libitum, postquam multa adiecit, multa detraxit, multa variavit, cetera omnia ubicumque invenirentur iussit incendi. Tunc et ille liber, quem superius in Syria remansisse retulimus, pariter combustus est. Voluit enim rex Elehegeig in hoc imitari Ozmen filium Hafen, cum esset probus et studiosior omnibus, licet curvus esset statura et gibbosus. Fecit autem de suo libro sex exemplaria, ex quibus unum misit in Aegyptum, alterum in Syriam, alterum in Civitatem, alterum in Mecham, alterum in Mesopotamiam, alterum in Albazara. Aliquando etiam venerunt ad istos multi de gente Elnehbeti, qui idolatrae erant, et simulantes se velle esse Saracenos ut legem eorum, si possent, adnihilarent, multa nihilominus in praedicta scriptura, ubicumque latenter poterant, modis omnibus lacerabant.

107 Quod si nulla alia varietatis huius scripturae causa fuisse videretur quam quod illi a quibus habebatur (scilicet, Hali et Ebubecr et Ozmen et Gomar) semper discordes fuerunt et inimici, sufficeret, dum pro certo constat singulos eorum pro sua intentione alterum adversus alterum in libro suo iuxta propriam voluntatem quicquid sibi placuit ad suae causae commodum vel addidisse vel minuisse vel variasse. Haec igitur et his similia, quae non a nobis vel a quibuslibet sed a maturis et doctis et veracibus viris qui omnia subtiliter et longo tempore investigaverant habemus, satis evidenter omni rationabili homini ostendunt quam nulla fide vel

he had all books, leaves of parchment, and scrolls gathered up and made into a single codex, and, at his own discretion, added, removed, and altered much, and had all remnants that could be found burned. It was at this time that the book that remained in Syria, as described above, was reduced to ashes along with the others. With this, King al-Hajjāj wished to follow in the footsteps of ʿUthmān b. ʿAffān, since he was morally upright and more learned than all the rest, despite having a curved stature and a hump. From his own copy he had six other copies made, one of which he sent to Egypt, another to Syria, another to Medina, another to Mecca, another to Mesopotamia, and another to Baṣra. At some point many of the Elnehbeti tribe, who were idolaters, arrived and pretended that they wished to become Saracens, in order that, if given the chance, they might reduce their law to nothing, and they mutilated much of the aforementioned scripture in every possible way, whenever they could do so unobtrusively.

Even if there would appear to be no reason for altering 107
this scripture other than that the people who were in possession of it (that is to say, ʿAlī, ʾAbū Bakr, ʿUthmān, and ʿUmar) were enemies and continuously at odds with one another, that would be sufficient. For it is certain that each of them added, removed, or changed at his own discretion, each in opposition with another, whatever he wished in his own copy to promote his own cause. These and similar things I have come by, not of my own invention or from just any person or other, but from experienced, learned, and truthful men, who have looked into the matter in detail and over a long period of time. To any rational human being they demonstrate with sufficient proof how little faith and

reverentia digna sit haec scriptura quae totiens aucta, totiens minuta, totiens innovata, totiens variata, totiens mutata, totiens dilacerata probatur. Viri certe probi Saraceni et qui satis inde dolebant mihi saepius hoc dixerunt quod tota Alcorani scriptura adeo commixta et confusa sit ut quicquid ibi est totum sine continuatione, sine compositione, absque omni verborum ordine, postremo absque ullo sensu vel ratione esse videatur, unde iterum atque iterum mirari non cesso te de hac scriptura dixisse quod talis nec ab hominibus nec a daemonibus fieri possit.

108 Nam si dixeris quia clara est in extraneis et exquisitis partibus, O quam scias scripturas Graecas clariores esse in suo eloquio, Hebraeas in suo, Latinas in suo, et de ceteris similiter. Si enim clara et copiosa est, ut tu dicis, quid necesse fuit ibi ex aliis linguis partes plurimas apponere, cum Arabicus sermo dives sit in omnium rerum nominibus? Quid faciunt illic verba Persica et barbara, ut est *elestebric,* vestimentum purpureum, et *taceit,* quae sunt conchae, et *abeiric,* quod est urceus, et multa talia?

109 Patet certe solam imperitiam et rusticitatem illi impedimento fuisse, cum Arabica lingua abundet in omnibus et ipse aliarum linguarum nomina emendicata ibi posuerit. Seque ipsum in hoc mendacissimum probat, cum postea dicatur ibi a Deo: *"Nos fecimus descendere Alchoran in puro sermone Arabico."* Miror autem quid illic tibi placere possit;

reverence this scripture is worth, since it is proven to have been augmented, abbreviated, renewed, changed, altered, and mutilated so often. Indeed, strict Saracens who were quite upset about this have frequently indicated to me that the entire scripture of the Qurʾān had been interpolated and jumbled to such an extent that everything in it appears to be without sequence, without arrangement, and lacking in any kind of ordered arrangement of words, and indeed, lacking in any kind of sense or logic. This is why, time and time again, I am continually amazed that you, speaking about this scripture, have asserted that such a scripture could not have been created either by humans or by demons.

If you were to say that this scripture is splendid in some unrepresentative and choice passages,—O!—you should know how much more splendid Greek scripture is in its own eloquence, and likewise the Hebrew and the Latin scriptures in their own eloquence. If it is splendid and rich, as you say, why was it necessary to bring to it so many expressions from other languages, since the Arabic language is rich in terms for all manner of things? What is the purpose of those Persian and barbaric words, as, for example, *al-istabraq,* a purple garment, and *taceit,* which are seashells, and *ʾabārīq,* which is a pitcher, and many other such things? 108

Certainly, it is clear that only lack of skill and education impeded Muhammad, since the Arabic language is plentiful in all things, because he himself inserted in it words borrowed from other languages. And he proves himself to be utterly untruthful, for afterward it is said by God: "I have made the Qurʾān descend in the pure Arabic language." I wonder what in it could be pleasing to you; for nobody has 109

nam, si eloquentia consideretur, nemo tam turpiter aliquid Arabice scripsit. Quantum enim ad sapientes Arabicos scriptores et praecipue ad poetam Amruhalcaiz, quem ipse etiam valde laudabat, et ad poetam Hannabiga vel ad alios multos, quid est totum Alchoran nisi digna risu barbaries?

110 Si vero sententiae perpendantur, ego nihil ibi video, si tamen esse potest aliquid, boni. Nam mala illic reperiri multa non dubium est, quod vel quilibet stultus similiter aut certe multo elegantius fingere non possit. Esto tamen, bona ibi videntur esse aliqua, sicuti, verbi gratia, ut aliquando ieiunetur, oretur, et ut fiant aliquae elemosinae. Et, O novitas rerum, nunc primum talia inventa sunt a Mahumet qualia, scilicet, ante ipsum nullus audierat. O quanto sanctius, quanto honestius, quanto rationabilius et Moses et Helias et alii prophetarum multi, Iohannes quoque Baptista, sed et ipse Dominus omnium Iesus Christus et ieiunaverunt et oraverunt et misericordias impenderunt, nosque ieiunare et orare et elemosinam dare ante prodigiosam prophetiam Mahumet infinitis retro temporibus docuerunt. Cesset, cesset Mahumet earum rerum velle videri magister primus, quarum nec dignus fuit in aliquo discipulus esse vel ultimus. Absit, absit a nobis talis praedicator ieiunii, qui post monstruosum ieiunium, sic omni libidini et ingluviei operam impendere praecipit ut non ad aliud videatur instituisse ieiunium quam ut postea voluptuosius et appetentius exerceatur omnium turpitudo libidinum.

111 Iam vero illud quod et tu mihi dixisti et ipse prius in eadem scriptura praedicavit, hanc scilicet scripturam talem

written anything in Arabic so foul in terms of eloquence. In comparison with the Arabic sages and especially the poet Imru' al-Qays, whom Muhammad himself praised greatly, and the poet Hannabiga, or many others, what is the entire Qur'ān but a laughable barbarity?

If, however, the ideas of the Qur'ān are considered, I see nothing good in it, if indeed it is possible for it to have any at all. It is without doubt that there are many evils that can be found in it, which any fool could come up with in a similar, and certainly much more eloquent, manner. Granted, there appear to be some good things in it, as, for example, that one ought to fast sometimes, that one should pray, and that some charity should be performed. What novelty! Now, for the first time, these things are invented by Muhammad, things which, indeed, nobody had heard before him. How much more piously, honorably, and reasonably did Moses, Elijah and many other prophets, as well as John the Baptist, but also Jesus Christ, Lord of all, fast, pray, and dispense mercy, and indeed teach us all to fast, pray, and perform charity, uncountable ages before that marvelous prophecy of Muhammad! Let him cease, cease to wish to appear to be the first teacher of such things, in any aspect of which he was not even worthy to be the last student! Let that type of preacher of fasting be far, far away from us! After an inhuman fast he taught that one should expend such attention on one's appetite and gluttony that he appears to have only instituted the fast in order that the foulness of every appetite might afterward be fulfilled with more pleasure and lust. 110

Now, with regard to what you said to me, and which Muhammad, too, said before in that same scripture, namely that this scripture is such that it cannot have been created 111

esse qualis nec ab hominibus nec a daemonibus fieri potest, certe satis ipse elegit quibus hoc diceret, rusticissimos videlicet et agrestes homines, qui et noviter de diversis sectis ad eum venerant, ipsamque etiam linguam Arabicam ignorabant. Ceterum, si hoc nobis exponere liceat, per omnia sic ei concedimus quod vere tam stulta, tam inhonesta tamque irrationabilis scriptura nec ab hominibus nec a daemonibus fieri potest. Puto enim quod etiam daemones talia scribere erubescerent.

112 Sane si tantum vult Mahumet gloriari de suo Alcorano, quanto magis gloriari possent alii quidam, quos te ignorare non puto, Muzeilema Helaifi et Aethiops Alahazbi et Talhata Ellecedi, qui eodem tempore aemulatione illius, ut et ipsi nomen sibi apud homines compararent, suum quisque Alcoranum fecerunt multoque honestiora et saltem in aliquo verisimilia conscripserunt. Sed quia non ex toto ventri et libidini frena laxabant, non tantos bestialium hominum greges asininos post se trahere potuerunt. Verumtamen rogo te ne, si aliquid liberius dixero et tibi expressius loqui voluero, arrogantiae hoc vel malitiae imputes.

113 Videtur enim mihi quod in scriptura Mahumet nihil aliud iam remanserit quod tibi placere debeat nisi forte illa consonantia, quae nescio quomodo alicuius gravitatis viro vel admirationi sit vel amori. Nam, ut eam pro nihilo habendam certissime noveris, mihi crede, cui dedit Deus inter alia per suam gratiam ut nemo magis Arabicae linguae morem et

either by humans or demons: he himself selected the people to whom he might say this, the simplest men and country folk, who had recently joined him from various sects and did not know the Arabic language. Furthermore, if I may be allowed to expatiate on this matter, in every aspect I concede to him that truly such a foolish, dishonest, and illogical scripture cannot have been created either by humans or demons. I think that even demons would be ashamed to write such things.

Indeed, if Muhammad wishes to take so much pride in 112
his Qurʾān, how much more pride could certain others take—I think you know them well: Musaylima l-Ḥanafī, al-ʿAnasī the Ethiopian, and Ṭulayḥa l-Asadī? Each of them created his own Qurʾān in the same period, in competition with him, so that they, too, might acquire a name for themselves among humankind, and they wrote much more honorably, or at least in some way truthfully. Yet, since they did not give complete free rein to gluttony and lust, they were unable to lead behind them such great asinine herds of beastly humans. In any case, I ask that you do not attribute it to arrogance or ill will if I speak too freely, or if I wish to speak to you too urgently.

It seems to me that there is now nothing left in the scrip- 113
ture of Muhammad that you ought to like—except, perhaps, its musicality, but I do not know how this could be a reason for wonder and appreciation to a man of any dignity. And that you might know all the more that this scripture deserves to be considered worthless, believe me, for through his grace, God has bestowed it upon me, among other things, that no other man has acquired a greater understanding of the nature of the Arabic language and all the

omnem quae in ea est vim sermonum et elegantiam assecutus sit. Hoc enim et ipsa patria nostra et civitas ab antiquo semper obtinuit ut neque Corais neque alia quaelibet Arabiae regio in aliqua sive linguae sive scientiae sive morum urbanitate se umquam illi comparare potuerit.

114 Nam et ipsi nobiles Chorais nostrorum filias civium olim uxores habere adeo pro magno ducebant ut ipse quoque Mahumet quartamdecimam uxorem inde acciperet, filiam Noem Alquindiam. Quae adversus eum propter stultitiam et insaniam eius aliquando irata, sic locuta fuisse refertur: "Modo," inquit, "praepostero ordine, filiae nobilium sub mercatoribus et mercennariis Corais, heu pro dolor, devenerunt!" Scias igitur quod apud Arabes consonantiae huiusmodi magis in usu sunt, utpote qui semper carminibus et poeticis cantilenis studere consueverunt. Unde nec mirandum est si Mahumet aliquid tale componere potuit, quod fere omnes tam nobiles quam ignobiles facere leve quid et quasi pro nihilo ducunt.

115 Si autem miraris quare tantum quibusdam haec scriptura placuerit, pro certo teneas nulli umquam nobili vel sapienti eam placuisse, sed miserrimo et imperitissimo vulgarium hominum generi, qui ab eo de locis silvestribus congregati, cum has primas litteras audissent, rei novitate stupefacti sacrilegas fabulas divina esse oracula crediderunt. Denique, cum et paupertate et assiduo ruralium operum labore confecti fuissent, cibi et potus, pretiosarum vestium, umbrosae

virtue and elegance of its idiom. For since antiquity my homeland and city has held on to the fact that neither the Quraysh nor any other region of Arabia has been able to match it in refinement of language, knowledge, or morals.

Indeed, long ago even the nobles of the Quraysh consid- 114
ered it so valuable to have the daughters of our citizens as their wives that even Muhammad took his fourteenth wife from among them, the daughter of al-Nuʿmān, of the tribe of Kinda. She is reported to have spoken to him in the following manner, angry with him because of his foolishness and madness: "Now, in a reversal of the normal order of things, the daughters of noblemen have ended up with the merchants and mercenaries of the Quraysh—how miserable!" You should know that among the Arabs harmonies of this kind are more commonly used, for they have always been accustomed to cultivate the diligent study of poems and poetic songs. For this reason it is not surprising that Muhammad was able to compose something of this kind, since nearly everyone—both nobles and those of low birth—considers to do so a facile and almost worthless feat.

If you wonder why some people liked this scripture so 115
much, you should know that it was never liked by anyone who was noble or wise, but only by the most miserable and ignorant sort of common folk, convened by Muhammad from forests, and when they heard these writings for the first time, they were amazed by the novelty and believed that these sacrilegious myths were divine prophecies. Moreover, since they were impoverished and exhausted from the toil of working the land, they swiftly followed Muhammad's every wish as though they were cattle when they heard about the blessings of food and drink, costly garments,

amoenitatis, vasorum spectabilium, uxorum insuper pulcherrimarum et infiniti concubitus aliarumque spurcissimi paradisi deliciarum, quas etiam te, pro dolor, enumerare non puduit, beatitudinem audientes seque ibi ex promissione Mahumet iam iamque futuros esse sperantes, ad omnia quaecumque voluit pecorini homines cucurrerunt. Inde est quod contra regem Persidis exiens sic adiutus est ab eis ut vinceret. Promiserat siquidem omnibus qui in bello ipso mori pro eo eligerent sui paradisi delicias. Quidam tamen magis idcirco pugnasse dicuntur ut hortos optimos quos in Perside viderant obtinerent, nam et illos se post victoriam daturum eis dixerat ut et in hoc saeculo et in futuro semper in hortis essent. Nosti autem Arabes quantum delectentur hortorum pulchritudine.

116 Sed dicis: "Non soli rustici illi sed et multi alii secuti sunt eum." Vere multi alii, sed pessimi et leccatores et qui, vel gravati aere alieno vel pro suis sceleribus morituri, hanc solam evadendi viam invenerant. Nam dic mihi, obsecro, quem umquam sapientem aut nobilem aut honestum ad Saracenitatem venire vidisti? Illi enim qui ex Iudaeis vel ex Christianis adhuc veniunt ad vos, absit ut aliqua provocati honestate hoc faciant; sed quia miseri et impudici legis suae regulas non ferentes ad latam et spatiosam viam, quam socius tuus docuit, se convertunt. Quod quibusdam maxime Christianis contingit, quorum lex caelestis et spiritualis omnia quae in mundo sunt contemni spe et amore visionis Dei aeternae praecipiens, dum carnales et fluxas infelicium mentes comprimit, statim ab ea diffugiunt, quia pugnare contra concupiscentias negligunt.

lovely shade, wondrous dishes, and on top of that the most beautiful women and endless sexual encounters, and other delights of this filthy paradise, and they were given hope by him that, any moment now, they would be there. Even you—how shameful!—were not embarrassed to name these delights at length. That is the reason why they helped him to be victorious when he marched against the king of Persia. To anyone who would choose to die for him in battle he promised the delights of his paradise. All the same, some are said to have fought rather in order to lay hold of the wonderful gardens which they had seen in Persia, for he had said that he would give those gardens to them, so that they might always live in gardens, both in this world and the next. You know how much the Arabs love the beauty of gardens.

However, you say: "It was not only country folk that followed him, but many others as well." True, many others, but only the worst people: lechers and those burdened by a debt or sentenced to die for their crimes, who found this to be their only recourse for escape. Now tell me, I beg you, what wise, noble, or honorable man have you ever seen join the Saracen faith? Those who, even now, join you from Judaism or Christianity should not be considered to do so out of honorable motives, but rather because they could not bear the rules of their faith; miserable and shameless as they are, they convert to the broad and wide path taught by your friend. This happens especially to certain Christians, whose heavenly and spiritual religion commands that everything in the world should be rejected out of hope and longing for the beatific vision of God. Because this religion constrains the carnal and fleeting minds of those who are miserable, they flee before it immediately since they do not care about resisting their lusts. 116

117 Hoc tamen certissime scias, quia neque Iudaei neque Christiani neque pagani, quocumque modo se exterius habeant, et si venientes ad vos de vestra secta se esse simulent, umquam ex corde vobiscum sunt. Simulant quidem se esse quod non sunt, ut vel, prout supra dixi, aliquod corporis evadant incommodum aut ut porcinis voluptatibus, quarum apud vos copia est, perfruantur. Adeo autem quicquid facitis pro nihilo ducunt ut saepe inter se loquentes Mahumet et legi eius maledicant nec dignum eum aliquando fuisse prophetia vel Dei lege affirment. Dicunt etiam quidam eorum Mahumet fuisse absque omni probitate vel nobilitate. Quidam vero, dividentes Spiritum Sanctum, dicunt partem eius habuisse Mosen, partem aliam Christum, reliquam vero partem nescio quem alium, non Mahumet. Ipsum enim nihil umquam boni habuisse contendunt.

118 Sane superfluum mihi videtur agere tecum de illis quae tuam non latent industriam, qualia sint apud vos et quam nullipendenda, scilicet diversitas in praeconio, celebritates exsequiarum, varietas in testimonio, orationes sollemnitatum, sollicita ad meridianam plagam conversio et modus legendi et modus discernendi similesque huiusmodi varietates, quae omnia in corde tuo quam nihil sint scio, cum haec sola superficie teneas, nec tamen propter gloriam et principatum, quem tenes, dimittere velis. Illud vero tam ego quam omnis qui audit et intelligit mirari possumus, quomodo illis, qui tot blasphemias in Deum et in sanctos eius prophetas in Alcorano legentes credunt, caelum non

This you should know absolutely for certain: nobody, whether Jew, Christian, or pagan, regardless of how they appear to be on the outside, even when they join you and pretend to be a part your sect, ever joins you out of sincerity. They pretend to be what they are not, perhaps, as I said earlier, to escape some kind of bodily discomfort or to enjoy the delights—fit only for swine—that are so abundant among you. Indeed, they disdain all that you do to such an extent that, when they are talking among themselves, they frequently curse Muhammad and his religion, and assert that he at no point was worthy either of prophecy or of God's law. Some of them even say that Muhammad lacked any kind of morality or nobility. Some, however, splitting up the Holy Spirit, say that Moses had a piece of it, Christ had another piece, and someone else—not Muhammad—had the remaining piece, for they claim that he never possessed any good quality. 117

It seems unnecessary to me to discuss with you, since your diligent mind is well aware, what your religious customs are like and how meaningless they are: the differences in the calls to prayer, the burial feasts, the different oaths, the prayers of feast days, the preoccupation with turning to the south, the manner of reading, the manner of interpreting, and similar divergences. I know how insignificant these things are to you in your heart, since you hold to them only superficially, and yet you are unwilling to abandon them because of the glory and rule you enjoy. However, we—I and anyone who hears and understands this—can all wonder how those who believe so many blasphemies against God and against his holy prophets when they read them in the Qur'ān, are not excluded from heaven, swallowed up by the 118

clauditur vel terra eos non absorbet aut daemones non arripiunt. Sed Deus Iudex iustus fortis et longanimis patienter sustinet, sciens eos non posse evadere iudicium suum, cum venerit reddere unicuique secundum opera sua.

119 Porro illud quod mihi scripsisti, antequam saecula crearet Deus scriptum fuisse in throno, "Non est deus nisi Deus, Mahumet nuntius Dei," unde acceperis aut ubi inveneris nescio, cum nec in Alcorano nec in alia qualibet ipsius inveniatur scriptura. Verumtamen ponamus ut alicubi hoc repertum sit. Velim ergo mihi dicas, si in throno scriptum est, quis hoc ibi scripserit? An aliquis scripsit hoc Deo? Sed quis posset scribere, cum necdum saecula creata essent? An Deus ipse sibi hoc scripsit timens, scilicet, perdere nomen suum, nisi illud scriberet? Quod satis absurdum videtur. Sed forsitan ideo scripsit ut angeli possent hoc legere? Et hoc non minus insulsum est sentire. Non enim per litteras loquitur Deus angelis, sed illuminatione praesentiae suae, quae illis ubique adest. Num praeterea propter homines scriptum est ut ipsi legerent et scirent? Sed homines in throno quomodo legerent? Restat ergo frivolum et vanum esse hoc, quod et te ipsum intelligere credo et te tibi ipsi scienter illudere, sicut quidam de sociis tuis dicunt, qui hoc pro nihilo habent, dicentes a Iudaeis confictum esse et inter alias fabulas mixtum ut risum de vobis toti mundo moverent.

120 Certe cum aliquis vult benedicere Mahumet et ultra modum laudare, hoc solummodo dicit: "Deus, tu benedic Mahumet, sicut benedixisti Abraham et generationi eius." Unde in libro eius scriptum est: *"O filii Israel, recordamini*

earth, or snatched away by demons. But God is a righteous, powerful, and patient judge, and knows that they cannot escape his judgment when he will come to render unto each in accordance with his deeds.

Moving on to what you wrote to me—namely that before 119
God created the earth there was written on his throne, "There is no god but God, and Muhammad is his prophet"—, I do not know where you heard or found this, since it cannot be found either in the Qurʾān or in any other writing of Muhammad. But let us assume that it is found somewhere. I would like you to tell me, if it is written on his throne, who wrote it there? Did someone write this for God? But who could have written it, since the world had not yet been created? Or did God himself write it, fearing that he might forget his own name if he did not write it down? This seems rather absurd. Perhaps he wrote it so that angels might read it? Yet this is no less foolish to think, for God does not address the angels with writing, but with the splendor of his presence, which is all around them. Surely, moreover, it was not written for humans, so that they might read it and know it? How would humans read it, located as it is, on the throne? It remains, therefore, that this is a ridiculous falsehood, and I believe that even you think this and are consciously fooling yourself, just as some of your companions consider this nonsense and say that it was made up by Jews and slipped in with other tales in order to stir up the whole world's laughter at your expense.

Certainly, when someone wishes to bless Muhammad and 120
praise him beyond measure, he merely says the following: "God bless Muhammad, just as you blessed Abraham and his generation." This is why it is written in his book: "O sons of

beneficiorum quae ego vobis exhibui, quia praetuli vos omnibus gentibus." Si ergo ita benedici Mahumet a Deo, sicut benedictus fuit Abraham et generatio eius, super omnes laudes et benedictiones, et si filii Israel praelati sunt a Deo omnibus gentibus, cum tamen nec Abraham nec generatio eius nomen habeant scriptum in throno, quomodo factum est ut nomen Mahumet, qui secundum hanc regulam ipso Abraham et generatione eius minor habetur, in throno Dei scriptum sit?

121 Denique invitas me ad quinque orationes et ad ieiunium mensis Ramazan. Ubi ego non tam tibi respondeo quam ut tu ipse tibi respondeas volo. Dixisti enim in tua exhortatione quod inter alia quae de nostra religione cognoveras etiam orationibus monachorum et ieiuniis interfueris, genuflexiones et instantiam deprecationum videris et cetera omnia, quae vere sancta et caelestia esse nullus negare poterit. Super animam ergo tuam hoc pono et teipsum iudicem facio, conferque, obsecro, studiose et diligenter orationes et ieiunia Christianorum et Saracenorum, et quicquid inde tibi ratio ipsa dixerit, hoc ego concedo. Scio namque pro certo quia, si quid iudicium rationis exigit, inde dicere volueris. Quantum ad ieiunia et orationes Christianorum, ieiunia et orationes vestrorum non solum ieiunia et orationes non esse clamabis, verum etiam quod tales sordes veris et sanctis servorum Dei virtutibus se comparare ullo modo ausae sint cum maxima indignatione ridebis.

Israel, remember the favors I have bestowed upon you, for I have placed you before all other nations." If therefore Muhammad is blessed by God in this manner, just as Abraham and his generation were blessed beyond all praises and blessings, and if the sons of Israel were placed before all other nations by God, how did it happen that the name of Muhammad, who, in accordance with this rule, is considered to be lesser than Abraham and his generation, was written on the throne of God, when neither Abraham nor his generation have their names inscribed on the throne?

Lastly, you invite me to participate in the five prayers and 121
the fast of the month of Ramaḍān. Concerning this, it is not so much that *I* will answer you, but rather I would like *you* to answer yourself. For you said in your exhortation that, among the other things you learned about my religion, you witnessed the prayers and fasts of monks, and observed the prostrations and the urgency of their supplications, and all other things, whose holy and heavenly nature nobody will be able to deny. It is on your soul that I place this, and it is you whom I make the judge: compare, I beg you, carefully and diligently the prayers and fasts of the Christians and Saracens, and whatever reason itself will tell you, this I will yield to you. I know for certain that, if the judgment of reason requires anything, you will be willing to speak of it. In comparison with the fasts and prayers of the Christians, not only will you say that those of your people are no fasts and prayers at all, but you will even laugh with great indignation at the fact that such foulness has dared to compare itself in any way to the true and saintly virtues of the servants of God.

122 Quod vero frequenti corporum lavatione hominem purificari creditis easque lavationes totiens frequentatis, hoc tibi respondeo quod Dominus meus in Evangelio suo Iudaeis similia facientibus et cur ipse vel discipuli eius talia non facerent conquerentibus ait: *"Quid prodest domui tenebrosae habere forinsecus lucernam ardentem, cum intus fuerit tenebrosa? Oportet ergo mundari mentes et corda a pollutione infidelitatis et ab inmunditia iniquitatis. Corpora vero quid prodest mundari forinsecus, si anima plena sit iniquitate?"* Unde iterum Dominus: *"Vae,"* inquit, *"vobis, hypocritae, qui similes estis sepulchris ornatis de foris, cum intus habeant cadavera. Ita vos quidem lavatis corpora vestra forinsecus et corda vestra polluta sunt iniquitate."* Quid ergo prodest lavare manus et pedes et extergere caput et insistere orationibus, cum conscientia cordis et mens et animus occupata fuerint in effusione sanguinis et diripiendis substantiis aliorum, uxoribus quoque et filiis captivandis? Vide igitur quomodo respondet illis Spiritus vivificans: Oportet enim hominem prius lavare interiora cordis sui et purificari a cogitationibus pessimis, quibus ingrediuntur mala in homine, sicque mundato animo et conscientia, laventur si placet et si necesse est etiam corpora.

123 Circumcisio vero quid ad vos pertineat scire non possum, cum nec Mahumet circumcisus fuerit, nec in Alcorano suo inde aliquid dixerit, nisi forte Abraham in hoc vos sequi dicatis. De quo superius ostendimus quod hereditas eius non vos sed Iudaei sint. Cum enim vos Ismaelis filios esse iactetis

As to the fact that you believe that man is fully cleansed by frequently bathing the body, and that you busy yourselves with those baths so often, I answer to you that my Lord said in his Gospel to those Jews performing similar activities and complaining that he and his disciples were not: "What use is there for a dark house to have a lantern burning on the outside when it is dark on the inside? One ought to cleanse the mind and heart from the defilement of unfaithfulness and the impurity of wickedness. What use is there in cleansing the body on the outside, if the soul is filled with wickedness?" And again the Lord said: "Woe to you, hypocrites, who are like tombs that are outwardly decorated, but are full of corpses within. So you also outwardly wash your body, while your hearts are defiled with wickedness." What use, therefore, is there in washing the hands and feet, wiping clean the head, and persisting in prayer, even though the heart's conscience, mind, and spirit are engaged in bloodshed, snatching away the possessions of others, and even in taking wives and children captive? See how the life-giving Spirit responds to them: man ought first to wash the inner recesses of his heart and to purge them of the basest thoughts through which evil enters into man, and when his spirit and heart have been cleansed in this way, let the body, too, be washed if he wishes and if it is necessary. 122

I cannot figure out how circumcision relates to you at all, since Muhammad was not circumcised, nor did he say anything about the matter in his Qurʾān, unless perhaps you maintain that you follow Abraham in this matter. I have demonstrated above that not you but the Jews are his legacy. Since you boast about being the sons of Ishmael, and since 123

et Abrahae dicatur a Deo, *"Non in Ismaele sed in Isaac reputabitur tibi semen,"* vos in semine Abrahae quomodo estis, qui ad Isaac nullomodo pertinetis? Si vero dicatis Christum fuisse circumcisum, quid ad vos, qui Christiani non estis? De cuius tamen circumcisione quam rationabilis fuerit, si vel digni essetis vel in aliquo ad eum pertineretis, plenissime responderemus. Nunc vero, cum nec Iudaei nec Christiani sitis, circumcisionem ubi invenistis? Nisi certe, quod valde credibile est, hoc etiam a Iudaeis libro vestro insertum sit ut, sicut de quibusdam Paulus Apostolus dicit, *"In carne vestra gloriarentur,"* dum vos more suo circumcidi facerent et suos in errore socios habere gauderent.

124 Quare etiam Mahumet porcum comedi vetuerit nescio. Nam et si Iudaei a porco et a quibusdam aliis prohibiti sunt, ratio certa apud nos est, quorum fidei lex illa militabat. Et licet nos modo illa corporaliter non servemus, ea tamen quae ibi significabantur spiritualiter implemus, quibus in Novo Testamento revelata sunt omnia per Christum, qui utriusque testamenti conditor est. Ipse enim dixit per apostolum suum: *"Omnia munda mundis"* et *"Nihil reiciendum est quod cum gratiarum actione percipitur."*

125 Illam vero turpitudinem quis audiens non exhorreat quam non erubuit Mahumet in Alcorano suo ponere, ut scilicet liceat viro, quandocumque voluerit, qualibet causa voluerit, uxorem repudiare, sed nisi prius alteri viro iungatur,

God said to Abraham, "Not in Ishmael, but in Isaac shall your seed be called," how are you of the seed of Abraham, who have no relation whatsoever to Isaac? If you were to say that Christ was circumcised, what is it to you, who are not Christians? I would tell you in full detail how reasonable his circumcision was, if you were worthy or had any relation to him. As it is, however, since you are neither Jews nor Christians, where did you get circumcision? Unless of course, as is perfectly believable, this, too, was inserted into your book by the Jews, as the apostle Paul says concerning certain individuals, "so that they might glory in your flesh," while they caused you to circumcise yourselves in accordance with their own custom, and rejoiced at having companions in error.

Moreover, I do not know why Muhammad prohibited 124
the consumption of pork. For even if Jews are forbidden from eating pork and some other things, we possess a certain rationale not to abstain, since that law of abstention fought against our faith. And even if we do not now observe those things according to the flesh, we still fulfill according to the spirit the things that are signified there—we, to whom all was revealed in the New Testament through Christ, who is the founder of both testaments, for he himself spoke through his apostle: "All things are pure to the pure," and "Nothing that is received with thanksgiving is to be rejected."

Who would not shudder upon hearing the foulness that 125
Muhammad did not shy away from placing in his Qurʾān, namely that a man is allowed to repudiate his wife whenever he wants, and for whatever reason he wants, but that he may not, even if he so wishes, recall her until after she has first

nec si velit, possit eam revocare? Hanc certe legem etiam bruta animalia, si loqui possent, turpissimam esse clamarent.

126 Quid est autem quod me, inter alia legis vestrae optima, etiam ad *alahagh,* hoc est, ad peregrinandum in domum Dei illicitam, quae est in Mecha, exhortatus es, ad proiciendos quoque lapillos et ad involutionem linteoli circa renes? Miror enim quod ita mecum loqueris ac si nunc me primo nosse inciperes. Numquid ego aut caecus aut surdus nuper effectus sum aut forsitan mutatus in puerum, cui sic illudere possis, ut modo primum discere incipiam inanes et fatuas superstitiones, quae nec rationem nec honestatem in aliquo habere probantur? Quasi vero nesciam quid sit et unde processerit vel qualiter ad vos ritus impius errorque stultissimus inter alia mala devolutus sit. Nonne haec est illa praeclara socii tui in idolorum destructione diligentia ut, cum a ceterorum cultu suos discipulos inhiberet, istud tamen in honore Veneris fieri apud Mecham suam permitteret? Quod quale sit vel a quibus ceperit, quoniam tu te ignorare simulas, audi.

127 Duarum quarumdam gentium Indiae, quae vocantur Zemchia et Albarahimia, antiqua consuetudo fuit nudos et decalvatos, magnisque ululatibus personantes, simulacra daemonum circuire, angulos quoque osculari et proicere lapides in acervum, qui quasi pro honore diis exstruebatur. Inde enim est quod in libro Salomonis dicitur: *"Qui proicit lapidem in acervum Mercurii."* Faciebant autem hoc bis in anno, sole scilicet existente in primo gradu Arietis et rursum cum esset in primo gradu Librae, hoc est, in initio veris et

been wedded to another man? Surely even the brute animals, if they could talk, would cry out that this is a most shameful law.

What was the reason that, among the other excellent elements of your religion, you also urged me to participate in the *ḥājj,* that is the pilgrimage to the forbidden house of God in Mecca, and in the casting of the stones and in wrapping a piece of linen around the loins? I am surprised at the fact that you speak to me as if you are only now becoming acquainted with me. Surely I have not recently become blind or deaf, or perhaps changed into a child, whom you may fool in this manner, in order that I may now, for the first time, begin to learn your empty and foolish superstitions, which are proven to possess no rational or honorable element whatsoever? Indeed, as if I do not know what the nature of your ungodly religion and most foolish error is, where it came from or how it ended up among you, along with other evils! Was not your friend so famously diligent in destroying idols that, while keeping his followers from the worship of other idols, he allowed that of Venus to take place at Mecca? And since you pretend not to know, hear what that worship is like and from whom he took it. 126

It was an ancient custom of two certain peoples of India, known as the *Zemchia* and the *Albarahimia,* for nude and shorn men to encircle effigies of demons, while resounding loudly with great shrieks, and also to kiss the corners and to cast stones in a heap, which was piled up in honor of the gods, as it were. This is why it is said in the book of Solomon: "He who casts a stone in the heap of Mercury." They would do this twice a year, when the sun enters Aries and again when it enters Libra, that is to say, at the start of spring 127

autumni. Haec ergo consuetudo cum ab Indis ad Arabes descendisset eamque suo tempore apud Mecham Mahumet in honore Veneris celebrari reperisset, sic illam manere praecepit, cum tamen cetera idolatriae praestigia removisset. Illud vero soli Veneri in illa celebratione dicitur exhiberi solitum ut lapilli retro, hoc est, sub genitalibus membris, proicerentur eo quod Venus illis maxime partibus dominetur. Unde adhuc ita fit in domum Dei, quam tu vocas "illicitam," id est, ubi nihil licet nisi quod sacrum est. Verumtamen, cum olim a nudis ex toto hominibus semper fieri soleret, non tulit hoc humana verecundia sed instituerunt aliqui ut proiectores lapidum parvo saltem linteolo renes obtegerent, ne homines denudati omnino canum impudentiam imitarentur.

128 Hanc ergo insaniam merito creditur Mahumet salvam et incolumem, cum reliquas daemonum culturas cessare praeciperet, dimisisse, ne dominam suam Venerem, in qua se esse potentissimum ipse iactabat, penitus sine honore relinqueret. Pro quo beneficio talem illi gratiam Venus rependit ut ad eum totam huius honoris gloriam referri, utpote ad singularem amicum, aequanimiter sustineret, dummodo vos non Veneri sed ipsi prophetae eius hoc obsequium impendatis. Quod apud quosdam vestrum tantae stultitiae deputatur ut vir prudens Gomar, filius Hata, cum ad osculandos lapides, quod ante alia Mahumet et fecerat et fieri iusserat, aliquando accessisset, sic locutus fuisse dicatur: "Ego scio quia lapides istos osculari nec obest nec prodest, sed quia sic

and autumn. Since this custom came to the Arabs from the Hindus, and was found by Muhammad to be celebrated at Mecca in worship of Venus, he ordered it to remain as it was, even though he eradicated all the other delusions of idolatry. The following custom, however, is said only to be allowed to be openly displayed in veneration of Venus, namely that rocks be thrown backward, that is, below the genitals, because Venus has particular influence over those parts. And this is why this still takes place in the house of God, which you call "forbidden," that is, where nothing is allowed except what is sacred. Yet, even though this used to always be performed by completely naked men, human modesty could not bear this but instead some people ordained that the throwers of stones should at least cover their loins with a small piece of linen, to prevent the naked men from completely imitating the shamelessness of dogs.

Muhammad is rightly believed to have left this insanity 128
whole and unaltered, even though he ordered all other worship of demons to cease, so that he might not leave his mistress Venus, with respect to whose domain he boasted that he was extremely potent, entirely without worship. In return for this favor, Venus repaid him with such gratitude that she kindly allowed all honor of this worship to be attributed to him, as to a special friend, provided that you do not offer obedience to Venus but to him, her prophet. This is considered by some of you to be such foolishness that ʿUmar b. Khaṭṭāb, a wise man, when he once approached the stones in order to kiss them, which Muhammad had done himself and ordered to be done before the other things, is reported to have said the following: "I know that it is neither harmful nor beneficial to kiss those stones, but

fecit et fieri iussit noster propheta, facio, licet sit omnino inutile." Ecce quid est *alahagh* vestrum et *alchimar* et peregrinatio in Domum Dei Illicitam. Ecce ad quae sacra, ad quam festivitatem, ad quantae honestatis et utilitatis celebrationem amicos tuos invitas. Obsecro, carissime, ut et nobis in hoc et tuae quoque verecundiae amodo parcas, nec homines ad huiusmodi spurcitias sed magis porcos, si ita volueris, advoca.

129 Unum autem quid verissimum in tua laudatione dixisti, quod scilicet mira ibi fieri videantur. Et vere mira ibi non solum videntur fieri, sed fiunt quando rationabiles homines, in bestialem sensum mutati, ista quae narravimus et similia faciunt. Non enim hoc facere possent homines, nisi prius ab humanae rationis iudicio in pecualem animalitatem converterentur. Verum, ne dicas nos serio non ludo tecum agere debere, dimittamus paululum ioca et quod ad rem pertinet disseramus.

130 Quaero igitur a te quae sunt illa mirabilia quae ibi fieri vidisti vel audisti. Nam, si me interrogares de locis vel ecclesiis Christianorum tale aliquid, non unum ego sed mille tibi loca enumerare et ostendere possem, in quibus caeci visum, surdi auditum, muti loquelam, paralytici (vel quolibet alio modo claudi) gressum recipiunt; ad ultimum, ubi omnium generum languores et incommoda sive animarum sive corporum depelluntur; ubi etiam saepe, quod maius est, ipsi mortui resuscitantur, et hoc non aliquibus exterioribus adiumentis

because our prophet did so and ordered it, I do it, even though it is completely useless." See what your *al-ḥājj* and *al-jimār* and pilgrimage to the Forbidden House of God amounts to! See to what sacred rites, to what festivities, to what celebration of honor and benefice you invite your friends! I beg you, dear friend, to spare both us and your own modesty in this matter from now on, and not to urge humans toward such filth, but preferably to urge pigs, if you really want to.

However, you said one thing in your praise that is very 129
true, namely that it seems to you that wondrous things take place there. Indeed, wondrous things do not only seem to take place there, but do take place, when rational men, with their sensibilities transformed into those of beasts, do the things I told of and similar things. For men could not do this, unless they had first been transformed from the judgment of human reason into the beastly nature of cattle. However, to prevent you from saying that I should be serious with you and not jest, let us leave, for a little while, the jokes behind and discuss what is relevant to the matter at hand.

I ask you, what miracles have you seen or heard there? If 130
you were to ask me the same thing about Christian sites and churches, I would be able to list and demonstrate not one but a thousand sites, where the blind have regained sight, the deaf have regained hearing, the mute their speech, the paralyzed (or those crippled in some other way) their ability to walk, where, in sum, all manner of enfeebling afflictions of mind and body are expelled, and, an even greater feat, where even the dead are brought to life. This is a gift from God and from the saints who died because of their justice

sive quolibet genere medicinae humanae, sed fide et oratione et pura cordis devotione id apud Deum et sanctos pro iustitia et vera pietate mortuos impetrante.

131 Tu ergo, si umquam vel semel huiusmodi virtus aliqua in illa, quam domum Dei dicis, facta sit, enarra. Et si saltem unum quid tale ibi aliquando factum mihi ostendere potes, concedo vera esse quae dicis. Sed quoniam scio te id nullo modo posse, non enim illud tacuisses, si haberes, quando me invitans et illa mirabilia narrans nihil habuisti quid diceres nisi quia lapilli proiciuntur, quod non virtutis divinae miraculum sed diabolicae impuritatis constat esse deliramentum, cur illa loca sacrata etiam dixeris responde. Quod si nec ad hoc respondere vales, immo quia non vales, restat ut et nos de nostrorum sanctitate locorum, quia tu de vestrorum quid dicas nihil habes, aliquid ostendamus.

132 Nec tu (quem Deus salvet) obsecro, putes vel scire te praesumas quicquid in sacrosancta Christianorum religione pie et sancte agitur, non dico in Arabia, in Aegypto, in Graecia vel Armenia, sed in toto, qui ei subiectus est, orbe terrarum, pro eo quod te, sicut in tuo scripto dixisti, aliqua clericorum seu monachorum loca vidisse vel colloquia expertum esse contigit. Si enim hoc putaveris, ita eris sicut ille qui mare quidem esse audiens quod numquam viderit, cum ei aliquis parum aquae marinae in vasculo ostenderit, totum se mare vidisse iactat et dicit: "Ecce quam parvum est mare, quod tam magnum esse audieram."

and true piety, a gift merited by faith, prayer, and the heart's pure devotion, not by any external aids or any kind of medical treatment invented by humans.

Tell me, then, if any such miracle has ever, even once, occurred in that place you call the House of God. If you can demonstrate to me even one such occurrence, I will admit that you are telling the truth. However, I know that you are in no way able to do so, for you would not have kept silent about it if you were, when you were inviting me and telling me about the wonders of your religion and there was nothing for you to mention except that people cast stones, which is clearly not a miracle of divine virtue, but rather a madness of devilish baseness. Tell me, why do you even call those sites sacred at all? And if you cannot even answer this—indeed, because you cannot—it remains for me to show you an example of the holiness of our sites, since you have nothing to say about yours. 131

You (may God save you) should not think, I beg you, or presume that you know every pious and saintly activity that takes place in the sacred religion of Christians, and I do not mean just in Arabia, Egypt, Greece, or Armenia, but in the entire world subject to it, just because you, as you wrote in your letter, happened to have seen the abodes of certain clerics and monks, and to have struck up conversations with them. If you were to think this, you would be just like the person who, upon hearing about the existence of a sea he has never seen, when someone shows him a bit of seawater in a little vessel, boasts of having seen the entire sea, and says: "See how small the sea is, which I had heard was so great!" 132

133 Ita et tu, carissime, non quia paucos monachos seu clericos et loca eorum vidisti et aliqua fortasse non intelligens de scripturis Dei legisti, idcirco omnia Christianorum sacra et supercaelestia opera inspexisse, mysteria cognovisse, sacramenta intellexisse praesumas. Sic enim sunt ea quae vidisti, licet tamen videre, nisi credantur, nihil proficiat. Nam et ipsum Dominum Iesum Christum multi viderunt, quibus nihil profuit, quia non crediderunt. Sic omnino quae vidisti sunt ad comparationem eorum quae in Christiana religione per totum orbem terrarum geruntur, sicut parva aquae guttula totius maris inmensitati comparata.

134 Quae enim lingua dicere vel quis sermo explicare sufficiat illam quam Deus Ecclesiae suae quamvis adhuc peregrinanti, gloriam et gratiam contulit? Non enim, sicut tu forte existimas, tota sanctae Christianitatis gloria, honor, et magnificentia in paucis Syriae vel Armeniae monachis continetur, sed in imperiis, in regnis, in provinciis, in civitatibus, in turbis denique omnium gentium, linguarum, populorum, in magisteriis et professionibus omnium bonorum studiorum, in usibus pulcherrimis et honestissimis diversarum observationum, in caritate et susceptione et relevatione peregrinorum, egentium omniumque desolatorum, in sancta castitate et patientia innumerabilium diversae aetatis et sexus, clericorum, monachorum et virginum, in doctrina et conversatione castissima sanctorum episcoporum et abbatum aliorumque variae professionis, in una fide et caritate rectorum sive magistrorum, in fide et devotione populorum, in oboedientia et subiectione imperatorum, regum,

So should you, too, dearest friend, not assume, just because you saw a few monks or clerics and their abodes, and read some things of the scriptures of God, which you perhaps did not understand, that you, therefore, have witnessed all the sacred works from above the heavens, have uncovered their mysteries, and have understood their sacraments. The things you have seen are such that, though you were allowed to witness them, they are of no benefit unless they are believed. For many saw the very Lord Jesus Christ, yet it was of no benefit to them, since they did not believe. It is exactly the same with the things you witnessed: in comparison with what is practiced in Christianity throughout the entire world, those things are like a small drop of water being compared to the immeasurable sea. 133

What language or idiom could suffice to describe the glory and grace God has bestowed upon his Church, though it is still on its pilgrimage? The entire glory, honor, and magnificence of the sacred Church is not, as you perhaps think, limited to the few monks in Syria or Armenia, but is in the empires, kingdoms, provinces, and cities—in short, in the collective masses of all nations, tongues, and peoples; it is in the teaching and instruction of all good endeavors; in the most noble and honorable practices of the various observances; in charity and the taking in and sheltering of pilgrims, of those in need, and of all those abandoned; in sacred chastity and the suffering of countless individuals of various age and gender, of clerics, monks, and virgins; it is in the teaching and chaste lives of saintly bishops, abbots, and others of different professions; it is in the singular faith and charity of instructors and teachers, in the faith and devotion of the masses, in the obedience and deference of emperors, 134

consulum omniumque quae sub caelo sunt potestatum, dignitatum, nobilitatum; postremo in signis et prodigiis et sanitatibus, quae per puras et sacras servorum Christi orationes saepissime ostenduntur, ubi et promissiones eius tam efficaciter et evidenter implentur ut vere appareat eum numquam ab Ecclesia sua recessisse, qui cum corporaliter recederet dixit ei: *"Ecce ego vobiscum sum usque ad consummationem saeculi."* Certe in his et huiusmodi sacris operibus et mirabilibus rebus quanta sanctitas, quanta munditia, quanta honestas loca, domos, ecclesias, monasteria, basilicas, altaria, sacrificia Christianorum possideat, exornet, illustret, illuminet, apertissime demonstratur.

135 Denique invitas me ad viam Dei, quae est expeditio contra adversarios et incredulos et participatores, scilicet, in ictu gladii et populatione et devastatione, donec ingrediantur in fidem Dei et testificentur quia non est deus nisi Deus et quia Mahumet servus eius et nuntius, aut reddant tributum subiecti. O tu prudens et sapiens, an voluisti me invitare ad opus diaboli, in quo nulla misericordia est, qui infudit iram suam in Adam et in generationem eius, de quibus plures elegit infundens in eis furorem suum et, implens eos sua nequitia, fecit eos sibi arma? Ipsi vero sunt qui subiacent nutui eius et supplent voluntatem eius, et oboedientes ei in gladio et direptione et depopulatione perficiunt ea quae sibi placent.

136 Modo obsecro te ut dicas mihi quomodo possunt continuari verba tua. Nam multum discrepant, cum dicas hoc contra tuam scripturam, quam credis esse a Deo, quae ita

kings, consuls, and all other magnates, dignitaries, and nobles under the heavens; finally, it is in the signs, miracles, and healings so often demonstrated through the pure and saintly prayers of the servants of Christ. In this his promises are fulfilled with such great effect and in such plain sight for all to see, that it truly seems that he has never left his Church, as he said when he was leaving his body behind: "See, I am with you until the consummation of the world." Certainly, through these and similar sacred works and miracles it is most clearly shown what great saintliness, what great purity, and what great nobility possesses, adorns, illuminates, and lights up the sites, houses, churches, monasteries, basilicas, altars, and offertories of the Christians.

Finally, you invite me upon the path of God, which is the 135
campaign against opponents, infidels, and traitors—that is to say, a campaign of striking down with the sword, of plundering and sacking, until they proceed to faith in God and testify that there is no god but God and that Muhammad is his servant and messenger, or until they render tribute as subjects. O prudent and wise man, did you wish to invite me to take part in the work of the devil, who has no compassion, and who poured his wrath into Adam and his generation, many of whom he has chosen to pour his rage into and, filling them with his wickedness, has fashioned into weapons for himself? It is they who submit to his command and fulfill his wishes, and obeying him they satisfy their own desires with the sword, plundering, and sacking.

Now I ask you to tell me how your words are able to fit 136
together. For they are greatly at odds with one another, since you speak in contradiction to your scripture, which you believe to come from God, which says the following:

dicit: *"Sit in eis signum quod me ad bonum advocet ita ut iubeant congrua et prohibeant mala. Ipsi equidem sunt beati."* Rursum dicit: *"Non est tuum iustificare eos sed Deus iustificet quem vult."* Deinde subiungit: *"Nam si Dominus tuus vellet, omnes qui in terra sunt crederent. Tu autem quare compellis homines ad credendum, cum nulla anima credat nisi nutu Dei?"*

137 An non vides quomodo contrarium est huic verbo quod iterum scribit dicens: *"Dic, o vos homines: 'Iam veritas venit a Domino vestro. Qui autem iustificatus fuerit, sibimet iustificabitur; qui autem in errore permanserit, suae animae nocet. Ego autem exactor vester non sum.' Sequere quod tibi a Deo inspiratur et patienter age, donec iudicet Deus. Ipse est enim in iudicibus melior."* Rursum in alio loco: *"Nam si vellet Deus tuus, omnes homines unam plebem faceret, sed non desistent a diversitate nisi cui Deus miserebitur."* Item dicit: *"Missus est hominibus pariter in pietate et misericordia."* Qualis misericordia habetur cum effusione sanguinis et latrocinio et praeda? Licet autem Iudaei scripturam tuam dicant sibimet in multis esse contrariam, ego tamen eam non vocabo tam mirabili nomine, sed dico: aut tuum certe verbum sibi est contrarium aut tu mentiris ea quae tibi indesinenter imponis. Oro enim te, quae est via diaboli nisi homicidia et furta et praeda? An poterit hoc aliquis contradicere?

138 Si autem iterum opposueris nobis Mosen, quoniam ipse cultores idolorum expugnaverit, recordare illa miracula et prodigia quae legisti eum fecisse in Lege, et videbis quod

"Let them have a sign that pronounces me to be an advocate of what is good, so that they may command what is right and forbid evil. Indeed, they are fortunate." Elsewhere, it says: "It is not up to you to justify them, but let God justify whom he wishes." Then it adds: "For if your Lord would wish it, all who live in your land would believe. Why then do you compel men to believe, even though no soul believes but at the behest of God?"

Do you not see how contradictory to this he is when he 137
writes elsewhere: "Say, O you men: 'Now the truth has arrived from your Lord. He who will be justified, will be justified unto himself; but he who will remain in his sin, will harm his own soul. However, I am not your guardian.' Follow what has been inspired in you by God and be patient, until God may judge, for he is the best among judges." And in a different passage: "For if your God would will it, he would make all men into one nation, but none will abandon their differences, except those pardoned by him." He also says: "He has been sent to mankind with equal piety and compassion." What kind of compassion does one consider this to be when it comes with bloodshed, robbery, and looting? Although Jews might say that your scripture is greatly self-contradictory in many aspects, I will not go so far as to give it such an extraordinary title, but I say to you: either your words are greatly self-contradictory, or you lie about the things with which you are constantly deceiving yourself. I ask you, what is the path of the devil if not homicide, thieving, and looting? Could anyone claim otherwise?

If, however, you once again use the example of Moses 138
against us, that he, too, subdued idolaters in battle, recall those miracles and portents you read about him performing

iustum est credere illum ex praecepto Dei hoc fecisse. Similiter de Iosue filio Nun, cui sol et luna stetere. Quae miracula, cum fieri non possint nisi ab electis Dei, credimus quod quicquid fecerunt iussu Dei factum sit. Tu autem quod signum aut quod miraculum ostendis socium tuum fecisse, quod sit ei in testimonium unde credamus ei, cum suum proprium non sit nisi occidere homines et latrocinari et diripere aliena et captivare parentes cum liberis? Quod semper quidem malum est, sed multo magis quando fit contra populum Dei, qui non habent aliud munimen nisi cultum Dei, implentes mandata eius et caerimonias et, ingredientes recte in fide eius et in Christum eius credentes, timent eum sicuti oportet. Ipse enim direxit eos in viam aequitatis, quorum facies candidae sunt in hoc saeculo et in futuro. An non sufficit tibi nisi nuncupes eam viam Dei? Absit hoc a Deo ut talis sit via Dei aut quisquis talia iusserit sit de plebe aut de electis eius, quanto minus de prophetis. Deus enim nulla nisi opera sanctorum diligit.

139 Quid dicam de diversitate ista? Dixisti enim, "Nulla violentia in fide." Et iterum in Alcoran dixit Deus illis quibus lex data est: *"De ignorantibus legem dimisi eos. Si autem effecti fuerint Saraceni, iustificabuntur. Quod si noluerint, ad te nihil aliud pertinet nisi annuntiare illis."* Item dicit: *"Nam, si Deus vellet, non essent diversi ad invicem, posteaquam testimonia venerunt illis. Diversi quippe fuerunt, ex quibus alii crediderunt, alii non;*

in the Law, and you will see that it is right to believe that he did so at God's command. Likewise with Joshua, son of Nun, for whom the sun and moon stood still. Since those miracles could not have been performed by anyone other than God's elect, we believe that whatever they did, they did at God's command. What sign or miracle can you demonstrate that your friend has performed that might serve him as a testimony for us to believe him, when his characteristic behavior was to kill men, steal and plunder another's possessions, and take parents captive along with their children? This is always evil, but all the more so when it happens against the people of God, who have no other protection except the worship of God, fulfilling his commands and rites, and while they walk upright in their faith in him and believe in his Christ, they fear him as they should. For it was he who steered them on the path of justice, and their faces are resplendent in this world and the next. Or is it not sufficient for you if you do not call it the path of God? Far be it from him for the path of God to be such, or for whoever commanded such things to be of his people or of his elect, let alone of the prophets. For God loves nothing but the works of the saints.

What can I say about this contradiction? You said, "There 139
will be no violence in faith." And again, in the Qur'ān God said to whom the law had been given: "I have separated them from those who do not know the law. However, if they have become Saracens, they will be justified. But if they do not want to, your only duty is to convey the message to them." And elsewhere: "If God willed it, they would not be divided among one another, after the testimonies came to them. Indeed, they were divided from one another, for some

nam si vellet Deus, non essent diversi. Deus enim quaecumque voluerit facit." Item in alio loco, *"O vos infideles,"* rursumque discernens dicit, *"Ego habeo fidem et vos fidem."* Iterum subsequitur dicens: *"Nolite disceptare cum legem habentibus nisi in his quae benigne habentur."*

140 Tu autem indesinenter vocas ad percutiendum homines gladio et praeda et captivitate et pessundatione, donec ingrediantur ad fidem tuam. Qua ergo ex duabus sententiis tuis redarguam te? Prima an secunda? Cum non possis defendi eo verbo ut dicas mandatum quidem primo scriptum fuisse sed postea cessasse, non enim potes discernere ea quae cessavere ab his quae videntur manere. Fortassis enim ea quae putas non cessavere sed manent.

141 Si igitur fateris te hoc ignorare et tua scientia nullatenus comprehendi, nec potest hoc ulla ratione probari, nobis necesse non est de hoc amplius tractare. Nos autem nihil consecuti sumus in hoc nisi quia probavimus temetipsum tibi contradicere et tua verba adnihilare, tuamque prolocutionem evacuare, et conditionem disrumpere, cum dixeris socium tuum cum misericordia et pietate pariter ad homines venisse et nullam violentiam in fide esse; et post invitasti nos ad percutiendum homines in gladio eorumque facultates diripere atque omnia pessundare, donec violenter ad tuam fidem veniant tuisque legibus inviti subiciantur et coacti tuum testimonium testificentur.

of them believed, some did not; if God willed it, they would not be divided, for God does whatever he wishes." And in another passage, making distinctions again, he says, "O you unbelievers! I have my religion, and you have your religion." And he follows it up with: "Do not debate with the People of the Book, except on those matters that are dealt with in a kind manner."

You, however, continuously call upon others to strike 140
men with the sword, to afflict them with looting, captivity, and ruin, until they enter into your religion. With which of your two statements should I refute you? The first or the second? Especially since you cannot defend yourself with the statement that this commandment was first written down but later ceased to be valid, for you cannot separate those that are no longer valid from those that appear to remain. Perhaps those things you thought were no longer valid have instead abided.

If, therefore, you admit that you do not know this and 141
cannot grasp it with your intellect in any way, and that you are unable to prove it by any means, it is unnecessary for me to discuss this any longer. I have gained nothing by this except that I have proven that you contradict yourself, annul your own words, make your own argument void, and disprove your own way of life, since you said that your friend came to men with equal measure of compassion and piety, and that there was no violence in your religion; afterward you invited me to strike men down with the sword and to snatch away their possessions, and to bring them to ruin, until they join your religion by these violent means and are unwillingly subjected to your laws and forced to bear witness to your testimony.

142 Verumtamen, cum hactenus in incerto simus, nec possis nobis respondere vel discernere quid horum sit verum aut falsum, dum nescis quid iussum sit manere aut cessare, manifesta ratione concluditur utrumque incertum et falsum esse. Quia quod videtur tibi verum et debere teneri, fortasse illud est quod iussum est cessare. Et hinc satis probatur quod numquam talia iusserit Deus, quae sic facile debeant immutari. Tu autem numquam legisti in divina scriptura aliquos ad Deum violenter conversos, nec praeceptis eius gladio, direptione, captivitate, sicut tuus socius fecit et iussit, oboedire coactos esse. Scis etiam quod ea omnia, quae a Mose vel ceteris prophetis facta vel iussa sunt, probant eos a Deo venisse.

143 Multi certe olim haeretici fuerunt, quorum tamen nullus nec gladio nec aliqua coactione aliquem ad suam sectam pertrahere conatus est. Ex quibus unus, nomine Daradast Graecus, errore deceptus dixit venisse super se in monte Celen visionem divinam. Tunc advocavit regem Zebeizib omnesque qui cum eo erant ad suam sectam, decipiens eos falsis miraculis et magicis figmentis. Faciebat enim equum quasi mori et postea resurgere. Aliud quoque simulavit miraculum, recitans eis quandam orationem in qua diversitas omnium linguarum haberi videbatur, quam scripsit in duodecim milia pergamenis, cui nomen imposuit *Hortus,* id est *Codex Fidei.* Illi autem, qui hunc librum habent, cum interrogantur quae sit expositio eius, ignorantiam confitentur. Similiter fecit et Helbidius Indus, qui cum ostenderet eis

Nevertheless, since I am still in uncertainty, and you are unable to respond to me or to decide which of these is true and which is false, since you do not know which of them has been commanded to abide and which to be void, one can conclude with good reason that each is dubious and false. Indeed, perhaps that which appears true to you and requiring observance is what has been commanded to be void. Hence there is sufficient reason to conclude that God never commanded such things, which are liable to being altered so easily. You have never read in the divine scripture that anyone was converted by violence, nor that anyone was forced to obey his commandments by means of the sword, through plundering, or captivity, as your friend did and commanded. You also know that all the things that were done or commanded by Moses or the other prophets prove that they came from God. 142

Certainly, there were once many heretics, yet none of them attempted to draw anyone to his own sect by means of the sword or any other form of coercion. One of them, a Greek by the name of Zoroaster, claimed, deceived by error, that a divine vision came upon him on Mount Sīlān. He then called King Zebeizib to his sect, and all those who were with him, beguiling them with false miracles and magical fictions. For example, he supposedly killed a horse and later resurrected it. He also feigned another miracle, reciting to them a certain speech that appeared to contain all the different languages and which he wrote down on twelve thousand leaves of parchment, giving it the title *Hortus,* that is *The Book of Faith.* But when those in possession of the book were asked about its interpretation, they confessed their ignorance. The Hindu Helbidius did something similar when he 143

quasi avem quandam praemaximam volantem circa occasum solis, habentem in utero puellam clamantem et dicentem, "Scitote quia quaecumque vobis Helbidius annuntiaverit vera sunt," multos seduxit. Haec sunt machinationes et seductiones pseudoprophetarum, qui nomen prophetiae sibi assumunt.

144 Quicumque enim voluit inducere homines ad veritatem sive ad mendacium, non potuit hoc facere sine aliqua vel vera vel saltem verisimili praedicatione, et illud quidem quicquid sit permanere videtur usque ad examinationem. Sed postquam diligenti investigatione discussum fuerit, secernitur verum a falso. Omnes autem sive haeretici sive quolibet alio errore decepti praeter socium tuum ita fecisse noscuntur. Ipse enim ad suam sectam non ita homines, hoc est, non sola arte calliditatis aut ingeniosa loquacitate, sed gladio et violentia et oppressione et depopulatione coegit. Numquam enim auditum est ab aliquo quod ille dicebat hominibus: "Quicumque non confitebitur me prophetam esse Domini saeculorum, gladio illum feriam ego, et omnes quicumque de mea progenie sunt similiter facient, et domum eius diripiam et omnem familiam eius captivitate affligam." Hoc totum sine ratione et veridica locutione fecit socius tuus, ad cuius sectam me invitare non erubescis.

145 Advocatio vero Domini nostri Iesu Christi, qui est creator omnium rerum et mundi vivificator, cuius nomen sit benedictum et excelsum, qualis sit non est modo necesse tibi exponi, maxime cum tu omnia te legisse dixeris et propria cognitione cuncta comprehendisse.

led many astray by supposedly showing them a gigantic bird flying in the west, with a girl in its belly that cried out and said: "Know that all that Helbidius has proclaimed to you is true!" These are the tricks and seductions of the false prophets, who lay claim to the title of prophet for themselves.

Whoever wished to lead men either to truth or falsehood 144
was not able to do so without some kind of true prophecy—or at least one with an ounce of verisimilitude—and this prophecy, whatever it is, appears tenable up until closer examination. But once it has been analyzed with careful scrutiny, truth is separated from falsehood. All—heretics or those deceived by some kind of error—are known to have acted in this fashion, except for your friend. For he did not draw men to his sect in this manner, that is to say, merely by the skill of his cunning or ingenious facility with words, but with the sword, with violence, with oppression, and with plundering. Never before had anyone heard that which he used to say to people: "Anyone who will not confess that I am the prophet of the Lord of the world I will strike with the sword, and anyone of my kin will do the same, and I will plunder his house and afflict his entire family with captivity." All of this your friend did without proof or truthful proclamation, and yet you are not ashamed to invite me to his sect.

It is not necessary to explain to you the nature of the 145
message of our Lord Jesus Christ, who is the creator of all things and the life-giver of the world (may his name be blessed and raised up high)—especially since you claimed to have read it all and to have understood it all with your own intellect.

146 O tu (quem Deus salvet), numquid decet tuam prudentiam seu generis nobilitatem et consanguinitatis generositatem invitare me ad haec horribilia, hominem scilicet qui omnia quaecumque socius tuus dixit aut scripsit investigavi atque diligenter inspexi, qui super omnia et ante omnia indesinenter et sine intermissione nocte ac die verba Domini nostri Iesu Christi meditari non cesso. Ipse est consolatio mea, spes mea, et refugium meum, mihique misericors et propitius. Ipsum ego cotidie in sancto Evangelio audio dicentem: *"Estote misericordes sicut et Pater vester misericors est, et cum omnibus hominibus benefacite, ut sitis similes Patri vestro caelesti et misericordi, qui solem suum oriri facit super bonos et malos et pluit super iustos et iniustos."*

147 An aestimabas me caecitate obductum a tramite veritatis recedere et converti ad illa quae errori subiacent? Dominus Iesus Christus cotidie mihi praedicat ea quae tu novisti et legisti de benedictionibus in sua scriptura positis, in quarum deliciis sum nutritus et beneficiis auctus. Quae beneficia ita influxerunt membris et visceribus meis, donec effecta sunt cum sanguine sanguis et cum medullis medullae et cum ossibus ossa, in qua pietate creverunt mihi et capilli et cutis et caro.

148 Tu ergo existimasti me ab ista dulcedine posse averti et effici in effigie daemonum, qui effusione sanguinis delectantur, ut interficiam generis mei filios et progeniem Adam patris mei, qui factus est ad imaginem et similitudinem Dei? Quae omnes creaturas praecellit, cui angeli caelestes adsunt defensores, cuius obsequio caelestia et terrestria parata sunt

O you (may God save you), surely it does not befit your wisdom, your noble lineage, or the excellence of your relatives, to invite me to these dreadful things—me, a man who has investigated and carefully looked into everything your friend has said or written, and who continues, before all other things, to be mindful of the words of our Lord Jesus Christ, without cease or pause, day and night. He is my comfort, my hope and my refuge, and he is compassionate and favorable toward me. I hear him say daily in the sacred Gospel: "Be compassionate just as your Father is compassionate, and do well unto all others, so that you may be like your heavenly and compassionate Father, who causes the sun to rise for both the good and the wicked, and sends rain on both the just and the unjust." 146

Did you think that I was so blind as to stray from the path of truth and to convert to things which are erroneous? The Lord Jesus Christ tells me every day those things (which you know and have read) about the Beatitudes in his scripture, in whose delights I have found nourishment and by whose acts of kindness I have grown. Those good deeds have flowed into my limbs and into my innards, until they became blood of my blood, marrow of my marrow, and bone of my bone, and with this piety my hair, skin, and flesh grew. 147

Did you think, then, that I could be turned away from that sweetness, and made like the demons that delight in bloodshed, so that I would kill the children of my own flesh and blood and the offspring of my father Adam, who was created in the image and likeness of God? This sweetness excels beyond all other creatures, and the heavenly angels assist it as protectors, and in obedience to it all heavenly and 148

mala ab illo avertere et commoda exhibere, et hoc sine intermissione et fatigatione faciunt nocte ac die.

149 Ipse est enim dominator terrae, cuius regnum crevit et beatitudo, quando *"Verbum caro factum est et habitavit in nobis."* Tunc enim humanitas cum divinitate una persona effecta est. Tunc data est humanitati divinitas et potestas, virtus et aeternitas, quam angeli adorant et benedicunt et sanctificant nomen eius. Super haec omnia adiectum est illi sedere a dextris Dei in gloria virtutis eius. Illud enim corpus exaltatum est et elevatum super choros angelorum. Ipse est similis nostri et frater noster in natura hominis, et conditor et Dominus noster in substantia verbi. Cui data est omnis potestas in caelo et in terra ad exaltandum eum et glorificandum, et providentia omnis creaturae et resurrectio mortuorum et iudicare vivos et mortuos et angelos et homines et daemones. Videtur ergo tibi ut ego contra animam meam et praecepta Dei percutiam gladio et diripiam et pessumdem? Plane hoc multum distat a cultura Dei et longe est a mandatis et beneficiis eius. Hoc enim esset negare benignitatem eius et parvipendere clementiam et illi gratiarum actiones non reddere. Absit tam intolerabilis error a nobis et ab omnibus Dei fidelibus.

150 Si dixeris mihi, "Quoniam ipsum Dominum gloriosum et excelsum videmus mortificare et diversis langoribus interficere et calamitatibus et doloribus flagellare, quid prohibet te illi assimilari?," nos respondebimus tibi prompte et facile, non sicut tu respondisti de Spiritu, quando interrogatus

earthly things are prepared to turn away evil from it and to bestow favors upon it, doing so ceaselessly and tirelessly, day and night.

He is the ruler of the earth and his realm and blessing 149
grew when "the Word became flesh and dwelled among us." It is then that human and divine nature became unified in a single person, and human nature was granted divine power and eternal virtue, which the angels venerate and bless as they sanctify his name. In addition to all of this, he is allowed to sit at God's right hand in the glory of his virtue. For Christ's body is exalted and elevated beyond the angelic choirs, and he, our brother, is similar to us in his human nature, and our creator and Lord in the essence of the Word. Every power in heaven and earth is given to him to exalt and glorify him: providence over all of creation, resurrection of the dead, and judgment over the living, dead, angels, men, and demons. Does it seem likely to you, therefore, that I would strike with the sword, plunder, and cause ruin, against my very own soul and the commandments of God? Clearly this is greatly at odds with the worship of God and far removed from his commandments and favors, since this would be to deny his goodness and to despise his mercy, and would be a failure to render gratitude to him. Far be it from us, and all of God's faithful, to fall into such a grievous error!

If you should say to me, "Since we see your glorious and 150
exalted Lord killing and murdering men by means of various afflictions and bringing suffering from disaster and pain, what is to prevent you from being exactly like him?" I would answer you promptly and without difficulty, not the way you answered me concerning the Spirit, when, upon being asked,

dixisti Spiritum esse de creaturis Dei. Deus enim omnipotens, benedictus et excelsus, mortificat suos servos, non ut illis noceat neque ut aliquid mali eis ingerat. Quod si ita esset, nullatenus eos crearet. Creavit enim illos gratuita pietate et clementia et benignitate, cum fecit eos de nihilo esse aliquid et de non esse ad esse perduxit, sed ut illos transferat ab hoc mundo, quae est illis domus iniqua et pessima et labilis et instabilis et deficiens et non permanens, ad domum aeternitatis, quae indeficiens permanet. Numquid ille, qui aliquem transfert de civitate pauperrima et miserrima ad civitatem opulentam et deliciosam, dicendus est nocuisse illi aut iniuste egisse cum illo? Ille enim, qui eum transtulit, gratis cum eo bene egit.

151 Illud vero quod dicis, quia intulit eis Deus diversos langores et dolores, nos hoc tibi quare faciat exponemus. Voluit enim eos esse dignos mercede et retributione, utroque modo saluti eorum providens, sive sanitate sive infirmitate, utpote medicus sollers et clementissimus, qui dat infirmis potiones amarissimas eosque etiam, si necesse sit, cauterio urit et quaedam membra secat et incidit, prohibens eorum appetitus ab his quibus noxiae delectantur, agens cum illis clementer et benigne. Numquid ista faciens medicus propter odium facit aut inimicitiam an quia appetit sanitatem et incolumitatem ipsorum et ab illis langores auferre et relevare eos ab illa pessima et nociva habitudine qua detinentur ad prosperitatem et vitae dulcedinem?

you said that the Spirit is one of God's creations. For God is omnipotent, blessed, and exalted, and he subdues his servants, but not to harm them or to bring evil upon them. If that were the case, he would not have created them in the first place, for he created them out of love freely given, out of mercy, and out of kindness. When he created them out of nothing and brought them from nonexistence into existence, he did so in order to bring them out of this world, which is a wicked abode, evil, fleeting, fickle, imperfect, and transient, to the eternal abode, which is never wanting and everlasting. Surely he who brings someone from a greatly impoverished and miserable city to a wealthy and delightful city does not deserve to be accused of harming him or of having dealt unjustly with him? Indeed, the person who does so acted kindly to him out of his own free will.

As to what you said about God bringing various afflic- 151
tions and pains upon them, I will explain to you why he did so. He wished them to be worthy of reward and punishment, providing for their salvation in both cases, whether by healing or disease. Like a skilled and merciful doctor, who dispenses bitter medicine to those who are sick, and even, if necessary, cauterizes them and amputates and removes their limbs, he treats them kindly and mercifully when he takes away their appetites, in which they delight to their own destruction. When a doctor does these things, does he do so out of hate or hostility or because he strives for their good health and sound condition, and to alleviate their afflictions and to relieve them from that terrible and harmful state by which they are kept from wellness and the sweetness of life?

152 Si dixeris quia poterat bene facere cum illis sine tormentis et doloribus, dicemus tibi quia poterat etiam non creare mundum praesentem, sed futurum, pariterque etiam paradisum, in quo introduceret homines sine aliqua passione et sine ullo merito. Hoc enim totum illi possibile erat. Sed haec nostra in eum meditatio iniqua habetur. Poterat enim quilibet perversus dicere quia non debuit creare nisi unum mundum. Creavit autem omnipotens Deus, gloriosus et excelsus, hunc mundum et posuit eum domum labilem et passionis et pariter homines, qui debent eam aestimare non manentem et fugitivam. Praecipitur enim eis expectare illam ultimam domum atque mansuram, in qua aeternitas et pax et securitas est sine fine.

153 Si autem dixeris quod tuus iste socius, cui ascripsisti talia et quem nos sequi hortaris, gladio et direptione et captivitate transferat homines de malo ad bonum, plane bene et benigne facit, imitans, scilicet, Dei benignitatem et misericordiam, sed ipse certe ad hoc non fecit nec tale aliquid cogitavit nec in cor eius ascendit. Quaesivit enim suum commodum et honorem transitorium in hoc saeculo, nihil meditans de futuro. De hoc enim ut certum probetur dixit: *"Interficiam eos et affligam quousque aut me testificentur prophetam esse Domini aut tributum reddant subiecti."* Tu enim, si volueris, bene poteris cognoscere quoniam non transtulit illos ab eo in quo erant et quod apud ipsum infidelitas et participatio putabatur ad illud quod fides et veritas est, providens illis utilia et ea quae animae sunt necessaria, sed ad suum regnum temporale firmandum et principatum augendum, et hoc amore huius saeculi, sicut fecerant gentiles, qui

If you say that he could have treated them well without any pain and suffering, I will say to you that he could also not have created the present world, but the future one, and at the same time a paradise, in which he could bring men without any suffering and without any merit. All of this was possible for him. But these musings of ours concerning him are considered wicked. Indeed, any wicked person could say that he only needed to create one world. Yet omnipotent God, glorious and exalted, created this world and made it a fleeting abode of suffering, and at the same time he created humans, who should consider it not a permanent place but a transient one. For they are commanded to await that final and everlasting abode, in which there is eternity, peace, and security without end. 152

If, however, you say that your friend, to whom you have attributed such things and whom you are urging me to follow, brings men from evil to good by means of the sword, plundering, and captivity, then, indeed, he is good and kind, and imitates God's kindness and compassion, but it is certain that he did not do these things for this reason, nor did this occur to him or enter into his heart. Indeed, he was after his own profit and the fleeting honor of this world, having no concern for the future world. In order to provide definite proof of this, he said: "I will kill them and torment them until they either testify that I am a prophet of God, or render tribute as my subjects." If you so wished, you could easily see that he did not lead them out of what he considered unbelief and polytheism to faith and truth by supplying them with what is beneficial and what is necessary for the soul. Instead, he was intent on establishing his temporal rule and expanding his sovereignty, doing so out of love of this 153

ante fuerant, regnum sibi et gloriam huius mundi quaerendo.

154 Deprecor te (quem Deus salvet) nominare mihi illos, qui in fide Mahumet martyrium susceperunt. Quod si nec unum potes, quoniam vere nullus est, considera ea quae sunt illata Christi martyribus, non uni non duobus sed innumerabilibus, maxime a regibus Persarum et ceteris. Obsecro te, qui dicendi sunt martyres, isti qui pro Christi nomine gratis tradiderunt se morti, an tui socii, qui pro amore huius saeculi toto conamine certantes interficiuntur?

155 Nos enim certi et experti sumus quantum proni et alacres erant ad effundendum sanguinem suum pro Christo, filiorum quoque et filiarum suarum, sed et saeculum perdere et de suis omnibus nihil curare. Immolabant enim corpora sua Deo in decollatione et necis diversitate et passionum afflictione. Ubi enim unus interficiebatur, statim plures supervenientes martyrio sponte se offerebant.

156 Fertur enim quod quodam tempore cuidam regi Romanorum impiissimo, cum instanter ageret de interfectione martyrum eorumque innumerabiles trucidaret, dictum est: "O rex, certe quos putas interficiendo minui et consumi, inde magis augentur et multiplicantur." Dixit autem rex: "Quomodo potest hoc fieri?" Dixeruntque illi: "Heri occidisti tantos et tantos numero, sed in nocte multo plures, immo in duplum, Christiani facti sunt." At ipse: "Quae est," inquit, "huius rei causa?" Responderunt: "Quando enim poenis applicantur, dicunt se vidisse hominem de caelo

world, just as the pagans who lived before had done by seeking the dominion and glory of this world for themselves.

I beg you (may God save you) to name me any persons who have suffered martyrdom for their faith in Muhammad. If you cannot name even one, since there is truly no one, consider what was brought upon the martyrs of Christ—not just one or two, but countless individuals, and especially at the hands of the kings of the Persians, as well as others. Who deserve to be called martyrs, I beg of you: those who freely gave themselves over to death for the name of Christ, or your companions, who are killed fighting out of love for this world with all their might? 154

I know for certain and have experienced how readily and enthusiastically they shed blood for Christ, even that of their own sons and daughters, and abandoned this world and had no care for any of their possessions. Indeed, they offered their own bodies to God by decapitation, diverse manners of death, and the affliction of suffering. When one of them was killed, immediately more would come to offer themselves to martyrdom of their own accord. 155

The story goes that once, when a certain wicked king of the Romans persisted in killing martyrs and had slaughtered countless of them, it was said to him: "O king, those whom you thought could be diminished and eliminated by slaughter are increased and multiplied by this very action." The king, however, responded: "How can this be?" And they said: "Yesterday you killed however many, but during the night many more—indeed, twice the number—have become Christians." And he: "What is the reason for this?" They answered: "When they are afflicted with punishment, they say they saw a man coming from heaven, who gives 156

venientem, qui eos ad omnia pro Christo sustinenda corroborat." Tunc rex pepercit illis atque ab impietate sua paululum mitigatus iussit cessare tormenta.

157 Itaque considera quales erant isti in constantia passionis, in puritate mentis, in sinceritate fidei, quorum nullatenus animi deficiebant, cum gladiis et ignibus diversisque poenarum generibus cruciarentur. Suscipiebant enim supplicia nullo umquam taedio vel tristitia affecti, sed hilares gaudebant et exultabant in omnibus, scientes quod, si aliqua maestitudine pungerentur, contra semetipsos agerent, et quia sic oportebat eos pati pro nomine Christi et implere ea quae ipse fidem suam profitentibus praecepisset. Denique huius mundi gaudia pro nihilo computantes, ultro se morti ac suppliciis tradiderunt.

158 Quorum alii vivi excoriati, alii igne cremati, alii bestiis subministrati, alii gladio truncati, alii serris secti, alii truncatis manibus et pedibus Deo gratias referebant. Adeo autem alacres in suppliciis videbantur, ut quidam illorum in gravissimo tormento constitutus, cum interrogaretur utrum paene illius dolorem sentiret, ad dextrum latus sese subridendo convertens ita responderet: "Non solum nihil doleo sed et iuvenem hilari vultu mihi astare conspicio qui, candidissimo linteo sanguinem meum extergens, non cessat mihi subridere congratulans. Ita sum vero," inquit, "ac si alter pro me hoc totum sustineat." Nos autem illum procul dubio vera dixisse credimus, quoniam omnipotens Deus, benedictus et excelsus, suos electos gratiae suae muneribus accumulare non cessat.

them the strength to bear anything for Christ." Then the king spared them, and, his wickedness being assuaged for the moment, he ordered the torments to cease.

Consider, therefore, what constancy of suffering, what purity of mind, and what sincerity of faith were in those individuals, whose spirit was not lessened in any way when they were tormented with the sword, fire, and various kinds of afflictions. They accepted the punishments without ever being affected by any aversion or dejection, but they cheerfully rejoiced and exulted in everything, knowing that, if they were affected by any sadness, they would be a hindrance to themselves, since they had to suffer those things in Christ's name and fulfill what he had commanded to those professing their faith. Considering, at last, the joys of this world to be worthless, they voluntarily handed themselves over to death and punishment. 157

Some of them were skinned alive, others were burned in the fire, thrown to the beasts, beheaded by sword, cut by saws, or had their hands and feet amputated, but all gave thanks to God. They seemed so cheerful during their punishments that when one of them, who had been afflicted with the most severe torments, was asked whether he felt the pain of that punishment, he smiled, turned over on his right side, and responded: "Not only do I not feel anything, but I see a young man standing by me with a cheerful expression, who, wiping my blood away with a cloth of the whitest linen, does not cease to smile at me with encouragement. Truly, I feel," he said, "as if another person is suffering this on my behalf." I believe without doubt that he spoke the truth, since the omnipotent God, blessed and exalted, does not cease to heap up the gifts of his grace upon his chosen ones in abundance. 158

159 Si vero dixeris quare ille angelus, cui commissum erat eos animare et sanguinem eorum extergere, non eos ab ipsis suppliciis visibiliter eruebat ut videntes tortores illi converterentur et paenitentiam agerent, respondebimus tibi. Primo itaque scias quia omnipotens Deus (gloriosus et excelsus) si vellet omnes homines in fide colligere, possibile illi esset, sed, quando dedit eis liberum arbitrium, ita instituit eos ut, si bene agerent, sibi agerent, et si male, similiter, sicque retribueretur eis secundum quod sibi eligerent, pro bonis bona, pro malis mala. Quia non oportebat alium sibi ostendere quid eligerent quam seipsos, quibus data erat ratio, per quam bonum, si vellent, eligere possent. Alioquin unusquisque contra Deum excusationem haberet. Idcirco per manus sanctorum electorum suorum signa et prodigia eo tempore ostendit ut acceptio fidei perficeretur.

160 In aliis vero temporibus signa cessare ex maiori parte voluit, ut ostenderet eos posse recipere fidem, si voluerint. Nam si pro miraculis tantum ad Deum converterentur, quae merces esset illis? Sed dimisit eos secundum desideria cordis eorum, cum tamen ab electorum suorum defensione numquam destiterit ut ostenderet suam liberam potestatem et fructum rationis in homine, et posuit meditationem posteriorum in qualitate receptae suae fidei a devotione priorum et hoc libera voce et aperta ratione.

161 Oportet ergo unumquemque rationabilem scire nullum eorum qui convertuntur a quolibet genere vel voluntate et diversis fidei sectis ad hanc veram fidem posse transferri nisi

If, however, you ask why that angel, whose task it was to give them courage and wipe away their blood, did not rescue them from those torments in plain sight, so that the torturers, upon witnessing this, might be converted and do penance, I will answer you in the following way. In the first place, you should know that if the omnipotent God (glorious and exalted) wished to bring all men together in the faith, it would be possible for him, but, since he has given them free will, he has created them such that, if they do good, they do so for themselves, and likewise if they do evil. In this manner, all are repaid in accordance with what they have chosen for themselves: good for good, evil for evil. Since it would not be right for anyone but themselves to show them what they should choose, they were given a method by which they might choose good, if they so wished. Otherwise everyone would have an excuse against God. For this reason he showed them signs and miracles at that time through his chosen saints, so that they might accept the faith. 159

However, in other periods he wished for the greater part of his miracles to cease in order to demonstrate that they could accept the faith, if they so wished. For if people only turned to God because of miracles, what credit would accrue to them? But he gave them free rein in accordance with their heart's desires, though he never ceased protecting his elect to demonstrate his unrestrained power and the benefit of reason in man. He provided later generations with an example of faith, which they received from their devout forefathers with frank words and for a manifest reason. 160

Any reasonable person should know that of those who converted from various religious sects from any background or inclination, none could have been brought to this true 161

signis atque miraculis. Unde et virtus miraculorum adhuc manens in radice fidei hucusque non desinit. Cuius fructum cotidie oculis perspicimus, auditu percipimus, sensu cognoscimus, scilicet, illa mira quae prae manibus iustorum et castissimorum habentur in expulsione daemonum, in diversorum curatione langorum, per basilicas, per monasteria, per altaria quae in honore ipsorum fabricantur qui martyrii nomine digni sunt. Quaedam autem sunt in quibus sepulcra eorum, quaedam in quibus corpora, quaedam in quibus reliquiae continentur. Haec beneficia currunt ab oriente usque in occidentem, tam in regione Romanorum quam Syriae et Persidis et Aegypti atque Aethiopum et in insulis maris ac in omni orbe terrarum. Et hoc non potest latere neque fideles neque infideles neque magos neque haereticos.

162 Tuus autem socius vacuus et inanis ab his omnibus esse probatur, quoniam nullum istorum ei videre contigit praeter illos duos, quos tu nosti, scilicet, Sergium, qui se Nestorium dixit, et Iohannem, qui cognominatur Buhaire. Haec enim gratia non est nisi in fide universali, nec sibi hoc aliquis vindicat nisi populus Christianus. Haec est enim propria eorum hereditas permanens usque in finem saeculi. Quae praedicatio sanctior, quae lux splendidior, quae veritas manifestior quaerenti veritatem?

163 Cur non consideras hoc tota mente investigans et examinans sitque tota intentio toto conamine a profundo miseriae ad singularem salutis huius portum cito confugere? Quis dignior est nomine martyrii: aut quis probatur mortuus fuisse in via Dei, ille qui nolens adorare solem et lunam, ignem et aquam et simulacra lignorum et auri et argenti et cetera portenta gentilium, cui etiam multa promittebantur ut

faith without signs and miracles. Hence the virtue of miracles even now does not cease to remain at the root of the faith. We see its fruit daily with our eyes, hear it with our ears, perceive it with our mind, specifically, those miracles performed by the hands of the righteous and the most chaste, in exorcising demons, in curing various afflictions, in churches, monasteries, and altars constructed in the honor of those worthy of the title of martyr. Some contain their tombs, some their bodies, their relics. Their good deeds range from east to west, in the land of the Romans as well as Syria, Persia, Egypt, Ethiopia, the islands of the sea—in short, in the whole world. This cannot have gone unnoticed by the faithful or the unfaithful, magicians or heretics.

Your friend, however, is proven to be lacking in and de- 162
void of all of these things, since he never got a chance to see any Christians except for those two, whom you know: Sergius, who called himself Nestorius, and John, called Baḥīrā. This grace is only in the universal faith, and nobody can claim it for himself but the Christian people, for this is their inheritance, enduring unto the end of times. What message is more sacred, what light is brighter, what truth is clearer to those who seek the truth?

Why do you not focus upon this diligently and carefully 163
with your whole mind, and why are you not completely intent on fleeing quickly from the sea of misery to the only safe haven with all your might? Who is worthier of the title of martyr: one who is proven to have died on the path of God, who was unwilling to worship the sun and the moon, fire and water, as well as idols of wood, gold, and silver, and the other fabrications of the pagans; to whom much was promised in order that he might worship them, but who

ea adoraret, omnia quae possidebat pariterque filios et filias et uxorem et parentes omnes contempsit et semetipsum Deo sacrificium obtulit—an ille qui toto nisu processit aliena diripere, homines interficere, parentes cum liberis captivare, mulieribus castitatem eripere ceteraque nefanda et diabolica perpetrare? Talem vero expeditionem socius tuus viam Dei appellare non erubuit. Deinde dixit: *"Qui occidit vel occiditur in tali expeditione paradisum sine dubio consequetur."*

164 Modo teipsum constituo iudicem. Tu autem, sicut oportet, iustum iudicium profer. Numquid fur cuiuslibet domum fodiens, si paries super eum rueret, aut in puteum caderet, immunis esset a peccato, aut si paterfamilias eum occideret, numquid tuo iudicio homicida propter hoc haberetur? Ego quidem puto, te iudice, non sic putari debere. Quomodo ergo credendi sunt possidere paradisum illi qui in expeditione tui socii vadunt ad furandum, ad devastandum, ad captivandum, insuper ad occidendum homines securos, innocentes, sine ulla sollicitatione in suis domibus quietos, quos numquam viderant nec videri ab eis poterant? Nec suffecit socio tuo de tali iniquitate non solum non paenitere et ad Dominum converti nisi insuper talem expeditionem viam Dei vocaret et sic insano ore clamaret: *"Qui occidit vel occiditur in tali expeditione paradisum sine dubio consequetur."* Quod si tu etiam tale iudicium dederis, diabolus, qui ab initio humani generis inimicus extitit, peior te non erit.

165 Ego tamen scio quod tua prudentia et sollertia prohibet

scorned all he possessed, as well as his sons, daughters, wife, and parents, and offered himself as a sacrifice to God—or he who expended every effort to plunder another's possessions, to kill people, to take parents captive with their children, to rob women of their chastity, and to commit other godless and diabolical acts? Yet your friend was not ashamed to call such a campaign the path of God. Then he said: "He who kills or is killed in such a campaign will, without doubt, win a place in paradise."

Now I make you the judge. Offer a just judgment, as is 164
proper. If a thief were to break into someone's house, and the wall collapsed on him, or he fell into a well, surely this would not absolve him from sin, or if the head of the household were to kill him, surely you would not judge him to be guilty of homicide because of this? It is my opinion that, even with you as judge, this is not the view that ought to be held. How then are they expected to win a place in paradise who go on a campaign of your friend to steal, plunder, take captive, and, on top of that, to kill without provocation untroubled, innocent people, who are at peace in their own homes, whom your companions had never seen, and who could not have been seen by them? It was not enough for your friend not to repent for such wickedness and not to turn to the Lord, but he also went so far as to designate such a campaign "the Path of God" and to cry out with raving tongue in the following manner: "He who kills or is killed in such a campaign will, without doubt, win a place in paradise." If you, too, were to pronounce such a judgment, the devil, who has been man's enemy from the beginning, would be no worse than you.

But I know that your prudence and cleverness prevent 165

te talia iudicare. Puto enim te omnium quae scripsi fidem et certitudinem nullatenus ignorare et me tibi sufficienter respondere. Nisi enim sperassem de tui sensus perfectione tuaque mirabili in rebus consideratione atque praeclara verborum discussione—immo inter certum et dubium subtili discretione—nequaquam tecum in omnibus sermonibus meis superioribus tam communis et securus fuissem. Te autem reminisci decet familiaritatis et securitatis quam mihi in tuo libello exhibuisti, quamque licet ego prius non expetissem, cum gaudio tamen suscepi. Et quoniam multum rogare visus es ea quae apud nos habentur, certa tibi ratione exponi, visum est mihi primo quidem propter ipsam veritatem non tacere, deinde tuis sicuti amici interrogationibus respondere.

166 Nos autem, quod scripsimus, non scripsimus ex invidia vel ex indignatione neque iniquo et odioso proposito, sed causa disputationis, ad quam tu nos provocasse videris, compulit nos pauca de multis in medium proferre. Nam, si voluissemus e contra uti res exigeret respondere, sermo noster aliter se haberet et adversus plura et maiora quae praetermissimus, multo plenius multoque vehementius ageremus, quod non metu sed ratione et amore dimisimus. Te vero non decet irasci neque de praeteritis quae in hoc libello scripta sunt, neque de futuris, si qua adhuc scribenda sunt, quae nihilominus ad respondendum, secundum quod tuus liber exigit, elegimus. Nostra enim verba tam aperta et clara sunt veritate subnixa ut nec tu nec alius eis iuste contradicere possit, nisi forte quis aut scienter aut ignoranter a

you from making such judgments. I think you are well aware of the reliability and truth of all that I have written, and that I have responded to you adequately. If I did not trust in the excellence of your good sense, your wondrous ability to consider things, and your splendid ability to analyze words—indeed, to make subtle distinctions between certainty and uncertainty—I would never have been so open and unworried in all of my earlier conversations with you. It befits you to recall the friendly and carefree nature you showed to me in your little book, and though I did not seek it first, still I received it gladly. And since you seemed to ask urgently for a clear and rational exposition of our customs, I decided, first, that because truth itself was in question I should not be silent, and, second, to respond to your inquiries as though they were a friend's.

What I wrote, however, I did not write out of ill will or 166
indignation, nor with a wicked and hateful purpose, but the discussion, to which you seem to have invited me, prompted me to offer a few thoughts about many subjects. For if I wished, on the contrary, to answer in the manner that this matter required, my speech would have been different, and I would have dealt in much more detail and much more vigorously with many greater topics that I omitted—and I did so not out of fear but because of reason and love. You should not grow angry either about things in the past that were written in this little book, or about future things, if any will yet be written, which I nevertheless have chosen in my response to you, since this is what your book requests. My words are so perspicuous and clear, supported as they are by truth, that neither you nor anyone else could rightly contradict them, except perhaps for the person who, knowingly or

tramite veritatis devius modum discretionis servare nescierit. Noster quidem ignis latebat in lapide, sed tua chalybe excussus coactas erupit in flammas.

167 Quo circa tam tibi quam omnibus qui meum scriptum viderint, plane et fiducialiter loquor, quoniam illa ad quae me invitasti de rebus labilibus et fugitivis tam stulta et inania sunt ut etiam, si aeterna essent, nullatenus homo rationabilis ea deberet appetere vel suum ad haec animum inclinare, praesertim cum sint communia asinis et canibus et porcis sive ceteris animalibus, in quibus nihil est aliud quam comedere et bibere et concumbere. Hic etenim mundus, qui maxime per ista miseros decipit, apud rationabiles homines cum omnibus suis illecebris pro nihilo deputatur, qui sollerter ac veraciter cuncta eius blandimenta et gaudia fugitiva et misera esse considerantes seque ab ipsius laqueis viriliter excutientes, Christi Domini vera et sempiterna bona in futuro saeculo promittentis sacrosanctis vestigiis adhaeserunt. Istis etenim tuis inordinatis admonitionibus nemo dignus habetur, nisi qui suae carnis miseriae subiacens pronus et praeceps ad quaelibet libidinis incitamenta, sicut equus et mulus, fertur et rapitur. Ego autem non puto te credere me ad talia anhelare.

168 Utinam scirem unde me voluisti irretire his talibus laqueis pessimis et caenulentissimis in quibus mergitur ac delectatur cuius natura in nullo a pecorum similitudine discernitur. Sapientes vero ac rerum causas subtiliter perpendentes ab omnibus illis, quae tu pro magno munere in libro tuo promittis, longe distare videntur. Illi enim indesinenter toto nisu per Dei gratiam elaborant concupiscentias et vitia

unknowingly wandering from the path of truth, does not know how to use a measure of discretion. My fire was, to be sure, hidden in a rock, but it was forced to burst into flames once it had been struck by your sword.

I spoke plainly and faithfully to you and all those who will 167
read my writings, since the transient and fleeting topic to which you have invited me is so foolish and idle that even if it were eternal, a rational man should never seek these things nor focus his mind on them, especially since they are shared with asses, dogs, pigs, and other animals who do nothing but eat, drink, and copulate. This world, that deludes wretches with those things above all, is deemed worthless by rational men, along with all of its enticements. With special insight they are able to see that all its attractions and joys are fleeting and miserable, and, vigorously freeing themselves from its traps, they follow closely in the hallowed footsteps of Lord Christ, who promises true and eternal goods in the next world. Indeed, nobody considers themselves worthy of your inappropriate urgings, except for those who are subject to the misery of the flesh, and are carried and dragged head over heels toward all manner of lustful attractions, just like horses or mules. I, for my part, do not think that you believe that I desire such things.

I wish I knew why you wish to ensnare me in traps so evil 168
and full of filth that only those whose nature is no different from that of cattle find pleasure in being submerged in them. Indeed, those who are wise and capable of carefully weighing the causes of things appear to be greatly removed from everything you are promising as a rich reward in your book. For they strive unceasingly and with all of their effort, as well as the grace of God, to blot out all lust and carnal

carnis extinguere et ut etiam quod naturaliter superfluum habetur in corpore possit auferri, sanctissimo castimoniae studio seipsos non desinunt castigare. Deus enim non creavit hominem ad hoc nec in Die Iudicii ad huic simile resuscitari faciet.

169 Tu autem in libro tui socii scis hoc scriptum esse: *"Nos non ad aliud homines et daemones creavimus nisi ad colendum nos."* Numquid non vides socium tuum verbis suis esse contrarium, cum dicit "creavimus ad colendum," deinde aversus solvit pactum et destruit aedificium, praecipiens uxores tres vel quattuor ducere et ancillas quantaecumque inveniri poterunt unumquemque sibi applicare, insuper et more pecudum comedere et bibere absque ordine omnique moderationis discretione?

170 Capitulum vero repudii et licitae revocationis hic ponerem nisi et prolixus esse timerem et librum meum verbis inhonestissimis sordidare refugerem. Referrem quoque qualiter Deus per Ieremiam aliosque prophetas ob hoc maxime contra populum suum se iratum esse mandaverit. Tu autem scis quam detestandum atque horribile sit hoc apud omne genus humanum, nam et ipsi gentiles, qui filios suos idolis immolabant, hanc turpitudinem omnimodis abhorrebant. Ego autem confundor talia nominare et scribere.

171 Illud vero quod mihi aliquando dixisti et me tuis minis verberasti, fiducialiter in Christo agens, non timeo. Dixisti enim mihi: "Considera, quaeso, diligenter et hanc iniuriam tibi inferre noli neque quod noceat provocare." Audi ergo Dominum Iesum Christum in suo evangelio mihi dicentem: *"Nolite timere eos qui occidunt corpus, animam autem non possunt*

vices, and they also do not refrain from chastising themselves out of the holy desire for chastity, so that even what is considered naturally excessive in the body might be eradicated. Since God did not create man for this, he will not cause him to be reborn into something similar to this on the day of judgment.

But you know that the following is written in your friend's 169
book: "I created humans and demons for no other purpose than for them to worship me." Do you not see that your friend contradicted his own words when he said, "I created them to worship," and then turned around and broke a truce, razed a building, and ordered men to have three or four wives, as well as many slave girls as could be found, and for every man to be selfish, and to eat and drink as do cattle, without any kind of order or modicum of moderation?

I would add at this point the *sūra* on divorce and remar- 170
riage if I did not fear to be verbose and to besmirch my book with utterly dishonorable words. I would also tell you how God conveyed through Jeremiah and the other prophets that he was wrathful with his people on these grounds above all. And you know how despised and abhorred this is among the entire human race, since even the pagans, who were accustomed to sacrifice their own children to idols, shuddered at this kind of shamelessness in every way. But I am too appalled to mention or write about such things.

I do not fear what you said to me earlier, nor the threats 171
you leveled against me, since I trust in Christ. For you said to me: "Consider carefully, I ask you, and do not bring this harm upon yourself, and do not invite what could hurt you." Listen to the Lord Jesus Christ, saying in his gospel to me: "Do not fear those who kill the body, for they cannot kill the

occidere, sed potius eum timete, qui potest et animam et corpus perdere in Gehennam." Ego igitur securus et constans scio et credo quia nullus in animam meam potestatem habet nisi Dominus meus Iesus Christus (cuius nomen sit gloriosum et benedictum), qui in me abundare fecit iustitiam et misericordiam et benignitatem et clementiam domini mei *Emirhelmomini.* Nam et ego et mei similes, qui eius vel longe vel prope familiaritate gaudemus, sub umbra alarum ipsius in securitate et aequitate atque benignitate manemus. Omnipotens Deus retribuat illi aeternitatem in regno caelorum et communionem habere cum sanctis et electis suis post longum aevum in abundantia bonorum et gaudio et tranquillitate vitae. Ille clementer nos exaudiat. Amen.

172 Praeterea dixisti mihi: "Haec est fides nostra et haec est lex nostra, in qua tu, cum ingressus fueris et nostra testificatione testificatus, eris nostri similis et particeps nobiscum in gloria, scilicet, et in hoc saeculo et in futuro." Sed quid rursus tibi respondeam de fide et lege tua? Iam enim taedet me totiens repetere quod mihi satis expresse et intelligibiliter iamdudum videor explicasse.

173 De gloria vero, quam mihi pollicitus es, scio equidem quod magnum tibi Deus dederit principatum, quem in domo generis tui posuit, unde precor Deum ut illum tibi per multa tempora servet. Gloriam enim futuri saeculi, quam similiter promisisti, nullus nisi bonis operibus promeretur. Fertur enim quod tuus socius dixerit: "O filii Abdemenef, nihil subtraham vobis de his quae iusserit Deus. Nolite venire ad me cum vanitate, aliis venientibus cum opere. Bonitas vestra apud Deum est timere illum." Si autem hoc dixit, iam tibi gloriam futuri saeculi abstulit, nisi bona opera

soul; rather, fear him, who is able to bring both soul and body to ruin in Gehenna." Thus I am free from care and steadfast, and I know and believe that no one has any power over my soul except my Lord Jesus Christ (may his name be glorious and blessed), who has brought the justice, compassion, kindness, and mercy of my lord the *ʾamīr al-muʾminīn* upon me. For I and similar persons enjoy his familiarity near or far and reside under the protective shadow of his wing in a carefree, just, and friendly environment. May the omnipotent God grant him eternity in the kingdom of heaven and the right to hold communion with saints and his elect, after a long lifetime in the abundance of goods and a joyful and peaceful life. May he hear our prayers with mercy. Amen.

You also said to me: "This is our faith and this is our law, 172
and if you enter into it and testify by our testimony, you will be like us and share with us in glory, in both this world and the next." What can I respond to you concerning your faith and law? I am getting tired of repeating over and over what I seem to have already explained to you clearly and comprehensibly enough.

Concerning the glory you promised me, I am well aware 173
that God has given you a great realm, which he has placed in the house of your family, and so I pray to him that he may keep it safe for many ages. The glory of the future world, which you have also promised to me, cannot be earned by anyone except through good works. Your friend is reported to have said: "Sons of ʿAbd Manāf, I will not take from you any of the things God has commanded. Do not come to me with idleness, while others come with action. The measure of your goodness before God is to fear him." But if he said this, he has already taken from you the glory of the future

facias. Nos vero non invenimus electos Dei nisi illos qui non in genere, non in nobilitate, non in dignitate huius saeculi gloriabantur sed nobilitas eorum in futuro per bona opera nunc habetur. Tu ergo et alii, si feceritis quae Deo placent, gloriam illam invenietis.

174 Mihi autem absit gloriari generis nobilitate vel parentum generositate, licet mea generatio sit super omnes Arabum generationes, sicut notum est nobis et parentibus et avis nostris. Nullus enim ignorat qualiter se reges Quindae habuerunt, quantumque ceteros Arabes dignitate et gloria superaverunt. Nos tamen nihil aliud dicimus nisi quod Paulus Apostolus praedicator veritatis dicit: *"Qui gloriatur, in Domino glorietur."* Haec est enim perfectio nobilitatis et gloriae. Nec nos aliam quaerimus nobilitatem nisi fidem Christianitatis, quae est cognitio Dei. Per ipsam enim dirigimur ad omne opus bonum, per eam Deum in veritate cognoscimus, eiusque proximi et domestici facti sumus. Ipsa est enim porta quae ducit ad vitam et ab infernali cruciatu defendit.

175 Quod iterum dicis quia socius tuus dicturus sit Deo in die iudicii, cum unusquisque occupatus fuerit de seipso, "Plebs mea, plebs mea, domus mea, domus mea," pro nulla alia deprecor te: et qualiter exaudietur oratio eius? Oculi tui soporati sunt et bene vidisti? Istae certe sunt fabulae senum et promissiones mulierum et spei fallacia. Possibile est enim omni falso prophetae talia de se confingere. Ego autem credo et non dubito quod Dominus noster Iesus Christus venturus est iudicare vivos et mortuos, de quo tua scriptura testificatur quoniam ipse est excellentissimus omnium in hoc saeculo et in futuro, et nullus gloriosus nisi ipse solus. Et

world, unless you perform good works. I have not found anyone to be a chosen one of God except for those who did not take pride in their lineage, nobility, or the dignity of this world—instead, their future glory is thought to consist in the good works they do now. You and the rest, if you do what is pleasing to God, will find that glory.

May I never take pride in the nobility of my family or of 174
my parents, even though my lineage is superior to that of all the Arabs, as is known to me, my parents, and my grandparents. Everyone knows what the kings of Kinda were like, and how greatly they surpassed all other Arabs in dignity and glory. I will mention nothing else except what the apostle Paul, preacher of truth, said: "Let him who glories glory in the Lord." For this is the perfection of nobility and glory. And I do not seek any other nobility but the faith of Christianity, which is to know God. For through it we are directed toward every good work, and through it we truly know God, and have become his neighbors and intimates, for it is the gate that leads to life and protects from hellish torment.

As to your claim that on judgment day, when each will be 175
concerned with himself, your friend will speak to God, "My people, my people, my house, my house," I ask you, on behalf of the very same house: how will his speech be heard? Your eyes were sleeping and yet you saw well? Surely those are the tales of old men, the promises of women, and the deception of hope. For it is possible for any false prophet to make up such things about himself. But I believe and do not doubt that our Lord Jesus Christ will come to judge the living and the dead, about whom your scripture attests that he is the most exalted of all in this world and the next, and no one except him alone is glorious. And truly he is the judge of

vere ipse est iudex omnium hominum et ipse in die iudicii retribuet unicuique secundum opera sua, aliis bona, aliis mala. Ipse habet examen iustum, qui non declinat in iudicio nec personas accipit. Ipse discernet in illa die inter homines aequitate et iudicabit iustitia.

176 Cum igitur tua scriptura tale testimonium Christo perhibeat et quia ipse est spiritus Dei et Verbum eius, quare non adquiescis mihi amicabiliter te exhortanti et non declinas ab hac spe falsa et iniqua dimittens ista vanissima et ridicula et sequens ea, quae te oporteret facere, opera bona? Et cur non adquiris tibi viaticum, dum manes in hac domo, ut sit tibi salus et refugium in illo terribili die? Cave, obsecro, et fuge ab illa stulta et vana securitate et a verbositate segnium et insipientium et diligenter age de salute animae tuae.

177 Terminus enim iam instat et mors prope est ad standum in conspectu Iesu Christi, sicuti testatur tua scriptura indubitanter hoc esse, quando iudicium dabitur vera discussione, ubi nulla excusatio, nulla paenitentia erit, loqui enim non poterunt, quanto minus excusare se. Tu vero time Deum in anima tua et scias quia timor Dei melior est omni negotiatione, unde habebis lucra sine pecunia. Nam et tu, sicut dicis, vidisti illam instantiam monachorum et nulla voce poteris evadere iudicium Dei, cum sis undique veritate conclusus, eo quod scientia et intellectus tibi naturaliter data sint. Nulla enim occasio vel excusatio tibi remansisse videtur.

178 Illa enim facilia et levia, quae in fide tua et lege commemorasti, quomodo et qualiter possunt fieri? Heu, quam male

all men and on judgment day he will render to each according to their works, to some good, to some evil. He has a just scale, which is not skewed in its judgment, nor does it show partiality. He will distinguish between men on that day with fairness and judge with justice.

Since your scripture offers such a report about Christ, 176
and since he is the Spirit of God and his Word, why do you not give in to my friendly exhortation and turn away from this false and wrongful hope, laying aside those idle and laughable things, and pursue those good works, which you ought to perform? And why do you not seek provisions for your journey, while you remain in this abode, so that you may have safety and refuge on that terrible day? Be careful, I beg you, and avoid that foolish and idle carelessness, and the long-windedness of the sluggish and the imprudent, and take good care for the safety of your soul.

The end is near and death is close by, when we are to 177
stand before Jesus Christ, as your scripture in no uncertain terms attests, when judgment will be passed in true discrimination, when there will be no excuses, no repentance, for they will not be able to speak, let alone excuse themselves. Fear God in your heart, therefore, and know that the fear of God is better than any business transaction, since you will have profit without money. You too, as you say, have witnessed the perseverance of monks, and you will not be able to escape the judgment of God with any words, since you are surrounded on all sides by the truth, for knowledge and understanding have been given to you by nature. No opportunity to excuse yourself will be left to you.

How and in what fashion can those shallow and petty 178
things which you related as being part of your faith and religion take place? Alas, how badly is your soul tricking you,

blanditur tibi anima tua, cum Dominus meus Iesus Christus in suo sancto evangelio inter alia dixerit: *"Cum feceritis omnia quae praecepta sunt vobis, dicite: 'Servi inutiles sumus, quod debuimus facere fecimus;'" "Arta est enim via quae ducit ad vitam et pauci sunt qui vadunt per eam, quam lata et spatiosa est via quae ducit ad mortem et quam multi sunt qui incedunt per eam."* Vide autem quam contraria sint haec verba illis facilibus et levibus fidei tuae, quae consentiens carnalibus affectibus hominum, inmoderate uti mulieribus iussit dicens, "Coite cum quantiscumque vultis de mulieribus," et alia his similia, quae prolixitas prohibet numerari.

179 Adiutorium sit a Domino super omnibus quae tibi impressa sunt et in animo tuo informata, quae tu aestimas certa et indubia, cum sint tibi naufraga et periculosa. Quomodo latere te potuit haec falsa esse et inania? Ego autem deprecor Deum, qui iustificat errantem et ad viam aequitatis dirigit, ut illuminet te splendore scientiae suae ut iustificari valeas et a densitate tenebrarum huius erroris emergere. Oportet enim me hoc facere pro te specialiter et pro aliis omnibus generaliter. Hoc enim lex et regula Christianitatis iubet. Oratio namque perfecta est orare pro omnibus hominibus pariter ut iustificet eos Dominus et aperiat oculos interiores eorum, auferens ab eis errorem incredulitatis, donec cognoscant Dominum et de peccatis suis paeniteant. Et quicumque iustificatus fuerit, confirmet Deus iustificationem eius. Omnipotens Deus, o amice carissime, impleat tibi hoc et omnibus amicis et fratribus nostris sua virtute et potentia.

when my Lord Jesus Christ says in his sacred gospel, among other things: "When you have done all that is commanded to you, say: 'We are useless servants, because we have done what we were supposed to do,'" and "Narrow is the path that leads to life, and few are they who travel by it, but how wide and broad is the path that leads to death, and how many are they who travel by it!" See how these words contradict those shallow and petty tenets of your faith that catered to the carnal lusts of men when it commanded them to make immoderate use of women, saying "Copulate with however many women you wish," and other similar things, which my fear of verboseness prevents me from enumerating.

May the Lord aid you in all that has been taught to you 179
and instilled in you, which you consider to be certain and without doubt, even though it is ruinous and dangerous to you. How can it have gone unnoticed by you that these things are false and vain? I pray to God, who sets right those who wander off and directs them to the path of righteousness, to illuminate you with the splendor of his knowledge, so that you may be pardoned and able to escape from the deep darkness of this error. It is proper that I do so, for you in particular and for all others in general. For this is commanded to me by the law and rule of Christianity. The ideal prayer is to pray for all men equally that the Lord pardon them and open their inner eyes, removing from them their error of unbelieving, until they acknowledge the Lord and repent their sins. Whoever will be pardoned, let God sanction his pardon. May omnipotent God, dearest friend, fulfill this for you and for all our friends and brothers, by his virtue and power.

180 De hoc etiam nolo tacere quod hortaris me dicens: "Desine ab errore et infidelitate qua detineris, et ab eo quod dicis Patrem, Filium, Spiritum Sanctum, et a cultura crucis, quae nec obest nec prodest." De infidelitate et errore saepe et aperte superius diximus, quae ob prolixitatem et taedium legentis reiterare nolumus. Iam enim manifeste et rationabiliter ostendimus ad quem nostrum magis haec duo verba pertineant, error, scilicet, et infidelitas, nec necesse est ut inde ulterius sermones multiplicemus.

181 Si vero dixeris ea quae dicta sunt commixta esse et obscura, scio vere illud quod non intelligis apud te obscurum esse et indiscretum, sicut scriptum est: "Quod ignorat quis inimicum est illi." Absit a te, opitulante Deo, stultitia. Non est hoc sicut tu aestimas (quem Deus salvet). Ne facias tibi rogo pro velle iudicium dum contradictor defuerit. Scito enim illud, quod tu obscurum dicis et commixtum et indiscretum mysterium esse, quod angeli ministrantes et prophetae missi desideranter exquisierunt, quibus vix aliquid parum inde arcana contemplatione scire concessum est. Unde prorsus nihil intelligi posse existimes nisi fide et humili cordis ad Deum conversione et ab omni carnalium desideriorum sorde purgata intentione. Nam nec ipsi sancti prophetae hoc plene intelligere potuerunt, donec venit Dei Filius dilectus et revelavit illud suis electis apostolis et inundavit illos scientia aperiens hoc illis Spiritu suo Sancto aperte et manifeste, cum diceret: *"Ite et advocate homines ad cognitionem veritatis certam atque perfectam, quae est Pater et*

I also do not want to keep silent about your exhortation to me: "Desist from the error and unbelief in which you are trapped, and from what you call the Father, Son, and the Holy Spirit, and from the veneration of the cross, which neither helps nor hinders." I have previously spoken to you often and openly about this faithlessness and error, which I do not care to repeat, to prevent wearing down the reader with verboseness. I have already demonstrated clearly and reasonably to which of us these two words, error and faithlessness, apply more; it is unnecessary to reiterate talk of this anymore. 180

If, however, you say that I have spoken ambiguously and vaguely, I know for certain that what you do not understand is vague and ambiguous only to you, as it is written: "That which someone does not know is hostile to him." May foolishness be far from you, God willing! Things are not as you (may God save you) think they are. I ask you not to give the judgment you wish while your opponent is absent. You know that what you call an ambiguous and vague mystery has been sought with great zeal by angelic servants and God-sent prophets, to whom it has just barely been granted to know a little about these things through mystical contemplation. For this reason you should know that nothing can be understood except through faith and the humble devotion of the heart to God, and through an intention cleansed of any kind of filthy carnal desire. Indeed, not even the holy prophets were able to understand this fully, until the beloved Son of God came and revealed it to his chosen apostles, and made them overflow with knowledge, granting them open and clear access to it by means of the Holy Spirit, when he said: "Go and call mankind to a certain and complete knowledge 181

Filius et Spiritus Sanctus." Apostoli vero susceperunt hoc ab eius ore sacratissimo et tradiderunt nobis, qui fideliter in Christum credimus. Nos autem suscipientes illud ab apostolis in signis et prodigiis usque ad finem saeculi in eo permanebimus.

182 De cultura vero crucis quam nec obesse nec prodesse dicis, cum adoramus eam et osculamur et ab ipsa benedicimur, respondeo quia non sine causa et ratione hoc facimus. Ideo enim facimus quia Dominus noster Iesus Christus in ea mortem passus est, quae est causa nostrae salutis et redemptionis ab interitu et errore. Huius beneficii gratia apud nos non potest comprehendi sermone nec digna glorificari veneratione. Crux etenim sancta ad hoc exemplum praefigurata est et oculis nostris praeparata ut nos moneat et hortetur ad orandum, venerandum, et glorificandum illum, qui pro nobis in ea suspensus est.

183 Nec, sicut tu putas, lignum ibi adoramus vel veneramur. Si enim pro ligno adorando hoc faceremus, nequaquam crucem de auro vel argento aut lapidibus pretiosis vel qualibet alia materia nobis fabricaremus. Unde probamus nos neque lignum neque aurum neque argentum neque aliud quidlibet in cruce adorare nisi Christum pro nobis in ea passum, cuius passio gloriosa per crucis imaginem nobis repraesentatur.

184 Si enim humana lex iubet honorari ea quae regis sunt et ea quae ad eum pertinent glorificari maximeque nomen et imagines eius venerabiliter adorari, quanto magis honorari, glorificari, et adorari debet crux sancta, in qua Christus humani generis redemptor pependit. Nam et nostri temporis homines huius consuetudinis morem honestissimum imitantes manus eorum et pedes osculantur, immo quod maius est, humiliter eos adorant. Quare ergo redarguimur adorare

of truth, which is the Father, the Son, and the Holy Spirit." The apostles received this from his hallowed mouth and delivered it to us, who believe faithfully in Christ. Since we received this from the apostles by means of signs and miracles, we will remain faithful in him until the end of times.

With regard to the veneration of the cross, which you say 182
neither helps nor harms, I answer that, when we adore it, kiss it, and are blessed by it, we do not do so without cause or reason. We do so because our Lord Jesus Christ suffered death on it, which is the cause of our salvation and redemption from our own death and error. The kindness of this favor to us cannot be expressed in speech or glorified with worthy reverence. The holy cross was prefigured for this example and shown to our eyes to urge and encourage us to pray, venerate, and glorify the one who was crucified on it for us.

And we do not, as you think, worship and venerate the 183
wood. If we were to worship it for the sake of the wood, we would not fashion a cross out of gold, silver, gems, or any other material. Thus we prove that we worship not the wood nor the gold nor the silver nor anything else on the cross but Christ, who died for us, whose glorious suffering is represented to us through the figure of the cross.

If the human law orders us to honor that which belongs 184
to the king and to glorify what is his, and to worship his name and images with special veneration, how much more should the holy cross on which Christ was crucified as redeemer of the human race be honored, glorified, and worshipped? Even men of our age imitate this most honorable custom by kissing the hands and feet of kings, and—which is an even greater good—they worship them humbly. Am I

crucem, quae regis nostri pro nobis mortui singulare signum est?

185 Et si prophetae convenientes et exultantes Arcam quam Moses, iubente Domino, aedificaverat adorabant, quid nos facere convenit de cruce redemptoris nostri, cuius mysterio et Arca illa et Tabernaculum et omnia legis illius instituta et sacrificia militabant? Quod autem in Arca Mosi crucis mysterium lateret, satis ipse Moses ostendit, quando in deductione eius et a castris elevatione dicebat: *"Exsurge, Domine, et dissipentur inimici tui."* Et cum reduceretur ad castra et in suo loco collocaretur iterum dicebat: *"Revertere, Domine, ad milia et ad decem milia filiorum Israel."* Quod etiam Iosue et Samuel et David ostenderunt, quando eam ducentes et reducentes in signis et mirabilibus adoraverunt, glorificaverunt, cantantesque ante eam in laudibus Dei exultaverunt. Numquid isti, quando haec faciebant, lignum adorabant et non magis Deum in hoc se toto pietatis affectu glorificare credebant? Nos igitur eorum exempla sectantes multo dignius et honorificentius crucem Domini Dei nostri et adoramus et honoramus et glorificamus.

186 Cur in te (quem Deus salvet), tanta hic oblivio praevalet ut tanto studio Saracenitati patrocineris et Heleisimin defendere cures, cum velle eos fulcire nihil aliud tibi sit quam a via veritatis deviare et a proposito iustitiae, in quo gloriari solebas, divertere et contra hoc quod ore protulisti et lingua confessus es iniuste agere? Nonne tu es ille qui narrare nobis solitus eras, quomodo te virtus sanctae crucis liberaverit, quando fugiens illum quem tu scis cecidisti de mula et

then criticized for worshipping the cross, which is a unique symbol of our Lord's death for us?

And if the prophets gathered in jubilation to worship the 185
Ark, which Moses built at the Lord's command, what ought we to do with respect to the cross of our redeemer, whom the Ark, the Tabernacle, and all of the commandments and sacrifices prescribed by his law serve and prefigure? Moses himself demonstrated sufficiently that the mystery of the cross lay hidden in the Ark, when, in leading it ahead and raising it aloft from the camp, he said: "Rise, Lord, and may your enemies be confounded!" And when it was brought into camp and set in its place, he said: "Return, Lord, to the thousand and ten thousand sons of Israel!" Joshua, Samuel, and David also demonstrated this, when they brought it out and led it back with signs and miracles, and worshipped and glorified it, singing in the praise of God and exulting before it. Surely, when they did these things, they were not worshipping the wood, but rather believed that they were glorifying God with this feeling of piety? Following in their footsteps, we worship, honor, and glorify the cross of the Lord our God in a much more worthy and honorable manner.

Why is there in you (may God save you) such confusion 186
that you defend the Saracen faith with such zeal and are so concerned with defending the Hāshimites, since to wish to support them is the same as deviating from the path of truth and turning away from the pursuit of justice, about which you are accustomed to boast, and to unjustly go against what you professed with your mouth and declared with your tongue? Are you not the one who used to tell me how the virtue of the holy cross freed you when, fleeing from the one you know, you fell from your mule, and on a different occa-

iterum, quando pergens ad Gomar Alachabarha obviam venit tibi ille qui obviam venit, et quando pergebas in Civitatem et occurrit tibi leo? Numquid ista omnia tradidisti oblivioni et quomodo cum inclamares memoriam et signum sanctae crucis liberatus sis? Quare ergo tu (quem Deus salvet) tam mirabile beneficium denegas et mala pro bonis restituis? Non enim decet te hoc, si fidem diligis et veritati consentis.

187 Tu enim scis quoniam nos omnes Christiani non colimus crucem, sed quae in cruce est Dei gloriam et virtutem. Credimus enim illam causam esse nostrae salutis. Numquid non saepe de hoc contendimus et tu conclusus es veritate? Quare ergo te avertisti ab eo quod probabile et certum extitit apud te? Expecto certe tamen quia quandoque, auxiliante Domino, melius videbis, et procul dubio salvus eris.

188 Inde vero quod mecum bene egisti ut me ab igne liberari velles et mihi aeque ut tibi consultum esse optasti. Secundum quod exterius sonare videtur, gratias ago; secundum vero quod in veritate habetur, tu potius eas mihi debes. Tu enim (quem Deus salvet) attende, quoniam si intelligere volueris, meus sermo et exhortatio tibi ad salutem. Tua vero verba et invitatio mihi ad perditionem si, quod absit, tibi adquiescere vellem. Nonne tu cotidie postulas in quinque orationibus tuis ut dirigat te Deus in viam rectam, quae est via eorum cum quibus Deus ab initio bene egit et quibus minime irascitur et in errore non sunt? Nam, si tu in errore non es vel errare non times, quid necesse est hanc orationem facere?

sion, when you were on your way to ʿUmr al-Karj and one you know crossed your path, and when you were on your way to Medina and you came upon a lion? Did you forget all of this, as well as how you were freed when you invoked his memory and the sign of the holy cross? Why then do you (may God save you) reject such a miraculous boon and exchange good things for evil? This does not befit you, if you love faith and submit to the truth.

You know that all of us Christians do not worship the 187
cross, but God's glory and virtue that are in the cross, for we believe that it is the cause of our salvation. Have we not debated about this often, and are you still shut off from the truth? Why then did you turn away from what was probable and certain within you? But I am patient, since with God's aid you will one day amend your views, and, without doubt, will be saved.

For this reason I thank you for being so kind to me as to 188
wish to free me from the fire, and for wishing that I be taken care of as well as you. In accordance with what appears to be expressed superficially, I thank you; but in accordance with what is held to be true, it is rather you who owes me gratitude. You (may God save you) should pay attention therefore, since if you are willing to understand, my speech and exhortation will facilitate your salvation. Your words and invitation, on the other hand, will facilitate my damnation if—God forbid!—I were willing to assent to you. Do you not ask daily in five prayers for God to set you on the right path, which is the path of those to whom God has acted kindly from the beginning, with whom he is not angry, and who are not in a state of error? For if you are not in a state of error, or are not afraid to be in error, what need is there to make this prayer?

189 Ostende, quaeso, mihi qui sunt hi in quorum via vis esse, cum iactes te fore de meliori populo qui in hoc saeculo visus est. An cultores idolorum sunt isti? An Iudaei, de quibus dicit socius tuus quia ipsi sunt praecipue quibus irascitur Deus? De cultura vero idolorum, quod erratica sit, ipsa tua scriptura dicit, cum loquitur Deus ad Mahumet, quem ab errore idolorum iustificasse se dicebat, ita: *"Nonne tu in errore fuisti et iustificatus es?"* Ille enim nec Iudaeus nec gentilis tantum sed gentilis et idolorum cultor extitisse probatur. Si autem dixeris viam eorum rectam qui dicunt mundum istum nec incepisse aliquando nec finiendum esse, qui sunt haeretici mundani, vel illorum qui sunt Georgiani et Samaniani et Brahamiani, dicemus tibi quia numquam socius tuus eorum sectas approbavit, nec viam alicuius eorum rectam fuisse dixit.

190 Cum igitur nec Iudaei nec gentiles nec idolorum cultores nec haeretici in via recta sint, restat ut Christianos intelligamus, cum quibus Deus ab initio bene egit et quibus minime irascitur et in errore non sunt. Vides ergo quia hoc deprecaris in oratione tua ut Christianus sis? Ipsi enim vere in via recta sunt, qui prae manibus habent lumen evangelii et iustificationem eius, quibus perfecta scientia Dei data est in verbo et spiritu et mandata caelestia et spiritualia habent. Ego prorsus nihil profero quod ignores, sed quod scis reminisci te facio. Numquid negare poteris hoc nostrum ius proprium esse, scilicet, lumen evangelii et iustificationem eius, cum socius tuus hoc in sua scriptura testificetur et omnes populi et linguae et diversae sectae hoc nobis attribuant et

Show me, I ask you, who are these persons on whose path 189
you wish to be, since you boast that you are part of the best people seen in this world. Are they worshippers of idols? Are they Jews, of whom your friend says that they are the ones with whom God is especially wrathful? Your very own scripture declares that the worship of idols is wrong, when God says to Muhammad, whom he declared to have set aright from the error of idolatry: "Were you not in error and set aright?" For it is certain that he was not just a Jew, not just a pagan, but a pagan and an idolater. If, however, you say that the right path is that of those who claim that this world has neither beginning nor end, who are worldly heretics, or the path of those who are Georgians or Samanians or Brahmins, then I will say to you that your friend has never approved of their sects, nor did he ever say that the path of any of those is the right one.

Since therefore neither the Jews, pagans, idolaters, nor 190
heretics are on the right path, it remains for us to see that it is the Christians who are on it. God has been kind to them from the beginning and is not angry with them, and they are not in a state of error. Do you see, then, that in your prayer you are praying to become a Christian? For they who have the light of the gospel and its justification in their hands, to whom the perfect knowledge of God has been given in the word and in the spirit, and who possess the heavenly and spiritual commandments truly are on the right path. Certainly, I tell you nothing you do not know, but I cause you to remember what you already know. Surely you cannot deny that this is our rightful patrimony, specifically, the light of the gospel and its justification, since your friend attests this in his scripture, and all peoples, languages, and various sects

sic esse affirment? Hoc, rogo, diligenter attende et sollerter meditare, ut sis tibi ipsi propitius et adquiescens veritati tuae conscientiae satisfacias. Omnipotens Deus te inspiret et consilium tibi bene agendi tribuat et ad viam, quae sola recta est, perducat.

191 Illud quoque quod dixisti mihi: "Scribe illa quae tuae fidei sunt et quae vera probantur apud te ut videam et satisfaciam veritati"; tanto citius et perfectius te implere oportet quanto ceteris prudentior es et ea quae te legisse asseris nunc etiam per me, sicut postulasti, plenissime audiens nihil superest quam ut facias quod promisisti, satisfaciens, videlicet, veritati. Rationabiles quippe et sapientes, quanto studiosiores et subtiliores sunt in inquirenda et cognoscenda veritate, tanto facilius atque libentius cognitae et inventae adquiescere debent. Ratio enim examen Dei est et linea aequitatis.

192 Nos igitur sub imperio Dei incipientes obnixe deprecamur misericordiam eius ut in cor tuum ascendat et tuae animae oculos aperiat, sensumque tuum illuminet ut consideres ea quae nobis impertitur Spiritus Sanctus, opitulante Deo, ad salutem animae tuae et in hoc saeculo et in futuro. Quod etiam illis omnibus concedat, qui hunc librum legerint et his quae sunt in eo crediderint.

193 Oportet ergo nos primitus mundare corda et purificare auditus et honestis sermonibus sanctificare labia ad praedicandum et ad disserendum ea quae sacrae annuntiationis sunt, et ad proferendum testimonia prophetarum, quibus Deus mysteria sua contulit et sua visione locutus est, de

grant this to us and confirm that it is so? Pay careful attention to this, I ask you, and contemplate this intelligently, so that, in accepting the truth you may treat yourself kindly and satisfy your conscience. May omnipotent God inspire you, grant you the intention of doing well unto yourself, and lead you on the only path that is right.

This, too, you said to me: "Write to me about those ele- 191
ments of your faith that you consider to be proven true, so that I may consider them and carefully consider their truth." You should fulfill this request all the more quickly and fully since you are more prudent than all others; and now that you have heard those things that you claim to have read, also through me, as you requested, it remains for you to do as you promised, and to carefully consider their truth. The more devoted to learning rational and wise men are, and the more precise they are in examining and investigating the truth, the more easily and willingly should they assent to it when they have found it and taken notice of it. Reason is the scale of God and his measuring stick.

Novices under the rule of God like me obstinately be- 192
seech his compassion to rise into your heart and open the eyes of your soul and to enlighten your mind, so that, with God's help, you may look upon that which the Holy Spirit grants to us, for the benefit of your soul's salvation both in this world and the next. And may he also grant this to all who will read this book and believe the things in it.

We must first therefore cleanse our hearts and purify our 193
ears and consecrate our lips with honorable speech for preaching and discoursing on what is part of the sacred message, and for declaring the testimonies of the prophets, on whom God bestowed his mysteries and to whom God spoke

adventu filii sui dilecti, qui est Verbum eius creans omnia, quomodo assumpturus esset corpus humanum fieretque una persona Deus et homo. Voluit enim Deus angelos et homines et daemones illum audire eique parere et satisfacere humanitati assumptae in eum ut scirent homines ea locutione, qua locutus est ad eos manifeste, Deum esse unum et tribus personis trinum, id est, Patrem et Filium et Spiritum Sanctum, unum Deum perfectum. Simulque ut impleret suae benignitatis propositum, revelans illis mysterium quod in abscondito erat, ut sermo eius manifestus esset hominibus et inexcusabiles essent et evacuarentur verba dicentium: "Nullam scientiam dedit nobis." Nulla enim excusatio remansit deneganti veritatem, dicente Paulo Apostolo: *"Ut omne os obstruatur et subditus fiat omnis mundus Deo."*

194 Iacob ergo, cum filios suos moriens benediceret et ea quae unicuique eventura erant in novissimis annuntiaret, sic inter alias Iudam, de cuius semine Christus descendit, allocutus est dicens: *"Iuda, tibi subiacebunt fratres tui et manus tua erit super umeros inimicorum tuorum teque adorabunt filii patris tui. O Iuda, catulus leonis, de interfectione surrexisti, dormisti et ascendisti. Non auferetur tibi regnum nec propheta deficiet a te, donec veniat qui est expectatio Gentium et ipsi erit regnum aeternum."*

195 Considera (quem Deus salvet) in hoc spiritualiter oculis iustitiae et aequitatis et diligenter perpende quod hic sub mysterio latet, sed credentibus et intelligentibus patet. Patet enim hoc singulariter pertinere ad Dominum nostrum Iesum Christum, qui de Iuda processit et cui filii Israel

in their visions about the coming of his beloved son, who is the Word that created all, and about how he would take up a human body and how God and man would become one person. For God wished for angels, humans, and demons to listen to and obey him, and to revere the human form he had taken up, so that men may know by that statement, which he clearly enunciated to them, that God is one and threefold in three persons, that is, the Father, the Son, and the Holy Spirit—one perfect God. He also revealed to them the hidden mystery to fulfill his kind intention so that his words might be known to everyone and they might have no excuse, and so that he might invalidate the words of those who say: "He has not given us any knowledge." No excuse remains for those who deny the truth, as the apostle Paul says: "In order that he might close every mouth and the entire world might become subject to God."

When Jacob blessed his sons on his deathbed, and proph- 194
esied what would happen to each in the future, he addressed Judah, from whose seed Christ descended, in the following manner: "Judah, your brothers will submit to you, and your hand will be on the shoulders of your enemies, and the sons of your father will worship you. Judah, lion's cub, you have risen from death, you slumbered, and you rose up. Your kingdom will not be taken from you, nor will a prophet abandon you, until the arrival of him who is the hope of the Gentiles, whose kingdom will be eternal."

You (may God save you) should regard this with the spiri- 195
tual eye of justice and fairness and consider carefully what is hidden here in a mystery but is clear to those who believe and understand. For it is clear that this only applies to our Lord Jesus Christ, who proceeded from Judah and to whom

venientes ad vocationem eius subiecti sunt. Romani quoque inimici Iudaeorum iam subiecti sunt ei et super collum eorum facta est manus eius et ipse est, qui ascendit de interfectione, id est, surrexit a mortuis, et adoraverunt eum filii Israel, id est, apostoli et discipuli sui. Ipse quoque catulus est leonis, quia filius est fortissimi et gloriosissimi Dei. Regnum vero non defecit a filiis Iudae nec cessavit prophetia in illis, praedicando adventum ipsius salvatoris et redemptoris mundi, donec venit ipse et implevit omnes annuntiationes prophetarum et tunc desiit regnum ab eis et cessavit prophetia. Gentes autem et populi et nationes ingredientes in advocationem ipsius combusserunt idola et templa daemonum et iustificati sunt, et ita completa est prophetia Iacob. Post adventum vero Christi nullus propheta a Deo missus est, sicuti nec post adventum regis alicuius temporalis ad annuntiandum eum venire aliquis debet, quia stultissimum esset.

196 Zacharias quoque propheta sic de ipso dicit: *"Laetare vehementer, filia Sion, et exulta, filia Hierusalem, ecce rex tuus venit tibi mansuetus sedens super pullum asinae et ipse destruet naves de Ephraim et disperdet equos de Hierusalem et confringet arcum dimicantium et annuntiabit Gentibus pacem."* Hoc totum completum est in adventu Domini, qui venit cum humilitate et pace, et adventus eius extitit Hierosolymis, quae est Sion. In cuius adventu omnia quae parata erant ad proeliandum et ad dimicandum contrita et adnihilata sunt et ablata sunt odia et discidia quae inter homines erant. Ipse quoque sedit super pullum asinae et pacem omnibus annuntiavit et heredes fecit eos vocationis suae et filios regni caelorum.

the sons of Israel came and submitted when he called them. Even the Romans, enemies of the Jews, are now subjected to him, his hand is on their neck, and he is the one who has risen up after being slain, that is to say, he rose from the dead, and the sons of Israel worshipped him, that is, his apostles and disciples. He, too, is the lion's cub, since he is the son of the strongest and most glorious God. The kingdom did not abandon the sons of Judah, nor did prophecy cease among them, preaching the arrival of the savior and redeemer of the world, until he came and fulfilled all prophecies of the prophets, and then the kingdom abandoned them, and prophecy ceased. The Gentiles, peoples, and nations then came in answer to his call and burned the idols and temples of demons and were justified, and so Jacob's prophecy was fulfilled. After the arrival of Christ, no prophet was sent by God, just as after the arrival of some earthly king it would be incredibly foolish and unnecessary for anyone to announce his coming.

The prophet Zechariah also spoke about him: "Rejoice 196
greatly, daughter of Zion, and exult, daughter of Jerusalem: Behold, your king, well-disposed to you, comes seated on the foal of a she-ass, and he will sink the ships of Ephraim and destroy the horses of Jerusalem and shatter the bow of those fighting, and proclaim peace to the Gentiles." All of this was brought to fulfillment with the coming of the Lord, who came with humility and peace, and his arrival took place in Jerusalem, which is Zion. All that had been prepared for fighting and doing battle was crushed and reduced to nothing by his arrival, and hate and discord among men were done away with. He, moreover, was seated on the foal of a she-ass, proclaiming peace to all, and made them heirs to his preaching and children of the kingdom of heaven.

197 Sed et David rex et propheta sic ipsum introducit loquentem: *"Dominus dixit ad me: 'Filius meus es tu, ego hodie genui te. Postula a me et dabo tibi gentes hereditatem et ponam terminos tuos fines terrae.'"* Numquid (quem Deus salvet) ad aliam quamlibet advocationem vel fidem congregatae sunt gentes et populi a finibus terrae et ab insulis maris et a variis linguis et locutionibus nisi ad fidem Christi, qui est filius Dei dilectus? Rursum David: *"O vos, reges, intelligite et, o iudices terrae, scitote et servite Domino in timore et suscipite eum cum tremore. Suscipite filium ne forte irascatur."* Quod est dicere, suscipite ea quae filius tradet vobis, qui est Christus. Ipse enim loquetur vobis et docebit vos labiis suis et lingua. Quod si eum audire nolueritis, disperdet vos ira sua. Iudaei quippe, quibus hoc annuntiatum est, et noluerunt recipere Christum, ab ira eius dispersi et consumpti sunt, quibus etiam regnum abstulit in hoc saeculo et misericordiam in futuro.

198 Itemque ipse David: *"Dixit Dominus domino meo: 'Sede a dextris meis.'"* In quo loco tu (quem Deus salvet) scito David habuisse mysterium, quod necesse est scire omnibus in hoc libro diligenter considerantibus. Mos apud Hebraeos a tempore Mosi fuit ut litteris quibus nomina divina scribuntur nihil aliud scribatur. Istae litterae erant in duabus tabulis, quas tradidit Deus Mosi. Istis proprie litteris scriptum est: "Dixit Dominus domino meo." Considera et intuere quoniam hoc magnum mysterium est, siquidem eodem modo hoc et apud Iudaeos et apud Christianos habetur, quamvis

Even King David portrays him as saying: "The Lord said to me: 'You are my son, I have begotten you today. Ask it of me, and I will give you the nations in your inheritance and make the ends of the earth your boundaries.'" Surely you (may God save you) do not think that the nations and peoples from the ends of the earth and the islands of the sea, and of various tongues and manners of speech were gathered for any other calling or faith but for the faith of Christ, who is the beloved son of God? Again, David said: "O kings, understand, and O judges of the earth, know and serve the Lord in fear and receive him with trembling! Receive the son so that he may not become wrathful." This is to say: Receive that which the son, who is Christ, will deliver to you; for he will speak to you and teach you by his own mouth and tongue. But if you will not listen to him, he will destroy you with his wrath. Indeed, the Jews, to whom this has been announced, and who were unwilling to accept Christ, have been scattered and annihilated by his wrath, and from them was taken the kingdom of this world and mercy in the future world. 197

David also said: "The Lord spoke to my lord: be seated at my right hand side." You (may God save you) should know that David placed a mystery in that passage, and all who study this book carefully ought to know this. It was customary among the Hebrews, from Moses's time onward, that nothing else be written with the letters in which the sacred names were written. Those letters were on the two tables that God delivered to Moses. It is with those very letters that the phrase is written: "The Lord spoke to my lord." Regard and behold how great a mystery this is, that this is interpreted in the same way by both Jews and Christians even 198

sint discordes et inimici adinvicem. Item ipse, *"Dominus prospexit de excelso sancto suo, Dominus de caelo in terram aspexit ut audiret gemitus captivorum et solveret compeditos a morte,"* id est, a morte peccati, quod est cultus idolorum, et desperare de promissione vitae aeternae, quam annuntiavit nobis Iesus Christus vivificator mundi, et quam dabit nobis in die iudicii ut meditetur *"in Sion nomen Domini,"* id est, nomen Patris et Filii et Spiritus Sancti, quod est nomen ipsius gloriosissimi Domini veraciter et perfecte. *"Et laudes eius in Hierusalem, cum congregatae fuerint omnes gentes et regna ad serviendum Domino,"* haec est, Hierusalem domus sanctificationis, in qua congregatae omnes gentes meditantur nomen Patris et Filii et Spiritus Sancti et laudant nomen Christi diversis modis et glorificant cum variis modulationibus, diversis linguis et peregrinis locutionibus, nocte ac die, non declinantes neque cessantes a cultu Dei et divinum pensum sine intermissione implentes. Veniunt enim ad eam ex cunctis regionibus longe positis et ab universis finibus terrae. Vaticinium ergo David impletum est, cui non potest contradicere nisi caecus corde et insipiens.

199 Unde Isaias dicit: *"Confortate manus fatigatas et genua debilia roborate. Dicite: pusillanimes confortamini et nolite timere. Ecce Deus caeli veniet et salvabit vos. Tunc aperientur oculi caecorum et aures surdorum et tunc saliet sicut cervus claudus."* Tu autem (quem Deus salvet) in libro tuo legis quoniam Christus fecit haec omnia et quia ipse est Spiritus Dei et Verbum.

though they are in disagreement and hostile to one another. He also said, "The Lord gazed from his sacred lofty heights, looked down from heaven on earth to hear the groans of the captives and free them from the chains of death," that is, from the death of sin, which is to worship idols and to despair of the promise of eternal life proclaimed to us by Jesus Christ, who gave life to the universe. He will grant it to us on the day of judgment so that he might contemplate the "Lord's name on Zion," that is, the name of the Father, the Son, and the Holy Spirit, which is truly and completely the name of the most glorious God. "And his praise will be in Jerusalem, when all the nations and kingdoms will be gathered to serve the Lord," that is, Jerusalem, home of holiness, in which all nations will gather to contemplate the name of the Father, the Son, and the Holy Spirit, and to praise the name of Christ in various ways, and to glorify him with diverse tunes, in various languages, and in foreign idioms, night and day, without turning away or abandoning the worship of God, and fulfilling their sacred duty without interruption. They come to this abode from all distant regions, and from all the ends of the earth. David's prophecy, therefore, has been fulfilled, as none except the fool and blind of heart can deny.

On this, Isaiah says: "Rest your tired hands and 199
strengthen your weak knees. Say: comfort the weak of heart and do not fear. Behold, the God of heaven will come and save you. Then the eyes of the blind and the ears of the deaf will be opened, and the cripple will leap forth like a deer." In your book, you (may God save you) read moreover that Christ was the one who did all these things, and that he is the Spirit of God and the Word, for Christ said to the

Christus enim claudo dixit, *"Surge, tolle grabatum tuum, et ambula,"* et statim surgens ambulavit. Et ipse dixit surdo et muto, *"Audies, loqueris,"* et solutum est vinculum linguae eius et locutus est et apertae aures eius et audivit. Ipse quoque fecit caeco nato sine oculis oculos de luto, cum in terram spueret et fecisset lutum de sputo et liniret oculos eius, et vidit et sanitas ibi perfecta est. Sic prophetae annuntiavere quod Christus postea adimplevit.

200 Rursum Isaias de nativitate Christi: *"Audite, inquit, domus David: ecce virgo concipiet et pariet filium et vocabitur nomen eius Emmanuel, quod interpretatur 'nobiscum Deus.'"* Et in alio loco: *"Puer nascetur nobis et parvulus dabitur nobis et erit regnum eius super umeros eius et nomen eius Mirabile, Consiliarius, Deus, Fortis, cuius regnum erit firmum sine fine, et sedebit super solium David patris sui ut confirmet illud et corroboret in iustitia et iudicio, et ipsi servient reges et adorabunt eum gentes."* Quid manifestius sive veracius hoc? Haec sunt prophetiae de nativitate Christi salvatoris mundi. Voluimus et alia addere testimonia, sed renuentes prolixitatem ista tibi collegimus.

201 Verumtamen quia vos Saraceni magnum vos putatis habere refugium et consolationem et cavernam ad protegendum vos, quando dicitis nos scripturas corrupisse et a tramite veritatis eas distorsisse, ego, si mihi aurem accommodare velis, in veritate respondeo quia numquam tam horrificum tamque a vero alienum verbum dixistis nec tam inanem et vanam obiectionem Christianis imposuistis. An vos ignoratis discordiam et discidium inter nos et Iudaeos

cripple: "Rise, take your cot, and walk!" And immediately he arose and walked. He also said to the deaf and mute, "You will hear, you will speak," and the bond of his tongue was removed and he spoke, and his ears were opened and he heard. He also fashioned eyes out of mud for the blind man who was born without eyes, when he spat in the dirt and made mud with his spit and smeared it on his eyes; the man saw, and his healing was complete. In this way did the prophets proclaim what Christ later brought to fulfillment.

Isaiah says about the birth of Christ: "Listen, house of 200
David: behold, a virgin will conceive and bear a son, and his name will be Emmanuel, which means 'God is with us.'" In another passage: "A boy will be born to us, and a small child will be given to us, and his kingdom will be on his shoulders, and his name will be Wonder, Counselor, God, Strong, whose kingdom will be steadfast without end, and he will be seated on the throne of David his father, in order to strengthen and fortify it with justice and judgment, and kings will serve him and the nations will worship him." What is clearer and truer than this? These are the prophecies concerning the birth of Christ, savior of the world. I would like to add even further testimonies, but to avoid verboseness I have excerpted these alone.

However, since you Saracens think you have a great re- 201
course, a comfort and shelter, to protect yourselves by claiming that we have corrupted the scriptures and caused them to deviate from the path of truth, I respond to you truthfully—if you will lend me your ear—that you have never spoken such dreadful and such untrue words, nor have you ever lodged such an idle and futile objection against Christians. Are you unaware of the disagreement and

ab adventu Domini usque in finem saeculi, quantumque odiunt Christum Dominum et vituperant, quem nos Deum colimus et adoramus? Qui tandem eamdem scripturam omnem Veteris Testamenti, quam habemus et credimus esse veram et laudamus et approbamus, ipsam habent omnino similiter et laudant et approbant sine diminutione et corruptione, nec illi unam litteram vel syllabam mutaverunt, nec addiderunt, nec minuerunt, nec nos similiter. Tu ergo convictus veritate nihil residuum habes contradictionis vel refragationis, cum ego inimicum meum in testimonium accipiam. Ubi est ergo corruptio et mutatio, cum impossibile pro certo fuisset duas tam sibi inimicas gentes in eadem scriptura, pro qua etiam inter eos tota discordia est, sic pariter concordare, si ibi aliquis aliquid corrupisset?

202 Si vero etiam nobis obicias quod scripturam sancti evangelii mutavimus et corrupimus et non est sicuti descendit, dicemus tibi: ostende nobis originem sanctam atque perfectam, quae nec corrupta sit nec mutata ab eo quod primitus extitit. Sed cum aliam demonstrare non possis nisi illam, quae toto terrarum orbe ab universali ecclesia pariter una eademque in omnibus habetur et venerabiliter tenetur, cur nobis tantam falsitatem obicitis?

203 Tu enim scis scripturam evangelii a sanctis apostolis Ecclesiae traditam, qui locuti sunt diversis linguis, prout Spiritus Sanctus dabat eloqui illis, cum congregati pariter viderunt caelum apertum et super capita uniuscuiusque eorum lingua ignis erat, et loquebantur variis linguis, quousque omnes qui erant ex diversis regionibus in Hierusalem

conflict between us and the Jews, since the coming of the Lord until the end of the world, and how much they hate and speak ill of Lord Christ, whom we worship and venerate as God? Indeed, the same Old Testament that we have, believe to be true, praise, and approve of, they likewise have, praise, and approve of, without abbreviation or corruption; and they have not changed, added, or removed a single letter or syllable, nor have we. Defeated by the truth, there is nothing left for you to object to or contest, since I can adopt even my enemy as my witness. Where is that corruption and alteration, since, if anyone had corrupted anything, it would have been impossible for two peoples, so greatly opposed to one another, to be in such harmony in the same scripture, on which there is complete disagreement even among themselves?

But if you also accuse us of having corrupted and distorted the scripture of the sacred gospel, and that it is now not as it was when it came down to us, I will say to you: show me the sacred and perfect origin, which is neither corrupted nor altered from what it first was. And since you cannot show me anything else besides that which is considered and held on to with veneration in the same and identical way by each church in the entire earth, why do you accuse us of such falsities? 202

For you know that the scripture of the gospel was transmitted to the Church by the holy apostles, who spoke in different tongues, just as the Holy Spirit granted to them when they were gathered together and saw the heavens open. Above the head of each was a tongue of flame, and they spoke in different tongues, until all those who were from different regions came to them in Jerusalem, and each 203

convenerunt ad eos, et unusquisque cognovit linguam suae regionis et admirabantur super hoc. Apostoli vero postea dispersi sunt per universum orbem evangelizantes evangelium diversis linguis et locutionibus. Et habuit unaquaeque gens evangelium in sua lingua, iuxta quod unusquisque apostolus commisso sibi populo praedicavit. Nullusque in eo aliquid alteri dissonum vel adversum scripsisse invenitur.

204 Dic ergo mihi quis potuit colligere evangelium ab universis mundi partibus et ad suum libitum mutare vel corrumpere consentientibus omnibus, quae sub caelo sunt, linguis et gentibus? An poteris dicere quod universae nationes et gentes, quae minime se alterutrum intelligunt, reges quoque et principes, qui saepe inimici habentur ad invicem, non divinae fidei sed humanae gloriae causa certantes unanimiter convenerunt ad corrumpendam scripturam Dei, quam susceperant signis et virtutibus et prodigiis? Quod nullatenus ab aliqua rationabili mente suscipitur. An forsitan ideo scriptura etiam nostra tibi corrupta videtur, quia tuam totiens mutatam, totiens corruptam, totiens diverso modo laceratam non ambigis? Absit hoc a scriptura Dei, quam Spiritus Sanctus sicut similem ubique tradidit, ita ubique similem conservavit.

205 An tua scriptura idcirco corrumpi non potuit, quia, scilicet, magnis et divinis mirabilibus signis quoque et prodigiis a Mahumet confirmata sit? Sed hoc pro certo nusquam probatur, maxime cum ipse in Alcorano dicat non sibi datum esse signum aliquod facere. Scriptura vero divina tam Novi quam Veteris Testamenti signis et miraculis antea inauditis confirmata omnibusque populis et gentibus uno eodemque

recognized the language of his region, and they were amazed at this. The apostles then dispersed over the entire world to preach the gospel in different tongues and languages. And every nation had the gospel in its own language, in accordance with what each apostle preached to the people that had been entrusted to him. Not one of them is found to have written in it anything that is in discord or at variance with another apostle.

Tell me, then, who could have gathered the gospel from 204
all the parts of the world and altered it as he wished, or corrupted it with the assent of all tongues and nations that exist under the sun? Are you capable of claiming that all nations and peoples, who are unable to understand each other, including kings and princes, who are often considered to be hostile to one another, gathered together in their fight not on behalf of the divine faith but on behalf of human glory, in order to corrupt God's scripture, which they received with signs, virtues, and miracles? No rational mind accepts this claim. Or does our scripture appear corrupt to you, because you have no doubt that your own scripture was so often altered, corrupted, and mutilated in different ways? Far be this from God's scripture, which the Holy Spirit preserved just as it had been transmitted to every place.

Or was your scripture unable to be corrupted because, as 205
you claim, it was supported by the great and divine signs and miracles of Muhammad? But nowhere is this proven to be true, especially since he himself says in the Qur'ān that it has not been granted to him to perform any sign. The divine scriptures of both the Old and the New Testament are considered to be supported by signs and miracles previously unheard of and delivered intact to all peoples and nations in

modo commendata integra similisque in toto mundo habetur et usque in finem saeculi ita habebitur. Cui etiam in hoc tua cum sit tamen sibi paene ubique contraria testificatur dicens: *"Si ambiguus fueris de his quae descendere fecimus super te, interroga eos qui legunt legem ante te. Iam tibi veritas a Deo tuo venit. Noli ergo esse de illis qui non crediderunt signis Dei, ne forte damneris."*

206 Et in alio loco: *"Quoniam habent sapientiam Legis et evangelii et quia sicuti oportet illa recitant credunt illis, et qui noluerunt credere in illis damnandi sunt."* Perpende (quem Deus salvet), quomodo socius tuus testificatur nobis asserens nos recitare sicut oportet, et iubens interrogari nos et auscultari et suscipi. Et quemadmodum scripturam illam corruptam esse astruis, cui Mahumet tuus tale testimonium perhibuit? Vel quare teipsum tibimet contrarium non intelligis, cum aliquando dicas nos habere veram et certam lectionem, aliquando vero nobis ascribas corruptionem et mutationem? Quod certe falsum et vanissimum est. Cum itaque huic nostrae assertioni nec tu nec aliquis contradicere possit, quare factus es segnis et stolidus obiciens nobis falsa et inania?

207 Considera, quaeso, diligenter: qui nostrum magis videantur scripturam falsam et corruptam habere? Nos, qui eam sanam et sinceram accepimus a sanctis hominibus in signis et prodigiis, quae contra usum naturae habentur et quae ab hominibus nisi operante Deo fieri numquam potuissent, in

the same way in the whole world, and they will be considered so until the end of the world. Your scripture even bears testimony to this—though it contradicts itself almost everywhere—when it asserts: "If you have doubts concerning the things I have made descend upon you, consult those who read the law before you. The truth has already come to you from your God. To avoid being damned, do not be one of those who did not believe the signs of God."

And in another passage: "They believe because they have 206
the wisdom of the Law and gospel, and because they recite them as is proper, and those who did not want to believe will be damned." You (may God save you) should consider your friend's testimony when he asserts that we recite as is proper, and orders you to consult us, to listen to us, and to welcome us. How can you claim that our scripture is corrupt, when your very own Muhammad gave you such a testimony? How can you not see that you are contradicting yourself, when at one point you say we have a true and unquestionable reading, and at another point you charge us with corruption and alteration? This is undoubtedly false and utterly groundless. Since neither you nor anyone else could deny this statement of mine, why are you so slow and dimwitted that you charge me with false and groundless accusations?

Consider, I ask you, the following carefully: which of us is 207
more likely to have a false and corrupt scripture? We, who have received a whole and unblemished scripture from holy men with signs and miracles, which are considered to be contrary to the usual course of nature, and which could never have been performed by humans except through the agency of God, through which miracles various nations,

quibus diversae nationes et gentes et linguae et affectus et consilia unum idemque sentiunt; an vos qui suscepistis scripturam Mahumet sine aliquo veri indicio, sine certa locutione, quam more poetarum ipse sibi ad libitum suum confinxit et unius tantum parvae gentis linguae contradidit, unamquamque illius irrationabilis et turpissimi scripti sententiam miraculum vocans volensque eas comparare Rubro Mari diviso, resurrectioni mortuorum, diversae quoque curationi languorum aliisque innumeris et excellentissimis Dei miraculis, quam etiam tradidit hominibus vanis et mendacissimis ac inter se sic inde discordantibus ut unusquisque eam postea iuxta sui cordis intentionem mutaret, corrumperet, augeret, minueret et sicut superius ostendimus, omnino pro velle suo varie laceraret? Plane ipse suae scripturae probus et idoneus testis est cum dicit: "Nisi meam scripturam susceperis et credideris eam a Deo saeculorum descendisse et me prophetam missum a Deo confessus fueris, diripiam omnem substantiam tuam, uxorem, et filios et filias tuas captivitati subiciam et teipsum interficiam." Et idcirco miseri homines minis et terrore coacti susceperunt iniquam legem sine sensu et ratione.

208 Sed redeamus ad praeclara de Domino nostro prophetarum oracula et de annuntiatione eius ad Virginem, prout ipse dederit, eloquamur. Deus itaque misericors et propitius humano generi elegit de genere Adam, quem sua manu creavit et sua imagine decoravit suaque similitudine omni creaturae praefecit, puellam virginem, pudicam, honestam, sanctam, sinceram prorsus sine macula et reprehensione, quam sibi providit ut Verbum suum in ea poneret, quod

peoples, languages, dispositions, and ideas are in harmony; or you, who have received your scripture from Muhammad without any proof of its veracity, without any clear language, which he, in the manner of poets, made up as he liked and delivered to the insignificant language of only one small people? He called every sentence of that irrational and shameless writing a miracle, which he wanted to compare to the parting of the Red Sea, to the resurrection of the dead, as well as to the healing of various afflictions and numerous other most splendid miracles of God. He even delivered this scripture to the most idle and dishonest men, who are in such disagreement with one another that, afterward, each of them altered, corrupted, extended, and shortened it in accordance with his own agenda, and, as I have demonstrated above, completely mutilated it as he wished. Clearly, Muhammad himself is a reliable and ideal witness to his own scripture when he says: "If you will not accept my scripture and believe that it came down from the God of the world, and if you will not confess that I am a prophet sent by God, I will snatch away all of your possessions, deliver your wife and children into captivity, and kill you." For this reason miserable men were forced by threats and terror to accept this unjust law without any sense or reason.

But let us return to those celebrated prophecies of the 208
prophets about our Lord, and let us speak about his message to the Virgin, as he himself delivered it. God, merciful and well-disposed to the human race, chose a chaste, honorable, saintly, and pure virgin maiden without any blemish or fault from the line of Adam, whom he created with his own hands, fashioned in his own image, and, placed at the head of all creation in his own likeness, and he arranged to place his

humanum corpus et animam ex ea perfecte susciperet, et Verbum caro fieret.

209 Misit ergo ad eam Gabrielem magnum inter angelos principem, quem huius annuntiationis fidelem nuntium fecit, dansque illi hanc gratiam prae ceteris angelis, commisit ei hoc sacrosanctum mysterium et misit eum ad praeelectam puellam de stirpe Adae, nomine Mariam, matrem Domini Iesu Christi. Qui cum venisset a Deo ad annuntiandum et praedicandum ei, honorificans eam, dixit: *"Ave, benedicta inter mulieres, Dominus noster tecum."* Considera etiam (quem Deus salvet) quomodo dicat Gabriel ad virginem, "Dominus noster tecum," et non, "Dominus tecum," dans scilicet intelligi Christum et suum et omnium esse Dominum angelorum. Quis est Dominus angelorum nisi Dominus hominum et universae creaturae? Ipse est enim Verbum Dei vivi et aeterni, quo creavit caelum et terram et omnia quae in eis sunt.

210 Prosequitur dehinc angelus ad Mariam, *"Ecce concipies et paries filium et vocabitur nomen eius Iesus";*—quod interpretatur 'salvator'—*"hic erit magnus et filius Altissimi vocabitur et dabit ei Dominus Deus sedem David patris eius,"* id est, Verbum, quod est Deus, dabit assumptae humanitati sedem David patris eius. Quia humanitas assumpta est de corpore Mariae, quae est de stirpe David. Subiungit angelus dicens: *"Et regnabit in domo Iacob in aeternum."* Cumque annuntiasset ei, admirata est in sermone eius et respondit sic: "Quomodo fiet hoc, quoniam non tetigit me homo?" Et angelus dixit ei: *"Spiritus Sanctus veniet tibi et virtus Altissimi obumbrabit tibi et*

Word in her so that it might receive a perfect human body and soul from her, and so that the Word might become flesh.

For this reason he sent to her Gabriel, a great prince 209
among the angels, and made him the faithful messenger of this message, granting him this grace before all other angels, and entrusted to him this sacred mystery and sent him to the chosen maiden of the line of Adam named Mary, the mother of the Lord Jesus Christ. When he had come from God to announce and preach to her, he said while honoring her: "Greetings, blessed among women, our Lord be with you." You (may God save you) should notice that Gabriel says to the virgin, "Our Lord be with you," and not, "The Lord be with you," indicating that Christ is his Lord, as well as that of all the angels. Who is the Lord of the angels if not the Lord of men and all creation? For he is the Word of the living and eternal God, in which he created heaven and earth, and all that is in them.

The angel then continues to Mary, "Behold, you will con- 210
ceive and bear a son, and his name will be Jesus";—which means 'savior'—"he will be great, and he will be called the son of the Highest, and the Lord God will grant to him the throne of his father David," that is to say, the Word, which is God, will give the throne of its father David to the human form he had taken up—for it was taken up from the body of Mary, who is of the line of David. The angel then adds: "And he will rule over the house of Jacob for eternity." When he had delivered the annunciation to her, she wondered at his speech and responded the following: "How will this happen, since no man has touched me?" And the angel said to her: "The Holy Spirit will come to you, and the virtue of the Highest will cover you, and so it will come to pass that

sic erit quod nascetur ex te sanctum et vocabitur Filius Dei." Deinde sequitur dans ei indicium, quo fidem eius augeret et non dubitaret. *"Ecce,"* inquit, *"Elisabeth, cognata tua et ipsa concepit filium in senectute et sterilitate."*

211 Recordare, obsecro, quantum socius tuus hoc Verbum laudaverit, secundum quod ei retulerat monachus philosophus, de quo praediximus. Dicit enim in sua scriptura quoniam angeli dixerunt: *"'O Maria, Deus elegit te et super omnes mulieres exaltavit te. O Maria, adhaere Deo, quoniam Deus annuntiabit tibi Verbum suum, cuius nomen est Christus Iesus, filius Mariae, excellentissimus inter sanctos et in hoc saeculo et in futuro, et loquetur hominibus in cunabulis et senex praeerit iustis.' Et illa dixit: 'Quomodo erit mihi filius et non tetigit me homo?' Respondit ei angelus: 'Sic faciet Deus quodcumque voluerit, et cum proposuerit aliquid facere, dicit illi rei quam vult facere, "Esto," et statim est. Et docebit illum Deus scripturam et sapientiam et legem et evangelium et mittet eum nuntium filiis Israel ut dicat eis: "Ego vobis a Domino vestro porto signa, quoniam ego creabo vobis de luto similitudinem avis et insufflabo in eum et erit avis, et curabo surdum et mutum et leprosum et mortuos suscitabo nutu Dei et annuntiabo vobis quae manducabitis et bibetis et reponetis. Hoc signum magnum vobis si credideritis et indubitanter habueritis ea quae prae manibus habeo legis et evangelii, ego vobis de quibusdam prohibitis licita faciam."'"*

212 Hoc est verbum tui socii et testimonium eius. Ipse enim subiecte atque libenter confessus est veritatem. Numquid

sanctity will be born from you, and it will be called the Son of God." He followed this up with proof, to further her faith in him and so that she might not doubt. "Behold," he said, "Elisabeth, your kinswoman, has conceived a son despite being old and barren."

Recall, I ask you, how much your friend praised this Word, in accordance with what the philosopher-monk had told him, about whom I spoke earlier. Your friend says in his scripture that the angels said: "'O Mary, God has chosen you and exalted you above all other women. O Mary, cling to God, for God will announce to you his Word, whose name is Jesus Christ, son of Mary, most exalted among the saints, both in this world and the next; he will speak to men while still in his swaddling clothes, and, like an old man, he will preside over the just.' And she said: 'How will I have a son, since no man has touched me?' The angel answered: 'God will do whatever he wishes, and when he has decided to do something, he says to the thing he wishes to do, "Be," and immediately it comes into existence. And God will teach him the scripture, wisdom, law, and gospel, and he will send him as a messenger to the sons of Israel so that he may say to them: "I bring you signs from your Lord, for I will create for you out of mud the likeness of a bird, and I will breathe onto it and it will be a bird, and I will heal the deaf, mute, and leprous, and I will resurrect the dead at God's command, and I will announce to you what you will eat, drink, and set aside. If you believe this great sign and hold without doubt to the law and gospel I present to you, I will grant for you that some things that are now forbidden will be allowed."'" 211

These are the words and testimony of your friend. He himself confessed the truth humbly and willingly. Surely you 212

scis (quem Deus salvet) aut reminisci poteris in aliqua scriptura adversariorum aut in tua, quam tu asseris esse veram, tale novum et insigne miraculum, quale hoc huius annuntiationis, quod in sancto evangelio legitur et in tua lege scriptum habetur?

213 Deinde abiit electa Maria ad matrem Iohannis benedicti filii Zachariae, cui nomen erat Elisabeth, eratque ipsa et vir eius steriles et iam processerant in diebus multis, et ipsa conceperat filium Iohannem. Cumque percuteret Maria fores domus illius et salutaret eam secundum solitum morem, exultavit gaudio et laetitia in utero matris suae Iohannes, et exclamavit mater eius voce magna dicens: *"Unde hoc mihi ut veniat mater Domini mei ad me? Procidit autem infans filius meus in utero meo et exultans nimis adoravit."*

214 Tuus item socius de Zacharia sic loquitur dicens: *"Oravit Zacharias Dominum suum et dixit: 'Domine, da mihi a te progeniem optimam quoniam tu es exauditor deprecationis.' Et statim angeli vocaverunt eum, cum staret ille in oratione in templo et dixerunt ei quoniam 'Annuntiamus tibi fidelem in Verbo Dei et Domino,'"* id est, in Christo Domino in quem credidit Iohannes; ipse est enim Verbum Dei et Dominus filiorum Adam. Nos scimus quoniam fidelis iste non pertinet nisi ad Iohannem, et Verbum Dei non pertinet nisi ad Christum Iesum, quoniam Iohannes numquam dictus est Verbum Dei. "Propheta" vero et "fidelis inter iustos" est de nominibus Iohannis. Tu vero si nolueris mutare haec verba a modo suae qualitatis, scies pro certo quid ista significent.

215 Deinde apparuit stella in regione Persarum magis, significans nativitatem regis magni, cuius regni non erit finis, illius

(may God save you) are familiar with, or can recall from some scripture of your opponents or from your own which you claim to be true, a miracle as novel and remarkable as the annunciation, which is read in the Holy Gospel and is contained in your law?

Then Mary, the chosen one, went away to the mother of 213
John, the blessed son of Zechariah, whose name was Elisabeth, and both she and her husband were barren and were already advanced in age, and yet she had conceived a son called John. When Mary knocked on the door of her house and greeted her as usual, John leaped with joy and happiness in the womb of his mother, and she cried out loudly: "How has it come to pass that the Lord's mother comes to me? For my infant son has fallen down in worship in my womb and adored him with great joy."

Your friend, likewise, says the following about Zechariah: 214
"Zechariah prayed to his Lord and said: 'Lord, grant me your excellent offspring, for you answer prayers.' Immediately the angels called to him, while he was still in prayer in the temple, and they said to him, 'We announce to you one who is faithful in the Word of God and in the Lord,'" that is to say, in the Lord Christ, in whom John believed; for he is the Word of God and Lord of the sons of Adam. We know that that faithful one was none other than John, and the Word of God none other than Jesus Christ, for John was never called the Word of God. However, "prophet" and "faithful among the just" are among the epithets of John. Unless you wish to alter these words from their meaning, you will know with certainty what they mean.

Then a star appeared to the magi in the land of the Per- 215
sians, signifying the birth of a great king whose rule will

enim est regnare veraciter. Sapientes vero terrae illius praescientes hoc annuntiaverunt illum in scripturis suis et praedixerunt horam nativitatis eius, dantes illis indicium et signum apparitionem stellae, et praeceperunt eis venire ad signum et procidentes adorare eum. Illi vero non cessaverunt expectare et aspicere hoc, donec venit hora in qua apparuit stella, quae erat indicium nativitatis Iesu Christi Domini. Venit autem stella de regione Persarum in Hierosolymam, quae est regio Iudaeorum, donec videretur astrologis, qui sequebantur, se stare supra locum suum, et implentes morem obsequii solverunt debita procidentes et adorantes eum. Tunc videntes quod expectabant et consecuti quod desiderabant certi, exultantes in propria reversi sunt.

216 Apparuit vero angelus in ipsa nocte in qua natus est Dominus Iesus Christus multitudini pastorum qui vigilabant super greges suos. Et cum vidissent lucem magnam, audierunt sibi dicentem: *"Ecce evangelizo vobis gaudium magnum, quod erit vobis pariter et toti mundo. Quia natus est vobis hodie salvator et omni generi humano, qui est Christus Dominus, in civitate David. Et hoc vobis indicium et signum erit: cum veneritis ad locum, invenietis infantem pannis veteribus involutum et positum in praesepio."* Et subito apparuerunt illis turbae exercitus angelorum volantes inter caelum et terram, cantantes et psallentes voce magna, et laudabant Dominum dicentes: *"Gloria in excelsis Deo et in terra securitas et pax et spes bona hominibus pariter."* Pastores autem abeuntes ad locum festinanter,

know no end, for it is his role to rule truly. The wise men of that land had predicted this and announced him in their scriptures, and predicted the hour of his birth, giving to the Persians the appearance of a star as proof and a sign, and they ordered them to come to the sign, to fall down before him, and to worship him. And they did not cease to expect him and to look forward to the hour when the star would appear, which was a sign of the birth of the Lord Jesus Christ. The star came from the land of the Persians to Jerusalem, which is the land of the Jews, until it seemed to the astrologers who were following it that they were standing right at the site of the star, and fulfilling their traditional obeisance, they paid their due respects and fell down and worshipped him. When they had seen what they had been awaiting, and had received what they had desired without doubt, they rejoiced and returned to their own land.

On the night that the Lord Jesus Christ was born, an an- 216
gel appeared to a group of shepherds who were keeping watch over their flocks. And when they had seen a great light, they heard someone saying to them: "Behold, I bring you the good news of a great joy, which will be yours as well as the entire world's. For today a savior was born to you and to the entire human race, who is the Lord Christ, in the city of David. And this will be proof and a sign to you: when you come to the place, you will find an infant wrapped in old swaddling clothes and placed in a crib." And suddenly there appeared to them throngs of the angelic host, flying between heaven and earth, singing and chanting loudly and praising the Lord, saying: "Glory to God in the highest, peace and harmony on earth, and good hope to all men equally!" The shepherds hurriedly left for the place, and

invenerunt illud quod dixerat illis angelus et fidem adhibentes crediderunt et annuntiaverunt ea quae ab angelis audierunt, et audientes omnes admirabantur. Haec est annuntiatio et nativitas Domini nostri Iesu Christi compendiose descripta.

217 Cum autem pervenisset ad aetatem triginta annorum, et Iohannes filius Zachariae iuxta flumen Iordanis apparens praedicare hominibus et baptizare coepisset, lavans eos in aqua fluminis, venit ad baptismum. Cumque vidisset Iohannes Dominum Iesum venientem ad se dicit ei: "Necesse est mihi manibus tuis lavari et merito a te baptizari, et tu venis ut baptizeris a me?" Cui respondit Christus: *"Sine modo, sic enim oportet nos implere benedictionem."* Et non destitit urgens eum, donec baptizavit eum. Et, baptizato eo a Iohanne, apertum est caelum et vidit ipse et qui aderant Spiritum Sanctum descendentem in specie columbae et audierunt vocem magnam clamantem et dicentem: *"Hic est filius meus dilectus, in quo mihi complacui."* Et resedit columba super caput eius. Et miratus est Iohannes et omnes qui erant cum eo.

218 Deinde coepit praedicare et advocare homines ad iustificationem et paenitentiam, docens eos renuntiare mundo et cavere ab illo, et dimittere parentes et filios et substantias et appetere opera iustitiae et declinare a peccatis et fugere discordias et invidiam et dolum et reddere bona pro malis et oblivisci talionem et dimittere omnibus et facere cum omnibus quod melius et benignius est, dicens illis quod sic appropinquatur Deo, et faciens eos unanimes exhortabatur eos declinare a malo et facere bonum, quoniam ad hoc creati sunt, et quia ipse retribueret illis magnae retributionis praemium in domo aeternitatis, ubi vita non finitur et opes non

found all as the angel had told them; then they believed and announced what they had heard from the angels, and all who heard were amazed. This is, in short, the annunciation and nativity of our Lord Jesus Christ.

When Jesus had reached the age of thirty years and John, 217 the son of Zechariah, had begun to appear alongside the river Jordan to preach to mankind and baptize by washing them in the water of the river, he came to be baptized. When John saw Lord Jesus coming toward him, he said to him: "It is necessary for me to be washed by your hands, and it would be right for me to be baptized by you, and you are coming to be baptized by me?" To which Christ responded: "Permit it now, for in this way must we fulfill the blessing." And he did not cease to urge him, until he baptized him. When he had been baptized by John, the heavens opened and he, as well as those with him, witnessed the Holy Spirit descending in the form of a dove, and they heard a loud voice cry out: "This is my beloved son, in whom I am pleased." And the dove descended upon his head. John, and all those with him, marveled at this.

Then he began to preach and to call men to justification 218 and repentance, teaching them to renounce the world and to be wary of it, to leave behind their parents, children, and possessions, to seek the works of justice and to avoid sin, discord, envy, and subterfuge, to return good for evil and to forget vengeance, to forgive all, and to do unto others what is best and most kind. And he said that in this way one could reach God, and he made them all like-minded and urged them to avoid evil and to do good, since they were created for this purpose, and he said that he was the one who would reward them greatly in the house of eternity, where life does

deficiunt. Et dicebat eis se venturum post resurrectionem mortuorum ad iudicium, et quia operibus bonis pervenitur ad regna caelorum et operibus malis ad submersionem in ignem aeternum. Cuius dictis et promissionibus signa magna et prodigia et virtutes inenarrabiles dabant fidem. Talia enim erant quae faciebat, qualia nisi a Deo fieri non possunt.

219 Erat enim perfectus in simplicitate et benignitate et mansuetudine et humilitate, fugiens dolum et odium et superfluitatem et omnem nequitiam et huius saeculi potestatem et superbiam et elationem, ostendens dilectionem et misericordiam et benignitatem et clementiam omnibus hominibus pariter. Et quicquid ab eo postulabatur, clementer impendebat, non quaerens temporalia munera, nec aliquam retributionem mundanam, sed agere gratias Deo et laudare illum et credere in eum, qui promissum suum adimplevit, quod per prophetas suos promiserat, et perfecit benignitatem et misericordiam suam humano generi, quando misit Verbum suum assumere ab eis corpus et eripuit eos ab errore diaboli et potestate mortis et docuit eos unum Deum esse in Trinitate perfectum, id est, in Patre et Filio et Spiritu Sancto, ut confirmati tali cognitione merito possiderent vitam aeternam in regno caelorum.

220 Haec est autem prima advocatio ipsius. Dicebat enim: *"O vos, homines, paenitentiam agite, appropinquavit enim regnum caelorum."* Sic in auribus eorum memoriam paenitentiae intulit et resurrectionem mortuorum et iudicium, quod ignorabant, illis ostendit. Et fecit eos regnum caelorum appetere et opera quibus illud mererentur ingredi affectare, et a peccatis in quibus conversabantur declinare, et ad paenitentiam

not end and riches do not run out. And he said to them that he would be coming to judge after the resurrection of the dead, and that one might reach the kingdom of heaven by good works, and be immersed in the eternal fire by evil works. Great signs, miracles, and indescribable virtues lent credence to his words and promises. For such were the things he did, that they could not occur except through God.

He was perfect in his simplicity, kindness, meekness, and 219
humility, avoided subterfuge, hate, excess, all manner of wickedness, worldly power, pride, and vanity, showing love, sympathy, kindness, and mercy to all men in equal measure. Whatever was asked of him, he granted mercifully. He did not seek temporal gifts nor any worldly repayment other than to thank, praise, and believe in God, who fulfilled his promise, which he had made through his prophets, and who completed his kindness and compassion toward the human race when he sent his Word to assume a body from among them, saved them from the deception of the devil and the power of death, and taught them that there is one perfect God in a Trinity—that is, in the Father, the Son, and the Holy Spirit—so that they, strengthened by this knowledge, might deservedly possess the eternal life in the kingdom of heaven.

This was his first message. For he said: "O men, repent, 220
for the kingdom of heaven is near!" In this way, he instilled into their ears the thought of penitence, and showed them the judgment and the resurrection of the dead, which they did not know. He also made them seek the kingdom of heaven, and to pursue works by which they might earn it, and to leave behind the sins in which they spent their lives,

converti, per quam dimittuntur crimina atque peccata. Ieiunans etiam quadraginta diebus et quadraginta noctibus ieiunium instituit. Cui agonizanti contra calliditatem diaboli angeli ministrabant. Et ipse autem dicebat, *"Non in solo pane vivit homo sed in omni Verbo Dei,"* quod significat habitudinem vitae nostrae post mortem. Statim quippe ut resurrexerimus a mortuis, auferetur a nobis necessitas cibi et potus terreni.

221 Deinde instituit mandata et monita spiritualia, docens eos divinas leges, quae Deum decent, et iussit eos fugere carnalia et adhaerere spiritualibus, et dixit eis: *"Audistis quia dictum est antiquis: 'Non occides, qui autem occiderit, occidatur.' Ego autem dico vobis quia omnis qui irascitur fratri suo reus erit iudicio. Qui autem dixerit fratri suo 'racha,' reus erit concilio, qui vero fratrem suum nocuerit aut laeserit reus erit Gehennae ignis."* Et item: *"Sol non occidat super unumquemque vestrum fratri suo iratum."*

222 Et item: *"Cum orare coeperis et recordatus fueris quia frater tuus habet aliquid adversum te, dimissa oratione statim vade humiliter reconciliari fratri tuo, et sic redi ad orationem."* His et huiusmodi exhortationibus nequitiam odii et occasiones furoris exclusit. Iterum dicit: *"Audistis quia dictum est antiquis: 'Non moechaberis.' Ego autem dico vobis: Qui viderit mulierem ad concupiscendum eam, iam moechatus est eam in corde suo. Et item*

and to turn to repentance, through which trespasses and sins are forgiven. He also instituted the fast by fasting for forty days and forty nights, and the angels assisted him in his struggle against the devil's cunning. He also said, "Man lives not by bread alone, but by every Word of God," which signifies the state of our life after death. For as soon as we have been resurrected from the dead, we will no longer need earthly food and drink.

Then he instituted spiritual rules and commandments, 221
teaching them the divine laws which are proper to God, and commanded them to avoid the flesh and to cling to the spirit, and said to them: "You have heard it said to the ancients: 'Thou shalt not kill; whosoever has killed shall be killed.' But I say to you that all who become angry at their brothers will be found guilty in judgment. Whoever says to his brother, 'Good-for-nothing!' will be found guilty in the council, but whoever harms or wounds his brother will be condemned to the fire of hell." He also said: "Let not the sun go down on any of you while you are still angry with your brother."

He also said: "When you have started to pray and remem- 222
ber that your brother has something against you, interrupt your prayer and go immediately with humble heart to be reconciled with your brother, and then return to your prayer." With these and similar exhortations did he banish the wickedness of hate and all occasions for wrath. He also said: "You have heard it said to the ancients: 'Thou shalt not commit adultery.' But I say to you: Whoever has looked upon a woman with desire has already committed adultery with her in his heart. Elsewhere it was said to the ancients:

dictum est antiquis: 'Qui dimiserit uxorem suam, faciat illi libellum repudii.' Ego autem dico vobis: Nemo uxorem dimittat nisi causa fornicationis. Si aliter fecerit, occasionem adulterii dabit, et qui repudiatam duxerit et ipse moechatur."

223 Et item: *"Dictum est antiquis: 'Non periurabis in iuramento.' Ego autem dico vobis non iurare omnino neque per caelum, quia thronus Dei est, neque per terram, quia scabellum est pedum eius, neque per caput tuum, quia non potes unum capillum facere album aut nigrum, sed sit sermo vester: est est, non non. Si quid amplius est, a malo est."* Item *"Audistis dictum esse antiquis: 'Oculum pro oculo et dentem pro dente et vulnus pro vulnere.' Ego autem dico vobis non reddere malum pro malo et qui te percusserit in maxillam praebe ei et alteram, et qui abstulerit tibi tunicam tuam, adde ei et pallium, et qui angariaverit te mille passus, vade cum eo et alios mille."*

224 Et item: *"Omni petenti te tribue et tibi maledicenti benedicito et nocenti benefacito et non salutantem salutato."* His etiam sermonibus sacris abscidit occasionem altercationis et abstulit odia mala, quae inter homines evenire solent. Et fecit eos unanimes ac sibi invicem proximantes, emolliens duritiam et crassitudinem cordis eorum et fecit homines invicem fratres in longanimitate et misericordia.

225 Et item: *"Audistis quia dictum est: 'Diliges proximum tuum et odio habebis inimicum tuum.' Ego autem dico vobis: Diligite inimicos vestros, benefacite his qui oderunt vos et eritis filii Patris vestri*

'Whosoever shall cast out his wife, let him give her a notification of divorce.' But I say to you: Let no one cast out his wife, except for the reason of adultery. If anyone does otherwise, he will give her occasion for adultery, and he who marries a divorced woman will also commit adultery."

He also said: "It was said to the ancients: 'Thou shalt not 223
commit perjury.' But I say to you that you should not swear by the heaven, for it is the throne of God, nor by the earth, for it is his footstool, nor by your own head, since you cannot make a single hair white or black. Instead, let your language be thus: yes, yes, no, no. If anything else is added, it is a part of evil." He also said: "You have heard it said to the ancients: 'An eye for an eye, a tooth for a tooth, and an injury for an injury.' But I say to you that you should not return evil for evil, and if someone strikes you on the cheek, present to him the other cheek as well, and if someone has stolen your tunic, give him your mantle as well, and if one has compelled you to go a thousand paces, go with him for another thousand."

He also said: "Offer yourself to anyone who seeks you, 224
bless the one who curses you, do well unto the one who harms you, and greet the one who does not greet you." With these sacred words he eradicated all occasions for strife and eliminated all evil hatred that commonly arises among men. And he created harmony among them, and made them draw near to each other, softening the insensitivity and rudeness of their hearts, and made men brothers to each other, acting with patience and sympathy.

He also said: "You have heard it said: 'You shall love your 225
neighbor and hate your enemy.' But I say to you: Love your enemies, do well unto those who hate you, and you will be

caelestis, cum secundum opera eius feceritis. Ipse enim pluit super iustos et iniustos et solem suum oriri facit super bonos et malos." Et item: *"Si bene feceritis tantum his qui vobiscum bene egerint, quam mercedem habebitis? Nonne et perversi hoc faciunt?"*

226 Deinde de eleemosyna sic dicit: *"Noli facere eleemosynam coram hominibus, ut videaris ab eis, sed cum facis eleemosynam, nesciat sinistra tua quid faciat dextera tua."* Et item: *"Cum oraveris, noli protelare orationem sicut hypocritae faciunt, prolongantes orationem coram hominibus, et augent preces ut honorificentur ab illis. Ego autem dico vobis: Quicumque vestrum oraverit, intret cubiculum suum et, clauso ostio, oret Patrem suum in abscondito, et Pater eius caelestis, qui scit secreta, reddet illi."* Et item: *"Cum ieiunaveritis, nolite ieiunia vestra patefacere hominibus nec facies vestras immutare, sed quicumque ex vobis ieiunaverit, faciem suam lavet et caput suum ungat et sit hilaris, ne videatur hominibus ieiunans sed Patri suo caelesti, qui reddet illi secundum quod videt in eo."*

227 Et item: *"Nolite thesaurizare vestros thesauros in terra, ubi tinea et fur et putredo timetur. Thesaurizate autem vobis thesauros in caelo, ubi neque aerugo nec fur nec tinea demolitur; ubi enim sunt thesauri vestri ibi est et cor vestrum."* Item: *"Non potest servus duobus dominis servire. Aut enim unum eorum odio habebit et alterum diliget, aut unum sustinebit et alterum contemnet. Sic nec vos Deo servire potestis et vestris substantiis."*

children of your heavenly Father, for you will act in accordance with his deeds. For he rains on both the just and unjust, and lets the sun rise on both the good and the evil." He also said: "If you only do well unto those who have done well unto you, what reward will you receive? Do not also the wicked do this?"

About charity he says the following: "Do not perform 226
charity in the presence of others, in order to be seen by them, but when you perform charity, may your left hand not know what the right hand is doing." He also said: "When you pray, do not extend your prayer as the hypocrites do, dragging out their prayers in the presence of others, and embellishing their prayers in order to receive praise from them. But I say to you: Let anyone of you who prays enter his private room, close the door, and pray to his Father in secret, and his heavenly Father, who knows all secrets, will reward him." He also said: "When you fast, do not reveal your fasts to others, and do not change your countenance, but if anyone of you fasts, let him wash his face, oil his hair, and be cheerful, so that he may seem to fast not to men, but only to his heavenly Father, who will reward him in accordance with what he sees inside him."

He also said: "Do not hoard your treasures in the earth, 227
where there is the threat of the moth, the thief, and rot. Rather keep your treasures in heaven, where neither rust, nor thief, nor moth threatens; for where your treasure is, there is your heart." He also said: "A servant cannot serve two masters. He will either hate one of them and love the other, or put up with one and hold the other in disdain. Likewise you, too, cannot serve both God and your possessions."

228 Item: *"Ego autem dico vobis: Quaerite primum ea quae sunt spiritus, qui est plus quam corpus, et cum perfeceritis ea quae debetis et acceptabiles fueritis et digni, merito adicientur vobis victus et vestimenta, quibus corpora vestra refici poterunt, et quicquid vobis necessarium fuerit in hoc saeculo dabitur vobis. Et scitote quia anima plus est quam corpus, et corpus plus quam vestimentum. Et respicite volatilia caeli, quae non serunt neque metunt neque congregant aliquid in horrea, et Pater vester caelestis praebet illis victum. Amen, dico vobis quoniam vos meliores illis estis apud Deum. Nolite sollicitari de corporibus vestris quomodo sustententur. Sollicitudo enim victus corporis vobis ablata est, si impleveritis ea quae instituta sunt vobis. Sit sollicitudo vestra in illis quibus appropinquatur Deo, et nolite cogitare de crastino, quia non estis creati ad crastinum; crastinum enim vobis creatum est. Sed qui creavit crastinum victum in eo vobis dabit."*

229 Item: *"Nolite excedere iustitiam et fraudare in iudicio. In quo enim iudicaveritis iudicabimini, et in qua mensura mensi fueritis remetietur vobis. Et ne aliquis fratri suo dicat, 'Quoniam in oculo tuo palea habetur,' sed consideret primum ligna quae sunt in oculo suo, et mox educere studeat. Et cum ea eduxerit, tunc licet ei considerare et educere paleam de oculo fratris sui."*

230 Et item: *"Date et dabitur vobis, et benefacite vobis adinvicem, et benefaciet vobis Pater vester caelestis. Et scitote quia si fueritis filii Patris vestri caelestis, quicquid ab eo petieritis, dabit vobis. Si enim cuiuslibet filius patrem suum petit panem, numquid lapidem*

He also said: "But I say to you: Seek first the things of the spirit, which is greater than the body, and when you have fulfilled your debts and have become acceptable and worthy, then will you deserve to receive food and clothing to sustain your bodies, and all that you need in this world will be given to you. Know also that the soul is greater than the body, and the body greater than clothing. Consider the birds in the sky, which neither sow nor reap, nor gather anything in a barn, and yet your heavenly Father provides food for them. Amen, I say to you that you are better than those creatures in God's eyes. Do not worry about sustaining your bodies. The worry of sustaining your bodies has been lifted from you, if you will fulfill what has been commanded to you. Let your worries instead be focused on those things by which one may reach God, and do not think about tomorrow, for you were not created for tomorrow; tomorrow was created for you. And he who created tomorrow will provide food to you tomorrow." 228

He also said: "Do not depart from justice or deceive in judgment. For you will be judged by the judgments you make, and you will be measured by the measure you have taken. Let no one say to his brother: 'There is a speck in your eye,' but let him look first at the logs in his own eye, and then focus on removing them. And when he has done so, then he may regard and remove the speck from his brother's eye." 229

He also said: "Give, and you will receive; do well unto one another, and your heavenly Father will do well unto you. And know that you will be the children of your heavenly Father, and whatever you will ask of him, he will give to you. If a son asks his father for bread, surely he will not give him a 230

dabit illi, aut si piscem, numquid serpentem dabit illi? Aut si ovum petit, numquid dabit ei scorpionem? Si ergo vos non potestis dare filiis vestris noxia cum a vobis petunt panem aut piscem et cetera, quanto magis Pater vester non nisi bona dabit petentibus se?" Item: *"Quicquid volueritis fieri vobis ab hominibus, et vos facite illis, et ne faciatis hominibus nisi quod vobis fieri vultis."* Haec est enim perfectio benedictionis et voluntas Dei benedicti et excelsi.

231 Sed si quis dixerit quare Dominus Iesus Christus nuncupaverit Deum Patrem hominum, dicemus ei quoniam Christus Dominus saeculorum voluit homines adhaerere oboedientiae Dei, et ut sit eorum oboedientia erga Deum magis amore et dilectione quam formidine et timore, et ut corda ipsorum in Deo per caritatem uniret, odiumque ab eis averteret et gloriationem carnalis generationis auferret, fratresque et amicos, utpote unius Dei patris per adoptionem filios se esse scientes, in unam spiritus societatem efficeret, sicuti naturaliter unius patris et unius matris filii fratres habentur. Et ita oportet eos esse in omnibus quae ad Deum pertinent. Non sicut tuus socius, qui discordias inter homines seminavit et odia plantavit in cordibus eorum, cum diceret: *"O vos qui credidistis, quoniam de uxoribus vestris et filiis erunt qui vos odio habebunt; cavete ab illis."*

232 Tu ergo diligenter attende quantum differt inter praecepta Christi et tui socii, cum tuus socius iubeat homines interfici et substantias eorum diripi et filios cum parentibus captivitate affligi et diversa illicita ubique fieri et coitus

rock, or if he asks for a fish, surely he will not give him a snake? Or if he asks for an egg, surely he will not give him a scorpion? If, therefore, you are unable to give your children harmful things when they ask you for bread, fish, and similar things, how much more will your Father give only good things to those who ask him?" He also said: "Whatever you wish to be done to you by others, do so unto them, and do not treat others in any other way than you yourself wish to be treated." This is the highest blessing and the will of the blessed and exalted God.

But if someone asks why the Lord Jesus Christ called God the Father of men, I will answer him that Christ, Lord of the world, wanted all men to be obedient to God, and their obedience to God to be out of love and affection rather than dread and fear. And he wanted to unite their hearts in God through love, and to take away from them hatred and the celebration of bodily procreation. He also wanted to make them brothers and friends in a spiritual fellowship, just as children by nature of one father and one mother are considered brothers, since all realize that they are children by adoption of the Father, the one God. This is how they should act in all that pertains to God. Not like your friend, who sowed discord among men and planted hatred in their hearts when he said: "O you who have believed, be wary, for those who will hate you will come from among your wives and children." 231

Consider carefully how much the teachings of Christ differ from those of your friend, since your friend orders that men be killed, that their possessions be snatched away, that their children suffer captivity along with their parents, that various unlawful things take place everywhere, and that 232

mulierum iugiter exerceri. Luxuriosus enim spem exercendae libidinis miserrimis hominibus tribuit, ita sibi eos allicere studens, dum non ignorat quam sit humana natura prona ad malum et facilis, maximeque ad ea quae carnis sunt. Et ideo non satis ei visum est amplificare hoc illis in hoc saeculo sed etiam in futuro, dicente ipso in Alcoran quoniam in paradiso virgines sunt, quas nemo hominum vel daemonum violavit. Et ista misera et stultissima verba tantum repetit et revolvit, donec cordibus amentium et insipientium inhaesere.

233 Cum enim carnalia desideria affectarent et beluinis voluptatibus subiacerent, quicquid eis dixit cum magno gaudio suscepere, et adquiescentes illi miserrimae fidei se subdiderunt, putantes illam domum esse tanquam in hoc saeculo. Absit hoc a fidelium cordibus ut in paradiso, in quo erunt homines similes angelis, aliquid carnale vel inhonestum fieri possit.

234 Tuus autem socius non fuit ausus vocare homines ad ea quibus Iesus Christus suum populum invitavit, cum diceret: "estote similes Patri vestro caelesti et Pater vester caelestis faciet vobis quaecumque sunt utilia." Nam qui facit bona et reddit bona pro malis similis est Patri caelesti proculdubio et quasi natus ab eo. Ipse enim est misericors et propitius, super omnia gloriosus et excellentissimus, et non est Deus nisi ipse solus. Ipse bonitate et benignitate sua creavit nos, et ipse potentia sua pascit et reficit nos et ditat nos et peccata nostra dimittit et stultitiam nostram tolerat. Non festinat ad condemnamdum nos propter peccata nostra in hoc saeculo, sicuti pius et clemens pater in filiis. Sed aliquando

there be constant sexual activity with women. Being a lustful man himself, he provided the most miserable men with the hope of fulfilling their lust, intending to draw them to him, since he was not unaware how prone and disposed human nature is to evil, and especially to the things of the flesh. And for this reason he deemed it sufficient to increase these practices for them not only in this world alone, but also in the next, since he says in the Qurʾān that there are virgins in paradise, whom no man or demon has violated. He repeated and reiterated those miserable and utterly foolish words incessantly until they penetrated the hearts of the stupid and foolish.

Since they lusted for carnal desires and were subject to 233
beastly pleasures, they received with great joy whatever he told them, and submitting to him, they gave themselves up to that most miserable religion, thinking that the future abode would be like the one in this world. Far be it from the hearts of the faithful that anything carnal or dishonorable could happen in paradise, where men will be like angels.

However, your friend did not dare to call men to the 234
things that Jesus Christ urged his people to do, when he said: "Be like your heavenly Father, and your heavenly Father will do all that is beneficial to you." For he who does good and returns good for evil is without doubt like the heavenly Father, and his son, as it were. For he is merciful and kind, glorious above all and most exalted, and there is no God but him alone. He created us out of his own goodness and kindness, and with his own power nourishes, comforts, and enriches us, forgives our sins, and puts up with our foolishness. He does not hasten to condemn us for our sins in this world, like a dutiful and sympathetic father to his

arguit et flagellat nos, ostendens erga nos suam clementiam et misericordiam ut corrigamur et iustificemur. Quis igitur ita dignus est paterno nomine sicut omnipotens Deus, gloriosus et excelsus?

235 Vita vero Domini Iesu et conversatio, sicut ex parte iam diximus, certissimam fidem dictis eius et monitis faciebat. Erat enim indesinenter ieiunans et orans non habens domum vel hospitium nec expensas ad victualia nec vestimenta praeter duo, quibus induebatur. Dixit enim ei quidam: "Magister, ubi habitas?" Respondit ei dicens: "Volucres caeli nidos habent et ferae foveas; ego autem nullam mansionem habeo. Ubicumque fuero, hospitium meum est, et quando quaesieris me, cito invenies." Numquam enim locutus est vanitatem aut mendacium nec admisit peccatum aut fecit contra iustitiam, nec aliquem vituperavit nec alicui crimen imposuit, nec aliquem derisit vel maledixit, nec petentem a se reppulit, nec sperantem in se misericordia defraudavit, nec a clamante aurem suam avertit, sicuti annuntiaverant prophetae de ipso.

236 Quae omnia confirmavit signis et prodigiis, scilicet, mortuos suscitando, infirmos curando, daemones expellendo, caecos illuminando, surdos et claudos et paralyticos sanitati restituendo et cetera omnia faciendo, quae numerari non possunt, sicuti est satiare quinque milia hominum de quinque panibus et duobus piscibus, remanentibus inde duodecim cophinis plenis. Et clamare daemones expulsos ab hominibus: *"Tu es Christus filius Dei, ut quid venisti perdere nos?"* Et de aqua facere vinum in nuptiis Iohannis filii Zebedaei, et pueros laudare illum dicentes, *"Benedictus qui venit in nomine*

children. However, he does chide and strike us from time to time, showing us his sympathy in order to correct and justify us. Who then is as worthy of the title of father as omnipotent God, glorious and exalted?

Now the life and ways of Lord Jesus, as I have told you in 235
part, lent the greatest credence to his words and teachings. For he fasted ceaselessly and prayed, having no home or lodging, no funds for provisions, nor any garments, other than the two he wore. Someone said to him: "Master, where do you live?" He responded: "The birds in the sky have nests and the beasts have dens, but I have no dwelling. Wherever I am, there is my lodging, and when you seek me, you will quickly find me." Never did he speak vainly or utter a lie, nor did he commit sin or act unjustly, nor did he ever blame anyone or falsely accuse anyone of a crime, nor did he ever mock or curse anyone, nor did he send away those who sought him, nor did he ever cheat those hoping for mercy from him, nor did he ever turn his ear from those calling him, just as the prophets had prophesied about him.

All of this he confirmed with signs and miracles, such as 236
resurrecting the dead, healing the sick, exorcising demons, giving sight to the blind, restoring the deaf, crippled, and paralyzed to health, and doing many other things that are impossible to enumerate, such as feeding five thousand people with five loaves of bread and two fishes, while twelve full baskets were left over. There is also the fact that the demons, after they had been exorcised from humans, cried out: "You are Christ, Son of God, why have you come to destroy us?" There was the turning of the water into wine at the wedding, as related by John, son of Zebedee, and children praising him, saying, "Blessed is he who has come in

Domini," et ambulare super undas maris et imperare ventis et tempestatibus et procellis. Sed et transformari ante apostolos in monte, Mose et Elia cum eo loquentibus, et mulierem a fluxu sanguinis tactu fimbriae liberare, multaque etiam alia quae et ante mortem eius et resurrectionem et post ab illo facta sunt. Ex quibus plura intermisi, fugiendo prolixitatem.

237 Tuus vero socius testificatur illi dicens in Alcorano Deum sic esse locutum: *"Dedimus Iesu filio Mariae testimonia et munivimus eum Spiritu Sancto."* Numquid dubitat in istis divinis operibus nisi qui sibi noxius est et obcaecatus invidia vel furore? Nam quicumque contulerit opera Christi et praecepta eius, quae supra diximus, operibus et monitis tui socii, cito apparebit illi veritas et manifestabitur lumen a tenebris. Nulla enim opera hominum possunt conferri operibus Christi, quia ipse est gloriosior et excelsior omnibus. Oportet ergo credi et sine dubio intelligi ista opera esse impossibilia hominibus nec in virtute hominum posse constare. Opera vero tui socii quilibet rusticus vel pessimus facere potest et ab omnibus in omni tempore fieri possunt.

238 Si vero adhuc contradicens dixeris quod et Moses et alii talia multa fecerunt quae non possunt fieri ab hominibus, dicemus tibi quod vere Moses et alii quaedam similia signa fecerunt, sed non imperando solummodo et praecipiendo sicut dominus, sed rogando et supplicando sicut servi. Dominus autem Iesus Christus, qui est filius Dei dilectus, propria sua virtute fecit mirabilia et manifesta opera. Ipse est enim Verbum, per quod creata sunt omnia.

239 Qui etiam assumpsit sibi in apostolos homines idiotas et

the name of the Lord," and the walking on water and the commanding of the winds, storms, and gales. But there was also his transfiguration before the apostles on the mountain, while Moses and Elijah spoke with him, and the freeing of the woman from her hemorrhage when she touched the fringe of his robe, and many other things that were performed by him both before and after his death and resurrection. To avoid verboseness, I have left out many of them.

Your friend bears witness to him, claiming in the Qurʾān 237
that God said the following: "I have given testimonies of Jesus, son of Mary, and protected him with the Holy Spirit." Surely only a person who is harmful to himself and blinded by envy or rage has doubts about these divine acts? Whoever compares Christ's deeds and teachings, which I have mentioned above, with those of your friend, the truth will soon be clear to him, and light will be cast on the darkness. For no human acts can be compared to those of Christ, for he is more glorious and exalted than all others. Undoubtedly one should believe and understand that those deeds are impossible for humans and not within human capability. However, even the worst country bumpkin could perform your friend's deeds, which can be done by anyone at any time.

But if you were to object that both Moses and the others 238
did many such things, which cannot be done by humans, I will say to you that truly Moses and others performed similar signs, but not by commanding and ordering like a master, but by asking and begging like servants. The Lord Jesus Christ, who is the beloved Son of God, performed all miracles openly by his own virtue. For he is the Word, through which all things were created.

Yet he received as apostles uneducated and inexperienced 239

imperitos sine sapientia et scientia, absque generositate vel nobilitate, egentes sine substantia, et misit eos praedicare veritatem in universo mundo et aperuit corda eorum et illuminavit eos lumine scientiae suae et praevaluerunt scientia sua omnibus philosophis et sapientibus et prudentibus, et subiecti sunt eis reges et principes et omnis potestas et regnum et nobilitas et generositas saeculi, oboedientesque illis in omnibus, ipsorum dominio mancipati sunt.

240 Omnia vero ista facta sunt absque compulsione, absque violentia, absque proelio, absque potestate, absque pretio vel munere, absque seductione vel calliditate, absque eloquentia vel aliqua humana persuasione; denique sine ulla quae in hoc mundo fit arte vel altitudine, sed divinis signis et mirabilibus, quodque mirabilius est, paupertate, ieiuniis, nuditate, contumeliarum et opprobriorum, verberum quoque et diversorum cruciatuum, ad ultimum vero, mortium durissimarum patientia et humilitate.

241 Quorum doctrina omnes gentes et populi per universum orbem terrarum recedentes a cultura idolorum et ad fidem Dei undique concurrentes combusserunt idola, templa everterunt, carnalia desideria, honores, et potentias huius saeculi abiecerunt et conversi sunt ad ieiunium, ad orationem, ad eleemosynas, ad cilicia, ad monachatum, ad spem futurae resurrectionis, oboedientes et humiliter confitentes se fuisse filios diaboli et tenebrarum. Nunc autem gaudentes et exultantes esse filios Dei et lucis aeternae participes et coheredes.

242 Miserat enim eos ipse Dominus dicens illis: *"Ite et advocate omnes gentes ad vitam aeternam et annuntiate illis*

men without any wisdom or knowledge, without any dignity or nobility, impoverished and without possessions. He sent them to preach the truth throughout the whole world, and opened their hearts and filled them with the light of his knowledge, and with his knowledge they were superior to all the philosophers and wise and learned men. Kings, princes, and all authorities, governments, dignitaries, and nobles of the world were subjected to them and, placed under their rule, obeyed them in all things.

All of these things, however, were done without force, violence, battle, power, bribe or gift, seduction or cunning, without eloquence or any kind of human persuasion. In short, they were done without any kind of skill or authority of this world, but through divine signs and miracles, and, what is even more wondrous, with poverty, fasting, bareness, and the humble forbearance of insults and abuses, even of lashes and various tortures, and, in extreme cases, of the harshest deaths. 240

It was through their teachings that all the pagans and nations throughout the entire world abandoned the worship of idols and, entering the faith of God from every direction, burned idols, sacked temples, did away with carnal desires, honors, and authority of this world, and converting to fasting, prayer, charity, simple clothing, monasticism, and the hope of the future resurrection, they displayed obedience and humbly confessed that they had been the children of the devil and of darkness. Now, however, they rejoice and exult to be the children of God, and the sharers in and heirs to the eternal light. 241

For the Lord had sent them himself, saying: "Go and call all nations to the eternal life and announce to them the 242

resurrectionem mortuorum et iudicii diem et quod resurgent mortui in corpore et in anima et liberabuntur a captivitate mortis. Et ut hoc certum teneatis dedi vobis virtutem ad facienda miracula et prodigia et sanitates, et vos non accipiatis propter hoc aurum vel argentum nec aliquid transitorium, sed sicut gratis accepistis ita gratis resuscitate mortuos in nomine meo et imponite manus infirmis et curabuntur." Illi autem imitantes eum et praecepta eius implentes faciebant haec omnia in nomine eius, et annuntiantes misericordiam et remissionem peccatorum vocabant omnes ad doctrinam suam et spem vitae aeternae.

243 Postea volens modum humilitatis implere, tradidit se manibus impiorum, donec implentes desiderium suum posuerunt eum in cruce vivum, in qua ipse dicebat: *"Pater, dimitte illis, quia nesciunt quid faciunt."* Et sic postquam crucifixerunt eum, mortuus est. Deinde positus est in sepulcro et mansit in eo usque ad diem tertium, in qua resurrexit a mortuis et apparuit mulieribus quae venerant videre sepulcrum. Deinde apparuit apostolis in Galilaea et postea in cenaculo, ubi erant congregati, deinde in via duobus euntibus in castellum, deinde in litore discipulis piscantibus, deinde per dies quadraginta in multis argumentis apparuit eis et locutus est de regno Dei et promisit eis Spiritum Sanctum.

244 Tandem vero quadrigesimo die, videntibus cunctis, ascendit in caelum et ipsi aspicientes ad portas caeli viderunt angelos descendentes et dicentes: *"O vos, homines, quid aspicientes admiramini et quid obstupescitis? Ecce Iesus Christus ascendit in caelum corporeus gloriosus et sic proposuit venire in*

resurrection of the dead and the day of judgment, and that the dead will be resurrected in body and soul and will be freed from the bonds of death. And so that you might know this for certain, I have given you the power to perform signs, miracles, and healing, and you must not accept gold, silver, or anything transitory in return, but, just as you have freely received, so must you resurrect the dead freely in my name, and lay your hands on the sick, and they will be healed." They imitated him and fulfilled his commands, doing all of these things in his name, and, by announcing the mercy and forgiveness of sins, they called all to his teachings and to the hope of eternal life.

Afterward, wishing to fulfill the measure of humility, he 243
delivered himself to the hands of the wicked, who fulfilled their desires and placed him alive on the cross, on which he said: "Father, forgive them, for they know not what they do." And so, after they crucified him, he died. Then he was placed in a tomb and remained there until the third day, on which he rose from the dead and appeared to the women who had come to visit the tomb. Then he appeared to the apostles in Galilee, and afterward at the banquet where they had gathered, then on the road to two travelers going to the fort, then on the shore to his disciples, who were fishing, then for forty days he appeared to them in various ways and spoke to them about the kingdom of God and promised them the Holy Spirit.

Finally, on the fortieth day, as witnessed by all, he as- 244
cended to heaven, and while they looked on, they saw angels descending to the gate of heaven and saying: "O you, humans, why do you wonder and marvel at what you see? Behold, Jesus Christ has ascended to heaven, glorious in his

novissimo tempore et videbitur in illa hora de caelo descendere, sicut modo eum videtis ascendere." Mons autem ille unde ascendit est in Syria et vocatur Mons Oliveti, unde nullus dubitat.

245 Tuus autem socius sic in Alcorano dicit ad Iesum in persona Dei: *"O Iesu, ego faciam te mori et exaltari et purificari ab his qui non crediderunt in te, et proponam credentes in te his qui non crediderint, usque in diem iudicii. Deinde ad me revertemini et iudicabo inter vos de eo quod eratis diversi. Qui autem non crediderint, praeparabo illis grave tormentum in hoc saeculo et in futuro et non habebunt defensores. Qui autem crediderint et bene fecerint, retribuam illis mercedem suam. Et Deus non diligit impios. Hoc proferimus tibi de signis et memoria prudenti."* Quaero igitur a te (quem Deus salvet), qui sunt qui crediderunt nisi Christiani? Et qui non crediderunt nisi Iudaei? Hoc enim testimonium est tui socii pro Deo, sicut tu asseris. Sed tu modo animadverte et temetipsum exhortare ut, ista discernens, non declines a veritate, quoniam si satisfeceris cito quod verum est tibi videbitur et apparebit tibi lumen et indicia veritatis.

246 Post ascensionem vero Domini Iesu decimo die, cum essent apostoli congregati in cenaculo, ubi solebant commorari cum eo, audierunt vocem magnam et venit super eos virtus Spiritus Sancti, qui est Paraclitus, et facta est super unumquemque eorum quasi lingua ignis et coeperunt loqui lingua regionis in qua venturi erant ut praedicarent Christum salvatorem et liberatorem mundi et advocarent illam

bodily form, and thus does he plan to return at the End of Days, and as you have just witnessed him ascend, so will he be seen to descend from heaven at that hour." The mountain from which he ascended is in Syria, and is called the Mount of Olives, about which no one has any doubts.

Your friend, however, speaks to Jesus in the Qur'ān in the 245
person of God: "O Jesus, I will let you die and exalt you and purify you from those who did not believe in you, and I will prefer those who believe in you to those who did not, until judgment day. Then you all will return to me and I will judge between you on the matter by which you differ. For those who did not believe, I will prepare severe torments in this world and the next, and they will not have anyone to protect them. However, I will pay just rewards to those who believed and performed good deeds. God does not love the impious. This I reveal to you from signs and from well-informed memory." I ask you (may God save you), who are those who believed, if not the Christians? And who are those who did not believe, if not the Jews? For this is the testimony of your friend on behalf of God, as you claim. In light of these things, you should take good care now, and urge yourself not to depart from the truth, for if you make amends quickly, then the truth will be seen by you, and the light and signs of truth will appear to you.

After the ascension of Lord Jesus on the tenth day, while 246
the apostles were gathered at supper, where they were accustomed to spend time with him, they heard a loud voice, and above them came the power of the Holy Spirit, the Paraclete. A tongue of flame, as it were, appeared above each of them, and they began to speak in the language of the lands to which they would travel to preach Christ, savior and liberator of the world, and to call those lands to the faith of

regionem ad fidem Christianitatis, linguis eorum loquentes et ostendentes illis mirabilia signa. Et ex illa hora dispersi sunt apostoli in regiones ad quas missi erant. Quibus data est notitia sermonis illarum regionum, et scripserunt divinam scripturam diversis linguis aspirante Spiritu Sancto cuius vestigia permanent firma et stabilita in saecula saeculorum.

247 Et nos in eo quod ab eis accepimus nec auximus nec minuimus nec mutavimus nec corrupimus. In hoc enim vivimus et in hoc moriemur et in hoc in die resurrectionis resurgemus. Nec facimus sicut discipuli socii tui, qui non destiterunt post mortem eius ab effusione sanguinis et a direptione domorum et regionum devastatione et violare uxores et filias alienorum et captivare innocentes et dilacerare eos; et ita in talibus horribilibus habentur usque huc. Unde dicebat Gumar filius Hatap: "Quicumque habuerit vicinum ex alia tribu, neccesitate cogente, vendat eum," et alia multo peiora.

248 Si dixeris quare monachi hodie non faciunt signa et miracula, sicuti faciebant apostoli euntes per regiones ad advocandos homines, respondebimus tibi quia euntes apostoli per regiones ad vocandos homines, ut confiterentur divinitatem Domini nostri Iesu Christi, necesse habuerunt facere signa et miracula saepius atque frequentius ut probaretur advocatio eorum esse vera et ut advocati scirent et intelligerent ad quid vocarentur.

249 Monachi vero hodie non ita sunt missi vocare ad fidem, quamvis multa signa fiant per eos in occulto, ut sciatur ista

Christianity by speaking in their languages and showing them miraculous signs. And from that moment the apostles dispersed into the lands to which they had been sent. To them was given the knowledge of the languages of those lands, and they set down the divine scripture in different languages with the inspiration of the Holy Spirit, whose traces remain fixed and unchanged until the end of times.

What we have received from them we have not aug- 247
mented, abbreviated, altered, or corrupted. For by this we live and by this we die, and by this we will rise again on the day of resurrection. We do not act like the disciples of your friend, who did not desist from bloodshed after his death, nor from plundering houses, laying waste to lands, violating the wives and daughters of others, and taking captive the innocent and wounding them; and in such horrifying activities they persist even now. This is why ʿUmar b. al-Khaṭṭāb said: "Let whoever has taken captive a neighbor from another tribe sell him, if the need arises," and many much worse things.

If you ask why monks today do not perform signs and 248
miracles, as the apostles used to do when they traveled through lands to call upon men, I will answer you that it was necessary for the apostles to perform signs and miracles more often and frequently, when they traveled to lands to urge men to proclaim the divinity of our Lord Jesus Christ. This was so that their calling might be proven to be true, and so that those who had been called might know and understand to what they were being called.

Today, monks are not sent on a mission to call others to 249
the faith in the same way, although many signs occur through them in secret, so that it might be known that the ability to

beneficia non ex toto discessisse a fidelibus Christi. Sed et, cum necessitas cogit, fiunt ab eis signa etiam in aperto, quorum plura nota sunt per diversa loca in universo orbe. Nam, si monachis datum esset a Deo omnes mortuos resuscitare cunctosque languidos relevare, nullus moreretur nec mundus finiretur. Fiunt tamen per monachos multa signa operante divina clementia, ut augeatur fiducia eorum in eo quod sunt laboris et cruciatus et instantiae, et sciant quantus sit ordo eorum apud Dominum suum, in cuius potestate consistunt et cui serviunt die ac nocte. Etenim si quis ad eos venerit corde perfecto, pura mente, sana fide, humili supplicatione, sciat se exaudiri a Deo et adipisci quod petierit orationibus et benedictionibus eorum. Quod si cotidie fierent signa, sicut olim fiebant tempore apostolorum, quae merces esset Christianis de fide sua?

Nunc autem exercetur fides eorum per bona opera, non per signa, quae quidem primitus fuerunt necessaria ut fidem susciperent. Iam vero non sunt, quia confirmata et roborata fide bonis operibus tantummodo ea exercere debemus, quae nos ad id quod credimus ducant. Et non desiderare miracula facere, quibus nulla merces adquiritur in futuro et periculum vanitatis cito incurritur in hoc saeculo. Nec debent homines ut pecudes esse, quibus semper necesse est novis ad oboediendum cogi incitamentis, sed ut rationabiles et sapientes, quod eis semel signis divinis et certissimis indiciis traditum et confirmatum est, illud firmissime credere, fortissime tenere et in eo usque ad finem perseverare oportet.

grant these favors has not entirely departed from the faithful of Christ. Yet, when the need arises, signs occur through them even in public, many of which are well-known in different places all over the world. For if it had been granted by God to monks to resurrect all of the dead and heal all of the sick, no one would die, and the world would not end. Still, many signs occur through monks by the agency of divine mercy, so that the faith of men may be increased due to the toil, suffering, and urgent prayer of monks, and so that men may know how great the monastic order is before God, by whose power they exist, and whom they serve day and night. Indeed, if anyone were to come to the monks with a perfect heart, a pure mind, with faith intact, and humble supplication, he should know that he will be heard by God and that he will gain what he has sought by their prayers and blessings. But if signs were to take place every day, just as they once did in the time of the apostles, what reward would there be for Christians for their faith?

250 Now however, their faith is expressed by good works, not by the signs that were necessary in the beginning in order that they might accept the faith. But now they do not occur, because we should only do the things that lead us to what we believe, with our faith being reinforced and strengthened by good deeds. And we should not desire to perform miracles, by which no reward is gained in the future, and by which only the risk of vanity in this world is quickly incurred. Nor should people be like cattle, which are always in need of new goads to make them obey, but they should instead be like rational and wise men, and have unshaking belief in what has once been delivered and confirmed to them by divine and indubitable signs, and hold to it most strongly, and persist in it until the very end.

251 Ego tibi expressius declaravi gesta Domini mei Iesu Christi et quaedam de Actibus Apostolorum, a quibus istam fidem in qua stamus suscepimus. Collige modo de his quae tibi placuerint, ad ea quae retines, et utere satisfactione et noli animam tuam suo iure fraudare. Nam, si adquiescens vocem meam audieris et meae exhortationi animum tuum dederis, dimittens stultitiam et amentiam, venies ad evangelii lumen et ad splendorem fidei Domini nostri Iesu Christi. In quam illuminatus si credideris, possidebis regnum Dei. Time ergo illum, qui potestatem habet in corpore et in anima tua, qui potest misereri tui et recipere te, sicuti suscipitur filius errans et profugus, et tunc eris acceptabilis Deo. Tu enim scis quod nullam excusationem poteris habere apud Deum, habens, scilicet, cognitionem et intellectum et liberum arbitrium a Deo datum, praesertim cum multos praecellas sapientia et scientia.

252 Noli, dilecte mi, noli negligenter tecum agere. Noli parvipendere ea quae tibi scripsi vel oblivioni tradere. Noli gloriari in hoc saeculo vel exultare in divitiis eius nec submergi voluptatibus eius. Mundus enim periculosus est, labilis, exitiosus omnibus in se confidentibus et se in illum praecipitantibus. Considera igitur et animadverte, antequam veniat humana sors, et meditare in his, quae scripsi tibi et apertius declaravi, utens canone iustitiae et examine aequitatis. Elige veritatem et adhaere illi et avertere ab iniquitate et fugito illam et cave a rebus falsis et illicitis.

253 Seduxerunt enim homines stultos et ignaros, qui sine sensu et ratione habentur. Non est hoc de illis quae debent

I have told you in plenty of detail the deeds of my Lord Jesus Christ, and some things about the acts of the apostles, from whom we have received the faith in which we stand. Take what is pleasing to you and add it to what you already have, lay claim to satisfaction and do not deprive your soul of its own right. For if you will listen to my words with assent and focus your mind on my exhortation, setting aside all foolishness and madness, you will reach the light of the gospel and the splendor of the faith of our Lord Jesus Christ. If you are enlightened and come to believe in it, you will possess the kingdom of God. Fear the one who has power over your body and soul, who can have mercy on you and receive you, just as a wandering child that has run away is taken up, and then you will be acceptable to God. For you know that you will not have any excuse before God, since you possess knowledge, understanding, and free will granted to you by God, and especially since you are superior to many in your wisdom and knowledge. 251

Do not, my dear one, do not behave carelessly with yourself. Do not consider what I have written to you to be of little worth, or consign it to forgetfulness. Do not glory in this world or rejoice in its riches or immerse yourself in its pleasures. For the world is dangerous, fleeting, and deadly to all who trust in it and throw themselves on it. Pay close attention therefore and, before your human destiny arrives, meditate upon the things I have written to you and openly told you, using the rule of justice and the scales of fairness. Choose the truth and stay with it, turn away from wickedness and avoid it, and be wary of false and unlawful things. 252

For they have led astray foolish and ignorant men, who are considered lacking in all sense and reason. This is not 253

parvipendi et negligenter considerari. Est enim in quo diligenter et intente meditari debes die ac nocte. Hoc equidem exigetur a te in die qua nullam excusationem habere poteris coram iusto iudice. Scito autem quoniam qui negaverit errorem et crediderit in Christum columnae firmissimae adhaerebit, magnoque et mirabili munimine protegetur, et nullus a gratia Dei fraudabitur qui nihil aliud quaesierit nisi appropinquare Deo.

254 Ego itaque tota diligentia exhortatus sum te et omnes, qui meum libellum perspexerint nihil apud me de necessariis retinens. Deprecorque Deum ut nos in viam suam dirigat suisque praeceptis subiectos et oboedientes faciat et ab omni iniquitate liberet et in regno suo cum electis suis collocari iubeat. Amen.

255 Scriptor huius libri dicit: Testificatur mihi Deus vivus aeternus et filius eius dilectus et Spiritus Vivificans, qui scit animarum mysteria et quem non latent abscondita cordium, quod propositum meum non extitit respondere viro qui me ad loquendum provocasse videtur, aliud quam ut ostenderem omnibus quid in sua secta et in nostra lege contineretur, nec putaremur a minus doctis et imperitis esse in errore et in caecitate infidelitatis, in qua habentur ceteri qui in Christum non credunt.

256 Mea itaque voluntas et conamen in hoc opusculo non aliud extitit nisi confortare et illuminare corda credentium, ut, si quidem fidelis fuerit lector et robustus in fide, fidelior amodo sit atque robustior. Si vero minus fortis aut forsitan ex toto debilis, fidei vires, quas sive sua negligentia sive alterius perfidia depravatus amiserat, iterum fortius resumat.

one of those things that deserves to be despised and ignored. In fact, it is something that you should meditate upon carefully and closely, day and night. For this is what will be demanded of you on the day when there will be no excusing yourself to the righteous judge. But know that he who has rejected error and believed in Christ will cling to the steadiest column, and will be protected by a miraculous fortification, and no one who has sought only to reach God will be deprived of the grace of God.

I have urged you earnestly, and all those who will look at 254
my booklet, not keeping to myself anything that is vital. I pray to God to direct us on his path, and to make us subject and obedient to his commandments, and to free us from wickedness and to have us placed in his kingdom with his chosen ones. Amen.

The author of this book says: The living, eternal God, his 255
beloved Son, and the Life-giving Spirit, who knows the mysteries of the soul and before whom the secrets of the heart do not remain hidden, bear witness to me that my purpose did not consist in responding to the man who appears to have challenged me to speak, but to show to all what is contained in his sect and in our religion, and not to appear to the less expert and ignorant to be in the blind error of unbelief, as all others are who do not believe in Christ.

My wish and effort in this book has been none other than 256
to comfort and enlighten the hearts of the believers, so that, if the reader is faithful and firm in his faith, he will from now on be more faithful and firmer in his faith. But if he is less strong, or perhaps entirely weak, and has lost the powers of his faith, either by his own negligence or through the treachery of someone else, let him resume his strength the more

Quae enim divitiae sunt meliores vel quae opes excellentiores quam ut sciat homo Deum suum fide sancta et sana, et leges et caerimonias quibus ei pure ac devote serviat?

257 Qui, postquam dedit nobis fidem, qua in eum crederemus, addidit nobis baptismum dicens: *"Nisi quis renatus fuerit ex aqua et Spiritu Sancto, non potest introire in regnum Dei."* Hic est baptismus, quo baptizati liberamur ab igne inextinguibili. Tertium nobis pignus et magni amoris indicium Dominus noster omnipotens dereliquit, sacri, scilicet, corporis et sanguinis sui mysterium. Quod qui sincera mente et recta fide et corde optimo susceperit, numquam ambiguitatis stimulis vulnerabitur, quoniam in hoc mysterio unum cum Christo efficimur, sicut ipse in evangelio dicit: *"Qui manducat carnem meam et bibit sanguinem meum, in me manet et ego in eo, et habebit vitam aeternam. Et qui manducat me, ipse vivit propter me et dimittuntur omnia peccata eius."* Adiecit etiam nobis opes quae computari non possunt, scilicet, docens nos praecepta utilia et divinas leges, quibus translati sumus a potestate diaboli et ab operibus corporis, ut coniungeremur caelestibus et mundissimis angelis, imitantes eos in cultu et laude et sanctificatione nominis Dei die ac nocte.

258 Quae ergo vox resonans et lingua loquens poterit reddere gratiarum actiones pro istis beneficiis, vel quae vis aut virtus poterit esse nobis ad aequiperandam benignitatem ipsius? Cur non cogitamus in hoc? Nam et si duplicem vitam in hoc saeculo viveremus, non poteramus pervenire digne ad laudem unius beneficiorum suorum. Super omnia vero beneficia quae nobis contulit, est spes futurae resurrectionis post mortem et renovationis post vetustatem et regnandi post huius exilii miseram et calamitosam peregrinationem.

vigorously. What riches are better, or what wealth is more outstanding than for man to know his God with saintly and intact faith, as well as the laws and rituals with which to serve him purely and devoutly?

After he granted us faith, with which we might believe in 257
him, he also gave us baptism, saying: "If anyone has not been reborn from the water and Holy Spirit, he will not be able to enter the Kingdom of God." This is the baptism, by which we are freed from the inextinguishable fire. Our omnipotent Lord also left us a third pledge and proof of his great love for us: the mystery of his sacred body and blood. Whoever accepts it with a pure mind, correct faith, and the best of hearts, will never suffer the pangs of doubt, since by this mystery we are made one with Christ, as he himself says in the gospel: "Whoever eats my flesh and drinks my blood remains in me, and I in him, and he will have the eternal life. Whoever eats me lives through me, and all of his sins are forgiven." He also bestowed on us innumerable riches; teaching us, for example, useful precepts and divine laws, through which we have been transferred from the power of the devil and the fleshly works, so that we may join the heavenly and most pure angels, imitating them in worship, praise, and sanctification of the name of God, day and night.

What voice and tongue could return gratitude for those 258
favors, either by calling out or by speaking, or what power or virtue could we have to equal his kindness? Why are our thoughts not on this? Even if we would live lives twice as long in this world, we would not be able to praise even one of his gifts sufficiently. On top of all the gifts he bestowed on us, there is the hope of future resurrection after death, and of revitalization after old age, of ruling after the miserable and disastrous pilgrimage of this exile.

259 Nos ergo deprecamur supplicantes Dominum nostrum Iesum Christum et salvatorem mundi ut impleat suam gratiam et perficiat suam benignitatem super patrem nostrum Adam et super filios eius pariter, et baptizentur vivi et mortui misericordia eius, et dimittat illis peccata et crimina sua et faciat venire super populum suum pacem et salutem per quattuor mundi cardines, et impleat promissum suum, quo pollicitus est liberare nos a diabolo et ab omnibus calliditatibus eius. Et illuminet nos lumine claritatis suae et sit nobis clemens et propitius et custodiat nos auxilio suae sanctae crucis, et non auferat a nobis beneficia sua, sed confirmet ea in nos. Et memoriam sanctae crucis exaltet, et nomen eius sublimet, et faciat eam refugium confugientibus ad se et calamitatem patientibus, et omnem tristem faciat gaudere et maestum laetari.

260 Et prolonget vitam nostri regis in perfectiori gratia, in altiori gloria, in ampliori incolumitate, in sublimiori securitate. Et permanere faciat honorem suae successionis, et praevalere donet adversario suo, et inimicum suum confundat, et liberet eum ab hoc, unde sollicitus est et pavet in hoc saeculo et in futuro. Ipse est enim aequus in plebe sua et defensor illius, misericors et benignus ac benivolus et propitius illi. Ipse retribuit bona bonis et mala temperanter malis. Ipse tractat omnia suavitatis amplitudine, doctrinae multitudine, sapientiae magnitudine, mentis honestate et animi serenitate et vitae benignitate. Retribuat illi Deus pro his omnibus maiora et meliora quam ceteris principibus.

261 Et quidem oportuisset me in tali opere uti partibus orationis dignioribus et altioribus ac subtilioribus, quae difficiles sunt ad intelligendum et quibus utuntur philosophi

We pray therefore to our Lord Jesus, savior of the world, and beseech him to fulfill his grace and bring to completion his kindness toward our father Adam and his children in equal measure, to baptize both the living and the dead with his mercy, to forgive them their sins and crimes, to let peace and salvation come over his people throughout the four corners of the world, and to fulfill his pledge, in which he promised to free us from the devil and from all of his tricks. And may he enlighten us with the light of his brilliance, may he be merciful to us and kind, may he protect us with the aid of his holy cross, and may he not deprive us of his favors, but bestow them to us. And may he exalt the memory of the holy cross, and raise its name aloft, and make it the refuge for all who flee to him and suffer disaster, and may he cheer up all the wretched and lift up the sorrowful. 259

And may he prolong the life of our king in more perfect grace, in more lofty glory, in greater health, and in more sublime peace. And may he make permanent the honor of his successors, and grant him to be superior to his enemy, to put his foe to shame, and may he deliver him from the cause of his worry and fear in this world and the next. For he is kind to his people, and he is their protector, being merciful, kind, friendly, and favorable to them. He returns good for good and evil sparingly with evil. He treats all things with abundant pleasantness, much learning, great wisdom, honesty of mind, calmness of spirit, and kindness of character. May God recompense him for all of this with greater and better rewards than to other rulers. 260

Indeed, in a work of this nature I should have availed myself of more dignified, elevated, and refined parts of speech, which are difficult to understand and are used by the Greek 261

Graeci in suis opusculis et etiam haeretici Christiani, qui praecipitantur ad diversas sectas, qui tempus occupant prolixitate sermonis, revolventes genera et species, et differentiam et proprium et substantiam et accidens et ad aliquid et qualitatem et quantitatem et cetera, propositionem quoque et assumptionem et conclusionem. Sed haec et huiusmodi minus et apostolicae doctrinae et evangelico sermoni conveniunt.

262 Si vero aliquis argumentari voluerit, dicens antiquos patres, qui sunt columnae fidei et fundamenta Ecclesiae et munimenta Christianitatis, quorum orationibus custodimur, his et similibus verbis uti in suis disputationibus, dicemus illis quidem hoc fuisse necessarium, qui contra subtiles et eruditos homines, licet haereticos, loquebantur. Nos autem et inter vulgares sumus, et secta quam impugnamus adeo rationis est expers ut omnino indigna sit aliqua rationis subtilitate convinci. Nonne superfluum esset loqui verba profunda et disputatoria hominibus non intelligentibus? Et ideo nos libellum istum simplicibus et notis sermonibus explicuimus, ut facile et a quibuslibet possit intelligi.

263 Nam si quis talis est ut sciat aut velit exercere ingenium in definitionibus philosophiae et regulis dialecticae, scire etiam propositiones universales et particulares et disputandi multifariam artem interque verum et falsum subtili indagatione discernere, accedat ad alium nostrum librum, quem contra Arium rebellem conscripsimus, qui stulte et inmoderate Verbum Dei creatum fuisse asseruit. In eo

philosophers in their treatises, and even by Christian heretics, who rush headlong toward various sects and fill the time with their verbosity, ruminating upon genus and species, difference and property, substance and accident, purpose, quality, quantity, as well as major and minor premise, and conclusion. However, these and similar things are less fitting for apostolic teachings and the language of the gospel.

But if someone should wish to debate, and object that 262
the ancient fathers, who are the columns of the faith, the foundations of the Church, and the fortifications of Christianity, and by whose prayers we are protected, used these and similar words in their disputations, I will say to them that this was necessary, since they were speaking against subtle and learned men, even though they were heretics. I however am among the common folk, and the sect that I am fighting against is bereft of reason to such an extent that it is completely unworthy to be defeated by any kind of subtle argumentation. Surely it would be unnecessary to speak profound and argumentative words to men who do not understand them? It is for this reason that I have composed this booklet in simple and common language, so that it may easily be understood by anyone.

And if anyone is the type of person who is knowledgeable 263
or wishes to exercise his intellect with philosophical definitions and dialectical rules, or even to know universal and particular propositions, and the multifarious art of disputation, or to differentiate between truth and falsehood with subtle analysis, let him go to another book of mine, which I wrote against the heretic Arius, who foolishly and unrestrainedly claims that the Word of God was created. In the

quippe libro et modos philosophiae et multa sanctorum praeclara verba posuimus.

264 Dominus autem sua magna pietate et misericordia confirmet nos in fide Christianitatis, quae est pars eius, quam sibi elegit et praeelegit, detque nobis suam gratiam et benedictionem et respiciat nos oculis misericordiae et pietatis suae, quando ante conspectum eius in die iudicii venerimus, cum venerit discernere inter veritatem et mendacium. Et faciat nos in regno suo consortes electorum suorum.

265 O tu, fidelis in Christo, qui confiteris divinitatem eius, confidens in misericordia ipsius, glorificans crucem eius, credens in Patrem et Filium et Spiritum Sanctum, unum Deum, non dubites te in magno munimine esse, sciens te epulaturum in domo aeternitatis, in divitiis, quas *"nec oculus vidit nec auris audivit nec in cor hominis ascenderunt, quas praeparavit Deus diligentibus se"* et oboedientibus et credentibus. Nec dubites te futurum esse domesticum angelorum in illo gaudio ineffabili, ubi videbis faciem Domini nostri Iesu Christi salvatoris mundi. Et scias te ponendum ad dexteram eius, quando astabunt omnes homines ante eum, et faciet stare electos suos ad dexteram suam et impios ad sinistram, sicuti dixit—et verbum eius verum est. Si enim puram fidem in eum habueris et voluntati eius subiectus et oboediens fueris et praecepta eius custodieris et ea quae in sacro evangelio sunt adimpleveris, tunc animam tuam et corpus ab inferno liberabis, in quo diabolus et angeli eius et omnes infideles et negantes Christi divinitatem eiusque advocationi contradicentes et praecepta eius respuentes et legem eius pro nihilo computantes sine fine trudentur. Deprecor te, quicumque hunc librum legeris, ut misertus mei ores pro me ad Dominum, qui laboravi nocte ac die ad hoc opusculum

same book I also included philosophical expressions and many celebrated words of the saints.

May the Lord strengthen us with his great piety and 264
mercy in the faith of Christianity, which is a part of him, which he chose for himself and preferred, and may he grant us his grace and blessing, and may he regard us with eyes of pity and kindness when we come before him on judgment day, when he will come to separate truth from falsehood. And may he make us consorts of his elect in his kingdom.

O you, faithful one in Christ, who professes his divinity, 265
trusting in his mercy, exalting his cross, believing in the Father, the Son, and the Holy Spirit as one God, do not doubt that you have great protection, knowing that you will feast in the eternal abode, among riches that "no eye has seen and no ear has heard, and that have not entered man's heart, which God has prepared for those who love him," and obey and believe in him. And do not doubt that you will be a member of the angelic household with great, inexpressible joy, where you will look upon the face of our Lord Jesus Christ, savior of the world. And you should know that you will be placed at his right hand, when all men will stand before him, and he will make the elect stand at his right hand and the unfaithful at his left, just as he said—and his word is true. For if you have pure faith in him, and obey and submit to his wish, and keep safe his teachings, and fulfill what is in the sacred gospel, then you will free your soul and body from hell, into which will be thrust forever the devil and his angels, and all the unfaithful and those who deny Christ's divinity, oppose his call, reject his teachings, and deem his law worthless. I beg you, whoever reads this book, to have pity on me and to pray for me to the Lord, as I have toiled day

faciendum, quaerens retributionem et appropinquare Deo et aliquam utilitatem facere hominibus.

266 Cum vero pervenissent istae duae epistolae ad Emirhelmomini Elmemun, iussit et Christianum et Maurum venire ante se et utriusque epistolam recitari et non destitit intente et diligenter audire donec perlectae sunt. Et dixit Mauro: "Utinam non provocasses illum, nec hoc certamen cum ipso committeres. Tu enim sciebas eum doctum et prudentem in omnibus. Nunc enim nihil ei respondere possumus." Dixitque iterum Emirhelmomini Helmemun: "Nos scimus esse duas fides, unam istius saeculi et alteram futuri. Fides vero et institutio huius saeculi est quam dedit Daradast. Fides autem futuri saeculi est quam dedit Christus (orationes Dei super eum). Fides autem sana est unitas quam dedit Mahumet noster propheta (oratio Dei super eum et salus). Ipsa est fides quae continet in se utriusque fidei modos, scilicet et istius saeculi et futuri. Sit nobis Deus adiutor et protector et procurator benignus in omnibus. Amen."

and night to compose this little work, seeking as my reward to reach God and to create something of some use to people.

When these two letters had reached the *ʾamīr al-muʾminīn* 266
al-Maʾmūn, he ordered both the Christian and the Moor to come before him and for each letter to be read aloud, and he did not cease to listen closely and carefully until the letters were read all the way through. He said to the Moor: "I wish that you had not challenged him, and that you had not fought this battle with him. For you knew that he was learned and knowledgeable in all things. Now I am unable to respond anything to him." Then the *ʾamīr al-muʾminīn* al-Maʾmūn spoke again: "I know that there are two faiths: one of this world and another of the next. The faith and foundation of this world is what Zoroaster gave. The faith of the next world is what Christ gave (may God's prayers be upon him). The correct faith is the unity given by our prophet Muhammad (may God's prayer and salvation be upon him). This is the faith that contains both facets of each faith, that is, the faiths of this world and the next. May God aid, protect, and oversee us kindly in all things. Amen."

BOOK OF NICHOLAS

INCIPIT LIBER NYCHOLAY, QUI DICITUR MACHUMETUS: QUOMODO CHRISTIANAM LEGEM SUBVERTIT ET CREDULITATEM SARACENORUM FECIT.

Legimus in historiis Romanorum quod Nycholaus, qui Machometus dicitur, unus fuit de septem diaconibus cardinalibus Ecclesiae Romanae. Hic cum esset in grammatica, dialectica, et astronomia doctus ac in factis saecularibus eruditus et omnes diversas linguas loqui sciret, et neccesse esset ut post Constantini Imperatoris baptismum universis mundi nationibus evangelium manifestum fieret, Agabitus Summus Pontifex, qui tenebatur senectute decrepita, cum omnium cardinalium voluntate, Nycholaum in suum successorem elegit. Erat enim consuetudo antiquitus observata quod, sicut Petrus Apostolus fuit a Iesu Christo electus, et Petrus elegit Clementem, ita unusquisque papa, dum credebat mori, unum de cardinalibus eligebat successorem sibi. Et sic factus fuit Nycholaus in Hispaniam et Barbariam apostolicae sedis generalis legatus.

2 Qui cum universas regiones ad quas missus fuerat ad fidem Catholicam convertisset et fere totus mundus baptizatus fuisset, universalis Ecclesia, quae post passionem Iesu Christi in persecutione fuerat apostolorum et aliorum Christianorum usque ad tempora Constantini per trecentos annos et amplius, postquam Constantinus baptizatus et mundatus fuit a lepra, iterum in prosperitate maxima per alios trecentos annos fuit usque ad tempora Machometi.

HERE BEGINS THE BOOK OF NICHOLAS, WHO IS CALLED MUHAMMAD: HOW HE SUBVERTED THE CHRISTIAN RELIGION AND CREATED THE FALSE BELIEF OF THE SARACENS.

We read in the histories of the Romans that Nicholas, who is called Muhammad, was one of the seven cardinal deacons of the Roman Church. Since he was learned in grammar, dialectic, and astronomy, well versed in secular history, and knew how to speak every different language, and since after Emperor Constantine's baptism it was necessary for the gospel to be made manifest to all the nations of the world, Pope Agapetus, suffering from feeble old age, chose Nicholas to be his successor with the consensus of all the cardinals. For it was a custom that had been observed since ancient times that, just as the apostle Peter was chosen by Jesus Christ, and Peter chose Clement, so each pope, when he believed he was about to die, would choose one of the cardinals to be his successor. And so Nicholas was made the general legate of the apostolic see to Spain and Barbary.

When he had converted all of the regions to which he 2
had been sent to the Catholic faith, and when nearly the whole world had been baptized, the apostolic Church, which after the passion of Jesus Christ had suffered the persecution of its apostles and many other Christians for more than three hundred years until the time of Constantine, experienced great prosperity for another three hundred years, from the period after Constantine was baptized and cleansed from leprosy until the time of Muhammad.

3 Sed cum adhuc Nycholaus esset in legatione sua, Agabitus Papa obiit et fuit cum debitis exequiis tumulatus. Unde quia corpus papae defuncti, sicut moris est, in tumulo claudi non debet nisi alius papa succedat et faciat absolutionem defuncto, Iohannem, titulo Sancti Laurentii in Damaso presbyterum cardinalem, in summum pontificem elegerunt, et hoc fecerunt quia erat in senectam et senium et potius de morte quam de vita sperabant ipsius.

4 Miserant enim sollemnes nuntios ut Nycholaus Romam rediret; grandis enim erat via, magis equidem quam unius anni in eundo et redeundo iter habebat. Aestimabant tunc cardinales ut papa senior interim moreretur. Sed qui fuerat in cardinalatu debilis et macilentus, confortatus et inpinguatus est in papatu.

5 Adveniente igitur Nycholao, omnes cardinales ei obviam exiverunt, et licet de papa ab ipsis facto valde indignatus fuisset, tamen indignationem eius multum mitigaverunt praetendentes sibi excusationem initam cur fecerunt. Ad haec insuper unanimiter promiserunt quod absque cogniventia ipsius et sine voluntate eius nihil penitus facere vel ordinare debebant.

6 Et accedens cum cardinalibus ad ipsum papam nullam ei reverentiam fecit. Sed "in corde et corde loquebatur contra ipsum verba dolosa" et quod in eius praeiudicium in apostolatum assumpsisset. Cum haec et hiis similia, increpando eum iugiter, non cessaret loqui, summus pontifex dixit ei quod ad Curiam non accederet nisi vocatus, quia ipsum in senectute sua nimium infestabat. Quare Nicholaus accensus ira, cum nimio furore respondit: "Ego ostendam tibi, Iohannes, qui diceris papa Romanus, quis inter me et te maior

But while Nicholas was still occupied as a legate, Pope Agapetus died and was buried with the proper rites. Since the body of a deceased pope must not, as is the custom, be interred in a tomb before another has succeeded as pope and performed absolution for the deceased, they chose John, cardinal bishop of the titular church of San Lorenzo in Damaso, and they did so because he was already advanced in old age, and so they hoped that he would die rather than remain alive. 3

They sent an official message saying that Nicholas should return to Rome; for the road to travel was long, and the journey would last more than a year in both directions. The cardinals estimated that the elderly pope would die in the meantime, but he who had been weak and gaunt as a cardinal, was strengthened and fattened as a pope. 4

So when Nicholas arrived, all of the cardinals came to meet him, and although he was greatly indignant about what they had done concerning the papacy, still they mitigated his indignation considerably by explaining their motivation for doing what they did. In addition to this, they unanimously promised that they would do or arrange nothing at all without his permission and will. 5

When he visited the pope with the cardinals, he paid him no respect. He spoke "deceitful words to him from the heart" and said that he had received the Apostolic See at his own peril. While he kept uttering these and similar words and reproached him without cease, the Pope said to him that he must not come to the Curia unless summoned, since he was proving to be a great vexation to him in his old age. Incensed, Nicholas responded with great rage: "I will show you, John, who call yourself the Roman Pope, which of us 6

erit in universo circulo orbis terrae." Et audientibus cardinalibus iratus recessit et ad domum suam se reduxit.

7 Unde post modum cogitavit quomodo Christianam religionem subverteret et novam sectam inveniret, praemeditatus fuit in corde suo contra Romanam Ecclesiam maximam controversiam tali modo. Fecit sibi maximum pergamenum inveniri et optime praeparatum et magnis litteris deauratis ipsum scripsit, incipiens: *"In principio creavit Deus caelum et terram."* Item quomodo fecit hominem Adam de limo terrae et qualiter propter praevaricationem et inoboedientiam de paradiso vitae ad mortem saeculi expulsus fuit. Item quod dixit homini Deus: *"Terra es et in terram reverteris et postquam morieris reverteris ad paradisum et vita vives et ultra non morieris."*

8 Docuit etiam quod mulier esset subdita homini et quod homo apprehenderet tot mulieres quot posset nutrire, et quot apprehenderet mulieres in uxores tot reciperet in paradiso merita, tribuens auctoritatis doctrinam, sicut scriptum est: *"Apprehendent VII mulieres virum unum in die illa dicentes: 'panem nostrum comedemus et vestimentis nostris operiemus, tantummodo invocetur nomen tuum super nos, aufer opprobrium nostrum.'"*

9 Igitur sacerdotibus inhibuit confiteri delicta, docens quod ex confessione multa mala orta et perpetrata fuissent. Et scripsit dicens quod omnipotenti deo omnia sunt manifesta. Affirmavit etiam quod Verbum Dei natus homo ex Maria Virgine, qui Deus est Iesus Christus, dixit peccatoribus et leprosis: *"Ite, ostendite vos sacerdotibus,"* et dum irent

will be greater across the entire earth's globe." As the cardinals listened to this, he angrily left and returned to his house.

Afterward he thought about how he might subvert the Christian religion and found a new sect, and devised in his heart a great controversy against the Roman Church in the following way: he had a very large piece of parchment brought to him and carefully prepared, and wrote on it with great golden letters, starting: "In the beginning, God created heaven and earth." Similarly he wrote how God created the man Adam from the earth's clay, how he was banished from the paradise of life to death in the world on account of his deception and disobedience, and how God said to man: "You are earth, and to earth shall you return, and when you have died, you will return to paradise and live, and you will not die." 7

He also taught that woman is subject to man, and that a man may take as many women as he is able to feed, and that as many women as he takes as wives, so many will he receive in paradise as rewards. He supported this with doctrinal authority, as it is written: "And in that day seven women shall take hold of one man, saying, 'We will eat our own bread, and wear our own apparel; only let us be called by thy name, to take away our reproach.'" 8

For this reason, he prevented the confession of sins to priests, teaching that many bad things have arisen from and have been perpetrated by confession. He wrote that all things are known to the omnipotent God. He confirmed that the Word of God became man by being born from the Virgin Mary, which god is Jesus Christ, and said to the sinners and lepers: "Go, show yourselves to the priests," and 9

non ad confitendum sed ad ostendendum mundati sunt. "Quare creator omnipotens vult et praecipit ut in corde paeniteamini, quia scriptum est: 'Et tu remisisti peccatum meum.'" Scripsit et docuit psalterium Daviticum de verbo ad verbum, sicut Iudaei et Christiani habent. Ipse enim bene noverat tamquam qui cardinalis et omnibus facultatibus eruditus erat.

10 Constituit et docuit unusquisque Saracenus antequam intraret ecclesiam mixitam abluere debeat de aqua manus et faciem et dicat: "Miserere mei, Deus, secundum magnam misericordiam tuam, lava me, Domine, ab iniquitate mea et a peccato meo munda me." Et iniunxit nudis pedibus intrent Saraceni mixitam. Nec debent in ipsam spuere propter aliquam neccesitatem, et si iniret neccesitas, exire debet ab ecclesia. Talis consuetudo data est Saracenis.

11 In pergameno scriptum erat quod Deus omnipotens Mahumet de nuntio suo mandavit ut multas gentes aquireret et ipsas Saracenos nominaret, id est, filios Sarae satos, exponens eis quod Sara fuit uxor Abrahae et quod Deus constituit Abraham patrem multarum gentium, et ita sunt Saraceni filii Abrahae nominati. Docuit quod omnes Saraceni mixitam cum cera et oleo honorarent et illuminarent, et sacerdotibus suis, id est, sancta conservantibus, de omnibus quae possident certum, quasi bis deo debitum, certis temporibus offerant, et triginta diebus continue ieiunare Saracenis instituit, et in rotatione lunae de mense Martii celebrare Pascha, in quo quilibet Saracenus, si possibilitatem habet, unum arietem occidat, sicut Abraham arietem de mandato Dei occidit et immolavit. Voluit et ibi dixit ut

that, when they went to priests not to confess but to show themselves, they were cleansed. "This is why the omnipotent creator wishes and commands you to repent in your hearts, for it is written: 'And you have forgiven my sin.'" He copied and taught David's psalter word for word, just as the Jews and Christians have it. For Nicholas knew it well, being a cardinal and having been instructed in all disciplines.

He instituted and taught that every Saracen should 10
cleanse defilement from his hands and face with water before entering the mosque and say: "Have mercy on me, God, in accordance with your great compassion, and cleanse me, o Lord, from my wickedness and wash away my sin." And he added that Saracens must enter the mosque with bare feet. Also, they must not spit in it for any reason, and if nature should call, one must leave the mosque. Such is the tradition given to the Saracens.

On the parchment was written that the omnipotent God 11
commanded his messenger Muhammad to acquire many followers and to call them "Saracens," that is to say, children born of Sarah. And he told them that Sarah was the wife of Abraham, and that God made Abraham the patriarch of many nations, and so the Saracens are called children of Abraham. He taught that all Saracens should beautify their mosques by lighting candles and oil lamps, and offer at fixed times to their priests, that is, those who guard the holy rites, a fixed amount from all that they possess, as if given twice to God. He also ordered the Saracens to fast for thirty days continuously, and to celebrate Easter on the lunar cycle in March, in which every Saracen, if he has the means to do so, should kill one ram, just as Abraham killed and sacrificed a ram at God's command. He also wished, and said so in his

omnes pelles arietum Saraceni portent ad mixitam et dent sacerdotibus suis, et carnes comedant et pauperibus partem faciant iuxta possibilitatem suam.

12 Omne ieiunium et quando ieiunant per totum diem observare ieiunando mandavit, dicens non est verum illud quod dicitur . . . Ieiunant tantum die, non ieiunant si in ipso die comedunt. Transacto vero die, postquam sero venerit, de omnibus quae Deus eis dederit et habere potuerint comedant.

13 Vinum autem non bibunt quia, sicut scriptum est: "Vinum apostatare facit sapientem," unde maledixit omnibus qui bibunt vinum in die. Si vero bibant vinum in noctem propter dormitionem non incurrant maledictionem. Sicut ipse Mahumetus aquam pigmentis et speciebus confectam bibebat, ita Saraceni divites et potentes aquam quasi xerubium confectam bibunt. Multae provinciae sunt in occidentalibus et aquilonis partibus in quibus homines cervisiam de frumento, pomeratam de pomis, et medonem de melle, diverso modo aquam conficiunt et ipsam pro vino bibunt. Et ideo Machometus exinde sumpsit materiam ut aquam Saraceni bibant, quae etiam in regnis et provinciis meridianis sine difficultate potest haberi.

14 Scripsit insuper et praecepit ut corpora defunctorum sepeliantur in locis in quibus haberetur aqua et ibidem cineritia eorum fiant, docens quod sicut aqua surgit de terra, ita anima surget de corpore et revertetur ad patriam paradisi, de qua Adam primus homo expulsus fuit. Docuit et praecepit ut omnis homo circumcidatur et postquam fuerit circumcisus debeat statuto tempore ieiunare.

writing, that all Saracens carry the rams' skins to the mosque and give them to their priests, and eat the meat, giving part of it to the poor in accordance with their means.

He also ordered them to observe every fast, and that, 12
when they do so, they must fast all day long, saying that is not true what is said . . . They fast only during the day, they do not fast if they eat at any point during the day. When the day is over, however, when evening has arrived, let them eat from all that God has given them and that they have been able to acquire.

They do not drink wine, however, since it is written: 13
"Wine causes the wise man to apostatize," which is why he cursed all who drink wine during the day. Yet if they drink wine at night to fall asleep they do not incur his reproach. Just as Muhammad himself used to drink water mixed with various spices, so do the wealthy and powerful Saracens drink water made into a spiced drink. There are many lands in the west and north in which people make beer from wheat, cider from apples, and mead from honey; they mix water in different ways and drink it instead of wine. This is where Muhammad got the idea of telling the Saracens to drink water, which even in the southern kingdoms and provinces is not hard to come by.

He also ordered them in his scripture to bury their dead 14
in a place where there is water, and to keep their ash deposits there. He taught them that just as water rises up from the earth, so will the soul rise up from the body and return to paradise, its homeland, from which Adam, the first man, was banished. He also taught and prescribed that every man must be circumcised, and after he has been circumcised he must fast for the appointed time.

15 Docuit etiam Saracenis firmiter credens quod verbum omnipotentis Dei, Christus, de Maria Virgine natus fuit et ipse inter nos homines factus est homo. Ipse debet de quadraginta annis mundum iudicare et omnes homines sub sua potestate . . . Deinde, sicut Adam mortuus fuit, morietur et ipse. Adiunxit quod quicumque nascitur morietur, adhuc: *"Omnis caro faenum."*

16 Postquam omnia ordinando scripsit, iter arripuit et ad illos quos ab idolorum cultura ad Christianam fidem revocaverat fuit reversus. Convocans ad se omnes maiores natu congregavit per eos gentes et concilium celebravit apud Marrocos, ubi venire fecit universos pontifices et praelatos quos ipse constituerat. Et elevatis manibus intuens in caelum oculis iniunxit omnibus quod diligenter ipsum audirent. Qui locutus est dicens: *"Filii universae carnis, audite et intelligite omnia quae Deus caeli et terrae creator fecit mihi propter vos. Dum ego vellem Romam redire et appropinquarem ei, audivi vocem dicentem mihi: 'Revertere ad populum meum quem seduxisti.' Audiens quidem vocem et nihil videns tremefactus in terram cecidi: 'Ego ostendam tibi quid te oporteat facere.' Et ego dixi: 'Quis es, Domine, et quid iubes me facere?' Et ipse dixit ad me: 'Ecce do tibi legem meam scriptam digito meo non in lapide, sicut per Mosen famulum meum Iudaeis dedi, qui lapideum cor habuerunt, sed in pergameno arietis quem sacrificavit et obtulit mihi Abraham senex fidelis. Et portes praeceptum meum omnibus gentibus et dedicaris omnipotentis Dei nuntius.' Statimque charta cecidit super me et lumen recepi et reversus sum ad vos in laboribus, ieiuniis et orationibus multis, unde quod Deo placuerit fiat, et quod ante factum est destruatur, quia 'a Deo factum est et est mirabile in oculis nostris.'"*

With firm belief, he also taught the Saracens that Christ, the Word of the omnipotent God, was born of the Virgin Mary and became man among us. He will judge the world in forty years and all men under his power <* * *> Then, just as Adam was mortal, will he too die. He added that, so far, whoever is born will die: "All flesh is dry grass." 15

When he had written all of these instructions down, he set out to travel and returned to those whom he had converted from idolatry to the Christian faith. Summoning all the elders, he gathered the people with their help, holding a council in Marrakech, where he had all bishops and prelates whom he had consecrated gather. Raising his hands he turned his gaze to the sky and bade all to listen to him carefully. He said: "Children of every race, listen and understand all that God, creator of heaven and earth, has done for me on your behalf. When I wanted to return to Rome and was approaching it, I heard a voice saying to me: 'Return to my people that you have led astray.' Hearing a voice and being blinded, I trembled and fell to the ground. 'I will show you what to do.' And I said: 'Who are you, Lord, what do you command me to do?' And he said to me: 'Lo! I give you my law, written with my own hand, not on stone, as I have given through my servant Moses to the Jews, who had a heart of stone, but in parchment made of ram's hide, which Abraham, faithful in his old age, sacrificed and brought to me. You must carry my commandment to all nations, and you will be declared the messenger of the omnipotent God.' Immediately the parchment fell on me, and I regained my sight, and I returned to you with labor, fasting, and many prayers, so that what God has decided may be done, and what was done before may be destroyed, for it is God's work and it is miraculous in our eyes." 16

17 Et praecepit quod omnes calices, vestimenta sacerdotalia et pannos altarium et evangelia et alios libros praelati venderent, et ad ipsum pecuniam reportarent. Tantam quidem pecuniam congregavit ex venditione rerum et veneratione legis et institutione pontificum, qui dicuntur caxisi, qua omnes nobiles milites faciebat et populares cotidie vicissim ad prandium invitabat, multis pauperibus porrigebat pecuniam et multas mulieres pauperculas maritabat. Gaudium et laetitiam cum omnibus semper habebat, gaudebat cum gaudentibus et flebat cum flentibus, omnia quae habebat pauperibus dabat, die et nocte orationibus vacabat et omni die ieiunabat et ita faciebat quod omnes verum Dei nuntium ipsum esse credebant.

18 Et quia fidem habebant in eum fides operata fuit quibusdam infirmis. Habent enim Saraceni scriptum quod duos leprosos mundavit, unum caecum illuminavit et quattuor paralyticos sanavit. Et ideo Saraceni post deum omnium vivificatorem ipsum adorant apud Baldacca. Ubi credunt quod in sexta feria, iam lucis orto sidere, fuit Machumetus mortuus et assumptus in caelum. Affirmant etiam quod quaedam discipula eius nomine Charufa incantavit pedem dextrum ipsius ad deum et ad omnes angelos qui ipsum elevaverant et ferebant in caelum, misericordiam invocando quod pes pro reliquiis in manibus eius remiserit.

19 Quare fecerunt arcam deauratam et in ea posuerunt pedem ipsum balsemando et aromatibus involvendo, et ita omnibus Saracenis caput est Baldacca sicut Roma caput est Christianis. Et sicut omnes Ecclesiae Romanae subiacent dignitati, sic omnes mixitae Saracenorum Baldacae sunt subditae potestati. Apud Romam est summus pontifex

And he ordered the bishops to sell all chalices, priestly 17
vestments, altar cloths, gospel books and other books, and to bring him the proceeds. He gathered a great sum of money by selling things, through the worship of his religion, and by instituting priests, who are called *caxisi,* and with these funds he made all the nobles into soldiers, invited the common folk—each in turn—to a meal every day, gave money to many poor people, and married off many impoverished women. He also shared joy and happiness with all, rejoicing with the happy and weeping with the sad, and gave all that he had to the poor, and spent day and night in prayer, fasting every day, and behaved in such a way that all believed him to be the true messenger of God.

Since they had faith in him, their faith was effective for 18
certain people who were ill. For the Saracens have it written that he healed two lepers, gave sight to one blind man, and healed four cripples. This is why Saracens worship him in Baghdad, second to God, giver of life to all. They believe that on a Friday, when the star of light appeared, Muhammad died and was taken up to heaven. They also claim that a certain woman, a disciple of his by the name of Carufa, consecrated his right foot to God and to all the angels who lifted him up and carried him to heaven, invoking God's mercy in leaving the foot behind in her hands as a relic.

For this reason they made a gilded casket and placed the 19
foot in it, after wrapping it in balsam and other balms, and so Baghdad is the capital for all Saracens, just as Rome is for the Christians. And just as all churches are subject to the dignity of Rome, so are all Saracen mosques subject to the power of Baghdad. In Rome there is the highest bishop of

Christianorum et apud Baldaccam summus pontifex Saracenorum et vocatus est califfus.

20 Omnes Saraceni peregrinationem faciunt ad Mecham et adorabant ibi pedem in arca, pedem Machumeti. Arca vero in aere detinetur suspensa et trahitur a tribus magnis lapidibus calamitis in catenis pendentibus super eam, non est enim ex illa parte deaurata arca, quam superius calamitae tangunt. Credunt multi simplices Saraceni quod non artificiose sed potius virtuose illud sit factum.

21 Quemadmodum Christiani papam Romanum credunt vicarium Iesu Christi, sic Saraceni credunt califfum de Baldacca esse vicarium. Et sicut Christiani credunt Iesu Christum filium Dei fuisse, sic Saraceni credunt Machumetum fuisse nuntium et prophetam altissimi creatoris et fieri salvi per ipsum ante Deum.

22 Machumetus vixit in hoc seculo LX annis et mensibus septem. Ipse fecit in Maroco imperatorem Saracenorum qui dicitur miramulus Maximitus. Coronavit in Barbaria et Arabia et Armennia et Chaulandia et Turchia triginta et duos reges. Constituit in partibus orientalibus potentes principes qui dicuntur soldani: soldanum de Caro Babylonie et soldanum Alexandrie, soldanum de tractu Ierusalem, soldanum de Alap et de Tuneo et soldanum de Damasco, et constituit sub poena maledictionis perpetuae quod universi observent legem quam dedit eis Deus per Machumetum nuntium suum, et qui legem ipsam dimiserit decapitetur.

23 De cunctis autem offensionibus quas Saraceni faciunt, sicut distinxit et scripsit, verberibus corriguntur et recipiunt pro unoquoque delicto sui plus et minus verbera numerata. Inhibuit et mandavit quod nullus Saracenus caecari

all Christians, and in Baghdad there is the highest bishop of all Saracens, who is called the caliph.

All Saracens make a pilgrimage to Mecca, where they 20
worship the foot in the casket, the foot of Muhammad. The casket, however, is suspended in the air, pulled by three large magnetic stones hanging above it by chains; for the casket is not gilded at the point touched by the magnets from above. Many simple Saracens believe that this is done not by craft but by miraculous power.

Just as Christians believe the Roman pope to be the vicar 21
of Jesus Christ, so do Saracens believe the caliph of Baghdad to be a vicar. And just as Christians believe Jesus Christ to have been the Son of God, so do Saracens believe that Muhammad was the messenger and prophet of the most exalted creator and that through him they will be saved before God.

Muhammad lived in this world for sixty years and seven 22
months. He appointed the emperor of the Saracens in Morocco, who is called *miramulus* Maximitus. He crowned thirty-two kings in Barbary, Arabia, Armenia, Chaulandia, and Turchia. In the eastern lands he appointed powerful rulers who are called sultans; a sultan of Cairo, of Alexandria, of the area surrounding Jerusalem, of Aleppo, of Tunis, and of Damascus. He also decreed under penalty of eternal excommunication that all must observe the religion which God gave them through his messenger Muhammad, and that anyone who apostatized would be beheaded.

Saracens are punished by lashes for all the offenses they 23
commit, in accordance with what he determined and set down, and they receive a greater or lesser number of lashes for each offense. He ordered that no Saracen be blinded or

seu immutilari debeat, sed si fuerit gravis offensa aut proditio decapitetur. Et mandavit quod singuli Saraceni litteras addiscerent ut praecepta legis legant et intelligant.

24 Dicunt et in lege eorum scriptum est quod Machumetus habuit tres uxores et ex omnibus filios masculos fecit, sed nullus filiorum eius ad duodecimum annum pervenit, mortui quidem fuerunt nec ad annos discretionis pervenerunt. Corpora filiorum vero et uxorum apud Baldaccam sepulta sunt, ubi cum reverentia requiritur omni die.

25 Postquam vero omnia sicut dictum est ordinavit, placuit ei ut apud Baldaccam sedem suam poneret, ubi viam fuit universae carnis ingressus. Sed, sicut asseritur, Carufa, quae dicta est Machumeti discipula, nimis erat pulchra et virum nobilem maritum habebat, sed cum maritus eius nomine Marzucus ipsam suspectam haberet et fingeret se iter arripere, dum nocturno tempore clam rediret et inveniret Machumetum et Carufam pariter commisceri, statim Machumetum occidit et ne ipse Marzucus interficeretur a populo machinatus est cum Carufa consilium quod ab angelis fuit Machumetus portatus in paradisum et pes eius, sicut dictum est, remansit in manibus Charufae discipulae eius.

26 Et ita Marzucus et Charuffa collegerunt a Saracenis maximae quantitatis pecuniam et ex ea maximam construxerunt ecclesiam quam vocant Saraceni Machumeti Meccam. Et sicut Christiani dicunt quod fundatores ecclesiae habent ius patronatus in ea, ita Marzucus et Caruffa et omnes qui de eorum consanguineitate fuerunt semper in ipsa mixita ius patronatus habuerunt et de proventibus et oblationibus medietatem percipiunt omni die. Aliam vero medietatem charissi, presbyteri, et canonici mixitae inter se dividunt.

mutilated, but if the offense were serious or amounted to treason, then he should be beheaded. He also ordered that all Saracens must learn to read, so that they might be able to read the precepts of their religion and understand them.

They say, and so it is written in their scripture, that Muhammad had three wives and had sons from all of them, but that none of them reached the age of twelve, but died before reaching the age of reason. The bodies of his sons and wives are buried in Baghdad, where they are sought out every day with reverence. 24

After he decreed everything, as has just been said, he decided to establish his throne in Baghdad, where he went the way of all flesh. Now it is claimed that Carufa, the aforementioned disciple of Muhammad, was exceedingly beautiful and had a noble husband. Her husband, however, who was called Marzucus, suspected her and pretended to go on a trip. When he secretly returned at night and found Muhammad and Carufa engaging in intercourse, he immediately killed Muhammad and, to prevent himself from being killed by the people, he devised a plan with Carufa, claiming that Muhammad had been carried to paradise by angels, and that his foot, as was mentioned earlier, remained in the hands of Carufa, his disciple. 25

In this way Marzucus and Carufa collected a great amount of money from the Saracens, and with it they built a very large church, which the Saracens call Muhammad's Mecca. And just as Christians say that the founders of a church have the right of patronage to it, so did Marzucus and Carufa and all of their kinsmen always have the right of patronage to that mosque, and every day they receive half of all the proceeds and donations. The other half is divided among the *charissi,* priests, and canons. 26

27 Et nota quod post mortem Machumeti quidam consobrinus Carufae Buzacannus nomine a sociis Machumeti qui archadi, id est, cardinales erant, fuit electus et factus papa, id est, califfus. Qui statim congregavit omnes principes, id est, soldanos Saracenorum, et praecepit eis ex parte Dei omnipotentis et sicut Machumetus nuntius eius scripserat, ut contra Leonem tertium, Romanorum Imperatorem, qui apud Constantinopolim morabatur, per mare exercitum facerent. Sed cum Constantinopolim concesisssent, infra urbem ipsam centum hominum fame et pestilentia perierunt, et Saracenorum maxima multitudo in mari periit.

28 Sed ex alia parte dictus califfus Maximitum in Hispaniam fecit transferre cum innumerata multitudine Saracenorum. Qui contra Karolum Magnum, filium Pipini, cum uxoribus et filiis parvulis regnum Franciae invaserunt quasi habitaturi, et ex tunc usque nunc humani generis inimicus non cessavit ad Tartara secum animas ducere. Infiniti et innumerabiles ex utraque parte homines interierunt et adhuc interire non cessant, dum Saraceni et Christiani, ac si non essent humanae creaturae, se ad invicem destruerunt. Omnes tamen unum deum creatorem caeli et terrae adorant, Christiani, Iudaei et Saraceni, et omnes salvari indubitanter credunt. Amen.

Note that after the death of Muhammad, a certain nephew of Carufa by the name of Buzacannus was elected and made pope, which is to say, caliph, by the companions of Muhammad who were *archadi,* or cardinals. He gathered rulers, that is to say, the sultans of the Saracens, and ordered them on behalf of the omnipotent God, just as Muhammad his messenger had written, to form an army to go across the sea against the Roman emperor Leo III, who resided at Constantinople. But when they arrived at Constantinople, a hundred men died of hunger and disease at the foot of the city, and a greater mass of Saracens perished at sea. 27

In the other direction, the caliph had Maximitus cross over to Spain with an innumerable host of Saracens. They invaded the kingdom of the Franks, fighting against Charlemagne, son of Pippin, intending to live there with their wives and small children, and from that point onward, even up until today, the enemy of the human race has not ceased to bring souls to hell with him. Countless and innumerable men from both sides have died, and even now continue to die, while Saracens and Christians destroy each other, as though they were not of the human race. Yet all worship one God, creator of heaven and earth—Christians, Jews, and Saracens—and all believe without doubt that they will be saved. Amen. 28

WHERE WICKED MUHAMMAD CAME FROM

HIC INCIPIT QUALITER INIQUUS MAHOMETUS VENIT ET A QUIBUS ET QUO MODO PROCESSIT.

Fuit in diebus apostolorum vir nomine Nicolaus per omnia reprobus et maledictus: de septem tamen diaconibus unus erat, sicut et Iudas traditor ex Christi discipulis unus exstiterat. Hic post obitum beati Clementis Papae, qui tertius a Petro beato rexit monarchiam et cathedram digne sedit apostolicam, nisus est pro suo posse illam adipisci, licet indigne, quia non verebatur stimulos et reprehensiones suae pravae conscientiae, sed, sicut Simon magus, infideli amaritudine Spiritus Sancti, conatus est adrequirere se esse papam propter suam malitiam.

2 Sed misericors Deus qui suam semper protegit et defendit ecclesiam, noluit tam iniquo pastori et sponso adultero eam dare. Qua de causa praedictus Nicolaus ira maxima commotus a consortio sanctae Ecclesiae est sequestratus et pessimus effectus haereticus. Dicebat siquidem quod apostoli, quando praeceptum dederunt fidelibus ut omnia omnibus essent communia propter pauperum substentationem, quod etiam uxores deberent in eadem esse communione: videlicet ut qui uxore careret ad proximi sui licite uxorem accederet. Et haec omnia profano et truculento animo

HERE BEGINS THE ACCOUNT OF WHERE WICKED MUHAMMAD CAME FROM AND AMONG WHOM AND HOW HE ROSE TO PROMINENCE.

In the days of the apostles there was a man by the name of Nicolas, who was false and wicked in every way; nonetheless, he was one of the seven deacons, just as the traitor Judas had been one of Christ's disciples. After the death of blessed Pope Clement, who was the third after the blessed Peter to govern as head of the church and honorably occupy the Apostolic See, this Nicolas attempted as much as he could to obtain the See, though he was not worthy, since he did not fear the pricks and admonitions of his guilty conscience, but rather, just like Simon Magus, he tried, with bitter infidelity to the Holy Spirit, to become pope, because of his wickedness.

But God, who always protects and defends his church, in 2
all his mercy did not wish to give it to such a wicked shepherd and adulterous bridegroom. The aforementioned Nicolas was moved to great anger because of this and was separated from the community of the sacred Church and became the worst heretic. He said that the apostles, when they commanded the faithful that all possessions must be held in common in order to support the poor, also commanded that wives should be held in the same way: clearly in order that he who did not have a wife might lawfully approach the wife of his neighbor. All of this he said with the

loquebatur ut infamiam in ecclesiam sanctam poneret et fideles quos posset propter hoc scandalum ab ea divideret.

3 Non solum enim haec sed multas alias blasphemias et scandali verba de suo spurcissimo corde invenit. Et alios multos perditos quos habebat discipulos docuit, et sic adversus catholicam Ecclesiam diaboli malitia armavit. Siquidem inter ceteros suae malitiae discipulos insignis exstiterat unus nomine et natione Maurus. Hic namque ab eo omnes didicerat artes et praecipue perditam et non nominandam nigromantiam plane et perfecte ad suam noverat perditionem. Ad cumulum omne etiam perditionis—ut suam perfecte damnaret animam in infernum flammae—omnium quoque generum noverat linguas.

4 Denique sancta Ecclesia cernens maledictum Nicolaum tanta adversus eam furere insania, fidelium etiam supplicum metuens periculum, facto synodo, illum de errore convenit, et cum se defendere non posset, coram omnibus excommunicato et a fidelium consortio separato, eum in quandam turrem Romae percludi fecit, in qua vitam Nicolaus brevi tempore durans, fame et siti, ut erat dignus, infeliciter periit.

5 Quod cernens praedictus Maurus suus nefandissimus discipulus, monachi accepto habitu, ascendens in navi fugam petiit. Arabicas demum ad partes pervenit, in quibus partibus maxima erat civitas in Arabia radice montis posita, quae etiam ad apostolorum praedicationem noviter ad Christi fidem erat conversa. In hoc siquidem monte impius ascendens Maurus quasi heremita coepit habitare; et, etsi multa iniqua

unholy and savage intent of bringing disgrace on the sacred church and separating as many of its faithful as he could through this scandal.

He conceived not only these things but many other blasphemous and scandalous words in his most vile heart. He also instructed many other wicked people, who were his disciples, and in this way did the devil's wickedness arm him against the catholic Church. Among the disciples of his wickedness there was one who stood out, who was Maurus both by name and ethnicity. He had learned every art from him, and knew above all that damned and unspeakable art of necromancy, which he learned thoroughly and completely—to his own damnation. To make his damnation complete, and in order that he might utterly doom his soul to the fires of hell, he also knew all manner of languages. 3

The sacred Church, seeing at last that that accursed Nicolas was raging against it with such great madness, and fearing the danger to its faithful suppliants, convened a synod and accused him of error, and when he was unable to defend himself, he was excommunicated in the presence of all and removed from the community of the faithful, and he was locked up in a certain tower in Rome, in which Nicolas prolonged his life for a little while until he died miserably, as he deserved, of hunger and thirst. 4

When the aforementioned Maurus, his most heinous disciple, saw this, he took up a monk's garb, boarded a ship, and took to flight. At last he arrived in the Arab lands, where there was a great city at the foot of a mountain, which had recently converted to the faith of Christ at the preaching of the apostles. Maurus the impious climbed this mountain and began to live as though he were a hermit, and to live off 5

religione, fructibus tantum et herbis cum aqua praedictam coepit vitam ducere.

6 Quod videntes illius civitatis homines coeperunt illum habere in magna veneratione et quod a deo illum credebant missum esse ad eorum regionem. Ipse tamen infelix agebat amaritudine ut excitaret in sanctam Ecclesiam nefandissimum spurcissimorum errorem et vindicaret sui perditi magistri mortem. Siquidem, ipso ita cogitante et taliter in supradicto monte versante, accidit quadam die ut quendam cerneret puerorum camelos in monte pascentem, quem ad se vocavit. Noverat autem per astronomicam artem ipsum virum per quem suae nequitiae posset implere propositum. Igitur cum praedictus puer vocatus venisset ad eum, coepit illum fructibus et delicatis cibis ad sui dilectionem adducere, et cum eo saepe et saepius confabulare, ut per singulos dies sic agendo suam normam, plenus ea posset adquiescere.

7 Denique transacto parvo tempore, cum vidisset puerum ad intellectualem sensum pervenisse, vocavit eum ad se. Ait ille secrete: "Fili, audi consilium meum et camelos tuae dominae, quos custodis, relinque mihi, quod a Deo hoc est. Et ego te docebo et faciam te unum de principibus mundi maiorem esse." Quo audito, iuvenis maximo gaudio est repletus, et, relictis camelis, factus est eius discipulus. Denique erat valde ingenio docibilis et intellectu subtilis: vocabatur etiam Maometo.

8 Igitur praedictus et maledictus Maurus coepit illum studiose scientiam et literaturam omnium linguarum docere; et ita coepit, operante diabolo quo plenus erat, praedictus

of fruits and herbs alone, with water, according to his religion, although it was very wicked.

When the people of that city saw this, they began to treat 6
him with great reverence because they believed that he had been sent to their region by God. Yet that miserable man planned with bitterness in his heart to stir up an unspeakable heresy of the vilest people against the holy Church, and to avenge the death of his damned master. Now it happened, while he was engaged in these thoughts and living on the aforementioned mountain, that one day he saw a boy leading camels to pasture on the mountain, whom he called over; for he knew by means of the art of astronomy that he was the one through whom he could bring his wicked plan to fruition. When the boy whom he had called came to him, he began to win him over to his affection with fruits and delicacies, and to hold more and more frequent conversations with him, in order that by thus living his rule day by day, he might fully become accustomed to it.

After a short time had passed, when he saw that the boy 7
was old enough to understand, he summoned him. He said in secret: "Child, listen to my plan and leave to me the camels of your mistress, over which you keep watch, for this commandment comes from God. I will instruct you and make you one of the greatest rulers of the world." When the youth heard this, he was filled with joy and, leaving his camels behind, became his disciple. He was highly susceptible to teaching and his intellect was keen; he was called Muhammad.

Accursed Maurus eagerly began to teach him science and 8
literature of every language; and so Muhammad, at the instigation of the devil who filled him with his presence, began

Maometo cotidie in malo proficere; cumque per tempus maximum eum iam cerneret doctrina suae nequitiae perfectum, coepit ei revelare suum malignum propositum. Acceptis duabus virgis, eas decorticavit et unam earum albo, aliam omni colore variavit; et vocato puero, praecepit ei dicens: "Tolles has virgas et perge ad gregem dominae tuae; et inde cum in calore coitus vaccas perspexeris esse, eas effer, et ipsae concipient ad illarum similitudinem; cumque pepererint vitulos, accipe, et columbam etiam, parvam et totam albam, quaerere stude; et his omnibus inventis, ad me festina redire."

9 Perrexit ergo iuvenis, et virgis secum acceptis et studiose, ut est iussus, malignis sui magistri oboedire praeceptis; atque omnia quae sibi fuerant iussa complens, acceptis secum quae quaesierat, ad suum magistrum redire quam citius potuit festinavit. Quo dum pervenit, ei magister suus praecepit quatinus in terra, accepto sarculo, latam satis et profundam faceret foveam. Qua expleta, album ibi fecit deponi vitulum et praecepit ut ab aliquo ei cibum non praeberetur, nec etiam potum nisi a solo Maometo.

10 Alium vero vitulum diversis coloribus ornatum praecepit in pueri semper comedere sinu; similiter etiam columbam ad suam faciebat dexteram cotidie comedere auriculam. Pergebat denique inimicus Maometo cotidie ad foveam tauri, et arreptis eius cornibus, ludendo illum prosternebat in terram. Similiter et taurus aliis diversis coloribus variatus cotidie, iam mansuetus, pergebat comedere in gremio eius. Sic et columba erat docta, et consueta volabat cotidie per omnia montis loca, et rediebat ac residebat in dextro humero maledicti iuvenis: sic semper cibum accipiebat ab aure sine metu.

to make daily progress in evil; and when, after a great amount of time, Maurus saw that he had become an expert in his depraved teachings, he began to unveil his wicked plan to him. Taking two rods, he stripped the bark off and painted one white, the other various colors; he summoned the boy and told him: "Take these rods and go to your mistress's herd; when you see that the cows are in heat, bring forth the rods, and they will conceive in accordance with their likeness; and when they have borne calves, take them, and look for a dove, small and completely white; when you have found all of these things, hurry back to me."

The youth went forth and took the rods and eagerly obeyed the wicked commands of his master, as he was told; and when he had done all that he had been told and brought with him the things he had searched for, he hurried back to his master as quickly as he could. Upon his arrival, his master told him to take a hoe and make a wide and deep ditch in the ground. When it was finished, he had the white calf lowered in it and gave orders that it must not be given food or drink by anyone but Muhammad alone. 9

He ordered that the other calf, which was covered in many different colors, always be fed in the boy's lap; likewise he had the dove fed every day next to the boy's right ear. The enemy Muhammad went forth every day to the bull's pit and, taking him by the horns, wrestled him to the ground in play. Likewise the other, many-colored bull went to the boy's lap every day to be fed, having become tame. So, too, had the dove been taught to fly over every part of the mountain every day and to return and perch on the accursed boy's right shoulder; in this way it always received food from the boy's ear without any fear. 10

11 Transacto itaque tempore non parvo, rex supradictae civitatis simul et pontifex cum regibus et principibus uno defuncti sunt in anno. Interea iuvenis iniquus cum praedictis animalibus ad congruam pervenerunt aetatem. In monte supradicto denique rege mortuo maximum inter cives de Christi lege per diaboli immissionem ortum iam est scandalum. Unde et inter eos periculosum factum est divortium. Etenim quia erant nec firmi et nondum Spiritus Sancti gratia in fide confirmati, eorum exientibus medicis, ab ea sunt velociter divisi.

12 Quapropter discessio inter eos erat maxima. Dicebant namque iuvenes senioribus quod "hanc legem sustinere nequimus eo quod ieiuniis plurimis secundum eius praecepta adimplere non valemus; vigiliis immoderatis continentiisque superfluis nos gravare non desinunt, et haec omnia sustinendo omnino imbecilles nos existimus." Ex contrario seniores respondebant dicentes: "Nequaquam omnino iustum est ut ad pristinam legem redeuntes more canum reverti videamur ad vomitum; siquidem omnino nullam invenire legem potuerimus nisi istam qua salvari possimus." Et adversus iuvenes dicebant: "Etsi iustum est ad pristinam nos redire legem, tamen quia istam non valemus sustinere, oportet profecto aliam quaerere ut Deo valeamus servire et ea quae ipse ad nostram creavit utilitatem, uti valeamus libere."

13 Denique in hunc modum altercantibus iuvenibus et senioribus, seniores accepto consilio dixerunt intra se: "Quare tantum volumus sustinere dispendium, cum nihil sit periculosius quam civile bellum? Siquidem nobis melius videtur ut pergamus ad Dei servitium et super hanc rem habeamus

After a considerable amount of time had passed, the king of the city, as well as the bishop, along with all the other kings and nobles, all died in one year. The wicked youth, in the meantime, reached the appropriate age along with the animals. After the death of the king, a great scandal arose on that mountain among the citizens concerning the religion of Christ—a scandal caused by the devil. For this reason, a dangerous schism occurred among them. Since they were not yet secure and confirmed in the faith by the grace of the Holy Spirit, they quickly departed from the faith when their physicians left. 11

For this reason a large group apostatized; for the youths said to the elderly: "We cannot bear this religion, since we are unable to complete the many fasts according its precepts; they do not cease to burden us with extreme vigils and unnecessary restraints, and by suffering all of this we become completely enfeebled." The elderly, on the other hand, responded: "It is utterly unjustified for us to return to our former religion, so that we appear to go back to our vomit like dogs; indeed, we will be unable to find any other religion that can save us but this one." To this the youths said: "Although it is right for us to return to our former religion, still, because we cannot bear this one, we should find another one so that we may be able to serve God, and freely make use of the things that God has created for our benefit." 12

While the youths and the elderly were arguing in this way, the elderly took counsel and said among themselves: "Why are we willing to suffer such a great loss, since nothing is more perilous than civil war? It seems preferable to us to continue to serve God and to hold counsel on this matter." 13

consilium." Igitur vocatis iuvenibus seniores dixerunt: "Quare, fratres, inter nos lites et divisionem facimus? Secundum Evangelium 'omne regnum in se ipsum desolabitur.' Sed venite potius et accipiamus salubre consilium: pergamus ad Dei servum Maurum, quem veraciter credimus esse Catholicum, et eum inter nos constituamus iudicem, ut quodcumque ille decreverit, nos firmiter impleamus et suo consilio causam nostram absque ulla retractione feliciter et pacifice compleamus."

14 Quod audientes iuvenes libenter adsensum praebuerunt et se ad iudicium maledicti Mauri esse velle annuerunt. Statimque ipsi cum senioribus ad montem pergere coeperunt. In quo ascendentes ecce primum Maurum una cum nefando Maomet simul invenerunt. Ascenderunt ergo senes et praedicto Mauro ita dixerunt: "Venerabilis pater, credimus te profecto Christi veracem esse civem et in hanc regionem ad nostram missum salutem et praecipue ob hanc causam praesentem. Nunc autem tuam deposcimus sanctitatem et exoramus paternitatem ut nobis salubre consilium des super hanc maximam, quam pro peccatis nostris patimur, confusionem."

15 Quibus ille, ut erat felle amaritudinis plenus, quippe enim contra sanctam Catholicam Ecclesiam semper gestabat animum, tale eis dedit responsum: "Filioli mei, hoc consilium quod a me petitis, non unius diei est vel tridui, et non potest ab aliquo corporeo homine praeberi, nisi sola aspiratione Dei. Qua de re ad vestram civitatem revertimini et inter vos pacem habeatis et post octo dies ad me iterum venitis. Ego iterum Deum exorabo pro vobis, et quicquid mihi praeceperit, vobis, cum ad me reversi eritis, indicabo."

Therefore the youths were summoned and the elderly said: "Why, brothers, do we create strife and discord among ourselves? According to the Gospel, 'every kingdom turned against itself will be made desolate.' But come, let us take up this salutary counsel: let us go to Maurus, God's servant, whom we truly believe to be a Catholic, and let us appoint him to judge between us, so that whatever he decrees we will fulfill to the fullest, and through his counsel may we end our dispute in a happy and peaceful way without any reluctance."

Upon hearing this, the youths eagerly agreed and said 14
that they would be willing to submit themselves to the judgment of accursed Maurus. Immediately they set off for the mountain together with the old men. When they had climbed it, they found, first of all, Maurus, together with Muhammad. The old men climbed up and spoke to Maurus: "Venerable father, we believe firmly that you are a true citizen of Christ, and that you have been sent to this land of ours for our salvation, and above all on account of our dispute. We now beseech your holiness and beg you, father, to provide us with salutatory counsel on this great matter of confusion, which we suffer for our sins."

Filled as he was with gall and bitterness, for he always 15
bore a grudge against the holy Catholic Church, he gave them the following response: "My dear children, the counsel you seek from me is not the work of a single day or even of three, nor can it be given by a mortal man, but only by divine inspiration. Return to your city, therefore, and make peace among yourselves, and come back to me after eight days. I will beseech God for you, and I will relate to you upon your return whatever He commands me."

16 Quod audientes pariter omnes dixerunt et ad suam civitatem reversi sunt. Denique iniquissimus Maurus, vocato ad se Maometo, die septimo dixit ei: "Extrahe taurum album de fovea et permitte eum ire per multa loca singula; impletisque utribus quinque aqua limpidissima eos in fovea naviter collocare stude. Et in superficiem terram impone ut cum populus venerit et <sitim maximam> prae calore . . . ceperit, post tauri victoriam accepto tuo ordine percutiam foveam, et sic utribus ruptis, miraculose videaris de arida humo ducere aquam."

17 Factum est autem complerentur dies octo: populus omnis ad montem ascendit et nefandissimum Maurum ut eis responsum, uti promiserat, redderet, rogare coeperunt plurimum. Quibus ille ait: "Carissimi filii, vos mihi vestrum exposuistis negotium insuper et ad aliam legem praeter quam habetis inveniendam a me petistis consilium, quod omnino vobis dare non debeo, nec possum, quia ego Christianus sum et Christo servus; et si vobis ut aliam legem inveniretis, consilium darem, ipsum dominum offenderem et legem quam Ecclesia sua per sanctos apostolos constituit, transgrederer, unde et maledictionibus legis subiacerem. Sed quia scriptum est: 'Omne petenti te tribue' et quod 'gratis accepistis gratis date,' quia 'sermo non peribit a propheta, nec consilium a sapiente,' vobis consilium secundum Dei praeceptum dare cogor. Quapropter pro certo quia omne corpus quod caret capite, nunquam omnino potest esse in pace vel etiam in modico proficere, nunc igitur fideliter consulo quatenus, inter vos accepto consilio, regem constituatis, et sic

When they heard this, all agreed and returned to their 16
city. The wicked Maurus finally summoned Muhammad on the seventh day and said to him: "Take the white bull from the pit and allow him to roam about; after filling five jugs with the clearest water, take care to place them skillfully inside the pit, covering them with dirt, so that, when the people come and have grown <very thirsty> because of the heat, I will strike the pit, after you have obtained victory over the bull when this sequence of tasks has been accomplished, and when the jugs have burst, you will appear to bring forth water from the dry earth in a miraculous fashion."

It came to pass that the eight days had come to an end; 17
the entire people climbed the mountain and began to ask the wicked Maurus again and again to give them a response, as he had promised. He said to them: "Dearest children, you have explained to me your problem and have asked me for advice about finding a religion different from the one you have; but this is something that I must not do, nor am I able to, since I am a Christian and a servant to Christ; if I were to advise you to find a different religion, I would offend the Lord and transgress the religion which his Church has instituted through the holy apostles, and so I would be subject to religious damnation. However, since it is written, 'Give to every man that asks of you,' and 'freely give what you have freely received,' for 'the word shall not perish from the prophet, nor counsel from the wise,' I am, in accordance with God's precepts, compelled to give you advice. Since it is certain that any body that lacks a head can never be entirely at peace or make even a little progress, I advise you now to take counsel among yourselves and appoint a king,

demum cum Dei adiutorio legem et aliam quam cupitis, precante capite, levius et melius invenire poteritis."

18 Quo audito consilio, omnes unanimiter ei responderunt: "Venerande pater, nos regem leviter habere nequimus eo quod noster rex obiit sine heredibus et nullus est eius; unde et magnates inter se propter regnum maximam habent litem, ita quod nullus alteri concedere vult coronam." Quo audito, Maurus sic respondit: "Fratres mei, super hoc negotium ego vobis facile et optimum dabo consilium. Ecce enim Deus qui nullam suarum creaturarum vult perire et qui magis leges propter homines quam homines propter leges voluit constituere; unde in quacumque lege ei voluerit homo servire, eum non dedignatur suscipere; et ideo vobis in hunc montem pro vestra pace et salute ingentem taurum dignatus est mittere; et quare vobis consulo, omnes ut iuvenes fortiores et potentes cum tauro luctantes pugnetis, et quicumque eum in terra proiecerit, illum vobis regem constituatis, et sic eius consilio et adiutorio quidquid facturi eritis, feliciter peragatis."

19 Igitur omnibus placuit consilium et unanimiter praebere adsensum ad expugnandum taurum. Siquidem armati iuvenes unus post alterum eum insequebantur, sed ab ipso percussi propter eius maximam fortitudinem singuli in terra prosternabantur. Cumque ab eo omnes essent victi, dixerunt infelicissimo Mauro: "Pater, vide quia nullus nostrum per Dei voluntatem hunc taurum potest superare. Rogamus ergo vos ut vestrum discipulum adversus illum debeatis dirigere: forsitan tuis orationibus Deus ipsi victoriam dignabitur praebere." Quibus ille respondit: "Fratres, quomodo potest hoc fieri cum discipulus meus simpliciter in Dei servitio sic mittatur et pugnam vel . . . nullam unquam . . . sit expertus."

and then, when your head prays for it, you will more easily and better be able to find, with God's aid, the different religion you desire."

Upon hearing this advice, all replied to him unanimously: 18
"Venerable father, we cannot have a king as easily as that, since our king passed away without any heirs, and so he has no heir; the nobles have a great conflict among them because of this, since no one is willing to concede the crown to another." Having heard this, Maurus responded: "My brothers, I will give you simple and excellent advice on this matter. Indeed, God wishes none of His creations to perish and rather instituted laws for mankind than mankind for laws; for this reason He will not refuse to accept man, whatever religion he chooses to serve Him in; therefore He has deemed it worthy to send to you on this mountain a giant bull, for your peace and salvation. I advise you, therefore, to let every strong and able youth wrestle with the bull, and whoever throws it to the ground, him you must appoint your king, and then, with his advice and assistance, you will accomplish successfully whatever you undertake."

This advice was pleasing to all, and they unanimously 19
consented to fight the bull. One after another, the armed youths chased after it, but when they were struck by it, each was thrown to the ground on account of its formidable strength. When all had been defeated by it, they said to the ill-fated Maurus: "Father, see, by God's will, none among us is able to defeat the bull. We ask you, therefore, to send your disciple against him; perhaps, with the help of your prayers, God will deem him worthy to bestow victory upon him." He responded: "Brothers, how could this be? For my disciple

Et illi: "Ita esse dicimus, Pater, quia—volente Deo—obtinebit de tauro victoriam propter orationem tuam sanctam."

20 Cum ergo diu in hac perseverarent supplicatione, nefandus Maurus perditum Maomet ad se vocavit; factaque super oratione, daemon statim in eum ingressus est, qui cum eo usque in finem vitae suae perseveravit. Denique oratione peracta et maledicta benedictione a suo magistro accepta, adrectus a daemone ad taurum accessit arreptisque eius cornibus sicut eum in foveam mittere consueverat, ad unum tractum ipso sponte decadente in terra, eum, videntibus cunctis, prostravit; tamque magna victoria cunctus populus regem sibi illum constituit; denique populus prae maximo calore . . . erat enim aestas, hora sexta diei quando parata est victoria et populus etiam felix maxima exultavit laetitia, et merito; et illa hora qua Christus crucifixus est et sancta contristata Ecclesia est, cum concussa sunt etiam omnia elementa, populo reprobo de sua perditione trista, ut ita dicam, accidit laetitia.

21 Igitur postquam iniquus Maomet rex est constitutus, cernens populum propter pugnam tauri nimium fatigatum et quod propter maximum calorem siti anxiavit, accepto bordone ad praedictae foveae accessit locum et oratione simulata, valido in eam bordonem finxit, ruptisque utribus, aqua insuper faciem terre exivit. Quod cernens populus coepit valde mirari et prae gaudio facti mendaciis miraculi, omnes

is simply given in the service of God and has never experienced any combat." And they said: "Yes, father, this is what we mean, since—God willing—he will be victorious over the bull through your holy prayers."

When they continued to persist in their request for a 20
long time, wicked Maurus summoned damned Muhammad. After a prayer, the demon immediately entered him who continued to remain with him until the end of his life. When the prayer was completed, and he had received a cursed blessing from his master, guided by the demon he went to the bull and took it by the horns, just as he had been accustomed when casting him into the pit. At a single pull it fell to the earth of its own accord, and Muhammad laid it low on the ground as everyone was looking on. Because of such a great victory, they all appointed him their king. Then they grew thirsty because of the great heat, for it was summer and the victory had been won at noon. The exceedingly happy people rejoiced greatly, and rightly so: for at that hour at which Christ was crucified and the holy Church grieved, when all creation was shaken at its core, a tragic joy, as it were, befell this people who were at fault for their own damnation.

When wicked Muhammad was appointed king, seeing 21
that the people were greatly exhausted because of the struggle with the bull, and that they were suffering from thirst because of the extreme heat, he took a staff and went to the location of the pit, where he pretended to pray, then powerfully struck the staff inside the pit, breaking the jugs so that water flowed out on the surface. Seeing this, the people began to wonder greatly, and out of sheer joy for the miracle that had been performed through trickery, all began to

ex aqua illa coeperunt communicare; et quicumque etiam terram aqua infusa poterat tangere, se beatum esse dicebat.

22 Peracto itaque diabolico mysterio, accepto etiam secum tauro, populus perditus una cum rege, iniquo taeterrimo Mauro in monte relicto, ipsi descenderunt in plano; ingressique civitatem, taurum epulari coeperunt in nefando convivio quod et fecerunt per dies octo. Die vero nono nefandus rex Maomet, deadunato in ecclesia universo populo, facto etiam sermone pestifero, locutus est ei dicens: "Fratres mei, vos, video, me regem constituistis ut vobis legem leviorem praebeam, qua et Deo servire et saeculi deliciis uti possitis libere. Sed hoc omnino non est hominis. Non enim homo vivens super terram ex suo corde legem potest constituere aliquam nisi plenius in se habuerit gratiam. Quapropter vobis iubeo in ecclesia perseverantes per quinque dies orationibus vacetis devote. Ego vero ad magistrum meum ascendam in monte et eum rogabo quatenus ipse qui cotidie cum angelis loquitur et Deum videt saepius, vobis de caelo mittat legem qua et ipsi valeatis placere et in praesenti saeculo de bonis adeo nobis a Deo collatis diligenter quaeratis gaudere."

23 Et hiis dictis, populo in ecclesia relicto, solus ad montem profectus est. In quo dum perveniret, ad nefandum Maurum, suum impium magistrum, discipulus iniquus accessit et de abominabili et haeretica inventione tractare coepit, acceptaque charta maxima ingentem tomum fecerunt; et ideo de Veteri et Novo Testamento composuerunt iniquum

partake of that water. All who were able to touch the ground that had been flooded by the water claimed to have been blessed.

After this devilish mystery had been consummated, the damned people, along with the king, took the bull with them, leaving behind the wicked and vile Maurus on the mountain, and descended onto the plain; when they had entered the city, they began to feast on the bull in an unholy banquet that lasted for eight days. On the ninth day, the wicked king Muhammad addressed the entire people, which had gathered in the church, and said to them in a poisonous speech: "My brothers, I see that you have appointed me your king in order that I may provide you with an easier religion, in which you may be able to both serve God and freely enjoy the delights of the world. This, however, is not right for man. A man who lives on earth cannot institute a religion of his own will unless he possesses greater grace. For this reason I order you continuously to pray with devotion in church for five days. I will climb up the mountain to my master and ask him, since he daily converses with angels and frequently beholds God, to send down to you from heaven a religion in which you can both please him and seek with diligence to rejoice in the goods of this world that God has bestowed upon you." 22

When he had said this, he left the people behind in the church and set off for the mountain alone. When he arrived there, the wicked disciple went to wicked Maurus, his ungodly master, and began to discuss with him an abhorrent and heretical invention, and, taking a large piece of parchment, they put together a huge tome. They created a wicked heresy by combining elements from the Old and New 23

errorem tali modo: denique de Vetere testamento circumcisionem et prophetas, libros Regis et Registros acceperunt, tantum de Novo Psalterium et quaedam evangelia. Sanctam autem Trinitatem verbo tantum confitendam et corde omnino negandam obscurissimo modo scripserunt. De cibis illud quod in Actibus Apostolorum scriptum est tenuerunt, videlicet quando linteum de caelo quattuor initiis submissum omnibus animalibus plenum et Beato Petro ab angelo reverenti comedere est dictum: "quod Deus sanctificavit, tu ne commune dixeris."

24 Siquidem formam beatissimi taliter composuerunt ut cotidie, cum ingredi deberent in synagogam ad blasphemandum Deum potius quam adorandum, lavarent exterius omnia illa membra quibus potest aliquid committi peccatum. Et hac lavatione salvari se credunt, et ut satisfacerent eius voluntati, ex spurcissima luxuria ut sues infectae, ita ipsi volutantur cotidie. Et dedit eis licentiam accipiendi tot uxores cum suis dotibus quot possent sustentare cum eorum heredibus: aliam licentiam etiam abominandus Maomet a se ipse illis concessit. Etenim cum contra adversarios facto exercitu longe vel prope proficiscerentur, eis mulieres secum ducere prohibuit et quod obsint plurimum et in bello debilitant hominem. Unde cepit eos invicem habitu et more sodomitico, quod ipsi nefandissimi non solum in bello sed etiam omnes agunt tempore tranquillo. Porcinam namque carnem sicut alia cibaria primitus comedebant; sed cur eam dimiserant, circa finem plenius dicemus. Nunc autem ad proposita respondeamus.

Testament in the following way: they took circumcision and the prophets, the books of Kings and Chronicles from the Old Testament, and only the Psalms and certain gospels from the New Testament. In the most abstruse way they wrote that the Holy Trinity must be confessed in words only and be utterly denied with the heart. Concerning food, they hold to what is written in the Acts of the Apostles; namely, the passage in which a great sheet was lowered from heaven by its four corners, filled with every kind of animal, and the venerable angel told blessed Peter to eat: "What God has cleansed, do not call common."

They construed the example of that most blessed one in 24
such a way that every day, when they had to enter the church—more to blaspheme God than to worship him—they washed on the outside all those body parts with which a sin could be committed. They believe that they are saved by this cleansing, and, in order to fulfill Muhammad's wish, they wallow daily in the filthiest lust like muddy swine. He gave them permission to have as many wives (along with their dowries) as they could support, together with their heirs. That execrable Muhammad also gave them permission for something else, which he came up with by himself: when he had formed an army and they set off to march against their enemies, far or near, he forbade them to bring their wives along with them, both on the grounds that they would be greatly in the way and that they weaken a man's strength in war; in this way, he tricked them into mutual homosexual activity and behavior, which all of those most wicked men practice not only in war but also in peace. At first they used to eat pork, just like any other foods; but the reason why they have abandoned it I will tell you more fully at the end. Now let us deal with the topic at hand.

25 Eius vero quem nos Christiani diem dominicum custodimus et Iudaei Sabbato vocant, ipsi, ut et nos et illos viderentur traxendare, medium elegerunt diem custodiendum, videlicet diem Veneris: et merito Venerem colunt qui Veneri id est luxuriae incessanter dediti sunt. Itaque his omnibus ita rite paratis, acceperunt praedictum tomum qui his nefandis praeceptis scriptum est, et cornibus alterius tauri diversorum colorum aptaverunt cum litteris aureis et bene formatis factis. Et sic iniquus Mahummet, accepta sui perditi magistri maledicta benedictione, sequente secum tauro, tomo in suis cornibus composito, de monte descendit et civitatem ingressus ad ecclesiam in qua populus orantem dimiserat, venit.

26 Quem dum cerneret populus venientem, maximo cum honore ei obviam exivit. <Mahummet> illum salutans eos concedere iussit. Statimque hic in medio eorum apparuit hoc blasphemum et dixit: "Audite, fratres et filii: quinque dies sunt hodie quod ego montem adscendi et venerabilem magistrum inveni; ut a deo vobis postularet, obnixe plurimum rogavi, et sic tandem a deo ipso me duce legem congruam vobis accipere meruit, sed illam mecum ferre modo non detulit, quia omnipotens Creator eam vobis per suum angelum mittere placuit, ut sciatis vere quia non ab homine nec per hominem, sed a deo per angelum nobis est data, et credatis firmiter quia haec sola lex est illi placita et coram ipso accepta."

27 Et hoc dicens, illis omnibus eum adorantibus et gratias

For the Lord's day, which we Christians keep on Sunday, 25
and which the Jews call Sabbath, they have chosen to keep the middle day, that is to say, Friday, in order that they may appear to outdo both us and them; and rightly do they worship Venus, since they are perpetually given over to Venus, that is to say: lust. When they had duly prepared all of these things, they took the tome in which they had written those unspeakable commandments, and attached it to the horns of the other, spotted bull, and wrote elegant letters in gold on it. After receiving the cursed blessing of his damned master, wicked Muhammad took the bull with him, with the tome arranged on its horns, and descended the mountain; entering the city, he went to the church from which the people had let him leave to make his request.

When the people saw him coming, they went out to greet 26
him with the greatest respect. Muhammad greeted them and ordered them to stand back. Immediately this blasphemous entity appeared in their midst and said: "Listen, my brothers and children: today it is five days since I climbed the mountain and found my venerable master. I beseeched him with great insistence to make his request to God on your behalf, and so at last he was worthy to receive from God, under my guidance, a religion befitting you. But he did not now bestow it upon me to deliver it, since the omnipotent Creator decided to send it to you through his angel, so that you might know truly that it is given not by man or through man, but by God through an angel, and so that you may believe firmly that this religion alone is the one that pleased him and was approved before Him."

When he had said this, he ascended his throne, while all 27
of them worshipped him and gave thanks to him, shouting,

referentibus ac "vivat rex!" clamantibus, ipse in solio suo rescendit. Et ecce taurus, quem ante civitatem, cum de monte descenderet, in loco secreto relinquerat, per magicam artem ab eo vocatus, daemone illum ducente, portans tomum explicatum atque extensum in suis cornibus ecclesiam statim est ingressus. Quem cernens populus surgens velociter, illum, ut quem credebant angelum, ut iniquus Maomet dixerat, ei prosternens se in terra adoravit protinus.

28 Deinque taurus, ut ante erat consuetus, iniquo rege in suo solio sedente, ad eum accessit et caput suum ubi consueverat comedere, in eius gremio reclinavit. Illum vero tomum de eius cornibus reverenter explicans eum coram omni populo legit et verba scripta erroris eis intimavit et adiecit dicens: "Noveritis, fratres, quia haec verba <quae> legitis a Dei ore sunt scripta. Ideo a me nec ullo aliquo homine perfecte nequeunt esse intellecta. Quapropter Deum devote exorate quatenus angelum suum alium ad me dignetur mittere, vobis videntibus, <qui> haec verba mihi possit exponere." Hoc dicente, taurus suo iussu recessit et versus montem se recepit. Et ecce columbam quam in sua aure docuerat comedere, in medio populi statim apparuit et per totam ecclesiam volare coepit, et sic demum ad umerum iniqui regis Mahummet recedens resedit. Ac in eius aure dextra rostrum tenens grana frumenti quae ibi invenit comedit et recedit.

29 Tunc Maomet daemone arreptus ut taurus et rubicundus oculis, ore, manibus, etiam manibus et pedibus tortis et quasi totus quadam paralysi resolutus, in pavimento diu est

"Long live the king!" And lo! the bull, which he had left outside the city in a secret spot when he was coming down from the mountain, was summoned by him by means of the art of magic, guided by a demon, and, bearing the scroll open and unrolled on its horns, immediately entered the church. When they saw it, the people rose up quickly and, prostrating themselves on the ground, immediately worshipped it, since they believed that it was an angel, as wicked Muhammad had said.

Then the bull, as it had been accustomed, went to the 28
wicked king who was seated on his throne, and laid its head in his lap, where it had grown accustomed to be fed. Taking the scroll from its horns and solemnly unrolling it, he read it out loud in the presence of all, sharing with them its heretical words, and added: "You should know, brothers, that these words you read have been written down from the mouth of God. Because of this they cannot be completely understood by me or any other man. Pray to God with devotion, therefore, that he may see fit to send me another angel to explain these words to me while you are present as witnesses." As he was saying this, the bull left at his command and turned back to the mountain. Lo, the dove, which he had taught to feed from his ear, suddenly appeared in the midst of the crowd and began to fly throughout the entire church, settling at last to perch on the shoulder of the wicked king Muhammad. Taking with its beak the grains which it found on his ear, it fed and then left.

Muhammad was then seized by a demon, just like the bull 29
had been, and his eyes, mouth, and hands grew red, and his hands and feet twisted, and he as if rendered completely helpless by a kind of paralysis writhed on the floor for a long

volutatus. Quod cernens populus nimio timore confusus fortiter coepit clamare. Familiares sui accipientes linteum eum coeperunt festinanter operire. Involutus namque linteo et resumpto flatu coepit eis daemoniaca aspiratione verba legis quasi ab angelo sibi exposita aperire. Siquidem quotienscumque prophetam se simulabat et populum docere volebat, et taliter ei contingebat. Et sic a daemone vexabatur et a suis famulis linteo involvebatur, et quicquid tunc phantastice et fabulose dicebat, a misero populo scribebatur.

30 Quadam namque die cum vexaretur a daemone coepit mendaciora loqui et mentitus est se usque ad septimum caelum ascendisse et dominum omnium creatorem propriis oculis vidisse. Agebat namque: "Ego cum caelum ascenderem, in primo Mosen inveni et eum ut pro meo populo deum exoraret rogavi, et ille dixit mihi: 'Vade tu primus et ego post te veniam et tecum Dominum deprecabor. In secundo invoca Gabrielem qui semper extitit magister meus et docet me de omnibus quae sum locutus.' Et eum similiter sum deprecatus, et dixit mihi respondens: 'In tertia invoca Iesum.' Siquidem inveni Iesum fratrem meum et similiter rogavi eum, et ipse promisit se mecum venturum. Et statim cum eo et duobus aliis una accessimus in septimo caelo ante Deum: in quo tam immensa erat claritas ut nullus vestrorum nisi solus deus Iesus, qui est verbum et anima eius, posset videre eum.

31 "Gabriel vero accedens nuntiavit ei adventum nostrum.

time. Upon seeing this, the crowd was filled with great fear and began to exclaim loudly. Members of his household took a sheet of linen and quickly began to cover him. When he had been wrapped in the sheet and resumed breathing, he began to reveal to them, with the help of demonic inspiration, the words of the law, as though they had been expounded to him by an angel. Whenever he pretended to be a prophet and wished to instruct his people, the same happened to him. Then he would be tormented by a demon, wrapped in a sheet by his servants, and whatever fantastic and fabled words he spoke would be copied down by his miserable people.

One day, when he was tormented by a demon, he began to 30
utter something even more deceptive, and falsely claimed that he had ascended all the way up to the seventh heaven and had seen the Lord Creator of all with his very own eyes. He claimed: "When I was going up to heaven, I found Moses in the first heaven, and asked him to pray to God on behalf of my people, and he said to me: 'Go in front, and I will follow behind you, and I will beseech the Lord together with you. In the second heaven you must call upon Gabriel, who has always been my master and taught all that I have spoken.' I implored him in the same way, and he answered me: 'In the third heaven you must call upon Jesus.' So I found Jesus, my brother, and requested the same of him, and he promised that he would come with me. And immediately afterward I went together with him and the two others to go before God in the seventh heaven; there was such a brilliant splendor there that not one of you, except for Jesus, being God, as well as his Word and soul, could see Him.

"Gabriel approached and announced our arrival to him. 31

Et ille dixit: 'Quid petit nuntius meus fidelis et dilectus Maomet?' Et ille una cum Iesu et Mose dixerunt ei: 'Domine, fidelis tuus frater noster Mahummet et nos similiter cum eo oramus te populo tuo ut constituas eis quot et quibus horis persolvere debeant laudem sanctissimo nomini tuo.' Et ille ait: 'Accedat ad me fidelis meus Maomet.'

32 "Et cum accessissem ante pedes eius, ipse ad me confortandum simul et laetificandum praecepit lunam ingredi per unam meam manicam et transire per aliam. Quo facto, ait mihi: 'Vade et dic populo tuo ut mihi per diem et noctem decies persolvant laudem.' At Iesus, Moses et Gabriel oraverunt eum dicentes: 'Domine, multum est, quia populus est debilis et non valet sustinere impositionem tanti oneris. Sed si placet tibi, altissime Maiestati, quinquies per noctem et diem persolvant laudem tuo nomini.' Et Dominus ait: 'Ita fiat ut vos decrevistis fieri.' Et ecce enim quali modo, quam sancto et venerabili labore, quam pia etiam altissimarum et sanctarum personarum prece de caelo vobis detuli praeceptum qualiter per diem et noctem deo valeatis persolvere obsequium. Et postea quicquid agere vultis de vestris voluntatibus, vobis licitum sit."

33 His itaque gestis, iniquus Mahummet, postquam nefandam legem volentibus eam recipere tradidit—namque in principio nulli vim fecit—postmodo civitatem in duas partes divisit et Saracenos quasi dominos intra, domos Christianorum et Iudaeorum extra in burgo habitare fecit. Denique, postquam populum aliquantulum acquisivit, facto exercitu, alias nationes coepit expugnare et quoscumque

And he said: 'What asks Muhammad, my faithful and beloved messenger?' He said to him, together with Jesus and Moses: 'Lord, your faithful Muhammad, our brother, beseeches you, and we along with him, to establish for your people how often and at what hours they should render praise to your most holy name.' And he said: 'Let Muhammad, my faithful servant, approach me.'

"When I had approached his feet, in order to comfort me 32
and bring joy to me, he ordered the moon to enter through one of my sleeves, and to pass through the other. After this, he said to me: 'Go and tell your people to render praise to me ten times every day and night.' Jesus, Moses, and Gabriel, however, beseeched him and said: 'Lord, that is too much, since the people are weak and unable to bear the weight of such a great burden. However, if it pleases you, most exalted majesty, let them render praise to your name five times every day and night.' And the Lord said: 'Let it be as you have decreed.' Behold in what manner, with what holy and venerable effort, with the aid moreover of what pious prayers of most exalted and holy persons I have brought down to you a precept from heaven, commanding you how you may manage to render obeisance to God day and night. After you have done so, let it be granted to you to do whatever you wish."

After this was done, wicked Muhammad handed this un- 33
speakable law over to those who were willing to receive it—for at first, he did not impose any violence on anyone—and then divided the city into two parts, and let the Muslims live inside like lords, situating the dwellings of the Christians and Jews outside it in a separate neighborhood. Then, when he had acquired somewhat of a following, he formed an

obtinere poterat timore ensis per vim ad suum profanum errorem eos converti compellabat.

34 At ipse nequissimus Maomet, licet vitiis omnibus plenam et magicis viribus fultam turpissimam semper vixerit vitam, reginam et omnium vitiorum dominam et praecipuam et principaliter in suo nequissimo animo constituerat luxuriam. In tantum ut non solum perditas Saracenas, sed etiam fideles Christianas et abominabiles Hebraeas ab sua coinquinatione nunquam transire permittebat immunes, et non solum harum generationum feminas, sed etiam iuvenes et pueros aequali sorde maculabat. Hic itaque iniquus cum talis existeret et tam turpissimam vitam duceret, quotienscumque ad suum pergebat abominabile adulterium perpetrandum, hic—pro nefas!—dicebat se ire ad caelum cum deo locuturum; et quandoque per quinque, per octo, nonnunquam etiam per quindecim dies solus in suo tali turpissimo vacabat stupro. Et cum revertebatur ad populum (quod adunabat eum in sublimi palatio), et statim arreptus a daemone secundum suam iniquam consuetudinem aliquod fingebat, simulabat prophetiam, et sic semper in malo expendebat suos perditos et obscuros dies.

35 Veniamus ergo tandem ad narrationis metam et dicamus quali modo suam perditam fecerit finem. Siquidem, ut supra diximus, Christianis et Iudaeis simul in burgo habitantibus, quia Christiani secundum eorum morem porcos secum habebant et saepius contingebat, eo quod porci ingrederent domos Iudaeorum, inter eos et Christianos iurgium; unde Christiani omnes acceperunt consilium et facta . . . quadam platea spatiosa quae erat inter eos et . . . Iudaeos posita maxima et spatiosa, congregatis porcis in unum, noctu

army and began to attack other peoples, and to force as many as he could to convert to his unholy heresy by fear of the sword.

Although the wicked Muhammad himself lived a vile life filled with every sin and dependent on magical arts, he made lust the queen and mistress of all sins, which held special sway over his depraved mind. He did this to such an extent that he not only did not allow damned Muslim women but also faithful Christian and abominable Jewish women to pass by free from his filth, and he besmirched with equal filth not only the women of these peoples, but also their youths and boys. This wicked man, since he acted in this way and led a most disgraceful life, whenever he went to commit his abominable adulteries, said—for shame!—that he was going to heaven to converse with God; and sometimes he occupied himself alone in such utterly disgraceful adulteries for five, eight, or sometimes even fifteen days. When he returned to his people (for he would convene them in his lofty palace), he would be seized by a demon and would make something up, as was his wicked custom, and would pretend to emit a prophecy, and in this way he spent all of his damned and dark days in evil. 34

Let us come now to the conclusion of the story and tell how he came to his damned end. Since, as I have said above, the Christians and Jews lived in the same neighborhood, and the Christians customarily kept pigs, frequent arguments arose among them when the pigs entered the houses of the Jews. All the Christians, therefore, decided to create a very large square situated between them and the Jews, and gathered all of the pigs, which were enclosed in that place at 35

ponebantur et claudebantur in illum locum, die vero ducebantur extra civitatem longius et pascebantur in maximum pratum.

36 Igitur his ita se habentibus, accidit quadam die ut Maomet videret pulcherrimam Hebraeam quam statim concupivit et ad eam suum nuntium direxit. Hebraea vero erat nimis agitata et mali negotii plena. Quae cum audisset nuntii verba, ea respondit dicens: "Quae sum ego et quod genus meum est ut non impleam domini mei regis et prophetae mandatum? Vade et dic: ea fiant secundum suum beneplacitum. Unum tantum rogo eum, verbum ut dignetur facere quatenus non in die sed in nocte ad me velit venire, eo quod timeam obprobium generis mei et confusionem meae legis." Igitur reversus nuntius nuntiavit haec domino suo.

37 At ille laetus effectus disposuit a qua nocte deberet pergere ad satisfaciendum spurcissimo suo animo. Siquidem, ut non vituperaretur suum iniquum ministerium nec probaretur eius flagitium, solus semper sine comite ad tale consueverat ire negotium. Hebraea siquidem, postquam suo nuntio tale dedit responsum, vocavit ad se omne genus suum et super hanc rem cum eis habuit consilium. At illi dixerunt ei: "Soror nostra, hoc erit nostrae legis maximum improperium et nobis omnibus inevitabile periculum. Tamen quid tibi faciemus? Nullum tibi valemus dare adiutorium, quia ipse est dominus omnium et nos omnes timemus eius gladium."

38 Illa vero dixit eis: "Miror, fratres mei, valde de vobis quod in tam gravi causa omne vestrum defecerit ingenium et nullum mihi liberationis in propriis potestis dare consilium. Sed ego vobis patefaciam de hac re meum animum et faciam tale factum ut ego remaneam impolluta et vobis istud non

night, and from where they were brought out by day quite far outside the city to graze out on a very large meadow.

Now these things being as they were, it happened one 36
day that Muhammad saw a very beautiful Jewish woman, and immediately began to lust after her, and sent a messenger to her. The Jewish woman was greatly disturbed, but was ready with an evil deed. When she heard the words of the messenger, she answered: "Who am I, and of what lineage am I to refuse to fulfill the command of my lord, king, and prophet? Go and say to him: let it be as you wish. I ask him one thing only, that he deign not to come to me during the day but only at night, since I fear the reproach of my people and the transgression of my religion." The messenger returned and reported this to his master.

Muhammad rejoiced and made plans for which night he 37
would go to satisfy his vile passion. He was accustomed to always engage in such business alone without any companion, so that his wicked ministry not suffer insult, and so that his crime not be proven. The Jewish woman, however, after giving this response to his messenger, convened all of her people and consulted them on this matter. They said to her: "Sister of ours, this will be a great reproach to our religion, and an unavoidable danger to all of us. Yet what are we to do? We are unable to provide any aid to you, since he is the lord of all, and all of us fear his sword."

She said to them: "I am greatly surprised at you, my 38
brothers, that all of your talents have failed me in such a grave matter, and that you are unable to provide me with any plan of rescue by your own means. I will tell you my thoughts on this matter, and I will do what needs to be done so that that I may remain unpolluted, and that there be no

sit obprobrium et insuper etiam omnes evadamus periculum." At illi dixerunt ei: "Scimus quia, mulier sapiens et filia sapientium parentum, adiuvet Deus tuum propositum et det tibi et nobis suum auxilium. Tamen rogamus te ut nobis exponas quo modo exponere tam fortem et difficilem causam debeas."

39 At illa dixit eis: "Audite me, fratres, et omnes unanimiter meo consilio adquiescite. Et in tali nocte arma vestra arripite, ad me venite et in loco quod vobis constituero absconsi manete et ego vobis signum dabo; quod postquam ipse venerit et ad me ingressus fuerit, vos, audito signo, statim exite et accedentes absque ullo timore nihil dicentes eum interficite. Et quiquid vobis mali de hac re contigerit super me ponite." Quod et factum est.

40 Venit siquidem iniquus Mahomet nocte qua proposuerat ad Hebraeam et, ut erat propositum, occisus est a suis parentibus antequam tangeret eam. Parentes vero ei statim, ut interfecerunt, ipsa Hebraea suggerente eius sinistrum pedem absciderunt et reliquum cadaver iniquum in cloaca porcis proiecerunt. Qui statim ab eis ita comestus est ut nec pillus de eo unquam fuerit inventus. Et haec est causa odii inter Saracenos et Iudaeos. Et propter hanc causam abominabuntur comedere porcos, quod in principio electos habebant cibos. Quia in tanto Saraceni maledicunt eos ut non liceat eis neque aquam bibere nisi maledixerint eos, aut maledicunt donec vivunt. Praedicta ergo Hebraea pedem nequissimi Mahumet accipiens sale illum et aliis aromatibus condivit, in panno serico involutum studiose in sua eum arca locavit.

reproach to you—and, in addition, that all of us will avoid danger." They said to her: "Wise woman, and daughter of wise parents, we know that God will aid your plan and grant His assistance to both you and us. Nevertheless, we ask you to explain to us how you will set out such a bold and difficult enterprise."

She said to them: "Listen to me, brothers, and give your 39
approval to my plan—all of you. Take up your arms on that night, and come to me at the place that I will determine for you, and remain hidden there until I give you the signal; after he arrives and has come to me, quickly, upon hearing the signal, leave your position and approach him without any fear and kill him, without saying a word. Whatever harm shall come to you on this account you may pass on to me." And so it happened.

Wicked Muhammad came on the night he had agreed 40
upon with the Jewish woman, and, as was planned, was killed by her relatives before he could lay a hand on her. As soon as her kin had killed him, they cut off, at the Jewish woman's suggestion, his left foot and cast the remainder of the wicked corpse into the sewers for the pigs. He was immediately devoured by them, so that not even a single hair of his was ever found. And this is the reason for the hate between the Muslims and the Jews, and for this reason do they abhor to eat pork, which before they had considered a choice meal. The Muslims curse them so much that they are not allowed even to drink water unless they have first cursed those Jews, or they curse them for as long as they live. Now the Jewish woman took the foot of the wicked Muhammad, treated it with salt and other preservatives, then carefully wrapped it in a silk cloth and placed it in her safe-box.

41 Denique Saraceni videntes quod eorum rex et propheta plus quam solito redire tardabat, coeperunt inter se quaerere ubi posset esse et timebant ne forte ei aliquid adversitatis accideret. Cumque inter se plurimum exitarent et quod de eo actum esset penitus ignorarent, post expectationem quinque mensium habuerunt inter se consilium et coeperunt eum quaerere in domibus concubinarum suarum. Cumque diu quaererent, pervenit ad aures eorum quod istam diligebat suprascriptam Hebraeam. Qui statim armati cum maximo furore perrexerunt ad eam et dixerunt ei: "Nisi statim ostendis dominum et regem et prophetam nostrum, interficiemus te et genus tuum totum."

42 At illa dixit eis: "Domini mei, revera sciatis quia me dominus rex dilexit et ad me in tali nocte secrete venit ac mecum simul in lecto cubavit. Cumque nos sopori dedissemus, a Deo missi venerunt angeli et eum per bracchia accipientes levare coeperunt. Ego autem hoc sciens futurum quod a me deberet requiri, eius sinistrum pedem tenui. Angeli vero ad se illum trahebant sursum, et ego similiter deorsum. Et sic per totam noctem pugnantes, circa auroram tandem angeli sua multitudine, quia fortiores me erant, corpus acceperunt, pedem maxima vi ex corpore disiunctum mihi derelinquerunt. Quem propter vestrum honorem conditum aromatibus in hoc pretioso involvi panno et in meo honorifice reposui scrinio. Et ite: habetis quod vestrum est. Accipite eum et, diligenter custodite ac iuxta mandatum domini vestri illum silvestro camelo imponite et reprimite. Quem sequentes

When the Muslims finally noticed that their king and prophet was slower than usual in returning they began to inquire among themselves where he could be, and they feared that something bad had happened to him. While they were greatly troubled among themselves, and were completely ignorant of what had happened to him, they held counsel after waiting for five months, and began to look for him in the houses of his concubines. When they had searched for a long time, a report reached them that he had been in love with the aforementioned Jewish woman. They immediately went to her, armed and with great rage, and said to her: "If you do not immediately show us our lord, king, and prophet, we will kill you and your entire people." 41

She, however, said to them: "My lords, in truth you should know that the lord king loved me and came to me in secret on one of those nights and slept with me in my bed. When we had surrendered ourselves to sleep, angels came, sent by God, and took him by the arm and began to lift him up. Knowing full well that this would happen and that I would be required to produce him, I held on to his left foot. The angels, however, pulled him up toward them, and likewise I pulled him down. Struggling in this way through the entire night, the angels finally took his body with their multitude around dawn, since they were stronger than I, but left his foot to me, which had become separated from the body owing to the great force. Out of respect for you I preserved it with spices and wrapped it in this precious cloth, and respectfully kept it in this case of mine. Go now, you have what is yours. Take it and watch over it with care, and, in accordance with the command of your lord, place it on a wild camel and fasten it. Follow the camel and, wherever the 42

in quo loco se camelus proiecerit, ibi sepulcrum ipsius de adamantino lapide facite et pedem illuc debito cum honore locate. Et sic demum adorantes eum ad loca vestra redite, et de cetero peregrinatio gentis vestrae illuc fiat omni tempore."

43 Quo viso complentes fecerunt omnia quae illos iusserat Hebraea. Et posito in supradicto monte arduo et influcoso loco, reversi sunt unusquisque ad locum suum. Et sic crescente eorum populo usque in hodiernum diem tenent et venerantur et colunt errorem iniquum.

44 Et ecce quali modo iniqua Ismaelitarum secta per diaboli operationem fuerit inventa.

EXPLICIT VITA MALA, ID EST, VITA SARACENORUM, FACTA PER OPERATIONEM DIABOLI.

camel will cast itself down, there you must build a tomb for Muhammad out of adamantine rock, and you must place the foot in it with due dignity. When you have worshipped him in this way, return to your homes; let there be from now on always a pilgrimage of your people to that site."

When they laid eyes on the foot, they did all that the Jew- 43
ish woman had ordered them. When they had placed it on the aforementioned mountain, in a steep and barren place, all returned each to his own home. Their people keep growing even to this day, and they hold fast to the veneration and worship of this wicked heresy.

And this is how the wicked sect of the descendants of 44
Ishmael was invented through the agency of the devil.

HERE ENDS THE EVIL LIFE, THAT IS, OF THE SARACENS, WHICH WAS CREATED THROUGH THE AGENCY OF THE DEVIL.

Abbreviations

Bischoff = Bernhard Bischoff, "Ein Leben Mohammeds (Adelphus?) (Zwölftes Jahrhundert)," in *Anecdota Novissima: Texte des vierten bis sechzehnten Jahrhundert* (Stuttgart: A. Hiersemann, 1984), 106–22

Cambier = Guy Cambier, *Embricon de Mayence. La vie de Mahomet.* Collection Latomus 52 (Brussels: Latomus, Revue d'études latines, 1962)

D'Ancona = Alessandro d'Ancona, "Il tesoro di Brunetto Latini versificato," *Atti della Reale Accademia dei Lincei,* Classe di scienze morali, storiche, e filologiche 4:1, 285 (1888): Appendix 1:152–55

ES = *Apology of al-Kindī,* Letter of the Saracen *(Epistula Saraceni)*

Gil = Juan Gil, *Corpus Scriptorum Muzarabicorum* (Madrid: Instituto Antonio de Nebrija, 1973), 1:483–86, 2:709–10

González Muñoz, *Exposición* = Fernando González Muñoz, *Exposición y refutación del Islam: la versión latina de las epístolas de al-Hāšimī y al-Kindī* (Coruña: Universidade da Coruña, Servizo de Publicacións, 2005)

González Muñoz, "*Liber Nycholay*" = Fernando González Muñoz, "*Liber Nycholay.* La leyenda de Mahome y el cardenal Nicolás," *al-Qantara* 25 (2004): 5–43

Jacobsen = Peter Jacobsen, Review of Guy Cambier, *Embricon de Mayence. La Vie de Mahomet, Mittellateinisches Jahrbuch* 3 (1966): 274–78

Mancini = Augusto Mancini, "Per lo studio della legenda di Maometto in Occidente," *Rendiconti della R. Accademia nazionale dei Lincei, Classe di scienze morali, storiche e filologiche* 6 (Issue 10, 1934): 325–49

P = Pisa, Biblioteca del Seminario 50, fols. 81v–85r

Qualiter = *Where Wicked Muhammad Came From* (*Qualiter iniquus Mahometus*)

RC = *Apology of al-Kindī,* Reply of the Christian *(Responsum Christiani)*

Wolf = Kenneth B. Wolf, "The Earliest Latin Lives of Muḥammad," in *Conversion and Continuity: Indigenous Christian Communities in Islamic Lands, Eighth to Eighteenth Centuries*, ed. Michael Gervers and Ramzi Jibran Bilkhazi (Toronto, 1990), 89–101. Repr. in *Medieval Iberia. Readings from Christian, Muslim, and Jewish sources*, ed. Olivia Remie Constable (Philadelphia, 1997), 48–50

Note on the Texts

In the Latin texts, we have implemented a classicizing orthography for the benefit of the reader, in accordance with the mission of the Dumbarton Oaks Medieval Library. This means that, with the exclusion of proper names, the spelling of words has been modified to classical norms: for example, *ae* diphthongs have been restored where medieval practice tended to favor a spelling with *e,* while *ci* resulting from palatalization has been restored to *ti.*

History of Muhammad and *Tultusceptru* from the Book of Lord Metobius

The Latin texts were first edited by Manuel Díaz y Díaz in 1970 and later by Juan Gil in 1973. The editions and translations presented here are adapted from those kindly placed at our disposal by Kenneth B. Wolf: "The earliest Latin lives of Muḥammad," in *Conversion and Continuity: Indigenous Christian Communities in Islamic Lands, Eighth to Eighteenth Centuries*, ed. Michael Gervers and Ramzi Jibran Bilkhazi (Toronto, 1990), 89–101. Repr. in *Medieval Iberia. Readings from Christian, Muslim, and Jewish Sources*, ed. Olivia Remie Constable (Philadelphia, 1997), 48–50.

Anastasius the Librarian, *Chronicle* of Theophanes

The text printed here is a short selection from a Latin translation of the Greek text of Theophanes the Confessor's *Chronographia* made by Anastasius the Librarian (d. 879). The Latin presented is that of the edition by Carolus de Boor from 1885. The Latin text dealing with the life of Muhammad most recently appeared in Di Cesare, *The Pseudo-historical Image,* 52–54.

Embrico of Mainz, *Life of Muhammad*

The Latin text printed here is adapted from the critical edition of Guy Cambier from 1962. Suggestions of Peter Jacobsen in his review of Cambier's edition, almost all of which I have adopted, resulted in improvement of the text and punctuation. Cambier based his edition on sixteen extant manuscripts of varied date and provenance, but he followed most closely the readings and orthography of a Berlin manuscript: Preussische Staatsbibliothek, Phil. 1694. For his edition, Cambier was significantly indebted to the 1935 critical edition of Fritz Hübner.

Embrico's *Life of Muhammad* was published for the first time in 1708, under the title *Carmen de fraudibus Mahumeti* ("Poem on Muhammad's trickery"), along with other works by or attributed to Hildebert of Lavardin, in an edition by Antoine Beaugendre, which was reprinted in the *Patrologia Latina* in 1854.

Walter of Compiègne, *Poetic Pastimes on Muhammad*

The Latin text of Walter's *Poetic Pastimes* is adapted from R. B. C. Huygens's second edition of the poem, which ac-

companied an edition of the Old French romance based on it: *Le roman de Mahomet de Alexandre du Pont,* ed. Yvan Lepage (Paris, 1977). This edition is based on two manuscripts in the Bibliothèque Nationale, Paris, Latin 8501 A, fols. 23–32 (= A), and Latin 11332, fols. 1–28 (= B), as well as on a third manuscript discovered by E. Pellegrin in the Vatican Library, Reg. lat. 620, fols. 33–48v (= R), which contains only three-quarters of the poem. A previous 1956 edition also by R. B. C. Huygens was based on only the first two manuscripts. The first edition of the poem, by Édélestand du Méril, appeared in an anthology of popular medieval Latin poetry in 1847.

Although in other works in this volume biblical names have generally been standardized to the spelling of the Stuttgart Vulgate, in this poem the non-Vulgate spelling *Moyses* has been retained in order to preserve the meter. The abundance of passages written in paratactic style, featuring a large proportion of simple sentences without subordination, can sometimes make it difficult to punctuate the text in accordance with modern conventions.

Adelphus, *Life of Muhammad*

The only known manuscript of this work, Trier, Stadtbibliothek 1897 (18), was discovered by Bernhard Bischoff in the early 1980s. Bischoff dated the manuscript to the mid-twelfth century. The text of this *vita* is adapted from Bischoff's 1984 edition. To provide a solid text for translation, choices have been made among conjectures offered by Bischoff. The paragraph division in the Latin text in this volume consists of shorter units than that of Bischoff's edition, and the numbering has been modified accordingly.

Apology of al-Kindī

The *Apology of al-Kindī* is one of the texts that was translated into Latin from Arabic in the years 1142 to 1143 at the initiative of Peter the Venerable, collectively known as the *Toledan Collection* or *Islamo-Latin Corpus.* As part of the *Corpus,* the *Apology* circulated together with the first Latin translation of the Qur'ān made by Robert of Ketton, and a lengthy extract of it was included with the *editio princeps* of this translation published by Theodor Bibliander in Basel in 1543.

The first critical edition of the *Apology* was made by José Muñoz Sendino in 1949 on the basis of two manuscripts: Oxford, Corpus Christi College 184, and Paris, Bibliothèque nationale F 6064. Rather than wishing to present an exhaustive edition of the text, Muñoz Sendino was motivated first and foremost to make the text available to the scholarly community, especially given that Ugo Monneret de Villard had earlier assumed this text to be lost (Muñoz Sendino, "Al-Kindi," 339–40). The year before, Marie Thérèse d'Alverny had published on a still earlier manuscript from the middle of the twelfth century: Paris, Bibliothèque de l'Arsenal 1162 ("Deux traductions," 96). In a subsequent study, d'Alverny cataloged all known manuscripts of the *Apology* and concluded that the Arsenal manuscript, like all other extant manuscripts containing the *Toledan Collection,* was copied from a lost exemplar at Cluny ("Quelques manuscrits de la 'Collectio Toletana'").

The text of Muñoz Sendino was based on two incomplete manuscripts and has since been supplanted by that of Fernando González Muñoz, published in 2005. González Mu-

ñoz provides a full critical edition along with a Spanish translation based on all eleven manuscripts, including the glosses found in the various manuscripts, which have been omitted here for the sake of brevity.

The text presented in this volume is that of González Muñoz, although some minor typos have been corrected, and punctuation has been altered silently in some cases. In a few instances I have chosen to depart from González Muñoz's text and to adopt a slightly different reading, as indicated in the notes to the text. Finally, for the purposes of this volume it has been necessary to divide the text into chapters more evenly; for those readers who wish to consult the text of González Muñoz, a concordance will be made available on the Dumbarton Oaks Medieval Library website.

Book of Nicholas

The *Book of Nicholas* is transmitted in two manuscripts: Paris, Bibliothèque nationale lat. 14503 and Vatican, Reg. lat. 627, although only the first contains the text in its entirety. The text presented here largely corresponds to that edited in 2004 by Fernando González Muñoz, who also provides a Spanish translation and a discussion of the place of the *Book of Nicholas* in the literary tradition of lives of Muhammad.

Unbeknownst to González Muñoz, the text of the *Book of Nicholas* as it appears in the Paris manuscript had already been published in 1888 in the appendix of a study by Alessandro d'Ancona, who did not, however, give any commentary or translation, nor did he offer many emendations. In a

few places, his transcription of the manuscript differs from that of González Muñoz. After a fresh consultation of the manuscript, I have determined that most of these readings are the result of faulty transcription and have opted not to record these in the notes to the text; in a few instances, however, d'Ancona offers a preferable reading, which I have adopted.

Where Wicked Muhammad Came From

This text is based on the edition of Augusto Mancini made in 1934. The sole manuscript in which this text appears is from the fifteenth century, from the Dominican Convent of St. Catherine in Pisa: Pisa, Biblioteca del Seminario 50, fol. 81v–85r (= *P*). The manuscript was heavily used, as indicated by the many erasures and corrections made by later hands. In several instances, the text as it stands is not meaningful, resulting in emendations and omissions as indicated in the notes to the text. Unless otherwise noted, I have silently accepted all conjectures and emendations proposed by Mancini.

Notes to the Texts

History of Muhammad

2 <e> *Gil*

Tultusceptru from the Book of Lord Metobius

1 <in> inpudicitiis *Gil*

2 <cui> *Wolf*

3 doctore meo *Yolles*: doctorem meum *Gil*

4 situ leila citus est *corrupted text*
ad perditionem *Yolles*: et perdictjone *Gil*

Embrico of Mainz, *Life of Muhammad*

58 nos *Jacobsen*: hos *Cambier*

67 hinc *Ziolkowski*: hic *Cambier*

94 blanditus *Jacobsen*: blanditur *Cambier*

114 hoc *Jacobsen*: haec *Cambier*

275 hoc *Jacobsen*: haec *Cambier*

552 protervus *Jacobsen*: proterus *Cambier*

732 quae *Jacobsen*: quod *Cambier*

756 facias *Jacobsen*: facies *Cambier*

759 parebit *Jacobsen*: patebit *Cambier*

908 quod *Jacobsen*: quid *Cambier*

960 meritis *Jacobsen*: meretis *Cambier*

998 iamque *Jacobsen*: iam *Cambier*

1002 quod *Jacobsen*: quid *Cambier*

1030 et *Jacobsen*: sed *Cambier*

1040 gemit *Jacobsen*: gemens *Cambier*
1045 animam *Jacobsen*: animum *Cambier*
1076 fecerat *Jacobsen*: fecit hic *Cambier*
1121 quacumque *Jacobsen*: quocumque *Cambier*

Walter of Compiègne, *Poetic Pastimes on Muhammad*

190 *Lacuna, most likely due to censorship. See Notes to the Translations.*

Adelphus, *Life of Muhammad*

2 utpote qui *Shanzer*: utpote quia *Bischoff*
12 ei qui hoc te munere *Weiss*: civi qui hoc te munere *Bischoff*

Apology of al-Kindī

Reply of the Christian

120 benedictiones *Yolles*: benedictiones est *González Muñoz*
121 quid *Yolles*: quod *González Muñoz*
158 responderet *Yolles*: respondit *González Muñoz*
196 Hierosolymis *Yolles*: a Ierosolimis *González Muñoz*
207 illius *Yolles*: illis *González Muñoz*

Book of Nicholas

6 cardinalibus *D'Ancona*: cardinabus *González Muñoz*
11 exponens *Yolles*: et ponens *González Muñoz*
12 potuerint *D'Ancona*: potuerit *González Muñoz*
13 quae *Wetherbee*: quam *González Muñoz*
meridianis *Shanzer and Ziolkowski*: meridie non *González Muñoz*
14 revertetur *Wetherbee*: revertitur *González Muñoz*
15 annis *Yolles*: annos *González Muñoz*
16 Statimque *Yolles*: Statim qui *González Muñoz*
17 qua *Yolles*: que *González Muñoz*
22 Turchia *D'Ancona*: Cinthia *González Muñoz*

Where Wicked Muhammad Came From

3 natione *Yolles*: rationaliter *Mancini*: natiter *P*

4 fame *P*: fama *Mancini*

5 monachi *Yolles*: monacho *Mancini*

6 puerorum *Yolles*: dictorum puerorum *Mancini*

11 exientibus medicis *Yolles*: . . . exientibus medicis *Mancini*

16 <sitim maximam> *Yolles*: siti maxima *Mancini*

calore . . . ceperit *corrupted text omitted*

17 cogor *Yolles*: cogor vobis *Mancini*

19 vel . . . nullam unquam . . . sit expertus *corrupted text omitted*

24 longe *Yolles*: lege *Mancini*

26 Mahummet *Yolles*: Maurus *Mancini*

28 adiecit *Yolles*: abiecit *Mancini*

<quae> legitis *Yolles*: legitis quod *Mancini*

vobis videntibus *Yolles*: pro vobis videntibus *P, marked as corrupt by Mancini*

<qui> *Yolles*

exponere *Yolles*: ea ponere *Mancini*

30 mendaciora *Yolles*: mendaciorem *Mancini*

31 meus *Yolles*: mens *Mancini*

32 pia *Yolles*: pium *Mancini*

35 quadam platea *Yolles*: in quadam platea *Mancini*

inter eos et . . . Iudaeos posita maxima et spaciosa, congregatis *Yolles*: inter eos et . . . congregatis *Mancini*: inter eos et firma clusum̄ et Iudeos posita maxima et spaciosa *P*

39 absconsi *Yolles*: absconse *Mancini*

40 abominabuntur *Yolles*: abominabitur *Mancini*

eos *Yolles*: eos Christianos *Mancini*

43 viso *Yolles*: visa *Mancini*

44 Ismaelitarum secta *Nallino, Mancini in critical apparatus*: ysura helitarum facta *Mancini*

Notes to the Translations

History of Muhammad

1 The Byzantine emperor Heraclius (610–641 CE).

Isidore of Seville (bishop in 600–636 CE).

The Visigothic king Sisebut (612–621 CE).

Euphrasius was a martyred first-century bishop of Roman Iliturgi whom legend associated with the so-called seven apostolic men who were commissioned by Peter and Paul to proselytize in Spain. Iliturgi was near modern-day Andújar in Andalucía, Jaén province.

Leocadia was an early fourth-century virgin martyr venerated in Toledo.

2 The widow referred to is Khadīja.

3 "For behold . . . the burning wind": Habakkuk 1:6–8.

Theodore, the brother of Emperor Heraclius.

4 The title of the second *sūra*: *al-Baqara* (the cow).

Sūra 29: *al-ʿAnkabūt* (the spider).

The hoopoe bird is mentioned twice in Sūra 27: *al-Naml* (the ant).

The frog is mentioned in Sūra 7: *al-ʾAʿrāf* (the heights).

Sūra 12: *Yūsuf* (Joseph).

Zachary, the father of John the Baptist, and Mary appear in Sūra 19: *Maryam* (Mary).

5 Zayd's wife's name was Zaynab.

Qurʾān 33:37: "And when thou saidst unto him on whom Allah hath conferred favor and thou hast conferred favor: Keep thy wife to thyself, and fear Allah. And thou didst hide in thy mind

that which Allah was to bring to light, and thou didst fear mankind whereas Allah hath a better right that thou shouldst fear Him. So when Zeyd had performed the necessary formality (of divorce) from her, We gave her unto thee in marriage, so that (henceforth) there may be no sin for believers in respect of wives of their adopted sons, when the latter have performed the necessary formality (of release) from them. The commandment of Allah must be fulfilled." (Pickthall)

Tultusceptru from the Book of Lord Metobius

1 Hosius of Córdoba (257–359 CE) was a prominent advocate of orthodox Christianity during the Arian controversy. He was exiled but ultimately recalled after agreeing to adopt a compromise formula produced at the Council of Sirmium in 357.

This first sentence is incomplete, one of a number of indications that whoever transcribed it into the Codex of Roda had difficulty reading the exemplar from which he was working.

"Satrap" is here a generic term referring to a provincial governor of the Persian Empire.

Erribon is a version of the Greek name for Yathrib (Medina).

The syntax of the relative clause is unclear; perhaps, as suggested by Winthrop Wetherbee, *dedi* is to be construed like the verb *donare,* which takes an accusative of the person (in this instance the genitive *quorum*) and an ablative of the thing given.

The angel's directive is based on Ezekiel 2:3–5 (where the prophet is being sent to the wayward Israelites) and John 20:27 (the concluding line of the "doubting Thomas" episode). See González Muñoz, "La nota del códice de Roda."

2 *Ocim* is also rendered *Ozim* later on. It may be derived from Hāshim, the name of Muhammad's great-grandfather and by extension the name of the Prophet's clan. Or it could be the epithet *ʿaẓīm* (great), as suggested by Hoyland, *Seeing Islam as Others Saw It,* 516.

The Latin is unclear and likely corrupt or incomplete; possibly, *satrapum* should be construed as a genitive with *eorum,* but then

the sentence lacks an antecedent for the prepositional phrase *ad quem*.

4 This appears to be a garbled representation of the Islamic call to prayer *(ʿadhān)*, corresponding to the following sections: *Allāhu ʾakbar Allāhu ʾakbar* (God is most great); *ʾashhadu ʾan lā ilāha* (I bear witness that there is no god); *Muhammad rasūl Allāh* (Muhammad is the messenger of God); *situ leila citus est* is the only part that is unaccounted for. See Hoyland, *Seeing Islam as Others Saw It*, 515.

The "sheaves for burning" alludes to the Parable of the Tares in Matthew 13:30 or to the sheaves of the Philistines in Judges 15:5.

Anastasius the Librarian, *Chronicle* of Theophanes

1 Byzantine calculation placed the year of the world's creation at 5509 BCE.

Heraclius was a Byzantine emperor (610–641 CE) who led several successful campaigns against the Sassanids, only to lose the regained territories to the Muslims.

The pope referred to must be Pope John IV, who was actually elected in 640 CE. The mention of Pope John IV was an addition of Anastasius the Librarian; Theophanes listed the regnal years of the Byzantine emperor and of Muhammad (listed as *Arabōn archēgos*, "leader of the Arabs"), and the pontifical years of the bishops of Constantinople, Jerusalem, and Alexandria.

Theophanes places Muhammad's death in the year 6122 since the creation of the world and 622 since the birth of Christ, corresponding to the year 629/30 in the Gregorian calendar. Muhammad's death is traditionally dated to the year 632.

2 Like many later traditions, Theophanes claims that Muhammad was murdered. For Muslim traditions on the Jews as early followers of Muhammad, see Ibn Hishām, *Sīrat Rasūl Allāh*, trans. Alfred Guillaume, *The Life of Muhammad: A Translation of Isḥāq's Sīrat Rasūl Allāh* (Oxford, 1967), 239–41, 246–70.

3 This genealogy accords with Arabic traditions on the ancestry

of the principal tribes of Arabia, and probably derives from an Arabic source (Conrad, "Theophanes and the Arabic Historical Tradition," 11–16).

The tribe of the Midianites is frequently mentioned in both the Bible and the Qur'ān; here, "Midian" probably indicates the area inhabited by the northern Arab tribes in the south Syrian desert, as opposed to "Joktan," which must refer to the southern tribes. In the Bible, Joktan is the great-great-grandson of Noah's son Shem (Genesis 10:25; 1 Chronicles 1:19), who in Arabic traditions is brought into connection with Qaḥṭān, or the group of "pure" Arab tribes from the southern region of the Arabian Peninsula (Conrad, "Theophanes and the Arabic Historical Tradition," 11–12). The Ḥimyarites (or Homerites in Greco-Roman historiography) established the kingdom of Ḥimyar in ancient Yemen.

5 Instead of describing the man as an adulterer, most of the Greek manuscripts simply read "a certain monk, exiled for false belief." Four manuscripts, however, among which an early copy dating to the tenth century, contain the reading of *moichos* (adulterer) instead of *monachos* (monk), indicating that Anastasius must have based his Latin translation on a manuscript of this tradition (see Mango and Scott, *The Chronicle of Theophanes Confessor,* 465–66). The reading of *moichos/adulterer* leads to a much more vicious version of the life of Muhammad by injecting adultery into the mix and may have influenced later accounts such as *Where Wicked Muhammad Came From* (see below).

6 This conversation may be loosely based on some early Muslim traditions on the life of Muhammad, in which a monk recognizes the signs of prophethood in Muhammad; see Ibn Hishām, trans. Guillaume, 82.

The Greek text describes the monk-figure as a "pseudo-abbot" *(pseudabbā)*.

Yathrib is the pre-Islamic name of the city Medina.

8 The David referred to is David Tiberios (631–641 CE), son of Heraclius by his niece Martina.

The Constantine mentioned here must be Constans II. Actually born in 630 rather than 632, he was the son of Constantine III (also known as "Heraclius the New Constantine"), was baptized as Heraclius, and reigned as Constantine from 641 to 668.

Sergius I was patriarch of Constantinople from 610 to 638 CE.

Embrico of Mainz, *Life of Muhammad*

12 The verb *desipere* can refer to mental defects of stupidity or of insanity.

19 Avernus is the name of a lake near Puteoli (mod. Pozzuoli), thought to be the entrance to the underworld. Throughout the poem Embrico uses numerous pagan designations for the underworld, its topographical features, and its ruler to represent Christian concepts of the hell and the devil. These include Dis (173, 987, 998), Pluto (1007), Orcus (1045), Tartarus (1000), and Styx (1041).

24 Compare Zechariah 14:6.

26 Compare Isaiah 34:9.

27 Compare Isaiah 66:24; Mark 9:43, 45, 47.

43–72 In these lines Embrico describes Islamic attitudes toward paganism.

47 Here I have followed the punctuation, and hence interpretation, of González Muñoz (pp. 100–101).

69–70, 88, 120, 196, 394, 663, 698, 1020 The Latin term for the vice that Embrico attributes to the mage and to Mammutius throughout the poem is *perfidia.* This vice is the opposite of *fidelitas,* the virtue of faithfulness or loyalty. In this poem in general, it is not so much a question of loyalty to other humans as loyalty to God, adherence to correct belief in religion. Hence, I have translated *perfidia* uniformly throughout by "faithlessness" in order to echo the uniform resonance of this term in the Latin text. Especially here where Muhammad is said to occupy the throne of *perfidia,* after the worship of pagan gods yielded, it seems it could even mean "false belief."

73 On Godebold see Introduction.

81–82 It was commonplace for medieval writers to make affected declarations of modesty.

111–16 Here and below (ll. 685–91) Embrico turns on its head a *topos* of Latin *vitae* of popes and prelates known as *non currens sed tractus.* In official biographies, church officials must be portrayed as attaining high office not by racing in ambition toward it but rather as dragged by others against their will.

117 Proverbs 24:12.

121–24 Theodosius I (347–395 CE, r. 379–395), much admired in the Middle Ages for establishing orthodox Christianity as the official religion throughout the Roman Empire. Saint Ambrose, bishop of Milan and Doctor of the Church (340–397 CE). On the anachronism see Introduction.

207–8 On the consul in Libya, see note to 398 below.

220 "Mammutius": In accordance with the setting of events in the Christianized Roman province of Libya, Embrico gives Muhammad a Roman-sounding name, which is changed to Mahumet only toward the end of the poem's narrative, when he becomes a religious leader.

263 Erichtho, the fiercest witch in Thessaly, a region of Greece known in antiquity for its witches. Erichtho is an important character in Lucan's *Civil War,* 6.508–830, a popular school text in the Middle Ages, where she uses black magic to resurrect a dead soldier in order to predict the outcome of the battle.

265 A classical locus for witches who conjure down the moon and stars from the sky by magic is Horace's Epode 5.45–46. This trick is also alluded to in the passage from Lucan in the previous note.

303–5 As Cambier points out (*Embricon de Mayence*, 7), the scene in which the Khadīja figure asks the mage for advice about whether she should marry Mammutius clearly recalls the legend of Baḥīrā.

371–86 This detailed description known in classical poetics as an ekphrasis demonstrates Embrico's affinity with classical poetic tradition.

388 Scholars have sometimes expressed consternation that the political organization of Embrico's Libya features both a consul and a king (e.g., Tolan, *Sons of Ishmael*, 7). In order to resolve this apparent contradiction, González Muñoz (*Mahometrica*, 111). suggests that the consul (who is also referred to as "the rich man") is not to be understood as the imperial governor of Libya, but rather as a local nobleman. The interpretation of Gonzalez Muñoz is supported by the fact that Libya would need to be an independent kingdom in order for Muhammad to set up his theocracy there, and whereas the consul is a minor detail, the kingdom is the subject of the whole remainder of the poem.

422–23 This inscription is taken word for word from the inscription on the tomb of Holy Roman Emperor Otto I (912–973) in the Cathedral of Magdeburg, a detail that suggests that the author is German.

460 Compare Mark 3:24–26.

503–5 Compare Matthew 21:6–7.

609 The Bacchants, known for ecstatic dance, were priests, priestesses, or followers of the Roman wine god, Bacchus.

634 Cassius Scaeva, a centurion of proverbial bravery who continued to fight in spite of multiple wounds, his shield pierced 120 times or more (*Civil War* 3.53; Valerius Maximus 3.2.23; Suetonius, *Caesar* 68; Cicero, *Letters to Atticus* 14.10).

640 "Mirror" here means "example."

685–91 See note to lines 111–16.

743–48 Here the poet's use of irony reaches its peak.

813–36 Here the poet lists forms of martyrdom of the Christian martyrs under Muslim rule in North Africa, much as the martyrs under Roman rule. He probably based this on reports of martyrs under Arab rule in Spain.

821 "conquered worldliness"—by dying a martyr's death.

837 Compare Romans 12:19.

881 The mage knew in advance, that is, by magic.

905 The Plow (or Bear) is the Big Dipper.

907 The unyielding stars are the so-called fixed stars, to be contrasted with the wandering stars, which were actually planets.

905–33 This passage may contain allusions to the *miʿrāj,* or Muhammad's ascent to heaven via a ladder. Various traditions, drawing on Qurʾānic passages and ḥadīth, sprang up; in 1264, Bonaventura of Siena translated into Latin one such narrative under the title *Liber scale* (Book of the ladder) from a now-lost Castilian version, which in turn was translated from a lost Arabic account (the so-called *Kitāb al-Miʿrāj*). Despite Cambier's attempts to argue that Embrico drew on an oral version of the *Kitāb al-Miʿrāj* (*Embricon de Mayence,* 27–30), the narrative as preserved in the later Latin translation does not bear any particular resemblance to Embrico's passage. See also the note to *Qualiter* 30–32.

914–15 Embrico could have taken this opportunity to lambast the Muslim concept of heaven, widely considered sensual and materialistic by Christian critics; however, here it is not at odds with the Christian one.

920 Compare John 3:16.

925–26 These difficult lines are taken, probably correctly, by González Muñoz (p. 155), to refer to the inclusion of all humanity in the Muslim religion, discussed in the following paragraphs of the poem.

929 On the chosen people, compare 1 Peter 2:9.

959 Compare Lucifer's hubris at Isaiah 14:12–14.

965–72 Here Embrico depicts Islamic ritual ablutions and prayer with repetitions. Muslim ablutions are often criticized in Christian polemics as merely superficial. Here, however, as Tolan accurately comments, Embrico takes his criticism to a satirical extreme, in that the ablutions give a "blanket license for sin." (Tolan, *Sons of Ishmael,* 16). See also Daniel, *Islam and the West,* 235–36.

971 Here, Mammutius names himself "Muhammad," the name that he uses when he becomes a religious leader.

976 A highly ironic detail. After Muhammad's brief mention of the prayer and ablutions, he cannot instruct them further, because the time for doing whatever gives pleasure today is running out!

985 Juno's love under Jove may refer to the clamor of Juno's anger at Jupiter's adulteries; as Winthrop Wetherbee suggests to us, a meteorological explanation is also possible, since in medieval tradition (represented, e.g., in Augustine's *City of God* 7.10–11 and Martianus Capella's *The Marriage of Philology and Mercury,* 149) Jupiter represents the ether and Juno the atmosphere, the mixture of which could cause the thunderstorm here.

1045 Orcus is a synonym for Dis, Roman god of the underworld.

1115–39 This is the earliest written version of the legend of Muhammad's floating tomb, which later was disseminated throughout the Christian world. The ekphrasis of the temple borrows language from the ekphrasis of the sun god's temple in Ovid's *Metamorphoses* 2.1–18. Embrico probably encountered the magnet trick in patristic writings such as Rufinus, *Church History* 2.23, and especially Augustine, *City of God* 21.6. For additional precedents, including pre-Christian ones, see Alexandre Eckhardt, "Le cercueil flottant de Mahomet," 79–81. For the adaptation of this passage by Walter of Compiègne, see *Poetic Pastimes* at 1061 to 1074.

1121 Marble from the Greek island of Paros particularly prized for sculpture.

1124 The workmanship speaking as if it were alive is an elaboration of a classical commonplace: in Ovid, *Metamorphoses* 2.5, *Tristia* 2.336; Martial 8.50.7; passages courtesy of Ratkowitsch, "Grab des Propheten."

1137–39 As Ratkowitsch points out ("Grab des Propheten," 240), Marbod of Rennes's popular lapidary (§19, PL 171 1752A), which she sees as a source for this passage, associates magnets and magical arts. Compare the note to the parallel passage in Walter of Compiègne, *Poetic Pastimes,* n. 1071 below.

Walter of Compiègne, *Poetic Pastimes on Muhammad*

9–10 On the thorn and the grape, see Augustine, *In Iohannis Evangelium tractatus* 44.6, ed. Radbodus Willems, Corpus Christianorum: Series Latina 36 (Turnhout, 1954), 401, 415.

21 Idumean is the Greek form of the Hebrew demonym Edomite. In biblical texts, Edom, or Idumea, was a kingdom that bordered Judah on the south and was largely hostile to it during the Old Testament period.

22–24 Since in Islamic tradition Muhammad is unlettered, it is unusual to present him as a person with great knowledge of the liberal arts in Christian accounts of the prophet's life. See Daniel, *Islam and the West*, 107–8.

51–52 Compare 2 Corinthians 6:14–15.

52 Belial is another name for Satan.

63 Compare Romans 2:29; Acts of the Apostles 7:51; Deuteronomy 10:16 and 30:6.

65 Compare 1 Corinthians 15:45.

73 As Huygens notes, this seems to allude to the proverbial wisdom of the common medieval school text, *Distichs of Cato* 1.14b: "Do not believe other people about you more than you believe yourself."

83 Tyrian purple, produced from certain species of Mediterranean shellfish, was the most expensive, prestigious dye in the ancient world (see Mark Monaghan, "dyes and dying," in *The Cambridge Dictionary of Classical Civilization,* ed. Graham Shipley, John Vanderspoel et al. [Cambridge: Cambridge University Press, 2006], 292).

93 Compare Isaiah 40:23.

99 Compare Psalms 13:1 and 13:3, 52:4; Romans 3:12.

105 Antiochus IV of Syria (r. 175–164 BCE) appears as a villain in the deuterocanonical book of Maccabees because he outlawed traditional Jewish religious practices. This religious oppression provoked the Maccabees to rebel successfully, and they went on to found the Hasmonean dynasty in Judea.

107 Compare John 16:33.

111–14 On Lazarus and the rich man, see Luke 16:19–25.

115 Emperor Nero's persecution of Christians is described in Tacitus's *Annals* (15.44).

Decius's short reign (249–51 CE) included an edict forcing Christians throughout the empire to make pagan sacrifices.

Maximian (286–305 CE) is mentioned because he shared power with Diocletian, a notorious persecutor of Christians whose name would have been more difficult to fit into the verse structure.

Dacianus was a Roman official who, according to hagiographical writings, served under Diocletian and Maximian and was responsible for the death of Spain's protomartyr Vincent of Zaragoza (dramatized in Prudentius, *Peristephanon* 5), and of many other Christians in Zaragoza and Barcelona.

121–22 Compare Isaiah 66:24 and Mark 9:43–44.

147–48 Whether an action is "honorable" and "expedient," as criteria for ethical decision-making, is the subject of Cicero's *On Duties,* used as a manual in medieval schools.

169–70 The "colors" of rhetoric are principles taught in medieval schools.

Cicero's Latin style was highly esteemed, and he was the author of *On Invention,* used to teach rhetoric in the medieval schools. An additional rhetorical handbook used in the medieval schools, the *Rhetoric for Herennius,* was incorrectly attributed to Cicero in the Middle Ages.

190 The Latin distich is missing its pentameter. The lacuna has been considered a possible act of censorship, since it may have described older men's supposed lack of sexual prowess.

201 "A sow teaches Minerva" is a common Latin saying.

355–70 Compare Genesis 9:20–27.

359–60 Compare Genesis 6:12–18.

371 Compare John 8:34.

449–50 See Luke 1:26–38.

480 Compare 1 Corinthians 10:6.

498 "[Christ] broke them down [the regions of Tartarus] and returned with the spoils:" This line refers to the legend of Christ's harrowing of hell, with the "spoils" being the souls of the righteous who died before his act of salvation.

500 See John 20:27.

503–4 See Mark 16:15–19.

509 See Acts of the Apostles 2:1–4.

659 As Huygens points out, the wording of this line reflects the prohibition of joking in the cloister in the Rule of Saint Benedict 6.

666 Here, the Roman gods Ceres and Bacchus represent bread and wine. Compare Virgil, *Eclogues* 5.79. As Ratkowitsch observes, as well as being invoked in prayer by farmers (as in the Eclogue passage), these gods also represent the substances used for Holy Communion in the mass: "Grab des Propheten," 246.

675–90 This sequence of events in the narrative clearly shows influence of Theophanes's *Chronicle,* chapter 6.

728 Compare Proverbs 13:24.

799 "created all things with a word" or "created all things with the Word," that is, with Christ.

799–801 Here, the poet adopts the language of Boethius in the verse passages of *The Consolation of Philosophy,* 3 meter 9.1–3, when speaking of God.

833–34 On Moses receiving the law written by God's finger, see Exodus 31:18.

885–978 As Lepage points out (*Le roman de Mahomet de Alexandre du Pont,* 244), Walter's account of the war between Muslims and Persians is fictional. In fact, the Muslims conquered Sassanid Persia in 642 under the Caliph ʿUmar b. al-Khaṭṭāb, ten years after Muhammad's death.

904 The Parthians were famous in antiquity for a military technique by which they feigned retreat while turning to fire arrows at the enemy from horseback.

947 On Peter weeping: Matthew 26:75; Mark 14:72; Luke 22:62. On the blessed thief: Luke 23:39–43.

948 See Matthew 9:9.

955 See Jonah 3:5–10.

1029–30 Compare Job 1:19.

1055–62 In keeping with his generally more positive portrait of Muhammad, Walter does not incorporate the legend of Muhammad's ignominious death by pigs that his predecessors Embrico of Mainz and Guibert of Nogent, and contemporaries such as Adelphus, recount.

1061–74 The floating tomb passage recalls Embrico's complete ekphra-

sis; see Embrico's *Life of Muhammad,* 1115–39 and note. Walter, however, adds the inaccurate information that Muhammad is buried at Mecca, when in fact Muhammad is buried in Medina in a mosque called *al-Masjid al-Nabawī* (The Mosque of the Prophet).

1071 In Embrico's *Life of Muhammad*, the tomb of Muhammad is said to be kept floating by a magnet (see note to Embrico at ll. 1137–39). Walter of Compiègne's adaptation replaces the magnet with a diamond. Although today we do not think of diamonds as having magnetic properties, there is a tradition on the diamond's magnetic properties going back to Pliny's *Natural History* (37.61), passing through Isidore of Seville's *Etylmologies*, and repeated in Marbod of Rennes's popular lapidary, §1 (Ratkowitsch, "Grab des Propheten," 250). All ancient and modern sources listed by Ratowitsch in connection with the magnetic powers of the diamond consider that the diamond *(adamas)* has greater magnetic properties than the magnet *(magnes)* itself. Ratkowitsch interprets Walter's use of the diamond instead of the magnet as an act of literary one-upmanship.

1077–80 The portent is that *moechia,* the Latin word for "adultery," sounds like *Mecha,* the Latin name of the city of Mecca. This polemical "etymology" was also used in the thirteenth century by Mark of Toledo, who notes the similarity between *moecha,* the Latin word for "adulteress," and the name of the city of Mecca in his *Preface* to his Qur'ān translation (http://grupsderecerca.uab.cat/islamolatina/content/prologus-marci-toletani-alcorano).

1083–86 Compare Genesis 11:9.

1087 Although the poet refers the reader to Moses, presumably to attest the darkening of the Egyptians' hearts, the etymology is taken from Jerome, *Liber interpretationis hebraicorum nominum,* ed. P. de Lagarde, Corpus Christianorum. Series Latina 72 (Turnhout, 1959), 66.28–29, 73.14, and 77.25.

ADELPHUS, *LIFE OF MUHAMMAD*

1 The laborious writers of epic cycle are used as a negative literary example at Horace, *Art of Poetry,* 136.

2 Tolan plausibly takes the sound of the Saracens calling with their voices to be the sound of the voice of the muezzin making the call to prayer (*Saracens,* 138), which typically captured the attention of Christians in cities with an Islamic population (see also *Sons of Ishmael,* chap. 10).

On the man born of a handmaid, see Galatians 4:29.

3 The false etymology in which "Saracen" is derived from "Sarah," Abraham's wife, goes back at least as far as Jerome (and is thus pre-Islamic), who presented it as a false claim to legitimacy of the descendants of Ishmael, the son of Abraham's concubine Hagar. See Jerome, *In Hiezechielem,* ed. François Glorie, Corpus Christianorum: Series Latina 75 (Turnhout, 1964), 335, and for a discussion Beckett, *Anglo-Saxon Perceptions,* 93–95. Muslims claim descent from Ishmael, Abraham's firstborn son, in the Qur'ān. In the Qur'ān the servile status of the mother and even her name are not mentioned.

4 Peter (apostle) as bishop of Antioch is to be found in Eusebius, *Ecclesiastical History* 3.36.2.

On tares among the wheat, compare Matthew 13:25–30.

"enemy of the human race": An epithet of the devil. Adelphus tends to refer to the devil by his epithets rather than explicitly, as below in paragraphs 6, 7, 13, and 23.

"after my departure, voracious wolves will appear among you, dangerous wolves": See Acts of the Apostles 20:29.

"Catch for me the little foxes that destroy the vineyards": See Song of Songs 2:15.

5 On knowledge beyond what one should know, see Ecclesiastes 7:17 and Romans 12:3.

On the wolf in sheep's clothing, see Matthew 7:15.

On evil discourse that corrupts good customs, see 1 Corinthians 15:33.

On the grape bruised by the grape and the herd falling by the scales of one pig, see Juvenal 2.79–81.

On a fearful, vastly deserted place, see Deuteronomy 32:10.

6 On the last state of the man, worse than his first, see Matthew 12:44 and Luke 11:24–26. In the passage alluded to here, Jesus

speaks of an unclean spirit leaving a man only to return accompanied by seven even more wicked spirits.

The line of verse at the end of paragraph 6 is taken from Horace, *Epodes* 5.67, in which a group of witches pursue an old man with magic spells, attempting to mangle a boy for use in their potion. Compare also Horace, *Satires* 1.8.22.

"I will return to the house which I have left": see Matthew 12:44.

7 On Muhammad's learning, Adelphus makes much use in this life of the uncommon Greek loan word *mathēsis,* which is the equivalent of Latin *disciplina* (learning). This learning is interpreted by Tolan (*Saracens*, 142) and Bischoff ("Ein Leben Mohammeds," 111) as Muhammad's prior knowledge of black magic, but it seems it could also be his prior knowledge in combination with his capacity to learn from Nestorius.

"Our deceiver" refers to the devil.

9 On prophets not accepted in their own country, see Luke 4:24; Mark 6:4; Matthew 13:57.

12 On the last state worse than the first, see note to paragraph 6.

13 The "clever craftsman" refers to the devil.

14 On the ministry to the thirsty, see Exodus 17:6.

On the works of darkness, see Romans 13:12.

15 On the letters written by God's finger, see Exodus 31:18.

24 "This was so that his fall would be the more severe:" That is, God's reason for allowing Muhammad's ascent was in order to make Muhammad's fall more severe.

25 The "stumbling block of souls" is another epithet of the devil.

Apology of al-Kindī

[*Prologue*]

1 The ʿAbbāsid caliph al-Maʾmūn (813–834). The untranslated *Emirhelmomini* represents *ʾamīr al-muʾminīn,* a customary title used by caliphs that means "commander of the faithful." A gloss in one of the manuscripts writes: *rex credencium* ("king of the believers," see González Muñoz, *Exposición,* 1).

The Latin *Maurorum* (Moors) was used to refer to the Muslims of the Maghreb and al-ʾAndalus; it is used here and throughout as a synonym for *Saracenus* (Saracen) and indicates the Andalusian context in which the translator was working.

Kinda was a prominent tribe, originally from the south of the Arabian Peninsula, that established a kingdom in central Arabia.

Letter of the Saracen

3 "I am merciful . . . toward men": Qurʾān 9:128.

5 The Arabic original speaks of "love for one's neighbors" *(maḥabbat al-qarīb)*. The source for this statement is unclear; González Muñoz (*Exposición*, 154) proposes a *hadīth* in al-Bukhārī, *Ṣaḥīḥ, Kitāb al-ʾImān* 17, ed. Muhammad Muhsin Khan (Riyadh, 1997), vol. 1; see Tartar (*Dialogue,* 86n4) and Bottini (*Apologia,* 42n5) for other suggestions.

6 Here, as throughout, the translator has rendered the Arabic *Muslim* as "Saracen," as was common practice among Latin Christian authors.

"The people of Abraham are perfectly Saracen": compare Qurʾān 2:135.

"They who believed . . . were Saracens": compare Qurʾān 43:69.

"He was . . . purely Saracen": compare Qurʾān 3:67.

7 "Only debate . . . in a kind and peaceful manner": Qurʾān 29:46.

In Islam, the "People of the Book" *(ʾAhl al-Kitāb)* refers to the Jews, Ṣabians, and Christians, who have received a revealed scripture (Qurʾān 2:62, 5:69, 22:17).

8 "They who are with God are Saracens": Compare Qurʾān 3:19.

"He who pursues any faith but that of the Moors . . . will be condemned in the future": Compare Qurʾān 3:85.

"O . . . fear him and do not die unless you have become Saracens": Compare Qurʾān 3:102.

10 The Pentateuch, or first five books of the Bible, was frequently referred to as the "Law" or the "Law of Moses," given that the

Ten Commandments and the various laws in Deuteronomy and Numbers were considered the core of these books. See also *RC* 6, 30, 138, 206.

As González Muñoz points out ("La versión latina," 35), the translator appears to have misread the Arabic *ṣafā* (rock) for *ṣafāʾ* (brightness). The author is referring to Simon Peter, compared to a rock by Jesus in Matthew 16:18.

For the seventy disciples, see Luke 10:1.

"Bishop Timothy" presumably refers to Timothy I (d. 823), patriarch (known technically as catholicos) of the East-Syrian Christian church in Baghdad. His most celebrated work is a debate with the ʿAbbāsid caliph al-Mahdī on the merits of Christianity and Islam. The translator's decision to render the Arabic *jāthlīq* (for catholicos) as *episcopus* (bishop) could be an attempt to strip the text of its Eastern Christian elements, as could be the addition of a statement by the Christian in which he identifies himself as catholic (see *RC* 38).

11 "King Marcian" refers to the Roman emperor Marcian (450–457), who convened the Council of Chalcedon in 451. The Arabic references the debate between Nestorius and Cyril of Alexandria, Nestorius's opponent at the First Council of Ephesus in 431; anachronistically, the translator replaced Cyril with Arius (ca. 250/56–336), a notorious heretic in the Christian tradition who emphasized the divinity of the Father over that of the Son, arguing that Christ was created by the Father.

The first group of heretics, here called "Romans" (that is, Byzantines), is that of the Melkites, named thus for their recognition of Emperor (*malik* in Arabic) Marcian's edict in 451 condemning monophysitism. In a misreading of the Arabic, the translator also includes the followers of Jacob of Bardaeus ("Jacobites") in this group and mentions them again as being part of the second group (see next note).

The second group is a combination of followers of Cyril of Alexandria (d. 444), followers of Jacob Bardaeus (d. 578), and followers of Severus of Antioch (d. 538), who rejected the confes-

sion of the Council of Chalcedon condemning monophysitism, or the tenet that Christ has a single, perfect nature (as opposed to the orthodox position of separate human and divine natures). A pro-Jacobite revision has replaced the mention of Jacobites here with that of Nestorians, and vice-versa below (Georges Troupeau, "al- Kindī, ʿAbd al-Masīḥ," 121).

The third group are followers of Nestorius (ca. 386–451), who rejected the use of the term *theotokos* (Mother of God) for the Virgin Mary and were considered by many to deny Christ's divinity. The Muslim's excessive praise of the Nestorians in this passage could be evidence that the Christian author (whether or not he authored both letters or only the reply) may have had ties to the "Nestorian" Christian community (better known as the East-Syrian Church). However, the comment that the Nestorians are "akin to you" is not found in the Arabic text.

13 The Latin reads *participatores* to refer to polytheists, a rather clumsy translation of *mushrikūna,* used in the Qurʾān (see, for example, 98:1). A gloss on 29 explains that the Muslims call the Christians *participatores,* because they give God "participants" in the form of Christ and the Holy Spirit.

The reference to the Quraysh as believing in "three persons in God," or a Trinity, is not in the Arabic. Van Koningsveld ("The Apology," 74–75) suggests that this is "an early pro-Christian interpolation." González Muñoz ("La versión latina, 32–33), however, points out that the translator has misconstrued the Arabic of the Muslim, who uses the term *mushrikūna* to refer only to the Quraysh when they were polytheists, not to the Christians; in effect, therefore, the Latin is paradoxically more anti-Christian than the Arabic.

Quraysh was the tribe of Muhammad.

14 The word *qurʾān* means "recitation" in Arabic; naturally, this is an addition of the Latin translator, which accords with the title given to the Qurʾān by Robert of Ketton in his translation: *Lex Mahumet pseudo-prophete que arabice Alchoran, id est, collectio preceptorum vocatur* ("The law of the pseudo-prophet Muhammad,

which is called *al-Qur'ān* in Arabic, that is, 'collection of precepts'"). Robert's gloss of the title as a "collection of precepts" stuck (see Peter the Venerable, *Summa totius haeresis,* trans. Irven M. Resnick, *Writings against the Saracens* [Washington, D.C., 2016], 35 and n. 26 for Robert of Ketton; Riccoldo of Montecroce, *Contra legem Sarracenorum,* ed. Jean-Marie Mérigoux, "L'ouvrage d'un frère Prêcheur florentin en orient à la fin du XIIIe siècle. Le 'Contra legem Sarracenorum' de Riccoldo da Monte di Croce," *Memorie Domenicane* 17 [1986]: 1.47–48), and provided polemical fodder to Nicholas of Cusa, who viewed the Qur'ān as a haphazard collection of elements drawn from the Hebrew and Christian bibles and assembled by human rather than divine agency (*Cribratio Alcorani*, ed. Hervé Pasqua, *Le Coran tamisé* [Paris, 2011], 1.24).

"Let the polytheists . . . and they are not prideful": Qur'ān 5:82.

16 These monastic times of prayer are collectively known as the Divine Office, with the hours here referred to corresponding to prime, terce, sext, none, and either matins or vigils. The sacrifices refer to the bread and the wine of the mass.

The meaning of *pedes suos adaptant* is unclear; perhaps, as González Muñoz suggests (*Exposición*, 159), a rhythmical striking of the ground with the feet is meant.

20 For God as singular and indivisible, without wife or child, see Qur'ān 112:1–4, 72:3.

21 For Muhammad as "seal of the prophets" *(khātam al-nabiyyīn),* see Qur'ān 33:40. For these epithets of Muhammad, see Qur'ān 9:33 and the comments in Tartar, *Dialogue*, 94; Bottini, *Apologia*, 53; and González Muñoz, "La versión latina," 36. The medieval gloss on this passage runs: "Muhammad is called the possessor of the rod because he always carried a rod in his hand, which he said had been brought to him from heaven. He is also the possessor of the camel on account of the camel that spoke with him. He is the possessor of the well because he promised a shell of infinite capacity in paradise, from which all could drink without ever emptying it."

22 For the claim that the Qur'ān could not have been created by mankind or jinn (here, "demons"), see Qur'ān 17:88, and also *RC* 107 below.

23 "There is no god but God, and Muhammad is the prophet of God": Qur'ān 2:255.

This confessional formula is known as the *shahāda* (testimony) in Islam; the decision to translate *Allāh* with *Deus* has led confused medieval readers, who considered this a tautology, to produce ingenious alternatives, such as *non est Deus nisi Mahomet nuncius eius* ("There is no God but Muhammad, His messenger"). See the glosses in González Muñoz, *Exposición*, 10, and the discussion in González Muñoz, "La versión latina," 38.24. The source of the remark about camels has not been identified—see González Muñoz, *Exposición*, 162n59.

25 For the "night of predestination," conventionally known as *laylat al-qadr* (night of decree), see Qur'ān 97:1–3.

26–27 "I have written. . . . These are the commandments of God": Qur'ān 2:183–87.

26 *Al-furqān* (the standard) refers to the notion of the Qur'ān as the standard of good and evil; see Qur'ān 25:1–11.

28 The Arabic reads *ḥarām,* which can mean both "sacred" and "forbidden," much like the Latin *sacer.* Three manuscripts read *angelus* (angel) for *angulus* (corner), feeding into Western conceptions of Islamic idolatry; see the discussion in González Muñoz, "La versión latina," 38.

31 "When they will have armlets of gold . . . their garments will be made of silk": Qur'ān 22:23.

Electrum is an alloy of gold and silver.

"and they will say: Thanks to God, who has taken away our tribulation": Qur'ān 35:34–35.

"They will have continuous nourishment. . . . They will have women with comely eyes": Qur'ān 37:40–49.

"They will have dining rooms. . . . Never will God's promise fail them": Qur'ān 39:20.

"and it will be said to them . . . among gardens and springs'": Qur'ān 43:68–71.

"They will be clothed in garments which surpass all other clothing. . . . This is the gracious gift of your God, for it is a great liberation": Qur'ān 44:51–57.

32 "The best things will come in the end to those who fear God. . . . At no point will they run out of sustenance there": Qur'ān 38:39–54.

33 "There are two flowing springs in it. . . . Truly, the works of your God will always remain": Qur'ān 55:50–78.

The refrain in the Qur'ān actually reads: "Which is it, of the favors of your Lord, that ye deny?" (Pickthall).

34 "Those who fear God will be led to paradise . . . 'peace to you and be comfortable, enter and remain here forever'": Qur'ān 39:73.

35 "I have let them encounter joys and delights. . . . There is a spring in it called 'clearness,'": Qur'ān 76:11–18.

36 "To those who fear God and who are set free will be given orchards. . . . This is the recompense of your Lord, which is the greatest gift of all": Qur'ān 78:31–36.

37 "We were once kind. . . . For he is great and merciful"'": Qur'ān 52:17–28.

38 "Let dwellings in the paradise of delight be given to . . . who are of the first-comers and of those who come last": Qur'ān 56:11–40.

40 In both the Bible and the Qur'ān, Gehenna, from the Hebrew "valley of Hinnom," formerly a site of the worship of Moloch, came to indicate a place of punishment by fire.

In the Qur'ān, the *zaqqūm* is a tree in hell, the bitter fruit of which serves as punishment. See Qur'ān 37:62–66 and 44:43–46.

41 "Those who do not believe in God's miracles and prophets . . . will be upon their own heads, with nobody there to aid them": Qur'ān 3:21–22.

42 "Those who do not believe in God and his prophets . . . certainly are infidels, for whom eternal torment has been prepared": Qur'ān 4:150–51.

43 "Those who do not believe will suffer Gehenna without end.

They will die and yet they will not be freed from torment": Qur'ān 35:36.

"The tree *zaqqūm* is given to the impious as their delight. . . . they will experience again and again the punishments of hell": Qur'ān 37:62–68.

"Woe to them, of the fire and extreme evils, which they will suffer in hell": Qur'ān 38:55–56.

"Above and below there is gloom, fire, and darkness": Qur'ān 39:16.

"On the day of resurrection . . . those who do not believe our signs and deserve to be condemned": Qur'ān 39:60, 63.

44 "Those who did not believe will be rounded up and cast together into hell. . . . These are the dwellings that have been prepared for the prideful": Qur'ān 39:71–72.

"And those who were submerged in the fire . . . and again be vexed by it": Qur'ān 40:49–50.

45 "The impious will suffer unbearable torment . . . and casting fearful glances as they hide": Qur'ān 42:44–45.

"The godless will remain in the torment of Gehenna. . . . He said: 'So you will remain without end'": Qur'ān 43:74–77.

"The tree *zaqqūm* is the food of the sinners. . . . These are the deeds which you will perform": Qur'ān 44:43–50.

46 "Bring bitter water . . . For they loved what deserved God's wrath and spurned his grace, and did not receive any benefit from their actions": Qur'ān 47:15, 26–28.

"'Go forth. . . . so that they might have some excuse": Qur'ān 77:29, 34–36.

47 "Remind him again and again, for it is beneficial for believers to be reminded": Qur'ān 51:55.

50 The direction of prayer in Islam, here referred to as being "to our south," is toward the *Ka'aba* in Mecca and is known as the *qibla.*

51 "Persist in your prayers and pay the *zakāt*": Qur'ān 2:43.

Zakāt, or the practice of almsgiving, is one of the five pillars of Islam.

52 The translator has tendentiously rendered the Arabic *mā 'aḥbabta* ("as you wish," or "whom you wish," as Tien translates

[399]) with *quantum volueris* ("as many as you wish"), feeding into Christian prejudices and misunderstandings regarding Muslim polygamy. The statement probably loosely refers to Qur'ān 4:3 (see also *RC* 178 below).

The phrase *unius cuiuslibet tuitione* has no equivalent in the Arabic, and it is unclear what the sense is.

"I do not forbid a dismissed wife from being recalled": compare Qur'ān 2:230.

54 "You will not be judged. . . . perhaps you will honor him": Qur'ān 5:89.

55 The *ḥājj*, or pilgrimage to Mecca, is one of the five pillars of Islam, and it must be undertaken at least once.

Romeria, preserved in modern Spanish, is an uncommon word in medieval Latin for pilgrimage, although *romeus* for "pilgrim" does occur, deriving from Rome as a popular destination of pilgrims.

"This is what people owe God . . . which is to depart for the house": Qur'ān 3:97.

57 "God has no mercy on the polytheists except for those he wishes": Qur'ān 4:48.

58 "How mistaken are they. . . . The impious will receive no aid'": Qur'ān 5:72.

59 "How mistaken are they who claim that God is threefold. . . . Behold, therefore, what signs he has given to them, in order that they might believe": Qur'ān 5:73–75.

61 For the "People of the Book," see note on *ES* 7.

"For the People of the Book and the polytheists . . . this is for those who fear God": Qur'ān 98:6–8.

62 "You are better than all people . . . and treated with compassion": Qur'ān 3:110.

64 "Do nothing violently in faith": Qur'ān 2:256.

Reply of the Christian

5 For the Saracen's statements on Abraham, see *ES* 6.

"When you stand . . . inspiration will be given to you on what you should say": Luke 12:11–12.

6 The pre-Islamic idol al-ʿUzzā is not mentioned in Genesis; for Abraham's departure from Ḥarrān, see Genesis 11:31, 12:4, 15:4–6.

"he believed in God and it was imputed unto him for righteousness": Genesis 15:6; 1 Maccabees 2:52; Galatians 3:6; James 2:23; Romans 4:3.

7 On God's command to Abraham to sacrifice Isaac, compare Genesis 22:2.

9 For the passage of Moses and the burning bush, see Exodus 3–4. *Ehiehas Rahieh* appears to be a corruption of the Hebrew *ʾEhyeh ʾasher ʾEhyeh* (I am who I am).

"The God of Abraham, the God of Isaac, and the God of Jacob": Exodus 3:15.

13 "and it was credited to him as righteousness": Romans 4:31; Maccabees 2:52.

14 "Say: 'I have been given commands in order that I might be the first one to be a Saracen,' and do not be one of the polytheists": compare Qurʾān 6:14.

The translator has consistently rendered *Islām* as *Saracenitas,* or "Saracenhood," which, for clarity, I have translated as "the Saracen faith."

16 The author engages in a discussion of the unity of God by using terms proper to dialectic or logic, arguing that there are three ways in which "one" can be understood: in reference to genus, species, or number. These were properties used by dialecticians to describe things, ultimately going back to the ten categories enumerated by Aristotle. The discussion bears a close resemblance to an early ninth-century work on the Trinity by the Jacobite Ḥabīb b. Khidma ʾAbū Rāʾiṭa al-Takrītī (d. after 828), which was probably the source for the author of the *Apology*. See Graf, *Geschichte*, 2:136–38; Griffith, "The Prophet Muḥammad," 106; Samir, "The Earliest Arab Apology," 111n237.

18 The Latin here accurately reflects the Arabic but must necessarily be emended, as González Muñoz (*Exposición,* 184n176; see also "La versión latina," 35) explains. The idea is that the property of number is something that can be predicated only of creation, not of God.

The idea seems to be that to say that something is "one" (or any number) means that it participates in the overarching genus that is "number"; since God cannot be said to be a species of a larger genus, this cannot be predicated of God.

19 It is unclear what the Latin translator meant by "those things," but he seems to have misunderstood the Arabic, where the subject is God.

21 The discussion of the Trinity in terms of substance *(substantia)* and persons *(personae)* stems from early Christian theological debates on the nature of the Trinity.

22 As the sum of an odd and an even number, the number three is considered by the Christian to be a perfect and all-encompassing number.

25 The statements asserting that God has no equal refer to Qur'ān 112.

As the author will explain below, he held these Jews to be fellow conspirators of Muhammad, even though they were not contemporaries of each other. ʿAbd Allāh b. Sallām was a Jew from Medina who converted to Islam during the life of Muhammad (Ibn Hishām, trans. Guillaume, 240–41); Kaʿb al-ʾAḥbār was a Jew from Yemen who converted to Islam during the Caliphate of ʾAbū Bakr (632–634) or ʿUmar b. al-Khaṭṭāb (634–644) (Schmitz, "Kaʿb al-ʾAḥbār," 4:316–17); Wahb b. al-Munabbih, also a Jew from Yemen, lived a generation later, around 646–728 (Ibn Hishām, trans. Guillaume, xv).

30 "Let us create a man in our image and likeness": Genesis 1:26.

"It is not good that man is alone. Let us create a helper like him": Genesis 2:18.

"Behold, Adam has been created like one of us": Genesis 3:22.

"Come, let us go down and confound their language": Genesis 11:7.

31 " God is one, singular, and whole": Qur'ān 4:171.

32 "We say to you, Nebuchadnezzar": Daniel 4:28.

"But I will bring some water and may your feet be washed, and rest yourselves under the tree": Genesis 18:3–4.

33 "Listen, Israel: The Lord your God is one God": Deuteronomy 6:4.

"By the word of the Lord . . . all the host of them by the breath of his mouth": Psalms 32:6.

"May God bless us, our God, may God bless us": Psalms 66:7–8.

"And now the Lord and his Spirit have sent me": Isaiah 48:16.

34 The Muslim made no accusation in his letter of Christian corruption of biblical texts. However, an accusation that a faction of the People of the Book (which group is not specified) "corrupted" or "distorted" (*yuḥarrifūna*[*hu*], the same root used by the Christian) the revelation given to them does occur in Qur'ān 2:75, 5:13, 5:41. For another discussion of Muslim accusations of Christian corruption of the biblical text, see *RC* 201–5. See also *RC* 102 and 105 (and later 206–7), where the Christian applies similar terminology in discussing the transmission of the Qur'ān. For introductions to *taḥrīf* doctrine in polemics, see Thomas, "The Use of Scripture"; Reynolds, "On the Qur'anic Accusation"; Nickel, *Narratives of Tampering*.

35 "Holy, holy, holy Lord God of hosts, all the earth is filled with his glory": Isaiah 6:1–3.

37 "How wrongly do they believe . . . beseeching God to forgive them?": Qur'ān 5:73–74.

38 The reference to Catholicism is an interpolation made by the translator, to "Catholicize" the text, as pointed out by Van Koningsveld, "The Apology," 74. Unaware of the fact that this is a Latin interpolation, Muñoz Sendino falsely believed that this proved that the author was a Catholic Christian ("Apología," 400, and see Caskel's review of Sendino, "*Apologia del Christiamismo,*" 154).

Marcion (ca. 85–160) was bishop of Sinope and propagated a dualist worldview, in which the wicked God of the Old Testament was responsible for the creation of matter, and the God of the New Testament governed the spiritual. González Muñoz suggests (*Exposición*, 191) that the threefold division presented here may go back to John of Damascus (*De haeresibus* 42), who claimed that Marcion's doctrine posited three principles: good, justice, and evil. Since the Arabic speaks only of "beings/entities" *(akwān),* the description of these principles in

terms of "spheres" appears to be an invention of the translator, perhaps conflating Marcionism with the celestial spheres of ancient philosophy (Pythagorism in particular).

39 "Do not say or think that there are three gods . . . surely it will be to your benefit": Qurʾān 4:171.

42 Muhammad was first taken in by his grandfather ʿAbd al-Muṭṭalib and, after his death, raised by ʾAbū Ṭālib.

"Were you not an orphan and taken in? . . . and were you not made wealthy?": Qurʾān 93:6–8.

43 The father of Khadīja is traditionally known as Khuwaylid b. ʾAsad.

47 "How did . . . two men put to flight ten thousand?": Deuteronomy 32:30.

48 For Joshua's encounter with the angel, see Joshua 5:13–16.

49 The reference to the Qurʾān here, which does not contain this version of the Exodus story, is absent from the Arabic, although Qurʾān 7:136 does allude to the drowning of Pharaoh. The biblical passage (Exodus 14:19–20) mentions only an unnamed angel who guides the Israelites.

50 For the passage of Samuel and the she-asses, see 1 Samuel 9:20, 10:2. The highly unusual form *asinabus* (after the model of *animabus, deabus,* and *filiabus*) occurs four times in Peter the Venerable's treatise against Judaism: *Adversus Iudeorum inveteratam duritiem,* ed. Yvonne Friedman, Corpus Christianorum. Continuatio Mediaevalis 58 (Turnhout, 1985), 3.147, 192, 214, 233.

51 *Probitates* here translated sarcastically, as González Muñoz did. Another option would be to emend the text to *improbitates,* as supported by some manuscripts.

52 Bābik, or Atābik al-Khurramī, led a religious and social movement in the early ninth century. After eluding ʿAbbāsid authorities for twenty years, he was crucified by Caliph al-Muʿtaṣim in 838. Samir ("La version latine") sees the fact that Bābik is still spoken of as being at large as an argument to date the composition of the Arabic text before the year 838.

54 This seems to be a paraphrase of the statements made by the Muslim at the opening of his letter; see *ES* 3.

56 As pointed out by González Muñoz, *Exposición*, 197n247, *Phenica* is a misreading of the Arabic, which refers to the Jews of Banū Qaynūqāʿ in Medina. See Ibn Hishām, trans. Guillaume, 363–64.

57 The passage referred to is Luke 22:49–51, where Jesus heals a slave of the high priest after one of his supporters had struck off the slave's ear.

The passages of angelic protection alluded to are 1 Kings 19:1–18 and Daniel 6:14–24.

58 These purported claims of Muhammad are not in the Qurʾān, although they can be found in *ḥadīth,* or traditions on the life of Muhammad.

For the passage about Muhammad's stamina (here equaled to that of thirty men, not forty), see al-Bukhārī, *Ṣaḥiḥ, Kitāb al-ghusl* 268, ed. Khan, vol. 1.

For the passage on Muhammad's delight in fragrances and women, compare al-Bukhārī, *Ṣaḥiḥ, Kitāb al-ghusl* 267, ed. Khan, vol. 1.

59 The first passage from the Qurʾān has been grossly misunderstood by the translator, who missed the imperative *amsik* (hold on to, keep), translating it as a first-person singular, and rendered *zawj,* referring to "wife" here (like "spouse," it can refer to both husband and wife) as "husband." This episode is particularly favored among Christian polemicists, who see it as evidence that Muhammad invented divine authority to justify his pursuits (see Daniel, *Islam and the West*, 119–20).

"For the one to whom I have given favor. . . . fear God all the more": Compare Qurʾān 33:37.

"Once Zayd, her husband . . . for God's order is a predestined decree": Qurʾān 33:38.

60 This episode, too, was popular among Christian authors, who relished in recounting the scandal. The words *libidini dedita* and *qui et consuetudinarium cum ea stuprum gerebat, ipso Mahumet sciente et consentiente* are not in the original and must have been inserted by the translator in an effort to tarnish the reputation of Muhammad as much as possible (see Daniel, *Islam and the*

West, 123). The Qurʾānic passage referred to here is likely the *Sūrat al-Nūr,* which focuses on adultery (see especially Qurʾān 24:11–16). A later Latin gloss remarks about this passage: *non reperio ista verba in Alchorano meo* (I do not find these words in my Qurʾān), indicating that readers were reading the *Apology* side by side with the Qurʾān (see González Muñoz, "La versión latina," 37).

61 The translator has grossly misunderstood this passage and added a few fanciful details of his own. The Arabic relates that when ʾUmm Salama refused Muhammad's advances, he stated that he would remove from her all jealousy; apparently she had claimed to be jealous, being afraid that, in competing with Muhammad's other wives, she and her children would not be cared for sufficiently. The translator seems to have construed the Arabic *ghayrā* (jealous) as a proper name and constructed a fanciful account of adultery around it; in reality, ʾUmm Salama was a widow when she married Muhammad. This would also explain the word *seducta* (seduced), which is nowhere to be found in the original (the word that it should be translating is *makhzūmiyya,* or "belonging to the tribe of Makhzūm").

For this anecdote about Ṣafiyya, see al-Shāṭiʾ, *The Wives of the Prophet*, 178–81.

Ezudeit was not one of the wives of Muhammad: the translator has misunderstood the Arabic, construing this as another person, when it actually gives an alternate name for Fāṭima as "Amra, daughter of Yazīd (Ezudeit)."

62 "He that is married cares . . . how he may please God": 1 Corinthians 7:32–33.

"But I want you to be without worry": 1 Corinthians 7:32.

"No man can serve two masters . . . and despise the other": Matthew 6:24.

66 "Behold a virgin shall conceive, and bear a son": Isaiah 37:38, 7:14.

For the prophecies about the destruction and the restoration of the Temple, see Jeremiah 26:30.

Daniel 2:5, 9:24–27.

69 For the stories being alluded to here, see Qurʾān 7:73, 11:61–68, 26:141–59 (the people of Thamūd and the camel), 105 (sūra of the Elephant).

71 What is passed off as a quotation from the Qurʾān about Muhammad's lack of miracles is actually a paraphrase in the Arabic of Qurʾān 17:59.

The appeals to reason and authority here and below (*RC* 75) are not in the Arabic; it is tempting to see in such instances the hand of Peter of Poitiers (see Introduction).

72 "God has not given you the power to kill . . . on account of their wickedness and impiety": Deuteronomy 9:4–6.

77 For other sources of the story of the wolf, see Platti, "Criteria for Authenticity," 14.

The story of the ox is not otherwise attested; for other testimonies of the story of the sheep, see Platti, "Criteria for Authenticity," 14–15; the story of the tree is in Ibn Hishām, trans. Guillaume, 80.

78 For the story of Zaynab bint Ḥārith and the poisoned lamb, see Ibn Hishām, trans. Guillaume, 516. The translator appears to have misread the name of Zaynab's husband, Sallām b. Mishkam, as "Muslim."

79 On the miracles of Elijah and Elisha, see 1 Kings 17:8–24; 2 Kings 4:18–37, 13:20–21.

81 Muhammad b. ʾIsḥāq (d. 767 or 761) gathered oral traditions to write the most important biography of Muhammad, known as the *Sīrat rasūl Allāh* (Life of the messenger of God); this particular episode, however, is not to be found in his writings, although a similar story can be found in al-Bukhārī, *Ṣaḥīḥ, Kitāb al-wuḍūʿ* 195, ed. Khan, vol. 1.

This quotation is otherwise unknown, but compare Qurʾān 9:29.

82 Again, this quotation is unattested.

83 Nothing is otherwise known about this authority. The Arabic refers to an authority named Ḍamrān (Tartar, *Dialogue*, 167).

84 Compare this account of Muhammad's death with those of al-Bukhārī, *Ṣaḥīḥ, Kitāb al-Maghāzī* 4431–32, 4442, ed. Khan, vol. 5.

June 8, 632 CE.

88 It is unclear to whom the Christian refers, possibly the biographer Ibn Hishām or one of his followers. The reference to the "Law" (the Qurʾān or perhaps Islamic law) is not in the Arabic.

90 For John the Baptist as the last of the prophets, see Matthew 11:11–13.

91 "whose God is their belly, and whose glory is in their shame": Philippians 3:19.

93 Compare the Sermon on the Mount in Matthew 5–7.

95 The first Qurʾānic quotation (2:23) is somewhat garbled from the original, which reads, "And if ye are in doubt concerning that which We reveal unto Our slave (Muhammad), then produce a sūra of the like thereof, and call your witnesses beside Allah if ye are truthful" (Pickthall).

In this second quotation from the Qurʾān, the original (59:21) reads that the mountain would be "rent asunder by the fear of Allah" (Pickthall).

Exodus 14; Joshua 10:12–13; Luke 8:54; John 11:43.

97 Tihāma is a region in the Arabian Peninsula along the coast of the Red Sea.

The parenthetical remark on "Nestorian heretics" is not in the Arabic; the Latin, therefore, adds a polemical tone to the passage by describing Sergius's sect as one of heretics. Marie-Thérèse d'Alverny erroneously adduced this comment as evidence that the author of the Arabic could not have been a Nestorian ("Deux traductions," 88).

For the saying that Christian monks and priests are not arrogant, see Qurʾān 5:82.

98 For these three Jews, see §25. For the idea that Jews inserted elements into the Qurʾān, compare Roggema, *The Legend of Sergius Baḥīrā,* 269.

100 "The Jews say: 'Christians are nothing.' Christians say: 'Jews are fools'": Qurʾān 2:113.

The Qurʾānic quotation states that Jews and Christians tell one another that they "have nothing to stand on."

Referring to the *Sūrat al-Naml* or *Sūra of the Ant* (27), *Sūrat al-Naḥl* or *Sūra of the Bee* (16), and the *Sūrat al-ʿAnkabūt* or *Sūra of*

the Spider (29); the extant Arabic manuscripts do not mention the *Sūra of the Ant.*

102 As pointed out by González Muñoz (*Exposición*, 215n348), the Latin translator has rendered as names the various materials on which the Qur'ān was transmitted: *Zaheftin* for *ṣaḥīfa* (leaves), *Azihbin* for *jashab* (wood), *Hatuhil Enhail* for *jarīd al-nakhl* (palm branches), and *Hazim Elquef* for *ʿaẓm al-katif* (bone).

Ibn Masʿūd was a companion of Muhammad. His text of the Qur'ān left out Sūra 1, 113, and 114. For the source of this quotation, see Bottini, *Apologia*, 162n266.

104 The variant readings mentioned here obviously do not occur in the Arabic version, where the examples given are not, as González Muñoz (*Exposición*, 216n361; "La versión latina," 35–36) points out, so much lexical as phonetic variants (see Introduction).

'Abū al-Sarāyā's sack of Mecca occurred in 815; its mention here is perhaps another indication that the text dates to the ninth century.

105 There is no *Sūra of the Ox* in the Qur'ān; the Arabic refers to the *Sūrat an-Nūr* or *Sūra of Light* (24). González Muñoz suggests ("La versión latina," 34–35) that a scribe wrote *bovis* (ox) for *lucis* (light).

There is no *Sūra of Sentences* in the Qur'ān; the Arabic refers to the *Sūrat al-Aḥzāb* or *Sūra of the Combined Forces* (33). Caskel ("*Apologia del Christiamismo,*" 157) suggests that the translator confused *al-Aḥzāb* with *al-Ḥizb,* meaning "formula."

The *Sūra of the Heights* (7) and the *Sūra of the Spoils of War* (8), respectively.

The sections here called *al-muʿawwidhatāni* (the two protective sūras) refer to the last two sūras of the Qur'ān (113 and 114).

The *Sūrat al-Qunūt* and the *Sūrat al-Mutʿa* translate to the *Sūra of Obedience* and the *Sūra of Enjoyment*, respectively.

106 Tartar (*Dialogue*, 191) suggests that this is a corruption of the Arabic *al-buhut,* or "the deceitful ones."

107 The Christian refers to *ES* 22.

108 For examples of the word *al-istabraq,* see Qurʾān 18:31, 44:53, 76:21. Abel ("L'Apologie," 513n70) argues that it is of Abyssinian rather than Persian origin.

The original word referred to by *taceit* is unclear.

For the word *ʾabārīq,* see Qurʾān 56:18.

109 "I have made the Qurʾān descend in the pure Arabic language": Qurʾān 12:2.

Imruʾ al-Qays was a famous pre-Islamic poet (ca. 500–550) of the tribe of Kinda. According to a disputed *ḥadīth* recounted by Ibn al-Kalbī, Muhammad had said that "Imruʾ al-Qays is honored in this world but forgotten in the next. On the Day of Judgment, he will carry the banner of the poets and lead them into Hell." See Makkī, "Imruʾ al-Qays," 222.

It is uncertain to whom the name "Hannabiga" refers; it does not occur in the Arabic; González Muñoz (*Exposición*, 219n390) suggests al-Nābigha al-Jaʿdī (d. ca. 683), a late contemporary of Muhammad. I would propose instead to identify this person with the more famous al-Nābigha al-Dhubiyānī (ca. 535–ca. 604), a poet and friend of Imruʾ al-Qays who features in the ninth-century history of Arabic poetry by Ibn Qutayba (828–889): *Kitāb al-shiʿr wa-l-shuʿarāʾ* (The book on poetry and poets). See Ibn Qutayba, *Kitāb al-shiʿr wa-l-shuʿarāʾ,* ed. M. J. de Goeje (Leiden, 1902).

111 The Latin *fieri* is present tense, but the sense would require a past tense. See also below in the same paragraph.

112 Musaylima al-Ḥanafī, who claimed to be a prophet in Yamāma, in central Arabia, was defeated by the Muslims in the Battle of Aqaba in 632; al-ʾAswad al-ʿAnasī, who claimed to be a *kāhin,* or visionary poet, started an uprising in Yemen against Medina and was executed in 632. González Muñoz (*Exposición*, 220n395) suggests that the Latin *aethiops* may refer to *ʾaswad,* or "black"; Ṭulayḥa al-ʾAsadī also claimed to be a *kāhin* and led an uprising after the death of Muhammad.

Samir ("La version latine," 49) points out that this attack does not occur in the Arabic.

114 Her name was ʾAsmāʾ bint al-Nuʿmān, of the tribe of Kinda.

The Latin skips an entire section on the tribe of Kinda, renowned for poetry, and awkwardly moves ahead to the discussion of harmony and musicality in the Arabic language.

119 On the inscription on the throne of Allāh, see *ES* 23. Reference to the inscription on the throne is also made by Eulogius of Córdoba, *Memoriale Sanctorum*, 1.12, 5–19, ed. Juan Gil, *Corpus Scriptorum Muzarabicorum* (Madrid, 1973), 1:378–79, and see the discussion in González Muñoz, "La versión latina," 27–28.

120 "O sons of Israel . . . I have placed you before all other nations": Qur'ān 2:47.

122 "What use is there for a dark house . . . if the soul is filled with wickedness?": Matthew 15:1–2, 23:25–26.

"Woe to you, hypocrites . . . your hearts are defiled with wickedness": compare Matthew 23:27–28.

123 "Not in Ishmael, but in Isaac shall your seed be called": Genesis 21:12.

"That they might glory in your flesh": Galatians 6:13.

124 "All things are pure to the pure": Titus 1:15. This letter, in which Paul warns against Jews imposing "Jewish myths" (such as circumcision and dietary laws) upon Christians (Titus 1:10–15), is particularly relevant to the passage at hand.

"Nothing that is received with thanksgiving is to be rejected": Timothy 4:4.

126 This passage, which does not occur in the Arabic (see González Muñoz, "La versión latina," 32) is a pre-Islamic motif that occurs in Western literature at least as early as Jerome, who writes in the *Life of St. Hilarion,* ed. A. A. R. Bastiaensen and J. W. Smit, *Vite dei Santi del III al VI secolo*, 4:72–142 (Milan, 1975), at 108: "They worship Venus on account of Lucifer, to whose worship the Saracen people is dedicated." The Venerable Bede echoes this phrase when commenting on the "Star of Rompha" in Acts of the Apostles 7:43 (*Expositio Actuum apostolorum. Retractatio in Actus apostolorum*, ed. M. L. W. Laistner and D. Hurst, Corpus Christianorum: Series Latina 121 [Turnhout, 1983]): "This indicates Lucifer, to whose worship the Saracen people was dedicated for the sake of honoring Venus." The mo-

tif reoccurs in Peter Alfonsi's *Dialogus contra Iudaeos* (ed. Mieth, 98; trans. Irven M. Resnick, *Dialogue against the Jews* [Washington, D.C., 2006], 156): "A purity resulting from the ablution of the members, however, was important to the worshipers of the planet Venus, who, wanting to pray to her, prepared themselves as if they were women, coloring their mouths and eyes. He [Muhammad] commanded this for the reason that he became king at the minute of the planet Venus." See for a more extensive discussion, Septimus, "On the cult at Mecca."

127 The Arabic speaks of *al-shamsiyya,* or "worshippers of the sun," and *al-barāhima,* or "Brahmins."

"Who casts a stone in the heap of Mercury": Proverbs 26:8.

128 This quote of ʿUmar b. Khaṭṭāb, the second caliph, is recounted by al-Bukhārī, *Saḥīḥ, Kitāb al-ḥājj* 1597, ed. Khan, vol. 2.

Al-ḥājj refers to the pilgrimage to Mecca, one of the five pillars of Islam. *Al-jimār* refers to the small pebbles used in the ritual stoning of the devil as part of the proceedings during the *ḥājj.* The Forbidden House of God is a somewhat literal rendering of the Sacred Mosque *(al-Masjid al-Ḥarām)* in Mecca.

129 The Christian refers to *ES* 28.

134 "See, I am with you until the consummation of this world": Matthew 28:20.

136 "Let them have a sign. . . . Indeed, they are fortunate": Qurʾān 3:104.

"It is not up to you to justify them, but let God justify whom he wishes": Qurʾān 2:272.

"For if your Lord would wish it . . . at the behest of God?": Qurʾān 10:99–100.

137 "Say, o you men . . . for he is the best among judges": Qurʾān 10:108–9.

"For if your God would will it . . . except those pardoned by him": Qurʾān 11:118–19.

"He has been sent to mankind with equal piety and compassion": Qurʾān 9:128.

139 "There will be no violence in faith": compare Qurʾān 2:256.

See *ES* 64. The famous phrase from the Qurʾān (2:256) that

"there is no compulsion in religion" is not accurately represented in the Latin, where *violentia* is more akin to "violence."

"I have separated . . . your only duty is to convey the message to them": Qur'ān 3:20.

"If God would will it. . . . God does whatever he wishes": Qur'ān 2:253.

"O you unbelievers! I have my religion, and you have your religion": Qur'ān 109:1 and 6.

"Do not debate . . . except in those matters that are dealt with in a kind manner": Qur'ān 29:46.

143 The Arabic does not contain the description of Zoroaster as Greek.

"King Zebeizib" refers to Vishtaspa, patron of Zoaraster, as noted by González Muñoz (*Exposición*, 234n463).

The title of this work is *Zandawastā* in Arabic; Caskel ("*Apologia del Christiamismo,*" 157) suggests that the title was confused with the Arabic *bustān,* or "garden"; González Muñoz (*Exposición*, 234n465) adds that the Latin translator might have resorted to using *hortus* (garden) in the way that it was commonly used for titles of medieval texts to indicate a miscellany.

The name "Helbidius" refers to Buddha (Arabic: *al-Bud*) but would have been associated by a Western reader with Christian heresy, as it resembles the name Helvidius (or Elvidius), an infamous fourth-century heresiarch (see González Muñoz, "La versión latina," 36), who denied the doctrine of Mary's perpetual virginity and is also discussed by Peter the Venerable, *Contra sectam Saracenorum*, Prol. 7.

144 As González Muñoz (*Exposición*, 234) points out, the phrase "and anyone of my kin will do the same" does not occur in the Arabic, while the entire quote is not found in either the Qur'ān or in the Hadīth.

146 "Be compassionate just as your Father is compassionate . . . and sends rain on both the just and the unjust": Matthew 5:44–45; John 1:14.

149 "The Word became flesh and dwelled among us": John 1:14.

153 “I will kill them and torment them until they . . . render tribute as my subjects”: Qurʾān 9:29.

156 The origin of this story is unknown.

161 The Byzantines, who considered themselves a continuation of the Roman Empire, are meant here.

162 The Arabic clearly indicates that no Christians entered the land of Muhammad except for Sergius-Nestorius and John-Baḥīrā; the Latin ambiguously states *istorum* (those people).

Sergius-Nestorius and John-Baḥīrā seem to be a doubling of the Sergius-Baḥīrā figure who appears under various names in earlier traditions (see Introduction). It is possible that the second person is a reference to John of Antioch, a contemporary of Nestorius and patriarch of Antioch (d. 441).

163, 164 “He who kills . . . win a place in paradise”: Qurʾān 4:74, 22:58–59.

168 Instead of “naturally excessive,” one could alternatively understand “to exceed the bounds of nature,” as González Muñoz has it (*Exposición*, 242), but the Latin would not seem to support this.

169 “I created humans and demons . . . for them to worship me”: Qurʾān 51:56.

170 For the “*sūra* on divorce and remarriage,” see Qurʾān 2:226–42, 65:1–7. A *sūra* is a chapter of the Qurʾān, although there is no *sūra* dedicated to this topic, as the Christian claims.

Deuteronomy 24:1–4; Jeremiah 3:1.

171 The Christian paraphrases the words in *ES* 50: “No one will harm you, no one will vex you, no one will reproach you, no one will bring injustice upon you.”

“Do not fear those who kill the body . . . who is able to bring both soul and body to ruin in Gehenna”: Matthew 10:28.

172 See *ES* 49.

173 For this quotation attributed to Muhammad, compare al-Bukhārī, *Ṣaḥīḥ, Kitāb al-Waṣāyā* 2753, ed. Khan, vol. 4.

ʿAbd Manāf was the great-great-grandfather of Muhammad.

174 “Let him who glories glory in the Lord”: 1 Corinthians 1:31.

175 For the Muslim’s statements on Judgment Day, see *ES* 50.

178 "When you have done all that is commanded to you . . . we have done what we were supposed to have already done'": Luke 17:10.

"Narrow is the path that leads to life . . . and how many are they who travel by it!": Matthew 7:13–14.

The Christian makes a tendentiously incomplete reference to Qur'ān 4:3, in which Muslims are permitted to marry up to four women (compare also *ES* 52): "And if ye fear that ye will not deal fairly by the orphans, marry of the women, who seem good to you, two or three or four; and if ye fear that ye cannot do justice (to so many) then one (only) or (the captives) that your right hands possess" (Pickthall).

180 See *ES* 57.

181 "Go and call mankind . . . the Son, and the Holy Spirit": Matthew 28:19–20.

185 The Ark of the Covenant housed the stone tablets containing the Ten Commandments; the Ark in turn was kept in a portable temple known as the Tabernacle.

"Rise, Lord, and may your enemies be confounded!": Numbers 10:35–36.

"Return, Lord, to the thousand and ten thousand sons of Israel!": Joshua 7:6.

186 "Hāshimites" refers to the tribe of Muhammad, as well as that of the Christian's addressee.

ʿUmr al-Karj refers to a Nestorian congregation in al-Karj, near Baghdad.

188 This refers to the opening of the Qur'ān, known as *al-Fātiḥa,* which is recited at the start of each prayer.

189 "Were you not in error and set aright?": Qur'ān 93:7.

For *haeretici mundani,* the Arabic reads *Dahriyya,* which refers to a sect that believed in the eternity of the world; this elusive philosophical sect has frequently been associated with Qur'ān 45:24 (see Goldziher and Goichon, "Dahriyya," 2:95–97).

Georgiani reads as *Ḥarnāniyya* in the Arabic; they were a group in Ḥarrān known as Ṣabians, whose religious practices are unclear, but apparently contained Neoplatonic elements.

Samaniani is *Sabāʾiyya* in the Arabic; they were a sect named after ʿAbd Allāh b. Sabaʾ, who believed in the divinity of ʿAbd Allāh b. ʾAbī Ṭālib (one of the companions of Muhammad) and that he would return at the end of times (see Tartar, *Dialogue*, 243n58; Bottini, *Apologia,* 226n381; González Muñoz, *Exposición*, 250n532). The translator probably took *Samaniani* from Jerome, who mentions a group called the *Samanaei* in connection with the Brahmins in *Adversus Iovinianum,* 2.14.17.

191 See *ES* 63.

193 "In order that he might . . . become subject to God": Romans 3:19.

194 "Judah . . . until the arrival of him who is the hope of the Gentiles, whose kingdom will be eternal": Genesis 49:8–10.

196 "Rejoice greatly . . . and proclaim peace to the Gentiles": Zechariah 9:9–10.

Ephraim was one of the sons of Joseph and the ancestor to one of the twelve tribes of Israel.

Zion is one of the mountains in Jerusalem, often used to refer to the city itself.

197 "The Lord said . . . make the ends of the earth your boundaries'": Psalms 2:7–8.

"O kings. . . . Receive the son so that he may not become wrathful": Psalms 2:10–12.

198 The phrase "The Lord spoke to my lord" occurs in Psalms 110:1; Matthew 22:44; Mark 12:36; Luke 20:42; Acts of the Apostles 2:34.

"The Lord spoke to my lord: be seated at my right-hand side": Psalms 109:1.

"The Lord gazed . . . and free them from the chains of death": Psalms 101:20–22.

"Lord's name on Zion": Psalms 101:22.

"And his . . . kingdoms will be gathered to serve the Lord": Psalms 101:22–23.

199 "Rest your tired hands . . . and the cripple will leap forth like a deer": Isaiah 35:3–6.

"Rise, take your cot, and walk!": John 5:8.

"You will hear, you will speak": Mark 7:32.

200 "Listen, house of David . . . 'God is with us'": Isaiah 7:13–14.

"A boy will be born to us . . . and the nations will worship him": Isaiah 9:6–7.

201 The Christian means here the accusation in the Qurʾān (but absent from the Muslim's letter) that the Christians corrupted or tampered with scripture (the so-called charge of *taḥrīf*). See note to *RC* 34.

205 "If you have doubts . . . believe the signs of God": Qurʾān 10:94–95.

206 "They believe . . . and those who did not want to believe will be damned": Qurʾān 2:121.

207 The quotation "If you will not accept my scripture . . . and kill you" does not occur in the Qurʾān.

209 "Greetings, blessed among women, our Lord be with you": Luke 1:26–28.

210 "Behold . . . the Lord God will grant to him the throne of his father David": Luke 1:31–32.

David was the second king of Israel and Judah, and in the New Testament he is considered the ancestor of Jesus.

"And he will rule over the house of Jacob for eternity": Luke 1:32.

The "house of Jacob" refers to the descendants of Jacob, Patriarch of the Israelites.

"The Holy Spirit will come . . . will be called the Son of God": Luke 1:32–35.

"Behold . . . has conceived a son despite being old and barren": Luke 1:36.

According to the Gospel of Luke, Elisabeth was the mother of John the Baptist, who later announced the arrival of Jesus.

211 The Christian refers to the monk Sergius-Nestorius, as related in *RC* 97.

"'O Mary, God has chosen you. . . . some things that are forbidden will be allowed to you'": Qurʾān 3:42–50.

I have chosen to interpret *senex* predicatively here, "like an old man." For the *puer senex* motif, prevalent in hagiography, see

E. R. Curtius, *European Literature and the Latin Middle Ages*, trans. Willard R. Trask (Princeton, 1953), 98–101.

213 "How has it come to pass. . . . For my infant son has prostrated in my womb and worshipped him with great joy": Luke 1:39–44.

214 "Zechariah prayed . . . in the Word of God and in the Lord'": Qur'ān 3:38–39.

216 "Behold . . . an infant wrapped in old swaddling clothes and placed in a crib": Luke 2:10–12.

"Glory . . . and good hope to all men equally!": Luke 2:14.

217 The quotation attributed to John the Baptist is a paraphrase of Matthew 3:13.

"Permit it now, for in this way must we fulfill the blessing": Matthew 3:14. Note that in most editions, the Bible reads "justice" (or "righteousness") for "blessing."

"This is my beloved son, in whom I am pleased": Matthew 3:17.

220 "O men, repent, for the kingdom of heaven is near!": Matthew 4:17.

What is described as a "fast" here refers to the observance of Lent, a period of roughly six weeks during which Christians practice penance, self-denial, and repentance of sins.

"Man lives not by bread alone, but by the whole Word of God": Matthew 4:4.

221 You have heard . . . whoever harms or wounds his brother will be condemned to the fire of hell": Matthew 5:21–22.

"Let not the sun go down . . . while you are still angry with your brother": Ephesians 4:26.

222 "When you have started to pray . . . then return to your prayer": Matthew 5:23–24.

"You have heard . . . he who marries a divorced woman will also commit adultery": Matthew 5:27–28, 5:31–32.

223 "It was said. . . . it is a part of evil": Matthew 5:36–37.

"You have heard . . . go with him for another thousand": Matthew 5:38–41.

224 "Offer yourself . . . and greet the one who does not greet you": Luke 6:30.

225 "You have heard . . . the sun rise on both the good and the evil": Matthew 5:43–45.

"If you only do well. . . . Do not also the wicked ones do this?": Matthew 5:46.

226 "Do not perform charity in the presence of others . . . your left hand not know what the right hand is doing": Matthew 6:2–3.

"When you pray . . . heavenly Father, who knows all secrets, will reward him": Matthew 6:5.

"When you fast . . . reward him in accordance with what he sees inside him": Matthew 6:16–18.

227 "Do not hoard your treasures in the earth . . . for where your treasure is, there is your heart": Matthew 6:19–21.

"A servant cannot serve two masters. . . . you, too, cannot serve both God and your possessions": Matthew 6:24.

228 "But I say to you. . . . he who created tomorrow will provide food to you tomorrow": Matthew 6:25–34.

229 "Do not depart from . . . and remove the speck from his brother's eye": Matthew 7:1–5.

230 "Give. . . . only good things to those who ask him?": Matthew 7:7–11.

"Whatever you wish . . . than you yourself wish to be treated": Matthew 7:12.

231 "O you . . . will come from among your wives and children": Qur'ān 64:14.

234 For these sentiments, see Matthew 5:48, 6:14.

235 Compare the passage in Matthew 8:19–20.

236 For the episode of the loaves and the fishes, see Matthew 14:13–21; Mark 6:31–44; Luke 9:12–17; John 6:1–14.

"You are Christ . . . why have you come to destroy us?": Mark 1:23–24; Luke 4:33–34.

The episode of the wedding at Cana is recounted in the Gospel of John (2:1–11), who is here identified with the apostle John, son of Zebedee.

"Blessed is he who has come in the name of the Lord": Matthew 21:15–16; Mark 11:9; Luke 19:38; John 12:13.

For the episode in which Jesus walks on water and calms the storm on the Sea of Galilee, see Matthew 14:22–34; Mark 6:45–53; John 6:15–21.

For the episode in which Jesus becomes radiant and speaks with the prophets Moses and Elijah (known as the Transfiguration of Jesus), see Matthew 17:1–8; Mark 9:2–8; Luke 9:28–36.

For the episode in which Jesus heals a sick woman, see Luke 8:43–47.

237 "I have given . . . and protected him with the Holy Spirit": Qurʾān 2:87, 253.

242 "Go . . . and lay your hands on the sick, and they will be healed": Matthew 10:7–9.

243 "Father, forgive them, for they know not what they do": Luke 23:24.

For these episodes, see Matthew 28:17–20 and John 20:19; Luke 24:13–35; John 21:1–14; Acts of the Apostles 1:2–8.

244 "O you . . . so will he be witnessed to descend from heaven at that hour": Acts of the Apostles 1:9–12.

The Mount of Olives, from the summit of which Christ is believed to have ascended, is not in Syria but in Jerusalem (as the Arabic original correctly states).

245 "O Jesus. . . . I reveal to you from signs and from well-informed memory": Qurʾān 3:55–58.

246 "Paraclete," from the Greek for "advocate" or "helper," is commonly used to refer to the Holy Spirit, as in John 14:25.

247 ʿUmar b. al-Khaṭṭāb was the second caliph. On the origin of this saying, see Bottini (*Apologia*, 268).

257 "If anyone . . . will not be able to enter the Kingdom of God": John 3:5.

"Whoever eats my flesh. . . . all of his sins are forgiven": John 6:55–58.

255–65 This section is absent from most of the Arabic manuscripts, although it is contained in the two oldest manuscripts, which were copied from a now lost twelfth-century manuscript (González Muñoz, *Exposición*, xxii, xlii–xliii). Marie-Thérèse

d'Alverny argues on the basis of this passage (and particularly the nonextant work against the teachings of Arius mentioned in 263) that the author was a Jacobite or a West Syrian Christian philosopher ("Deux traductions," 87–96). Most likely, however, the passage is a later accretion (see Introduction).

265 "such as no eye . . . has prepared for those who love him": 1 Corinthians 2:9.

[*Epilogue*]

266 The final adjudication in favor of Islam is not in the Latin text; it has been erased in the oldest manuscript (see Introduction).

Book of Nicholas

1 Constantine the Great (r. 306–337), legalized Christianity with the Edict of Milan in 313 and was baptized on his deathbed, according to tradition.

It is unclear which pope is meant here: Agapitus I was pope from 535 to 536, while Agapitus II was pope from 946 to 955. As González Muñoz points out ("*Liber Nycholay*," 28), there is some evidence that the latter was meant: the pope's successor is named as a certain John (see n. 10 below: Agapitus II was succeeded by John XII, while Agapitus I was succeeded by Silverius); the chronicle of Johannes Ruffus, moreover, which occurs immediately before this text in the Vatican manuscript, refers to Pope Agapitus II as the one who appointed Nicolas as his successor, "also known as Muhammad." The chronology is difficult to reconcile with the reference below (see 2) that the events took place three hundred years after Constantine's legalization of Christianity (that is, in 613).

3 The titular church of San Lorenzo in Damaso in Rome had been elevated to a basilica by Pope Damasus I (366–384), whose name has been associated with it ever since. The mention of this church may provide evidence of a compositional context in Rome.

6 For the phrase "deceitful words from the heart," compare Psalms 11:3.

7 Maribel Fierro's suggestion ("La visión," 156) that the Qur'ān described in the *Book of Nicholas,* written with letters of gold, refers to a manuscript associated with the founder of the Almohads, the Mahdī Ibn Tūmart, is farfetched; rather, the passage goes back to Embrico of Mainz's depiction of Qur'ānic revelation (ll. 671–78). Compare also *Qualiter* 27.

"In the beginning, God created heaven and earth": Genesis 1:1.

"You are earth . . . and you will not die": Genesis 3:19.

8 "And in that day . . . take away our reproach'": Isaiah 4:1.

9 "Go, show yourselves to the priests": Luke 17:14.

Compare Psalms 31:5, which reads: *et tu remisisti impietatem peccati mei* (and you forgave the impiety of my sin).

10 Compare Psalms 50:3–4. The person addressed by Nicholas is possibly John XII, who succeeded Pope Agapitus II in 955.

11 For the false etymology in which "Saracen" is derived from "Sarah," Abraham's wife, see Adelphus's *Life of Muhammad,* n. 3.

This summary of Islamic practices contains some accurate elements. The "double tribute" to God may refer to the *zakāt,* or giving of alms; the reference to the thirty-day fast is accurate and alludes to the month-long fast of *Ramaḍān;* the sacrifice in imitation of Abraham's sacrifice refers to the annual *ʿīd al-aḍḥā* (Feast of the Sacrifice).

12 The argument between the youth and the older citizens draws heavily on Embrico, *Life of Muhammad,* ll. 569–78, as discussed in Cambier, "L'épisode des taureaux dans la Légende de Mahomet (ms. 50, Bibl. du Sém. de Pise)," 231–32.

13 Compare Ecclesiasticus 19:2; *Rule of Saint Benedict* 40:7.

The word *xerubium* is otherwise unattested, but presumably derives from the Arabic *sharāb* (beverage), whence the English "syrup"; González Muñoz translates it as "*agua sazonada a manera de jarabe*" (water seasoned in the manner of syrup; see "*Liber Nycholay*," 17).

15 "All flesh is dry grass": Isaiah 40:6.

16 Compare Nicholas/Machometus's account of his vision on the way to Rome with that of Saul on the road to Damascus, as described in Acts of the Apostle 9:1–16.

Compare the issuing of divine commandments in Exodus 31:18; Deuteronomy 9:10.

For the Jews' "heart of stone," compare Ezekiel 11:19, 36:26.

"Children of every race. . . . God's work and it is miraculous in our eyes": Psalms 117:23; Matthew 21:42.

17 It is uncertain where the author got the otherwise unattested term *caxisi.* González Muñoz suggests ("*Liber Nycholay,*" 33) that it could refer to the *qādīy* (judge); another possibility is that it is somehow derived from the Arabic plural form of *qiddīs* (a Christian saint), *qiddīsūn.*

18 The name *Charufa,* which alternatively appears as *Charuffa* and *Carufa,* may, as suggested by González Muñoz ("*Liber Nycholay,*" 36), ultimately be derived from a misunderstood reference to the patricians *(shurafāʾ)* of Mecca, or alternatively be a corruption of the name Khadīja, Muhammad's first wife.

The phrase *Iam lucis orto sidere* recalls the hymn that opens with the same words, used in the Roman Breviary at the Office of Prime.

I have rendered the verb *incantare* as "to pray"—not an uncommon medieval Latin usage (see Blaise, *Lexicon, incanto* 2). González Muñoz proposes ("*Liber Nycholay,*" 39) to render it as "to snatch, confiscate," as an extension of its usage "to auction" (Blaise, *Lexicon, incanto* 3) that is preserved in the Italian *far incanti,* and provides for him further evidence for the Italian origin of this version of the life of Muhammad. However, this translation fits awkwardly with the prepositional phrase starting with *ad* that follows.

For the motif of Muhammad's right foot being left behind, compare *Qualiter* 25, where instead the left foot remains, and Guibert of Nogent (*Dei gesta per Francos,* ed. Huygens, 1.386–401), where only the ankles are spared by the devouring pigs. Like González Muñoz ("*Liber Nycholay,*" 18), I have translated *pes*

(foot) here as though it were accusative, as the sense requires it to be the object of *remiserit*.

20 The depiction of Muhammad's tomb, suspended in midair by magnetic force, resembles the extended descriptions of Embrico of Mainz (1115–46) and Walter of Compiègne (1059–74).

22 The fanciful *miramulus* probably represents a contraction of the customary title of caliphs, *amīr al-muʾminīn* (commander of the faithful). It is uncertain who is meant by *Maximitus*. See also note 28 below.

It is unclear to which place *Chaulandia* refers. By *Turchia* is probably meant the remnant of the Seljuk Sultanate of Rūm in Anatolia, so referred to also by the traveler William of Rubruck in the years 1253 to 1255 (*The Mission of William of Rubruck*, trans. Peter Jackson [London, 1990], 61). González Muñoz, who read *Cinthia* instead of *Turchia* ("*Liber Nycholay,*" 13), suggested that the word was a corruption from *Syria*.

Here the author means not the Mesopotamian city but the fortress of Babylon near Cairo.

25 *Marzucus* is an Italian name and can also refer to the rampant lion on the Florentine coat of arms *(Marzocco),* as pointed out by González Muñoz ("*Liber Nycholay,*" 36). It may offer further proof that the text, or at least this version of it, was composed in Italy.

For the motif that only Muhammad's left foot remained behind, compare 18 above, where the right foot instead of the left remains, and see note.

26 These *charissi* could be the same as the *caxisi* mentioned in 17. González Muñoz suggests ("*Liber Nycholay,*" 33) that it could refer to the *Quraysh,* the tribe of Muhammad entrusted with guarding the Kaʿaba.

27 *Archadi* presumably derives from the Arabic *al-qādīy,* or "judge."

These "companions of Muhammad" presumably refer to the *ṣaḥāba* (companions) of Muhammad in Islamic tradition.

It is unclear to whom the fictional name *Buzacannus* refers, but the defeat of the Byzantine navy took place during the Caliphate of Sulaymān b. ʿAbd al-Malik (715–717).

The emperor in question is Leo III the Isaurian, Byzantine emperor from 717 to 741.

28 The person called *Maximitus* is possibly Mūsā b. Nuṣayr (d. 716), the governor of the province of *Ifrīqiya* who oversaw the Islamic conquest of Spain, or to ʿAbd al-Raḥmān al-Ghāfiqī, the general who led an army across Spain into modern-day France, where he was defeated by Charles Martel at the Battle of Tours in 732.

I have translated the nonexistent form *destruerunt* as though it read *destruunt* (they destroy), as the sense requires.

Where Wicked Muhammad Came From

1 Clement I was pope from 92 to 99.

Simon Magus is a magician described in Acts of the Apostles 8:9–24 as asking Peter to bestow upon him the Holy Spirit in return for payment; for this reason the practice of simony (the "buying" and "selling" of ecclesiastical offices) is named after him. The author clearly considers this practice to be a betrayal of the Holy Spirit.

3 *Maurus* is Latin for Moor, usually referring to the Muslim inhabitants of North Africa and Iberia, although the term was also used to refer to Muslims more generally. Mancini conjectures *rationaliter* from the manuscript's reading of *natiter,* arguing that this refers to the "sinister" reputation of the Moors to a Western European audience in the Middle Ages. Apart from the obvious problems associated with this interpretation, there also is no evidence of *Maurus* carrying this prejudiced connotation in earlier medieval Latin. The reading *natione* would appear to make much more sense, as the author is explaining that this particular person is called *Maurus* while also being a Moor.

5 Note the sarcastic reference to Maurus's "religion," which is no religion at all.

8 This passage bears close similarities to Genesis 30:30–42, where Jacob uses rods to separate his flock.

11 The physicians spoken of here are probably the apostles mentioned in 5.

13 See Matthew 12:25; Luke 11:17. The full text of the passage quoted is: *Omne regnum divisum contra se desolabitur* (every kingdom divided against itself will be made desolate).

17 This passage is a patchwork of Luke 6:30, Matthew 10:8, and Jeremiah 18:18.

This last quotation comes from Jeremiah 18:18, where it is spoken by people planning to bring false charges against Jeremiah. The ambiguity of this verse may have been intended to undermine Maurus.

18 A noun, such as "heir" or "son," must have dropped out in the Latin.

20 For the motif of Muhammad as possessed by a demon, compare *Tultusceptru* and Walter of Compiègne, lines 48 and 49.

21 The rare word *bordo* indicates a type of pilgrim's staff; see Blaise, *Lexicon, "bordo."*

23 For some reason, the Psalter is described here as belonging to the New Testament rather than the Old.

For this passage, see Acts of the Apostles 11:5 and 9, where, however, it is a vessel *(vas)* that descends from heaven, which is then compared to a sheet.

24 The sense of *cepit eos invicem* (or perhaps *coepit,* "began," with a missing infinitive) is unclear.

25 The meaning of the otherwise unattested verb *traxendare* is obscure, though perhaps related to the Italian *trascendere* (to transcend, go beyond).

For the trope that Muslims are worshippers of Venus, see *RC* 126 and note.

26 The manuscript reads *Maurus,* but this is clearly a mistake, since Maurus remained behind on the mountain; I have replaced it instead with "Muhammad," as the sense requires.

30–32 This episode resembles the account found in the *Kitāb al-Miʿrāj,*

or *Book of the Ladder,* which describes Muhammad's voyage to the various spheres of heaven and hell. The Arabic original is lost, but thirteenth-century Latin and Old French translations are extant. The Latin translation was made in 1264 by Bonaventura of Siena at the court of Alfonso X and may have implications for the dating of this text (see Introduction).

32 The episode of the moon passing through Muhammad's sleeves also occurs in Peter Alfonsi's *Dialogus contra Iudaeos* (ed. Mieth, 96; trans. Resnick, 153).

36 The unnamed Jewish woman resembles to some extent the character Carufa/Charufa in the *Book of Nicholas.*

40 I have struck from the text a nonsensical reference to Christians, since the passage deals with a conflict between Muslims and Jews (see Notes to the Texts).

The motif of Muhammad being devoured by pigs (which is then offered as the explanation for the Muslim abstention from eating pork) first occurs in Embrico of Mainz's *Life of Muhammad* (see ll. 1045–46, 1091–110 and note).

42 This appears to be a fanciful explanation for the Muslim practice of *hājj,* or yearly pilgrimage to Mecca during the month of Ramaḍān.

43 The strange and otherwise unattested *influcoso* might be a corruption from *infructuoso* (barren).

44 For the term "Ishmaelites," compare the full title of Peter the Venerable's polemical summary of Islam: *Summa totius haeresis ac diabolicae sectae Saracenorum sive Hismahelitarum* (Overview of the entire heresy and diabolical sect of the Saracens or Ishmaelites). The emendation was proposed by Mancini's colleague and well-known orientalist scholar Carlo Alfonso Nallino, but it was not adopted by Mancini (see Mancini, 349, and Notes to the Texts).

The sense of the explicit is obscure; most likely, a genitive noun such as *prophetae* (prophet) or *regis* (king) directly preceding *Saracenorum* (of the Saracens) was omitted by the scribe.

Bibliography

Editions and Translations

History of Muhammad and *Tultusceptru* from the Book of Lord Metobius

Díaz y Díaz, Manuel. "Los textos antimahometanos más antiguos en códices españoles." *Archives d'histoire doctrinale et littéraire du Moyen Age* 37 (1970): 149–68.

Gil, Juan. *Corpus Scriptorum Muzarabicorum,* 1:483–86, 2:709–10. Madrid: Instituto Antonio de Nebrija, 1973.

Wolf, Kenneth B. "The Earliest Latin Lives of Muḥammad." In *Conversion and Continuity: Indigenous Christian Communities in Islamic Lands, Eighth to Eighteenth Centuries,* edited by Michael Gervers and Ramzi Jibran Bilkhazi, 89–101. Papers in Mediaeval Studies 9. Toronto: Pontifical Institute of Mediaeval Studies, 1990. Repr. in *Medieval Iberia. Readings from Christian, Muslim, and Jewish sources,* edited by Olivia Remie Constable, 48–50. Philadelphia: University of Pennsylvania Press, 1997.

Anastasius the Librarian, *Chronicle* of Theophanes

The Chronicle of Theophanes Confessor: Byzantine and Near Eastern History AD 284–813. Translated by Cyril Mango and Roger Scott. Oxford: Oxford University Press, 1997.

de Boor, Carolus. *Theophanis Chronographia.* 2 vols. Leipzig: Teubner, 1885.

Embrico of Mainz, *Life of Muhammad*

Beaugendre, Antoine. *Carmen de fraudibus Mahumetis.* In *Venerabilis Hildeberti primo Cenomanensis episcopi deinde Turonensis archiepiscopi opera tam*

edita quam inedita: accesserunt Marbodi Redonensis episcopi ipsius Hildeberti supparis opuscula, 1277–95. Paris, 1708. (= *Patrologia Latina* vol. 171, cols. 1343–66.)

Cambier, Guy. *Embricon de Mayence. La vie de Mahomet.* Collection Latomus 52. Brussels: Latomus, Revue d'études latines, 1962.

González Muñoz, Fernando. *Mahometrica. Ficciones poéticas latinas del siglo XII sobre Mahoma,* 97–167. Madrid: Consejo Superior de Investigaciones Científicas, 2015.

Hübner, Fritz. "Vita Mahumeti." *Historische Vierteljahrschrift* 29 (1935): 441–90.

Walter of Compiègne, *Poetic Pastimes on Muhammad*

du Méril, Édélestand. *Poésies populaires latines du moyen age,* 379–415. Paris: F. Didot, 1847. Repr.: Bologna 1969; Geneva, 1977.

González Muñoz, Fernando. *Mahometrica. Ficciones poéticas latinas del siglo XII sobre Mahoma,* 173–241. Madrid: Consejo Superior de Investigaciones Científicas, 2015.

Huygens, R. B. C. "*Otia de Machomete.* Gedicht von Walter von Compiègne." *Sacris Erudiri* 8 (1956): 287–328.

———. "*Otia de Machomete.*" In Yvan Lepage, *Le roman de Mahomet de Alexandre du Pont: 1258: édition critique précédée d'une étude sur quelques aspects de la légende de Mahomet au Moyen Age.* Paris: Klincksieck, 1977.

Adelphus, *Life of Muhammad*

Bischoff, Bernhard. "Ein Leben Mohammeds (Adelphus?) (Zwölftes Jahrhundert)." In *Anecdota Novissima: Texte des vierten bis sechzehnten Jahrhundert,* 106–22. Stuttgart: A. Hiersemann, 1984.

González Muñoz, Fernando. *Mahometrica. Ficciones poéticas latinas del siglo XII sobre Mahoma,* 259–289. Madrid: Consejo Superior de Investigaciones Científicas, 2015.

Apology of al-Kindī

Bottini, Laura. *Apologia del cristianesimo.* Milan: Jaca book, 1998.

González Muñoz, Fernando. *Exposición y refutación del Islam: la versión la-*

tina de las epístolas de al-Hāšimī y al-Kindī. Coruña: Universidade da Coruña, Servizo de Publicacións, 2005.

Muir, William. *The Apology of al Kindy: Written at the Court of al Mâmûn (A.H. 215; A.D. 830) in Defence of Christianity against Islam.* London: Smith, Elder, 1882.

Muñoz Sendino, José. "Al-Kindi, la apología del cristianismo." *Miscelánea Comillas,* XI and XII (1949): 337–460.

Tartar, Georges. *Dialogue islamo-chrétien sous le calife Al-Ma'mūn (813–834). Les Épîtres d'Al-Hāshimī et d'Al-Kindī.* Strasbourg: Université des Sciences Humaines de Strasbourg, Faculté de Théologie Protestante, 1977.

———. *Dialogue islamo-chrétien sous le calife Al-Ma'mûn (813–834): les épîtres d'Al-Hashimî et d'Al-Kindî.* Paris: Nouvelles éditions latines, 1985.

Theodor Bibliander. *Machumetis Saracenorum principis eiusque successorum vitae ac doctrina ipseque Alcoran,* 2:2–20. Basle, 1543.

Tien, Anton. *ʿAbd Allāh ibn Ismāʿīl al-Hāshimī ʾilā ʿAbd al-Masīḥ ibn Isḥāq al-Kindī wa-Risālat al-Kindī ilā al-Hāshimī (The Apology of El-Kindi: A work of the ninth century written in defence of Christianity by a Arab).* London, Turkish Mission Aid Society, 1880. Repr. Cairo, 1885, 1912.

———. "The Apology of al-Kindi." In *The Early Christian-Muslim Dialogue: A Collection of Documents from the First Three Islamic Centuries, 632–900 A.D.*, edited by N. A. Newman, 355–545. Hatfield, Pa.: Interdisciplinary Biblical Research Institute, 1993.

Book of Nicholas

d'Ancona, Alessandro. "Il tesoro di Brunetto Latini versificato." *Atti della Reale Accademia dei Lincei,* Classe di scienze morali, storiche, e filologiche 4:1, 285 (1888), Appendix 1: 152–55.

González Muñoz, Fernando. "*Liber Nycholay.* La leyenda de Mahome y el cardenal Nicolás." *al-Qantara* 25 (2004): 5–43.

Where Wicked Muhammad Came From

Mancini, Augusto. "Per lo studio della legenda di Maometto in Occidente." *Rendiconti della R. Accademia nazionale dei Lincei, Classe di scienze morali, storiche e filologiche* 6 (Issue 10, 1934): 325–49.

Secondary Sources

Christian Muslim Relations: A Bibliographical History. Edited by David Thomas and Barbara Roggema. 6 vols. Leiden: Brill, 2009–2014.

Di Cesare, Michelina. *The Pseudo-historical Image of the Prophet Muhammad in Medieval Latin Literature: A Repertory.* Berlin: De Gruyter, 2011.

The Encyclopaedia of Islam: Second Edition. Edited by H. A. R. Gibb et al. Leiden: Brill, 1960–2009.

Encyclopédie de l'Islam: nouvelle édition établie avec le concours des principaux orientalistes. 6 vols. Leiden: E. J. Brill; Paris: G.-P. Maisonneuve et Larose, 1960–1989.

Abel, Armand. "L'Apologie d'al-Kindī et sa place dans la polémique islamo-chrétienne." In *Atti del convegno internazionale sul tema: L'oriente cristiano nella storia della civiltà,* 501–23. Rome: Accademia internazionale del Lincei, 1964.

Adamson, Peter. *al-Kindī.* Oxford: Oxford University Press, 2007.

al-Shāṭi', Bint. *The Wives of the Prophet.* Translated by Matti Moosa and D. Nicholas Ranson. Lahore, Sh. Muhammad Ashraf, 1971.

Arnaldi, Girolamo. "Anastasio bibliotecario, antipapa." In *Enciclopedia dei Papi,* 1:735–46. Rome: Istituto della Enciclopedia italiana, 2000.

———. "Anastasio Bibliotecario." In *Dizionario biografico degli Italiani,* 3:25–37. Rome: Istituto della Enciclopedia italiana, 1961.

Beckett, Katharine Scarfe. *Anglo-Saxon Perceptions of the Islamic World.* Cambridge: Cambridge University Press, 2003.

Bishko, Charles. "Peter the Venerable's journey to Spain." In *Petrus Venerabilis 1156–1956. Studies and Texts Commemorating the Eighth Centenary of His Death,* edited by Giles Constable and James Kritzeck, 152–75. Studia Anselmiana 40. Rome: Herder, 1956.

Blaise, Albert. *Lexicon Latinitatis Medii Aevi: praesertim ad res ecclesiasticas investigandas pertinens = Dictionnaire latin-français des auteurs du Moyen-Age.* Turnhout: Brepols, 1975.

Bottini, Laura. "*The Apology of al-Kindī.*" In *Christian-Muslim Relations,* 3:585–94.

Burman, Thomas E. "The Influence of the Apology of Al-Kindi and the Contrarietas Alfolica on Ramon Lull's Late Religious Polemic, 1305–1313." *Mediaeval Studies* 53 (1991): 197–228.

Cambier, Guy. "Embricon de Mayence (1010?-1077) est-il l'auteur de la Vita Mahumeti?" *Latomus* 16 (1957): 468–79.

———. "Quand Gautier de Compiègne composait les Otia de Machomete." *Latomus* 17 (1958): 531–39.

Caskel, Werner. "*Apologia del Christiamismo* [sic] *by al-Kindi:* José Muñoz Sendino." *Oriens* 4:1 (1951): 153–58.

Cerulli, Enrico. *Nuove ricerche sul Libro della Scala e la conoscenza dell'Islam in Occidente.* Vatican City: Biblioteca Apostolica Vaticana, 1972.

Colbert, Edward P. *The Martyrs of Córdoba (850–859): A Study of the Sources.* Washington, D.C.: Catholic University of America Press, 1962.

Conrad, Lawrence I. "Theophanes and the Arabic Historical Tradition: Some Indications of Intercultural Transmission." *Byzantinische Forschungen* 15 (1990): 1–44.

Conterno, Maria. *La "descrizione dei tempi" all'alba dell'espansione islamica: un'indagine sulla storiografia greca, siriaca e araba fra VII e VIII secolo.* Berlin: De Gruyter, 2014.

Cutler, Allan. "*Peter the Venerable and Islam* by James Kritzeck." *Journal of the American Oriental Society* 86: 184–98.

d'Alverny, Marie-Thérèse. "La connaissance de l'Islam en Occident du IXe au milieu du XIIe siècle." In *L'occidente e l'islam nell'alto medioevo: 2–8 aprile 1964,* 2:577–602. Spoleto: Presso la sede del Centro, 1965. Repr. in *La connaissance de l'Islam dans l'Occident médiéval,* edited by Charles Burnett. Aldershot: Variorum, 1994.

———. "Deux traductions latines du Coran au Moyen Age." *Archives d'Histoire Doctrinale et Littéraire du Moyen Âge* 16 (1948): 69–131.

———. "Quelques manuscrits de la 'Collectio Toletana.'" In *Petrus Venerabilis 1156–1956. Studies and Texts Commemorating the Eighth Centenary of His Death,* edited by Giles Constable and James Kritzeck, 202–218. Studia Anselmiana 40. Rome: Herder, 1956. Repr. in *La connaissance de l'Islam dans l'Occident médiéval,* edited by Charles Burnett. Aldershot: Variorum, 1994.

d'Ancona, Alessandro. *La leggenda di Maometto in Occidente.* Roma: Salerno editrice, 1994 (1889).

Daniel, Norman. *Islam and the West: The Making of an Image.* Oxford: Oneworld, 1993.

Doutté, Edmond. *Mahomet cardinal.* Châlons-sur-Marne: Martin frères, 1899.

Dronke, Peter. "La sessualità in Paradiso." In *Comportamenti e immaginario della sessualità nell'alto medioevo: 31 marzo–5 aprile 2005,* 303–21. Settimane di studio del Centro italiano di studi sull'alto medioevo 53. Spoleto: Fondazione Centro italiano di studi sull'alto Medioevo, 2006.

Echevarria, Ana. "*Liber scalae Machometi.*" In *Christian-Muslim Relations,* 4:425–28.

Eckhardt, Alexandre. "Le cercueil flottant de Mahomet." In *Mélanges de philologie romane et de littérature médiévale offerts à Ernest Hoepffner,* 77–88. Paris: Les Belles Lettres, 1949.

Fahd, T. "*Nubuwwa.*" In *Encyclopedia of Islam: Second Edition,* 93–97.

Fierro, Maribel. "La visión del otro Musulmán: el *Liber Nicholay* y la revolución Almohade." In *Fronteras en discusión,* edited by J. Martos Quesada and M. Bueno Sánchez, 143–61. Madrid: A. C. Almudayna, 2012.

Forrai, Réka. "Anastasius Bibliothecarius and His Textual Dossiers: Greek Collections and Their Latin Transmission in 9th Century Rome." In *L'Antiquité tardive dans les collections médiévales: textes et représentations, VIe–XIVe siècle,* edited by Stéphane Gioanni and Benoît Grévin, 319–35. Rome: École française de Rome, 2008.

Goldziher, I., and A. M. Goichon. "Dahriyya." In *Encyclopaedia of Islam,* 2nd ed., 2:95–97.

González Muñoz, Fernando. "Consideraciones sobre la versión latina de las cartas de al-Hašimi y al-Kindi." *Collectanea Christiana Orientalia* 2 (2005): 43–70.

———. "Dos versiones tardías de la leyenda de Mahoma. La *Vita Mahometi* del ms. *Pisa,* Biblioteca del Seminario 50 y el tratado *Sobre la seta mahometana* de Pedro de Jaén." In *IV Congresso Internacional de Latim Medieval Hispânico: Lisboa, 12–15 de outubro de 2005,* edited by Aires Augusto Nascimeto and Paulo Farmhouse Alberto, 591–98. Lisbon: Centro de Estudos Clássicos, 2006.

———. "*Liber Nycholay.*" In *Christian-Muslim Relations,* 4:650–53.

———. *Mahometrica. Ficciones poéticas latinas del siglo XII sobre Mahoma.* Madrid: Consejo Superior de Investigaciones Científicas, 2015.

———. "La nota del códice de Roda sobre el obispo Osio y el monje Ozim." *Collectanea Christiana Orientalia* 10 (2013): 51–63.

———. "La versión latina de la 'Apología de al-Kindi' y su tradición textual." In *Musulmanes y cristianos en Hispania durante las conquistas de los*

siglos XII y XIII, edited by Miguel Barceló Perello and José Martínez Gázquez, 25–40. Bellaterra: Universidad Autónoma de Barcelona, 2005.

Graf, Georg. *Geschichte der christlichen arabischen Literatur.* 5 vols. Vatican City: Biblioteca Apostolica Vaticana, 1944–1953.

Griffith, Sidney H. "The Prophet Muḥammad, His Scripture and His Message, According to the Christian Apologies in Arabic and Syriac from the First Abbasid Century." In *La Vie du prophète Mahomet: colloque de Strasbourg, octobre 1980,* 99–146. Paris: Presses universitaires de France, 1983. Repr. in *Arabic Christianity in the Monasteries of Ninth-Century Palestine,* I. Aldershot: Variorum, 1992.

Haddad, Rachid. *La Trinité divine chez les théologiens arabes: 750–1050.* Paris: Beauchesne, 1985.

Hotz, Stephan. *Mohammed und seine Lehre in der Darstellung abendländischer Autoren vom späten 11. bis zur Mitte des 12. Jahrhunderts: Aspekte, Quellen und Tendenzen in Kontinuität und Wandel.* Frankfurt am Main: Lang, 2002.

Hoyland, Robert. *Seeing Islam as Others Saw It: A Survey and Evaluation of Christian, Jewish, and Zoroastrian Writings on Early Islam.* Princeton, N.J.: Darwin Press, 1997.

Jacobsen, Peter. Review of Guy Cambier, *Embricon de Mayence. La Vie de Mahomet, Mittellateinisches Jahrbuch* 3 (1966): 274–78.

Klueting, Edeltraud. "Quis fuerit Machometus? Mohammed im lateinischen Mittelalter (11.–13. Jahrhundert)." *Archiv für Kulturgeschichte* 90 (2008): 283–306.

Kritzeck, James. *Peter the Venerable and Islam.* Princeton, N.J.: Princeton University Press, 1964.

Makkī, al-Tahīr ʾAḥmad. "Imruʾ al-Qays." In *Arabic Literary Culture, 500–925 (Dictionary of literary biography* 311), edited by Michael Cooperson and Shawkat M. Toorawa, 212–24. Detroit: Thomson Gale, 2005.

Margoliouth, D. S. "The Discussion Between Abu Bishr Matta and Abu Saʿid al-Sirafi on the Merits of Logic and Grammar." *The Journal of the Royal Asiatic Society of Great Britain and Ireland* (1905): 79–129.

Massignon, Louis. "al-Kindī, ʿAbd al-Masīḥ." In *Encyclopedie de l'Islam,* 2:1080–81.

Millet-Gérard, Dominique. *Chrétiens mozarabes et culture islamique dans l'Espagne des VIIIe–IXe siècles.* Paris: Etudes augustiniennes, 1984.

Monneret de Villard, Ugo. *Lo studio dell'Islām in Europa nel XII e nel XIII secolo.* Vatican City: Biblioteca Apostolica Vaticana, 1944.

Moos, Peter von. "Literarkritik im Mittelalter: Arnulf von Lisieux über Ennodius." In *Mélanges offerts à René Crozet à l'occasion de son 70e anniversaire par ses amis, ses collègues, ses élèves et les membres du C.E.S.C.M.*, edited by Pierre Gallais and Yves-Jean Rion, 2:929–35. Poitiers: Société d'études médiévales, 1966.

Neil, Bronwen. *Seventh-century Popes and Martyrs: The Political Hagiography of Anastasius Bibliothecarius.* Turnhout: Brepols, 2006.

Nickel, Gordon D. *Narratives of Tampering in the Earliest Commentaries on the Qur'ān.* Leiden: Brill, 2011.

Platti, Emilio. "Criteria for Authenticity of Prophecy in ʿAbd al-Masīḥ al-Kindī's *Risāla.*" In *Books and Written Culture of the Islamic World Studies Presented to Claude Gilliot on the Occasion of His 75th Birthday,* edited by Andrew Rippin and Roberto Tottoli, 3–25. Leiden: Brill, 2015.

Prutz, Hans. "Über des Gautier von Compiègne 'Otia de Machomete': Ein Beitrag zur Geschichte der Mohammedfabeln im Mittelalter und zur Kulturgeschichte der Kreuzzüge." *Sitzungsberichte der Bayerischen Akademie der Wissenschaften, phil.-hist. Klasse* (1903): 65–115.

Ratkowitsch, Christine. "Das Grab des Propheten. Die Mohammad-Dichtungen des Embricho von Mainz und Walter von Compiègne." *Wiener Studien* 106 (1993): 223–56.

Reynolds, Gabriel Said. "On the Qurʾanic Accusation of Scriptural Falsification (taḥrīf) and Christian Anti-Jewish Polemic." *Journal of the American Oriental Society* 130 (2010): 189–202.

Roggema, Barbara. *The Legend of Sergius Baḥīrā: Eastern Christian Apologetics and Apocalyptic in Response to Islam.* Leiden: Brill, 2009.

Rotter, Ekkehart, and Franz, Staab. "Anhang: Der Autor Embricho." In *Auslandsbeziehungen unter den salischen Kaisern. Geistige Auseinandersetzung und Politik,* edited by Franz Staab, 123–37. Speyer: Verlag der Pfälzischen Gesellschaft zur Förderung der Wissenschaften in Speyer, 1994.

———. "Embricho von Mainz und das Mohammed-Bild seiner Zeit." In *Auslandsbeziehungen unter den salischen Kaisern. Geistige Auseinandersetzung und Politik,* edited by Franz Staab, 69–137. Speyer: Verlag der Pfälzischen Gesellschaft zur Förderung der Wissenschaften in Speyer, 1994.

Samir, Samir K. "The Earliest Arab Apology for Christianity (c. 750)." In *Christian Arabic Apologetics During the Abbasid Period, 750–1258,* edited by Samir K. Samir and Jørgen S. Nielsen, 57–114. Leiden: Brill, 1994.

———. "La version latine de l'Apologie d'al-Kindi (vers 830 ap. J.-C.) et son original arabe." In *¿Existe una identidad mozárabe? Historia, lengua y cultura de los cristianos de al-Andalus (siglos IX–XII),* edited by Cyrille Aillet, Mayte Penelas, and Philippe Roisse, 33–82. Madrid: Casa de Velázquez, 2007.

Schmitz, M. "Kaʿb al-ʾAḥbār." In *Encyclopaedia of Islam,* 4:316–17.

Septimus, Bernard. "Petrus Alfonsi on the Cult at Mecca." *Speculum* 56:3 (1981): 517–33.

Sommerlechner, Andrea. "Ein stadtrömische Kaiser-Papst-Geschichte zu Ehren von König Manfred: der *Liber de istoriis* des Frater Johannes Ruffus." *Römische historische Mitteilungen* 42 (2000): 245–306.

Southern, Richard. *Western Views of Islam in the Middle Ages.* Cambridge, Mass.: Harvard University Press, 1962.

Stella, Francesco. "Le versificazioni latine delle vita di Maometto: dall'antiagiografia al romanzo picaresco." In *Dichten als Stoff-Vermittlung: Formen, Ziele, Wirkungen: Beiträge zur Praxis der Versifikation lateinischer Texte im Mittelalter,* edited by Peter Stotz, 119–50. Zürich: Chronos, 2008.

Thomas, David. "The Use of Scripture in Christian-Muslim Dialogue." In *The Bible in Arab Christianity,* edited by David Thomas, 179–96. Leiden: Brill, 2006.

Tolan, John V. "*Iniquus Mahometus,* 'Deceitful Muḥammad.'" In *Christian-Muslim Relations,* 4:654–56.

———. *Saracens. Islam in the Medieval European Imagination.* New York: Columbia University Press, 2002.

———. *Sons of Ishmael: Muslims through European Eyes in the Middle Ages.* Gainesville: University Press of Florida, 2008.

Treadgold, Warren. *The Middle Byzantine Historians.* Houndmills: Palgrave Macmillan, 2013.

Troupeau, Georges. "al- Kindī, ʿAbd al-Masīḥ." In *The Encyclopaedia of Islam,* 2nd ed., 5:120–21. Leiden: Brill, 1960–2009.

van Koningsveld, Pieter S. "La apología de Al-Kindî en la España del siglo XII. Huellas toledanas de un 'Animal Disputax.'" In *Estudios sobre Alfonso VI y la Reconquista de Toledo. Actas del II Congreso Internacional de*

Estudios Mozárabes (Toledo, 20–26 mayo 1985), 3:107–29. Toledo: Instituto de Estudios Visigótico-Mozárabes, 1991.

———. "The Apology of Al-Kindî." In *Religious Polemics in Context: Papers Presented to the Second International Conference of the Leiden Institute for the Study of Religions (Lisor) Held at Leiden, 27–28 April, 2000*, edited by T. L. Hettema and A. van der Kooij, 69–92. Assen: Royal Van Gorcum, 2004.

Vitelli, Camillo. "Index codicum latinorum qui Pisis in bybliothecis Conventus S. Catherinae et Universitatis adservantur." *Studi italiani di Filologia classica* 8 (1900): 321–427.

Wattenbach, Wilhelm. "Lateinische Gedichte aus Frankreich im elften Jahrhundert." *Sitzungsberichte der königlichen preussischen Akademie der Wissenschaften zu Berlin* 27 (1891): 97–114.

General Index

For poetry, numbers refer to line numbers of the original text; for prose, numbers refer to paragraph numbers. The primary texts are abbreviated as follows: *Hist.* (*History of Muhammad*), *Tult.* (*Tultusceptru*), *Theo.* (*Chronicle* of Theophanes), *Embr.* (Embrico of Mainz), *Walt.* (Walter of Compiègne), *Adel.* (Adelphus), *Prol.* (Prologue to the *Apology of al-Kindī*), *ES* (*Letter of the Saracen*), *RC* (*Reply of the Christian*), *Epil.* (Epilogue to the *Apology of al-Kindī*), *Nich.* (*Book of Nicholas*), *Qualiter* (*Where Wicked Muhammad Came From*).

Index of Scriptural Citations

The Bible

The Qur'ān